Nepal

Nepal

A History from the Earliest Times to the Present

AXEL MICHAELS

OXFORD
UNIVERSITY PRESS

OXFORD
UNIVERSITY PRESS

Oxford University Press is a department of the University of Oxford. It furthers the University's objective of excellence in research, scholarship, and education by publishing worldwide. Oxford is a registered trade mark of Oxford University Press in the UK and certain other countries.

Published in the United States of America by Oxford University Press
198 Madison Avenue, New York, NY 10016, United States of America.

CIP data is on file at the Library of Congress
ISBN 978-0-19-765093-6

DOI: 10.1093/oso/9780197650936.001.0001

Printed by Sheridan Books, Inc., United States of America

Contents

Preface vii
Acknowledgments ix
Glossary xi
On the Spelling and Pronunciation of Indian and Nepalese Words xvii
Chronology xix

Introduction—Nepal in the Making 1

1. The Country 10
   Infrastructure 11
   Mountains 13
   Earthquakes 16
   Water Resources 21
   Forests and Holy Trees 25

2. The Population 29
   Migration 31
   Social Structures and Hierarchies 34
   The Position of Women 39
   Nepal as a Multi-ethnic State 49

3. The Religions 52
   Buddhism 53
   Hinduism 61
   Religious Syncretism and Tolerance 81

4. Scattered Power and Petty Kingdoms: The Country before the Fourteenth Century 84
   Prehistory 84
   The Kirāta 85
   The Licchavi and Ābhīra Gupta Period 87
   The Early Medieval Period 95
   The Khasa-Malla in Western Nepal 99
   The Petty Kingdoms 102

5. Divided Rule: The Malla Kingdoms, Thirteenth to Eighteenth Century 105
   The Malla Rulers 106
   The Urban Culture of the Newars 114
   The Three Royal Cities of the Kathmandu Valley 124

6. From Gorkha to Nepal: The Śāha Monarchy, 1768/69–1846 136
Pṛthvīnārāyaṇa and His Followers 136
The Consolidation of Gorkhali Power 142
Anglo-British Encounters 145
Sino-Tibetan Encounters 153

7. Patrimonial Rule: The Rāṇā Period, 1846–1951 160
The Kũvara Rāṇā, 1846–85 162
The Śamśera Rāṇā, 1885–1951 166
Landholding and Agriculture 169
Labor and Slavery 180
Economy and Trade 191
The Legal and Administrative System 194
Education and Traditional Learning 202
Healing Systems and Shamanism 204
Hunting and Elephants 209
Rāṇā Architecture 211
The Legacy of the Śāha and Rāṇā Periods 214

8. From Monarchy to Republic, 1951–Present 217
The Restoration of the Śāhas 217
The Maoist Insurgency 223
The Decline of the Monarchy and the Emergence of Democracy 226
Power and Authority: King, Prime Minister, and Maoist Leader 236
Administration and Law 243
Public Education and Media 246
Public Health Care 248
The Urbanization and Cultural Heritage of the Kathmandu Valley 249
Literature, Art, and Music 253

9. Alliances and Resistance: Ethnic Groups and Their Histories 262
The Tarai: From Mithila to the Madhesi Uprising 264
The Sherpa 269
Mustang 276
The Kiranti (Rai-Limbu) in Eastern Nepal 280
From Empire to Nation State 284

Conclusion 290

Appendix 1. An Essay on the Sources of Nepalese Historiography 295
Appendix 2. Lists of Rulers, Prime Ministers, and British Envoys 313
Notes 323
Bibliography 343
Index 385

Preface

Nepal is a country with a cultural, religious, and socio-political diversity that is second to none. According to the 2021 Census, it is home to 142 castes or ethnic groups and 125 languages within five different language groups, and to a plethora of literatures and historical documents in different languages (Sanskrit, Maithilī, Nevārī, Nepālī, Tibetan). The Buddha was born in what is now Nepal, but until the mid-twentieth century it exalted in being the only Hindu kingdom of the world. It is still a stronghold of Tantric traditions, shamanism, and many other folk religions. Hardly a day goes by without elaborate festivals being celebrated and large rituals being performed, including animal sacrifices, the worship of a girl as a living goddess, and (until a century ago) widow burning. At the same time, great tolerance is practiced among these religions, and religious wars have been as good as unknown. Until 1951 Nepal was closed to the world, landlocked between the strongest Asian powers, India and China (Tibet). In some periods there were almost eighty different principalities on the territory, among them the mysterious and legendary Mustang and Sherpa realms. Each region has its own fascinating local history, but since the eighteenth century everything has been bundled into a contentious national history, a consensus version of which is still being fought for, as the Maoist insurgency against the government of Nepal (1996–2006) and the royal massacre (2001) have painfully demonstrated. Still, the Himalayan country is inhabited by an endearingly friendly population and offers uniquely rich and impressive architecture, art, and handicrafts; an exceptional landscape; the greatest biodiversity on earth; and the world's highest mountains.

This small but highly complex country truly deserves a new history that covers all these features and more. The historiography of Nepal has its beginnings—non-indigenous ones—in the seventh century with Chinese pilgrims who came to northern India and Lumbini, if not to the Kathmandu Valley. It continued only much later with Catholic missionaries in the seventeenth and eighteenth centuries, and in the nineteenth and twentieth centuries with the publishing of what are still important standard works—for instance, Sylvain Lévi's *Nepal: Etude historique d'un Royaume Hindou*

(1905–8), Dilli Raman Regmi's multivolume history of Nepal (1960, 1965–66 and 1975), and Mahesh Chandra Regmi's *Landownership in Nepal* (1976) and *Land Tenure and Taxation in Nepal* (1978). Other seminal works include Mary Slusser's two-volume *Nepal Mandala: A Cultural Study of the Kathmandu Valley* (1982) and John Whelpton's *A History of Nepal* (2005), which focuses on the nineteenth and twentieth centuries.

Why then another history of Nepal? This work synthesizes the large amount of recent research in various areas, including what has been written, often in the Nepālī language, by learned Nepalese scholars. Decisive sources are newly accessible documents of the long nineteenth century including the first legal code of Nepal (the comprehensive [Mulukī] Ain of 1854), which began with the conquest of the Kathmandu Valley by the Śāha dynasty in 1768/69 and ended with the fall of Rāṇā rule in 1951.

This book is a cultural history, which means that it encompasses different histories and temporalities. It provides an overview of major themes, areas, and periods in the history of Nepal. It attempts to convey the country's complexity and diversity; the histories of its regions; the different political currents and forms of political organization, the fluid and multiple identities, the cross-border, transcultural, transreligious, and economic entanglements; and the mobile ways of life, many taking place in marginal zones, transit regions, and enclaves.

Acknowledgments

This book would not exist without the work and publications of other researchers. I would like to mention a few scholars from whom I have learned more than one can find in their books and articles: architectural historian Niels Gutschow, anthropologists Martin Gaenszle, András Höfer, Michael Oppitz, Charles Ramble, Anne de Sales, and Prayag Raj Sharma, Indologists Bernhard Kölver († 2001), Siegfried Lienhard († 2011), and Alexander von Rospatt, art historian Mary Slusser († 2017), Nepalese scholars Mahes Raj Pant, Hemraj Shakya († 2010), and Gautam Vajracharya, and the scholars of Newar culture and history David Gellner, Kamal Prasad Malla († 2018), and Gérard Toffin. I count myself fortunate that many of these colleagues, with whom I usually became acquainted with in Nepal, have become friends.

I thank the following friends for having read parts of this book and contributing much to its improvement: David C. Andolfatto, Martin Gaenszle, David Gellner, Niels Gutschow, Nina Mirnig, Marcus Nüsser, Michael Oppitz, Joanna Pfaff-Czarnecka, Charles Ramble, and Alexander von Rospatt. Their advice and criticism have meant a great deal to me, particularly since a reading of original texts or a view of things in situ was out of reach, most prominently with regard to Tibetan sources and the high mountain regions. I also benefitted from the detailed criticism of two anonymous reviewers, one of whom pushed me to revise the structure of the book.

I likewise owe a debt of thanks to those who worked with me in my Heidelberg Academy project "Documents on the History of Religion and Law of Pre-modern Nepal" and the ARCADIA-funded "Nepal Heritage Documentation Project": Manik Bajracharya, Christiane Brosius, Simon Cubelic, Rajan Khatiwoda, Astrid Zotter, and Christoph Zotter. Without their help, discussions, and critical reading of individual chapters, this book would not have been possible.

While I was originally writing this Preface, I received the sad news that my old friend Laxmi Nath Shrestha passed away on September 3, 2020. He not only taught me Nepālī and Nevārī but also helped me to understand many things that are written between the lines of this book.

I thank Niels Gutschow, Stanisław Klimek, Michael Oppitz, Perdita Pohle, Ashesh Rajbanshi, Raju Roka, and Thomas Schrom for their kind provision of photographs, and Nils Harm for drawing the maps. Last but not least I thank Douglas Fear for the English translation, Philip H. Pierce for his exceptionally thorough revision, and Susan Ferber for her meticulous editorial work and many substantial improvements as well as Jaqueline Pavlovic and Katherine Ulrich for the excellent copy-editing.

By awarding me the Manfred Lautenschläger Research Prize, the Manfred Lautenschläger Foundation provided important support in procuring sources and checking them. Finally, I have profited from the German Research Council, which funded many projects over the years, and I am very grateful for this.

Very special thanks go, as always, to Christiane Brosius, who shares my life and love for Nepal.

* * *

This book is based on an English translation of *Kultur und Geschichte Nepals*, published in 2018 by the Kröner-Verlag, Stuttgart. Even though the core of the present book remains the same, I have revised the structure and several chapters, shortened the text, and added further material and references.

Glossary

adhiyā (adhiyā̃) The system under which harvest yields are shared equally between the tenant and the feudal lord

ahiṃsā The commandment not to harm sentient beings

***Ain* (of 1854)** Nepal's first major legal text (and a constitution of sorts), promulgated by Jaṅga Bahādura Rāṇā

amālī A junior district official in the Śāha und Rāṇā periods furnished with administrative and legal powers

ānā A currency unit, 1/16 of a rupee

Aśoka An Indian ruler (ca. 269–32 BCE)

Avalokiteśvara The Bodhisattva of universal compassion; also called Karuṇāmaya

bāhāḥ A Buddhist monastery, originally for married monks

bahī A Buddhist monastery, originally for unmarried monks

Bahun (*bāhuna*) A Parbatiyā (Khasa-Arya) Brahmin

Bajracharya (*vajrācārya*) A Buddhist priestly caste among the Newar; also called (Nev.) Gubhāju

bhāradāra ("Bearer of the burden") A designation for former high-ranking officials and palace counselors

Bhojapurī A language spoken in the central Tarai

Bhoṭiyā (Bhoṭe) A Nepālī designation for Tibetans and Tibetoid groups, and for Tibetan culture and languages, often used disparagingly

birtā Generally tax-free land

Bodhisattva Beings who have attained enlightenment but renounce entry into *nirvāṇa* to help others to salvation; worshiped as "gods," they stand between "saints" (*siddha*) and the Buddha

Brahmin (*brāhmaṇa*) The highest of the four traditional Hindu "caste classes" (*varṇa*), traditionally priests and scholars

caitya A Buddhist domed building, a *stūpa*

cautariyā In the pre-Rāṇā period: noble members of the king's council; in the Rāṇā Period: an honorary title for relatives of the royal house

Chhetri (Chhetrī, Kṣatriya) The dominant Khasa-Arya caste, often referred to together with the Bahun

Chitrakar (*citrakāra*) The Newar painter caste

Darbar (*darabāra*) A palace

Dasaĩ The ten-day festival in the autumn during which the killing of the buffalo demon Mahiṣa by Durgā is celebrated and many animals are sacrificed

dharma The traditional Hindu rules that embody law and custom

dharmādhikārin (also *dharmādhikāra*) A religious court judge

dharmaśāstra The traditional textbooks of law and custom

dvāre An official overseeing land-related matters; a village official who had policing powers; a constable

Gahrwal A district in the Indian Himalaya, previously occupied at times by Nepal

Gopālarājavaṃśāvalī A chronicle dating from the end of the 14th century

Gorakhanātha A Hindu saint (ca. 11th/12th century), the eponym of Gorkha

Gorkha (Gorkhā) The city in Central Nepal that was the original seat of the Śāha dynasty; also a designation for Nepalese soldiers

Gorkhali (*gorkhālī*) A person from Gorkha; another name for the Khasa-Arya and for the Nepālī language

Gũlā/Gumla A holy month for Newar Buddhists (straddling July and August)

Gurung An ethnic group prominent in the midwestern mountain region

guṭhī A foundation organized to promote a particular religious aim and that earns revenue from tax-exempt land to do so

hulāka The government's postal and dispatch service

Indo-Parbatiyā Members of castes who originally came from India and who speak Nepālī as their mother tongue

jāgira Land given as compensation, *jāgiradāra* being the holder of such land

Jaisī Descendants of a Brahmin male and a Brahmin widow

jāta/jāti A lineage, a caste group, an ethnic group

Janajāti The ethnic population collectively

jhārā Bonded labor

Jyāpu A Newar farmer

kājī A minister or senior official

Kaliyuga The current and worst of four world ages

kamaiyā A bonded laborer

Kanaphaṭṭā Members of the sect of the same name, probably founded by Gorakhanātha

Khas / Khasa / Khaśa An old name for Chhetris; a name for the Chhetris in western Nepal and for the Nepālī language (*khasakurā*)

Khasa-Arya (i.e., the same as Indo-Parbatiyā) Members of castes who originally came from India and who speak Nepālī as their mother tongue

kheta Irrigable land suitable for growing rice

kipaṭa Municipal land belong to ethnic groups, especially in eastern Nepal

Kiranti / Kirā̃tī A population group in eastern Nepal; the collective name for Rai-Limbu and other groups, and for their languages

Kirāta / Kirā̃ta (also Kirātī) The name for the putative indigenous population of Kathmandu Valley

Kshatriya (*kṣatriya*) The second of the four traditional Hindu "caste classes" (*varṇa*): aristocrats and warriors

Kumārī Coka A government office responsible for finances and accounting

kuta A lease arrangement wherein the tenant had to deliver a fixed sum or a fixed amount of harvested crops

Kũvara The surname of Jaṅga Bahādura Rāṇā

Lakṣmī (lit. "good fortune, wealth") The Hindu goddess who brings good fortune; Viṣṇu's consort

lālamohara A royal decree

lāmā A Tibetan monk or priest; a clan name among the Gurung, Magar, and Tamang

Licchavi A dynasty that lasted from the third to eighth century

Limbu A population group in eastern Nepal

liṅga A phallic symbol for Śiva

Magar A population group in the middle and western mountain regions

Maharjan A Newar farmer

Mahāyāna (lit. "Great Vehicle") A Buddhist tradition based on the Bodhisattva ideal and Bodhisattva worship

Maithilī The language of the inhabitants of the region originally called Mithila in the Tarai and northern Bihar

Malla The title of a ruler; the name of a dynasty that ruled the Kathmandu Valley from the thirteenth to eighteenth century

maṇḍala (lit. "circle") A circular diagram subject to various interpretations

mantra A ritual formula

matavālī / matuvālī A drinker of alcohol; a name applied to certain alcohol-drinking castes

Mithila A region in south-eastern Nepal and northern India

mukhtiyāra In the pre-Rāṇā period: premier or chief minister; in the Rāṇā Period: prime minister and *kamāṇḍara-ina-cīpha* (commander-in-chief) or title of a regent

mūlacuka The main courtyard of a palace

Mulukī Aḍḍā (after Candra Śamśera, the Mulukī Bandobasta Aḍḍā) A government office concerned with domestic and legal matters, directly under the prime minister

murī A volumetric measure (about 87.23 liters)

Nepāla The indigenous name for the Kathmandu Valley

Nepālālikabhūpavaṃśāvalī ("Chronicle of the Kings of Nepal") A Buddhist-Hindu chronicle from the nineteenth century

Newar A population group mainly settled in the Kathmandu Valley

Nevārī The Tibeto-Burman language spoken by the Newar

Padmasambhava (lit. "The Lotus-born One") A Buddhist master of the eighth/ninth century, regarded by many as the founder of Tibetan Buddhism

Pahāḍī (lit. "hilly") the Hill Brahmin and Chhetri culture

pajanī A list of posts and salaries confirmed or revoked at an annual hearing in the palace

pākho Dry land on which mainly corn, millet, and dry rice are grown

Panchayat (*pañcāyata*) Village or city councils which represented the country in parliament instead of parties in the years 1962–90

Pandit A traditionally educated scholar

Parbatiya (*parvatiyā / parvatīya / parvate*) A member of a caste (especially Bahun, Thakuri, and Chhetri) that speaks Nepālī as their mother tongue

Paśupatinātha (lit. "Lord of the Animals") An epithet of Śiva and the name of the national temple dedicated to him

pāṭī An open arcaded edifice, usually consisting of one story, where people rest and gather

pāthī A volumetric measure (about 4.5 liters)

pradhāna The head of a city quarter; a tax collector

***prasāda* (lit. "favor")** An offering made to a god that is returned to the offering person

pūjā A ritual performed in worship of a god

Purāṇa Sanskrit texts containing myths and legends

raikara Land held in fief

Rajopadhyaya Newar Brahmins

Rajput (Rajapūta / Rājapūta) A Kṣatriya caste from Rajasthan

rājya Tax-free land granted to petty kings

Rāṇā A title and surname adopted by Jaṅga Bahādur Kūvara

ropanī An areal measurement (about 0.05 hectares)

Śāha The name of a dynasty that ruled intermittently between 1769 and 2008

Śamśera Rāṇā The clan that produced the prime ministers who ruled from 1885 to 1951

saradāra In the pre-Rāṇā period, usually a high-ranking military official; later also active in civilian matters

śāstra A textbook, typically written in Sanskrit

satī Widow burning; a widow who submits herself to such a death

sattala An arcaded building that provides shelter or a place to stay

sikhara **(*śikhara*, lit. "mountain peak")** A temple in the rising tower style of North Indian Hindu architecture

Singha Darbar (Siṃha Darabāra) The seat of the government of Nepal

sinu Meat from dead cattle

Śiva A major Hindu god

śivālaya **(lit. "seat of Śiva")** A Śiva temple or shrine; a *liṅga*

Shrestha (*Śreṣṭha*) A high, mostly Hindu Newar caste

Shudra (*śūdra*) The lowest of the four traditional Hindu "caste classes" (*varṇa*), including peasants, servants, and common artisans

stūpa A Buddhist domed building

sunā-birtā Private taxable *birtā* land

subbā The governor of a province; a high-ranking official, at times standing in for a *kājī*

Tamang An ethnic population settled in and around the Kathmandu Valley

Tantrism Esoteric traditions of Hinduism and Buddhism whose ritual practices include the offering of alcohol and blood sacrifices

Tarai (also Terai) The Himalayan foreland of Nepal

Thakuri (Ṭhakurī) The high Khasa-Arya caste from which most rulers traditionally came

Theravāda (in Nepal) A reform strand of Buddhism

Tharaghara The highest, most privileged castes (*thara*), namely Pāḍe, Pantha, Arjyāla, Khanāla, Rāṇā, and Bohorā; dignitaries

ṭīkā A red mark impressed on the forehead

tirtha **(*tīrtha*)** A place of pilgrimage

Tuladhar (Tulādhara) A Newar merchant caste

umarāu, umarāva A military commander, particularly in the mountain regions

Uray (Urāy) A collective name for several Newar castes, mostly craftsmen and traders

vaidya A doctor; a naturopath, usually with a grounding in Ayurveda

Vaishya (*vaiṣya*) The third of the traditional Hindu "caste classes" (*varṇa*), including merchants, skilled artisans, and large landholders, and in olden times also peasants

vajra A diamond scepter or thunderbolt as a Buddhist symbol of the permanence of the teaching

Vajracharya A Buddhist caste among the Newar, often priests

Vajrayāna A Tantric-Buddhist tradition, especially prevalent in Nepal

vaṃśāvalī **(literally "genealogy")** A chronicle

varṇa A caste class made up of caste groups, each with a particular assigned social status

On the Spelling and Pronunciation of Indian and Nepalese Words

Unless otherwise indicated or clear from the particular context, all foreign words are from the Nepālī language. The transliteration for this language is generally that used in the standard dictionary, *Nepālī Bṛhat Śabdakośa* (1995). For concepts and most historical names in Indian and Nepalese languages, diacritical marks that are important for scientific identification are used, and anglicized spellings avoided.

To put it in a somewhat oversimplified way, three rules in particular should be attended to in pronunciation:

- A horizontal stroke over a vowel signifies a long vowel (i.e., a vowel that is held roughly twice as long as a normal vowel).
- A dot beneath a consonant (except in the case of *ṃ*, which usually nasalizes the preceding vowel) signifies a retroflex pronunciation, in which the tip of the tongue is slightly bent up and back, as generally in English *r* at the start of a word.
- *S* with a diacritic – *ṣ*, *ś* – is basically pronounced like *sh* in English. For the purists in Sanskrit, *ṣ* is retroflex, rather close to English *sh*, while *ś* is between *sh* and *s*, as it is in Polish.

In the Nepālī language, a final consonant at the end of a word is usually written with an inherent short *a*, but the latter is not enunciated. "Jaṅga Bahādura Rāṇā" is thus pronounced Jaṅg Bahādur Rāṇā.

Historical personal names, theonyms and temple names, concepts, and terms from Indian and Nepalese languages, as well as technical terms, are all written with diacritical marks. Personal names from the mid-twentieth century onward, place names and river names, most institutions, and the names of castes or ethnic groups are written in their anglicized forms, the latter without the plural -*s*. Sometimes, however, place names designate both a settlement and a temple; if the temple (or the god worshiped there) is meant, then the diacritical marks are used; otherwise they are not used. Thus, we distinguish Changu Narayan (place) and Cāṅgunārāyaṇa (deity), or Budhanilakantha and Buḍhānīlakaṇṭha.

Chronology

ca. 450–380 BCE	The Buddha is born in Lumbini

The Licchavi (Third to Eighth Century)

464–505	Mānadeva I
605–621	Aṃśuvarman
12th–14th c.	Khasa-Malla in western Nepal

The Malla (Thirteenth to Eighteenth Century)

1200–16	Ari Malla I, the first Malla king
1349	Sultan Shams ud-dīn Ilyās of Bengal invades the Kathmandu Valley
1382–95	(Jaya) Sthiti Malla consolidates the Malla kingdom
1428–82	Yakṣa Malla unifies the Malla kingdom
1484	Division of the Malla kingdom into the three independent kingdoms of Kathmandu, Bhadgaon (Bhaktapur), and Patan (Lalitpur)
1533	Arrival of the migrating Sherpa in Solukhumbu

The Śāha (1768/69–2008)

1559	Dravya Śāha founds the Gorkha kingdom
1606–33	Rāma Śāha conquers Gorkha
1715	Beginning of the Capuchin mission in Kathmandu
1743	Pṛthvīnārāyaṇa Śāha ascends the throne of Gorkha
1744	Pṛthvīnārāyaṇa Śāha conquers Nuvakot
1766	Pṛthvīnārāyaṇa Śāha conquers Kirtipur
1767	Captain George Kinloch's unsuccessful expedition to help Kathmandu

1768–69	Pṛthvīnārāyaṇa Śāha conquers Kathmandu, Patan, Bhadgaon, and large parts of eastern and western Nepal
1788–89	1st war with Tibet to enforce the terms of the Treaty of Kuti (1775)
1791–92	2nd war with Tibet to enforce the terms of the Treaty of Kerong (1789), Chinese troops enter Nepal and reach down to Nuvakot
1793	Kirkpatrick's mission to Kathmandu
1802	Captain W. D. Knox establishes the Residency in Kathmandu while serving as the envoy of the East India Company
1806	Raṇabahādura Śāha is killed
1806–37	Bhīmasena Thāpā is prime minister

The Rāṇā (1846–1951)

1814–16	War with the British East India Company
1846–77	Jaṅga Bahādura Rāṇā is prime minister
1850	Jaṅga Bahādura Rāṇā visits Britain and France
1855–6	3rd war with Tibet
1856	The office of prime minister is made hereditary
1885–1901	Vīra Śamśera; the Śamśera Rāṇā seize and consolidate power
1901–1929	Candra Śamśera
1914–18	Gorkha regiments fight on the Allied side in WW I
1918	Opening of Trichandra College in Kathmandu
1920	Prohibition of the burning of widows
1923	Great Britain recognizes Nepal's independence
1924	Abolition of slavery
1932–45	Juddha Śamśera
1934	Severe earthquake in the Kathmandu Valley
1941	Execution of the "Four Martyrs"

The Resurgence of the Monarchy (1951–62)

1947	Foundation of the Nepali Congress in Indian exile
1948	First written constitution under Padma Śamśera
1950 (November 6)	Flight of King Tribhuvan to India

1951 (December 11)	Resignation of the last Rāṇā prime minister, Mohana Śamśera
1951 (February 2)	Return of King Tribhuvan
1951 (February 18)	Proclamation of a constitutional monarchy
1951 (March 30)	Adoption of an interim constitution
1953 (May 29)	First ascent of Mt. Everest by Tenzing Norgay and Sir Edmund Hillary
1955 (March 3)	Mahendra becomes king
1959 (February 12)	First democratic constitution
1959 (February 18)	Direct elections producing a Nepali Congress victory
1960 (December 15)	Dissolution of the Parliament by the king and dismissal of Prime Minister Koirala; prohibition of political parties

The Panchayat Period (1962–90)

1962 (December 16)	Enactment of the Panchayat constitution
1972 (January 31)	Birendra (Vīrendra) Śāha becomes king
1975 (February 24)	Coronation of the king
1979 (May)	Unrest at the lack of democratization
1980	Referendum on the Panchayat system narrowly retains it
1980 (December 15)	Introduction of a new "more democratic" Panchayat constitution
1981 (September 5)	Elections, with many Panchayat candidates losing
1989 (March 19)	Beginning of an Indian economic blockade

Constitutional Monarchy with a Multiparty System (1990–2008)

1990 (February 18)	Emergence of a broadly based movement for democracy, a "popular uprising" (*jana āndolana*)
1990 (November 9)	Enactment of a new constitution defining Nepal as a constitutional monarchy with a multiparty system
1990 (May 12)	Elections producing an absolute majority for the Congress Party and G. P. Koirala as premier
1992	Elections in which Congress wins a clear plurality of votes and an absolute majority in Parliament
1994 (November 15)	Elections producing a victory for the Communist Party of Nepal (Unified Marxist-Leninist) / CPN-UML; from November 30, the first communist minority government

1995 (June 6)	Dissolution of the House of Representatives by the king; reinstatement of the House of Representatives after a decision by the Supreme Court on August 28
1996 (February 13)	Beginning of a Maoist peasants' revolt in northwest Nepal
2001 (June 1)	Massacre in the Royal Palace; Gyanendra is crowned king on June 4
2002 (May 22)	Dissolution of the parliament; formation of a transitional government
2005 (February 1)	Gyanendra dismisses the government and takes all power
2006 (April 7)	Call for a general strike and protests to reinstate Parliament
2006 (November 21)	Agreement to end the civil war by G. P. Koirala and P. K. Dahal
2007 (January 15)	Interim constitution
2007 (December 24)	Seven-party government including the Maoists agrees to abolish the monarchy and declares Nepal a republic

Federal Democratic Republic of Nepal (2008–Present)

2008 (April 10)	Elections to a constituent assembly
2008 (May 28)	The Maoists win a majority in elections; dissolution of the monarchy; King Gyanendra leaves the palace on June 11
2008 (July 23)	Ram Baran Yadav (Nepali Congress) becomes the first president of the Republic of Nepal
2008 (August 15)	The Maoist leader Pushpa Kamal Dahal ("Prachanda") becomes the first prime minister of the republic
2008 (December 28)	270 of 329 MPs vote for a federal democratic republic
2013 (November 19)	New elections producing victory to centrist and right-wing parties
2015 (September 20)	New constitution promulgated to strong protests by minorities in the Tarai; India subsequently blocks the border for weeks
2017 (November/December)	The first elections on the basis of a democratic constitution; Communists and Maoists achieve a near two-thirds majority
2018 (February 15)	Khadga Prasad Sharma Oli becomes prime minister for the third time

2021 (July 13)	Sher Bahadur Deuba replaces Prime Minister K. P. Oli amid a constitutional crisis
2021 (August 18)	The largest party, Communist Party of Nepal-UML splits to form CPN (Unified Socialist, also Maoist Centre) led by former prime minister Madhav Kumar Nepal
2021 (November 11)	Nepal census begins
2022 (July–October)	Nepal severely hit by Corona and Dengue endemics
2022 (November 20)	New elections with Communist Party of Nepal-UML winning most votes
2023 (January 1)	Pokhara International Airport begins operations
2023 (January 10)	Prime Minister Dahal has gained a vote of confidence with 268 out of 270 votes in the 275-member House of Representatives.
2023 (March 9)	Ram Chandra Poudel of the Nepali Congress is elected 3rd President of Nepal

Nepal

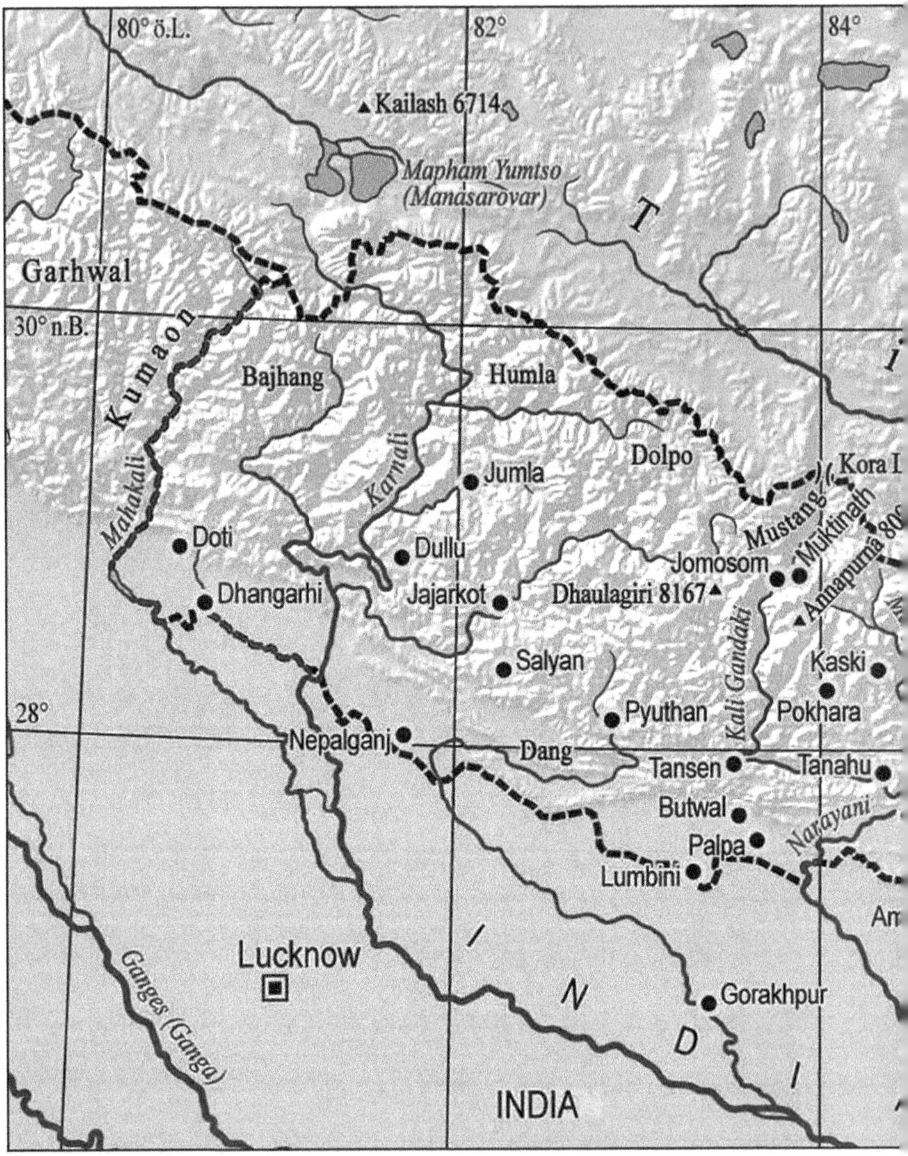

Nepal and Its Major Places. Map by Nils Harm.

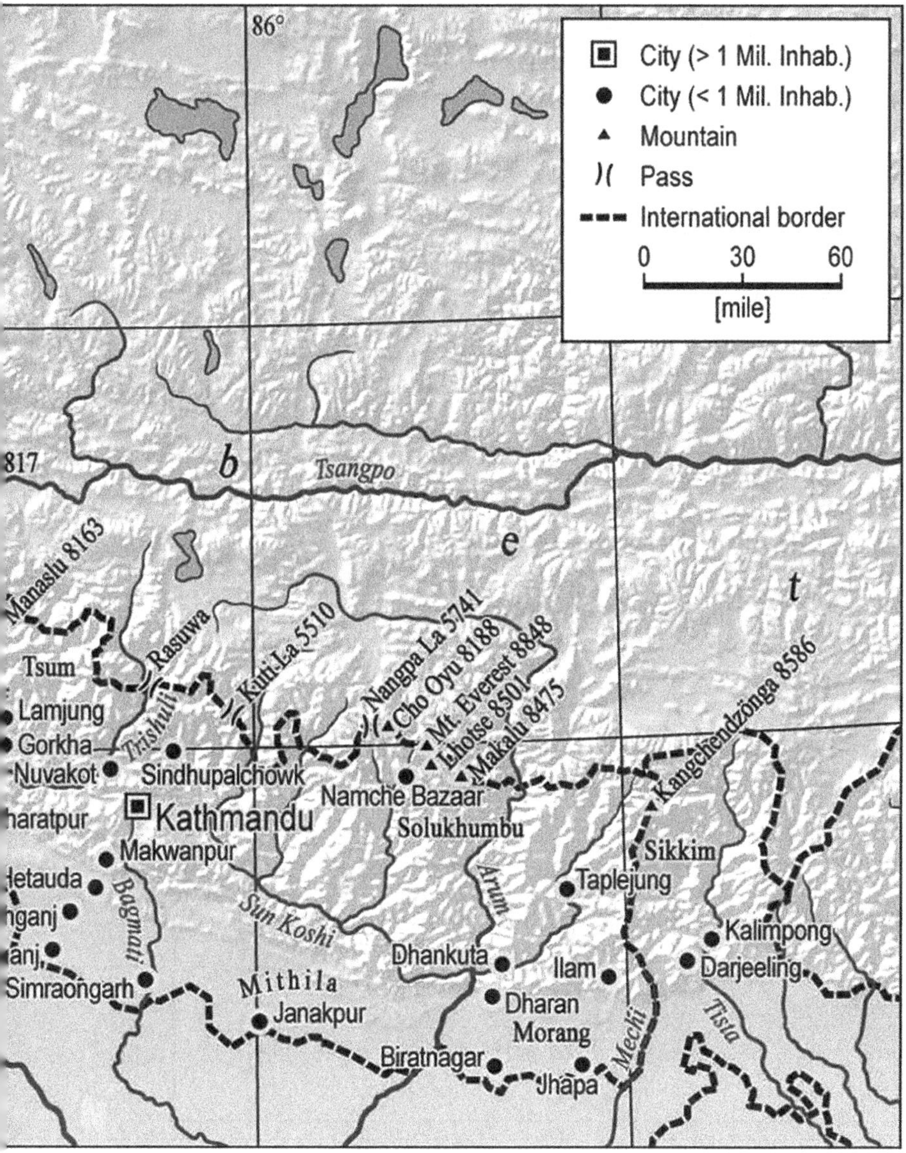

86°
City (> 1 Mil. Inhab.)
City (< 1 Mil. Inhab.)
Mountain
Pass
International border
0
30
60
[mile]
b
Tsangpo
e
t
Manaslu 8163
Rasuwa
Kuti La 5510
Nangpa La 5741
Cho Oyu 8188
Mt. Everest 8848
Lhotse 8501
Makalu 8475
Kangchendzönga 8586
Tsum
Lamjung
Gorkha
Trishuli
Nuvakot
Sindhupalchowk
Namche Bazaar
Kathmandu
Solukhumbu
Makwanpur
Bagmati
Sun Koshi
Arun
Sikkim
Taplejung
Kalimpong
Darjeeling
Dhankuta
Ilam
Dharan
Morang
Simraongarh
Mithila
Janakpur
Biratnagar
Jhapa
Mechi
Tista

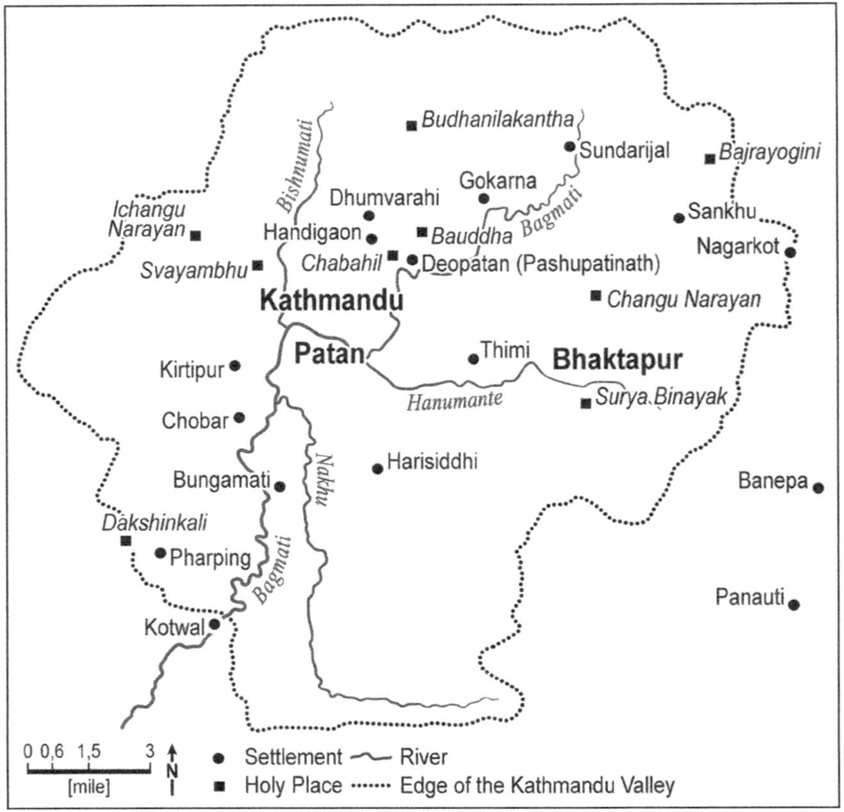

Kathmandu Valley. Map by Nils Harm.

Introduction—Nepal in the Making

In 1768, Pṛthvīnārāyaṇa Śāha, king of Gorkha, stood at the edge of the fertile Kathmandu Valley and asked:

> "Which is Nepal?" They showed me saying: "That is Bhadgaon (Bhaktapur), that is Patan, and there lies Kathmandu." The thought came to my heart that I might be the king of these three cities, why, let it be so.[1]

His court astrologer agreed, and one year later he had taken the valley, and thus the political and economic center of the country, which he did not call Nepal, a name commonly used for the Kathmandu Valley at that time, but Gorkhā Rāj (Kingdom of Gorkha).

Thus began, according to the *Divyopadeśa* (Holy Instruction), the history of the state of Nepal. In the years since, Pṛthvīnārāyaṇa has been regarded as the founding father of Nepal, and he is correspondingly honored with statues, street names, in school books, and on stamps, paintings, and visuals.[2] This heroization of Pṛthvīnārāyaṇa as the founder of the nation, and the unifier of the country associated with it, is among the great national myths of Nepal, firmly anchored in the mind of many Nepalese and propagated by some national historians.[3] In the nineteenth century Pṛthvīnārāyaṇa was hardly praised as the constructor of the nation, and up to the mid-twentieth century this idea is barely mentioned. It is said that Nepālī-speaking intellectuals in Darjeeling began to talk in such terms as a way of elevating their status in Indian society through association with a glorious past.[4] From 1951 on, the Śāha royals were all too glad to spread the story, having just retaken power over the country from the Rāṇā clan; they glorified Pṛthvīnārāyaṇa as the father of the nation,[5] and the cult reached a climax in 1967 with the publication of the biography of Pṛthvīnārāyaṇa written by renowned historian and literary scholar Baburam Acharya.

But where was this country exactly? In a map of 1838, published by the Society for the Diffusion of Useful Knowledge, Nepal shows up only as a diffuse image with hardly any clear limits. In Mitchell's *New General Atlas* of

Nepal. Axel Michaels, Oxford University Press. English language edition © Oxford University Press 2024.
DOI: 10.1093/oso/9780197650936.003.0001

1864, Nepal does not even appear as a state. In 1896, Herbert Hope Risley, the director of the Ethnographic Survey of India, could write that Nepal "is a kind of disputed land between Aryan and Mongol territory, which has the greater part of its population from Tibet and the intellectual and social leaders from India."[6]

To be sure, Pṛthvīnārāyaṇa did create a kingdom unified by power and military conquest, even though he primarily wanted to be victorious in battle and regarded as a first-class Kshatriya, or a member of an aristocratic and warrior caste. His kingdom controlled a large part of what is today Nepal, including important trade routes between India and Tibet, but he did not succeed in creating a society unified from the inside, with a single language or a common history; he certainly did not create a nation state. He had no vision of a united kingdom. Thus the narrative of a politically highly fragmented region developing into a unified, and thus modern, state does not hold true.

Knowing well that his country was "a yam between two rocks," as the *Divyopadeśa* says, Pṛthvīnārāyaṇa recommended a defensive position on the part of his country toward Tibet/China and British India. Nepal thus was (and remained until 1951) an isolated state. It did not participate in the global nation-forming process of the nineteenth century, even though it did successively adopt such national institutions as schools, universities, and a police force. Until the mid-twentieth century, the country was closed off to the outside world's great political, infrastructural, cultural, and religious reforms; the social and civil movements and forms of protest involving mass gatherings and publicity in new media; the rise of a new class of intellectuals; the embedding of the country in international organizations; and global competition. Nepal went its own way and only gradually was an attempt made to join the ever-changing modern world. That it was never colonized and was little exposed to international norms and values until 1951 meant that many unique social, religious, and cultural structures were preserved.

Nepal seemed to have somehow fallen by the wayside of the great wide world,[7] though it had not been pushed aside. As the world started to take notice of it, it continued to maintain its image as a far-distant, quasi-mythical land—at times as a Shangri-La, at other times as the Roof of the World—beyond the bounds of everyday life. Then too, and especially for India, it was the land that had preserved Hinduism pure, as it had not been conquered or even tarnished by the world of Indians, Chinese, or British, of Christians or Muslims. It presented itself as a living fossil, the last Hindu kingdom of the world, safeguarding elements from a time that had elsewhere moved on.

"The Last Hindu Kingdom of the World," or the Quest for Unity

From Pṛthvīnārāyaṇa Śāha's days and well into the twentieth century, all rulers pursued a political (but also a religious) strategy aimed at forming unity. They amplified the heterogeneous nature of the land that would, partly through Hinduization, become Nepal. The dogma of the last Hindu kingdom was used as the guiding principle for creating an identity for the young state. Certainly it was possible to forge a connection to old associations with the Khas-Arya, namely through the Nepālī language as a mother tongue of castes who originally came from India. Many inscriptions confirm that Nepal usually saw itself as a part of Āryāvarta, the holy Hindu subcontinent. At least as early as the fourth century the Kathmandu Valley, and later most other regions of Nepal, were in very close contact with the political, social, cultural, and scholarly world of India. These ties are not really surprising, since they were based to a large extent on the dominant influence of the Brahmins, their rituals, and Sanskrit texts, and the claimed origins of the Śāha and Rāṇā families in Rajasthan.

The close relationship to the southern neighbor, to the "Indosphere,"[8] is clear in Hindu (and in many Buddhist) rituals. These often begin with a ritual resolution, the *saṃkalpa*. Only then is individual religious merit possible. Such a *saṃkalpa* must consequently fulfill certain formal criteria, among them one of a spatial nature. Thus, a Nepalese collection of religious resolutions, the *Saṃkalparatnāvalī* (A Jewelled String of [Religious] Resolutions), published in 1923, contains the following formula for a *saṃkalpa*:

> A sample for the formulation of a *saṃkalpa*: *oṃ tat sat*. Today, in the second (half of the life) of Brahmā, in the Śvetavarāha eon (*kalpa*), in the Vaivaśvata period (*manvantara*), in the 28th *manvantara*, in the Kaliyuga, on the continent of Bhāratavarṣa, in the northern part (of it), in the holy field (*kṣetra*) of Paśupati, in Nepal, which falls within the Āryāvarta region.[9]

This formulaic text illustrates that almost every major Hindu ritual that takes place in Nepal is located by the Brahmin priest in Bhāratavarṣa (India) and that the Paśupatinātha temple is part of Āryāvarta, the holy subcontinent of India. Ruling dynasties intermarried with Indian families, and many advisors were called from India.[10] Nepal was a part of what Indologist Sheldon Pollock has called the hegemonial "Sanskrit-Cosmopolis," which comprised large areas of South, Southeast, and Central Asia from the fifth century on, and in which Brahmanical teachings spread through the medium of Sanskrit.[11] The Gorkhā Rāj, too, as Nepal was usually called under the Śāhas, regarded itself as part of its great southern neighbor. As late as 1951, Prime Minister B. P. Koirala said, at the opening conference of the Nepali National Congress, "Nepal and India are not two countries. . . . Today the political difference you find is basically the game of selfish diplomats and politicians."[12]

Anthropologist David Gellner quite rightly pointed out that Nepal cannot be reduced, as is often said, to the role of interface or cultural contact zone between the Indosphere (India) and the Sinosphere (Tibet/China).[13] Nonetheless the country has certainly acted as a catalyst for the spread of Brahmanical knowledge and, even more so, Buddhist teachings. As early as 1857, it was said in the report on Prince Waldemar von Preussen's journey to Nepal: "Nepal forms the transition from the Hindustanic to the Tibetan peoples, from the followers of Brahma to those of Buddha."[14] Generally, however, except for the few groups that live in the northern frontier regions, Nepal has always orientated itself toward the south, and today even those ethnic groups who live near the northern border increasingly do so too. Journeys to Tibet or the consumption of Tibetan-Chinese television programming, according to David Gellner, are both much less popular even among Sherpa or Tamang than a trip to India or a Hindi film.

This does not mean that Nepal was simply absorbed into India. On the contrary, Nepal has always been proud of its independence. This was reinforced in the eighteenth century by the fact that Nepal could regard itself as an especially hallowed land, as the true India (*asala hindusthāna*) that resisted decadent India (or Mughallana)—as Pṛthvīnārāyaṇa Śāha conveys in the *Divyopadeśa*. Seen from India, Nepal lay in the north, in the Himalaya, where Śiva has his divine seat. The more India was exposed to foreign influences, such as the Muslims, the Christian missionaries, and the Western world, and began to form itself into a secular state, the more Nepal touted itself as the last real Hindu kingdom on earth. Thus, Jaṅga Bahādura Rāṇā stylized himself as the defender of a "true" Hinduism against beef-eating Muslims and Christians. In the *Ain*, Nepal's first code, he emphasized that Nepal was the only country in the world where Brahmins, cows, and women were still protected:

> This is the only Hindu kingdom in the Kali era which has a Hindu king and whose *Ain* bans the killing of cows, women, and Brahmins; with a palace,

> [a location] in the Himalayas (*himavatkhaṇḍa*), the land of Vāsukī (i.e., the king of snakes), a pilgrimage place of Āryas that contains Paśupati's *jyotirliṅga* and the venerable abode (*pīṭha*) of Guhyeśvarī—such a land of merit is our own.[15]

In the end, such a self-image meant that those parts of Nepal that did not follow Hinduism, or did so only in a non-mainstream form, had to be Hinduized. At its core, then, the development of the state amounted more or less to the Brahmanical Hinduization of non-Hindu parts of the population, a process that started as early as the Licchavi and continued up into the Śāha and Rāṇā periods.

However, the Malla, Śāha, and Rāṇā rulers did not only promote and protect Hinduism. In many cases, they also supported Buddhist monasteries, mosques, ascetics, and lamas.[16] The claim to be a Hindu state was ideological, but one that was never put into consistent practice and never proved a fruitful basis for state-building. Nepal has never been and is not today a Hindu state; rather, according to the constitution, it is a secular and, at best, a multireligious state.

"The Garden for All," or Pride in Diversity

The great tale of Nepal united under the single roof of a Hindu kingdom was more a matter of ideological and symbolic appropriation by the ruling classes than the realization of a socio-religious ideal. Brahmins claimed that Buddhists were basically Hindus, while many Buddhists regarded only the Twice-born or upper classes as Hindus. In this way, a group could either inflate its own numbers to form a majority for itself or whittle away at others' to the same end. To be sure, among those brought into the fold under the cloak of such forms of appropriation were many ethnic groups who had adopted many rituals and teachings from both Hinduism and Buddhism and had melded them together. However, the Brahmanically proclaimed religious unity did not take hold in religious practice, especially not in the northern (often Tibetan Buddhist) areas or in the east, where, among others, tribal and shamanistic religions were practiced.

The Hinduization of Nepal, which was to be the harbinger of national unity, thus took place only very gradually and partially. Various religions, traditions, and cultures continued to flourish in the country. From this perspective, Nepal, at least in the eighteenth and nineteenth centuries, was a realm in the sense of an empire rather than a nation state, which is conventionally based on the idea of a common will and a common culture (e.g., a common language and literature)—a notion that in Nepal was introduced and only slowly propagated in the middle of the twentieth century, especially by King Mahendra. Pṛthvīnārāyaṇa built up his realm in an imperial fashion, conquering and repressing many a petty kingdom and principality. Only as a second step did he and his successors attempt the strategy of country-wide Hinduization by, for example, having temples built everywhere throughout the land for their patron deities and promulgating Dasaĩ as a national festival.

Despite Pṛthvīnārāyaṇa's partially successful conquest of petty kingdoms, many small rulers still held sway, especially in remote and rugged parts of the country. At the end of the eighteenth and beginning of the nineteenth century, there were somewhere between forty and fifty such rulers.

Pṛthvīnārāyaṇa attempted to unify this diversity of states under the umbrella of Hinduism, but only at the price of undoing his wish to make his kingdom a "garden for all groups" (*sabai jāta-ko phulabārī*):

> All [those] of this garden, high and low, belonging to the four *varṇas* and thirty-six *jāt* [castes], since it is a pure land of the Hindus, should not abandon the customary religion of [their respective] lineages.[17]

This garden comprised an incredibly rich number of religions, languages, ethnic groups, political systems, and social structures. Basically, he ruled over a patchwork kingdom always on the brink of falling apart.

Nonetheless, it proved possible to develop in a slow and continuous process a consciousness of Nepal as a state existing independently of the ruler of the moment. A feeling of belonging to the same country arose, extending from those living in the mountains, the Pahāḍī, to those living in the lowlands. The struggle against the British and the self-isolation vis-à-vis India and China contributed to the formation of a state identity, even though this unity was repeatedly called into question and no truly strong central government with a strong administrative infrastructure could be formed. The autonomy or indifference displayed by individual regions toward the state largely remained a latent feature of the Śāha and Rāṇā periods, resurfacing from time to time.

The strengthening of (the Hindu) religion during the Śāha and Rāṇā periods did not hinder modernization or the initial steps taken toward equal treatment under the law and state unity. This can be seen above all in the

Ain, which was the product of a feudal system of rule based on the dominance of the Bahun-Chhetri. It codified a measure of legal security, particularly equality before the law, if in rudimentary form, and thus worked to stem the arbitrariness of the feudal system. The theory propounded by Max Weber that modernization requires both the rational demystification of the world and secularization, cannot be confirmed in the case of Nepal, which has remained a thoroughly religious land throughout its process of modernization. Even during a strict lockdown due to Covid-19 measures, the Newar population in Patan persisted in pulling the Matsyendranātha chariot to its destination, risking clashes with the police and army.

Writing a History of Nepal

Given the complex emergence of Nepal as a state and its diversity, how does one write a history of Nepal? Doing so means facing a confusing mixture of far more than a hundred ethnic groups and as many languages; a plethora of religions great and small; places where development of the most modern sort stands opposite backward conditions; a country in which politics are conducted as often between the powers of India, China, and the "West" as in valleys nearly cut off from the world.

Most histories of Nepal follow a chronological orientation vis-à-vis the rulers of Nepal mainly because this is the stance that the written sources take.[18] There is hardly an inscription, colophon, or document that does not mention the current ruler of the time. Clearly it was important to people to record these things. This book is therefore first and foremost a political history too.

However, writing a history of Nepal depends not only on "facts," as the Nepalese chronicles themselves make abundantly clear.[19] These texts became more frequent with the spread of Islam in India and are intended to form a bond with the south, that is, India and the Great Tradition. They hardly distinguish between factual events, legends, genealogies, eulogies, and sagas. Their main purpose is to inflate the significance of the period or the historical persons being described. For example, there are the beginnings and origins, the divine creations, and the appearances of gods or their representatives (Brahmins and kings, both regarded as gods) on earth, or explanations of unusual places (especially where the gods reside) and natural phenomena (rain, earthquakes, etc.).

The *Gopālarājavaṃśāvalī* (Chronicle of the Gopāla Kings) calls itself a "report of events" (*bhūtavṛttānta*), and the Cambridge manuscript of the *Nepālikabhūpavaṃśāvalī* (Chronicle of the Kings of Nepal, commonly known as "Wright Chronicle") begins with a verse that speaks of "various past events" (Skt. *anekapūrvavṛttānta*). But many of these "events" owe more to a religious and literary imagination than to eyewitness accounts. Fact and fiction are not separated within the record of events in indigenous chronicles. The *Nepālikabhūpavaṃśāvalī*, for instance, is primarily a religious text that has been interwoven into the dynastic profile of various royal houses. It mainly has a legitimizing function, in that it highlights the miraculous deeds of the rulers, even though history as an arena of mastering circumstances is represented only to a limited extent in the Hindu chronicles.

These genealogies must therefore be understood as theological in character, bringing together cyclical and linear concepts of as well as Hindu and Buddhist ideas of time. Thus, the Buddhist *yuga* theory in the first chapter of the *Nepālikabhūpavaṃśāvalī*, in which the primordial Buddha (Ādibuddha) as the "savior" triggers the creation of the world (i.e., the Kathmandu Valley, or Nepāla), is based more on linear time, whereas the *yuga* concept of the eras is wholly Hindu and cyclically driven. The chronicle adapts to each of these contexts.

At the same time, the chronicles offer various explanations of the world and of notable places in it. Thus, the beginning of the *Nepālikabhūpavaṃśāvalī* is a Buddhist creation story taken from the *Svayambhūpurāṇa*; the middle part is primarily a Hindu panegyric of the site of that creation; and the last part becomes increasingly political and realistic and can almost be read as a historical narrative of events. These different genres do not exclude but supplement each other. In this way, a legendary account, such as the thousand-year rule of King Dharmadatta (*Nepālikabhūpavaṃśāvalī* 4.54), can be accompanied by precise regnal dates.

There exists, then, in Nepal a multifaceted consciousness of history as expressed in sundry historical writings alongside inscriptions, dated colophons, and coins, which has often been overlooked or downplayed. Even the editors of these texts dismissed the chronicles as sources of historically little value. In showcasing the cultural, social, and political diversity of Nepal and its historical sources, this book therefore contains not one but many entangled histories of various cultural and religious strands. It also investigates a number of key facets, or significant topics, in greater depth and considers them in a *longue durée* and different temporalities.

In this way, this book does not show the history as a one-dimensional, linear chronology, but as a conglomerate of very different interests and appropriation of historical events, which are put together in different forms to make many "ideas of Nepal" possible.[20] The question that arises and runs through this book is: How does Nepal deal with this exceptional diversity?

1
The Country

How did Nepal come to be? And what does "Nepal" actually mean?[1] For a long time it was assumed that the word is composed of the elements *ne* (derived from "Nemuni," the name of the legendary founder of Nepal) and *pāla* ("shepherd"), or that it derives from a Tibeto-Burman language, or else was related to *nevāra* (Newar). Recently, however, Sanskritist Diwakar Acharya has argued that *nepāla* is composed of (Skt.) *nīpa* (the name of a tribe mentioned in Vedic writings) and the (localizing) suffix *-āla*. This designation is also allegedly well documented in various texts with the derived (Prakrit) form *naivāla*. Acharya has thus concluded that the Nipa were the Ārya who migrated into Nepāla before the Licchavi during the first century and gradually became dominant in the Kathmandu Valley.

Regardless of origin and etymology, the first documented occurrence of "Nepal" can be found in an inscription of the Indian king Samudragupta from the fourth century CE. The name also shows up in Licchavi inscriptions—for example, in one from the year 512 CE—and as "Ni-po-lo"[2] in the *Dà Táng Xīyù Jì* (Great Tang Records on the Western Regions) of the Chinese monk Xuanzang (602 or 603–64.). In the Licchavi inscription, it seems to cover the territory between Nuvakot in the west, Dumja in the east, Chapaligaon in the north, and Tistung-Palung in the south, thus an area a little larger than the Kathmandu Valley. Of course, there was no question of a state within its modern boundaries at this point. For a long time "Nepal/Nepāla" referred only to the Kathmandu Valley; Licchavi designations of the country (*nepālarājya, nepālabhukti, nepālamaṇḍala*) refer only to this area. In 1860, the rulers in Nepal began to call their country the "state of Nipal," even though "King of Nepal" and "Rajah of Nipal" had already been used in the Sagauli Treaty with the East India Company, drafted in December 1815 and ratified on March 4, 1816.[3] Officially, though, the term Gorkhā was used not for the entire kingdom until the 1930s.[4]

Nepal. Axel Michaels, Oxford University Press. English language edition © Oxford University Press 2024.
DOI: 10.1093/oso/9780197650936.003.0002

Infrastructure

Nepal developed between the fertile Gangetic plains and the Himalaya (literally "place of snow"), the latter of which accounts for about one-third of the country's surface area.[5] It is thus a mountainous inland area with a singular topography,[6] reaching from 196 feet above sea level in the low-lying area of Kechana Kalan to the top of the highest mountain in the world, Sagarmatha/Chomolungma, better known as Mount Everest. Mountains and the water that flows from them have, therefore, shaped the country's history.

Despite its isolated—and in some parts inaccessible—location, Nepal, especially the Kathmandu Valley, has always been a transit area and a scene of cultural encounters between two large cultural and economic spheres of influence, the Indian and the Tibeto-Chinese cultures and religions. When the passes on the trade routes were open and safe in summer, the trans-Himalayan trade flourished and contributed to the growing wealth of the country. But for a long time, the rugged country favored even small areas of territorial power—petty states and isolated principalities—which, in the absence of a good transport infrastructure, were difficult to unite into what gradually became the present state territory of Nepal.

Nowadays the lowland, called the Tarai or Terai, forms Nepal's breadbasket, accounting for some 70% of its agricultural output. It also contains the largest amount of forested area in the country, where—despite heavy logging—tigers, leopards, elephants, rhinoceros, apes, and hundreds of bird species can still find in some measure an undisturbed biosphere. Above it, the central mountains rise to approximately 8202 feet: first the Siwalik Hills, and then the Mahabharat Range and the Churia-Gati Hills, in many of which fertile valleys lie, including the Kathmandu Valley. Towering above both are the slopes of the High Himalaya including its arid zones, which above 11,811 to 13,123 feet are no longer forested. Depending on the region, the climate may vary from subtropical during the monsoon season to regions practically free of precipitation.

The Tarai and parts of the central mountains tended to be settled more by hunter-gatherers, along with groups practicing slash-and-burn cultivation, who originally had no fixed area of settlement. From the 1950s onwards, when malaria was curbed, a mass migration from the hills to the Tarai took place. People in the central mountains engaged in trade and sedentary agriculture, traditionally on terraced fields with a complex system of irrigation. The Kathmandu Valley is not only a fertile agricultural region, but also a center for handicrafts and trade. In the high mountainous regions, animal husbandry and trade dominate, including trans-Himalayan trade. Some ethnic groups are semi-nomadic, moving to the lower parts of the country with their herds in the cold winter months.

Nepal is a medium-sized country. At 91,454 square miles its surface area is similar to Bangladesh or the state of New York. From east to west, it is on average 550 miles; from the north to the south, 119 miles. Around 27% of the country is agricultural land, 37% forest area, 12% pastureland, 3% water, and the rest frozen terrain or wasteland. Three-quarters of the population works in agriculture. Urbanization is rapidly increasing, but at 17%, the proportion of urban dwellers is still small. Houses in the countryside are generally modestly equipped: a living room and kitchen, sleeping areas, and perhaps a trunk or a cupboard. Less than half have running water, while some 67% have electricity, even if the supply is often interrupted; 64% use wood to cook, a little more than one-fifth use gas imported from India. Twenty-eight percent of houses have a corrugated iron roof, 38% have no toilet. Meanwhile, among the city dwellers 84% have mobile phones, and 23% (compared with 11% of the rural population) a computer.[7]

Only a few trunk roads (*rājamarga*) cross the country, mostly from north to south; they include the Tribhuvan Highway (117 miles), finished in 1956; the Araniko Highway (69 miles); the Mahendra (or East–West) Highway (749 miles); and the B. P. Koirala Highway (127 miles) from Dhulikhel to the eastern Tarai. During monsoon season these roads regularly flood, annually interrupting traffic. In cities, the sides of roads are rarely properly paved, leading to large amounts of dust. There is a railway 24 miles long in the Tarai, planned by Candra Śamśera in 1927 and built by the British, that once connected Raxaul and Amlekhganj before being shut down; and another line of 27 miles built in 1937 connects Janakpur and Jainagar. A transnational railway is planned between India and China, more than 80% of which would be through tunnels, although geologists believe that this is very unlikely to be realized. There are also plans for an express east–west road through the Kathmandu Valley and a similar road down to the Tarai—a much-debated project, as traditional settlements such as Khokana would have to make way for it. The most common means of transport are buses, among them many minibuses. A number of places can only be reached on foot, so that goods must be carried to them.

Nepal has forty-nine airports, but only ten runways are paved with asphalt. The Tribhuvan Airport in Kathmandu is the largest international airport, serving about three hundred international flights per week. It was built on the Gauchar Airport, an airfield on which the first plane landed in 1949, which was inaugurated in 1955 by King Mahendra. The first jet landed in Kathmandu in 1967. A second international airport has been built in the Tarai, and a third one in Pokhara.

Mountains

The Buddha's birthplace in the Tarai and the tall mountains climaxing with Mount Everest at the "top of the world" are Nepal's most notable selling points.[8] The country has over two hundred peaks higher than 6,000 meters (19,685 ft.) Of the fourteen over 8,000 meters (26,246 ft.) in height, eight lie in Nepal, with their crest lines reaching into India or China, so that they can be climbed from there, too. Only Manaslu, Annapurna, and Dhaulagiri lie completely within Nepalese territory.

The difference between above and below is a topologically fundamental one in Nepal. Above are the regions of tall snow- and ice-covered mountains; below—on the plains, in the broad valleys, along the foothills of the Himalaya, or the river basin of the Ganges and Brahmaputra—are the

Table 1.1 First Ascents of the Eight Highest Peaks in Nepal

Mountain	Height (ft.)	First Ascent	Climbers
Annapurna	26,545	June 3, 1950*	Maurice Herzog and Louis Lachenal
Mt. Everest (Chomolungma, Sagarmatha)	29,015	May 29, 1953	Sir Edmund Hillary and Tenzing Norgay
Cho Oyu	26,906	October 19, 1954*	Herbert Tichy, Sepp Jöchler, and Pasang Dawa Lama
Makalu	27,805	May 15, 1955	Jean Couzy and Lionel Terray
Kangchenjunga	28,169	May 25, 1955	George Band and Joe Brown; one day later, Norman Hardie and Anthony Streather
Manaslu	26,781	May 9, 1956	Toshio Imanishi and Gyaltsen Norbu
Lhotse	27,939	May 18, 1956	Fritz Luchsinger and Ernst Reiss
Dhaulagiri	26,794	May 13, 1960*	Kurt Diemberger, Max Eiselin, Ernst Forrer, Albin Schelbert, Nima Dorje, and Nawang Dorje

* without artificial oxygen supplies

fertile agricultural lands. Above is treeless, dry land (unless, as in the case of Mustang, it lies in a rain shadow); below are the forests, the jungles, and the rivers. Above, in summer, are the sparse alpine pastures for sheep, goats, and yaks; below are the rich pastures for cattle. Above one walks and climbs; below one walks and rides animals or vehicles. Above is the fairly egalitarian Tibetan Buddhist culture; below is Indian Hindu culture. Above, Tibeto-Burman languages dominate; below, Indo-European ones. Above are tribal groups and petty kingdoms; below is a hierarchical caste society within republics or large kingdoms.

The conquest of peaks began in earnest in the West with the ascent of Mont Blanc in 1786, and within a century, mountains had become natural cathedrals. Nepal's tall mountains were first climbed for the most part by foreigners, and only from the mid-twentieth century. This had less to do with the natives' lack of opportunity and access routes than with their cultural attitude toward mountains. When the British mountaineer George Mallory, who died attempting to conquer Everest, was asked about his reason for attempting the summit, he gave the famously answer: "Because it's there." A similar answer was elicited in 2011 from the Dalit Giri Bahadur Sunar: "Because no Dalit has ever yet climbed Everest."[9] Earlier it would never have occurred to anyone in the Himalaya to climb Everest (or any other mountain). Indeed, some of the peaks are regarded by those living near them as gods or the seats of gods and thus not to be set foot on; other peaks were simply snow and long remained nameless.

In the early days of mountaineering, the highest Himalayan peaks were approached not from Nepal but from Darjeeling or Tibet. The British, for example, attempted seven times to climb Everest from the north—with no success. On June 3, 1950, Frenchmen Maurice Herzog and Louis Lachenal became the first to ascend one of the highest peaks, Annapurna I. The Sherpa Ang Tharkay was supposed to accompany them to the top, but he begged off: "Thank you very much, *bara sahib* (great lord), but my feet are beginning to freeze; I'd better go down to Camp 4." During descent, Herzog lost all his fingers and toes; Lachenal for his part lost "only" his toes.

The biggest mountaineering attraction was of course Mount Everest, the highest mountain in the world, named in 1865 after the surveyor (Sir) George Everest, leader of the Great Trigonometric Survey of India and surveyor general of India.[10] He had an Indian team measure the mountain in 1848 and, as a result, established the peak's preeminence. In the language of the Sherpa, it is called Chomolungma (after Tibetan *Qomolangma*, Chinese [Mandarin pinyin] *Zhūmùlǎngmǎ*), "Goddess and Mother of the Landscape," while in the 1950s Baburam Acharya invented the Nepālī name Sagaramāthā, "Forehead (or throne) of Heaven" or "brow of the sky." According to recent calculations, officially announced in 2020 in a joint statement by the survey departments of Nepal and China, this mountain rises to 29,031.7 feet above sea level, making it higher than before the earthquake of 2015.

Attempts to ascend the peak began in the first half of the twentieth century, when climbers did so without oxygen. Most were in vain. In 1913, George Ingle Finch surreptitiously searched out a way to Everest through Tibet disguised as a pilgrim. The first expedition, in 1921, only reached the north saddle (23,182 ft.), but a year later, Finch and Charles G. Bruce managed to ascend to 27,493 feet. The legendary third expedition has become a part of mountaineering mythology, for nobody knows whether George Mallory and Andrew Irvine made it to the top or not. They were last seen on the north-east ridge at over 27,887 on June 8, 1924; Irvine was never found, while Mallory's corpse was only discovered in 1999 at 27,887 feet.

Five attempts followed after Mallory and Irvine's until May 29, 1953, at the climax of an ambitious, large-scale expedition, the New Zealander Edmund Hillary and the Sherpa Tenzing Norgay reached the peak. The report was held back a few days, because Hillary wished to make a gift of the news to Queen Elizabeth II on the occasion of her coronation on June 2. A photograph of the occasion shows only Norgay, who allegedly did not know how to use a camera and so could not photograph Hillary.

Clearly the ascent had been quite difficult. While Hillary in his memoirs describes how he pulled Tenzing up the last couple of miles, it was important to Norgay that no distinction be made between guide and guided. Whatever the case may be, the two men remained lifelong friends, and Hillary did a great deal for the Sherpa community during his lifetime.

Both the sensational first ascent of Everest and the first ascent without the aid of oxygen by Reinhold Messner and Peter Habeler on May 8, 1978, were global media events, not least because of Messner's philosophy of mountaineering as a minimalistic, environmentally conscious endeavor in pursuit of knowledge.

While serious mountaineers sought to try out new routes, other climbers aimed at setting new records. These included the youngest to ascend: Jordan Romera, thirteen years old; the oldest to ascend: Yuichiro Miura, eighty years old (the Sherpa Min Bahadur Sherchan, who wanted to recapture the title at the age of eighty-five in 2017, died at the base camp before he could do so); the first women: Pasang Lhamu Sherpa, who reached the summit in 1993, the

Korean Oh Eun-Sun (whose ascent has been contested), and the Spaniard Edurna Pasaban on May 17, 2010); the oldest woman: Tamae Watanabe, at the age of seventy-three; the first complete descent by alpine ski from the peak: Davorin Karničar; the most ascents: the Sherpa climbers Appa, Kami Rita, and Phurba Tashi, twenty-one times each; the fastest ascent: the Sherpa Pemba Dorje in 8 hours 10 minutes; and the first blind mountaineers: Erik Weihenmayer and Andy Holzer. The government in Nepal decided in 2017 not to continue to allow amputees or the blind to climb Everest and other mountains. Solo ascents are no longer permitted either.

The media have played up mountaineering records for all they are worth, leading to a remarkable commercialization of the sport, which in turn has led to a number of problems. The onslaught of would-be climbers since the 1980s, especially those wishing to ascend Everest, has reached a point that is now nearly impossible to control, owing to logistics and the proliferation of rubbish. By 1979, barely one hundred people had reached the peak; by June 2016, thanks to improvements in equipment, the number had jumped to 4,469. Up through 1979, some 282 people had died on Everest, of whom 114 were Sherpa; the death rate has, however, gone down since the 2000s to 1.7%. Journalist-chronicler Elizabeth Hawley recorded 794 fatal accidents on Everest up to 2005: 274 people were caught in avalanches, 263 fell to their death, and the rest died of lung and brain edemas, exhaustion, freezing, or falling rocks.[11]

Numerous films about Everest play on the risk of death in their titles. The first film, shot from an airplane by Geoffrey Barkas and Ivor Montagu and released in June 1934, had the innocuous title *Wings over Everest*, but the film triggered fears in Nepal that the flight had been responsible for the earthquake of that same year. Subsequent movie titles were more dramatic: Robert Markowitz's *Into Thin Air: Death on Everest* (1997), Reinhold Messner's and Peter Habeler's *Mount Everest—Death Zone* (2002), Barny Revill's *Everest: Beyond the Limit* (2006–7), and Victor Grandits's and Jessica Krauß' *Mount Everest—Der Friedhof meiner Freunde* (*Mount Everest—Graveyard of My Friends*, 2007).

Earthquakes

The tall mountains, impressive and a climbing challenge though they are, pose two major problems: earthquakes and water supply. The Himalayan mountain range is constantly being created by massive tectonic shifts, in the course of which the Indian Plate is pushing northward at a rate of 1.77165 inch per year, while being subducted under the much larger Eurasian Plate.[12] This has caused the Himalaya to attain its present heights within the last two million years alone. Even with an assumed rate of growth of only 0.79 inch per year, Kathmandu sat at an altitude of only 984 feet some 500,000 years ago. Plate movements of this kind, in which the rate of rise and the rate of erosion work against each other, occur under such extreme pressure that the stored tension must be released at some point. The earthquake of 2015 pushed Kathmandu around 5 feet to the south and raised it around 3.2 feet higher. Even Mount Everest was displaced by 1.18 inch toward the southwest.

This slow process never stops and leads to repeated strong earthquakes, the last ones having taken place in Nepal on April 25 and May 12, 2015. Before these, ten quakes with a magnitude greater than 7.3 on the Richter scale have occurred since 1255, most of them claiming several thousand victims. These numbers are to a certain extent estimates, since an exact measurement system has only existed since 1935, when Charles Francis Richter developed his scale. In Nepal, it is said that the country is rocked by an earthquake every hundred years. This rings true if based on the dates of heavy earthquakes: April and May 2015; January 15, 1934; August 28, 1917; August 26, 1833; July 1768; January 1681; June 1505; August 1408; and June 7, 1255.[13]

In 2015, the first earthquake reached 7.8 on the Richter scale and caused some 9,000 deaths; the second quake, at 7.2 on the Richter scale, claimed 150 more. Altogether, some 22,000 people were injured. Approximately 600,000 residences, schools, and over thirty World Cultural Heritage sites were almost completely destroyed.

Help was on the way relatively quickly, as many donations were gathered after the media reported the disaster. Immediately after the earthquake, the Indian government sent several aircraft with food, water, and rescue gear. In total, some three hundred aid organizations were involved. The donations promised by governments, not all of which materialized, climbed into the millions, in addition to private contributions never officially documented.

Despite the considerable volume of donations, only a small portion actually reached those affected, especially in the days immediately following the earthquakes, mainly due to logistical problems. For example, there were far too few helicopters, and only incomplete plans for emergency relief operations. Border problems with India posed further difficulties. Setting up

(a)

(b)

Figure 1.1(a) and (b) The Cāranārāyaṇa temple in Patan before and after the 2015 earthquake. Photos by Raju Roka.

the National Emergency Operation Centre and the Prime Minister's Disaster Relief Fund were lengthy processes, and reports of corruption and mismanagement accumulated.

After a year and much infighting among the political parties, the National Reconstruction Authority (NRA) was established and began by offering initially ₨ 30,000 for damage with proven cases of death, ₨ 15,000 for completely destroyed houses, ₨ 3,000 for damaged houses, and ₨ 10,000 by way of winter help. Later, those whose houses had been destroyed received on average ₨ 300,000. A Nepal Rural Housing Reconstruction Program was eventually set up. However, serious problems soon developed. First, the damage had to be estimated and eligibility cards had to be issued to the earthquake's victims. Then, paying out the money quickly proved problematic owing to the infrequency of bank accounts; many in the more remote regions had to undergo costly days-long treks to get payments and found long lines on their arrival. Most importantly, however, there was far too little financial support for the victims and too few qualified workers and craftsmen.

How did Nepalese in earlier eras deal with these traumatic experiences? How did they explain such disasters? When Lisbon was struck by a massive earthquake and subsequent tsunami in 1755, the catastrophe cast doubt on the Enlightenment's belief in progress, and theologians, too, were at a loss to explain it. Have there been similar reactions in Nepal?

The historical and textual material in Nepal available to help answer this question essentially comprises four categories: mythological texts, astrological texts, chronicles, and official documents. The encyclopedic *Bṛhatsaṃhitā* by the Indian scholar Varāhamihira (505–587) gathered together explanations for earthquakes. According to this text, huge animals, such as a monstrous tortoise that carries the Earth, winds that fight each other and then fall onto the Earth, the sins of humanity, unfavorable constellations of stars, and angry gods or demons are among the causes of earthquakes. Varāhamihira even developed his own seismology, which included a typology of earthquakes according to time of day, presiding divinity, constellation, prognoses for the week prior to an earthquake, effects on the population, the areas affected, and the duration.

But these texts are too general in nature to explain a particular event, as are the Nepalese chronicles, even if they more precisely recorded the events. For June 7, 1255, the *Gopālarājavaṃśāvalī*, which contains the earliest record of an earthquake in Nepal, notes:

> A gigantic earthquake took place on Monday, the third day of the waxing moon of the month Āṣāḍha in the year (NS) 375 . . . . The people had to leave their homes and live outside for a fortnight to a month. Many temples and houses collapsed during the honorable reign of (King) Abhaya Malladeva. A third of the population, beginning with the king, died.[14]

The *Nepālikabhūpavaṃśāvalī* lists, in addition, seven smaller earthquakes beginning in 1308. Apart from a couple of astronomical indicators, however, the chronicles simply report the earthquakes, briefly and without interpretation.

The first extensive report of an earthquake is from 1934, written by General Brahma Shamsher Janga Bahadura Rana. According to it, that earthquake measured 8.5 on the Richter scale, caused 8,519 deaths, and destroyed 207,704 houses. Aftershocks supposedly occurred for months afterward. The book offers statistics and reports on aid measures, voluntary help, strict punishment of plunderers, and the establishment of an assistance fund by the prime minister, into which he himself paid ₨ 300,000 and the queen contributed another Rs 100,000. Prime Minister Juddha Shamsher and King Tribhuvan survived, but two princesses did not. Communications were difficult and information nearly impossible to get. For days nothing could be reported, and news of the extent of the disaster was only heard from many mountain regions ten or more days later. Foreign help was firmly refused.[15]

The reasons the general gave are informative. Astrologers supposedly predicted it. Alternatively, the myth of an animal (in this case a snake or a fish) carrying the earth was brought into play, with the added factor that the increase of sinfulness among people on earth had made it too heavy for the animal. Some claimed that the foreigner flying over Mount Everest had triggered the earthquake. All in all, a doomsday mood prevailed. People dressed up in their finery, thinking that the end of the world was approaching.

Forces were of course mobilized to deal with the catastrophe. The prime minister promised to permit only one-story buildings and recommended building roofs out of flattened metal canisters, with no pillars and few windows. Foreign geologists were brought in from Kolkata and questioned. At the time, they knew little of the theory of plate tectonics, but they did advise the government to start using concrete in building. At the time, it was thought that reconstruction would take only five to seven years; it took much longer, and some monuments have still not been repaired.

This first historical report by General Brahma Shamsher does not reveal much about native explanations for earthquakes. This same is true of many historical documents, in which the material demands of victims make up most of the content.

Water Resources

Nepal's most important natural resource is water, with the country having one of the largest water reserves in the world. Among these is primarily the "Place of (eternal) Snow," the literal meaning of Himalaya, along with great quantities of rain water. There are an estimated 6,000 rivers and tributaries with a total length of some 28,000 miles. This Himalaya water flows through the Ganges-Brahmaputra system into the Bay of Bengal, or through the Indus system into the Arabian Sea.

This wealth of water could be one of the biggest generators of revenue for Nepal, given its necessity for hydroelectric energy, and thus for the export of electricity. However, the constantly repeated idea that Nepal has more water available than India is erroneous. The mountains store very little (and because of the climate crisis increasingly less) meltwater, so the large rivers to the south are full, but in villages on either side of them there is often a lack of water. Based on hundreds of thousands of satellite images, an international group of researchers has calculated that the glaciers in the Himalaya are melting twice as fast as before the turn of the millennium. This has devastating consequences for 1.6 billion people south of the Hindu Kush and the Himalaya.[16]

It is India above all that profits from Nepal's water. Seventy percent of the water in the Ganges in the dry season and 40% in the monsoon season comes from Nepal. With one-quarter of the population of India dependent on the Ganges, the water is needed to ensure irrigation and thus sufficient food for North India. Of course, India and Nepal have different interests: while India is interested in maintaining a constant supply, Nepal would like to build reservoirs and use the water to generate electricity to sell to India.

Not surprisingly, disputes arose relatively early over Nepal's wealth of water. Many Nepalese concluded that India was taking unfair advantage of Nepal in their treaties and agreements. Indeed, in 1927 India started building water reservoirs on the border to Nepal primarily for its own benefit. The Tanakpur Reservoir above all, built at the end of the 1980s, has led to considerable political turbulence since it was constructed, according to a secret convention, to a large extent on Nepalese territory. This agreement led to Nepal giving up water for free and having to pay to import electricity. Protests followed, with the Maoist rebels in particular repeatedly blaming the governments of Nepal for selling out.

Even before recent confrontations over some rivers having become open sewers, water has led to disputes throughout the history of Nepal. There was either too much water (the monsoon) and hence destructive landslips and floods, or too little (in the other months), so that droughts and even famines occurred. Nepal, then, has always depended on the wise and predictable regulation of water. Disputes over the irrigation of rice fields or over the lack of potable water and proper sewage systems are nothing new.[17]

In traditional Nepal, one counted primarily on the rain-giving deities and semi-deities, such as those living in the underworld, in lakes, or in springs—including snakes or serpents (*nāga*). The beginning of the monsoon after a hot, dry early summer was always a blessing. Indeed, with the heavy rains the vegetation changes nearly overnight. Everything becomes greener and more colorful, flowers bloom, drooping leaves and branches regain their shape, dry riverbeds become torrents, and everywhere frogs croak. Still, a monsoon that begins too early or too late, or comes on too strongly, can have disastrous consequences.

This anxiety about water is demonstrated in literature, art, and architecture, in myths and in rituals. The serpents play a central role in all of this. Regarded as water animals in the chronicles and other texts, they are considered protectors of the waters—in Classical Sanskrit it is always a plural, "waters" (*āpas*)—and have to be venerated and pacified. If this was not done, drought could be the consequence. The creation in myth of Nepāla, of the Kathmandu Valley, is owed to the serpents, for there, in mythical times, was a lake, the Kālīhrada (Lake of Kālī) or Nāgavāsa ("residence of serpents"), which was ruled by the serpents and their king, Karkoṭaka. When Mañjuśrī slashed the southeast mountain range with his sword, letting the waters drain off near Kotwal, the serpents were in peril. According to the *Svayambhūpurāṇa* and the chronicles, they were left with only scattered lakes and ponds, Taudaha ("serpent") Lake near Chobhar in particular, where the inhabitants built an underwater palace for Karkoṭaka. The place became a popular pilgrimage destination.

Such myths reflect people's fears of too much or too little rain. This is exemplified in what is told about the Bāhrabarṣa Ināra (Twelve-Year Well), in Musum Bāhāḥ, Kathmandu. According to legend, King Guṇakāmadeva spent twelve years there during a drought digging in order to reach the nether world, down to the serpent king Karkoṭaka. He was helped by the Tantric priest Śāntikara, who lived in a cave near the Svayambhū Stūpa. When they reached the bottom and Karkoṭaka appeared, the king and his priest sang 108 hymns in his honor. The serpent king was so overjoyed that he promised always to send rain when people sang him these songs. Thereupon Guṇakāmadeva had a shrine for Karkoṭaka—Nāgapura or Vāsīgāḥ--built on Svayambhū Hill close to Amoghasiddhi, who himself sits upon a serpent. A large mural in the Śāntipura temple, destroyed in the 2015 earthquakes, showed scenes from this myth. The unique form of serpent veneration is also reflected in the myth that the first waters sprang from Viṣṇu's navel, as imposingly expressed by the "Viṣṇu Sleeping on the Water" (Jalaśayana), also known as the "Viṣṇu Resting on a Serpent" (Śeṣanārāyaṇa), in Budhanilakantha.

Many rituals are dedicated, directly or indirectly, to serpents. Many occasions are highly visible, as on Nāgapañcamī, the "snake Fifth" of the month of Śrāvaṇa in the rainy season, when serpents are honored with milk and sweets, and paper images of them are displayed on house entrances. Snakes must have their portion, too, every time a house is built. On Sithinakha, the sixth day of the month of Jyeṣṭha, fountains and watering places are cleaned and honored, with snakes again receiving their due. On Janaipūrṇimā a metal sheath embossed with snakes is put over the *liṅga* at Patan's Kumbheśvara temple, which was built in 1392 and renovated in 1809; named "Lord of the Water Jar," this temple expresses its affinity with water and has an assumed underground connection to the holy lake of Gosainkund, so that believers can acquire religious merit by bathing in the water basin of Kumbheśvara without making a pilgrimage to the lake.

The Newar festival calendar as a whole is orientated toward the cultivation of rice, which depends on water, from the first sowing on Jyā Punhī (the full moon of the month of Āṣāḍha) and the planting of seedlings to the beginning of the harvest during Dasaĩ and its end on Lakṣmīcaturdaśī (Lakṣmī's Fourteenth) in the month of Kārttika. When Newar peasants honor frogs with rice and beans at the corners of a field and bury a frog figure of clay, during the monsoon on the fifteenth day of the bright half of the month of Śrāvaṇa, this connection between rain water and fertility becomes even clearer.

As snakes live in the underworld, they are regarded as animals that bring or protect wealth and jewels. Consequently, they are often shown with jewels. The *nāga* are rainmakers. This is what is exactly expressed during the

Rāto-Matsyendranātha festival, for according to legend Gorakhanātha sat meditating on serpents, resulting in a drought that lasted twelve years. It only rained again when he was induced to get up by a trick played by his teacher Matsyendranātha. At the climax of the chariot procession, which takes weeks, a small black shirt (*bhoṭo*)—a gift of the serpent king Karkoṭaka to a helper (Vaidya) for making his wife well again—is held up in public. On this day, it is believed, there must be rain.

Especially important, and hence meticulously decorated, are the many access points to water in Nepal: the steps down to rivers (*ghāṭa*), the water tanks (*kuṇḍa*, Nev. *pukhū*), the drinking water tanks (Nev. *jarūhiti*), the old draw wells (Nev. *tun*), or the step wells (*dhārā*, Nev. *hiti*) with crocodile-like water spouts (*makara*). These last are hybrid mythical creatures with the mouth of a crocodile or gavial and often are depicted with a snout rolled upward. This architecture is testimony to the significance of water as Nepal's most important natural resource.[18] The architecture exploits this wealth and the promise of fertility embodied by the connection between water and snakes. Thus, serpents embellish many temple entrances and tympana as door guards (Skt. *dvārapāla*), often in association with Garuḍa, who keeps the *nāga* under control by holding them in his mouth or claws.

Snakes above all serve as protective guards and givers of water in water architecture. For example, the hood of the world serpent Ananta protects the king on his throne, as can be seen in an example from the year 1666 in the Patan Museum; on the high column of Yoganarendra Malla at the city's Darbar Square; on ubiquitous oil lamps (Nev. *sukundā*); or in representations of the meditating Buddha being shielded by the serpent king Mucalinda. Friezes around temples or fountains display this motif, as at the "golden spout" (*sūndhāra*) in Bhaktapur constructed by Jagajjyotir Malla, and on many sculptures of *nāga* and aquatic figures (Skt. *jalamānuṣa*).

One element of water architecture consists of the serpent poles (*nāgakaṣṭha*) with stylized cobra heads in the middle of some pond—for instance, at Nāga Pokharī in Naxal (Kathmandu)—or the open step wells (*hiti*, *hitimaṅga*), such as Tusāhiti (Royal Bath) in Patan (enhanced by a statue of the king of the serpents, Nāgarāja) or, a few steps to the north, Maṇihiti. Among the oldest such step wells is this same Maṇihiti, incorporating fragments from the sixth century; one built in 1652 by Pratāpa Malla in the Mohanacuka of the old palace in Kathmandu; and the twelfth-century Lūhiti at Taumadhi Square in Bhaktapur. In step wells, the water generally flows from the mouths of *makara* waterspouts, of which there are fragments from the Licchavi Period, mainly from the seventeenth century. Their water serves religious as well as everyday purposes, for ritual baths are indispensable in the lives of Hindus and Buddhists. Such ablutions may be more or less symbolic, as when a priest or a believer lets a little water dribble over his head, but they may also involve bathing the entire body in step wells, rivers, or specially made ponds or tanks. The most prominent of such tanks is the Rānī Pokharī (Queen's Lake) in Kathmandu. Built around 1670 by Pratāpa Malla or perhaps by his wife, it receives water, as an inscription proclaims, from fifty-one *tīrtha*. It is said that Pratāpa Malla had the rectangular basin built to comfort his wife on the early death of her son Cakravartendra Malla, to commemorate and honor him in a shrine built in the middle.

Forests and Holy Trees

Around 5.5 million hectares, 35% of the area of Nepal, is dense forest. Tropical hardwood trees, such as *sāla* and various kinds of acacia, grow especially in the southern Himalayan foothills; in the central regions, pines and rhododendron come into the mix. The tree line lies between 1.8 and 2.4 miles.

The wood of felled trees is an important commodity, it is being used for firewood and house construction.[19] Many smaller trees, though, supply animal fodder. Large-scale logging was already being carried out in the Tarai during the Rāṇā Period and between 1950 and 1980. Because the technical equipment was not very good, most trees were felled with handsaws or axes, and the transport of larger ones had to be done with elephants, logging operations were mainly kept within bounds.

In addition, in the course of the nineteenth century a consciousness of the need to protect forests did develop, if mostly for commercial reasons. Thus, the *Ain*, which dedicates all of Article 32 ("On Cutting Trees") to logging and forestry, prohibits branches from being chopped off or trees being felled on someone else's land. Trees along roads, at springs, or beside water channels were also safeguarded. The sale of timber for personal benefit was prohibited since all land belonged to the state. Although wood could be collected without permission on rented land for building a house or creating a garden, it was forbidden to cut down a single tree in the Tarai between the Mahakali and Mechi rivers. In cases of violations, the timber was confiscated and the offender punished; the magnitude of the sentence depended on the category of land. The sale of timber was the responsibility of a single office, the

Kāṭhamahala (Timber Storehouse). In 1885, Prime Minister Vīra Śamśera issued further prohibitions, such as forbidding the setting of traps, hunting, or pasturing animals in forests, and collecting forest fruits. He relied upon special guards, some mounted on elephants, to ensure compliance.

Protection was also given to shade trees in villages, to forests near watering places or beneath possible landslides, and to holy trees, of which there are several in Nepal.[20] One such tree is the fig tree (Skt. *nyagrodha*, *Ficus bengalensis* Linn.), better known as the banyan tree. Owing to the belief that promises made under a banyan tree are indissoluble, it was a favored meeting place for merchants (Hindī *banyan*) to finalize business deals. The *nīm* tree (*Azadirachta indica* Linn.) has a special purifying function during the death ritual. The leaves of the pipal tree (*Ficus religiosa* Linn.) symbolize the Hindu trinity of Brahmā, Viṣṇu, and Śiva. The leaves of the bel tree (Skt. *bilva*, *Aegle marmelos* Linn.) are often attached to form sacrificial plates for rituals. The robust *sāla* tree (*Shorea robusta* Gaertn.) is used for the construction of wooden temples and for famed wood carvings. The nuts of the *rudrākṣa* tree (*Elaeocarpus sphaericus* or *granitus* Gaertn.), also known as the wood apple tree, are an absolute necessity in many Śaiva rituals and a popular gift to temples.

The usefulness of such holy trees works to weaken inhibitions against cutting them down.[21] General prohibitions against exploiting holy trees are decidedly rare. Something else must be present for a holy tree to be protected, such as a special occurrence, the tree's location, or an extreme degree of growth. Anyone who cuts down such a tree or injures it commits sacrilege. If holy trees are used as poles or branches in rituals—as in the Bisketjātrā in Bhaktapur, in the Indrajātrā festival in Kathmandu, and in the Triśūlajātrā in Deopatan near Kathmandu—then there is nothing to prevent them being felled.

There was no notion in Nepal until the mid-eighteenth century of holy forests being well-defined areas. But there was the idea of leaving certain areas mostly untouched for religious reasons or populating them with trees. Such areas are then occasionally called in Nepālī *dhārmika bana* (religious forest). Their size rarely exceeded 10 acres, and they were generally under the control of foresters, priests, religious organizations, or the state. Thus, a 1905 document orders that trees are not to be felled in such forests.[22] District officials, too, had to inquire at the palace first if they wished to fell any trees. Indeed, there are many documents seeking permission to fell trees for various purposes, such as building bridges or temples. Such permission was quite often refused. In 1803, for instance, Gīrvāṇayuddha Śāha retracted the right, originally granted by Pṛthvīnārāyaṇa, to collect firewood for a Devīnārāyaṇa festival.[23]

Religious woods or groves are either temple areas, such as the Mṛgasthalī (Gazelle Grove) at the Paśupatinātha temple, or gardens of the aristocracy. A document of Gīrvāṇayuddha Śāha from the year 1815 exemplifies this special form of forest protection. In it he orders the main priest of the Paśupatinātha temple to take only wood in the form of old and fallen branches for activities in the temple. Even in cases of widow burning, no branches were to be cut from trees. If there was an urgent and unavoidable need to do so, the work was to be carried out by legitimate loggers. Those who violated forest regulations, whether by force or acts of thievery, were to be punished. In this way, the priest was to be given the wherewithal to let the forest grow back again and protect it.

The document hardly revealed any knowledge of ecological processes so why did the king instruct the main priest of the national shrine to protect the trees? To answer this question, a second document is helpful. In 1847, King Surendra Śāha, the grandson of Gīrvāṇayuddha, wrote to his subjects that earlier kings had consulted with both native and foreign learned Brahmins to establish, with proof from textbooks, that all the trees in the woods around the Paśupatinātha temple were seers (*ṛṣi*) and wise men (*muni*). Whoever felled them would be committing a great sin. Not a piece of wood the size of a bamboo sliver was to be cut from them for firewood. Surendra emphasized again his grandfather's regulations and additionally ordered that a committee consisting of a forest inspector, a leading official, and a logger should be formed, which was to report to the prime minister regularly. The letter closes with the instruction to determine the largest quantity of wood permitted for the Paśupatinātha temple and other shrines, and for certain festivals as well.[24]

This document openly states that the forest must be protected because it is holy; it is holy because the trees themselves are holy beings. The reason for this is mythological. The woods must remain untouched, because one foundation myth of the temple has Śiva and Pārvatī, in the form of a gazelle buck and doe, retreating to its future site for a thousand-year coitus; when the god was discovered by other gods in the midst of this, he sprang to the other side of the Bagmati River, where the temple of the "Lord of the Animals" (Paśupati) was later erected.

It is typical of Indian and other religions to believe that trees are inhabited by spirits or ghosts, are seats of the gods, and that plants are to be regarded as immovable living things to which the pious, and especially the ascetic, must afford special protection. The Śāha documents, however, make it clear that no person was permitted to use any tree in the forest specified in them. According to the documents, the trees, like ascetics or holy men, are sacred, and are thus protected, even against being used for *sati*, supposedly a particularly meritorious kind of self-sacrifice. The resolution of the king of Nepal, then, stems from protecting the holiness of a temple area, not from ecological awareness.

2
The Population

Nepal's diversity can be observed in the unusually wide spectrum of ethnic groups and their cultures, social structures, languages, and religions. In 2021, around thirty million people are living in Nepal in 6.6 million households with an average size of 4.37 members. Around 400,000 people are added annually. The population density was, on average, nearly 198 persons per square kilometer, and highest in the Kathmandu valley at 301.[1]

The population groups in Nepal are now generally categorized as follows:

Bahun-Chhetri (according to the census of 2021: approx. 30%):[2] Indo-Nepalese group, also called Indo-Parbatiyā by foreigners or, officially since 1990, Khasa-Arya; e.g., Bahun (Hill Brahmins, the caste of priests and scholars), Thakuri, Khasa/Chhetri (from Skt. *kṣatriya*, originally the warrior class), and Sannyasi. These castes share many similarities in rituals and festivals, mostly speak Indo-Aryan languages (Nepālī, Hindī, or Bhojapurī), came originally in certain cases from India, and have settled for the most part in the Tarai and hill regions.

Janajati (approx. 30%): Ethnic groups speaking mostly Tibeto-Burman languages, such as Magar, Tamang, Rai, Gurung, Limbu, Chepang, Sunuvar, Thakali, and Thami; most live in the central belt. Hill Janajati are distinguished from Tarai Janajati (e.g., the Tharu). Among the Tibetan-influenced groups living in the high mountain regions are the Sherpa, Lopa, Humli, and Tsum. The Newar are included in the official list of Janajati, but other Janajati do not regard them as such because generally they are well off, are not oppressed, are relatively well represented in state jobs, and have an internal caste hierarchy.

Newar (approx. 5%): This is also a Tibeto-Burman-speaking population, which is listed here separately because of its historical importance and influential presence in the Kathmandu Valley, although it is sometimes counted among the Janajati.

Madhesi (approx. 25%): Groups living in the Tarai and speaking languages close to Hindī. The term "Madhesi" or "Madheshi" (from Skt.

Nepal. Axel Michaels, Oxford University Press. English language edition © Oxford University Press 2024.
DOI: 10.1093/oso/9780197650936.003.0003

madhyadeśa) has been in use since the 1950s and also designates Indians. It takes in many different groups, including Madhesi Janajati, but especially the Tharu, Danuvar, Dhimal, and Rajbanshi; individual castes such as the "twice-born" Brahmins, Rajput, Kayastha, and Baniya; and middle or lower-middle castes, such as Yadav; there are also Madhesi Dalits.

Others (approx. 5%): Groups with a special status, such as Tibetan refugees (called Bhote or Bhotiya), Muslims, Sikhs, or foreigners who are more or less permanent residents of Nepal.

Dalit (approx. 13%): Numerous "unclean" castes, which partly fall under the above-mentioned categories, set apart from one another according to profession; e.g., launderers (Dhobi), tanners and leatherworkers (Sarki, Chamar), and metalsmiths (Kami). For these castes the term Untouchable is used or the designation "Dalit," which in Nepal has been in use since the 1990s.[3]

The designations for social groups are, in general, originally castes that once correlated with a profession or are regional ethnic groups. The castes may, however, have acquired new names, such as Nepali, Kirata, or Sangam, which often blur their social or regional origins. In individual cases, such as the Newar or Tharu, the names comprise multiple castes.

Except in districts in far-western Nepal, Nepālī-speaking Brahmins, Thakuri, and Chhetri do not form the majority of the population, but since the other groups rarely form a political unit, they constitute a dominant minority and are able to determine how the country will be run to a great extent.

According to the census of 2021, the Chhetri form the largest caste group (16.45%), followed by the Brahmins of the Middle Hills (11.29%), the Magar (6.9%), Tharu (6.2%), Tamang (5.32%), Kami/Vishwakarma (5.08%), Muslims (4.86%), Newar (4.3%), Yadav (4.29%), and Rai (2.2%). However, these censuses are always to be taken with a grain of salt. In the *Nepālika-bhūpavaṃśāvalī* and other texts of the nineteenth century, 64 castes are listed. In 1966, one researcher counted 26 castes among the Newar alone; in the census of 1991, 60 castes and ethnic groups were counted, and in the Census 2021 it was already 142.[4] This disparity is the result of occupational changes and migration, and also of changes in claimed status. Altogether, then, the country is one of ethnic diversity, in which the Bahun-Chhetri form the largest and the Newar perhaps the most influential group.[5] The identity of people is orientated toward their caste (*jāt/jāti*), region (*deśa*), religion, and social status.

The Nepal Federation of Indigenous Nationalities (NEFIN), founded in 2003, listed fifty-nine Janajati in 2004, dividing them into ten endangered groups, twelve highly marginalized, twenty marginalized, and fifteen disadvantaged; two more developed groups, the Newar and the Thakali, were counted among the latter. Hardly anything has changed since, although the political representation of the Janajati in the parliaments after 1991 is not reflective of any particular discrimination against them, measured against their proportion of the population.

Migration

Where exactly the various groups came from is often very difficult to say and is much debated.[6] Linguistic relationships and myths or legends do provide some clues, however. The earliest settlers in Nepal were probably gatherers and hunters like the Kusunda, Raute, Tharu, or Santhali; all of these speak languages outside the Indo-Aryan or Tibeto-Burman language families.

The Tibeto-Burman languages spoken by some groups (e.g., Tamang, Gurung, Sherpa, or Magar) are an indication of these groups having come in from the north—the Magar, for instance, during the seventh to eighth century, and others much later (the Sherpa, for one, less than five centuries ago), although these groups often claim an early resettling in their oral traditions.[7]

The origins of the Newar are also uncertain, but it is now generally accepted that Newar society evolved before the Licchavi Period.[8] A derivation from the (South) Indian Nayar, sometimes proposed, is improbable, even if this group formed the greater part of the Chalukya army in North India. The Nevārī language first appears in writing in 1173 CE; the term "Newar," which is supposed to mean inhabitant of the Kathmandu Valley is not found in an inscription until 1654, but researchers have speculated that the Newar arrived much earlier in the Kathmandu Valley from the northern or eastern regions of the Himalaya, or that they are Austroasians who were later assimilated by the Kirāta.[9] Although Kirāta influence on the early inhabitants of the Kathmandu Valley is probable, the relationship of the Kirāta to the Licchavi and the Newar remains unclear, since too little is known of their language, their way of life, their society, and their religion. The Kirāti languages and Nevārī are at any rate very different.

Most other groups came at some time from the south or the west. The Bahun-Chhetri or Thakuri mostly arrived from the plains in India, sometimes claiming in their genealogies descent from prestigious Rajput families in Rajasthan. Dor Bahadur Bista, who traveled extensively through Nepal, writes, however: "In all my research I have been unable to discover any genuine evidence that any Thakuri (aristocratic) family has its origins in India."[10] He points out that the clan and tutelary deities of the Śāha Thakuri are "worshipped and cared for exclusively by Magars—by Brahmanic standards a polluted low caste ethnic group."[11]

The role of "Indian" Brahmins in bringing the Hindu caste system to Nepal has also been overstated. Although they spread all over the country, except for Mustang, they could not win over the majority of the population, who did not readily accept their purity and pollution norms. Only the powerful Jaṅga Bahādura Rāṇā managed to impose a caste structure on the country, one that turned many professions into impure alcohol-consuming castes, taking water from whom was not allowed. At the same time, the visible emblem of the higher Hindu castes was the Sacred Thread (*janeu*, *janai*), which is received during their initiation and then hangs for the rest of their lives above the left shoulder and under the right arm. One result of this increasingly dominant influence of the Bahun-Chhetri was a growing emphasis on the ethnicity of groups who did not benefit from this structure.

The situation in the west of Nepal is unique. Many Brahmins and other castes arriving there from India in the twelfth century in flight from the Muslims found the Khasa, who were also caste Hindus, although they were regarded by the Brahmins as being of lower status. This was particularly true of the so-called Matwali ("alcohol-drinking") Chhetri who were not accorded the status of other Chhetri despite wearing the Sacred Thread.

It has been conjectured that, probably already during the fifth century, the Khasa in western Nepal came not from the south but from the north, where they encountered Pahāḍī who, for their part, had come from Bengal. Prior to the Khasa, the Bengali Pāla dynasty had ruled much of the area in question. In the ninth or tenth century, the Khasa reached the Karnali Basin and the Brahmins and Chhetri (or Rajputs) there. They have influenced these groups more than the Tibeto-Burmese communities have and, in the process, probably contributed to Nepal's unique caste system, whose impulse is to integrate rather than exclude tribal groups from the hierarchical Brahmanical caste structure.[12] In the *Ain*, however, the Khasa became a population group among others within the Gorkha kingdom and are counted as alcohol drinkers. It is not entirely clear how this loss of status came about.

The history of (im)migration in Nepal thus shows that people populated the country from the north and south, those coming from the south or west probably arriving earlier and in greater numbers. Even today the border to India is permeable, while access to Tibet is more difficult due to the high mountains with few passes.

The majority of the population in the Tarai by contrast has been there since ancient times. Its population, too, is composed of high-caste Hindus, who deliberately distance themselves from the mountain dwellers as well as from Muslims and the Tharu (an ethnic group with several endogamous subgroups).

As the Kathmandu Valley became a political and economic center from the Licchavi Period onward, and especially under Malla rule, it drew migrants to it. Within the last few decades this has led to exploding urbanization. The Newar, the originally dominant population, have somewhat lost political ground as a result. Still, they have been able to maintain themselves in numerous sectors of cultural, economic, and political life thanks to a stable social system and a relatively high standard of education.

Compulsory labor in some parts of Nepal led to peasants leaving their land and starting new lives elsewhere, whether in Nepal or abroad. These people were among the first migrant laborers.[13] Already in 1872, Nepalese made up the majority of the population in Darjeeling. By the end of the nineteenth century, they formed the majority in Sikkim, too, and many settled in southern Bhutan, in addition to numerous Nepalese laborers in India and the Gorkha soldiers recruited for the First and Second World Wars. By 2019, an estimated five million Nepalese were working abroad in 2019, around half in India, and the rest in Saudi Arabia, Qatar, the United Arab Emirates, Kuwait, and Malaysia. Every year around 600,000 young Nepalese leave their country and return with new socio-cultural values. Every third household has a member who works in a foreign country. Still, the money earned by migrant laborers represents, alongside tourism, Nepal's biggest source of revenue. In 2013/14, thanks to their money transfers, migrant labor contributed nearly 30% to the GDP.

Due to geographical conditions, there has always been migrant labor in Nepal. There have always been many population groups in Nepal with members on the move to earn something for their families: semi-nomads from the high mountains to the valleys, traders shuttling between India and

China, watchmen in India, mercenaries or guards, pilgrims or monks, land laborers or tea pickers, household servants, and prostitutes as well.

Conversely, Nepal has always been a destination for immigrants, primarily Tibetan or Bhutanese refugees and Indian peasants in the Tarai. The Indian refugees came in the wake of the Muslim invasions of North India; the Tibetan refugees came in 1959 and after, following China taking control of Tibet. Since the 1990s, more and more Nepālī-speaking southern Bhutanese have fled to the eastern regions of Nepal, as Bhutan repressed them, forced them out, and refused to regard them as a part of the country. Today all these groups represent a visible cultural and economic force, and if they have achieved Nepalese citizenship, it was only after many attempts.

The unavoidable opening up of Nepal in the course of what is called globalization has caused new problems. When migrant laborers return from the skyscrapers of Doha to their cold huts, they are, it would seem, uprooted. Many such migrants have difficulty re-integrating, and want neither to remain at home nor to return abroad, left in new forms of transnational and transregional senses of belonging.

Social Structures and Hierarchies

Given these diverse population groups and their ways of life, it is impossible to draw a homogeneous picture of families and social structures in Nepal. It can perhaps be said that the extended family forms the most common social unit in Nepal. In cases where this extended family comprises several smaller families, it becomes something on the order of a joint family, in which several families live side by side, sometimes even constituting a connected household, whose head is generally the father or grandfather. This joint family is based on a common heritage and devotion to ancestors; shared possessions or mutual support; commensality (i.e., sharing cooked food); the joint raising of children (up to a point); and life-cycle rituals being performed together.

To discern somewhat more exact social segmentation requires further differentiation between estate (or caste class, *varṇa*) and caste (or caste group, *jāti*/*jāta*). In the traditional Hindu context, there is a hierarchy of professional classes or status (*varṇa*), according to which the Brahmin (Bahun) figures at the top as the priestly and scholarly class; they are followed by the

Table 2.1 The Caste System of the Khasa-Arya (Indo-Parbatiyā)

Bahun (Brahmin)
Chhetri, Thakuri (Kshatriya) (previously warriors, now engaged in various professions)
Ascetics, such as the Dasanami Sannyasis or Kanphata Yogis
Various merchant and craftsman castes (Vaishya)
Dalits (Shudra): Sarki (leather workers), Kami (blacksmiths), Sunar (goldsmiths), Pariyar/Damai (tailors)

Kshatriya (Chhetri) as the warrior or defensive class; then come the Vaishya as the peasant class, the nourishers; and finally, the Shudra, the class whose members mostly work as craftsmen and helpers. This socio-religious ideology of a class-based society, however, does not reflect reality and is certainly not true in Nepal's case. At best it provides a rough classification in a Brahmanically charged context.

Caste segmentation is a different matter. What passes for a "caste" (*jāti/jāta*) is a group displaying similarities in profession, names, and traditions, which sometimes may develop a political organization associated with their caste. A subcaste (also called *jāti*) fulfills the same criteria as a caste but is more limited regionally and linguistically. The subcaste, as a rule, forms the endogamic upper boundary; below it, clans (Skt. *gotra*, *varṇa*, *kula*, *sapiṇḍa*; Nev. *phuki*) intermarry, in which context fictional genealogical criteria, such as reference to a common ancestor, can be just as relevant as a blood relationship or a lineage with genealogically provable members. Both (sub)caste and joint family are characterized by cooperative help within the group in economic and religious matters; by shared marriage arrangements or participation in rituals for the dead; and by divinities of the quarter or the family being jointly honored during festivals.

Beyond these features, there is no generally uniform caste system for all Hindus or Nepalese, especially since groups living in the high mountain regions would themselves scarcely recognize one as such. Instead, there are several caste systems. Roughly, the system in the Tarai is more Brahmanical and orthodox, while the Khasa-Arya and, even more so, the Newar systems are more liberal. The layers and the hierarchy depend, therefore, on various factors and can be seen best in marriage alliances and notions of purity. The caste system in the Tarai is particularly strongly orientated toward the *varṇa* ideology, while the Newar caste system in the Buddhist town of Patan follows a different hierarchy, in which, for example, craftsmen enjoy a higher status.

Table 2.2 The Caste System in the Tarai

Brahmin
Kshatriya: Chhetri, Kayastha (scribes), Bhumihar (landowners)
Vaishya: Bania (merchants), Marvari (merchants)
Other "pure" castes: Kurmi (peasants), Ahir/Yadav (herders, milkmen), Koiri (vegetable sellers), Mali (flower sellers), Darji (tailors), Lohar (blacksmiths), Mallah and Kewat (fishers), Nai (barbers), Kumhar (potters), Halwai (manufacturers of sweets)
Impure, but "touchable" castes: Kalawar (traders, brewers), Dhobi (laundrymen), Teli and Kanu (oil pressers)
"Untouchables" (Dalit): Chamar (leather workers), Dushdh and Dom (basket weavers), Khatawe (laborers), Bhangi (sweepers)
Ethnic groups: Tharu, Dhanuk, Rajbanshi, Gangai, Dhimal, Kumal, Majhi, Danuvar, Darai

Table 2.3 Some Newar Castes and Their Traditional Occupations

1. "Pure" Castes
Rajopadhyaya (Hindu Brahmins), Vajracharya and Gubhaju (Buddhist priests), Shakya/Bare (Buddhist goldsmiths/traders and/or temple priests)
Chatariya (Kshatriya) Shrestha, many high-ranked clans such as Malla, Amatya, Pradhan, Maske(y), Rajbhandari (traders or government officials), Joshi (astrologers), Karmacharya/Achaju (Śaiva-Tantric priests)
Panchthariya Shrestha (Hindu traders and merchants)
Uray (Buddhist traders and merchants from Kathmandu): Tuladhar (traders), Tamrakar/Tamot (coppersmiths), Kansakar/Kasah (metal workers), and others
Jyapu/Maharjan/Dangol (peasants), Kumhah/Kumhar (potters), Avale (brick makers), Shilpakar/Lohakami (stonemasons)
Citrakar/Pum (painters), Tandukar/Khusah (palanquin bearers, peasants, musicians), Vyanjankar/Tepay (florists), Napit/Nau (barbers), Ranjitkar (dyers)
2. "Impure" Castes
Khadgi/Sahi, Kasai/Nay (butchers and/or drummers)
Kusle/Kapali/Jugi (musicians, tailors, specialists for the dead)
Pore/Dyahla/Pvah and Chyama (sweepers)

Nepalese, like nearly all people today, have different local, regional, and national identities. They are Nepalese in contrast to Indians or when the national team plays cricket against New Zealand. But when it is a matter of regional interests and "home," then they are Newar, Tamang, or Tharu. More significantly, they can be in different categories without finding this contradictory. They can see themselves both as members of a minority group and members of a dominant caste at one and the same time. Modern methods of registration disallowing multiple options in the census force them into narrow categories. It is thus true of Nepal (more so than of India) that ethnic groups and castes are not mutually exclusive. Already in the *Ain* of 1854, no distinction is made between either category, both being given the same designation, *jāti/jāta*.

Furthermore, many of the usual definitory criteria for an ethnic group—such shared things as names, ancestral myths, history, culture, attachment to a particular place, and a sense of solidarity—in Nepal do not always apply.[14] For example, the Newars have no common ancestral myth, and groups such as the Gurung, Magar, Rai, Thakali, and others who speak Tibeto-Burman languages do not form cultural or linguistically homogeneous ethnic groups. The ethnic groups are also bound to different degrees to the rule of the Khasa-Arya. The Magar and the Gurung felt more strongly bound, not least through their early integration into the army, than, for instance, the Limbu. This went so far as to lead British naturalist and scholar Francis Hamilton to predict in the early nineteenth century that the Magar would soon develop into a Khasa-Arya caste and that the Śāha were "in reality a Magar tribe."[15]

In the history of Nepal there have been two attempts to merge the various caste hierarchies into one system. The first stemmed from King Sthiti Malla (1382–95, commonly called Jayasthiti Malla), who, likely with the help of Brahmins, wrote a text, the *Jātamālā* or *Jātimālā* (Garland of Castes), that set forth eighty-two castes;[16] the text was later inserted into the *Nepālikabhūpavaṃśāvalī.*[17] According to this organizational scheme, at the top are ten Brahmin castes, while Jaisi Brahmins, astrologers, and other such mixed castes are categorized as "not to be revered." The Thakuri are treated as Kshatriyas, as are the Malla clans. The Newar castes are divided into the following subcastes or clans: four Jaisi, five Acharya (priests), four Vaidya (physicians), and thirty-eight Shrestha (mainly merchants). The Jaisi and Acharya were permitted to wear the Sacred Thread and to marry a Shrestha. Then thirty-six Shudra castes follow, including the Jyapu (Newar peasants) and Kumhar (potters). At the bottom of the hierarchy are the Untouchables, such as the cleaners (Pore) and leather workers (Chamar/Chamarkara), from whose hands one may not receive even water.

Sthiti Malla also established that sexual relations between high-caste women and lower-caste men were taboo according to Brahmanical legal rules (i.e., the Dharmaśāstra). It is further said that he issued various laws according to which a person might not change the profession ordained for his caste, and members of lower castes were to wear particular clothing and ornaments and live in particular kinds of houses. Kasai, for instance, were to

Figure 2.1 An Untouchable Pore carries the head of a buffalo to the music provided by butchers, 1988. The buffalo was sacrificed to the goddess Bhadrakālī. Photo by Niels Gutschow.

wear sleeveless shirts; the Pore, caps and traditional male clothing (*labedā-suruvāla*). The Kasai, Pore, and Kulu were not to roof with tiles, and everyone was to obey members of higher castes. The *Nepālikabhūpavaṃśāvalī* concludes Sthiti Malla's listing of the castes with these words:

> Thus establishing laws regarding the castes, lands, and houses, and composing the "Garland of Castes," King Jayasthiti Malla corrected the Hindu *dharma* of Nepal. He made his glories and name known.[18]

The second outline of a caste system stems from Jaṅga Bahādura Rāṇā's "constitution," the *Ain*.[19] In this text, the caste system is generally encapsulated by the standard formulation "four caste classes (*varṇa*) and thirty-six caste groups (*jāta*)," used by Pṛthvīnārāyaṇa Śāha. The number thirty-six, however, does not correspond with the social reality and probably stands simply for the totality of all castes, for in the *Ain* alone some seventy castes are mentioned. According to it, the caste hierarchy is divided into five groups:[20] (1) those who wear the Sacred Thread (*tāgādhārī*); (2) drinkers of alcohol who may not be enslaved (*namāsinyā matvālī*); (3) drinkers of alcohol who may be enslaved (*māsinyā matvālī*); (4) impure but touchable castes (*pāni nacalnyā choi chiṭo hālnu naparnyā*); and (5) Untouchable castes (*pāni nacalnyā choi chiṭo hālnu parnyā*). In this system, then, there is a basic differentiation between pure (1–3) and impure (4–5) castes, or between those from whom water (and cooked rice) may be accepted and those from whom it may not. The hierarchy of the *Ain* is thus essentially based upon four indicators of (im)purity: the Sacred Thread, alcohol, and the acceptance of or offering of cooked rice and water. The caste order based on these indicators is strictly hierarchical, with Brahmins at the top.

According to one's ideas of purity, boiled rice could be offered only in a hierarchical direction. A prohibition on accepting rice from someone could be issued for life, which meant that person's exclusion from the caste, or could be temporary, as in cases of impurity incurred in the context of birth or death.

The social hierarchy of the *Ain*, which was supported by corresponding rules of marriage, made ethnic groups into castes, who had to respect Brahmanical purity standards, occasionally under state monitoring. Many repressive measures, such as a hierarchical tax system, bonded labor, slavery, exclusion from educational institutions, lack of access to private credit, or exclusion from political participation, can be explained as a result of these social divisions.

The *Ain* had established that one's "profession is not determined by caste,"[21] but this rule had hardly any practical effect. Even after the official abolition of the caste system by the constitution of 1959, hierarchical relationships remained in everyday life. They can be seen in the hierarchical forms of sharing cooked food, the right to place a mark on someone else's forehead (*ṭīkā*), the exchange of gifts, the smoking of a hookah, and above all bodily contact. However, not all social relations are circumscribed by caste hierarchy. Other hierarchical forms of interaction and displays of power are defined more by residential proximity, education, status, or wealth.

The Position of Women

Hindu women live, as a rule, between two socio-religious ideals and roles. As their husbands' second half, according to Brahmanical thinking, they are to be, on the one hand, faithful wives, thus realizing the ideal of the goddess Sītā, the wife of Rāma, who was true unto death, or of Satī, whose self-immolation might have made her the model for the wife who burns alongside

Table 2.4 Hierarchy of the Castes (with traditional professions) and Ethnic Group Mentioned in the *Ain*

1. Caste Groups of the "Sacred Thread-wearers" (*tāgādhārī*)
   Upādhyāya Brahmins
   Devabhāju (Newar Brahmins)
   Brahmins of foreign kingdoms: Terhaūte Brahmins, Bhaṭṭa Brahmins, Marhaṭṭā-Brahmins, Nāgara Brahmins, Gujarātī Brahmins, Mahārāṣṭrīya Brahmins, Tailaṅgī Brāhmins, Dravidian Brahmins, Brahmins of Madhesa
   Asala Rājapūta, Rājapūta, Chhetri/Kṣatriyas ("warrior')
   Asala Jaisī Brahmins, Jaisī Brāhmins, Doṭyāla Jaisī, Jumlī Jaisī, Duī-Liṅga-Jaisī, Tīna-Liṅga-Jaisī
   High Newar castes such as the Tharaghara, Asala Śreṣṭha*
   Hamāla
   Bhāṭa/Bhāṭa Jaisī
   Some ascetic sects (such as the Jogī, Jaṅgama, Sannyāsī, Sevaḍā, Kanaphaṭṭā, Udāsī, and Baghara)
2. Caste groups of the "Non-enslavable Alcohol-drinkers" (*namāsinyā matvālī*)
   ▶ Guruṅga
   ▶ Magara
   ▶ Ghale
   ▶ Sunuvāra
   ▶ Limbu, Kirāta
   ▶ Newar castes from whose members water is acceptable
3. Caste groups of the "Enslavable Alcohol-drinkers" (*māsinyā matvālī*)
   ▶ Bhoṭe (ethnic groups who speak Tibeto-Burmese languages)
   ▶ Chepāṅa
   ▶ Danuvāra
   ▶ Hāyu
   ▶ Darai
   ▶ Kumāla
   ▶ Paharī
   Ghartī (descendants of freed slaves) from hill regions, also called Pāre Ghartī
   ▶ Lāpacyā (Lepcha)***
   ▶ Mājhī
   ▶ Ṭhokryā
   ▶ Galahaṭyā
   ▶ Newar castes from whose members water is unacceptable
4. Impure but Touchable castes (*pāni nacalnyā choi chiṭo hālnu naparnyā*) (according to *Ain* 160.17)
   Muslims (Musalamāna)
   Telī of Madhesa (oil sellers)
   Kasāī (butchers)
   Kusle (the Newar caste whose members brush and sweep courtyards in palaces, high-ranking officials' houses, or temples, and play musical instruments in temples)
   Dhobī (washermen)
   Kulu (leather workers)
   Christians, Mleccha (Europeans)
   Curaute (Muslim bracelet sellers, mainly in the Kathmandu Valley)
   Kalavāra (brewers, merchants)
   ▶ Mecyā****

Table 2.4 Continued

5. Untouchable castes (*pāni nacalnyā choi chiṭo hālnu parnyā*) according to *Ain* 160.17
Sārkī (tanners, shoemakers)
Kāmī (blacksmith)
Cunāro/Cunāra
Hurkyā
Damāĩ (tailors and musicians)
Gāine (singers, players of musical instruments, and beggars)
Bādi Bhāḍa (singers, dancers, and beggars)
Cyāmakhala (Newār scavengers)
Kaḍārā (stemming from unions between a Kāmī and Sārkī)
▶ Ethnic group

N.B. In this table, caste names are spelled with diacritics as they appear in the *Ain*.

* The *Ain* does not extensively spell out caste hierarchy among the Newar. It assigns to Hindu Newar priests (Devabhāju) and foreign (i.e., Indian) Brahmins the same rank (146.3) and delineates a brief hierarchy for the other Hindu Newar (145.7, 8, 9, 10); see Khatiwoda, Cubelic, and Michaels 2021: 32–33 for details.

** The caste status of these two groups, which are mentioned only once in the *Ain* (124.5), is not very clear, as they originally seem to have been categorized as enslavable. Cf. Höfer 1979a: 124.

*** The caste status of this group, only mentioned in *Ain* 89.49, is not clear.

**** The members of the Mecya caste were upgraded to a Water-acceptable caste in 1860 CE (cp. *Ain* 89.49).

her deceased husband.[22] These goddesses, like Śrī and Lakṣmī, guaranteed familial welfare and wealth. On the other hand, like the goddesses Devī, Kālī, Durgā, or the living goddess Kumārī, women are dynamic bearers of possibly dangerous creative and regenerative power (*śakti, prakṛti*), and as such they may bring misfortune when not honored and pacified by way of, for example, a marriage bond.

Various problem areas derive from this tension between the malign threat of an unmarried or impure woman and the benevolent role of women as sisters, virgins, or mothers. Thus, on the one hand, women in Nepal are dependent on male relations, may not occupy any high religious office, and are rarely ascetics. On the other hand, they are greatly respected and upon occasion venerated as healers or servants of the gods.

Food inequality, intermittent extreme household violence, and forced isolation when impure continue to be social problems. In the west of Nepal, despite a prohibition decreed by the highest court, menstruating women are still customarily banned from their houses and placed in huts (*chāupaḍī*), in the belief that during this period they make people and animals ill and spoil food. Female infanticide, child marriages, and dowry murders still occur occasionally, if not to the same extent as in India. The lack of educational opportunity is another form of discrimination: Only with the enactment of the *Ain* were men allowed to teach their wives "such skills as writing and reading."[23]

Women have many responsibilities for working the land. They cook, fetch water, feed the animals, and do field work. In 2006, 85% of all Nepalese women worked in the agricultural sector. In towns they receive jobs, since discrimination on the basis of gender has been forbidden by law since 1990. Thanks to quota rules, they make up nearly one-third of the representatives in parliament, but this does not mean that they take part any more intensively in political and social decisions on the village level.

In Hindu circles, a woman gains respect by marrying and bearing a son. She is also the one who prays at home and in the temple for her husband, and she performs domestic rituals. This is impressively demonstrated by women who spend the entire month of Pauṣa (January/February) reciting the *Svasthānīvratakathā*, a text in which the goddess Svasthānī fulfills wishes they have for their husbands and family, or when they undertake a pilgrimage for their husbands during the Tīj festival to the Paśupatinātha temple.[24]

The situation of women in Nepal can only be adequately grasped when considered against the historically bequeathed, socially and religiously based ideas of what women are, including factors of age, profession, sexuality, and caste. The position of a woman depends greatly upon how old she is, whether, for instance, she is a beloved young girl, a potential marriage partner, a mother, a widow, or a concubine. Not least important for a woman are the family relationships she is in: whether sister, wife, mother-in-law, grandmother, aunt, or daughter-in-law. Equally significant is whether she lives in a village or city, in the hills or in the Tarai, in a Bahun-Chhetri or a Sherpa family, and whether she is a Hindu, Buddhist, or Muslim by birth. Education, wealth, status, and her physical location (at home or in public) also count. Generally, it is said that Newar, Tharu, Kham Magar, Rai, Limbu, Sherpa, or Tamang women are treated on an almost equal level.[25]

The situation is different for Hindu women of the Bahun-Chhetri caste classes. For them the traditional *strīdharma* is relevant, a complex of social, religious, and legal regulations, summarized in a comprehensive collection of Sanskrit legal literature, the Dharmaśāstra (classical Indian law). The *strīdharma* texts, whose authors were male, deal with ritual tasks for women and other concerns of female life: purity, strength, love, pride, self-sacrifice, shame, happiness, personal wealth, and belonging. The view of a woman's status changes in tandem with these attributes. In the family household—where identity and status are not defined by profession and possessions—women command a strong position. There they are no longer merely helpless, repressed persons with no goals, power, or liberty.

Over the past few decades much has been done to improve the situation of women in Nepal. Child or forced arranged marriages are banned and have greatly decreased. Childbed-related mortality has gone down considerably, and the number of births per woman has dropped from 4.6 (1996) to 3.1 (2006). During the same period, the proportion of women and girls going to school increased from 32% (1996) to over 80%; today about as many girls as boys go through primary schooling. The proportion of women with access to information and media has also increased considerably, as has the proportion of female employment, although far fewer women work for a salary than do men. Still, around one-half of all women now have a say in important decisions, such as going to the doctor, large-scale purchases, and visits to their parental homes.

The Living Child Goddess (Kumārī)

A special form of the worship of goddesses pertains to Kumārī, literally "girl, young woman, virgin," who, probably since the early medieval period, conferred sacred authority upon the power of kings.[26] All girls in South Asia can be called by this Sanskrit word, but only a very few Kumārī are living goddesses chosen from among high Buddhist castes by a process of searching and testing. They have been revered as embodiments of the Goddess for centuries, particularly the Rājakumārī, the royal Kumārī, in Kathmandu.

The beginnings of the worship of prepubescent girls as living goddesses are unclear, as are its religious roots. Indications that the Kumārī were venerated in India as part of a cult of the virgin already existed in Vedic texts. The earliest indication in Nepal seems to be the Kumārī temple in Gache Ṭol in Bhaktapur, constructed in 868. The later chronicles yield further evidence. Thus, the *Nepālikabhūpavaṃśāvalī* reports that Lakṣmīkāmadeva, king of Kāntipura (Kathmandu) in the years 1024 to 1040, owed his wealth to Kumārī, and so established *kumārīpūjā*, the veneration of a virgin girl. In other sources, Sthiti Malla or Jayaprakāśa Malla are named as founders of the cult, while in Bhaktapur this distinction goes to Trailokya Malla. More recent findings indicate that the first permanent Kumārī was established a century earlier, during the shared rule of Rāya, Ratna, Rāma, and Ari Malla in Bhaktapur. In Kathmandu, Sūrya Malla called on Kumārī and Taleju to stand by him during attacks by King Mukuṇḍa Sena I of Palpa. In Patan, the Kumārī was chosen by the Hakha Bāhāḥ community.

Several "unique" Kumārīs (*ekāntakumārī*) are worshiped equally by Buddhists and Hindus, usually in Tantric form, at various places associated with the Newar. For Buddhists, she is an outward form of Vajradevī or Tārā; for Hindus, usually of Durgā or Taleju (the patron goddess of the Malla kings). Generally, a Kumārī appears during festivals as a member of a group (*kumārīgaṇa*). Monarchy and the worship of Kumārī were thus closely linked from the beginning, but the worship of Kumārī is not necessarily bound to the monarchy.

The royal Kumārī in Kathmandu, who resides in a house finished by Jayaprakāśa Malla on March 27, 1757, the Kumārī Chẽ, comes from the Buddhist caste of Newar goldsmiths (Shakya). In Bhaktapur and Patan, they may also come from the caste of Buddhist Vajracharya priests, and in villages sometimes from peasant castes (Jyapu). Until 2007, the Rājakumārī in Kathmandu was worshiped specially during a days-long city festival. On the last day, and as the culmination of the Indrajātrā in August/September, the king appeared and, in a non-public ritual in the Kumārī house, he received a kind of return offering (*prasāda*) from the child goddess, who also pressed the *ṭīkā* onto his forehead. With this ritual, Kumārī confirmed the power of the king for a further year. Pṛthvīnārāyaṇa Śāha himself is supposed to have gone to Kumārī on arrival in Kathmandu and to have received the *ṭīkā* from her. The last Malla king was thus deprived of power, which, according to the chronicles, had been foretold to him by the child goddess in a dream.

For the selection of a Kumārī, certain traditional rules must be obeyed, especially in the case of a royal Kumārī. In Kathmandu, she was chosen until 2007 by the domestic priest (*rājapurohita*) of the king and a Tantric Buddhist priest (*vajrācārya*). Since 2007 this has been done by the Guṭhī Saṃsthāna (a partly state-run institution for the administration and organization of religious foundations). The girl, who is often very young, must be sound in mind and body and, in the ideal case, fulfill thirty-two external conditions, including the breast and cheeks of a lion, the voice of a sparrow, and the eyelashes of a cow.

Besides external signs, there are also internal characteristics, such as the emanation of peace or fearlessness. A test of this characteristic is carried out on the royal Kumārī in Kathmandu. In the night of the eighth to the ninth day of the Dasaĩ festival, she is led through the courtyard of the temple of the

Figure 2.2 The Ekantakumārī of Bhaktapur during Dasaĩ, 1976. Photo by Niels Gutschow.

goddess Taleju, which is part of the palace complex. This temple is filled with bloody buffalo heads that have been sacrificed to the goddess, and she must show no sign of fear of them, which is interpreted as proof of her divinity. Crying is seen as a bad omen. Thus, as the *Nepālikabhūpavaṃśāvalī* reports, a group of Kumārī who had been gathered by Pratāpa Malla for his fatally ill wife could not come from Patan to Kathmandu because one girl, who embodied the goddess Māheśvarī, began to cry. The queen died a few days later. If the horoscope also satisfies favorable prerequisites, nothing stands in the way of the choice. A new Kumārī remains in her office, as a rule, until the occurrence of her first menstruation. Then she must abandon her throne.

The life of a Kumārī in village milieux (and in Bhaktapur) is for the most part fairly normal. She merely participates in certain festivals in a special ritual function. However, the Kumārī in Kathmandu and, to a certain extent, Patan may leave her house only for ritual matters, but even then she is carried, because she is not to walk on the impure ground. Separated from her family and the outside world, she spends nearly her whole childhood in a house of her own, sitting several hours a day on her throne, where she is repeatedly visited by ordinary people and also by politicians. She is given gifts and wish lists, and the donors are blessed by her in return. She then strews flower petals over the visitor and presses the *ṭīkā* on their forehead. Her task is to bring good fortune. Every move on her part is interpreted as a sign.

These circumstances have led more recently to legal complaints involving universal human and children's rights. Thus, it is claimed that Kumārī worship involves child labor and that those who keep her from the outside world are robbing the girl of her rights to a family and education. As a result, the royal Kumārī now receives private instruction.

Satī or Widow Burning

Women historically have had little recourse to law, and abuses were often the result. Among these was suttee (*satī*, literally "the pure [wife]"), the ritual burning of widows.[27] The term refers both to the immolated widow and to the action itself. This form of suicide, always contentious in South Asia, was especially widespread in Nepal's aristocratic circles. In 1819 Francis Hamilton wrote of *satī* that it was "more prevalent" among the higher castes of Nepal "than in any part of India where I have been, the vicinity of Kolkata excepted." Many documents of the Śāha-Rāṇā Period confirm this statement.[28]

The first inscription to deal with *satī* in South Asia is from Nepal, dating from the year 464 CE. It was a widespread practice at least from that time. According to the chronicles, for instance, the wife of Rāma Śāha and the younger wife of Narabhūpāla Śāha both followed their husbands onto the funeral pyre.[29] Of Bahādura Śāha, one of the sons of Pṛthvīnārāyaṇa Śāha, it is said that seven legitimate and two illegitimate wives were burnt with him. It was possible to prevent the pregnant mother of Raṇabahādura Śāha from committing *satī* after her husband had died, but she did so immediately after her son was born in 1775. Prime Minister Bhīmasena Thāpā is supposed to have forced the main wives of King Raṇabahādura Śāha, Rājeśvarī and Suvarṇaprabhā, to commit *satī* in 1806. Six years after the suicide of his mother, Gīrvāṇayuddha Śāha fulfilled her wish and donated land to the priest Paśupati Regmi.

To be sure, there are indications that some Rāṇā rulers opposed *satī*. Thus, physician Henry Ambrose Oldfield reported that Jaṅga Bahādura Rāṇā successfully prevented both his sister and the widow of his friend Barra Captain Singh from committing suicide. Beyond this, there were also cases that breach the guidelines for *satī* in the old Indian legal texts, the Dharmaśāstras. For instance, both the wife and the mother of Pratāpa Malla committed *satī* after his death, although only the wife was sanctioned to do so. When a concubine of Rājendra Śāha did so, or when a servant of Narabhūpāla Śāha had himself immolated together with the king's second wife,[30] it was, strictly speaking, forbidden.[31] The explanation in the *Gorkhārājavaṃśāvalī* is, however, enlightening: "For a wife, her husband is the master of her life, and for a servant the master is master of his life." By no means, in any event, did the husband's death always lead to his widow's immolation.

The most comprehensive and also the most precise legal text on *satī* comes from Nepal.[32] This is Article 94 of the *Ain*, entitled *Satī Jānyāko* (On practicing *satī*). The *Ain* had been commissioned by Prime Minister Jaṅga Bahādura Rāṇā, whose three wives would later have themselves immolated with him. In it, married women are permitted to commit *satī* if they are more than sixteen years old, their sons are over sixteen and their daughters over five, and when they have no other husband and are not pregnant. The decision has to be voluntary and must be carried out immediately. Coercion, drugging, or persuasion may not be used; indeed, every effort is to be made to dissuade the woman from any such intention. *Satī* is expressly forbidden in a remote region when the son or husband of a Brahmin woman has died. Those who drug a widow before her sacrifice, or use force to coerce her, or in cases where *satī* is committed for a man who is not her husband, persons are punished particularly harshly. The moral content of these rules is easy to interpret. The authorities wanted to make sure, under all circumstances, that *satī* be practiced voluntarily and for ethically noble reasons. Small children or other husbands were not to suffer from the widow's decision.

Two stages of self-sacrifice are legally significant with regard to sentencing: first, the ritual bath (*snāna*), by means of which *satī* is commenced, or else the breaking of the arm ring, by which the ritual decision to commit suicide is confirmed; second, igniting the funeral pyre. If the woman voluntarily stops the process, a payment of expiation must be made. Here, the moment at which the decision is made is of importance: it must be after the bath but before the lighting of the funeral pyre; after the bath, the breaking of the arm ring, and the lighting of the fire a reversion is not possible anymore.

These features mark the difference between ritual and physical death. Some sections stipulate whether, and under what conditions, rehabilitation (*patiyā*) in the form of re-integration into society may occur or not. If the widow has taken the bath and has already climbed onto the funeral pyre, but is then hindered from performing self-immolation, she receives *patiyā* for rice and water. This means being taken up again by the family and caste community. A slightly different case occurs if she jumps down or falls from the funeral pyre before it can be ignited. In such a case, it is presumed that the woman reverses her intention. She then receives *patiyā* for water only, but not for rice. This means the loss of her caste status.

In a ritual sense, the widow is already dead at the point when she makes the decision, expresses her intention, and confirms this with the ceremonial bath (water poured over her head and shoulders) or by breaking the arm ring. If she subsequently alters her decision, then re-integration into society is only possible through countermeasures. Water and fire are important in any kind of vow. Fire burns and water washes away any impurity. The performative unity of language and action in rituals—a ceremonially expressed decision, given added importance by water and fire—can neither be repeated nor repealed.

For this reason, it is impossible to ritually distance oneself from *satī*. It is impossible to remarry, since marriage represents a lifelong bond. If the pyre has been lit, there is no way for the widow to return to the family unit and to society. At the Paśupatinātha temple in Deopatan there is a doorway, the so-called Satīdvāra, which makes this ritual threshold visible. In the past, once widows stepped through it, they could not return. Up until a few years ago, tales were told in whispered tones about this or that old beggarwoman who allegedly had jumped from the fire and was unable to go back to her family.

On July 8, 1920, nearly one hundred years after the legal prohibition of *satī* in British India by Lord William Bentinck on December 4, 1829, the practice was forbidden in Nepal by Prime Minister Candra Śaṃśera.[33] It is stated that *satī* is not a strict religious duty; that it is practiced in order to attain certain goals, such as reaching heaven or attaining fame, but that these could be achieved by other means, such as chastity; that women do not understand the holy scriptures, especially the Veda, and so can easily be led astray; and that it is impossible to distinguish between what is genuine and what is fraudulent.

Nepal as a Multi-ethnic State

Not until the late 1980s and early 1990s did movements emerge that opposed the dominance of the Bahun-Chhetri, a dominance not only propagated but claimed. These movements opposed Nepālī being the only national language, and they opposed Hinduism as the state religion. Instead, they fought for a secular state that gave due consideration to the concerns of the ethnic groups, the Janajati.[34] In 1991, after the first "People's Movement" (*jana āndolana*), many ethnic organizations joined together in the Nepal Janajati Mahasangh (NEFEN, Nepal Federation of Nationalities; since 2003 known as the NEFIN, Nepal Federation of Indigenous Nationalities). Until then ethnicity (defining oneself through ethnic identity and the practice of ethnic culture) was, if anything, being suppressed.[35] After 1990 it was on the daily agenda, even though the constitution of 1990 forbade regional or ethnic political parties, which were perceived as a threat to national unity. From 2003 on seats in parliament were reserved for such parties. The questions now raised were ones of national representation and access to positions in state institutions.

Since the 1990s the term Janajati has been used for what were once called (primitive) tribes. NEFIN was of the opinion that Nepal consisted of such nationalities, which were not opposed to the concept of a nation but rather collectively made up the nation, despite the danger that individual nationalities could potentially form their own states. These debates, which were always discussed with great fervor every time the constitution was changed, have to do with Nepal's self-image as a nation. Hardly anyone today denies that Nepal is a unified country, but what defines its identity is a very controversial topic. Thus, the majority of Janajati refuse any Hindu definition of state, along with the Hindu system of caste classes and groups. NEFIN, on the other hand, does not accept any low-caste Hindus (e.g., Dalits), Christian, or Muslim minorities among its membership.[36] Instead, they regard themselves as the original inhabitants of Nepal. In reaction, caste Hindus (or Khasa-Arya) feel that they are misunderstood and being treated by NEFIN as second-class Nepalese.

This debate ran parallel with the Year (later Decade) of Indigenous Peoples declared by the United Nations in 1993. To be accounted one of the designated indigenous peoples suddenly mattered. Numerous aid and development organizations, as well as the World Bank, supported this development. NEFEN reacted immediately. In March 1994, the opposition defined the characteristics of an indigenous people of Nepal as:

1. having their own distinct language and cultural tradition, and beliefs based on animism (honoring ancestors and the land [or nature]), and in no case based on Hinduism;
2. being descended from the original settlers of the modern state territory of Nepal and having their own historical tradition, written or oral;
3. having been driven off their own, communally used land, or having been robbed of their right to use it;
4. being a social group traditionally based on equality (including of the sexes), and not on the Indo-Aryan hierarchy of the caste system;
5. and claiming, formally or informally, to be an "indigenous population group of Nepal."[37]

Under these conditions, NEFEN leaders were even prepared to accept the Chhetri into their organization, but only if these were ready to declare themselves Khasa until the mid-nineteenth century and to renounce Hinduism. In the end, NEFEN was an anti-Hindu, and in particular an anti-Brahmanical, organization.

Despite such movements, the dominance of upper-caste Hindus remained clear for all to see. They still held the majority of important posts in the government, parliament, and public administration. It was the Khasa-Arya, after all, who had defined Nepal as the last (or only) Hindu kingdom in the world and enshrined this in the constitution of 1990. For the Khasa-Arya, Nepal was a Hindu nation, not a diverse one in the process of creation. They were not concerned with diversity; they were concerned with unity and submission to their norms. Articles 2 and 11 of the 1990 constitution guaranteed religious freedoms and forbade forced conversion, but Nepal was still defined as a Hindu kingdom in Article 4. According to it, Nepal was "a multi-ethnic, multilingual, democratic, independent, indivisible, sovereign Hindu and Constitutional Monarchical Kingdom."

Even though the constitution of 2015 declares in its preamble that the "sovereign People of Nepal" have been protecting and promoting "social and cultural solidarity, tolerance and harmony, and unity in diversity by recognizing the multi-ethnic, multi-lingual, multi-religious, multi-cultural and diverse regional characteristics, resolving to build an egalitarian society founded on the proportional inclusive and participatory principles in order to ensure economic equality, prosperity and social justice, by eliminating discrimination based on class, caste, region, language, religion and gender and all forms of caste-based untouchability," social groups still argued about who had the right to define what and in what way, and who had the majority. The 2011 census designated 81.3% of the population Hindu, while the Janajati lay claim to 70% of the population, and the suppressed minorities united under the Utpidit Jatiya Utthan Manch (Forum for the Uplift of Oppressed Castes), founded in 1987, professed to represent 60% of the population. Does Nepal need to be a nation as defined in its constitution in order to better deal with its ethnic problems? If it wishes to become a strong state, must it sacrifice its heterogeneity? Can it afford to give ethnic minorities the consideration due them? How far must this nationalization and unification process go? These questions are at the center of many political debates.

3
The Religions

In Sanskrit texts, Nepal is frequently called a refuge for the gods. In fact, Nepal is full of numerous temples, statues, rituals, festivals, and forms of worship. This is a result of a mixture of Vedic, Paurāṇic, Tantric, Buddhist, and folk traditions.

Until 2008, Nepal was the last remaining Hindu kingdom in the world. Hinduism had been declared the state religion upon various occasions,[1] but the other religions and religious movements in Nepal had always continued to exist alongside it, despite hardly being mentioned in the official statistics. According to the census of 2021, 81.19% of the Nepalese population are Hindu, 8.21% Buddhist, 5,09% Muslim, 1.76% Christian 1.76%, and the rest belongs to another religion or call themselves atheists. There are, however, ethnic activists who complain that the proportion given for Hindus is inflated.[2]

It is sometimes difficult to date the emergence of religions and their rituals.[3] Roughly, Buddhism can be shown to have existed in Nepal around a century after the historical Buddha, that is, from the third century BCE; Vaiṣṇavism is documented from approximately the fourth century CE with the Cāṅgunārāyaṇa inscription of Mānadeva; and Śaivism appears no later than the sixth century in the Licchavi inscriptions. From the eighth and nineth centuries on, Hinduism manifests in the form of sectarian groups and related activities in several forms. The more recent chronicles report a historically apocryphal visit by the philosopher Śaṅkara at about this time. The early Tantric Nātha and Siddha cults show up in texts from the nineth to eleventeenth century;[4] the earliest Gorakhanātha or Gorakṣanātha inscription, in a cave in Pharping, dates, however, from the year 1391.[5] Nātha Yogīs, widespread in Nepal from the fourteenth century, but receiving patronage from the Malla kings only from the seventeenth century onward, clearly participated in the Gorkhali conquest of western Nepal.[6]

Islam appeared briefly in the fourteenth century,[7] when the army of the Muslim Ghurids penetrated Bengal from Delhi across the Gangetic plain,

Nepal. Axel Michaels, Oxford University Press. English language edition © Oxford University Press 2024.
DOI: 10.1093/oso/9780197650936.003.0004

and especially when Ghiyās-ud-dīn Tuglaq annexed the kingdom of Mithila in 1324/25, forcing Hara- (or Hari-)siṃha, the last king of Mithila, to flee to Bhaktapur in 1326. In 1349, Sultan Shams ud-dīn Ilyās invaded the Kathmandu Valley for only for a week. He is blamed for the destruction of many statues. During the rule of Ratna Malla, Muslims were permitted to settle in the Kathmandu Valley. From that time on, Muslim traders repeatedly wandered through the land, but unlike in the Tarai, where 97% of Nepalese Muslims now live, the Muslim influence in the Kathmandu Valley is not very significant.

The first Christian mission in the Kathmandu Valley was established in 1715 by Catholic Capuchin friars, but they were expelled by Pṛthvīnārāyaṇa Śāha. From 1951 to 1990 Christian missionaries were again allowed to perform social work, but proselytizing is still prohibited.

Buddhism

For Buddhists (and many Hindus, too), the history of Nepal begins in a distant time with the draining of the Kathmandu Valley by Mañjuśrī.[8] According to the *Nepālikabhūpavaṃśāvalī* and other chronicles, this Bodhisattva brought Buddhism to Nepal when the Kathmandu Valley was a lake in which serpents lived.[9] In the Golden Age, Vipaśvī Buddha, a transcendental Buddha of the past, threw a lotus seed into the lake, from which there arose a flame "that came into being by itself" (*svayambhū*). He was followed by three further Buddhas in the valley, and finally the Bodhisattva Mañjuśrī, who saw the light and produced a cleft in the hill at Kotwal, near Chobhar, with a blow of his sword, so that the water could drain away. A *stūpa*, Svayambhū, was erected over of the self-arisen flame, and later Buddha Śākyamuni spent time at it.

The Buddha

In fact, the earliest historical religious relics of Buddhism point to the existence of the historical Buddha Siddhārtha Gautama, who was born in the middle of the fifth century BCE within the territory now belonging to modern Nepal. His birthplace, Lumbini, located in the southern foothills of the Himalaya, has now become a world-famous and frequently visited

Buddhist pilgrimage site.[10] In Gautama's time, the place was surrounded by a fertile, albeit malaria-infested, region where rich harvests of rice could be planted.

The discovery of Lumbini is based on an inscription found there in 1896 that dates to sometime around the year of Aśoka's visit to the site in 249 BCE. Archaeologist Alois Anton Führer discovered it with the help of Nepalese archaeologists, among them General Khaḍga Śamśera Rāṇā, the palace's regional governor. The text reads:

> *When King Devanampriya Priyadarsin [= Ashoka] had been anointed twenty years, he came himself and worshiped (this spot) because the Buddha Shakyamuni was born here.*[11]

This was the first historical indication of the birthplace of the Buddha. Führer had traveled to the area where the Buddha is supposed to have spent his youth, on a mission for the British Archaeological Survey of India; there he also found four small ruined *stūpas*. A proper excavation took place three years later, on the basis of information he had provided.[12] Since Führer's day, further excavations have concentrated on the area around Lumbini. The most recent, under the direction of British archaeologist Robin Coningham, have brought a pre-Buddhist shrine to light, where a tree was honored but no sacrifices were made.

Lumbini was part of a patchwork of small kingdoms and "large empires" (*mahājanapada*). Searching for enlightenment, Gautama wandered through these countries and, as is well known, found enlightenment while meditating under a tree in Bodh Gaya near Varanasi. Kapilavastu was the capital of the small Śākya kingdom, which was tributary to the neighboring Kosala monarchy.

The many popular ascetic movements like the Buddha's were signs of their particular socio-economic circumstances. They arose in villages but grew in cities and market places that produced surpluses, were to a certain extent based on an individualism born of this prosperity, and led in turn to one's own search for spiritual enlightenment and knowledge. This escape from the world was motivated by the Buddha's teaching that the world's basic condition was suffering. The Vedic religion was, by contrast, a priestly religion, centered on sacrificial ritual, enshrined in the elitist Sanskrit language, and propagating a hierarchical social order, the caste system. The Buddha turned against such exclusivity, and his teachings soon spread.

From Mahāyāna to Vajrayāna

Buddhism rather abruptly collapsed in India at the end of the twelfth century, but it survived in Nepal and the wider Himalaya as Mahāyāna ("great vehicle") Buddhism, which developed differently from the Theradāda ("School of the Elders") or the monastic teachings of Siddhārtha Gautama. Five major changes are characteristic:

- Heaven instead of *nirvāṇa* or the idea of a heavenly world including a Buddhist cosmography that features a heavenly sphere of transcendence, a pure Buddha land, and paradise.
- From the Buddha to god or the idea of various phases of spiritual development. As Siddhārtha Gautama, the historical Buddha, an "enlightened monk" (*arhat*) or a Buddha remained a human being, but his spirit and knowledge already belonged to the heavenly world. This division permitted the worship of Buddhas such as Dīpaṅkara or Maitreya, the future Buddha. Configurations of Buddhas arose, too, such as the Five Transcendental Buddhas worshiped in the cardinal directions on a *stūpa*: Vairocana, Akṣobhya, Ratnasambhava, Amitābha, and Amoghasiddhi. Bodhisattvas are beings who have attained enlightenment but who forego the final reward, the entry into *nirvāṇa*, so they might help other beings toward enlightenment. Among these are Samantabhadra, Vajrapāṇi, Ratnapāṇi, Avalokiteśvara, and Viśvapāṇi, and, in Nepal, besides the Bodhisattvas of the eight cardinal those of the intermediate directions: Avalokiteśvara, Ākāśagarbha, Vajrapāṇi, Kṣitigarbha, Sarvanivaraṇaviṣkambhin, Maitreya, Samantabhadra, and Mañjuśrī.
- From self-abandonment to ritual or the unearthly Buddha becoming an object ritual worship: For example, the recitation of "'magic' formulae" (*dhāraṇī*) or the use of flowers or incense in the worship of statues and other images.
- From the search for enlightenment to ethics or the theory of the transfer of merit being extended and integrated into the concept of "compassion" (*karuṇā*).

These new developments—transcendency; multicorporality, such as the Buddha's three bodies; ritualization and deification of the Buddha; and the Bodhisattva ideal, which opened up another route to enlightenment alongside the monastic-ascetic ideal of *nirvāṇa—all* added the ethical impulse of Mahāyāna Buddhism. The presence of such a form of Buddhism in the Kathmandu Valley is well documented no later than the Licchavi Period. The valley thus became one of the first regions outside the Gangetic plain where Buddhism established itself. There is, for example, an inscription on a lotus plinth in Chabahil that mentions Mahāmuni (an epithet of the Buddha) and dates from the early fifth century. This inscription is remarkable not only because the donor expresses her wish to be born a man in the next life, but also because it is one of the earliest indications of a distinct form of Mahāyāna Buddhism.

Other evidence, such as a number of fairly securely dated Buddha and Bodhisattva statues, primarily of Avalokiteśvara, Vajrapāṇi, and Maitreya, dates from the middle of the sixth century. In a long inscription at a *caitya* in Patan dating from the end of the sixth or beginning of the seventh century, the singular Nepalese form of Mahāyāna becomes visible, since in it four (instead of the usual Five) Tathāgatas—Akṣobhya in the east, Amitābha in the south, Samantakusuma in the west, and Śākyamuni in the north—are praised together with eight high-ranking Bodhisattvas.[13]

Buddhism spread in parallel with Hinduism but was not always supported to the same extent by rulers. The inscriptions variously mention rulers making offerings to both Śiva and Viṣṇu, and donations to Buddhist communities, but they used no Buddhist symbols.[14]

The foundation of thirteen Buddhist monasteries is documented in the Licchavi inscriptions, most of them serving Mahāsaṅghika monks. The *Gopālarājavaṃśāvalī*, too, though only composed in the fourteenth century, credits various rulers with promoting Buddhism: Mānadeva I who supposedly founded Mānavihāra monastery; Aṃśuvarman, Rājavihāra; Vṛṣadeva, Svayambhū; and Dharmadeva, the Dharmadevacaitya in Chabahil. Aṃśuvarman allegedly repaired Guṃvihāra near Sankhu,[15] while the Buṅgajātrā (the Matysendranātha festival) is ascribed to Narendradeva.[16] Evidently, some Brahmins found that the fostering of Buddhism went too far; around 800 CE Buddhist shrines were apparently destroyed in Handigaon.

It was long thought that Buddhism first spread from Nepal to Tibet and China, but, in fact, it was transmitted in the middle of the first century through the Tarim Basin and the Gansu and Hexi corridors.

Starting in the sixth century, Mahāyāna Buddhism in the Kathmandu Valley developed into Vajrayāna Buddhism, which understood itself as a path to Buddhahood by implementing tantric methods to the Mahāyāna practices. It is first named in an inscription of Aṃśuvarman. The Vajrayāna adds to previous Buddhist movements the esoteric worship of Tantric deities (or Śakti or Prajñā) and considers itself a Tantric path to enlightenment that enables the acquisition of magical powers through initiations (*dīkṣā*). Hence the Vajrayāna goal of enlightenment is not so much *nirvāṇa* as (Nev.) *taray juye*, attainment of the Sukhāvatī heaven, the Pure Land of Amitābha or Buddhahood.[17] It is further characterized by its admixture of the teachings and cosmos of Hinduism, the worship of holy men and Bodhisattvas, the laicization of monasteries (perhaps from the twelfth century on), a hereditary priesthood, and the introduction of a caste framework, as well as many special rituals and festivals.

The Vajrayāna, whose texts were at first written in Sanskrit, but whose teachings were preached in Old Nevārī, at first spread among Newar Buddhist merchants and craftsmen, but it was not limited to Nepal. It spread early to Tibet, as Chinese sources from the seventh century and many manuscripts and sculptures, mostly influenced by the North Indian Pāla style, testify.

Although there is no inscriptional mention of Buddhism for four hundred years after the Licchavi inscriptions, we know from manuscripts and art objects that Buddhism continued to exist in the monasteries of the Kathmandu Valley. This is also true for the high mountain regions, such as Humla, Dolpo, Lo Mustang, Manang, Langtang, Helambu, or Solukhumbu. Magar, Gurung, Tamang, and Sherpa, most of whom live in Mid Hill regions and speak Tibeto-Burman languages, generally follow the Nyingma school and engage *lāmā* priests for their rituals.

Buddhism experienced new impetus when numerous refugees arrived in the twelfth century following the Islamic invasions of North India. Hundreds, perhaps thousands, of highly regarded scholars and students had to leave universities such as Nalanda, Vikramashila, Somapura, or Odantapuri when they shut down. Scholars and monks came in hordes with their patrons and pupils to Nepal. Patan in particular became a center of Buddhist scholarship and spirituality.[18]

The Blue Annals, one of the most important texts of Tibetan historiography, reports that a monk visited Nepāla as early as 755. Tibetan sources tell of famous monks, such as Dīpaṃkaraśrījñāna, better known as Atīśa, Jñānakara, and Vanaratna who went from India via Nepal to Tibet and of Tibetan holy men and monks who came to Nepāla. The monk Marpa learnt from native teachers in Pharping in 1065, and Dharmasvāmin supposedly spent a long time in the Kathmandu Valley. In the twelfth century, Tibetan scholar Ralo Dorje Drak experienced Patan as a Buddhist paradise filled with scholars and holy men.

In the monasteries of Patan, Buddhist texts were learnt by rote and repeatedly copied.[19] Among the early Buddhist manuscripts in Nepal are the *Prajñāpāramitā* (998 CE), a text on the life of the Buddha (*Lalitavistara*, 1036), the *Saddharmapuṇḍarīka* (1093), *Gaṇḍavyūha* (1166), *Kāraṇḍavyūha* (1196), *Kriyāsaṃgraha* (eleventeenth/twelfth century), *Avadānakalpalatā* (1302), *Gopālarājavaṃśāvalī* (fourteenth century), and the *Svayambhūpurāṇa*, probably from the fifteenth or sixteenth century. The *Nepālikabhūpavaṃśāvalī* reports that a *Prajñāpāramitā* manuscript was being preserved in Bu Bāhāḥ, having allegedly been brought there by Yaśodharā, a Brahmanical widow.[20]

The fifteenth-century *Guṇakāraṇḍavyūha* ("Set of Reliquaries of the Qualities [of Avalokiteśvara]") occupies a special place among the "Garland Texts" (*avadāna-māla*), which are dedicated to the consequences of actions in past lives. It contains fifteen stories about Avalokiteśvara, who appears in various forms, such as a seer or a bee, to help others to be reincarnated in the Sukhāvatī heaven and to attain full enlightenment. The metric text recurs to a prose text that is nearly a thousand years older, the *Kāraṇḍavyūha*, for which it was long mistaken. It is characterized by specifically Newar elements that, together with other factors, justify assuming a thorough reformation of Buddhism in the fifteenth century.[21] Among the elements are the language (a Newar-Buddhist Sanskrit) and special rituals, such as the widespread cult of the Bodhisattva Amoghapāśa (a form of Avalokiteśvara) or the *poṣadha* vows of fasting, central to the Buṅgadyaḥ procession.

Until the twelfth century, Nepalese Buddhism essentially followed Sanskrit models and was a part of Indian Buddhism, embedded in a supraregional system of places of pilgrimage, patronage, and identity. Between 1200 and 1450, this relation to India changed, not least because North India returned increasingly to its Brahmanical roots, partly in reaction to Islam, while Buddhism lost its legitimizing and protective function, which it had had in the Pāla Empire (750–1161 CE). This led to Newar Vajrayāna Buddhism losing its own legitimation, so it reformed itself in its own way by gradually entering into competition for royal patronage. It became more political and more ritualistic. "Before the Garland Texts [such as the *Guṇakāraṇḍavyūha*] we can speak of a Nepalese tradition within Indian Buddhism; after the Garland Texts, we must speak of a Nepalese Buddhism," says anthropologist and historian Will Tuladhar-Douglas.[22]

Another development was that the Bodhisattvas in the Kathmandu Valley more and more turned into regular gods. In the Mahāyāna hierarchy of beings to be worshiped, they stand between "holy men" (*siddha*) and the Buddha; they have reached the other side (i.e., heaven), but are not yet liberated (in *nirvāṇa*). They are also regarded as sons or emanations of the Five Transcendental Buddhas, who embody, among other things, the five elements of ether, air, fire, water, and earth. Female counterparts, the Buddhaśakti, are assigned to them, making the worship of female Buddhist deities, such as Tārā and Prajñāpāramitā, widespread in Vajrayāna and Newar Buddhism.

One of the best-known Bodhisattvas in Nepal is Padmapāṇi-Avalokiteśvara, also called Lokeśvara or Lokanātha ("ruler of the world"), who is also the patron deity of Tibet. Avalokiteśvara means literally "the god who looks down (*avalokita* + *īśvara*)" or the "Lord who observes the sounds (of the world) (*avalokite* + *svara*)," all expressive of his great compassion; another Buddhist name for him is Karuṇāmaya, "the compassionate one." His character and the religious mixture are particularly highlighted by the Rāto-Matsyendranātha festival, the outcome of which is the long-awaited rain he brings after the endless heat of summer. In this cult, an originally pre-Hindu and pre-Buddhist deity, Buṅgadyaḥ (literally "the god of Buṅga or present-day Bungamati"), has been conjoined with gods of both pantheons, for Avalokiteśvara is identical with Śiva-Lokeśvara or Matsyendranātha for Hindus.[23]

Another Bodhisattva, Mañjuśrī, is likewise associated with a Hindu deity, the goddess Sarasvatī who is regarded as his companion. Both are deities of wisdom and the arts; surprisingly they are seen in this case as actually identical, despite having different sexes.

Non-celibate Buddhism

From around the end of the twelfth century, a decline of monastic life set in,[24] even though some Buddhist communities lasted into the seventeenth century and new ones were created toward the end of the twentieth century under the influence of Tibetan Mahāyāna Buddhism or missionary Theravāda monks.[25] This brought primarily a hereditary priesthood and hereditary "monks" to the fore. Newar Buddhism has been called "Buddhism without monks," and it has introduced a kind of Buddhist caste system that still holds sway.[26] But this view fails to recognize that the heads of households of certain castes, such as the Shakya and the Vajracharya, could be monks who were members of a community (*saṅgha*) with the right and obligation to care for the esoteric deity of their monastery.

At the top of the Buddhist caste system are the Vajracharya who, apart from the caste initiation (Nev. *bare chuyegu*), also receive Tantric esoteric initiations (*dīkṣā*). In the fourteenth century, Sthiti Malla is said to have placed Buddhist priests on the same level as Rajopadhyaya Brahmins.[27] The Shakya, originally monks (*bhikṣu*) who derive their name from the clan of the Buddha, are equal to them in rank but do not receive higher Tantric initiations and are therefore not priests. Every male member of both groups becomes a monk during initiation, but only for four days. After this, each remains active in his monastic community for the rest of his life, even long after being married. Whoever wishes to become a Buddhist monk as an adult Newar, then, has to enter a Theravāda or Tibetan order. Shakya are also called Vandya or, in a phonological corruption of the term, Bare, and are often professional artisans.

This unique form of Buddhism in the Kathmandu Valley can also be observed in the fact that it is the only living Buddhist tradition that transmits its canonical texts in Sanskrit and in repurposed buildings, especially in 350 plus monasteries, which, however, are no longer used by celibate monks but by family clans, and in the increase in rituals with a simultaneous muffling of doctrine. These rituals are similar to "Hindu divine worship" (*pūjā*), and include, for example, regular worship of Buddhas and deities including the planetary gods (*navagraha*), calendric festivals, life-cycle rituals, chariot festivals, dances, vows (*vrata*), donations (*dāna*), and recitations of ritual texts, especially in the month of Gũlā, when texts such as the *Aṣṭasāhasrikā-Prajñāpāramitā*, a central text of Mahāyāna Buddhism, are read.

The life-cycle rituals (*saṃskāra*), in particular, show just how much Newar Buddhism followed Brahmanical archetypes, probably because Buddhist castes regarded them as a way to enjoy more respect at court, or to gain the privilege of supplying the court with goods, or even in order to fill positions at court.[28] Buddhist beings were worshiped and Buddhist ritual objects were used, but the actions were, for the most part, taken from Hindu ritual literature and practice. Many of these rituals included a modified fire ritual (*homa*). Quite distinct rituals developed in this process, such as the *ihi* ritual, in which girls are married to a *bel* fruit (wood apple), and the *gurumaṇḍalapūjā*,[29] which often frames life-cycle rituals and includes the worship of the Bodhisattva Vajrasattva, whom the Vajracharya priests regard as their "teacher" (*guru*).

Given the Buddhist doctrine of non-violence (*ahiṃsā*), the Vajrayāna participation in animal sacrifices is also quite unusual. Originally, Shakya and Vajracharya sacrificed ducks to Bhīmasena, but this was abolished in 1923, probably under the influence of Kyanche Lama. Nonetheless, a Vajracharya must often be present when clients wish to offer an animal sacrifice in a non-Buddhist context. Newar Buddhists are usually not vegetarians, and meat is important in many Vajrayāna rituals.

For Tibet and China, Nepal (or the Kathmandu Valley) was a Buddhist country from the fifteenth century, when contacts between Tibet and Nepal expanded, especially under Pratāpa Malla. Tibetan monks founded their own communities and built their own monasteries. Conversely, many Uray went to Tibet, where they had a higher status than in the Kathmandu Valley. Newar Buddhism has been preserved in its distinct form, but it has been joined by Tibetan Buddhism, which is concentrated around the Bauddha Stupa (also called Bodhnath or, in Nevārī, Khāsti Caitya). Bauddha, at forty meters in diameter, is the largest *stūpa* in the Kathmandu Valley. Its origins are ascribed by the *Nepālikabhūpavaṃśāvalī* to Mānadeva in the fifth century. According to Tibetan sources from the sixteenth century, a Tantric master of the Nyingma school unearthed the *caitya* out of rubble and sand at the start of the century. This is the reason why Tibetan monks started taking care of the shrine.

Taking together Nepal as the Buddha's country of birth, Newar Buddhism, and Tibetan Buddhism, which has gained a foothold among many ethnic groups in the mountain regions, one can say with some justification that Nepal is much more Buddhist than often appears when restricting one's view to its central belt (including the Kathmandu Valley) and to the Tarai.

Hinduism

Hinduism, in Nepal often called *parbatiyā* ("mountain people's") or *smārta* ("traditional") Hinduism, is a Brahmanically dominated religion in which traditionally five deities or some manifestation of them stand out: Śiva, Viṣṇu, Gaṇeśa, the Great Goddess (Mahādevī, Devī, Śakti, Kālī, et al.), and Sūrya (or a deity of one's own choosing). Correspondingly many different religious currents have developed: Śaivism, Vaiṣṇavism, Śāktism, Kṛṣṇaism, Rāmaism, and others.[30]

Parbatiyā or Smārta Hinduism is characterized primarily by its closeness to the Veda. This is shown in the Licchavi inscriptions, which frequently speak of Vedic deities, such as Indra, Sūrya, and Agni, so one must assume that there was a living Vedic tradition at that time.[31] Thus, Mānadeva praises his father for carrying out Vedic sacrifices and mentions Brahmins (*vipra*, *dvija*) in his Changu Narayana inscription (464 CE). Agni is still revered by Newar Brahmins as an undying fire in an Agniśālā in Patan.[32] Another ritual has to do with Indra, who appears in the Veda as the sun god and the king of the gods, but in India is no longer the object of much attention. In Nepal, he is mentioned in at least eight Licchavi inscriptions and honored in many statues. In the autumn, an eight-day festival in Kathmandu is dedicated to him. Indra came to Earth once in the form of a human in order to steal the heavenly *pārijāta* flower. He was detected and thereupon tied to a wooden post like a thief, the post later being called Indradhvaja. He was freed only with the help of his mother. It is this episode that is represented in the popular Indrajātrā, a procession and festival in Kathmandu.[33] Finally, for the life-cycle rituals, the Brahmanically informed populations generally follow a late Vedic model based upon the *Pāraskaragṛhyasūtra*, a manual of household rites from the Mādhyandina school of the *Vājasaneyisaṃhitā* of the White (Śukla) Yajurveda.[34]

Parbatiyā Hinduism owes its prevalence in the foothill region and the Tarai to various waves of immigration by Brahmins from numerous parts of India, along with its promotion by rulers.[35] Upadhyaya Brahmins or Brahmins from Kumaon are responsible for the Bahun-Chhetri, Mithila Brahmins for the Tarai, and Rajopadhyaya Brahmins for the Hindu Newar. They have not only significantly contributed to cultural and religious development and introduced the caste system but also competed to some extent with Newar Tantric Hinduism. To increase their status, other groups, ethnic or otherwise, often adopted elements of Smārta Hinduism, thus Hinduizing themselves to some extent.

In Licchavi inscriptions there is already mention of donations of villages to Brahmins and colophons of early medieval manuscripts name Brahmins from Gujarat, Kashmir, Bengal, or South India. But the large waves of immigration and the greater influences they brought first arrived in the fourteenth century, when Muslims penetrated Bengal and Harisiṃhadeva was forced to flee from Simraunagarh in the Tarai to Bhaktapur after being defeated by

Tuglaq in 1324. Subsequently, many scholarly Brahmins came from Mithila to Nepal, which is evident in the large number of extant manuscripts in Maithilī script and language. The *Nepālikabhūpavaṃśāvalī*, too, speaks of Sthiti Malla having brought five Brahmins from Mithila to the court at Kathmandu, a tradition continued by other Malla rulers.

During the Malla Period, Śaiva Tantrism and the worship of the goddesses held sway, with rulers providing strong support for these cults. The goddess Taleju (Tulajā) in particular, worshiped especially by the Tantric ritual specialists within palace circles, became the unrivalled goddess of the Malla, with many rituals for her clearly meant to underscore their claim to power. This is why the Śāha and Rāṇā carried on with this worship of Tantric-esoteric goddesses, while still stressing their connections to the exoteric Smārta goddesses. At the same time, Hinduism overlay many old gods and rituals, originally folk-religious in character, that had long been at home in the Kathmandu Valley. The Brahmins added their own accents to the worship of these deities by, for instance, overlaying and modifying the Hindu worship (*pūjā*) or the fire ritual (*homa*). For the Newar inhabitants of the Kathmandu Valley, the deities that protect the settlements and the valley are mainly Viṣṇu/Nārāyaṇa and Śiva/Paśupati, Bhairava, Durgā (also known as Bhagavatī), the Eight Mother Goddesses (Aṣṭamātṛkā) or Nine Durgās (Navadurgā), and Gaṇeśa.

The Śāha and Rāṇā propagated Hinduism as the national religion. After the *Ain* came into force, conversion to other religions was forbidden,[36] and after the 1935 revision of this text, when a distinction between "religion" (*dharma*) (for Hinduism) and "belief" (*mata*) (for Christianity and Islam) was introduced, missionary activity was also forbidden, which did not, however, stop Christian missionaries from continuing their activities in Nepal. Article 14 of the Constitution of 1962 states: "Everyone can profess their religion as traditionally handed down and can practice it according to tradition—with the proviso that nobody is permitted to convert anyone from one religion to another." In the Constitution of 2015 (Article 1), Nepal is called a secular state, but an accompanying annotation defines *secular* as "religious and cultural freedom," which includes the protection of religion and traditional rituals.

A neo-Hindu movement like the one in India hardly ever existed in Nepal, but in the last few decades groups such as the Hare Krishna followers have occasionally appeared, and there was a strong campaign by Kavi Prasad, who popularized the public recitation of devotional songs (*kīrtana*, *bhajana*) in the worship of Kṛṣṇa and Rāma.[37] The emergent middle class is not averse to turning to esoteric or neo-religious ideas and practices, or to outright secularism, promoted especially by the Maoists and social activists.[38]

The Śāha dynasty created unique religious tension, and even a rudimentary rivalry between Tantric Hinduism or Buddhism, on the one hand, and Parbatiyā Hinduism on the other, which escalated to more or less open conflict, for example during the festival for the goddess Vatsalā. For the most part, however, the religions and the various religious currents have co-existed peacefully.

Paurāṇic and Tantric Śaivism

The veneration of Śiva and his "family" in texts, *liṅgas* and statues, processions and festivals is known of in Nepal from early on, not least because it enjoyed royal protection.[39] Already in 605 CE, Aṃśuvarman felt himself favored from having touched the foot of Śiva-Paśupatinātha, which is a standard formulation in inscriptions down to Yakṣa Malla. The veneration Śiva enjoyed and the royal support for Śaivism had to do with Śiva's growing popularity in North India. In inscriptions, Śiva appears in a mild form as creator and preserver, but also as a powerful destroyer, and it is probably owing to this side of him that Paśupati became so important for the rulers. Another reason for the royal support may have been that Śaivism offered a special initiation for kings, including support for Śaiva devotees and ascetics, which did not oblige them to observe all the troublesome ritual practices, but which promised success in this life and salvation after death. Nonetheless, many Licchavi rulers were at the same time venerators of Viṣṇu and other gods. Aṃśuvarman, for example, the name of whose seat of power, Kailāśakūṭabhavana, indicates that he revered Śiva, equally supported both the Vaiṣṇava Cāṅgunārāyaṇa temple and Buddhist monasteries.

Both Paurāṇic and Tantric Śaivism are clearly set off against the Vedic traditions and, for the most part, are not recognized by "orthodox," Vedic Brahmins. Śaivism, consequently, has its own texts.[40] In some of these texts Śaivism's superiority to the Veda is emphasized, without completely rejecting the latter. In addition to the Vedic tradition, the need for Śaiva rituals and spiritual practices toward attaining enlightenment or supernatural powers is stressed. Moreover, many early Śaiva Tantric texts propagate or refer to cults in which the Śaiva practice of devotion is bound up with Vaiṣṇavism, the Dharmaśāstra, and Buddhism.

The most prominent shrine of Śiva is the Paśupatinātha temple in Deopatan, east of Kathmandu, known far beyond the borders of Nepal and the annual destination of thousands of Indian pilgrims and tourists.[41] This temple, in which Śiva is worshiped as a "four-faced" (*caturmukha*) *liṅga*, is surrounded by numerous temples, shrines, rest houses, bathing sites (*ghāṭa*) on the banks of the Bagmati River, shops, and residences.

It would appear that many ascetic followers of the Pāśupata cult once maintained the Paśupatinātha temple.[42] One indication of this are the many manuscripts belonging to the Śivadharma tradition, a lay movement within Śaivism that arose under the influence of the Pāśupata.[43] While the Pāśupata ascetics, known for dwelling at cremation sites and rubbing themselves with ashes from immolated corpses, had soteriological goals, the donation of *liṅgas* by lay followers served more worldly interests. Five Licchavi inscriptions show that the Pāśupata were a prominent community in the time of Aṃśuvarman, among them an inscription, dating from the year 489 CE, found in 1995 on the plinth of a vanished statue, and in which Śarvāṇī, a female consort of Śiva, who is known particularly among the Pāśupata under the name of Śarva, is praised.[44]

Besides these early Tantric references to the Paśupatinātha temple, a Paurāṇic foundation myth for the appearance of Śiva in Deopatan is related

Figure 3.1 Paśupatinātha temple with the Vatsalā temple (below) and cremation sites, 1981. Photo by Axel Michaels.

in the *Nepālamāhātmya*.[45] According to it, Śiva came to this area from Kāśī (Varanasi) and took on the form of a gazelle in order to romp with his consort Pārvatī, who also had the form of a gazelle, in the Mṛgasthalī ("gazelle grove"). As a result, though, the world descended into chaos, and so the other gods set out to find Śiva. When they finally succeeded, they asked him to give up his gazelle form, but he refused. They tried to catch him, but he sprang to the other side of the river, where his horn broke into four pieces and became a holy shrine in the form of the four-faced *liṅga*. Śiva was known from then on as Paśupati, the Lord of the Animals.

According to the chronicles, the Paśupatinātha temple was built in the third century. It is also mentioned as early as the seventh century in an interpolation of the Pāśupata version of the *Skandapurāṇa*.[46] The *Gopālarājavaṃśāvalī* names Ananta Malla as having renovated it and gilded the roof. Further innovations and renovations were undertaken by Śivasiṃha Malla and Pratāpa Malla, but above all by Bhūpālendra Malla, who had the main temple taken down in 1696 and rebuilt after 105 days. Afterward it has received many other donations that range from the gilding of small statues to extensive gifts of land and valuable paraphernalia. The gates in particular were repeatedly gilded or coated in silver: in 1814 the north portal, by Amara Siṃha Thāpā, four years later the south one by Bhīmasena Thāpā, and in 1834 the west portal by Kulānanda Jhā. The kings Mahendra and Birendra also gilded roofs or covered ceilings in silver. Between 1848 and 1870, some seven hundred statues along with votive temples and shrines were set up. Older, and ritually more significant, are the many temples and shrines to the goddesses, among them a local Navadurgā group: Vatsalā, Vajreśvarī (or Pigamāī), Jayavāgīśvarī, Bhuvaneśvarī, Rājarājeśvarī, Bālakumārī, Jhaṅkeśvarī, Koṭeśvarī, and Guhyeśvarī.

The *liṅga* cult can be shown to have come into existence in Nepal no later than the fourth/fifth centuries.[47] It is expressed by worshiping an abstract phallic symbol, which can have faces on each of four sides, representing various manifestations of the divinity, or only one bust, which represents Śiva as the First Yogī. Already in the early Licchavi Period, beginning with the Ratneśvara *liṅga* (477 CE), many members of the aristocracy and wealthy merchants set up votive *liṅgas* in the area around the Paśupatinātha temple, a tradition that has brought forth the largest corpus of inscriptions on *liṅgas* in South Asia and continued into the late nineteenth century.[48]

The largest *liṅga*, not only in Nepal but in all of South Asia, is the Virāṭeśvara (late fourth century?), which stands on a well at the Bagmati

River in front of the Rājarājeśvarī temple.[49] It is said of this well that one could once see one's future reincarnation in it. The chronicles report that the Licchavi king Śaṅkaradeva looked into it and saw a rat swimming below, whereupon he had the well covered over with a *liṅga*.

In the Śāha and Rāṇā periods, some votive *liṅga* structures donated in memory of someone deceased began to take on monumental proportions. The *liṅgas* are, to some extent, arranged in groups, such as the "Fifteen-*Liṅga* Group" (Pandhraśivālaya) on the eastern bank of the Bagmati River, which were set up after the Koṭa Massacre of September 14, 1846. In the courtyard of the Paśupatinātha temple there is even a temple, the Koṭiliṅgeśvara, with 1008 *liṅgas*, set up by Prātapa Malla in 1654.

Many Śaiva shrines and temples are associated with "processions" (*tīrthayātrā*). The biggest of these pilgrimages is the "Great Night of Śiva" (Mahāśivarātri) in February/March, when thousands of pilgrims, among them many ascetics, come to the Paśupatinātha temple to worship Śiva and to fast, some occasionally staying awake all night.[50] The festival, documented in India since the twelfth century, goes back to a myth that clearly shows the integration of non-Hindu layers of society into Hindu society, and thus the caste system: Once a hunter (a member of an impure caste) is supposed to

Figure 3.2 Virāṭeśvara, the largest *liṅga* at Deopatan, 2082. Photo by Axel Michaels.

have been hunting in the forest when nightfall overcame him. Fearing for his life, he climbed a pipal tree, taking some water with him. A little water kept dripping down throughout the night, and some leaves of the tree fell as well; this all landed upon a *liṅga* hidden in undergrowth. As the hunter had worshiped Śiva with leaves and water during his watch throughout the night, albeit unintentionally and unconsciously, he was taken up into the god's heaven.

In iconographic representations, Śiva is often shown as Umāmaheśvara with his long hair tied up on his head and in a peaceful embrace with his consort Pārvatī (alias Umā), or as Ardhanarīśvara (half Śiva, half Pārvatī). In these representations, his consort usually appears in her beneficent aspect. Her most frequent names are Pārvatī ("daughter of the mountain"), Umā ("dawn"), and Gaurī ("the golden one"). She can appear alone, as on a great Gaurī rock in the Bagmati River north of the Paśupatinātha temple, or together with Śiva.

Śiva is worshiped in the Kathmandu Valley in many other distinctive forms, for instance, as Lukumahādyaḥ, Nāsadyaḥ, or Bhairava, in which the relationship between Śiva and Pārvatī, owing to Tantric influences, is not always so harmonious.[51] In the Lukumahādyaḥ ritual, which is celebrated by the Newar when the courtyards are cleaned of rubble and rubbish on the fourteenth day of the dark half of the month of Caitra (March/April), the "Day of the Demon."[52] On this occasion, a small *liṅga* or an uncarved stone is brought out from beneath the rubbish or out of a hole and worshiped during the night. These stones are called Lukumahādyaḥ in Nevārī (probably "hidden Mahādeva"). According to orally transmitted myths, Śiva sought protection here because (depending on the source) wild goddesses, evil demons, or even ignorant Buddhists threatened to pollute him.

The god Nāsadyaḥ ("God of the Dance"), the Newar musicians' patron god, is a similar case that shows how pre-Hindu cult elements have become mixed with Śaivism. It is a god whose path one may not block, which is why slits are built into many walls and in special shrines, through which the god may pass without having to make a detour. Neither the cult nor its form originally had anything to do with Śiva. But Śiva is the "Lord of the Dance" (Nāṭyeśvara or Naṭarāja) in the high Indian tradition. Combining both gods raised the musicians' status. Thus the patron god received the name Nāsadyaḥ, the Nevārī version of Nāṭyeśvara.

Bhairava, too, a horrific and destructive form of Śiva, is sometimes simply a bare stone, even though he is mostly worshiped in statues or masks.[53]

He displays traces of pre-Hindu deities whose status rose in the course of Hinduization after receiving prestigious Sanskrit names. The Bhairava cult in the Kathmandu Valley, known from the Licchavi Period on, was given a big boost by Tantrism, particularly among the Newar, and above all when connected with the veneration of goddesses or *yoginīs*. Numerous Tantric texts, especially the *Brahmayāmala*, *Śrītantrasadbhāva*, and *Jayadrathayāmala*, bear witness to this cult. Bhairava is appeased by being given alcohol and blood sacrifices. Among the outstanding holy sites is the great statue of Kāla/Kālo ("black") Bhairava at Hanuman Dhoka, which was supposedly either erected or discovered by Pratāpa Malla in the seventeenth century, and the spot where officials were sworn in. Near Kāla Bhairava, and hidden behind a wooden lattice, stands Sveta ("white") Bhairava, donated in 1795 by Raṇabahādura Śāha; during the Indrajātrā procession, rice beer streams out of its mouth and is drunk by devotees. Other exceptional Bhairavas are the Pacali Bhairava in Kathmandu, whom the child goddess Kumārī visits to worship; the Nīlabhairava painting, renewed every twelve years, on the north side of the Jayavāgīśvarī temple in Deopatan; and the great Bhairava temple in Bhaktapur, the focal point of the Bisketjātrā festival.

A connection of Nepalese Śaivism to the Indian Śaiva Nātha movement is seen in the Gorakhanātha cult, which from the eleventh century on propagated a mixture of yoga practices and Śiva worship alongside esoteric teachings.[54] The holy man and ascetic Gorakhanātha (from Skt. Gorakṣanātha) is venerated in the form of his footprints at his own temples, for example, in Deopatan, Pharping, or Dathuṭol, and at the Kāṣṭhamaṇḍapa in Kathmandu. In the chronicles, he is regarded as a pupil of Matsyendranātha ("He Whose Lord, [Śiva,] Is the Indra [= Head] of Fishes"). In one myth it is said that he caused a drought of several years in Assam because he was sitting on rain-bringing serpents while meditating. On orders from king Narendradeva, the priest Bandhudatta Ācārya was sent with Matsyendranātha to Assam, where Gorakhanātha had to stand up out of respect for his teacher, thus freeing the serpents, who were then able to bring rain. In the annual Matsyendranātha procession (May/June), a small black "vest" (*bhoṭo*) is displayed, whereupon, many say, it must rain on this day.

This Matsyendranātha procession, which the *Nepālikabhūpavaṃśāvalī* ascribes to Narendradeva, again reveals a close link between Hinduism and Buddhism, because the Hindu Matsyendranātha is also the Buddhist Avalokiteśvara and Karuṇāmaya ("the Compassionate One") and the local god Buṅgadyaḥ ("the god from Bugā").[55] According to the *Gopālarājava ṃśāvalī*, Bugā, where the procession starts every twelve years, was a popular place of pilgrimage as early as the twelfth century. The veneration of Matsyendranātha is documented first in 1647 CE (NS 795), in an inscription of Śrīnivāsa Malla in Bugā, but could well be older. The Matsyendranātha temple in Patan (Ta Bāhāḥ) was constructed in the seventeenth century. Other manifestations of Matsyendranātha are, for example, the White Matsyendranātha in Kathmandu, the Red (Rāto) Matsyendranātha in Patan, and Mīnanātha in Patan.

The popular elephant-headed deity Gaṇeśa or Vināyaka ("the remover of hindrances") has quite a distinct character of his own in Nepal. He is the son of Śiva but also an independent deity within Śaivism, Śāktism, and Buddhism.[56] Among the oldest statues is the four-armed Gaṇeśa of the third century, beside a "rest house" (Nev. *phalcā*) at Su Bāhāḥ in Patan. Again in the case of Gaṇeśa, pre-Hindu characteristics are mixed in with what is perhaps the most popular benevolent god of India. In the Kathmandu Valley, however, he receives not only sweets but also Tantric blood sacrifices and alcohol to prevent calamities. Gaṇeśa, thus, protects nearly every crossroad, house, temple, or city quarter, and the entire Kathmandu Valley from four places: Bhaktapur (Sūryavināyaka), Chabahil (Candravināyaka), Kathmandu (Aśokavināyaka), and Chobhar (Jala- or Koināvināyaka).[57] Certain uncarved coarse stones are also designated as Gaṇeśa, in which the otherwise well-known elephant's head with its trunk can only be made out with a good deal of imagination. A particularly striking example is a Gaṇeśa in Kathmandu that one worships in case of toothache; this is done by hammering a nail through a coin into a wooden block, which in the course of the time got covered completely. Probably Gaṇeśa is venerated most often by the Newar in the Kathmandu Valley on "oil lamps" (*sukundā*) that contain a tiny image of Gaṇeśa, which must not fail to be present at any Newar Hindu ritual.

Śāktism

An important part of Tantrism is the worship of the Goddess (often called Śāktism).[58] In the Nepalese Pāśupata recension of the *Skandapurāṇa* (sixth/seventh centuries), the Goddess is already regarded as Śakti, the wild and at times threatening embodiment of the female cosmic energy of Śiva, and as Mahādevī, the "Great Goddess." As such, she can even subordinate Śiva to herself, so the pre-Hindu characteristics of such goddesses shine through all the more. Being considered as fearful and malevolent, it is necessary to pacify them lest epidemics, earthquakes, or bad harvests result. An example is Śītalā, the goddess of smallpox, of whom there is a life-sized statue in the Kumbheśvara temple in Patan. Her Buddhist counterpart is the *ajimā* ("grandmother") Hārītī, who has a much-frequented temple at the Svayambhū Stūpa. Of her it is said that she brings illness to children.

"Śāktism" denotes the Tantric veneration of such d goddesses; the term is generally associated with Śaivism and Buddhism, less so with Vaiṣṇavism, in which "mild" goddesses such as Lakṣmī, Sītā, or Sarasvatī are worshiped.[59] In contrast, the "wild" goddess in Śāktism appears in divine coitus, wears chains strung with the heads of decapitated men, or treads triumphantly on the bodies of demons or gods defeated by her, including Śiva. She appears as a "mother" (*-māī*) or as an *ajimā*, and often in groups of similar deities.

Frequently, these goddesses are local, pre-Hindu divinities who have been around since ancient times, and who sometimes keep their original names and function, for example, Lumādi (Bhadrakālī), Kanga Ajimā (Kaṅkeśvarī), Lutumarī (Indrayāṇī), or Pīgāmāī (Vajreśvarī). But often they have been overlaid by the Great Goddess, most prominently from the Kālīkula (the "Family of Kālī"). Among these are the goddesses Durgā, Bhadrakālī, Caṇḍī, and Śītalā, all regarded as aspects of Kālī. Kālī and Cāmuṇḍā, who in Nepal are iconographically hardly distinguishable, are often represented as a gaunt, haggard figure displaying flat, sagging breasts, chains of human bones, and serpents around her neck, while dancing on a corpse. They like to frequent cremation sites or similarly dark locations outside settlements. One of their favorite manifestations is as "Kālī of the south," Dakṣiṇakālī, who protects the Kathmandu Valley in that direction. Their small shrine, surrounded by images of other Mother Goddesses, is hidden in a gorge along a hill stream. It must have once been the seat of a pre-Hindu goddess who, as so often in the valley, only gradually became identified with the Great Goddess of the Hindu pantheon.

The earliest documented version in the Kathmandu Valley of the *Devīmāhātmya* (the "[Book] of the Splendour of Devī," also known as the *Durgāsaptaśatī* or *Caṇḍī*) goes back to the eleventeenth century. It is one of the most widespread Śākta writings in which the myths of Durgā and Kālī are summarized. The latter, for example, is found in a fourfold form: as Guhyakālī (or Guhyeśvarī), Vatsalākālī, Dakṣiṇakālī, and Kalaṅkīkālī, all also being sites famous for their animal sacrifices. Kālī/Cāmuṇḍā is also known in the Kathmandu Valley as Bhadrakālī, Kaṅkeśvarī, Svetakālī (also

Figure 3.3 The goddess Indrāyaṇī riding on her elephant, Gokarṇeśvara temple, 2014. Photo by Ashesh Rajbansh.

called Naradevī), or Raktakālī. The Kāpālikā sect of of the Śaiva-Tantric Mantramārga, who wore necklaces of human skulls and dwelt at cremation sites, worshiped Kālī in the same way as those who venerated her in her manifestation form in the *Devīmāhātmya*: as the goddess of deliverance and immortality.

The cult of the goddess Kubjikā is another ancient cult, which in India is as good as extinct.[60] According to some researchers, it supposedly arose in Nepal when Newar Rajopadhyaya Brahmins and priests of the Malla kings made this goddess their patron deity as many documents, beginning from the eleventeenth century, testify. Thus, in the colophon of the *Kularatnoddyota* there are indications that the manuscript was copied during the rule of Harṣadeva. A manuscript of the *Kubjikāmatatantra* was written a little later, in the twelfth century. From about the same time is the *Netratantra* (also known as the *Amṛteśatantra* or *Amṛteśapūjāvidhi*), which bears witness to the Tantric rituals of the early Malla Period.[61] It was copied for Ari Malla I by a pandit from Gujarat in 1216, shortly before the king's death. This text occupies a place between a Vedic Śaiva cult and the extreme Tantric Kaula cults. The worship of Kubjikā in Nepal is limited almost exclusively to the Newar.

One of the more frequent motifs is that of Durgā killing the demon Mahiṣa, which appears repeatedly on archways over temple entrances or on carved wooden roof struts. Durgā is thereby usually treading on the demon Mahiṣa, who has taken the form of a water buffalo terrorizing the world, and piercing him with a long spear. This motif comes to life when, in the autumnal Dasaĩ festival dedicated to Durgā, many Hindus sacrifice animals.[62] This festival, also known (especially in India) as Navarātra ("nine nights"), was the most important royal ritual from no later than the Malla Period onward. The Śāha rulers would later try to impose it on groups other than the Khasa-Arya, not least in order to create religious unity in the process of nation building.[63]

The manifestation of the Goddess as Taleju (Skt. Tulajā) is of great significance in Nepal, where she is primarily a protective goddess of the Malla rulers, known of at least as early as the fourteenth century and worshiped in secret rituals. Her mantra was supposed to guarantee the kings their power. In all three palaces of the Kathmandu Valley, the most magnificent temple (Kathmandu) or shrines in the main courtyard (Bhaktapur and Patan) are dedicated to Taleju. In Kathmandu, her temple overtops all other buildings.

Its inner sanctum is a closely guarded secret; it is said that it contains a cult image or a water jug (*kalaśa*), in which the goddess resides.

One can see from the cult, the mythology, the forms of veneration, and the iconography that it is always the one Goddess appearing in different manifestations. Certain groups of goddesses arranged in cosmic diagrams (*maṇḍala*) are basically also one and the same goddess. Thus, the "Eight Mothers" (Aṣṭamātṛkā) or the "Nine Durgā" (Navadurgā) turn up repeatedly, surrounding a settlement or a temple. In Bhaktapur, for example, these are shrines or temples of Brahmāṇi or Brāhmī (east), Māheśvarī or Rudrāyaṇī (south-east), Kaumārī (south), Vaiṣṇavī (south-west), Vārāhī (west), Indrāṇī (north-west), Cāmuṇḍā (north), and Mahālakṣmī (north-east). They each have their own Bhairava to accompany them. In the center, there is the ninth goddess, Tripurasundarī. In the Rājarājeśvarī temple in Deopatan, all nine goddesses may be seen together as statues.

The Goddess is represented under various names in less exalted places, too. Her temple or shrine usually lies outside any settlement, so that she can protect its inhabitants. As a rule, in the town itself a mobile cult image of her is kept in a special "god-house" (Nev. *dyaḥchẽ*); this image is brought out and carried along exactly established routes during special festivals, such as the one of Vatsalā (literally "small calf, the tender one").[64]

This goddess has a temple in Deopatan, steps away to the south of the Paśupatinātha temple, which has no panels in its doorways, for, as is told in local legends and lore, Vatsalā likes to inhale the perfume of the nearby cremation sites. This alone shows what sort of goddess she is. Her festival in March/April that lasts for nine days and eight nights includes many animal sacrifices and worshiping with alcohol. At the end of a night in which there are even ritual signs of former human sacrifices, believers bathe in rice beer flowing from pipes of the Vatsalā temple into the Bagmati River. Afterwards, around forty men carry the goddess in her mobile form in a processional litter to the main temple of Śiva/Paśupati. But he rejects the goddess because she has become unclean through the sacrifices, visible when the priests close the gates to the temple courtyard. Vatsalā is angry and threatens to leave Paśupati. The ritual participants then carry the litter to the outskirts of the city. Paśupati relents and has Vatsalā recalled full of remorse. In a three-day triumphal procession, in which the goddess is worshiped by every household along the processional route, she returns. When she finally reaches the Paśupatinātha temple, the god reconciles with her by giving her a red piece of cloth (presented by the chief priest) as a symbol of a sari. In this festival, the contrast between pure and Paurāṇic, Brahmanical Hinduism on the one side, and the "impure," Tantric, and local Newar Hinduism on the other side becomes a conflict, but it is ritually resolved in such a way that both sides can live together.

Vaiṣṇavism, Rāmaism, and Kṛṣṇaism

Among the earliest objects in Nepal are Vaiṣṇava sculptures.[65] According to recent research, it would appear that Vaiṣṇavism was generally much more widespread in the first half of the first millennium than has been assumed hitherto.[66] Viṣṇu is invoked already in the earliest Licchavi inscriptions. Thus, in the long inscription on a stele in Changu Narayan according to which Mānadeva I (464 CE) had two identical statues of Viṣṇu/Garuḍa set up for the soul of his mother Rājyadevī, representing the god Viṣṇu as he traverses the three worlds (the underworld, this world, and the next world) in three steps (*trivikrānta*, *trivikrama*). Similar statues from the seventh to nineth century stand at the Paśupatinātha temple (Tilganga) and in the Lazimpat quarter of Kathmandu.

Cāṅgunārāyaṇa ("Nārāyaṇa of the *cāgu* tree")[67] stands on a hill some 2.5 miles north of Bhaktapur.[68] It is surrounded by two-story buildings from the nineteenth century and contains the oldest sculptures in the Kathmandu Valley. The present temple dates from the beginning of the eighteenth century. Earlier renovations are mentioned in chronicles from the twelfth century and the years 1506, 1676, and 1694, the last two during the time of Queen Riddhilakṣmī and her underaged son, Bhūpālendra Malla, both commemorated with bronze effigies as donors on the west side of the building. During the inauguration, in 1704 or 1708, all three kings of the Kathmandu Valley were present.

The central cult image with Viṣṇu riding Garuḍa is probably from the fourth century. The life-sized Garuḍa in anthropomorphic form on the west side is possibly a likeness of Mānadeva. A similar stele in Handigaon is undated, but epigraphic criteria justify ascribing it to the time of Mānadeva or Vasantadeva.

Viṣṇu is often also called Nārāyaṇa or Hari. As such he appears as (Jalaśayana or Śeṣaśayana) Nārāyaṇa on a snake, lying in the original waters from which the world was created. A large statue of this sort, from the seventh century, is called Buḍhānīlakaṇṭha and located north of Kathmandu;

a further such statue is found in the royal palace at Hanuman Dhoka. They testify to the promotion of Vaiṣṇavism by Licchavi and Malla kings. In the Malla epoch, Vaiṣṇava inscriptions become fewer, but the popularity of Viṣṇu remained. This showed itself among the kings, for example, in the incorporation of the divine name into their own: from Viṣṇu Malla to the name of the last royal palace, Narayanhiti. The Śāha even regarded themselves as descendants of Rāma and incarnations of Viṣṇu.

Figure 3.4 Viṣṇu riding Garuḍa, Changu Narayan, 2014. Photo by Niels Gutschow.

Also popular are representations of Viṣṇu in his ten *avatāras*: Matsya ("fish"), Kūrma ("tortoise"), Varāha ("boar"), Narasiṃha, Vāmana ("dwarf"), Paraśurāma ("Rāma with an axe"), Rāma, Kṛṣṇa, the Buddha, and Kalkin (Viṣṇu riding on a white horse). A large statue of Varāha from the sixth century, for instance, stands in Dhumvarāhī (Dhumbarai). Hanumān, a god in the form of a monkey, also often appears at Vaiṣṇava shrines. He is extremely popular because he helped one of Viṣṇu's manifestations, the heroic god Rāma, over many difficulties.

Apart from the classical manifestations, Viṣṇu's emanations (*vyūha*) are often categorized into groups—for example, the Four Emanations (*caturmūrti* or *caturvyūha*) Vāsudeva, Saṃkarṣaṇa, Pradyumna, and Aniruddha, who can occasionally be seen on four-faced truncated columns. The conflation of manifestations or shrines is an essential part of the religious dynamics of Hinduism. These classificatory criteria play some role when it comes to organizing pilgrimages. As with Gaṇeśa, Kālī, or other gods, there is a single group of four associated Viṣṇu temples, the Four Nārāyaṇas; these are the Cāṅgu, Viśaṅkhu, Śeṣa, and Icaṅgunārāyaṇa temples.[69] The founders, according to the chronicles, were Haridattavarman (before the fourth century, not known from inscriptions) and/or Viṣṇugupta, to the latter of whom the foundation of the four Jalaśayana Nārāyaṇas is also ascribed.[70]

Rāma and Kṛṣṇa, although traditionally regarded as forms of Viṣṇu, established themselves early on as autonomous, powerful, and fervently worshiped deities. Even though Nepal has nothing close to India's manifold traditions of Rāma and Kṛṣṇa veneration, there are distinct independent developments. The content of the epic *Rāmāyaṇa* was known in Nepal already in the eighth century, as is clear from an inscription of Jayadeva II.[71] Names containing Rāma, such as Rāmadeva, are found in other Licchavi inscriptions, but the only early representation from this period is a relief of Rāma with Sītā near the Paśupatinātha temple, dated to the seventh century and stolen in 1985.[72] The next iconographic representations of Rāma stem from the seventeenth century only. Many manuscripts of the *Rāmāyaṇa* verifiably date from the twelfth century, the oldest being from 1154. Performances of the *Rāmāyaṇa* have been recorded for the Malla epoch and can still be watched in Patan.

Temples of Rāma, on the other hand, are rather rare in the Kathmandu Valley.[73] A temple on the east bank of the Bagmati River in Deopatan, locally called the Rāma or Rāmacandra temple, contains statues not of Rāma with his sons Lava and Kuśa, as often claimed, but of Viṣṇugupta and his sons. In the chronicles, the construction of the temple is ascribed to Sthiti Malla.

Nonetheless, this area is full of shrines dedicated to Rāma and his family, primarily set up by the Rāṇā; for example, there is a temple erected by Prime Minister Bhīma Śamśera containing statues of Rāma's family: Nārāyaṇa, Sītā, Lakṣmaṇa, Bharata, and Hanumān.

A Rāmacandra temple was constructed by Sanak Siṃha Lāhūrī Ṭaṇḍan Chhetri (or Khatrī) in 1871 in Battisputali near Deopatan, and another one in 1864 in Jaisideval (Kathmandu) by a certain Dharma Siṃha.[74] Further Rāma temples were built by the Rāṇā at the Ramghat in Bhaktapur (1927), at the Hanumanghat in Bhaktapur (1932), and at the Kalamochanghat and the Pancalighat in Kathmandu. This accumulation of Rāma temples clearly illustrates a trend that was even more pronounced in India: Rāma was steadily turning into one of the major gods of Hinduism. The political preferment shown him in India is verifiable for the Kathmandu Valley only in the nineteenth century and the first half of the twentieth.

It is a different story in Janakpur in the Tarai, named after King Janaka, where the well-known holy man Rāmānanda, a zealous worshiper of Rāma, allegedly lived. This city, also traditionally known as Janakapurdham,[75] lies hardly twelve miles from the Indian frontier and is one of the most visited places of pilgrimage in the country. Down to the middle of the twentieth century, however, Janakpur was a relatively unknown conglomeration of small villages and residences for sects. Janakpur owes its fame primarily to the strong support of Rāmānandī ascetics by the Sena and Śāha kings. Thus, according to the *Rāmāyaṇa*, the goddess Sītā is said to have been born in Janakpur. As in Ayodhya, fundamentalist Hindu fanatics repeatedly try to reinterpret mythological history as real history. The Rāmānandī, too, have no doubt that Sītā was born in Janakpur. According to their orally transmitted tales, the "historical" facts long remained hidden, but guided by divine inspiration they "rediscovered" the site in the late seventeenth century and built the first monasteries there.

Thus a hamlet in the middle of the jungle became a place of pilgrimage, which was supported from then on mainly by the Sena rulers of Makwanpur, who endowed the monasteries with land. When the Gorkha kings conquered Makwanpur, they continued the tradition. They granted land (*kuśabirtā*) without requiring anything back from the ascetics because they hoped to gain religious merit and protection for their kingdom, including protection from spirits, whom ascetics have the privilege from the gods of vanquishing.

Since the eighteenth century some 120 Vaiṣṇava temples have been built in the Janakpur area. The most important and popular one is the monumental

Jānakī temple in the center of town, built in a Mogul style of architecture and dedicated to Sītā. At this location, the Rāmānandī ascetic Sur Kisor supposedly discovered a golden statue of Sītā at the end of the seventeenth century. The current temple was only begun in 1911, greatly furthered by Queen Vṛṣabandhu Kūvarī of Tikamgarh in the former kingdom of Orcha (in the Indian state of Madhya Pradesh). The temple is also called Nau-lakh Mandir, literally the "900,000-Rupee Temple," this being the amount of the queen's endowment. The entrance displays this queen's coat of arms framed by two lions.

Nowadays pilgrims come in their hundreds of thousands to the various festivals having to do with the lives of Rāma and Sītā, especially their wedding day in November/December, Sītā's birthday in April/May, and Rāma's birthday (Rāmanavamī) in March/April. On the last of these days, the most visited place is the Rāma temple, the oldest temple in town, built by King Raṇabahādura Śāha in 1782 and renovated by Prime Minister Candra Shamsher in 1927.

Another god that became particularly popular in the Kathmandu Valley is Kṛṣṇa, a deity exhibiting both heroic and pastoral features.[76] His popularity is based above all on his romantic love relationship with Rādhā. The worship of Rādhā and Kṛṣṇa emphasizes aspects of such devotional abandon. They are prayed to in heartfelt forms, and the songs sung and poems recited to them are full of divine love (*bhakti*).

There are some indications of Kṛṣṇa veneration in the Licchavi inscriptions. Thus, Vāsudeva,[77] another name for Kṛṣṇa, appears in two inscriptions, while the Viśvarūpa statue in Changu Narayan dated to the eighth century, betrays familiarity with the *Bhagavadgītā*, a central text of Kṛṣṇaism.

In the Malla Period, the Kṛṣṇa temples were among the most active holy places, perhaps due to the influence of the Bengalese mystic Caitanya on the region of Mithila and on the Brahmins who streamed into the Kathmandu Valley. In the inner courtyard of the old palace of Kathmandu, for instance, there is an undated Kāliyadamana statue portraying Kṛṣṇa as a boy killing the serpent demon Kālīya; the art points to a date in the early Malla Period.

The many Kṛṣṇaite manuscripts reflect the popularity of this religious movement. Thus, a manuscript of the *Harivaṃśa* is preserved, dating to the year 1136/37 (Saṃvat 257), on which is depicted the kings Jitāmitra Malla of Bhaktapur, Nṛpendra Malla of Kathmandu, and various ministers making peace on the banks of the Bagmati River in 1674 CE.[78]

Kṛṣṇaism is visible, too, in the numerous statues and temples with representations, for example, of the cowherd Kṛṣṇa playing the flute. The most important promoter of Kṛṣṇaism was Siddhinarasiṃha Malla of Patan, during whose reign a Kṛṣṇalīlā painting was made showing thirty-one episodes in Kṛṣṇa's life, and who had the three-story Bālagopāla (or Kṛṣṇa) temple built across from the royal palace in the *śikhara* style, in imitation of a Kṛṣṇa temple in Mathura near Delhi—still today a vibrant building. On the first floor of this temple, the only one to attain supraregional significance, there are statues of Kṛṣṇa, Rukmiṇī, and Satyabhāmā, around whom a frieze depicting part of the *Mahābhārata* epic extends. On the second floor there is a Kāśīviśveśvara *liṅga* evincing a close association with Kāśī (Varanasi), as does the frieze with 108 miniature *liṅgas* similar to ones located in the holy surroundings of Varanasi. On the ground floor is a frieze going right around the temple and displaying episodes from the *Rāmāyaṇa*. The expensive temple was not undisputed, for in the foundation inscription there is mention of an insidious enemy.[79]

Because of this temple's radiant power and the authority enjoyed by Siddhinarasiṃha, additional royally promoted Kṛṣṇa shrines were built in Patan in the seventeenth and eighteenth centuries. One with three roofs was built by Kīrtisiṃha, an illegitimate son of Siddhinarasiṃha, in the quarter of Svotha in 1668. Further Kṛṣṇa temples in Patan are the Vaṃśagopāla temple in Kvā Bāhāḥ, the Lakṣmīnārāyaṇa-Kṛṣṇa temple, built in 1699 in the Nugah quarter, and the octagonal Cyāsiṃ-Deval at Mangal Bazar, which was erected in 1723 by a powerful daughter of Yoganarendra Malla. In addition, there are numerous private Kṛṣṇa temples, often built in the name of some deceased person—for example, one built in 1643 in the quarter of Ola, or the Vaṃśagopāla temple in the Gā Bāhāḥ quarter, constructed in 1727.

Kathmandu was not inferior to Patan when it came to constructing buildings consecrated to Kṛṣṇa. The octagonal Vaṃśagopāla temple at the royal palace in Kathmandu, which Pratāpa Malla had built in 1649, or the Gopīnātha pagoda temple, also built there probably in the mid-seventeenth century, are both outstanding. In Bhaktapur, royal patronage of Kṛṣṇa temples was lacking, so that only a few such shrines are found at the palace square. Nor did the Ghorkali promote Kṛṣṇaism.

Since the beginning of the twentieth century, the number of places where for the most part men meet to sing "devotional songs" (*bhajana*) has increased, quite often dedicated to Kṛṣṇa or Rāma.[80] Among these are the Jānakījīva Kuñja (or Hare Rāma Kuñja) in Deopatan, and the Śrī Śrī

Rādhā-Kṛṣṇa temple in Budhanilakantha, which is also a center for the growing International Society for Krishna Consciousness (ISKCON), which bases itself on the Gauḍīya movement in Bengal founded by Caitanya.

Religious Syncretism and Tolerance

It can be seen repeatedly that in Nepal various religious currents and movements (Vedic, Tantric and Smārta Hinduism; Tantric, Tibetan, and Theravāda Buddhism; local and clan religions) have become mixed with each other, or exist side by side, complementing each other. Extensive studies on ritual have shown how ritual elements, in particular, are reinterpreted and transferred. Several traditions, such as the esoteric Taleju or popular Svasthānī cults, have been preserved only in Nepal. The Kumārī cult and Nepalese Vajrayāna Buddhism (also called Newar Buddhism), too, are unique, the latter featuring Buddhist castes, a hereditary priesthood, and monasteries with no monks. Moreover, many gods appear together as witnesses in inscriptions—for example, on a copperplate dating to 1695 from Bhaktapur, the Buddhist Karuṇāmaya together with the Hindu Paśupatinātha, Garuḍa-Nārāyaṇa, Guhyeśvarī, Vajrayoginī, and Harasiddhi.[81]

Even as Hinduism was able to absorb non-Hindu deities, so too was Newar Buddhism able to absorb elements of Hinduism.[82] Representations showing the Buddha on his return to Lumbini also show him accompanied by Śiva, Viṣṇu, or Gaṇeśa; the Bodhisattva Mañjuśrī frees the Kathmandu Valley from the waters with the help of Gaṇeśa and the Nāga (serpents); Vajrapāṇi is looked upon as the Buddhist equivalent of the rain god Indra, and, together with the Nāgas, as guardians of the world; Bodhisattvas are regarded as beings higher than the Hindu gods. In Patan, Śrīnivāsa Malla had a golden window built in his palace showing many Hindu deities emanating from Avalokiteśvara.[83] Another example is the procession of Dīpāṅkara, the "light-maker" Buddha, who according to the *Buddhavaṃśa* appears as the first of twenty-four Buddhas that preceded the historical Buddha. In this text, he is described as the one who first lit the lamp (*dīpa*) of the Buddha's teaching (*dharma*). The Dīpaṅkara procession is a very long pilgrimage around and through the Kathmandu Valley, lasting between twenty-four and thirty-six hours. It is conducted only every nineteen years, on the occasion of a certain constellation of stars. The route the procession takes is nearly 37 miles in length and covers around sixty-eight places with 130 deities, one third of which are Buddhist.

Thus just as Buddhist deities can be integrated into the Hindu pantheon, as in the teaching of the *avatāras* of Viṣṇu, Newar Buddhism for its part has adopted many Hindu rituals and other features. In general, however, Hinduism is the more assimilative of the two religions. This doubtless has something to do with the kings being traditionally closer to the Hindu pantheon, and thus to a greater extent promoting it. After all, their family gods were all Hindu, and for that reason enjoyed special standing.

The demarcation lines between the gods are often blurred in rituals and festivals, but even more so in the myths.[84] For example, the goddess Vajrayoginī who, at her seat in the northeast of the Kathmandu Valley, is worshiped both as the consort of Śiva and as a Buddhist *yoginī*. Likewise, once a year the *liṅga* in the Paśupatinātha temple is worshiped as the Bodhisattva Avalokiteśvara, a crown of this Buddhist deity then being placed on it. Other examples of such syncretistic milieus in which unique forms of religious practice could develop are the Taleju and Kumārī cults or the Matsyendranātha festival, the worship of Avalokiteśvara as an emanation of Śiva among the Tamang Lamas, or the worship of Mañjuśrī as Sarasvatī.[85]

Correspondingly great tolerance reigns in questions of belief and religious views as well as in rituals. Family or clan tradition dictates which priest is called to perform rituals or which god is worshiped as the protective deity of the clan (*kuladevatā*), and it is largely an individual choice as to whether one goes to a temple daily or meditates, sings religious songs, acquires religious merit by worshiping the gods at home, or which god is declared to be "one's personal god" (Skt. *iṣṭadevatā*).

It is well known that in South Asia religious boundaries are often blurred and that religious identities may be multiple, syncretistic, or hybrid.[86] But this perception only arises if one assumes fixed religious boundaries.[87] Even if it can be witnessed in recent times that the boundaries between religions are indeed becoming clearer, the special feature of South Asian religions lies in their mixture of Hinduism, Buddhism, and popular religions, and also to some extent of Islam and Christianity. From the point of view of the Abrahamic religions, this means a certain lack of form and identity. From the South Asian point of view, however, the gods' ability to cross or abolish borders constitutes a veritable strength.

This is, for example, shown in the case of the goddess Guhyeśvarī, the "Goddess of the Hidden." Her main temple is located in Deopatan, northeast of the Paśupatinātha temple.[88] According to the late chronicles, it was Pratāpa Malla who discovered this seat of the goddess. The sanctum itself in the interior of the temple (closed to non-Hindus) gives rise to manifold speculation. It is a pit filled with water, which is given to the worshipers as *prasāda*. The hole is usually covered with a metal *śrīyantra* diagram in the form of a lotus, or with a vase or jar. Guhyeśvarī is said to be the oldest seat (*pīṭha*) of its kind in the Kathmandu Valley.

According to a Hindu legend, Pārvatī/Satī threw herself onto the sacrificial fire after her father insulted Śiva and refused to recognize him as her husband. The latter thereupon placed the corpse over his shoulder and wandered through the land. Parts of the corpse fell off along the way; her "hidden part" (*guhya*), that is, her anus or pudendum, landed in Nepal. Given her mysterious name, the question of who Guhyeśvarī actually is arises. This question is not easy to answer; there is great uncertainty with regard to her manifestations, the priests and worshipers who venerate her, and the myths and legends surrounding her. Thus, she is worshiped as the Vedic-Purāṇic goddess Pārvatī or Satī and consort of Śiva, an independent Tantric goddess, the Buddhist goddess Tārā, the *śakti* ("divine female power") of Avalokiteśvara or the Ādibuddha, and as a local goddess.

Despite this hybrid diversity, Guhyeśvarī is regarded as a strong goddess precisely because she can absorb all contradiction, because she basically has infinitely many identities, constantly transforms herself, and does not need to draw boundaries. The goddess has everything *in herself*. That is her strength. And this explains the diversity and strength of religious developments in Nepal. Given these religious identifications and entanglements, many borders and differences fade away, and we move from cultural difference to religious fusion. The story is often told: A Newar asked whether he is a Hindu or Buddhist may well answer "yes."

4

Scattered Power and Petty Kingdoms

The Country before the Fourteenth Century

How could Nepal come into being? The Himalayan region was not only rugged and difficult to access, but also politically and socio-religiously fragmented. Many petty kingdoms existed until the Śāha conquered the Kathmandu Valley—in some periods, almost eighty principalities. In relation to the total area of Nepal, each of these small states was on average no larger than about 1,120 square miles, including the often impassable and virtually uninhabitable mountain regions. These states were constantly changing, forming alliances and separating again, waging wars, and expanding or being swallowed up. This fact basically also applies to the Malla dynasty, which, however, differs from the previous petty kingdoms in that it is much better documented and was able to establish itself as a center of power in the Kathmandu Valley over five centuries.

Apart from the Licchavi dynasty with its 210 inscriptions, the sources until the fourteenth century are rather poor. No coherent overall picture of the country can be derived from them, especially since they almost exclusively concern the Kathmandu Valley and western Nepal. On occasion, however, smaller independent or tributary kingdoms with very limited spheres of power are mentioned. Sometimes they formed alliances, sometimes different rulers shared power. Only the Khasa-Malla in western Nepal undertook major conquests.

Prehistory

When the first people appeared in Nepal—and thus when the history of Nepal begins—cannot be definitely pinpointed.[1] The earliest traces of a hominid are those of *Ramapithecus* in the Satpati section of the Siwalik Hills near Lumbini, dating from between eight and fourteen million years ago, at a time when the Himalayas were probably no higher than 10,000 feet. The

Nepal. Axel Michaels, Oxford University Press. English language edition © Oxford University Press 2024.
DOI: 10.1093/oso/9780197650936.003.0005

spectacular discovery of a hand axe made by *Homo erectus* enabled archaeologist Gudrun Corvinus to show that archaic humans lived at least from the mid-Pleistocene (ca. 700,000–127,000 BCE) in the Himalayan foreland. Charcoal has been found in the prehistoric Kathmandu Lake, and although this cannot be ascribed with certainty to the human use of fire, that does seem likely. Large-scale slashing and burning implies that domestic animals were present from about 8,000 BCE. These are all merely scattered indications but taken together they make an early settlement of Nepal probable. Unfortunately, palynology (the study of particulate samples including pollen grains), which can often deliver important information about prehistoric settlement, has made little progress with regard to Nepal so far.

In a strict scientific sense, the prehistory of the Kathmandu Valley remains, therefore, somewhat nebulous. But this is not so in the chronicles of the nineteenth century, which extensively recount the country's creation in myths. Thus, the Hindu chronicles have the history of the Kathmandu Valley begin with the Paśupatinātha-Jyotirliṅga, a *liṅga* in the form of a ray of light. According to the Buddhist *Nepālikabhūpavaṃśāvalī*, the Vipaśvī Buddha is supposed to have planted a lotus seed in the middle of the lake covering the valley. This then changed into a burning flame, in which the form the primordial Buddha chose to appear. Only when the Bodhisattva Mañjuśrī had hewn a cleft in the hill at Chobhar could the water then drain out.

What is being reported here in mythic form is based on an actual phenomenon in the natural history of Nepal. The Kathmandu Valley, at its broadest some 18.6 miles wide, is filled with siliciclastic sediments that prove that this was once a lake that was filled with meltwater from the Himalaya.[2] The valley emptied, quite rapidly, in the Late Pleistocene. Whether the unusually large number of terms for fish in Old Nevārī as compared with modern Nevārī can be attributed to cultural memory dating back to this time remains an intriguing possibility.

The Kirāta

The chronicles list various dynasties that ruled before the Licchavi, the first historically comparatively well-documented one. Of these, only the Kirāta (also Kirãta, Kirātī, or Kiranti) have left any sort of imprint, having been mentioned in Indian sources as well.[3] Usually they are described, as in an inscription of Samudragupta (about 350–80 CE) in Allahabad, as a tribe or else as a partly nomadic people near the frontier that—as in the *Mahābhārata*—fight or otherwise come into conflict with the Indo-Aryans "because they neglected the rituals and did not seek out Brahmins," as it says in *Manu* (10.44). In the *Mahābhārata* an episode occurs in which Arjuna, in the form of a Kirāta, displays a miracle weapon—an incident that would later be worked into Bharavi's poem *Kirātārjunīya* (ca. sixth century). The Kirāta are described as having settled north of the Ganges plain and as being particularly good at building or improving caves and handling snakes. The name Kirāta was, in addition, a collective term for a whole group of non-Hindu tribes often named together with the Cīna (Chinese), the Niṣāda (hunters), or other tribes. This information, however, is far too imprecise to connect with the Kirāta named in the Nepalese chronicles. In any event, it seems probable that the Kirati, who today live in eastern Nepal, have something in common with the Kirāta named in Indian sources.

Before the Kirāta there were no political structures in Nepal that could have been called a state. Rather, the population was made up of small neighboring groups that were able to grow together as tribes over time. These were ethnic groups whose social stratification was rather weak, who were just barely sedentary (if at all), and who lived by slash-and-burn methods or as hunter-gatherers. There were no signs of rule under a person or governing body—a form that perhaps only developed with the Kirāta, but with certainty with the Licchavi in the Kathmandu Valley, and with the Śākya (the Buddha's clan) in what is now the Tarai.

The advanced culture of the Licchavi, the first dynasty in Nepal to rule over the Kathmandu Valley (from the third to the eighth century) did not appear suddenly. This is shown by non-Indo-Aryan elements in Licchavi inscriptions.[4] There nearly all personal names are in Sanskrit, but not many of the administrative terms, nor are nearly 80% of toponyms (place names and river names); some of the latter have variants still used in Nevārī, or also in Tamang or Limbu.

The lists of kings in the chronicles name between twenty-nine and thirty-two Kirāta rulers. Some of them are connected with the great Mahābhārata war, with the worship of Ādibuddha, or with Aśoka's visit to the birthplace of the Buddha in Nepal, but without presenting any evidence for this. On the contrary, the assumption that Aśoka, who ruled roughly between 268 and 232 BCE, visited Nepāla in the third century is highly suspect. It is almost impossible that he ever reached the Kathmandu Valley, although there are four undated (and perhaps undatable) *stūpas* named after him in Lalitpur, and there is the legend that his undocumented daughter Cārumatī supposedly married the Nepalese king Devapāla and founded with him both Deopatan and the monastery that gave its name to Chabahil. Whatever the case, the name "Nepāla" does not occur in the Aśokan inscriptions, nor did any name of a Himalayan region that could stand in for it. But Aśoka did come to Lumbini; this is certain because there is a pillar erected by him in 257 BCE. It is probable, too, that he sent missionaries to Nepāla.

Oddly, the name "Kirāta" occurs only twice in the Licchavi inscriptions—once in a Paśupatinātha inscription from 733 CE, where a man is described as "wearing the clothes of the Kirāta" (*kirātaveṣadhara*), meaning "ragged," and in the 748 CE Paśupati inscription of Vijayadeva, son of Jayadeva II, where they are described as fierce, intent on slaughtering people, arrogant, and unconquerable.[5] In any event, despite a lack of evidence for the original settlers of the Kathmandu Valley, it was very likely that the Kathmandu Valley was visited and surrounded by various tribes before the Licchavi arrived.

The Licchavi and Ābhīra Gupta Period

More solid evidence exists about the Licchavi, although it is peculiar that the chronicles, with the exception of the *Gopālarājavaṃśāvalī*, and even the inscriptions, make virtually no mention of their lineage name. There are two exceptions. King Mānadeva's daughter, Vijayavatī, called her father the "full moon in the firmament of the Licchavi lineage" (*licchavikulāmbarapūrṇacandra*) in 505 CE, and Jayadeva II, in his Paśupatinātha inscription of 733 CE, refers to over thirty generations of Licchavi and connects them directly to the solar dynasty (Sūryavaṃśa) in India. Although these lists begin with the creator divinity Brahmā, followed by the Sun (Sūrya), a historically credible period only begins with Jayadeva I, the thirteenth ancestor.

The Licchavi are known almost exclusively from their approximately 210 inscriptions. These contain information relating to social and religious life that was based to a great extent on caste-bound guilds (Skt. *goṣṭhī*, *gauṣṭhika*, later Nep. *guṭhī*) and the Buddhist monasteries. Part of the tax revenue of such institutions was used to organize festivals.[6] The inscriptions also contain testimony relating to the immolation of widows in South Asia and indications of great religious tolerance, a complex government apparatus, ascetics, and lay followers of Pāśupata, and much more.

Chinese sources also shed light on this period. As early as the end of the fourth century, Chinese pilgrims were traveling to India to see first-hand the land of the Buddha and to study his teachings.[7] However, they did not travel through Nepāla, but along the old Silk Road(s), entering India to the west of modern-day Nepal in what is now Pakistan. Among them was Faxian (ca. 337–422), who visited Lumbini and returned with 413 texts, many of which he himself translated into Chinese. These pilgrimages and expeditions increased in number especially during the Tang dynasty (618–907); they were comparable in the difficulty and dangers involved to the later medieval pilgrimages to Jerusalem. The opening up of the route through Tibet marked the beginning of profitable trade with Nepal, known from ancient times as the land of Buddha bronzes, woolen clothing, jewelry, and carvings.

The first Chinese pilgrim to mention Nepāla was Xuanzang (Hsüan-tsang). Although he never reached Nepāla, he knew enough to at least mention the Licchavi (Lichepo), especially their educated King Aṃśuvarman (Yangshufamo) and nearly two thousand monks in Nepal, together with their monasteries and temples.

Xuanzang also tells of a lake from which fire rose when people threw something into it. This is repeated by Wang Xuance (seventh/eighth century), who was probably the first Chinese person to actually visit Nepāla. The detail soon became part of a widespread cycle of legends and is illustrated in the caves of the ancient oasis city of Dunhuang in western China. It is related to the myth of the drainage of the Kathmandu Valley, as is the tale of an "isolated rock outcrop" in a lake, probably Svayambhū Hill. Indeed, recent research has shown that its *stūpa* stands on an outcropping that was probably a place where a goddess was worshiped in pre-Buddhist times, perhaps the neighboring goddess Hāratī/Hārītī.

Finally, Indian sources convey much information about the Licchavi. The Licchavi of the Kathmandu Valley likely had something in common with the Licchavi who are so often mentioned in early Indian sources before the modern era.[8] These were part of the Vajji Confederation, and their capital, Vaishali, was the center of what was one of sixteen great realms (*mahājanapada*). In the *Mahāparinirvāṇasūtra*, one of the major texts of the Mahāyāna, they are mentioned as *khattiyas* (from Skt. *kṣatriya*, "warrior, noble"), and in the *Arthaśāstra* as a group of tribes (*gaṇasaṅgha*). The Magadha king Ajātaśatru (ca. 492–460 BCE) is said to have driven them off to Nepal. Their origins remain obscure. Sometimes they are mentioned as tribal, sometimes as Indo-Aryan. Later rulers, particularly the Gupta (about

320–500 CE), influenced the early Licchavi dynasty. Candragupta I married Kumāradevī, probably a Licchavi princess; both of them are portrayed on a coin of their son, Samudragupta. But here, too, the Licchavi in question are unclear.

Even though social, cultural, and religious influence from India is clearly recognizable, the territory of the Licchavi in the Kathmandu Valley was probably never absorbed by any Indian power, and thus not by the Licchavi in India. It would seem to be more a matter of the wanderings of people, ideas, and objects rather than conquest. The most momentous ideology that the Licchavi, whether descendants of the Indian Licchavi or not, brought with them to Nepāla was the introduction of the hierarchical caste system, even though this is only weakly attested in inscriptions.

A rough sequence of the Licchavi dynasty is given in Appendix 2. In the chronicles are found sequences that diverge from it and from each other. The dates of those who ruled before Mānadeva are quite uncertain. Their deeds are recorded only in the chronicles, and many a ruler is known only by his name.

The first large datable inscription is that of Mānadeva I from the year 464/5 CE. In it, Mānadeva mentions his three predecessors, his grandfather Vṛṣadeva, his father Śaṅkaradeva, and the latter's son Dharmadeva, but not the dates of their lives or rule. On the basis of information in the inscription of Jayadeva II, who names thirty generations before himself, and the *Gopālarājavaṃśāvalī*, we may assume that the Licchavi era began toward the end of the second century. This is confirmed by a statue in the Kushana style supposedly representing Jayavarman. Bearing a Brāhmī inscription, it was excavated in 1992 by Tara Nanda Mishra along with further archaeological finds, among them Kushana coins, which also indicate an earlier date for the beginning of the Licchavi era.[9]

Mānadeva was apparently a strong ruler, something also emphasized in the large number of inscriptions that were made in the forty-one years of his reign. He conquered rebellious vassals in the east (the Kirāta?) and in the west "like a fearless lion with a waving mane," as is stated in the long Changu Narayan inscription. The exact extent of the Licchavi Empire is unclear. In the fourth century, the Gupta emperor Samudragupta mentions Nepal as a bordering tributary state, Licchavi inscriptions were found in Dumja east of Gorkha, and other sources such as Kalhaṇa's twelfth-century *Rājataraṅgiṇī* indicate that the sphere of power might have extended beyond the borders

Figure 4.1 Statue of King Jayavarman. 171 × 49 cm. 2nd century. National Museum. Photo by Niels Gutschow.

of the Kathmandu Valley. But Xuanzang's assumption that Nepāla territory already had the expansion of today's state is rather questionable.[10]

When Mānadeva's mother Rājyavatī, who was probably originally from India, wished to be immolated together with his father, who had seemingly died suddenly, he persuaded her to live. He then immediately set forth to battle, relieving his uncle on the way and conquering the city of Mallapurī (exact location unknown), and so fulfilling his duty (*ṛṇa*) toward his father. Despite these successes, the Licchavi must have ruled for the most part peacefully, for in no other inscription do they boast of subjected regions or people.

The inscription of 464 CE is also the first to deal with *satī* in South Asia.[11] On the west side of the great column, the inscription reads:

> But the queen, called Rājyavatī, the true wife of this king, who was about to follow him as Śrī and be his companion in the next life, in whom was born in this world a king of faultless character who forever pleases the world with beauty like the autumn moon, returned, and with a long sigh, her words faltering, her face covered with tears, said to her son affectionately:
>
> "Your father has gone to his place in the third heaven. O my son, of what use is my life now with your father gone? It has no purpose. Rule the kingdom, my son, for this very day I shall follow the path of your father. Of what use to me are these bonds fashioned of hope and varied pleasures? To live as if married without my husband is a false dream. I shall go."
>
> When she had finished, her son, his soul saddened and overcome by devotion, touched his head to her feet and said firmly:
>
> "Of what use to me are the pleasures and happiness of this world without you? I shall leave this life first. Only then will you go from here to heaven."
>
> When he had finished speaking, she stood there like a bird caught firmly by the snares of his words that came forth from his lotus mouth mixed with tears. Performing then herself with her pious son the rites for her dead husband, giving up ordinary life, with a heart made pure in every respect by fasting and abstinence, and giving alms to Brahmans for the increase of his merit, she remained through her love for him in a vow of chastity, like Arundhati herself.[12]

In this early poetic inscription, it is clearly a concern for Rājyavatī to sacrifice herself out of grief and love for her husband. Only her son's tears make her change her mind; she then takes the vow of *satī*, which entails living according to the rules of virtuous behavior, in chastity, poverty, and humility.

Mānadeva's other inscriptions are located on the pedestals of *liṅgas* and statues, and at least one is located in a Buddhist monastery.[13] During his time there is the first mention of Mahāyāna Buddhism.[14] The similarity in names suggests that he also founded the Mānagṛha palace,[15] which was probably in Handigaon and was the base of Licchavi rule through the eighth century.

Many Licchavi kings remain in the shadows due to lack of information. Only with Vasantadeva and especially with Aṃśuvarman who, together with

Śivadeva I, accounts for around one-fifth of all Licchavi inscriptions, do the lives of the Licchavi emerge.

Aṃśuvarman is described as relatively modest, caring toward people, and well educated. He always describes himself as one proud to feud with Śrī, the goddess of wealth; someone who places knowledge before possessions. According to the Chinese pilgrim Xuanzang, he even wrote a text on rhetoric, the *Śabdavidyā* ("Knowledge of Sounds [or Words]"). While he did not neglect other gods and Buddhism, he was a devotee of Śiva, and he introduced into inscriptions the symbol for Śiva's mount, the bull, and the nearly stereotypical formula, repeated until the recent past: "favored by the feet of glorious Paśupati."

Aṃśuvarman probably already possessed power under Śivadeva I before he became *sāmanta* (later *mahāsāmanta*), a prime minister of sorts. He was brought to the court so as to check the power of King Śivadeva I, power that he then secured to his own advantage. This practice of dividing power between two persons continues throughout the history of Nepal. Aṃśuvarman had a second palace built, Kailāśakūṭabhavana, which, with Mānagṛha, was to remain the center of rule for nearly a hundred years, but its location remains unknown despite archaeological research.

The Ābhīra/Āhīra Gupta, who between 506 and 641 first shared power with the Licchavi and then ruled independently, did not trace their lineage back to the sun, as did the latter, but to the moon. They show up in inscriptions first as functionaries. Thus, Virocanagupta was ambassador (*dūtaka*) for Vasantadeva, while others were the main treasurer (*mahāpratihāra*) or top army general (*sarvadaṇḍanāyaka*). Two inscriptions designate Bhaumagupta (567–ca. 590) as a former king, along with his grandson Jiṣṇugupta and his son Viṣṇugupta. The relation between the Ābhīra/Āhīra Gupta and the Indian Gupta is unclear, as is their origin. What is probable is a connection with the Gopāla, who are mentioned in the chronicles as the first kings. Around 641, the Ābhīra Gupta disappear from inscriptions; after this, only Narendradeva (also mentioned in Tibetan sources), his son Śivadeva II, and the latter's son Jayadeva II appear, all ruling from Kailāśakūṭa.

There is a remarkable inscription from Handigaon from the early sixth century.[16] It is written by Bhaumagupta's father Anuparama, who was probably not a king. The content is a hymn in very scholarly Sanskrit in nine different meters. The text shows good knowledge of Indian philosophical schools, especially the Mīmāṃsā, Vedānta, and Sāṃkhya/Yoga systems. As it venerates the Veda and the (*Mahā-*)*Bhārata* epic, it may have been directed against the Buddhists. Dvaipāyana, who is named as the author of the epic, is called upon directly as the protector of *dharma*, the comprehensive Brahmanical principle of law and custom, against Buddhists:

> If you had not been the upholder of it (i.e., of the threefold Vedic knowledge), [the Dharma] would not have been established today in the world, which Dharma is being denied by men who have resorted to extreme nihilism, through an opposition to the threefold (Vedic knowledge).
>
> [Having divided] the Veda, which was existing since the beginningless time but whose words were scattered about in speech, you kept it [systematically] asunder. [Now], how could the Vedas have existed here [in this world], if you had not composed the Bhārata epic and other (Puranic) texts?
>
> If you, who knows the reality of things and are intent on the well-being of the world, [had not upheld] the [true] Dharma in this way, by the evidence of valid arguments (*pramāṇaśuddhyā*), it (i.e., the true Dharma), being shaken up by those who abide by (another Dharma), [namely, the Buddhists], would not have continued. . . .
>
> Even though [killing of an animal] is the cause of destruction of life, it is not an offense if this [killing] is not [carried out] in a way other [than the one prescribed in Vedic texts]. You alone know [the scripture] properly; no other knower [of it] exists in the world.[17]

This inscription highlights that these early debates between Buddhists and Vedic Brahmins already concerned quite fundamental questions, and by no means did religious tolerance reign. That the debate in this case concerned animal sacrifice—Anuparama refers here to an exception in the regulations, which is also found in the *Law Book of Manu*—may indicate a Tantric background.[18]

The unique blend of Buddhism and Hinduism is also evident in the art and architecture of the Licchavi period. Thus, the erection of famous *stūpas* such as Svayambhū, Cābahila, and Bauddha (in Kathmandu, Deopatan, and Bodhnath respectively) can be credited to the rulers of the Licchavi period, as can the cult of the Bodhisattva Avalokiteśvara. According to a count made by Niels Gutschow, there are twelve *stūpas* from the Licchavi Period and 263 *caityas* that incorporate Licchavi fragments.[19] Whether the four *caityas* in the form of earthen mounds (*thudvan*), also called Aśoka *stūpas*, can be ascribed to the Licchavi Period is questionable. Early Buddha statues in a standing pose are located, among other places, in Chabahil, Bangemura,

Patan, and Handigaon (sixth century), and in Deopatan and the Vajrayoginī shrine (both eleventh century or earlier). A unique relief from between the sixth and seventh centuries depicting Māra's attack on the Buddha is now in the National Museum.

Some three hundred Hindu architectural fragments from the Licchavi Period, which are to some extent similar to North Indian Gupta architecture (third to seventh century), have been preserved.[20] The Paśupatinātha temple probably already existed in some form in the sixth century, since Licchavi inscriptions repeatedly invoke this god as the rulers' tutelary deity. It is also to be assumed that the Cāṅgunārāyaṇa temple dates back to this time, or even to the century before. An entire temple of the Licchavi Period has been preserved in Nepal only in the form of a small *śikhara* sanctuary from the seventh century at the Paśupatinātha temple, but the Jhokhang temple in Lhasa, too, still retains important period details.

Tibetan sources tell us that King Songtsen Gampo (Srong-brtsan-sgampo) called Nepalese architects to Tibet for construction work. The Licchavi were indeed known for their art and craftwork. Xuanzang admiringly reports on their jewelry, statues, temple pinnacles, and ritual objects. Hardly any of this is extant but the many Gupta- and Kushana-style stone sculptures and reliefs show their existence. Among them are the statue of King Jayavarman from the second century that has already been mentioned. Other examples are from the fourth or fifth century, statues of Viṣṇu represented as a dwarf, one of them (dating from 467 CE) at the Tilganga River near the Paśupatinātha temple, and another one, probably by the same hand, in Lazimpat (Kathmandu). The second oldest sculpture is a Bodhisattva Avalokiteśvara near the Central Jail in Kathmandu; this bears an inscription that indicates that it must be from the mid-sixth century.

Early Vaiṣṇava sculptures in Changu Narayan and Kathmandu date from the Licchavi Period too: among them, a Viṣṇu riding upon Garuḍa from the fourth century, in Changu Narayan Viṣṇu as a boar (Varāha) on the Dhumvārāhī shrine in Kathmandu, from the sixth century; and the Jalaśayana-Nārāyaṇa in Budhanilakantha, from 642 CE. The earliest statue of Kṛṣṇa is the serpent-slayer Kāliyadamana at the Hanuman Dhoka palace, dated to the seventh century.

Equally numerous are Śaiva statues, among them several of Umāmaheśvara: the oldest of these, in Patan, is from 573 CE; another one, in Deopatan, is probably from the seventh century. The approximately fifty Licchavi *liṅgas* in the Kathmandu Valley are difficult to date except when they bear an inscription, as numerous Licchavi *liṅgas* or their pedestals (*yoni*) do. The earliest *liṅga* stands in Lazimpat and dates from 466 CE.[21] Such unique *liṅgas* as the Virāṭeśvara at Rājarājeśvarī Ghāṭa (probably the largest *liṅga* in South Asia) and the single-faced Ekamukhaliṅga, both in Deopatan, are from the fourth or fifth century; the nearby Bhasmeśvara at the cremation site dates from 533 CE. Four-faced *liṅgas*, like the one in the sanctum of the Paśupatinātha temple, likely emerged in the course of the nineth or tenth century. One of them once stood near the Vatsalā temple in Deopatan; another is in the Kumbheśvara temple in Patan. Probably the first anthropomorphic statue of Śiva, dating from the sixth century, stands at the Bāghabhairava temple in Kirtipur. A Śaṅkara-Nārāyaṇa statue, half Śiva and half Viṣṇu, probably from the seventh century, is another example of syncretistic forms that bring together different religious currents.

The Licchavi enjoyed a largely peaceful time at least in the period between 600 and 733. Neither the Gupta (ca. 320–500) nor the Harsha dynasty (606–47) made attempts to conquer the Kathmandu Valley. It remains uncertain whether Nepal was at times subject to Tibet, as the Tibetans and Chinese both maintain.[22] The *Gopālarājavaṃśāvalī* does mention that Nepal was governed twice from Bhoṭa (Tibet or Banepa), but no Licchavi inscription confirms this. Equally uncertain is whether, in 641 CE, King Songtsen Gampo married the Nepalese princess Bhṛkuṭī, whose exact origins are unknown.[23] The Licchavi Period ended in an unspectacular way. The last mention is in the colophon of a manuscript from 878 CE.[24] A new and much more uncertain era, Nepāla Saṃvat, began on October 20, 879.

The Early Medieval Period

The centuries following the Licchavi Period up to the Malla kings have been characterized as a "transitional period."[25] They have sometimes been dubbed a post-Licchavi, pre-Malla, a medieval, or a Thakuri era. But *ṭhākura* is the title of a high-ranking man, not a dynasty; the Malla kings used this term too. Given the small number of historically reliable sources it is largely a black hole in Nepalese history. Only around ten inscriptions, with little connection to political events, have survived; there are no travel reports and only a very few architectural fragments. The chronicles are contradictory and unreliable with regard to an exact chronology. However, given the religious history sources, especially Buddhist ones and those from the Khasa kingdom in western Nepal, it seems unjustified to call a span of three hundred years a transitional period.

To be sure, there are hundreds of manuscripts, mostly Buddhist, whose colophons contain information useful for dating the rulers, even though the dynastic sequence is often unclear. The manuscripts are written in Sanskrit, but increasingly in two new scripts, called *rañjanā* (Skt.) and *bhujīmola* (Nev.), and, from 1173 on, in the Nevārī language. How reliable such colophons can be as a source for historical determination is exemplified by a collection of Śivadharma texts. There it is written:

> In the expired Nepalese year named "ether-planet-hand," in the month of Pauṣa and in the 15th lunar day in the bright [fortnight], on the day of the sun, when the king [was] the celebrated Rudradeva, who has obscured the rays of the moon through the breaking forth of [his] fame, the treatise on the doctrine of Śiva copied by a distinguished [scribe] named Rāma has been then concluded. Obeisance to Śiva! Oṃ, obeisance to Śiva![26]

Since there was a particular system for giving dates in years on the basis of groups of numerically related concepts (e.g., "planet" stands for nine, because there were nine recognized planets in South Asia), the manuscript can be dated to January 14, 1170. At the same time, King Rudradeva II's existence is confirmed. The manuscript contains a handwritten addition from the year 1651 stating that it was used during the reign of Pratāpa Malla for a public recitation.

Not only the lack of inscriptions but also the beginning of the new Nepāla Saṃvat (NS) era in 879 justifies the caesura.[27] This era is first found in a manuscript dating from 907 CE (NS 28), and there are only three further such sources until 979 CE. The transition from the Licchavi to the Early Medieval Period did not take place abruptly, though; overall conditions did not fundamentally change. Rather, numerous Licchavi administrators probably continued after the beginning of the new era. Licchavi kings may even have remained in power. At any rate, the names that occur in the two eras are hardly distinguishable from one other. The chronicles, too, are comparatively reticent about this transitional time. Only from the time of Sthiti Malla are there more exact sources again.

The Early Medieval Period evidently did not produce any powerful ruler. Instead, there were many minor rulers, who often reigned for only a short time. Gradually the system of rule was weakened to the extent that several city-state kingdoms emerged: Kathmandu, Bhaktapur, Lalitpur (Patan), Banepa, and others. Of these, Bhaktapur—which had fallen in 1147 to Ānandadeva I, who had a new palace built in Tripura at the western end of town—would become particularly powerful by the end of the fifteenth century. Apart from some unity within the Kathmandu Valley under a number of Malla rulers, this fragmentation of power was to continue until 1768/69, when Pṛthvīnārāyaṇa Śāha conquered the Kathmandu Valley.

Many institutions and distinctive features were taken over from the Licchavi Period: the name "Nepāla" for the Kathmandu Valley, the institution of temple communities (Skt. *goṣṭhī*) based on an endowment system, the monarchy, the special form of village administration, coinage, artisanship, and the co-existence of Buddhism and Hinduism. The dual form of rulership (*dvairājya*, *ubhayarājya*, *ardharājya*), too, was retained.[28] In some cases, the reigns of three different kings overlap. It is said of Guṇakāmadeva II that he established "his own rule," which implies that he had had to share power before.

Now and again concrete events are reported in the chronicles. According to them, Bhāskaradeva sold his father's crown and then went blind; Guṇakāmadeva I founded Kathmandu and generously endowed both Buddhist monasteries and the Paśupatinātha temple;[29] Śivadeva built a palace in Kirtipur; and Pradyumnakāmadeva re-introduced the custom of wearing a crown, suggesting that there were periods during which this symbol of power was not put on display.

As far as religion is concerned, there are increasing indications of Vajrayāna Buddhism coming into prominence. Many new monasteries were built, among them Kvā Bāhāḥ in Patan. These became centers that drew Indian and Tibetan monks and scholars wishing to study texts to the Kathmandu Valley. Śāntarakṣita, Padmasambhava, and Kamaśīla are all said to have spent some years studying in late eighth-century Nepal.[30] Apparently, many Buddhist refugees fled there when North India was being conquered by the Muslims.

Throughout this period, the production of Śivadharma texts continued unabated. Indeed, one of the first palm-leaf manuscripts is of this type, and one of the largest collections of such texts, is from Nepal. In them the names of Lakṣmīkāmadeva I (1024–39), Mānadeva, Śivadeva, and others are confirmed. Several kings made generous endowments to the Paśupatinātha temple. Thus, Guṇakāmadeva I donated silver covers for *liṅgas*; Śaṅkaradeva II, the Śaṅkareśvara temple; and Śivadeva, a golden roof. Indradeva and

Ānandadeva took the epithet "greatest venerator of Śiva" (*paramaśaiva*) into their titles, and the latter had himself initiated, along with four princes, into the Tantric Śaiva tradition.

The Early Medieval Period also gave rise to new religious phenomena. Holy men (*yogin, siddha*) said to have supernatural powers are mentioned repeatedly. The most prominent of these were Matsyendranātha and Gorakhanātha, whose historical authenticity, however, is unproven. The Avalokiteśvara/Buṅgadyaḥ cult also appeared during this period. In the late chronicles it is reported that the Indian philosopher Śaṅkara (eighth century) came to Nepāla and burned Buddhist books.

During this era, the continued excellence of craftsmanship is unmistakable, as evidenced for stone and bronze sculptures and Carbon-14-dated woodcarvings. According to the most recent knowledge, the erection of the Kāṣṭhamaṇḍapa, the central gathering hall in the center of Kathmandu, probably occurred during the Early Medieval Period. In the middle of the twelfth century, the Kāṣṭhamaṇḍapa's name started to be used for the whole surrounding quarter, and a couple of centuries later the entire town had acquired the name. According to the chronicles, however, Kathmandu was supposedly founded already in the tenth century by King Guṇakāmadeva I. The modern name Kathmandu derives from Kāṣṭhamaṇḍapa and dates back to the seventeenth century.

The architectural history of the Early Medieval Period is shrouded in darkness.[31] Only a few fragments have been preserved, but several fragments of wooden architecture have been dated to between the eighth and eleventh centuries by using the Carbon-14 method. On the basis of these results, there were presumably many more construction elements dating to pre-Malla times. Thus, the *caitya*, just 6.5 square feet, at Dhavalacaitya Vihāra in Kathmandu has niches in its outer walls containing tablets carved out of wood that display the female figures known as "carriers of wisdom" (Skt. *vidyādharī*), which have been dated to the tenth century. And the oldest carved wooden door, from the ninth century, is in the Mañjuśrī temple beside Kvā Bāhāḥ in Patan.[32]

The oldest monastery buildings have also been dated to the transition period, among them Uku Bāhāḥ and Itum Bāhāḥ in Patan, both with wooden carvings and struts from the ninth or tenth century. Other old monastery complexes include Yatkhā Bāhāḥ (with such carvings from the tenth or eleventh century) and Buṅga Bahī (in Bungamati).

Figure 4.2 Kāṣṭhamaṇḍapa, drawing by Rajman Singh, approximately 1844. Courtesy of the Royal Asiatic Society.

The Khasa-Malla in Western Nepal

The Kathmandu Valley was exposed to various formative influences from the south and the north during this period, even if it is not certain to what extent Tibet and the powerful Pāla dynasty of the eighth and twelfth centuries in northeastern India had an effect on Nepal. The influence of the South Indian Chalukya from Kalyani (tenth to twelfth century) is somewhat better documented. Thus, Someśvara I claims the conquest of "Nepāla" in an inscription from the year 1047.[33] The influence of Tirhut or Mithila is well documented. Its kings, since Nānyadeva (eleventh/twelfth century), attempted repeated plundering incursions into the Kathmandu Valley from their capital of Sīmarāmapura, modern Simraongarh, up to the beginning of the fourteenth century, but they were never able to establish a lasting presence.

The greatest influence can be seen in the comparatively large Khasa (or Khaśa) kingdom in the western Karnali basin, which included parts of southeastern Tibet and Kumaon.[34] Also known as the Dullu kingdom after its capital city, it flourished between the twelfth and fourteenth centuries under a

Malla dynasty, which shared only its name with the one in the Kathmandu Valley. Stretching from the Tarai through the Karnali basin in the west of Nepal up to southwestern Tibet, it incorporated parts of Kumaon, Garhwal, and Lo/Mustang.[35] It thus lay on one of the most important trading and pilgrimage routes from India to Tibet and China. The Khasa kingdom is also the cradle of Nepal's Pahāḍī or Khasa-Arya culture.

There are comparatively many sources for the historical development of the Khasa rulers. They primarily encompass roughly 150 stone inscriptions and copperplates, many in Sanskrit and early Nepālī, originally called Khasakurā.[36] Most of the inscriptions deal with gifts of land, but one inscription from Dullu contains a genealogy of the rulers, which generally aligns with the chronology in a Tibetan chronicle.[37] The Khasa are also mentioned in the *Mahābhārata*, some Purāṇas, and other Indian texts,[38] as well as in the *Gopālarājavaṃśāvalī* and the *Nepālikabhūpavaṃśāvalī*.[39] In addition, there are archaeological finds, in particular Buddhist sculptures, *stūpas*, columns, and other relics.[40]

According to the extensive column inscription of King Pṛthvīmalla in Dullu dating from the year 1357, Nāgarāja, who came from Tibet, supposedly founded the kingdom around the beginning of the twelfth century. However, two aristocratic families had already long ruled over the Karnali basin. One had its seat in Purang and controlled the area around Jumla; the other had its seat northwest of Mount Kailash in Guge and ruled over parts of southwestern Tibet. In the first half of the thirteenth century, both families unified large parts of western Nepal and West Tibet into a single economic area, the Khasa kingdom, with Semjā (now Sinja) in Jumla District as its capital city. Whether parts of the Tarai belonged to it is uncertain, although this is what Tibetan sources maintain.

Nāgarāja ruled from Dullu, contrary to an earlier view that Sinja was the summer residence and Dullu the winter one. Following him, were rulers whose names end in *-calla*, among them Krācalla (ca. 1218–55) and Aśokācalla (1255–78), and finally the Samudra lineage, whose names end with the title *malla*, for example Jitāri Malla (1288–99), Ripu Malla (1312–13), Akṣaya Malla (1313–21), Āditya Malla (1321–28), Puṇya Malla (1328–37), who allegedly conquered large parts of North India, and Pṛthvī Malla (1338–58), who supposedly retired to become a monk in old age. After this, the sources are silent, even the Tibetan ones.

The Khasa-Malla conquered smaller kingdoms in their region, among them Lo/Mustang, Kumaon, and Garhwal (conquered by Krācalla and

Aśokācalla), and some territory in Tibet and in the Tarai as far as Bodh Gaya. Between 1288 and 1334 they attempted at least seven invasions of or pilgrimages to the Kathmandu Valley, whose kings became to some extent tributary vassals. The *Gopālarājavaṃśāvalī* reports on these attacks as follows:

> The Khaśas entered (the Nepal Valley) from the west. In N.S. 408 (A.D. 1288), King Jayatāri (Jitārimalla) entered (the Kathmandu Valley) for the first time. The whole nation entered the forest after massacring eight hundred Khaśas at Svayambhū. Consequently, the Khaśas took to their heels. Peoples returned to their respective home and hearth. A year passed. In the month of Phālguṇa, Jayatāri entered again. He set villages on fire. He visited the Svayambhū Caitya, paid homage to the Lokeśvara of Bugma (Buṅga), pleased Paśupati (by offerings). In N.S. 409 (A.D. 1289) he returned back happily to his own country (Western Nepal).[41]

The kingdom, which had been held together by a largely unified language, collapsed no later than the reign of Abhaya Malla (grandson of Pṛthvī Malla) into independent small states, such as Doti, Jumla, and Bajhang. But signs of dissolution had already appeared with the expansion of the Muslims in North India. Thus, Nirayapāla proclaimed himself the ruler of an independent kingdom of Doti in 1352, and shortly thereafter Kumaon and southwest Tibet seceded once and for all from the Khasa kingdom. Occasionally the Malla rulers retreated to the small kingdom of Doti in the west. The Varman family, which had gained great influence through the prime minister Yaśodharma under Pṛthvī Malla, took over de facto power. In a 1389 inscription in Jajarkot, Malayavarman even assumed the title of "great king" (*mahārājādhirāja*). This power grab by the Varman clan was enabled by the decentralized system of Khasa rule. They created such high-ranking offices as governor (*mahāmaṇḍaleśvara*, *māṇḍalika*) and minister (*mahāmātya*, *amātya*) that administered the more remote parts independently. Often the occupants of such posts were brothers of the crown prince.

In Indian sources, the Khasa-Malla are often referred to as Ārya of the northwest Himalaya who did not follow the Veda or know to construct the altars for Vedic sacrifices, so they had a lower status. They had a reputation for having fewer misgivings about intercaste marriages and for fighting against the Pāṇḍava in the Mahābhārata struggle. It appears that the dominant Khasa aristocracy had had Brahmins come from India and settle there as a way to increase their prestige.

The Khasa-Malla ruled over a population that was influenced by Buddhism and that spoke Pahāḍī and Tibeto-Burman dialects. Among the more prominent were the Magar and the Gurung, who presumably had settled there even before the Khasa. But many of them took Khasa names, perhaps in order to obtain a post in the administration. They were often loyal soldiers.

As the Khasa controlled the trade between Tibet and India, they were invested in having good infrastructure. They thus seem to have ensured that roads were safe, bridges were built, and watering places for mules and other water facilities were available. To pay for those they also levied taxes, as one inscription makes clear.

In their inscriptions, Khasa aristocrats call on the great Hindu divinities Brahmā, Viṣṇu, Śiva, Gaṇeśa, and others, but inscriptions often begin with the Tibetan Buddhist mantra *Oṃ maṇi padme hūṃ* ("O jewel in the lotus"). In the course of their invasions of the Kathmandu Valley, they visited both Hindu holy places (e.g., the Paśupatinātha and Matsyendranātha temples) and Buddhist ones (e.g., the Svayambhū Stūpa). They also had important places of pilgrimage in their own kingdom—in particular, the three Vaiśvānara temples of Śīrasthāna, Nābhisthāna, and Pādukasthāna, in all of which an eternal flame was fueled by escaping gas. Pṛthvī Malla and other rulers repeatedly endowed these sacred sites with land and other gifts.

The Khasa were known for their cults centered on shamanic oracular priests (*dhāmī*, *dhāminī*), which were and still are particularly widespread among the Matwali Khasa.[42] Each *dhāmī* is associated with a single spirit and its shrine; he can be possessed by this spirit. In some cases, the spirit can be "inherited" and possess the son of a *dhāmī*. Particularly striking in the rituals is the worship of the Twelve Maṣṭā ("brothers"), during which tales (*parelī*) of the Maṣṭā are recited and oracles are delivered. At certain festivals, up to fifty *dhāmī* may come together, during which caste restrictions are as good as suspended.

The Petty Kingdoms

The Khasa-Malla kingdom was split up into twenty-two petty kingdoms (*bāisī rājya*) in the Karnali-Bheri region. Alongside them were twenty-four petty kingdoms (*caubisī rājya*) in the western Gandaki region. How such division came about is unknown, as are the names and historicity of these areas of rule. They included both small principalities and tributary petty kingdoms. The terms for these groupings only occur in documents from the eighteenth century. Thus, in 1774 King Pṛthvīnārāyaṇa Śāha felt threatened "by the other *caubisī*."[43] Different lists of the petty kingdoms were produced by various Britons in Nepal and by later chronicles. The first list was compiled in 1811 by Colonel Kirkpatrick, who had traveled inside Nepal in 1793, and next was compiled in 1819 by traveler and naturalist Francis Buchanan Hamilton.[44] The number of kingdoms varies between forty-six and seventy-eight, even more if the kingdoms west of the Mahakali River are added.[45] The Sena kingdoms in Palpa, Makwanpur, Tanahun, and Butwal sometimes show up also on lists. Furthermore, Banepa (or Bhonta), Nuvakot, and Dolakha were for some time independent principalities. Besides the petty kingdoms, there were only a few established independent regional powers in the middle of the eighteenth century, among them Sikkim and Bhutan.

The petty kingdoms were ruled by strongmen who either came from the lowlands or, in the case of Khasa or Magar rulers, from the hill regions. It is said that the Śāha (or Gorkha) rulers were themselves of Khasa or Magar origin,[46] although they claimed Rajput roots. According to the chronicles, they fled Rajasthan in the twelfth and thirteenth centuries before advancing Muslims. The new rulers settled mostly on land where they could cultivate rice or other crops, and so avoided conflict with the Tibeto-Burmese ethnic groups, who were more engaged in livestock farming and shifting cultivation.

The reasons for the fragmentation of the country are manifold: disputed succession, division of the domain among too many heirs, the rise of a powerful aristocracy (especially among the Malla kingdoms), migrations and separations, and political and family alliances.[47] It often made more sense to conquer a neighboring state without undermining its ruling structures there, and instead demand tribute payments. This resulted in alliances but hindered the formation of powerful states and centralization. In general, wealth meant land ownership, and the larger the territory, the more powerful the kings were. If they owned land in the fertile Tarai or had significant trade that brought in taxes, this was an advantage. However, a larger territory also meant more expenditure on the realm's security, for which the king was responsible according to Hindu norms. This could not be done by a standing army alone but required the willingness of its inhabitants to pay taxes and to make sacrifices in the form of compulsory labor. The peasants could keep moving since unused land could be claimed in many regions by anyone who wanted to cultivate it. If they were coerced or pressured too much, they simply migrated, which severely reduced land output. And the human-to-land ratio was so low that not many farmers could be called up for military service.

The petty kingdoms' judicial and administrative autonomy continued through the Śāha Period or, in the case of Mustang and Salyan, even into the Rāṇā Period. Thus individual tributary kingdoms were preserved within the Gorkha realm, although Pṛthvīnārāyaṇa Śāha attempted to construct a strong state, which he called a *dhuṅgo*, literally "stone."[48] The Gorkhali and Śāha that ruled over the Dullu kingdom occasionally after the collapse of the Khasa empire regarded themselves as legitimate successors to the once mighty Khasa and as descendants of Indian Rajputs, and commissioned Brahmin priests to integrate them into such genealogies. Consequently, they called their country Khasadeśa ("Khasa Land"). But these rulers had not yet gained power over the whole country and the Kathmandu Valley was first taken over by another dynasty, the Malla kings.

5

Divided Rule

The Malla Kingdoms, Thirteenth to Eighteenth Century

Along the entire stretch of the Himalaya between Burma and Kashmir there is only one single valley, the Kathmandu Valley, in which, over a thousand years ago, an urban culture was able to establish itself. This quite distinctive culture was and is marked by the Newar, who live there in compact settlements with an urban lifestyle.[1] They speak a Tibeto-Burman language, Nevārī, and have spread to other regions, such as Sikkim, Dolakha, and Bhojpur.[2] They differ from other ethnic groups in Nepal, too, in that they have their own script and an extensive corpus of literature.

The Hindu-Buddhist religion of the Newar is full of singular features from the perspective of religious history. For example, Buddhist priests (Nev. *gubhāju*) often work alongside Tantric Hindu priests (Nev. *ācājyu*; Skt. *karmācārya*, *rājopādhyāya*) in rituals. The cult of venerating the Kumārī, a living girl as a goddess, is unique, as is the meld of folk or vernacular religion, Hinduism, and Buddhism in the Buṅgadyaḥ/Karuṇāmaya/Matsyendranātha festival; this also holds true for the clan (*digudyaḥ*) and lineage (*āgādyaḥ*) divinities, the distinctive communal (*guṭhī*) system, and Vajrayāna Buddhism (also called Newar Buddhism), among whose characteristics are monastery-like structures without a community of celibate monks.

In the Kathmandu Valley, three kingdoms competed with each other for centuries but their spheres of influence did not much extend far beyond the borders of the valley. The sediments of a prehistoric lake offered favorable conditions for agricultural surpluses, and thus residents enjoyed a certain measure of wealth, even though Nepāla was repeatedly struck by earthquakes and droughts. Farmers settled in the city rather than outside it. The trade routes between India and China or Tibet ensured vibrant trade, for which there is evidence at least as early as 1000 CE. Newar painters, jewelers, and architects left their stamp on the arts of Tibet, and they worked at the imperial court in Beijing as well. All in all, craftsmen enjoyed a thriving business, one still evident in the Kathmandu Valley. Elaborate windows and doors

Nepal. Axel Michaels, Oxford University Press. English language edition © Oxford University Press 2024.
DOI: 10.1093/oso/9780197650936.003.0006

made by woodcarvers, magnificent bronze or brass statues, finely chased objects made by goldsmiths, and colorful paintings by thangka and miniature painters offer testimony to it.

The Malla Rulers

The Newar were ruled by different Malla clans from the thirteenth century until 1768/69. This Malla Period is often divided into an early (1200–1382) and a late (1382–1769) one, given that the sources increase considerably from the reign of Sthiti Malla (1382–95) on.

The name Malla (lit. "wrestler, victor") is therefore not that of a single dynasty. Even though it appears in earlier Indian sources and in Licchavi inscriptions,[3] half of the kings of the Early Malla Period added *malla* to their name. From Sthitimalla, *malla* forms a part of the kings' names.[4] Far more, however, of them called themselves names ending in *-deva*, "god." Whether the early rulers can even be called Malla is thus questionable. In western Nepal, the Khasa, who ruled from the eleventh to fourteenth century and occasionally undertook raids into the Kathmandu Valley, called themselves Malla too, but it is unlikely that they gave rise to the use of the Malla title in the Kathmandu Valley.

Initially, the sources for the Malla period are still primarily stone inscriptions, copperplates,[5] and palm-leaf manuscripts or palm-leaf rolls (with clay seals), most of which are land titles. The inscriptions are usually in the Nevārī language and script, or in a corrupt Sanskrit, and follow the Nepāla or Śaka era. Often the copperplates and the inscriptions on statues and ritual objects deal with land endowments or other gifts, dictating what is to be paid for with the harvest revenue: the regular worship of the gods (*pūjā*), the lighting of oil lamps on a balustrade around temples, performing animal sacrifices, playing music, holding a procession (*jātrā*), securing the livelihood of temple servants, or providing donations to ascetics. The texts repeat formulaically that those who do not follow the stipulations in question will be afflicted with the sin of killing a cow, a Brahmin, a woman, or a child. Increasingly, paper manuscripts begin to appear, among them a number of chronologically ordered diaries (Nev. *ghaṭanāvalī, thyāsaphu*) written in Nevārī in the seventeenth century or later and recording historical events. There are reports from Jesuits and other travelers as well. Along with all these, the chronicles continue to offer important information.

As in the Early Medieval Period, there was often no one ruler who controlled the entire valley; especially in the thirteenth and fourteenth centuries, power was often divided. Up to the mid-thirteenth century, Bhaktapur (Bhadgaon) in particular was strong, but so was Banepa on the eastern edge of the Kathmandu Valley—the "Banepa kingdom" (Bhoṭarājya). With Sthiti Malla, who ascended to the throne in 1382, this division of power changed. Down through the reign of Yakṣa Malla there were relatively solid power structures in place. Afterward dominion was divided among his three sons, and the three city-kingdoms of Bhaktapur, Kathmandu, and Patan were formed—a state of affairs that lasted until 1769. Often alliances arose between kings, who were related to start with. Sometimes the Malla rulers agreed among themselves to respect each other, not to disturb fixed borders, and to maintain peace and friendship. This the sons of Yakṣa Malla did, for instance, in a copperplate dating from 1548 at the Paśupatinātha temple.[6]

Apart from a few exceptions, if a king died he was succeeded by his first-born son, the crown prince. It was of little import whether this prince was legitimate or illegitimate by birth, as the example in Patan of Mahindra Malla, an illegitimate son of Yoganarendra Malla, shows. Polygamy was widespread to begin with, but often the king also had mistresses and concubines, some of whom attained considerable standing. Thus, Rājyalakṣmīdevī is mentioned on a coin, and so is a concubine alongside the later queen Ṛddhilakṣmī in an inscription by Pārthivendra Malla.[7] If the king had no son, his brother or the first son of his daughter succeeded him, as in the case of Lokaprakāśa in Patan (who ended up ruling only one year, 1705–6). There was generally no ostentatious coronation. Usually, a simple ceremony took place, at the climax of which the oldest king in the Kathmandu Valley or the court priest would press a *ṭīkā* onto the forehead of the successor, often before the dying monarch had even been brought to the cremation site.

The Malla Period was characterized by an autocratic system of administration, tailor-made for the (usually) three absolute monarchs of the Kathmandu Valley, although the balance of power was not always clear-cut, due to occasionally shared rule. The palace administration had not essentially changed since the Licchavi Period. The posts of personal secretary to the king, court priest-cum-astrologer, court physician, religious judge (*dharmādhikārin*), and chamberlain still existed. Newly mentioned personnel include gardeners and supervisors of slaves. The crown prince for his part played a larger role. Crown Prince Jayadharma Malla, for example, became prime minister under

Jayasthiti Malla, while Siddhinarasiṃha Malla and Bhūpatīndra Malla both transferred kingly power to their sons while still alive.

Intrigues and imbroglios were a common feature of the Malla administration. For example, the minister (Nev./Nep. *kājī*) Bhīma Malla became so beloved among the people, thanks to the revival of trade with Tibet, that Pratāpa Malla had him poisoned in 1642 out of fear of a conspiracy between him and the Tibetans. Bhīma Malla's wife is supposed to have been immolated with him, but only after pronouncing the curse that it would henceforth not pay to be loyal.

The Malla's sphere of influence reached beyond the valley to the Tibetan frontier and encompassed Deopatan, Gokarna, Changu Narayan and Sankhu. Patan included Godavari and Pharping, among other places. The Bagmati River formed a visible border between Patan and Kathmandu, but there were no clearly demarcated territories inside the valley. In other places there were provincial governors. An exchange of ambassadors was agreed upon with the Gorkha kingdom.

There is little documentation of any long wars between the city-kingdoms or with the surrounding kingdoms. As it was, the military and economic wherewithal for such would not have been sufficient. What did occur, rather, were skirmishes, scuffles, and brawls, in which the people joined in robustly. Sticks, spears, slashing knives (*khukurī*), and swords (*khaḍga*) were the available weapons; only rarely were there firearms. A standing army existed solely as a force to protect the king and, beyond that, to serve as a small infantry, but there was no cavalry. Equally absent was any kind of police, but there were palace guards (*koṭavāla*, *dvāre*). Large fortresses protecting against external attack did not yet exist in the Kathmandu Valley, but the cities and palaces were walled.

Kingship was expressed not so much by wielding instruments of power as by displaying symbolic and ritual strength. For example, a king might balance his own weight against an equivalent weight in gold and donate the latter to a temple, for gods had to be attended to or disaster threatened. In inscriptions, a king almost always called himself "ruler (lit. "god") of Nepāla" (*nepāleśvara*). Paśupati remained the tutelary or guardian deity of kings and thus of their kingdoms, but under Sthiti Malla at the latest the goddess Māneśvarī (later called Taleju), a form of Durgā and a tutelary deity of the Karnata dynasty, was revered by the palaces. As the absolute authority, kings decided all important matters affecting the country. Still, Malla kings were not ivory tower rulers cut off from reality. They often mingled with the people, especially at festivals. The means at their disposal were limited, since their territory was small. Even when they built comparatively large palaces and temples, they did not live in fairy-tale splendor.

The kings' power was repeatedly constrained by certain factors. For example, aristocrats and wealthy landlords were sometimes so strong that the king could not do much against their wishes in any real sense, despite the basic difference between rights of ownership and rights of usage.[8] There were various claims to land, ranging from the king as the feudal owner of all land, to landlords as title holders of land, down to the tenant farmer who worked the land. Land use rights could additionally be supplemented by further rights (rites of passage, water, fodder) or penal rights. These rights, which could be vested in rare cases in women, were documented in palm-leaf rolls sealed with the clay seal of the king and kept in what may be called a land registry office. A land tax (Skt. *mūlapiṇḍa*, *piṇḍakara*) had to be paid, which ended up in the palace. The right to work fields, called (Skt.) *karṣaka*, could be passed on to tenants.

The kingdom of a Malla king was divided into districts (*pradeśa*), which were governed by governors (*pātra*, *mahāpātra*), and regions or boroughs (*viṣaya*), which were governed by headmen (*pramukha*, *pradhānpātra*). Villages and town quarters had their own headmen. Out of this class there arose a new nobility no later than the thirteenth century (Nev. *bhāro*, *bhā*), which came to occupy important positions in the palace.

The Malla also developed criteria for land sale documents and for marking borders. These documents record information about the place, features of the landscape, the names of the buyer and seller, ownership and use rights, and the names of the witnesses and the scribe. Such criteria are also standard for more recent documents from the Śāha and Rāṇā periods.[9]

Taxes and levies made up one-sixth to one-quarter of the harvest. Besides these, there were special taxes on oil, fish, pigs, water buffalo, wood, and other goods. Extra taxes could be levied to raise funds for weddings of members of the royal family, for example. All state income went to the palace. The administrative supervision of temples lay generally with *guṭhīs* but sometimes with high-ranking palace officials. The supervision of water channels was the responsibility of a special official (*nirjharādhipa*, Nev. *dhalapā*).

The king presided over a "council of courtiers" (*bhāradārī*), whose rotating membership included members of respected families, the prime minister (*mūlakājī*, *mahāmantrin*, *mukhyamantrin*, *cautārā*; Nev./Nep *kājī*), and several functionaries. These meetings of the council where matters of the state were discussed took place at irregular intervals. One of the other functions of the kings was to preside over the justice system and to pass judgement, especially in cases of the five heinous crimes (killing a cow, a Brahmin, a teacher, a woman, or one's own father). Important ancillary figures were the religious judge (*dharmādhikārin*) and the royal priest (*rājapurohita*, *rājaguru*, *rājopādhyāya*), the latter of whom performed rituals, granted absolution, interpreted signs and stars, and advised the king.

The actual day-to-day business of government lay in the hands of a ministerial council (*sacivamaṇḍala*), consisting of the prime minister and a few other ministers (*amātya*, *pramāṇa*, *mantrin*, *kājī*). Still other ministers or feudatories (*viṣayādhipati*) were responsible for about eight districts (*viṣaya*), and other officials oversaw subdistricts (*deśanāyaka*, *dvāre*, *ṭolanāyaka*).[10] Both the prime minister and other ministers could be tasked with military operations, in which not only soldiers but also large parts of the male population might be mobilized. There was probably no large professional army prior to the seventeenth century. In times of war, a professional recruiting official (*umrāu*/*umrāva*) was deployed, who could also be assigned the task of leading military units. Army leaders (*senādhyakṣa*) are named in inscriptions, but the supreme command remained with the king. The guarding and maintenance of palaces and forts, which were under the command of a castle guardian (Nev. *kvāthanāyaka*), were precisely regulated, at least under Yakṣa Malla.

The people could force the king to dismiss obscure ministers or officials, as in the case of the minister Bhāgīrāma in Bhaktapur, who had to go, against the will of King Jitāmitra Malla, because the people blamed him for hardships resulting from a three-year blockade of Kathmandu. There is, however, no evidence that a king was ever decapitated. The greatest danger to kings was from within the palace and from his closest relatives.

* * *

Between the Mogul Empire to the south and the Chinese Empire in the north there were, then, three areas of theocratic rule in the Late Malla Period. One reason why they could exist so long was Nepāla's geographical remoteness, which discouraged distant rulers from conquering the Kathmandu Valley. Mogul rulers appear to have been content to receive elephants annually as tribute from Nepāla. The British in India and the Chinese, too, were disinclined to attempt any conquest of this rugged, inaccessible country.

Individual dynasties in the south, such as the Karnata in Mithila, claimed sovereignty over Nepāla, but with no lasting success.

Several raids into the Kathmandu Valley are nevertheless documented: by the Maithili (or Tirhutiyā) from the Tarai between 1244 and 1311; by the Khasa from the west, especially between 1287 and 1334; and finally, in 1349, the seven-day attack of Muslims under Shams ud-dīn Ilyās from Bengal.[11] While the Maithili and the Muslims plundered and destroyed many statues, shrines, and temples, the Khasa bowed down to Paśupatinātha and directed their attacks against the population. But the Kathmandu Valley, and thus Nepal, were never conquered by foreign rulers. Granted repelling attackers was often only possible with the help of allies. Thus, Ratna Malla was able to keep the Bhotia (Tibetans) at arm's length solely because the Sena rulers from Palpa sent soldiers to his aid.

But Nepal was not isolated. For Tibetans, the land represented a glorious past. They especially wanted to participate in the great learning of Nepalese and Indian scholars. Nepal was for them the land of Sanskrit texts and wise men, and later the land from which the Buddha came. Tibetan monasteries often traced the lineages of their abbots back to Indian scholars. Nepāla remained a refuge for both Buddhist monks and Hindu ascetics. The Hindu population of Nepal had always seen itself as a part of Āryāvarta, the blessed Hindu subcontinent, as can be seen in many inscriptions. From the Indian side claims were made on it until quite recently, because its independence was either doubted or not recognized. Almost as a matter of course Nepal was listed on maps of "Indian" places of pilgrimage, and indeed there was lively interaction between the two regions. Nonetheless, the *Himavatkhaṇḍa*, for example, which serially eulogizes the holy places of Nepal, is not a part of the "Indian" *Skandapurāṇa*, even though it is often referred to as such.

* * *

Individual rulers stand out among the multitude of potentates named in the chronicles and other sources. Rudra Malla, for instance, was not a king but rather an influential kingmaker at the court of Kathmandu; he presided over the Matsyendranātha festival and set up Ari Malla II as a largely ineffectual shadow king. He also granted the Mithila queen Devaladevī, widowed in 1326, asylum in Bhaktapur when the Muslims besieged her kingdom. She married her son Jagatsiṃha to Rudra Malla's daughter Nāyakadevī and arranged in 1355 for the couple's daughter Rājalladevī to marry Sthiti Malla, who probably came from Mithila and likely attained power only thanks to this marriage. Even fifty years after the wedding, his own sons still called him "Rājalladevī's husband." Sthiti Malla ensured that there was unity and stability, and he wrote the previously mentioned "Garland of Castes" (later embedded in the *Nepālikabhūpavaṃśāvalī*), in which eighty-two castes are listed in hierarchical order according to their professions.

Sthiti Malla probably attained power as early in 1372, but did not ascend the throne until 1382, after Arjunadeva died, though he had done his best to dismantle his predecessor's power step by step. He remained controversial, especially among influential nobles, first and foremost Jayasiṃha-Rāmavardhana, the powerful minister of Bhaktapur, who had himself declared king of Bhoṭarājya (Banepa) immediately after Sthiti Malla's death. Despite the concentration of Sthiti Malla's power—he was acknowledged as supreme ruler in the Kathmandu Valley by the other kings and by Patan's seven dominant noble families (*pātra*, *mahāpātra*)—he was surrounded by other potentates both within and outside the valley, primarily those in Nuvakot, Pharping, and (most persistently) Banepa, whose ruler was occasionally recognized by the Chinese Ming dynasty (1368–1644) as the actual ruler. Sthiti Malla, however, cemented his influence among the people by, among other things, renovating the Svayambhū Stūpa, spreading the Nevārī language, and establishing the cult of the goddess Degutale (or Taleju), the tutelary deity shared by the Malla rulers.

Yakṣa Malla succeeded to the throne in 1428. He defeated Banepa, conquered some areas outside the Kathmandu Valley, and also endowed many temples (such as the great Dattātreya temple in Bhaktapur), shrines, and water facilities. He passed on the throne to his sons (Ratna Malla, Rāya Malla, and Raṇa Malla) and a son of his daughter (Bhīma Malla), who at first ruled jointly in Bhaktapur and in various combinations in Patan. In 1484 Ratna Malla made Kathmandu into a state of its own, while Patan soon fell back under the control of local nobles and remained in their hands until 1597, when Śivasiṃha of Kathmandu took power there. Not until 1619, with the accession of Siddhinarasiṃha, did Patan become an independent kingdom.

Thus the three city kingdoms of Kantipur (Kathmandu), Bhadgaon (Bhaktapur), and Lalitpur (Patan) developed into the three power centers in the Kathmandu Valley, each with large palaces and temples for the goddess Taleju and other deities.[12] But borders and alliances formed anew over and over, as a chronicle (*Thyāsaphu B*) published by D. R. Regmi makes clear.[13] There it is said that in the month of Vaiśākha in the year 1699 (NS 819) Patan was isolated, but five months later all three city kingdoms re-established friendship; two years later, Bhaktapur was isolated, and a few months later it was Yoganarendra Malla, the king of Patan, who was. Kantipur and Patan formed an alliance in the month of Mārga three years further on; in the following month all three cities were friends. And so it went. The missionary Gruebner reported that Pratāpa Malla and Śrīnivāsa Malla formed an alliance in 1662 and fought victoriously against Jagatprakāśa Malla, king of Bhadgaon. A copperplate from NS 823 (1703 CE) contains an agreement between King Bhāskara Malla of Kathmandu and King Bhūpatindra Malla of Bhaktapur to maintain peace and amity, for which a security of 36,000 *mohara* had been deposited in order to guarantee compliance by the parties to it.[14] For major events such as the initiation of a crown prince, the wedding of a king, or the dedication of a temple, all three kings came together.

One of the strongmen of the Late Malla Period was Pratāpa Malla (1641–74), who first took over as a regent when his father Lakṣmīnarasiṃha obviously became a victim of dementia. He himself was probably not very educated, but boasted of fostering priests, holy men, scholars, and artists, some of whom he invited to come to Nepāla from India. Indeed, a few poems in inscriptions and esoteric texts are ascribed to him. The Kavīndrapura (or Madunāsadyaḥ) temple near the Kāṣṭhamaṇḍapa in Kathmandu was founded by Pratāpa Malla. The name of the building refers to him, as he styled himself the "king (or Indra) of poets" (*kavīndra*). Beside the temple are two inscriptions with poems by Pratāpa Malla, and in the *Nepālikabhūpavaṃśāvalī* it is stated:

> He pulled out the essence (*dhyāna*) of the Nṛtyanātha (sculpture) in a shrine inside an ancient liṅga-shaped temple near Kāṣṭhamaṇḍapa, prepared a beautiful sculpture, composed a poem, and had it engraved on a stone. He established the deity in a large *sattala*, named it Kavīndrapura, and called the deity Madu Nāsaladeva.[15]

Jagajjyotir and Bhūpatīndra Malla of Bhaktapur, along with Yoganarendra and Siddhinarasiṃha Malla of Patan, were, like Pratāpa Malla, among the more artistically or intellectually inclined kings. A Maithilī drama named *Paraśurāmopakhyānanāṭaka* was written by Bhūpatīndra Malla of Bhaktapur, for example.

When Pratāpa Malla died in 1674, rumors swirled about his cause of death, as usual with such events. Supposedly the Tantric goddess Harisiddhi had sat beside him in the form of a girl while he watched the famous Harisiddhi dances. Not knowing that the girl was a goddess, he did not pay her the respect she deserved, so shortly thereafter he fainted and never awoke. From that time on—so say the chronicles—no Harisiddhi dance was performed in Kathmandu, although they are documented shortly afterward during the rule of Nṛpendra Malla (1774–80).

Pratāpa Malla supposedly had eight sons, the oldest being Nṛpendra Malla, but regents governed de facto in Kathmandu for the next fifty years. As always in such uncertain times, questions of legitimacy and of successors' ages arose. In 1744 Nuvakot was taken by the Gorkhali, and in 1768 Pṛthvīnārāyaṇa Śāha conquered the Kathmandu Valley, thus ending Malla rule.

The Urban Culture of the Newars

Since the sixth century at least, the inhabitants of the Kathmandu Valley started developing a unique architectural culture, which reached its apex under the Malla kings in the sixteenth to eighteenth century.[16] Three competing royal towns, Kathmandu, Patan, and Bhaktapur, tried to outdo each other in architecture, art, and craftsmanship. Apart from these main cities, many smaller towns and settlements with similar building styles became vibrant or historically important ones: the town of Banepa, long an independent kingdom; Bungamati, for part of the year the home of Matsyendranātha, and the starting point of a procession inaugurating a newly constructed chariot for the deity; Kirtipur, the last town to be conquered by Pṛthvīnārāyaṇa, with its Bāghabhairava and Umāmaheśvara temples; Panauti, under Bhūpatīndra Malla the capital of a small kingdom, with a palace and an old Indreśvara temple; Sankhu, the seat of the important Vajrayoginī temple; Thimi, the potters' town between Kathmandu and Bhaktapur; and Nuvakot, the first seat of the Śāha kings outside Gorkha, but in which the kings of Kathmandu had already built palaces before Pṛthvīnārāyaṇa added his own with seven stories and three roofs.[17]

The Early Malla Period does not offer much in the way of architectural remains, but from the seventeenth century on there was a boom in construction that was unequalled in the Himalaya.[18] At the core of this intense activity was the rivalry of royal families to build imposing palaces (*darbāra*, a concept from the eighteenth century) and support temples and monasteries. Hundreds of temples and shrines, palace buildings, and monasteries were created over more than a century. Among the most important builders were Siddhinarasiṃha Malla (1619–61) in Patan, Pratāpa Malla in Kathmandu, and Bhūpatīndra Malla in Bhaktapur.

The most striking characteristics of this architecture are temples with tiered hipped roofs; large palace complexes in the center of the towns; private residential houses of brick with carved wooden windows and doors; Buddhist *stūpas* or *caityas* (Nev. *chibhāḥ*); monasteries and shelters for Hindu ascetics; open shrines or ones only half roofed over; step wells and other water architecture; platforms for rituals and dance; and arcade-like rest houses.

The holy places are often related to each other and laid out according to religious criteria. In Bhaktapur, for example, the Eight Mother Goddesses (Aṣṭamātṛkā) surround and delimit the old core of the town. Such spatial patterns form the basis of processions in which the group of deities as a whole is visited, and indeed every day numerous people complete the circuit of visiting every seat (*pīṭha*) of the Aṣṭamātṛkā in Bhaktapur. Other such patterns are, for example, the Four Nārāyaṇa (Cāṅgunārāyaṇa, Icaṅgunārāyaṇa, Śeṣanārāyaṇa, and Viśaṅkhunārāyaṇa) at places along the edge of the Kathmandu Valley; the four "Aśoka *stūpas*," mounds of earth placed about Patan; the Twelve Tīrtha and the seats of serpents that Buddhists visit on each eighth day of the waxing moon; the Nine Durgā (Navadurgā); and the Ten Mahāvidyā, personifications of the female divine power (Skt. *śakti*).

Everyday life in the towns of the Kathmandu Valley was shaped by the peasants who lived in them, by craftsmanship and trade, and, above all, by religion. There are countless small shrines, temples, and divine seats located in every inner courtyard, at every crossroads, and at thresholds of houses, often attracting more veneration than the great monuments in the palace squares.

Temples

In Hinduism, the gods can manifest themselves nearly everywhere: in temples and shrines, but equally as people, animals, or plants. The simplest form of representation is divine seats in the form of unworked stone. The stones can be large boulders or smaller, immovable rocks, or even movable ones, such as the "hidden Śiva" (Lukumahādyaḥ) in Newar inner courtyards or "clan deities" (Nev. *dugudyaḥ/digudyaḥ*) out in the fields. Often small stones flecked with vermilion can be seen in front of houses, on paths, or at

Figure 5.1 So-called Aśoka Stūpa (North) in Patan, 2010. Photo by Thomas Schrom. Nepal Heritage Documentation Project, NHDP.

roadsides. These divine seats, firmly anchored in the earth, which are called guards of the threshold, of the immediate surroundings, or of "crossroads" (Skt. *kṣetrapāla*), must be pacified. Sometimes such stones called in Nevārī *chvāsaḥ* or *pikhālākhu* are seats of certain deities and demons, which accept what is impure and unclean, such as cut hair, umbilical cords, or the clothes of a deceased person. Depending on the significance and the frequency of veneration, these simple seats, generally maintained by lower-caste people, can be extended into U-shaped, ornamented shrines. This is especially the case with the "seats" (*pīṭha*) of local (if increasingly Sanskritized) goddesses who also have a god-house within the town area, often indistinguishable from a normal Newar residence. In this "god-house" is kept a movable form of the goddess (a statue, pictorial representation, or mask).

In contrast to these Tantric *pīṭha* deities, the Hindu-Paurāṇic high gods require a roof over their heads.[19] This is usually a temple in the Newar context, regardless of the divinity's popularity. The largest type of temple is the so-called pagoda, a term adopted in the nineteenth century that is misleading since this style has no connection to East Asia and the name obscures the distinct, self-defining individuality of Newar architecture. These buildings with their tiered roofs are called *degaḥ* in Nevārī and *mandira* (or *devālaya*) in Nepālī; all of these words simply mean "god-house" or "temple." For Tantric divine dwellings, there are further terms, such as Nevārī *āgãchẽ* or *dyaḥchẽ*, which have much the same meaning.

As a rule, temples bear the names of the central divinity. In the interior is the sanctum, usually a statue, surrounded by other deities. This sanctum can be circumambulated in only a few temples. In 1627, Patan introduced exterior walkways around the Viśveśvara temple, and these rapidly became very popular. However, Hindu temples are not gathering places for believers but are instead intended to allow individuals or small groups to worship the gods directly.

At first, temples probably had only a roof over a square ground plan, with doorways on all sides. Upper stories are not normally accessible to believers; only in exceptional cases, such as the Bhīmasena temple in Patan, is the sanctum upstairs. During the Malla epoch, in an effort to make the holy buildings visible from afar, up to five roofs were added, tapering towards the top with no extra space that could be walked in. Most larger temples of the Malla period stand on a stepped foundation. In the middle of the seventeenth century, Kathmandu introduced just such a temple, the monumental Taleju, with a twelve-stepped foundation. The Nyātapola temple in Bhaktapur, built in only eight months in 1702, is even higher. Temples for goddesses and Bhairava often have a square floor plan and only one doorway: the Mahālakṣmī temple in Thimi (late seventeenth century), the Bālakumārī temple in Patan (1622, renovated in the eighteenth century), or the Bhairava temple in Bhaktapur (1717, rebuilt 1940). Three temples with an octagonal floor plan are dedicated to Kṛṣṇa.

Temples are made with fired bricks. Their roof tiles, the size of an adult's palm, are pressed into a ground of clay in overlapping fashion (a characteristic of Newar architecture), while wood is used for their columns, roof struts, tympana, and windows. Roof constructions with "eaves" (Nev. *yegāḥpākhā*) overhanging up to 31 feet are typical of houses, monasteries (Nev. *bāhāḥ*, *bāhāla*, *bahī*), two-story "communal gathering buildings" (Nev. *capāḥ*, Nep. *sattala*), and temples. The roof covering lies upon close-set rafters and purlins, which are supported by carved struts at 45° angle. These carved parts are made from the wood of sal trees (Skt./Nep. *śāla*, *Shorea robusta*), a tropical hardwood that used to be brought from neighboring valleys, but now grows predominantly in the foothills of the Himalaya.

Only a few ostentatious temples have roofs made of copper sheet metal, which, as in the case of Paśupatinātha, may be gilt as well. Nearly all of them have small bells at the edges of the roof that chime in the wind, and for special occasions they receive a reddish-golden banner that runs around the building. The roof is usually decorated with a "pinnacle" (*gajura*) of copper or brass, which can also be gilt. Over the one- to three-paneled doors is displayed, as a rule, a carved "tympanum" (*toraṇa*), while anthropomorphic figures of the river goddesses Gaṅgā and Yamunā are frequently carved into the doorframe. The typical lintel is extremely long and extends far past the doorposts. On the outer walls are niches containing wooden tablets with representations of various deities, often guardians of the universe. Stone lions or other mythical animals frequently stand guard outside the entrances. In front of Hindu temples, the mount and attributes of the deity in question are also exhibited: in the case of a Śiva temple, a Nandī statue and a trident; in the case of a Vaiṣṇava temple, the mythical bird Garuḍa and a conch shell. The Viśveśvara temple in Patan served as the prototype for more than three hundred temples. It also displays many iconographic innovations, such as dragons along the lines of the Chinese representations Newar craftsmen had become acquainted with in the course of their commissioned work abroad.

Arcaded resthouses (Nepa. *pāṭī*, Nev. *phalcā*) and other gathering buildings (Nep. *sattala*; Nev. sataḥ; Skt. *maṇḍapa*, *dharmaśālā*) are mostly intended as places to stay during rituals and are generally donated by private persons or *guṭhīs*. The ground floor of the *pāṭīs*, of which there are over five hundred in various forms and sizes, are usually open to the street and serve, among other things, as a place to prepare *guṭhī* feasts or occasionally store ritual objects. Many have been converted in modern times into residential or business buildings. These structures are recognizable, like shelters for ascetics (*maṭha*) and Buddhist monastery complexes, by their carved wooden windows and doors, or by their gilt roof spire. Among the larger gathering halls are the Kāṣṭhamaṇḍapa (approx. 1640) and the Kavīndrapura (1657, renovated in 1940, rebuilt in 1988) in Kathmandu, and the Dattātreya in Bhaktapur (sixteenth century, extended in the nineteenth century).

The curvilinear *śikhara* temple is a tower-like structure made of stone and brick, occasionally whitewashed, and usually ornamented on its outside surface.[20] This style, which came from India, has been widespread within the Kathmandu Valley and beyond since the sixteenth century. Among the earliest are the Narasiṃha temple (1589) and the Mahābauddha temple (1601), both in Patan. A further seventy-five *śikhara* temples were built until about 1870. One of the most outstanding is the Kṛṣṇa (or Bālagopāla) temple in Patan, built in 1637. It has three stories, all of which can be circumambulated on the outside. Kṛṣṇa has his seat on the first floor, and Śiva as Viśvanātha ("lord of the universe") on the second. This temple was the model for a series of similar temples, among them the second octagonal Kṛṣṇa temple south of the palace square, erected in 1723.

Palaces

Palaces offer further striking examples of Newar architecture. As centers of power, they were designed to appear ostentatious in conspicuous locations. The rulers' power was lent to them by the gods, or the former at least depended on the latter's benevolence. This is why there are always large temples in the immediate vicinity for the patron goddess of the Malla, Taleju. What the palaces before the Malla epoch looked like is not known, although Licchavi inscriptions name centers from which power emanated. How the layout of modern palaces was created during the Malla period can be seen in the repeated extensions of existing structures in Kathmandu well into the Śāha and Rāṇā periods.

The individual rooms of Malla palaces probably served as chambers for the king's clan, as administrative offices, and as servants' quarters. The palaces themselves are laid out, as a rule, around an inner courtyard. In the private areas are stepped fountains for supplying ritual water, as well as small temples or shrines. Many buildings are open to the courtyard on their ground floor. Receptions were presumably held in the inner courtyard itself, and judgments passed there, although the main inner courtyard may have been reserved strictly for rituals. The palaces have gardens, where the treasury building was also located. On the palace squares (Darbar Squares) outside these self-contained areas, but very close to the seat of power, stand a multitude of temples, both large and small, some of which were donated by the aristocracy and others by the rulers themselves.

Large bells, tall columns crowned with images of rulers, or (as in Kathmandu) a huge kettledrum endow these squares with a stately elegance, one without any military trappings. In contrast to the palaces the Śāha kings built in Gorkha or Nuvakot, those of the Malla were not fortresses or castles, but instead conveyed a mixture of openness and seclusion. The windows of Newar palaces (and houses) are always barred on the first floor, so that women in particular could see out without being seen themselves. The king, too, generally was exposed to public view only at festivals and rituals. Entry to the palace was strictly guarded, and only possible through a single main entrance. From the originally nine-story (now five-story), four-roofed Basantapur (or Nautale) tower, erected in 1770 by Pṛthvīnārāyaṇa, the whole town could be seen.

Nearly all kings and queens, and many ministers, have immortalized themselves in temples they have endowed, or else have had votive temples built in their memory to immortalize them. A few large temples were erected by private persons. It is interesting that even Lakṣmīdevī, the mistress of Raṇabahādura Śāha, was permitted to build a temple in memory of this king: the Lakṣmīśvara in Teku (1812/13). Many of the larger or especially elaborate temples are state temples, such as the Indreśvara in Panauti, the Yakṣeśvara in Bhaktapur, and the Nārāyaṇa temples.

Monasteries and Stūpas

A distinct architectural feature of Buddhism in Nepal is its roughly 350 former monasteries. King Siddhinarasiṃha Malla alone supposedly donated twenty-five monasteries to communities. Almost every fourth entrance into an inner courtyard in the old town of Patan leads to such a monastic complex, the earliest of whose buildings date to the seventeenth century. However, these are usually no longer shelters for Buddhist monks but more or less ordinary residences for extended Newar families, who nevertheless see themselves as a "community" (*saṃgha*). As in Kathmandu, the tradition in Patan distinguishes between "monasteries" (Nev. *bāhāḥ*) for "married monks" (*gṛhastha-bhikṣu*) and those (Nev. *bahī*) for originally unmarried monks. The "main monasteries" (*mū bāhāḥ*) have "branches" (*kacā bāhāḥ*). In some *bāhāḥ* there are only Vajracharya, and in others both Vajracharya and Shakya; in the older *bāhāḥ*, there are only Shakya.

Monasteries and Buddhist holy shrines generally include *stūpas*.[21] A *stūpa*, also called a *caitya* (Nev. *cibhāḥ*; Tibetan *mchod-rten*, pronounced roughly *chörten*), is a small domed structure that cannot be entered.[22] It consists of a substructure under a dome-like mound, inside which (in the case of large ones) there is a "central pole" (Skt. *yūpa*, *yaṣṭi*; Nev. *yaḥsī*) with a crest jewel on top; the pole has to be renovated whenever damaged by lightning or a storm. On the mound is placed a cube (Skt. *harmika*) and a finial with a varying number of rings, also conceived of as "parasols" (*chatra*). These elements have led to many interpretations—for instance, that the dome is to be understood as the "world egg" (*aṇḍa*, *garbha*) or primordial hillock, the pole inside as the axis mundi, or the parasols as symbolic of the king. A *caitya* can also be placed on top of a small shrine-like *śikhara* temple, as in the Mahābauddha temple in Patan. Nearly all *caityas* bear sculptures of the four Tathāgatas and Bodhisattvas on their sides, and most of them are votive *caityas*, erected in memory of deceased persons and for the builder's own salvation.

A particularly fine example of the architectural pattern of *stūpas* is the Svayambhū Stūpa, which is central to the history of Newar (and Tibetan) Buddhism.[23] According to legend, Mañjuśrī found a lotus at the present location of the Svayambhūcaitya (called Svayambhūnātha only since the last century) after he had slashed the surrounding mountains with his sword to drain the lake that once covered the Valley. A Mañjuśrī temple, also venerated by Hindus as the seat of Sarasvatī, the goddess of wisdom and the arts, stands to the west of the Svayambhūcaitya. Svayambhū is hinted at in an inscription for the first time in the fifth century, but the first mention appears in the *Red Annals* of Panchen Sonam Drakpa in the fourteenth century, which tells of the renovation of the central pole.

The present form of the *caitya* is probably the product of a comprehensive renovation in the year 1372. Since the eighteenth century the *caitya* has been called a *mahācaitya* ("great *caitya*"), the four eyes of which, placed in the crown of the dome, look in all directions and are visible from afar. The main access to the *stūpa* is an eastern stairway with 365 steps, along which stand several votive *caityas* and Akṣobhya statues from the early Śāha period. The symbolism of the *caitya* is much discussed and interpreted in manuscripts. A circular ground plan is the base of a hemisphere, flattened at the top, which represents the body of the Buddha and is a symbol of his perfection. A railing with 211 prayer wheels surrounds the dome, each one bearing the holy mantra *Oṃ maṇi padme huṃ* ("O jewel in the lotus"). In the early eighteenth century, niches were made in the *caitya* to accommodate the five transcendental Buddhas (or Tathāgatas) along with their guardian mounts by Bhāskara Malla, namely: In the east sits Akṣobhya on his elephant and Vairocana on his lion; in the south, Ratnasambhava on his horse; in the west, Amitābha on his peacock; and in the north, Amoghasiddhi on the heavenly bird Garuḍa. Between these transcendental Buddhas, which additionally embody the cosmic elements, are niches for their four correlating feminine aspects, the Buddhaśakti.

Thirteen parasols rise up above the cube. Donated by various communities on the occasion of a renovation, as old Newar drawings show, they are represented as a tapering series of discs symbolizing the stages on the way to perfection and enlightenment. The wooden pole in the center was replaced in 1817, while in 1918 the *caitya* was renovated in its entirety. Old records show that the pole retained its length of 72 feet, while the total height is just about 31 meters.

A large bronze vajra (Tibetan *rdo-rje*, dorje), dating from 1667 atop a large *maṇḍala* to the east of the *stūpa*, is from Pratāpa Malla. In Hindu mythology, a vajra is Indra's thunderbolt weapon, while in Buddhism it is a diamond scepter, a symbol of the indestructibility of the Buddha's teachings. Pratāpa Malla also erected two sacred buildings in the style of Hindu *śikhara* temples, Pratāpapura and Anantapura, named after him and his wife, but dedicated to esoteric deities of Vajrayāna Buddhism. Since the eighteenth century the *stūpa* has been sharing the hilltop with a Bhutanese monastery, and since 1962 with a Tibetan one (Tibetan *dgon-pa*, gompa), rest houses for visitors, lodgings for maintenance workers and guards, and souvenir shops. Among the larger buildings is a Tantric temple dedicated to the goddess Hārītī (or Śītalā), who protects against smallpox and childhood

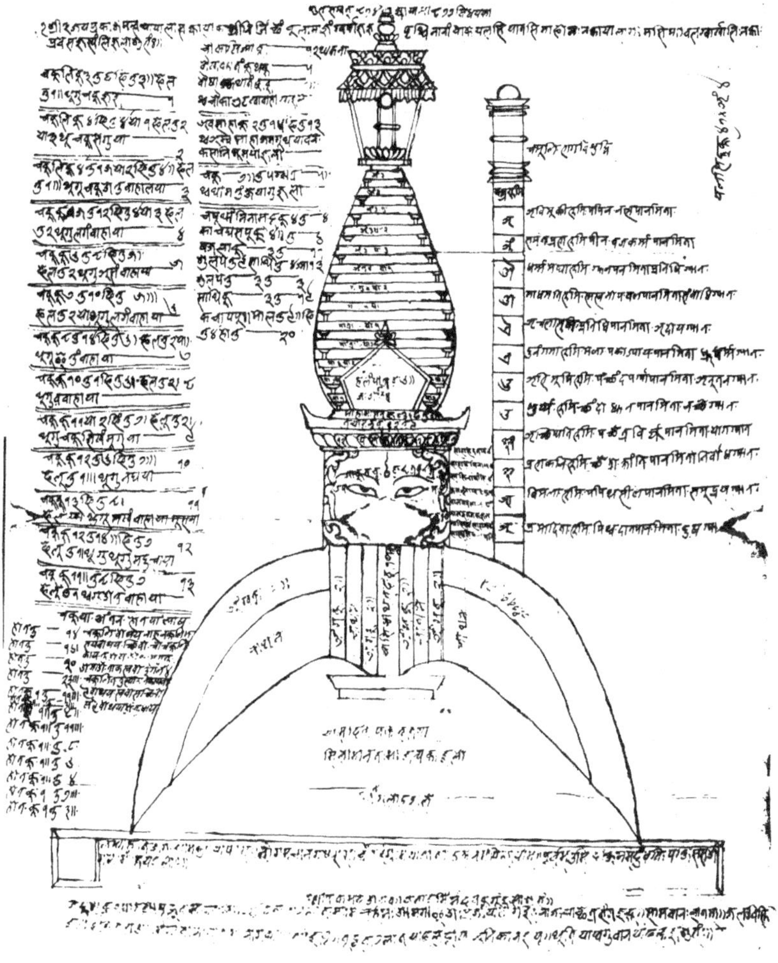

Figure 5.2 Drawing with dimensions for the reconstruction of the Svayambhū Stūpa, 1753–56. From Bernhard Kölver, *Re-building a Stūpa: Architectural Drawings of the Svayambhūnātha*. Bonn: VGH Wissenschaftsverlag, 1992.

illnesses, but who does not receive any blood sacrifices in her Buddhist surroundings.

To what extent the Vajrayāna regards itself as the culmination of Buddhism can be seen in the interpretation of the parasols of the Svayambhūcaitya. In India, the *stūpas* of the second century probably had only one such structural element; early buildings had three. Since the twelfth century Svayambhū has had thirteen. Doctrinal ascriptions of meaning to these parasols have been preserved in old architectural drawings and a number of Tibetan texts. The first ten of these structures correspond to the ten stages (*daśabhūmi*) on the path of a Bodhisattva:

1. the very joyous (*pramuditā*)
2. the stainless (*vimalā*)
3. the illuminating (*prabhākarī*)
4. the blazing (*arciṣmatī*)
5. the difficult to master (*sudurjayā*)
6. the facing manifest (*abhimukhī*)
7. the far-reaching (*dūraṅgamā*)
8. the immovable (*acalā*)
9. the [stage] of great wisdom (*sādhumatī*)
10. the [stage] of the cloud of dharma teachings (*dharmameghā*).

Other such explanations for the ten in number include the power arising from the ten knowledges (*daśajñānabala*). In the case of Svayambhū, the ten stages were chosen that must be traversed spiritually by anyone with an earnest aspiration to become a Buddha. The Newar Vajrayāna added another three stages, and correspondingly another three parasols. Clearly this was done in accordance with the *Dharmasaṃgraha*, a compendium of Buddhist concepts widespread in Nepal. This text attaches these three *bhūmi* to the ten such already in existence:

11. the totally enlightened (*samantaprabhā*)
12. the burning desire (*adhimukti*) [for enlightenment]
13. the vajra world, or one's consecration as a *vajrācārya*, a vajra master.

The *stūpa* thus gives visible expression to the fact that the Vajrayāna is understood as the culmination of the Mahāyāna's path of liberation.

The Three Royal Cities of the Kathmandu Valley

Of all three royal seats in the Kathmandu Valley, Bhaktapur, the "city of devotees," also called Bhadgaon, is the third-largest town.[24] It is located some ten miles east of Kathmandu on an old trading route between India and Tibet, which remains the main artery through town. Despite its urban image, until well into the 1970s only Newar peasants, the majority of them Hindu, lived in the dense old settlement. During the day the peasants went out to their fields, spread their rice and corn to dry, and let their chickens, goats, pigs, and cows wander through the town. At the markets and on the larger streets there was much going on, and during the night music sounded from the temples or rest houses (*phalcās*).

The town lived above all from its gods, represented everywhere in numerous temples, shrines, and sculptures. In *Mesocosm: Hinduism and the Organization of a Traditional Newar City in Nepal* (1990), American anthropologist Robert Levy describes that Bhaktapur as a sacred place that organizes itself around religious symbols. The gods are not in the beyond; they are here and now, in a mesocosm in the middle of it all right on earth; and in people, who to some extent embody them, and who are guarded and challenged by them. A large part of daily life is managed around them, as are the yearly cycle and the harvest cycle. Yet this was a town with an urban layout and culture, with a palace and its wider complex, and with many relations to other towns in the Kathmandu Valley and the surrounding region.

The center of Bhaktapur suffered very little congested urban development until recently, since through traffic circumvented it for the most part. Bhaktapur thus still offers a rare picture of a medieval town. It consists spatially of two areas, which are also socially distinct: an upper town in the east, and a lower town in the west. During certain festivals, such as the Bisketjātrā in the spring, these two areas collide in ritualized, and at times intense, combat. As in the other Newar towns in the Kathmandu Valley, open squares form the center of the twenty-four city quarters. They are particularly pronounced in Bhaktapur and often give the quarters their names. One very lively one is Potters Square, where potters' wheels are constantly turning and half-finished pottery dries or waits for the kiln. Pottery has an ancient pedigree in Nepal and is still practiced according to traditional methods in the Kathmandu Valley, mainly in Thimi and Bhaktapur.[25] The potters use hand-powered potters' wheels. Small plates, cups, bowls, pots, incense holders, lampshades, and also small figurines and gods are produced. The items are then set up on the ground to dry and, after a couple of days, are packed in straw and layered upon each other.

According to the chronicles, Bhaktapur was founded by King Ānandadeva I after he left rule of Kathmandu and Patan to his elder brother Narendradeva II. In the Early Medieval and the Early Malla periods, it came to be known by the name of Khopa. In the fourteenth century, Bhaktapur achieved dominance within the Kathmandu Valley under Sthiti Malla. Bhaktapur in fact grew out of several smaller settlements that united and expanded in the course of time, especially under Yakṣa Malla, who made the town his capital, and Jitāmitra Malla and Bhūpatīndra Malla. In 1769, Bhaktapur was conquered by Pṛthvīnārāyaṇa Śāha, who himself had lived for a time there with Raṇajit Malla.

In contrast to Kathmandu and Patan, the old palace in Bhaktapur is not in the center but at the northern edge of the old town. It is thus architecturally less integrated into town life, not surrounded by shops and workshops like its counterparts in Patan and Kathmandu. Nor can the palace be traced back to the Licchavi Period, although two fragments from it are from this time.

It is entirely possible that an earlier palace at the god-house of the goddess Tripurasundarī was the original center. The oldest architectural remains, in the form of a narrow doorway behind the Golden Gate, are from the fourteenth century, so the main courtyard likely also dates from this period, although the current configuration is from the time of Jitāmitra Malla. The first inscription, dated 1482, is from Yakṣa Malla, who in it donated a pot that is still used in the Dasaĩ festival. The first palace inscription, on a first-floor window, is from 1551. At the beginning of the eighteenth century, it was above all Bhūpatīndra Malla who extended and altered the palace. The central building of the broad palace complex, which was later used as the National Gallery, was only built around 1855. Aquarelles and drawings by Henry Ambrose Oldfield in the mid-nineteenth century show these buildings.

The palace, said to have once had twenty-nine courtyards, is similar to the one in Patan. Most courtyards were renovated by Pṛthvīnārāyaṇa Śāha and his son Pratāpa Siṃha in the late eighteenth century, and by Bhīmasena Thāpā around 1820. Two gilt windows and a number of murals, all from the seventeenth century, were made part of the building; outside in front of them stand statues of King Jitāmitra and his wife, dating from 1708/9. Taleju, the patron goddess of the Malla kings, was brought to the town at the beginning of the fourteenth century, there receiving her seat and her temple in the main courtyard, which is surrounded by several smaller courtyards and the royal bathing pool, Nāga Pokharī (or Nāgapukhū), built in 1678 by Jitāmitra Malla.

This temple complex was entered through the richly decorated "Golden Gate," Sunaḍhokā, which the last king of Bhaktapur, Raṇajit Malla, had set into the palace front in 1753, and adorned with the image of his preferred goddess. The inscription beside it forbids visitors from wearing shoes or carrying an umbrella when entering. The same ruler had a life-sized statue

Figure 5.3 The Palace Square of Bhaktapur. Drawing by H. A. Oldfield, 1853. 32.2 × 47.6 cm. Courtesy of the British Library.

placed on a column in front of this gate, namely one of his father, Bhūpatīndra Malla, displayed kneeling reverentially before Taleju under the protection of a parasol.

The palace complex basically consists of several palaces, whose functions are to some extent unclear. The façade of the eastern palace, built of red brick and restored in 2002–8, has fifty-five black wooden windows, in contrast to the Lāla Baiṭhaka to the west, plastered in white and with stucco decoration, which was erected by Bhūpatīndra and converted into a governor's seat in 1855 by Dhīra Śamśera. Further west is Siṃhadhvākhā Darbāra and the entrance to Basantapura Darbāra, which was built around 1660 by Jagatprakāśa Malla but has not been preserved.

As in the other royal cities, the kings did not build their temples only within the palace complex, but had shrines erected in the forecourt, too. Yet there are comparatively few monuments in Bhaktapur's palace square. As one can see in early drawings, though, it was once much more densely built up. The earthquakes of 1934 and 2015 destroyed a large number of the buildings. One testimony to this is the remains of a large Śiva temple called Silumahādyaḥ to the west of the palace, which collapsed in 2015 and has been reconstructed.

Kings had *liṅga* temples built—of which Yakṣeśvara is one, begun in 1478 and named after its originator, Yakṣa Malla—supposedly to allow for worship of Paśupati without taking the long journey to Deopatan. Above all, though, they had temples built in Bhaktapur for their preferred goddesses. This was the case with the temple in the *śikhara* style erected on a plinth and dedicated to the goddess Vatsalā in 1690 by Jitāmitra Malla, but it was partially destroyed in 1934 and collapsed completely in 2015.[26] This goddess, too, has another seat at the Paśupatinātha temple in Deopatan. These temples were for the most part meaningless to the populace, who seldom if ever visited them.

In contrast to the Darbar Square, Taumadhi Square is in the middle of the town, surrounded by old Newar houses and seen by traders and passers-by. It might appear that this square was more centralized than the palace square, but the idea of a town center here does not do justice to the polycentric nature of the population groups and the power relations between deities and people. Two temples collide with each other at Taumadhi Square: the tall, square Nyātapola temple and the nearby rectangular Bhairava temple. Nyātapola, constructed in 1702 by Bhūpatīndra Malla, presumably as a challenge to the Taleju temple in Kathmandu, is dedicated to his preferred goddess, Siddhilakṣmī. Nyātapola, which simply means "five-roofed (temple)," stands upon a five-stepped platform with four Gaṇeśa shrines at its corners, and its ascent is guarded by pairs of wrestlers, elephants, lions, mythical horses (Skt. *śārdūla*) with lion's claws, and two Tantric guardian goddesses, the lion-like Siṃhinī and tiger-like Vyāghrinī. This temple, too, was in a way a private temple of the king and thus little frequented.

The three-roofed Bhairava temple is the most important temple in Bhaktapur. Called Nāyo ("chief, leader"), it, too, was erected by Bhūpatīndra Malla in 1717, as an inscription on the north wall reveals. But this inscription also states that the temple "has stood here for a long time." Bhairava has his seat in the upper story, in the form of a stone regarded as the guardian of the town, while on the ground floor only a small, iconic representation of the god and of Nāsaḥdyaḥ, the god of music and dance, are worshiped. During the great festival of the New Year, Bisketjātrā, a Bhairava cult image is taken out of the temple and brought to a large processional chariot. He is followed by a smaller chariot carrying the goddess Bhadrakālī. Both chariots come to a halt on Taumadhi Square at the border between the upper and the lower towns. The square then becomes the stage for a performative town drama. At the start, men from both parts of town engage in a tug of war on long ropes during which longstanding fights between quarters often flare up. Often the upper town wins. Only when, days later, the chariots have reached a square in the south is the New Year ritually introduced by erecting a tall tree trunk.

These are the places in which religious life reaches its climactic moments. This applies, too, to the broad Tacapala Square at the town's eastern end of the old trading road through Bhaktapur. Its center is formed by the three-story Dattātreya temple, which is actually a *maṇḍapa* that, like the Kāṣṭhamaṇḍapa in Kathmandu, was originally a gathering place for ascetics. Its cella contains statues of the divine triad Brahmā, Viṣṇu, and Śiva. According to a fragmentary inscription, Yakṣa Malla erected the building around 1460, and Viśva Malla or Jitāmitra Malla rebuilt it in the middle of the sixteenth century. In the mid-nineteenth century the building was extended by a neighboring abbot, who added a porch in the west, two guardian figures (copies of the lowest pair of statues in front of the Nyātapola temple), and three columns with a Garuḍa, discus, and conch shell. In the west, the area is delimited by a rectangular, two-story Bhīmasena temple dedicated to a deified hero of the *Mahābhārata* epic of that name who is popular because of his feats of strength, and who in Nepal is the patron god of many trader castes. The second function of the great squares thereby becomes clear: trade. Where the gods stand or dance on special occasions is where vegetables and fruit, clothing, and tools are sold on normal days.

It is not surprising that business streets and places where trading is done are also magnets for ascetics, who depend on donations and contributions. Even as in Patan Buddhist monks have lived off that town's wealth, so too in Bhaktapur Hindu ascetics have gathered at Dattātreya, and at the Pūjārīmaṭha behind it, which was one of originally twelve shelters for pilgrims and ascetics, most of them Śaiva. These *maṭhas* are basically elaborate houses that integrate themselves into the townscape and thus, unlike temples, are not freestanding. They are testimony to the strong promotion of ascetics by the late Malla kings. The four-story Pūjārīmaṭha is the largest of its kind. It is surrounded by farmers' houses and served for a time as the center of administration of temple lands, but following its restoration in the winter of 1971/72 and 1987 it was converted into a crafts museum. The Pūjārīmaṭha is famous above all for the especially rich and delicate woodcarvings from the mid-eighteenth century on its doors and windows, among them the famous Peacock Window looking onto an alley in the eastern part of town. The restoration and reconstruction of this building was a wedding present from the Federal Republic of Germany to King Birendra.

Figure 5.4 Bhaktapur with a view of the palace (left) and the multi-roofed Nyātapola and Bhairava temples in the background, 1973. Photo by Niels Gutschow.

Another characteristic feature of Bhaktapur is the principal protection afforded by the Navadurgā ("Nine Durgā") and the Aṣṭamātṛkā ("Eight Mothers") to the town of Bhaktapur as a whole. The Aṣṭamātṛkā have their "seats" (*pīṭha*) in a ring about the core of the town; those of Mahākālī and Mahālakṣmī are particularly elaborate in design, and some of the seats have been roofed over in recent years. While the squares are oriented to linear structures, these goddesses embody the town's circular structure. This is visible when, during the Dasaĩ festival, many inhabitants of Bhaktapur go to all the shrines over eight days to pray to the goddesses for a successful rice harvest. Not only does each goddess have a permanent, unalterable seat at the edge of the town, but she also has a god-house within the town proper, indistinguishable, as a rule, from normal houses. Statues or masks of the goddesses are kept in the latter, "descending" from the upper floors on the occasion of a festival or procession so that they can be carried through the neighboring quarters. The Navadurgā, for example, have their god-houses in the eastern part of the old town, and these goddesses particularly express though their dances and rituals the link between linear and circular structures, and also the link to the outside world or the old area under Bhaktapur's control.

Palace and temple, streets and squares form the foundation of Bhaktapur's ritually shaped life. The town has changed little in this respect since Malla times. It has retained its individual character, something that can still be observed in the strong dialect of Nevārī spoken there. Most notably, however, its "agrarian citizens" have transformed pre-Hindu structures into a Hindu-Tantric town, all the while engaging in preservation. They have turned it into a town that is segmented into caste or social groups, yet remains communal, and is oriented for the most part toward the goddesses and Bhairava.

* * *

In contrast to Bhaktapur, Patan is laid out based the palace lying at a crossing of two axes whose end points are formed by the four mound-shaped Aśoka stūpas.[27] This place was probably the center of the settlement before the palace was constructed; at least the Old Nevārī name Mānigvala ("central place/square') seems to indicate this.[28]

Another early indication of the settlement of Patan, also called Lalitpur (Lālitapura) or in Nevārī, Yala, already points in this direction: an inscription from the year 570 CE found, together with fragments from the Licchavi Period, at the Maṇihiti step well in the northern part of the palace area. In addition, there is evidence of what was possibly an aristocrat's house at this place, namely in an inscription dating from December 26, 1414, on a *liṅga* excavated from the step well in 2008.

The core of the actual palace building was likely erected around 1627, when Siddhinarasiṃha Malla had it built on the occasion of the birth of his son Śrīnivāsa. According to the chronicles, the son made changes to the palace after his father's death, enhancing it, for example, with the tall Taleju temple. Apparently, large parts of it were destroyed in the earthquakes of 1681 and 1934, although it remained relatively intact during the earthquake of 2015. Around 1730, the entire front side was renovated and roughly acquired its modern appearance, with older elements being integrated into it. However, the central golden window (Nev. *lũjhyāḥ*), which the *Nepālikabhūpavaṃśāvalī* ascribes to Viṣṇu Malla, has more recently been dated only to the nineteenth century.[29] The twenty-first century brought further renovations and "improvements," some of which have been reversed by the Department of Archaeology and the Kathmandu Valley Preservation Trust. This is especially true of the southern courtyard containing the Royal Bath with its niches and sculptures, a step well that goes back to Śrīnivāsa Malla.

As in Bhaktapur, several temples stand in the forecourt, but in contrast to Bhaktapur they are not dedicated to Tantric goddesses worshiped by the kings. Instead, they are Vaiṣṇava and, to a lesser extent, Śaiva shrines, although the town itself, with its many monasteries, is conspicuously Buddhist. In neither the palace nor forecourt are there any Buddhist shrines.

The oldest temple in the palace square is the Cāranārāyaṇa ("Four Nārāyaṇa") temple, showing Viṣṇu in his four emanations (Skt. *caturvyūha*). The building was completely destroyed in 2015 but by 2019 had been rebuilt. The foundational inscription mentions Purandarasiṃha as the builder, a formidable noble (*mahāpātra*) who had usurped power for a time and ruled in Patan with his three brothers until 1597.

Patan experienced an upswing under Siddhinarasiṃha and his two successors, Śrīnivāsa and Yoganarendra Malla. Siddhinarasiṃha had the influential Viśveśvara temple (1627) built and, in the *śikhara* style, the popular Kṛṣṇa temple (1637), also known as the Bālagopāla temple. The latter was allegedly built after the king had seen Kṛṣṇa and Rādhā in a dream. His son Śrīnivāsa renovated the Viśveśvara and built the Maṇimaṇḍapa and the equally popular Bhīmasena temple (1681), at the inauguration of which all three kings of the Kathmandu Valley came together. This temple is maintained by Kapāliyogī (married Śaiva ascetics). Since the late Malla Period, Bhīmasena, one of the five brothers in the *Mahābhārata*, is regarded as a god of good fortune, trade, and love.[30] His statue is life-sized, and in his hand, he carries a club suggestive of his strength.

Yoganarendra, who can be seen with his two wives on a central column built in 1693 and re-erected in 2017, added the octagonal Taleju temple to the palace complex. The temple incorporates the square's great bell, donated by Viṣṇu Malla in 1737. Yoganarendra also instigated the renovation in 1694 of the Maṇihiti step well, containing three water spouts and two roofed platforms, of which one was reserved for coronations. The Kṛṣṇa temple, also called Cyāsī ("octagonal") Degaḥ, is a votive temple that the regent Yogamatī had built in commemoration of her son Lokaprakāśa, who died young. The Hariśaṅkara temple, named after a manifestation of Viṣṇu and Śiva, goes back to the same family: Yogamatī's sister Rudramatī had it built in 1706 for her father Yoganarendra. In the northern part of town stands the Kumbheśvara temple, which owes its present form to Yoganarendra. Apart from Nyātapola in Bhaktapur, this is the only temple in the Kathmandu Valley with five roofs.

If the palace in Bhaktapur lies on the spatial periphery, then the one in Patan, together with its Hindu surroundings, lies at the religious periphery.

The most striking characteristic in Patan is the number of Buddhist monasteries, whose courtyards are home to much of its social life. Here communal festivals, rituals, and meals are held, and badminton is played. Besides their iconographic program, the Buddhist structure of the former monasteries is expressed above all in their temples. To take one example, Kvā Bāhāḥ (or Hiraṇyavarṇa-Mahāvihāra), founded in 1206, boasts the town's largest membership, with over two thousand initiates, and is also very richly appointed. Many monastic inscriptions, the earliest from the late fourteenth century, testify to numerous donations to the monastery. Dubbed the Golden Temple, its dominant features are its sundry gilt statues and, above all, the three gilt copper roofs of the main shrine. The principal deity Akṣobhya (one of the five transcendent Buddhas) and Buddha Śākyamuni in his basic earth-touching posture have a place here. Both are often represented with identical iconographic characteristics, so that they cannot always be distinguished, especially when the statue is covered in ornamental objects. In the center of the courtyard is another temple with a gilt roof. A *caitya* from the Licchavi Period, it is a shrine of the community's clan deity. The courtyard is surrounded by an ambulatory with oil lamps, prayer wheels, and many shrines, among them four nearly life-sized Bodhisattva statues in the corners. Apart from the periodically changing human guardians of the gods, nobody lives in the houses around the courtyard, where holy texts are read or religious songs are sung.

In contrast to Bhaktapur and the Bisketjātrā, there is no square in Patan where the majority of the populace can gather and participate in mass events. The large, extremely significant Matsyendranāthajātrā, the biggest festival in Patan, takes largely place outside the old town and originally comes from Bungamati. Patan is a city of monasteries; Bhaktapur, on the other hand, has only two monasteries worth mentioning for its few Shakya and Bajracharya members. Patan is a town of communities, not of a community.

* * *

Kathmandu, also called Kantipur, is a mixture of Hindu Bhaktapur and Buddhist Patan.[31] The goddess Lakṣmī allegedly appeared to Guṇakāmadeva I in a dream and told him to build Kāntipura (Kānti being another name for Lakṣmī) at the place where the Bagmati and Vishnumati rivers come together. The town was to take the shape of a sword, as a painting from the nineteenth century shows.

The town was an old trading town and lies, like Bhaktapur, on the trade route between India and Tibet. Like Patan, it has many Buddhist monasteries, but nearly as many Hindu shrines. As the capital, Kathmandu developed in a more monumental style during the Śāha and Rāṇā periods, became much more densely settled, and architecturally was hit harder by the 1934 earthquake than the other royal cities. Until Kathmandu became the capital all the cities had been advancing along similar lines.

The core old town, which was once surrounded by a wall, goes back to the fifteenth century, when Kathmandu overtook the older town of Bhaktapur in terms of political significance and established itself as an independent kingdom under Ratna Malla.[32] No temples built by him have survived. Only under Mahendra Malla did any noteworthy amount of royal building activity begin, nearly a hundred years later than in Bhaktapur. This includes the stele in the forecourt of the palace with the four emanations of Viṣṇu, the Cāranārāyaṇa, dating from 1563. According to lists of historical events, this king built the great Taleju temple on a nine-step foundation in 1564, a sign of his power that was visible from afar. Legend has it that Mahendra used to go to Bhaktapur daily to worship Taleju there, but the goddess gave him a sign that he could also build a temple to her in Kathmandu, where she was to be venerated in the shape of a *yantra*, a magic diagram. Later Mahendra's great-grandson Pratāpa Malla and the latter's son, Pārthivendra, had many changes made to the temple, though the present temple was rebuilt around 1820.

The oldest parts of the palace complex were built under Mahendra Malla, who attracted many families to the town by giving them tax-free land. The palace, along with its forecourt and the surrounding temples, exhibits a mixture of architectural styles, and with its many courtyards (Nev. *cuka*) it is similar to the palaces in Patan and Bhaktapur. The most important of these courtyards are Mohanacuka, erected around 1650 and containing the Sūndhārā step well; Sundāricuka, created the same year, and displaying the previously mentioned Kāliyadamana statue from the seventh century; the main inner courtyard (Mūcuka), which was redesigned in 1708; and Nāsacuka, featuring a platform, renovated in 1826, on which the Śāha kings were crowned (in the Malla epoch, this had occurred in Mūcuka).

Outside the palace, Pratāpa Malla had the three-story Degutale temple built in 1670, to which another story was added in 1795; to the west, it is complemented by a large Sveta Bhairava mask, and to the east by a main gate (gilded in 1810) and a statue of Hanumān (erected by Pratāpa Malla in 1672) draped with a red cloth. This statue gives the whole area its name, Hanuman Dhoka ("Gate of Hanumān"). In the foundation of the northern wing, which contains thirty-four false arched windows, there is a rather long stone inscription in fifteen languages, intended to demonstrate that Pratāpa Malla was a ruler attuned to the outside world. He himself can be seen on a column erected in 1670 in front of the palace, together with his two queens and five sons. The construction of this plastered, three-story part of the palace complex was undertaken by Bhīmasena Thāpā in 1822, while the three-story building west of Degutale, whose ground floor is partially open, was built by Jaṅga Bahādura Rāṇā.

Apart from the Kāṣṭhamaṇḍapa, Kathmandu began later than Bhaktapur or Patan to construct monumental buildings, but it outdid both these towns and so flaunted itself as the center of the Kathmandu Valley, and even of Nepal as a whole. Kathmandu has the largest number of representative buildings and is the most regal of the towns. This can be seen in the Indrajātrā procession, dedicated to Indra, called king of the gods, which begins and ends directly at the palace, the human king having to present himself to the public on such occasions. It is also visible in the permanent seat of the Kumārī, the child goddess who ritually lends the king his power, being located next to the palace. In addition, Kathmandu had the most associations with holy shrines outside the old town, extending to Svayambhū and to Paśupatinātha. In many rituals, the sword of the king of Kathmandu is still visible today.[33]

Perhaps it is decisive for the three royal towns that urban societies developed in them that exude a certain openness and thus integrated many different people into them. At the same time, the three towns were also shaped by their gods, perhaps more so than by the kings, so they were able to preserve of their unmistakable unique characteristics.

6
From Gorkha to Nepal
The Śāha Monarchy, 1768/69–1846

How could Nepal's geographical-political potpourri of ethnicities, languages, and ways of life come together? Was it the heroic struggle of one individual? Or did other factors favor this merger? Why did the country need to unite in the first place? After all, there was not much to get out of it, hardly any mines or other riches. Apart from the few fertile valleys and the Tarai, the hill regions consisted mainly of land that was not easy to cultivate.

The Gorkha kingdom owed its pre-eminent position to Dravya Śāha, the founder of the Śāha dynasty who established his rule in Lamjung in 1559 and continued to reign until 1570.[1] He was almost constantly involved in wars with his neighbors and was never able to significantly extend his territory. Not until Rāma Śāha in the early seventeenth century could the kingdom expand to Nuvakot in the east, to the Marsyangdi River in the west, and to the Tibetan frontier in the north. Newar craftsmen from Kathmandu eventually settled in Gorkha and, most significantly, a process of Hinduization set in as the conquered areas came to be administered by Brahmins and Chhetri. Even though no military successes are documented for Rāma Śāha's four successors, this relatively small kingdom was able to bring nearly the entire region under its control by the end of the eighteenth century.

Pṛthvīnārāyaṇa and His Followers

The attention of the Gorkhali was directed above all toward the prosperous Kathmandu Valley. A first, unsuccessful attempt to capture Nuvakot a day's march away from it was undertaken by Narabhūpāla, but it was his son Pṛthvīnārāyaṇa who, in a long series of assaults, finally conquered the Valley.[2] In 1744, the twenty-one-year-old took Nuvakot, just one year after his enthronement, and then in 1748 Sindhupalchok and other areas in the east, having armed the population, practiced night attacks, set up weapons

Nepal. Axel Michaels, Oxford University Press. English language edition © Oxford University Press 2024.
DOI: 10.1093/oso/9780197650936.003.0007

stores along the way, and for the first time used firearms (mainly muskets). He succeeded, too, through night attacks and blockades, and by controlling the passes to Tibet and thus the trans-Himalaya trade. In August 1762 Makwanpur, to the south-west of the Kathmandu Valley, fell to him, giving him control over the main route to the Tarai. From then on it was only a question of time before he invaded the Kathmandu Valley, even though Jayaprakāśa Malla, the last Malla king of Kathmandu, in April 1767, asked the East India Company for support. British troops under Captain George Kinloch were sent in August 1767 to repel Pṛthvīnārāyaṇa's attacks, but also to secure the coveted trade route to Tibet for the Company.[3] However, they could only reach the forts of Sindhuli and Hariharpur, about 75 kilometers away from Kathmandu by mid-October before having to retreat due to heavy rains, swollen rivers, scarcity of grain supplies, and a great loss of soldiers and gunpowder but, above all, "a lack of intelligence about the terrain and his enemy."[4]

Thereafter, Pṛthvīnārāyaṇa was rather wary toward foreigners. He suspected the Capuchin monks, who had been received amicably by Pratāpa Malla, of having betrayed secrets to the British and in 1769 commanded them to leave the country. He remained distrustful of India, of the British there, and of Tibet and China. He did not permit any foreign traders into the country or anyone to wear foreign cloth. This affected primarily the Gosain, and also Kashmiri traders, who kept goods flowing between India and Tibet. "Do not let the merchants of India come up from the border. The merchants come to our country and let the people slip into poverty," he said in the *Divyopadeśa*.[5] Instead, he called on his compatriots to buy only wares from Nepal.

On March 17, 1766, Pṛthvīnārāyaṇa conquered Kirtipur to the west of Patan. This required several attacks. Father Giuseppe reports that the ruler commanded that the noses of all inhabitants be cut off, including those of children who no longer lay in their mothers' arms. The *Nepālikabhūpavaṃśāvalī* adds that this amounted altogether to 865 people, and it even gives the combined weight of the amputated noses. The large knives still hang in the Bāghabhairava temple of the city, which Pṛthvīnārāyaṇa wanted to rename Nāsakaṭapura, the "city of severed noses." Recently discovered evidence suggests that this incident may have actually happened. A document, either an original or an undated copy, in the possession of the late researcher Sukrasagar Shrestha, shows that those punished asked for the return of the land that, to add to their misery, had been taken from them.[6]

The conquest of the cities in the Kathmandu Valley occurred in stages and was only completed in 1769 after a long blockade, which is described in the colophon of a *Rāmāyaṇakathā* manuscript from NS 883 (1762 CE) to the effect that Pṛthvīnārāyaṇa had blocked the import of cotton, salt, and many other goods, so that these articles were hard to obtain and people were reduced to wearing rags.[7] Kathmandu fell on September 15, 1768, Patan on October 6, 1768, Thimi on April 14, 1769, and finally Bhaktapur on November 17, 1769. The last kings of Kathmandu and Patan were killed or tortured to death, while Raṇajit Malla, the last king of Bhaktapur, could escape to Varanasi. It therefore took twenty-five years, from the conquest of Nuvakot in 1744 to that of Bhaktapur, to consolidate rule over the Kathmandu Valley, the heart of Nepal in the making.

How small the scope of the conquest was is clearly shown by a count from that time: in 1769, Kathmandu had about 22,000 houses, Patan 24,000, and Bhaktapur 12,000.[8] Gorkha, for its part, is estimated to have had only 12,000 houses. With the exception of Kirtipur, the Kathmandu Valley had not resisted to Pṛthvīnārāyaṇa. It was weakened by the division into three areas of rule, put under kings who were either incompetent or young, or else, as in Patan (where the Pradhan clan was enormously influential), nearly powerless.

When Pṛthvīnārāyaṇa died on January 11, 1775, at the age of fifty-five, he left behind a notable legacy. His conquest of the Kathmandu Valley signified a paradigmatic shift:[9] a transfer of power from the Newar to the Khasa-Arya aristocracy, a suppression and overlayering of Newar culture, the introduction of new Hindu divinities along with a substantial increase in temple building, the promotion of Brahmin priests and festivals, the subordination of ethnic groups under Khasa-Arya rule through the establishment of a Hindu caste hierarchy, and the dominance of the modern Indo-Aryan language Nepālī over the Tibeto-Burman language Nevārī.

However, the question remains whether, and if so how, Pṛthvīnārāyaṇa Śāha managed to unify Nepal. He certainly united the country militarily, politically, and administratively, albeit with great regional differences, and not only through coercion, as the British at the time suggested.[10] Throughout this process, he was helped by the basic administrative structures set up by local rulers in the petty kingdoms. It is debatable whether the main motive for Gorkha's expansion was the desire for more land and power as to create a greater Hindu kingdom under a *hindupati rājā*, as stated in the *Divyopadeśa*.[11] There is no question that Pṛthvīnārāyaṇa Śāha was able, with a relatively small army—perhaps 8,000 to 10,000 soldiers[12]—both to bring large parts of present-day Nepal under his control and to protect his nascent state from takeover by other powers. This required diplomatic skill and a command of military tactics (e.g., blockades of settlements and trade routes, seizures of passes and mountain ridges, and night attacks), a well-trained soldiery, sufficient purchased or looted provisions (especially parched rice and corn, which could be easily stored), and effective military equipment (mainly *khukhurīs* and bows and arrows, but also rifles). Still, the best military preparation means little if the soldiers are not motivated. Pṛthvīnārāyaṇa Śāha was obviously able to convey his vision of a greater Nepal to his people; not without reason did historian Ludwig Stiller take this as a sign of his extraordinary stamina and high quality of leadership.[13]

On the other hand, some victories were relatively easy for Pṛthvīnārāyaṇa Śāha because of limited resistance. The parochial interests of petty kingdoms, including those in the Kathmandu Valley, outweighed any cohesiveness, and many inhabitants of the hill regions and the Kathmandu Valley did not have the military spirit the Gorkhali enjoyed in the form of their sometimes ruthless Magar and Khasa soldiers. As a result, there was insufficient preparedness, even though the conquest of the Kathmandu Valley took decades.

* * *

Pṛthvīnārāyaṇa Śāha's son, Pratāpa Siṃha, ruled for only two years. Under his leadership the collapse of the Śāha dynasty began, although this dynasty provided the head of state without interruption until 2006. Pratāpa Siṃha was the last king until Mahendra to ascend the throne as a mature man. After him, with the exception of Tribhuvan and Mahendra, the kings led a shadowy, marginal existence isolated from the people, always watched over by powerful regents or prime ministers, and finally completely enfeebled by the Rāṇā aristocracy and the *bhāradāras*, the nobility of basically a few powerful families: the Thāpā, Pā̃ḍe, Kũvara (Rāṇā), or Basnet. Pratāpa Siṃha's wife, Rājendra Rājyalakṣmī (or Rājendralakṣmī), became regent for eight years, for example, because her son, Raṇabahādura, was only two and a half years old. During her eventful and controversial regency, she conquered the Lamjung alliance of sway states and some eastern *caubisī* states.

After her death in 1785, Bahādura Śāha, Pratāpa Siṃha's brother and Raṇabahādura's uncle, and a rival of Rājendralakṣmī throughout her regency, took over power, becoming the *mukhtiyāra* after spending ten years in exile. By early 1790 he had conquered almost all the petty kingdoms, often by offering additional land to their rulers if they surrendered. He also made Palpa an ally by marrying Bidyā Lakṣmī, the daughter of its king, thus neutralizing a potential powerful enemy. Even such comparatively strong domains as Kaski, Lamjung, Makwanpur, Jumla, and Tanahu fell. In the western Himalaya, the Gorkhali oppressed kingdoms (in present-day India), made them vassals, or enslaved their populations. By the end of the eighteenth century the Gorkha kingdom thus had attained almost the whole of its modern territory, reaching to the west as far as Kumaon and Garhwal,[14] and in the east to Sikkim. However, a few small kingdoms, such as Jajarkot, Salyan, Palpa, and Mustang (Lo), long retained a certain degree of autonomy, and could only be incorporated as vassals. In a letter from 1769, Pṛthvīnārāyaṇa Śāha permits the king of Jajarkot to exercise capital punishment, deprive or restore caste membership, impose certain levies and fines, grant and confiscate *birtā* land, and keep the fees for stamping weights and measures. However, the subdued king had to pay a sum of 701 rupees when each new successor ascended to the Śāha throne.[15] Despite their autonomy the petty kingdoms were obliged to supply food and recruit men for the Gorkhali armies, to appear at certain events such as coronations or weddings, and to mourn the passing of the monarch in Kathmandu.

In February 1797, Raṇabahādura Śāha, the grandson of Pṛthvīnārāyaṇa, ordered Bahādura Śāha's imprisonment on suspicion of having conspired with China. The prisoner died two and a half months later at the age of thirty-nine.

After only two years of absolute power, Raṇabahādura Śāha abdicated in favor of his two-year-old son Gīrvāṇayuddha Śāha. The latter was the product of an affair, which shocked Kathmandu's upper crust, especially the minister (*kājī*) Dāmodara Pāḍe. Gīrvāṇayuddha's mother, Kāntivatī, after Rājarājeśvarī Devī and Suvarṇaprabhā Devī the third spouse (in fact, a concubine) of Raṇabahādura Śāha, was both a widow and a Brahmin from the Tarai. Raṇabahādura had thus broken important rules of caste and purity, yet he forced all *bhāradāras* to recognize the boy as king, even if, according to the line of succession, Raṇoddyota Śāha, the son of Suvarṇaprabhā, should have succeeded him. In 1799, following massive protests and the death of his concubine from smallpox, Raṇabahādura retired to the Paśupatinātha temple. In 1800, he went to Varanasi, where he lived as an ascetic with his first wife Rājarājeśvarī Devī and a few generals, among them the later powerful *mukhtiyāra* (a prime minister of sorts) Bhīmasena Thāpā.

In October 1801, Minister Dāmodara Pāḍe, by then the most powerful man in the Kathmandu Valley, took advantage of these events to sign an agreement with the East India Company. Among other things, the agreement provided for an exchange of ambassadors and stipulated that Raṇabahādura, still regarded by the British as king of Nepal, should receive landed estates so that he would remain abroad. Raṇabahādura, however, attempted to regain power and in 1804 succeeded to a limited extent by sending back Rājarājeśvarī, who managed, with the help of Dāmodara Pāḍe, to seize power as regent. Rājarājeśvarī immediately cancelled the agreement with the British, paid the debts accumulated by her husband in Varanasi, and saw to it that he returned. This is not what Dāmodara Pāḍe had wanted at all, and therefore he sent troops to stop Raṇabahādura. The soldiers, however, went over to the ex-king, and as soon as he reached the Kathmandu Valley he had Dāmodara Pāḍe arrested in Thankot. Raṇabahādura himself became the *mukhtiyāra*, a prime minister of sorts, and probably acted as regent too. He could not become king again after abdicating. In this confused transition from the eighteenth to the nineteenth century, there were sometimes three rulers: Dāmodara Pāḍe as the most powerful prime minister (*mūlakājī*), the regent Rājarājeśvarī, and Raṇabahādura, who still regarded himself as the actual ruler from his stronghold in Deopatan and who had Dāmodara Pāḍe beheaded on March 13, 1804.

The short rule of Raṇabahādura was characterized by further turbulence. He had all the tax-free *guṭhī* land brought under his control, for instance, and removed all children with smallpox from the Kathmandu Valley. Above all, he continually resisted the influence of Brahmins, whom he blamed for his fate of being exiled. To what degree Raṇabahādura occasionally went out of control is illustrated by a report by Captain W. D. Knox to the British governor general concerning his alliance with Kāntivatī:

> [Raṇabahādura Śāha] cut off the noses and ears of many of the Brahmins who officiated at the temples where prayers had been offered for the recovery of the Rannee [Kāntivatī]; he deprived others of their cast[e] by forcing the flesh of dogs and hogs into their mouths. . . . He directed the temple itself to be demolished, and the three companies of Sepoys, to whom he gave the orders, demurring at the sacrilege, he commanded scalding oil to be poured upon their naked bodies, feasting his eyes upon the sight of their sufferings.[16]

On April 25, 1806, Raṇabahādura was murdered by his half-brother Śera Bahādura.

In the course of these political disorders, Bhīmasena Thāpā became *mukhtiyāra* by violent means, following a massacre in which ninety-three courtiers of non-Thāpā origin suspected of conspiracy were executed, and Raṇabahādura's first two wives, Rājarājeśvarī and Suvarṇaprabhā, were forced to undergo self-immolation as widows. Raṇabahādura's fourth spouse, the twelve-year-old Lalitatripurasundarī, the niece of Bhīmasena Thāpā and a Thāpā herself, became, as queen, a shadow regent and also allegedly the concubine of Bhīmasena Thāpā, who would determine the fate of the country for over thirty years. King Gīrvāṇayuddha was then nine years old; he continued to be kept inside the palace, carefully shielded from politics.

In May 1806, the Gorkhali forces under *kājī* Amara Siṃha Thāpā continued their conquests westward up to the Sutlej River and the border of the kingdom of Lahore.[17] During his prime ministership Bhīmasena, having had to face war with the East India Company (1814–16), negotiated the Treaty of Sagauli.[18] He created the power structures that remained in place until 1951, ones in which the government was only nominally led by the king, while the real power lay with the prime minister (i.e., the *mukhtiyāra*). He dealt with all military and civil matters, and officials had to obey him. In 1835 Bhīmasena was made supreme commander of the army by a decree of King Rājendra Śāha, who was crowned in 1816 after the death of Gīrvāṇayuddha. Although the office of *mukhtiyāra* had not yet become hereditary, Bhīmasena ensured that his relatives were placed everywhere. He continued Gorkhali expansionist policies and came into conflict over frontiers, resulting in battles with the East India Company, which refused to accept that the petty kingdoms in the hills had land rights in the Tarai, and that therefore one government could exist within another.

The Consolidation of Gorkhali Power

The slow expansion of the kingdom of Gorkha—sometimes called unification,[19] sometimes conquest[20]—hardly changed daily life and social structures at all.[21] The Gorkhali created a kingdom with at first comparatively loose administrative and military apparatuses. Their strategy for ruling the country consisted of concentrating power in the Kathmandu Valley while initially leaving local polities largely to their own devices, save for matters relating to land grants, taxes, and tributary payments, and integrating certain ethnic groups into particular areas of activity including the military. As a consequence, the rural population experienced few changes, and their regional or ethnic traditions, festivals, and rituals were left in place.

Despite their military superiority, the Śāha were only able to unify the country because they did not exert an overabundance of pressure. Initially, the small Gorkha state had far too few well-trained civil servants to send to conquered regions. However, increasingly a network of overseers invested with administrative, fiscal, and judicial capacities—including ascetics—was established in the regions, partly through family kinship or other connections.[22] In return, these officials received land, cash payments, and honorary titles that raised their prestige. They also had the task of controlling abuse and corruption. As they acted on behalf of the king, they created an awareness of a higher power guiding the country und upholding standards of behavior. They possessed the right to complain about local officials, and local courts were established to adjudicate, so it was not uncommon for officials to be removed or punished.[23] This system was consolidated through the increased formulation of law into a large code, the *Ain*.

The decisive instrument of power, however, was access to land, for it was with land (of a type known as *jāgira*) that the Śāha compensated conquered petty kings and high-ranking soldiers. They could also take land away from one petty kingdom and give it to another, and they could adjust revenue from it depending on how heavy the burden of battle campaigns was. It was land that made the Śāha kings, along with prime ministers (or regents) and the army, strong. The Gorkhali also required compliance with certain principles—for example, "official help" in pursuing criminals or in military undertakings. Although Śāha and later Rāṇā rulers granted minor kings the right "to rule their territory and to enjoy it from generation to generation," as one standard formulation went, the latter were limited in their sovereign rights, that is, the right to do with the land as they pleased. The kings in Kathmandu could require gifts, labor services, and other obligations.

Another instrument of power that Pṛthvīnārāyaṇa Śāha and his successors knew how to use was the annual court day, when all high-ranking officials and soldiers had to appear in order to have their offices confirmed and to be registered in long "(pay) lists" (*pajanī*). On such occasions expressions of loyalty to the king could be demanded under threat of dismissal.

As of 1843 the Śāha court had more than a hundred officials working in the palace, the majority of them Brahmins and Chhetri.[24] The highest-ranking group consisted of members of certain "respected families" (*bhāradāra*). There was a sizable group of Brahmanical gurus, eight in number (mostly from the Pāṇḍe and Pauḍyāla clans), headed up by the *dharmādhikārin*, who also functioned as a religious judge. Some of them had the rank of "minister" (*mantrin*), while others were "royal priests" (*purohita*, *dīkṣāguru*, *rājaguru*) tasked with carrying out the rituals at court. The second sizable group was made up of "relatives of the king or prime minister" (*cautariyā*), who might also be governors of one of the twelve then-existing districts. The prime minister at that time was also a *cautariyā*. Other high administrative positions in the land were occupied by *kājīs* and *sardāras*, who functioned as governors or vice-governors, or else might occupy a position in the military. On a subordinate level, there were various officials with different functions: astrologers (*jyotiṣī*), chamberlains (*kapardāra*), treasurers (*khajāñcī*, *tahabiladāra*), male tutors (*dādā*) responsible for the education of the *bhāradāras*' sons and daughters, physicians (*vaidya*), envoys (*vakila*), guards and sentinels (*dvāre*, *koṭavāla*, *koṭe*), heads of various offices (*subbā*, *tharaghara*), judges (*diṭṭhā*, *bicārī*), translators (*munsī*), advisors and personal assistants (*jethābuḍhā*, *copadāra*), scribes (*khardāra/kharidāra*, *nausindā*), registrars (*bahidāra*), military officials (*umarāu*, *umarāva*), tax collectors (*pradhāna*, *bhansārī*), bodyguards (*sipāhi*), and various helpers (*ṭahaluvā*).[25]

Due to the inaccessibility of certain areas and the long distances within the growing kingdom, administrative tasks increasingly had to be delegated to provinces and districts. After Pṛthvīnārāyaṇa Śāha declared Kathmandu the capital of Nepal on March 21, 1770, he divided the country into twelve districts: four western ones (Gorkha, Sallyan, Nuvakot, Lamidanda), five eastern ones (Sindhupalchok, Kabhrepalanchok, Dolakha, Majhakirat, Pallokirat), and three southern ones (Makwanpur, Choudandi, Vijayapur Talahatti). By 1793, though, there were already seventeen districts, and under Bhīmasena Thāpā the number rose to thirty-nine (in individual documents, as many as fifty-two).

The "provincial governors" (*hākima*, *baḍāhākima*, *subbā*) were powerful personages responsible for supervising subordinate officials, maintaining law and order, collecting taxes and levies, and reporting to the palace in Kathmandu. At the beginning of the Śāha rule, petty kingdoms occupied a special position between those of provinces and districts, retaining as they did special rights with regard to taxation and adjudication. The administrative apparatus was geared, though, to rulers of petty kingdoms being increasingly replaced by provincial governors or other high officials. In petty kingdoms where this did not occur, the ruler enjoyed the same rights and duties as a *subbā* in the provinces.

The army was relatively small at the start of the nineteenth century. The first British envoy, Edward Gardner, counted 10,000 soldiers in 1815. However, this number probably referred only to the standing army; for military operations, many more thousands were quickly recruited. In December 1836 the Residency, as the seat of the British envoy was called up to 1923, reported to Fort William: "In 1817, the army on roll, was 10,000; in 1819, 12,000; in 1821, 14,000; in 1830, 15 to 16,000; and now it is 17,000."[26]

By the end of the nineteenth century, district administration had become much more centralized, comprising numerous military departments, the district court, the regional police headquarters, tax, finance, and accountancy sections, forestry (especially for felling and selling trees), the post office, communal work, elephant stables, the secret service, mints, and customs. Moreover, administration basically meant only military and tax administration. The state was not understood as an institution meant to see to the needs of the populace. There were, therefore, hardly any state welfare institutions for the normal citizen (hospitals, poorhouses, old age homes), hardly any educational institutions (schools, universities), and no substantial police offices. No ministry of social affairs or of education existed; nor did urban or traffic planning offices.

Anglo-British Encounters

By 1806 Nepal had reached its greatest extent of growth, an area which later was often called "Greater Nepal." In the west, it had conquered Garhwal and Kumaon and had advanced as far as Kangra, from where it was driven back out in 1809 with the help of Sikhs under Ranjit Singh; in the east, it had reached as far as the Tista River and Sikkim; in the north, it had temporarily overrun Shigatse and Tashilhunpo Monastery in Tibet; and in the south, had advanced far into the lowlands. It is little wonder that British India found this situation threatening. Again and again there were border disputes and confrontations, especially in the Oudh region, which in 1814 led to the Company and the Gorkha kingdom confronting each other militarily.[27] The casus belli was twenty-two villages near the present border around Butwal; both sides laid claim to them, and each accused the other of being predatory. The British regarded the villages as being within their territory; the Gorkhali based their claim on the fact that they were tributary to Palpa, which they had conquered in 1804.

In this war, there were 35,000 regular troops and 13,000 temporary ones on the British side, and 14,000 regulars (*bhārā*) and 28,000 conscripts (*jhārā*) on the Gorkhali side.[28] Both sides could fight only in the milder half of the year. The first campaign undertaken by the British, from October 1814 to March 1815, was successful but brought no victory, inasmuch as the Gorkhali did not sign an offered agreement, having set their hopes on help from China, but also because the war took place on three fronts and the British had difficulty finding their way in the mountainous terrain and underestimated the resistance of the Gorkha soldiers. Only after a massive increase in troop strength with more firearms and cannons did they succeed, under General David Ochterlony in the spring of 1816, in defeating the Gorkhali, and so were able to force the agreement upon them.

One of the main reasons for the war was probably that British India wanted to control the western trade routes to Tibet. There were, however, other reasons for this war, which was so significant historically for Nepal.[29] The Gorkhali needed ever more land in order to be able to pay their soldiers in the course of their conquests to the east and west. The standing army generally received *jāgira* land for their own use by way of a salary, but suitable land was becoming rarer. The British, in turn, who actually represented a trading company rather than some government authority, did not wish to let any state in South Asia become too large, having achieved the best results for their trade through a policy of *divide et impera* ("divide and rule"); in this way, they could conduct business with local large landowners or administrators without disturbance.

Above all, this was a conflict between two conflicting notions of territorial power and its limits. The British, who had been establishing a system of land registry in India similar to the one in their own country, wanted clearly defined borders. They thought, for example, that the simplest solution to the conflict would be to draw a border along the Siwalik Hills and allot all the land on the other side to Nepal. For the Rāṇā it was more important to control the land and exploit it. They understood land ownership as a hereditary right to land use, especially for the petty kings in the hills, who either occasionally used the land in the Tarai themselves or else collected tribute. The tributary duty could easily be required by two rulers from different territories at once. The Gorkhali took control over levies from the petty kings, either with or without force, claiming a sovereign right to them. Given their expansionist policy, the Gorkhali did not need border markers of the kind erected after 1816. The British, on the other hand, regarded such claims as encroachment. How different the positions were, and to what extent the two sides were talking at cross-purposes, is made clear by a letter of August 5, 1813, from (Gīrvāṇayuddha) Bikram Shaha, in which he reacts to previous correspondence with the governor general in Kolkata:

> This communication has excited my utmost astonishment. The fact is that territorial possession is not, by states, acquired by purchase. As the Honorable Company have by the grace of God established their dominion in Hindoostan by the power of the sword, so have I by the same means acquired possession of the hills *together with the low lands dependent* on the territories of former Rajahs, some of whom tamely submitted to my authority, while others were expelled for their conduct. Since the first establishment of the British authority in India and that of the Gorkha Government in Nipaul, however, such a principle of limitation as this, namely that the authority of such a one should extend as far as the Hills, and that the country below the hills should belong to such a one, *has never at any time formed the subject of a communication between the two states.* On the contrary, the principle which has from time immemorial obtained with both Governments is, that it should not be allowable for one state to exercise any kind of interference in those lands in which the other state had first established an authority.[30]

The problem was that neither the British nor the Gorkhali had documents, let alone maps, recording verifiable titles to land. The East India Company and the Gorkhali "claimed what the former rajas had claimed," as historian Ludwig Stiller put it.[31] It was clear that Nepal could hardly exist without the Tarai.

On December 2, 1815, a peace treaty was agreed in Sagauli (also spelled Sugauli), a village now in northern Bihar, and ratified on March 4, 1816.[32] A letter on March 13, 1816, addressed among others to General Bhīmasena Thāpā in Kathmandu, and delivered by state courier, contained a corrected draft of the treaty; six seals of the Nepalese military leadership certified it. In this treaty, Nepal's independent status was confirmed, but it had to accept a permanent British resident (without being allowed to send a Nepalese representative to Kolkata). The borders were drawn in such a way that Nepal lost one-third of its earlier area of influence (an area demanded back as "Greater

Nepal" only by present-day extreme nationalists). This included all previously held regions west of the Mahakali River (from Kangra to Kumaon and Garhwal) and east of the Mechi River (Sikkim, Morung), along with major parts of the Tarai, which was economically more damaging.[33] It thus amounted to a considerable loss, even though some of the Tarai was restored in December 1816 and in 1860.[34] The survival of the still young state was endangered, all the more so for deserving soldiers having received much land in the Tarai. For this the British paid compensation totaling 200,000 rupees annually. Nepal, however, lost 13.7% of its agricultural land area and 35% of its agricultural production.[35]

The British exercised two forms of power over territories in the seventeenth century: direct rule, as was the case in Bengal, and principalities or small kingdoms that recognized the suzerainty of British authorities but remained largely independent. Nepal was in a special position. The peace treaty had clear advantages for the British. They did not have to wage a long war with an uncertain outcome, had won territory, had come away with a trade route to Tibet through Kumaon and Garhwal, had gained direct influence in Kathmandu by means of the forcible acceptance of a British Residency, and had been able to fend off a threatening alliance among the Marathas, Sikhs, and Gorkhali. Nepal profited from the treaty insofar as it had established a reputation for itself as a country of hardy warriors and had formally achieved independence in its internal affairs, for the resident was not permitted to interfere in domestic matters and could move only within strictly supervised limits in the Kathmandu Valley. Bhīmasena Thāpā, who either surmised or knew that it was possible for the British to conquer Nepal, was able to boast in the subsequent years of guaranteeing of stability by warding off further British claims or even an occupation of the country, albeit at the price of isolating Nepal from the world.

In Nepal, people were henceforth split into camps. On the one hand, they wanted to keep the *firangis*, the British, out; on the other, they wanted the British as allies. Bhīmasena Thāpā did not have the full support of the *bhāradāras*, for the influential Pāḍe family, who were strictly against any British influence, repeatedly put pressure on him. Nonetheless, he retained his power until 1832, when the regent Lalitatripurasundarī died and the now adult son of Gīrvāṇayuddha, Rājendra Śāha, was increasingly attempting to achieve power. He was supported in this by the Pāḍe and other important families, and by Brian H. Hodgson, the British Resident.

The king first denied Bhīmasena the annual confirmation of his supreme command, and then on July 24, 1837, Bhīmasena was arrested on suspicion of having caused the sudden death of the seven-month-old prince, who allegedly had drunk poison intended for his mother, Saṃrājyalakṣmī Devī. Bhīmasena died two years later in prison, on August 11, 1839, under humiliating circumstances; it was reported to Brian H. Hodgson that he had committed suicide.[36]

The following years saw a rapid series of successive *mukhtiyāras*, disputes between the two wives of the king, and the constant fear that the British would use the situation to their advantage and occupy the country.

At a time when an anti-British mood held sway, and renewed conflict in the Tarai seemed likely, Resident Brian H. Hodgson kept attempting to exercise a moderating influence on the government, but in 1842, shortly before he left Nepal, he was ordered by the British governor of India, Edward Law, to keep wholly out of domestic politics. The Company had no desire to become further embroiled in military conflicts with Nepal, as the troops were needed for the conquest of Afghanistan. At least Hodgson was able to offer shelter to some of the people in the palace sympathetic to him before he finally retired from Nepal. Future British residents remained objects of suspicion.

In the same year, the incompetent and probably mentally impaired King Rājendra introduced shared rulership with his son Surendra and Prime Minister Phatte (Fateh) Jaṅga Cautariyā, and, on January 5, 1843, abdicated following a wave of protest against his style of rule. The junior queen Rājendra Rājyalakṣmī Devī assumed royal power and Māthabara Siṃha Thāpā, a nephew and one-time fellow prisoner with Bhīmasena Thāpā, became *mukhtiyāra*. On May 15, 1845, this new prime minister was murdered by a rising star in the army, Jaṅga Bahādura Kũvara (Rāṇā), himself a nephew of Māthabara Siṃha. This murder, which brought back Fateh Jaṅga Cautariyā as prime minister, was the harbinger of a new constellation of power.

Seen as a whole, the Gorkhali expansion was based on three principles more or less strictly adhered to: there was heavy exploitation in the form of revenue demands but no plundering or confiscation in conquered areas; local rulers, especially of petty kingdoms, remained instead of being driven out; and Gorkha hardly interfered with the cultural and religious customs of conquered regions. Regardless, the internal levers of power became too weak for the Śāha to retain their rule over Nepal in the long run.

The Gurkha Soldiers

The Treaty of Sagauli (1816) marked the birth of the famous Gurkha (or Gorkha or Gorkhali) regiments, who had become known as loyal warriors who would fight to the death.[37] General David Ochterlony, who in 1814 led the East India Company to a decisive victory over the Gurkha, had to learn the lesson that the Gurkha soldiers were at first superior within the terrain because they could easily get around infantry and blockades. Only when he applied his artillery did his own troops gain the advantage.

The Gurkha later fought in the Sepoy Rebellion of 1857 against the Indians, in the Boxer Rebellion in China (1899–1901), in the First and Second World Wars in Europe against the Germans and in Burma, and later in Kosovo and Syria. In the Falklands War, it is said that the Argentines dropped their weapons when they saw the Gurkha coming over the hills with their *khukurī* knives. Sir Ralph Lilley Turner, who served in the First World War in the 3rd Queen Alexandra's Own Gurkha Rifles, and who made a name for himself as a linguist and the author of several dictionaries of Indo-Aryan languages, praised the Gurkha with these words: "Bravest of the brave, most generous of the generous, never had country more faithful friends than you."[38]

To be sure, Nepalese had already served in Sikh regiments in the area around Lahore starting in 1809, which is why in Nepal soldiers serving in foreign military units are known as *lāhores* rather than Gurkha. *Lāhores* (roughly, "those who go to and come back from Lahore"), however, were not only soldiers but anyone who had some relationship with a foreign country and brought something back from there. The British called various ethnic groups Gurkha, especially the Gurung, Magar, and Khasa, and later also the Rai, Limbu, and Sunuvar, against whom the British fought in the war between the East India Company and Nepal in 1814–16. In 1892 the British resident Henry Wylie reported:

> The principal demand we make on Nepalis is for recruits, and this demand has been so fully met during the year under report that not only have we obtained the numbers required, (which for the regular army alone were close to 1,500 men), but commanding officers have been able to select men of the particular classes which they fancy. For this continued improvement in recruiting we have to thank Maharaja Bir Shamsher Jung, as it is only since his accession to power that we have succeeded in filling our ranks with the best classes of Gurkhas.[39]

The British thus created a social group and a designation for them that would not have existed otherwise, and so created the myth of a martial race.

The Gurkha—a name derived from the anglicized spelling "Goorkhas" for the Gorkhali who lived in the hills—have been seen from the British military perspective as courageous, fearless, extremely honest, and genetically predisposed to warfare. This reputation as courageous warriors was based on Orientalist presuppositions. Only in recent times have researchers begun to study the Gurkhas' tales and songs, to present this history from the viewpoint of the Gurkha themselves. Until the Anglo-Nepalese War, the Gurkha were seen by both the British and the Indian sepoys as barbaric and insolent, if also as particularly well suited for fighting. In an 1814 report to his government, Captain Hyder Young Hearsey wrote:

> [The Goorkhas'] commanders are ignorant, subtle, treacherous, faithless, and avaricious to an extreme. . . . Their sepoys [soldiers] are poorly armed . . . , wear little or no clothing, and very ill paid. . . . They are hardy, endure privations, and are very obedient, have not much of the distinction of caste, and are a neutral kind of Hindoo, eating in messes almost every thing they meet with, except beef. Under our Government and officers they would make excellent soldiers and numbers would, on the event of a rupture, join our standards for the sake of six rupees per month.[40]

Regardless of such a reputation preceding them, it was only in battle that the British really got to know the extremes of Gurkha resilience. And it was only after the British had developed their theory of a warrior race that the Gurkha become true allies. This "martial race theory" goes mainly back to Brian H. Hodgson.[41] Hodgson, in a speech given in 1833 shortly after his appointment as resident in Kathmandu, distinguished between the masculine energy of the Gurkha character and their love of exploits, on the one hand, and the superstition and lack of loyalty of Indian soldiers, on the other. The latter always "must bathe from head to foot, and make *púja*, ere they begin to dress their dinner, must eat nearly naked in the coldest weather, and cannot be in marching trim again in less than three hours."[42] They also supposedly regarded service with foreigners as wholly contaminating and unholy. The Gurkha, in contrast, were "by far the best soldiers in India," partially because the rough weather in the hills added to their toughness, ideas incorporated into military handbooks of the late nineteenth and early twentieth centuries. Accordingly, the Indians (feminine, soft, and submissive) were seen as no competition for the Gurkha (manly, loyal, and therefore the equal of Europeans).[43]

The Nepalese, beginning with Jaṅga Bahādura Rāṇā, were at first skeptical toward the enlistment, did not allow the British to establish recruiting offices on their territory, and occasionally prevented young men from crossing the border to offer their services. When the British wanted more soldiers in 1878, Jaṅga's successor, Raṇoddīpa Siṃha, promised a thousand men but sent half at number. Only under the Śamśera side of the Rāṇā clan did this negative attitude change. The Gurkha went on to become a popular transnational commodity. Thus, Candra Śamśera received 12,500 rifles in exchange for Gurkha between 1906 and 1908; between 1901 and 1913, over 24,000 were recruited, and in the First World War around 55,000 Nepalese soldiers fought for Great Britain, for which Candra received a million rupees annually. This sum increased to two million during the Second World War for 200,000 soldiers. Around 20,000 Gurkhas lost their lives in the First World War and 10,000 in the Second.

The popularity of this military service is generally exaggerated. On the one hand, many more men joined the Indian than the British Gurkha regiments; on the other hand, those who returned, while greatly admired, were often also accused of being unpatriotic accomplices of a colonial power. Above all, it was not free will that enabled such mass recruitments. Those who wanted to become Gurkha soldiers were generally peasants who had been driven from their homes by poverty and oppression. They had no innate interest in fighting; survival made them become mercenaries. Nor were the Gurkha always as decent and courageous as is made out. Reports of horrible torture are documented, as are reports on the fears Gurkha soldiers had of being killed in war.[44]

The history of the Gurkha has been whitewashed as a success story. The argument that the soldiers sent much money back to Nepal and thus improved living standards in their home regions is not true. For one thing, they did not receive the same pay as their British comrades in arms; for another, they received little or nothing by way of a pension. In addition, not all ex-soldiers never returned, and those who did often refused to live in villages any more, thus intensifying the rural exodus. In the whole, the British received cheap military labor, whereas Nepal, despite the modernization of its army and improved education for its soldiers, was left behind as an independent state, with many of the most physical men not available for its economic manpower.

Sino-Tibetan Encounters

The manifold connections between Nepal, Tibet, and China, which date back to the Licchavi Period and, linguistically, even further, were mostly of a peaceful nature: Songtsen Gampo married the Nepalese princess Bhṛkuṭī in 641 CE, pilgrims and monks visited the birthplace of the Buddha, old trading routes between India and Tibet/China passed through Nepal, and the famous craftsman Araniko worked at the emperor's court in the second half of the thirteenth century. Toward the end of the eighteenth century, however, these relations deteriorated, mainly due to a dispute over border and trade issues, and especially to the quality of coins manufactured in Nepal for Tibet.[45] This led to three wars between Nepal and Tibet, in 1788–89, 1791–92, and 1855–56.

Trans-Himalayan trade, principally involving the Sherpa, Thakali, and other hill groups,[46] was repeatedly hindered by these wars with Tibet. Probably the first contractual regulation of economic relations with a foreign country was signed by Bhīma Malla, who was the *kājī* under King Lakṣmīnarasiṃha Malla between 1615 and 1620. The treaty accorded Nepal the right to open thirty-two shops in Lhasa, each of which would revert to the Nepalese government upon the death of its owner. According to a report by George Bogle, the first British official in Tibet, Lhasa exported woollens, ponies, goats, sheep, musk, salt, borax, gold, silver, and paper to Nepal. In exchange, Nepalese traders brought cotton clothing, tobacco, knives, ivory, and statues to Tibet, along with rice and other cereals. The mainstay of the Tibet trade was the exchange of salt for rice.

Furthermore, it was agreed that the Kuti Pass would go to Nepal, that Nepal could send a representative to Lhasa and mint coins for Tibet (for which Tibet would provide the gold and silver), and that all trade with India would go through the Kathmandu Valley. An additional agreement had to do with the descendants of Nepalese men and Tibetan women, called Khacchara, who were regarded as Nepalese subjects but who received privileges in Tibet.[47] Some Nepalese traders took a Tibetan second wife in order to profit from their privileges.

As Tibet had no coins of its own, it imported them from Nepal. The Malla kings sourced the silver from Tibet, but minted the coins—especially the *mahendramallis* (later called *moharas*), named after King Mahendra Malla—from an impure alloy. It was a highly lucrative business for them (allowing them to partially finance their struggle against the Gorkhali), but one that increasingly caused distrust because trading conditions became unfavorable for both countries, including the many Newar merchants in Lhasa. The Śāha rulers inherited this problem and exacerbated the situation, inasmuch as Pṛthvīnārāyaṇa Śāha minted only pure coins struck with his name but refused to buy back any of the debased currency, which was still accepted in Tibet. The Tibetan government wanted to allow their use only if Gorkha bought back the old coins at their face value, which would have resulted in heavy losses for them.

Although in 1775 Pratāpa Siṃha, the son of Pṛthvīnārāyaṇa Śāha, negotiated better trade conditions with Tibet in the Treaty of Kuti, he did not solve the basic problem of the different currencies. This conflict led to ongoing disagreements regarding the status of traders, customs duties, trade routes, and borderlines, so that Bahādura Śāha, emboldened by all the successes against the petty kingdoms, in July 1788 invaded Tibet in order to enforce the terms of Treaty of Kuti. He occupied considerable parts of southern Tibetan territory. The Tibetans offered little resistance and so the war, in which the Gorkhali advanced as far as Shigatse, was quickly brought to an end with the Treaty of Kerung, signed on June 2, 1789.

The Tibetans then found themselves in a quandary. Nominally, they were a province of China, but de facto they retained their autonomy, which the Dalai Lama did not want to risk losing by calling on China for help. In September 1789 Nepal sent a goodwill mission to Beijing and demanded that the Tibetans compensate them for all the costs of the war, including losses due to the blockade of trade routes and currency differences. The Tibetans rejected this demand but acknowledged their culpability for the war, committing themselves to annual tribute payments of 50,001 rupees and leaving the Gorkhali with some territorial gains from the war. In addition, an exchange rate of 2:1 was agreed for the old and new *moharas*, along with further supplies of the coinage, while Nepal agreed to send a mission with presents to Beijing.

The Dalai Lama, however, stopped paying tribute after the second year. This led to the outbreak of Nepal's second war with Tibet in August 1791, when Raṇabahādura Śāha, or more properly speaking, his uncle the regent Bahādura Śāha, again invaded Tibet, captured Shigatse, and looted the monastery of the Panchen Lama, Tashilhunpo, which the Gorkhali army had reached on October 28. The Tibetan and Chinese soldiers again offered little resistance.

This was the moment when Tibet asked the Qing dynasty for support. Deciding to drive out the Gorkhali from Tibet, the latter began a punitive expedition into the heart of Nepal in mid-June 1792. Raṇabahādura Śāha was so afraid of China that he issued an executive order (*rukkā*) granting land for a ritual recitation at the time of the Chinese invasion, which ended in autumn 1792 in Nuvakot, a day's march from Kathmandu.[48] The fierce battle with thousands of casualties on both sides saw the Chinese troops confronted with strong counterattacks.[49]

The war did not have any clear victor, although both sides claimed to win. The *Nepālikabhūpavaṃśāvalī*, for instance, states: "[Raṇabahādura Śāha] killed the Chinese army. He thus caused the Chinese Emperor to praise him."[50] On the other hand, Wei Yüan writes: "Therefore, the rebels' [i.e., the Gorkhalis'] request for surrender was granted."[51] All in all, the result of the Sino-Nepalese war "can be best described as a stalemate."[52] The Chinese troops feared that they could not return to their homeland before winter made the Trans-Himalayan passes impassable—"Men going to and fro do not dare to utter a word, otherwise an avalanche 'as big as a house' would crush them to death."[53] As a face-saving outcome for both sides, on October 2, 1792, in Betravati[54] at the Trishuli River, a mile north of Nuvakot, Bahādura Śāha and the Qianlong Emperor (1711–99) agreed upon a peaceful settlement, if apparently not an official truce.[55] One part of this settlement redefined the tradition of diplomatic missions.

According to Chinese records, already from the eighth century onward Nepalese missions used to visit China with presents for the emperor. Between 1384 and 1427 five Chinese and seven Nepalese missions were sent to the other's court.[56] From 1792 on, Nepal was obliged to send missions every five years, a practice that continued until 1906.[57] Altogether eighteen such missions went to China: between 1792 and 1852 they were quite regular, but afterward only five missions followed.[58]

Such missions were headed by an officer of ministerial rank (*kājī*) and a *sardāra* as the leader and deputy leader respectively of a group of, on average, forty-five members (not including porters), all of whom were screened by the *amban*. The delegation also contained military officials (*subedāra*, *jamadāra*), interpreters, "local leaders" (*naike*), "official scribes" (*kharidāra*), cooks, and others. The more than 3,000-mile-long journeys were dangerous and normally lasted from one and a half to two years (the 1877 mission took five, and the 1894 mission seven years). Quite often members of the delegation and porters lost their lives; in three cases, even leaders died. There were many hindrances: Tibetan and Chinese officials, robbers and thieves, and the rough terrain and bad weather. According to Hodgson's papers the missions had to cross between 104 (or 106) and 652 rivers (with 607 bridges and 23 ferries).[59] Occasionally, they were stopped on suspicion of smuggling or spying, but according to diplomatic conventions they were allowed to trade and did not have to pay levies. Under Jaṅga Bahādura, opium became one of the most important commodities for trading.

It is often said that the Betravati agreement contained an understanding that obliged Nepal and Tibet to send presents every five years to the imperial court at Beijing. However, the original treaty is not extant, so that the exact wording of the contract, whether in Nepālī or in Chinese, is currently unknown. Possibly, the agreement did not take the form of a single document signed by the two parties but only through the exchange of letters.[60] But the leader of the Chinese troops wanted to make a treaty (*sandhi*) and wrote to the government of Nepal accordingly.[61] In 1909, Padma Jaṅga Bahādura Rāṇā, the third son of Jaṅga Bahādura, published a text of the treaty, but without any reference to an original document.[62] The Nepālī of this "treaty," summarized by Yogi Naraharinātha reads:

1. From now onwards, China (Cīna) shall remain as a father (*pitā*) of both Nepal and Tibet. Nepal and Tibet will behave towards each other as brothers.
2. The price of commodities looted in Lhasa shall be paid by Tibetan officials to the Nepalese after a proper investigation by the government of China.
3. Excluding armed soldiers, any Nepalese is allowed to cross the border to Tibet and China at any time, establish a workshop, or run a business.
4. If a quarrel breaks out between the two brothers [i.e., Tibet and Nepal] the representatives of both governments shall send a detailed report to Peking. The Peking Palace will make the final decision for solving the problem.
5. If a foreign power attacks Nepal, China shall support Nepal.
6. In order to respect and demonstrate a "father-son relationship," the two brothers (Nepal and Tibet) shall send products of their own country to China once every 5 years.
7. In return, China shall send presents (*kośelī*) to demonstrate friendship. China shall make all necessary arrangements for diplomats (of Nepal and Tibet) who come to or leave China.[63]

Section 6 speaks of "products of their own country" (i.e., Nepal and Tibet) but not, as most scholars write, "presents" or "gifts."[64] Nepal presented such products, but some of them came from India rather than Nepal, which China never objected to.[65] China always did insist, though, that the presents were worth much less than their own presents—a demonstrable claim by China of its superiority to Nepal. Such presents from China included brocade and silk garments, carpets, teapots and dishes, rosary beads, bags, and tea; for the penultimate mission (1894), the presents consisted of "a thousand taels of silver (£ 180), four complete suits of fur, and robes of wadded cotton and gauze for each member of the mission, along with silk pongees and gauze, Peking curios, and the like according to the rank of the recipient."[66] The presents from Nepal generally included tusks, coral pearls, gemstones, various cloths and garments, betel, nutmeg, cardamon, rhino horns, swords, and *khukurīs*. In the first mission the plan was to present an elephant, but the rough terrain of the Kuti Pass at the Tibetan border forced it to return.[67] The imbalance in this exchange was early noticed by the British: "The fact is that Sir Jang Bahadur's cupidity is the motive spring [sic!]. He sends Yak's tails and gets back gifts, *Pictai Vestis et auri*. He gives a trout and catches a salmon."[68]

In Nepalese documents, the products from Nepal were generally called in Nepālī *māmuli saugāta*, "ordinary presents," whereas the Chinese sources speak of "tribute" (Chin. *gòng*) that Nepal had to pay.[69] How could both sides live with such different understandings of central terms in their agreement? It seems that the linguistic difference was not perceived as an irresolvable problem but was instead intentionally maintained. For China it was absolutely necessary to regard and treat Nepal as a tributary state. The type of gifts and the asymmetrical form of their presentation, added to the accommodations in Beijing intended for tributary states, clearly demonstrate this hierarchy. However, the missions "were never accepted by the Nepalese as signifying or acknowledging a feudatory status. They were always regarded as goodwill delegations—gestures of friendship and respect."[70]

The Treaty of Betravati thus shows that the question of China's suzerainty over Nepal (and also Tibet) was viewed differently by the parties involved, when in fact there was no clear winner of the war and Nepal mattered little to China. Besides readjusting the border and fulfilling minor obligations (e.g., restoring what was plundered at Tashilhunpo Monastery), only the quinquennial missions stood as a serious burden for Nepal, and indeed one that the Gorkha government became increasingly reluctant to undertake.

China, on the other hand, never assisted Nepal militarily, not even in the Anglo-Nepalese War of 1814–16, even though military support was part of the treaty. This agreement proved quite harmless for Nepal, and in the end came to seem more like a gentlemen's agreement. It had a greater impact on Tibet, which had to accept powerful *ambans* and a reduction in the Dalai Lama's power.

This same view was expressed in 1877 by Thomas Wade, the British minister plenipotentiary in Beijing:

> As a tributary state, Nepal might be classed with Burma . . . in the habit of sending complementary tribute at intervals in token of amity and deference to a powerful neighbour, but the Chinese allow tribute missions to be made the opportunity of profitable transactions for the states which send them, otherwise the custom at present day would soon come to an end and it would be impossible now for the Chinese to enforce it afresh. The custom dates from time immemorial and has the effect of keeping an artificial importance for the Chinese throne which its military could never have gained for it.[71]

Nepal did not protest against the tributary status assigned to it by China. The main advantage it conferred was that the beneficial trade with Lhasa and China could be kept up, while the missions themselves received considerable wealth.

The catalyst for the Third Nepal-Tibet War (1855–56) was again the alleged bad treatment of Nepalese traders and disputes about the border. The settlement called for an annual tribute of a mere 10,000 rupees to be paid by Tibet, and for Nepal to relinquish its territorial claims. At the same time, Nepal received permission to set up a trading post in Lhasa. Although Nepalese businesses in Tibet were plundered or boycotted, trade still flourished. There were many further privileges such as no duties and no taxes being levied on traders.

In 1888, however, the trade route from Kalimpong in Sikkim through the Chumbi Valley to Tibet was opened. This enabled direct trade between British India and Tibet, in which Nepālī-speaking traders from Sikkim acquired an ever greater presence in this movement of Indian goods to Tibet. The British themselves were not allowed into Tibet; an attempt by the British military officer Francis Younghusband to form official trade relations failed in 1903. In the same year, following a rumor that Tibetan soldiers had stolen a herd of yaks from British Indian territory, Younghusband invaded Tibet. A horrible massacre ensued, as the Tibetans were hopelessly outclassed. In August 1904, Younghusband reached Lhasa, but no negotiations ensued, the Dalai Lama having fled to Mongolia. Still, the Tibetans were forced to hand over control of the Chumbi Valley to the British for seventy-five years and to permit free and unhindered access of a British trade commissioner to the country. As Nepal had supported the British mission with Gorkha soldiers, public opinion in Tibet turned increasingly against Nepal. Subsequently, the number of Nepalese traders in Tibet dropped from several hundred to a handful. In 1950, after the occupation of Tibet by China, Nepal lost its influence over Tibet almost completely.

7
Patrimonial Rule
The Rāṇā Period, 1846–1951

The night of September 14 to 15, 1846, was a fateful one for Nepal. A former servant who had risen to become an influential general, thanks to being the queen's lover, was murdered at evening prayer. That same night, the enraged queen had the entire court entourage gather the old royal palace in Kathmandu. Everyone of rank and good name in the Kathmandu Valley was to come to the "inner court" (*koṭa*) of the Hanuman Dhoka palace and military headquarters. The king too, with whom the queen had long since fallen out, was called upon to appear. She wanted the murderer found immediately. Among those gathered she thought she recognized the guilty party, a high courtier whom she had long found to be obnoxious. She gave her sword to a general and ordered him to decapitate the man then and there. The general looked helplessly at the king, but the king refused to confirm the death sentence without a court hearing. The general thereupon laid the sword at the feet of the queen. She demanded that her command be obeyed, since she had been made regent by the king himself and given all powers of command; but nobody obeyed her. In a frenzy, the queen commanded that the gates be kept closed until the murderer had been found. In fact, the headquarters was already surrounded by the troops of another general. A little later the *mukhtiyāra* arrived. The queen immediately turned to him and asked him to identify who had murdered her loyal general. But the prime minister, whose power had been seriously restricted by the lover-general, promised only to investigate the matter. Helpless, the queen retired with three ministers to an upper story of the palace. Suddenly, shots were fired. Suspicions were bandied about, sabers were drawn, firearms were loaded. The queen shouted that all her enemies should be killed. A massacre ensued from which only a few could flee.

On the morning of the next day, the courtyard was covered in corpses. Over thirty men, all of them senior officials and officers, among them the *mukhtiyāra*, lay dead, along with the sons of the highest-ranking families in

Nepal. Axel Michaels, Oxford University Press. English language edition © Oxford University Press 2024.
DOI: 10.1093/oso/9780197650936.003.0008

the country. There was only one victor: Jaṅga Bahādura Kũvara (who later received the title of Rāṇā), a general to whom the king had already entrusted two regiments and who had already risen within the governing council. That night, he was made *mukhtiyāra* by the queen and from then on had the fate of the country in his hands. The period of Rāṇā rule, which was to last for over a century, had begun.[1]

During the Rāṇā Period, important decrees (in the main *lālamoharas* and *rukkās*) were issued by the prime minister but had to be signed off on by the disempowered king.[2] This epoch was characterized by the concentration of power in the center, a hierarchical order, and the conjoining of military and civilian administration. At its core, the administration was directly modeled on the Mogul administration.

Table 7.1 Genealogical Table of the Kũvara Rāṇā and the Śamśera Rāṇā

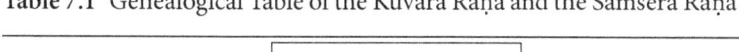

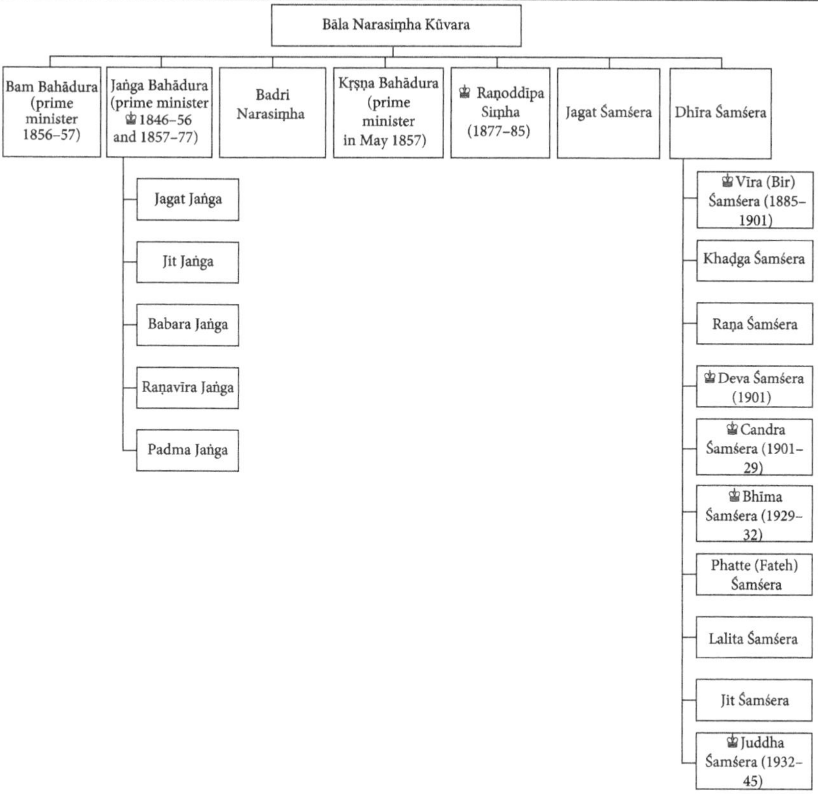

♔ = Prime Minister and Śrī-3 Mahārāja ("Thrice venerable great king"; the higher form of this title, Śrī-5 Mahārāja, was kept by the king)

The Kũvara Rāṇā, 1846–85

What happened on September 15, 1846, became known in the history books as the Kot (Koṭa) Massacre.[3] The lover was Gagana Siṃha Bhaṇḍārī, the queen was Rājyalakṣmī Devī, the second wife of King Rājendra Śāha, and the *mukhtiyāra* was Fateh Jaṅga Chautariyā. Those who survived the Koṭa Massacre, even the king and the queen, were soon just marginal figures on the political stage. Anyone who had ambitions in Nepal thereafter had to deal with Jaṅga Bahādura Rāṇā and his family.[4]

Reports of the massacre are contradictory, tainted by political bias and mutual accusations, and occasionally even forged. In addition, they were often recorded much later on the basis of hearsay, in some cases with the intention of condemning Jaṅga Bahādura Rāṇā. Many details of the massacre will never be known, such as whether it was a plot organized by Jaṅga Bahādura Rāṇā or others, or whether events simply spun out of control. Certainly, conflict between powerful family clans had contributed to an unstable situation, which Jaṅga Bahādura Rāṇā knew how to exploit to great advantage.

This power-hungry and exceptional ruler came from an influential military family. His father, Bāla Narasiṃha Kũvara, had killed the half-brother and murderer of Raṇabahādura Śāha, Śera Bahādura, on April 5, 1806, whereupon he was appointed minister and alone was permitted to carry a weapon in the private rooms at court.

Weapons and hunting had interested Jaṅga Bahādura from childhood. By nineteen he had already been accepted into the army. For a couple of years, he wandered around India and Nepal and repeatedly attracted attention to himself by performing feats of courage. He liked to impress Crown Prince Surendra by standing on the back of his horse and springing from a lofty height into a river, boasted of being able to tame elephants with his bare hands, and supposedly jumped with a parachute from the Dharahara tower in Kathmandu.[5] In 1840, he was promoted to captain of artillery; a year later, he became a personal bodyguard of Crown Prince Surendra; and in February 1842 he became a minister (*kājī*) in the Kumārī Coka, a general accounting office. But there he lost the favor of the *mukhtiyāra* Māthavara Siṃha Thāpā, whom from then on he opposed, if more in secret than openly. On May 17, 1845, he shot Māthavara on instructions from King Rājendra and afterward rose to become a powerful general, commanding three regiments. He remained loyal to the queen, in appreciation for which his brothers were accepted into the army.

Figure 7.1 Jaṅga Bahādura Rāṇā. Unknown photographer and date (from Wikipedia, CC-BY-SA-4.0).

Jaṅga Bahādura quickly overcame the initial mistrust of the British.[6] On the day after the Koṭa Massacre, he went to the sole remaining Briton in the Residency, Captain G. O. B. Ottley, and assured him that he wished to continue the friendly relationship with the British government.

From January 15, 1850, until February 6, 1851, Jaṅga Bahādura Rāṇā traveled by ship with a large entourage of about forty men (including his two youngest sons) via Kolkata to Europe, where he stayed until August.[7] There is a report of the journey by one of his traveling companions, entitled "The Journey to England" (*Belāyatyātrā*), which supposedly is based on a lost account that Jaṅga himself wrote.[8] The expensive trip on P&O Lines took the group to London, Plymouth, Birmingham, Edinburgh, Paris, and Marseille. Jaṅga was heartily received in London, as the first South Asian ruler to visit Great Britain. He wished to enjoy the country and become acquainted with it, but he also had three concrete aims. He wanted a treaty on the mutual exchange of prisoners; further, the removal of a prohibition on employing foreign experts that had been imposed after the Anglo-Nepalese War, and the right to communicate with London directly instead of via Kolkata. The prisoner exchange agreement was not signed until 1855. But with the second point he was immediately successful, so that the first technicians for road-building and irrigation systems soon entered the country.

The author of the "Journey" recorded how impressed Jaṅga Bahādura Rāṇā was by life in London, the cleanliness, the lack of political intrigues, the beautiful women and the splendor of society receptions, the composition of a "Nepaulese Polka" by the Austrian composer Johann Strauss, but above all by his treatment as an equal-ranking guest of state by Queen Victoria and France's president Louis Napoleon. He compared this with his reception by the Chinese emperor, whom one had to approach on one's knees, and where he had had to bring his own cushions to sit on at the emperor's feet.

When Jaṅga visited Parliament, he was astonished at the limited power wielded by the monarch. He went to the Royal Military Academy three times but was received only once by Queen Victoria and the Duke of Wellington. Jaṅga also visited the weapons manufacturer James Purdey & Sons and bought over thirty firearms and other military materiel,[9] weapons that were likely used primarily for hunting. In the mid-nineteenth century, the Nepalese army possessed only some three hundred rifles. It is said that Jaṅga wanted to size up the military strength of England with the idea of possibly even starting a war, but he soon realized that it was better to make friends with the British.[10] In 1857, he aided the British during the so-called Sepoy Mutiny in India in retaking Lucknow by sending about three thousand soldiers. The British thanked him by giving back parts of the western Banke, Bardiya, Kailali, and Kanchanpur districts in the Tarai that Nepal had lost under the Treaty of Sagauli in 1816 and by compensating for revenue losses. Although Jaṅga had a portrait of Queen Victoria hanging in his parlor, he remained mistrustful of foreigners. By preventing the construction of a road to India and permitting only a few outsiders to enter the country, he continued the isolationist policy of the Śāha rulers.

Jaṅga liked it so well in England that, for a time, he even considered standing down and staying there for two years. He also wanted to have his children raised in England, and then for them to return. Both wishes remained unfulfilled, and during a second similar journey in 1875 he fell from his horse in Mumbai and had to cut his trip short.

In Nepal, Jaṅga Bahādura Rāṇā soon had all political and legal power concentrated in his hands. On November 23, 1846, he sent King Rājendra and

Queen Rājyalakṣmī Devī into exile in India and made Surendra a puppet king. Jaṅga's power grab is evidenced in official documents of the king presumably dictated by Jaṅga. On May 5, 1849, Surendra conferred upon him the title Rāṇā and exempted him from death sentence.[11] With this decree, Jaṅga Bahādura and his family were practically placed on an equal footing with the king, for, apart from Brahmins, only the king was excepted from capital punishment.

On August 6, 1856, King Surendra granted Jaṅga Bahādura the title of Mahārāja of Kaski and Lamjung:

> Being the Maharaja of these places, you are authorized to prevent me from trying to coerce the nobility, the peasantry, or the soldiery, or from disturbing friendly relations with the Queen of England and the Emperor of China. . . . You will keep the people of your estates happy. When performing justice, you are granted the power to pass the death sentence. You are also granted the power, for the period of your lifetime, to execute anyone in my kingdom who tries to disturb the peace of your estates. All this will be enjoyed by you down to offspring of offspring.[12]

In this document, Surendra expresses Jaṅga Bahādura's superior power over him and officially confirms the hereditary nature of the office of prime minister. On June 28, 1857, King Surendra himself issued a document that practically sealed the end of Śāha rule:

> I have appointed Sri Sri Sri Maharaja Jung Bahadoor Ranajee to be the head (the Malik) of my Kingdom, and have invested him with the titles of Prime Minister and Commander-in-Chief; I have given him power to declare war, to make peace and to control the domestic arrangements of the State with full Military, Judicial, and Civil authority in all cases; he is empowered to appoint or dismiss from public offices, to control the Punjenee [*pajanī*], or periodical tenure of appointments and enlistments, and I have also delegated to him the powers of life and death. It will be his particular duty to keep up the friendship now existing between Nepal and the British and China Governments, as well as to preserve peace with Bhote (Tibet).[13]

However, without formally handing over the kingdom to Jaṅga Bahādura, the British were not willing to accept this instruction.

The political pecking order, then, was clearly dominated by the military, for after the prime minister followed the commander-in-chief, four commanding generals for the regions, and other generals, together with colonels and lieutenants. Most of these posts were filled by brothers of Jaṅga Bahādura, who wished thereby to ensure their mutual solidarity. Of course, fraternal strife was one of the most frequent types of family conflict in Nepal, and this arrangement, too, was fated to be short-lived.

The Śamśera Rāṇā, 1885–1951

After Jaṅga Bahādura's death during a hunting trip in the Tarai on February 25, 1877, his oldest surviving brother, Raṇoddīpa Siṃha, succeeded him, and also secured for himself the title of Mahārāja of Kaski and Lamjung, which Jaṅga had wanted to pass on to his son Jagat Jaṅga. As a result, strife with far-reaching consequences was created among the brothers, sons, and nephews of Jaṅga Bahādura—a conflict between the Kũvara Rāṇā (sons and direct relations of Jaṅga Bahādura) and the Śamśera Rāṇā (sons and direct relations of Dhīra Śamśera Rāṇā, Jaṅga's youngest brother).

Following the death of Dhīra Śamśera in October 1884, the Śamśera Rāṇā suspected Jagat Jaṅga of a plot to secure the premiership and had him arrested by the British in India. Jagat Jaṅga was able to return to Kathmandu in April 1885 and even to win the trust of Prime Minister Raṇoddīpa Siṃha, but his enemies struck in November 1885 and murdered Raṇoddīpa Siṃha, Jagat Jaṅga, and the latter's son, Juddha Pratāpa Jaṅga. Jaṅga Bahādura's four other sons fled, most of them to the British Residency. They cleared the path for the oldest son of Dhīra Śamśera, Vīra (Bir) Śamśera to seize power through a military coup. In the following years, Vīra Śamśera's brothers succeeded each other according to seniority, first (for four months) Deva, then Candra, Bhīma, and Juddha; and finally Bhīma's son Padma and Candra's son Mohana.

The Śamśera Rāṇā often spoke English and were not as mistrustful of the British as Jaṅga Bahādura Rāṇā had been. They even helped the British to increase the number of Gurkha regiments from five to ten. They also introduced certain modernizations. Deva Śamśera established primary schools, held court for the people, and encouraged them to suggest reforms. He founded the first public newspaper, the *Gorakhāpatra*, which would be the only newspaper in Nepal for thirty years. He was deposed, however, by his brother, who thought him too modern in outlook. Candra Śamśera, who had studied in Kolkata, established Nepal's first institution of higher learning, Trichandra College; brought electricity to Nepal in 1911; and prohibited widow burning and slavery. During his rule, a treaty was signed with the British on December 21, 1923, that affirmed Nepal's independence.

Candra could also be ruthless. He hardened the caste system, even within his own clan. Thus, he introduced the distinction among A-, B-, and C-class Rāṇā. An A-class Rāṇā was someone whose parents were of the same caste status and had married according to the full Hindu rites; only such progeny had a claim to the premiership. In the case of a B-class Rāṇā, the parents had not married with full Hindu rites, while the C-class comprised all illegitimate offspring. Candra's brother and successor Bhīma Śamśera was quick to flout this hierarchy, placing his own C-class sons and grandsons on the roll of succession. However, a whiff of favoritism and discrimination hung over the

Figure 7.2 Candra Śamśera Rāṇā, around 1920. Photo courtesy of Lakshmi Art. From Candra Śamśera, *Maharaja Chandra Shum Sher Jung Bahadur Rana's Appeal to the People of Nepal for the Emancipation of Slaves and Abolition of Slavery in the Country*. Kathmandu: Suba Pandit Rama Mani, 1925.

Rāṇā clan, which ultimately led to their fall from power, even as many B- and C-class Rāṇā from the mid-1930s on committed themselves to the democracy movement.

During Juddha Śamśera's rule, the great earthquake of January 15, 1934, struck, killing over seven thousand people. Juddha was in the Tarai hunting when it struck, and could only reach Kathmandu three weeks later, but he then rapidly organized reconstruction without foreign help. New Road in the old part of Kathmandu, very broad for the time, was built at his initiative. As soon as the hostilities of the Second World War commenced, Juddha Śamśera decided to ally with Britain and sent its Gurkha troops into battle.

By 1939 political opposition was forming, especially in eastern Nepal and in India, where some young Nepalese from influential families went to study. There they came into contact with India's independence movement. They admired Gandhi and Nehru and their struggle for democracy and wanted to establish free elections and a party system in Nepal, too. Owing to the censorship and strict military control of the country, however, they did not represent a true threat to the Rāṇā regime. Some opposition members were discovered and apprehended, and four of them were executed in January 1941: Dharma Bhakta Mathema, Shukra Raj Shastri, Dasarath Chand, and Ganga Lal Shrestha. These were Nepal's first martyrs. But at least two of the leading members of the oppositional Nepal Praja Parishad ("Nepal People's Assembly"), Tanka Prasad Acharya (later prime minister under King Mahendra) and Ramhari Joshi, survived because they were Brahmins and could not be executed according to Hindu law.[14]

Padma Śamśera, the son of Bhīma Śamśera, became prime minister in 1945. Demonstrating some understanding of the desire for change, he announced a new constitution on January 26, 1948, but Candra's eldest sons Mohana, Babara, and Keśara opposed him. Under the pretext of needing medical treatment, Padma flew on February 21, 1948, to India, and on April 30, Mohana became the next prime minister. The latter fought against the opposition, while at the same time ensuring good relations with Nehru, who was interested in a peaceful Nepal as a bulwark against China but also supported the social-democratic Nepali Congress. In any event, Mohana, the last Rāṇā prime minister, could no longer halt the forces in play.

In October 1946, the All-India Nepali National Congress was founded under the chairmanship of Dev Prasad Sapkota and with the backing of many students who had allied themselves in January 1947 with the All-India

Gorkha Congress operating out of Kolkata. Tanka Prasad Acharya formally became the first president, although he was still incarcerated in Kathmandu. B. P. Koirala became the party's actual leader. In the winter of 1950–51 the end of the Rāṇā era was at hand, not least owing to these activities across the border.

Despite the de facto coup of the Rāṇā, the king remained on the throne throughout the 109 years of that clan's rule. Although in 1856 Jaṅga Bahādura Rāṇā had the title of Mahārāja of Kaski and Lamjung (two Nepalese provinces) bestowed upon himself, making him a "maharaja prime minister" and the premiership became hereditary, the official title of the king of Nepal, *Śrī pāñca mahārājādhirāja* ("fivefold venerable king of the great kings"), was not awarded to him. The palace decrees bearing red seals (*lālamohara*) used for announcements and judgments continued to be issued in the name of the king. Yet it cannot be said that the Śāha king was a puppet, a king in name only. After all, he was regarded as a god, the incarnation of Viṣṇu, and thus responsible for the fate of the country in a way perhaps more meaningful to the people. In numerous public rituals and festivals related to the harvest cycle, he had to appear publicly in the palace and in temples, inaugurate proceedings, and either perform key ritual acts or have them performed.

Landholding and Agriculture

The Nepalese economy has traditionally been based on agriculture, inasmuch as Nepal's only appreciable resource, apart from water, has long been the land.[15] Until quite recently, over 90% of the population made their livelihood, either directly or indirectly, from agriculture. Two-thirds of farmable areas lie in the Tarai, where rice, corn, wheat, millet, soya, barley, jute, pulses, and vegetables are primarily grown. The remaining one-third is scattered throughout the central region, where similar items are produced, and throughout the mountainous regions, which offer pasturage for livestock (sheep, goats, yaks) and where potatoes, buckwheat, or barley can be grown. Owing to the rural exodus, however, agriculture in the higher mountain regions has shrunk greatly since the beginning of the twenty-first century.

For a long time, rulers could only acquire wealth by imposing levies on harvests, given that, until the mid-twentieth century, all land, including Rāṇā land, nominally belonged to the king or the state, which alone controlled the right to alienate land or bequeath it. The state drew three-quarters of its income from land revenue. These territorial rights constituted part of its sovereignty. The state did generally not hire and pay peasants to work the land; rather, it sublet the land to selected persons who did their own hiring, and who as a rule had to pay taxes on it, whether in cash or kind, or who were exempt from such taxes, as compensation for their labors or special services. This developed into a complex system of feudal, patrimonial land use rights with corresponding administrative and fiscal obligations. All of this provides the key to comprehending how the Gorkhali and Rāṇā rulers established and maintained their power and were able to found and extend the state of Nepal.

During the Śāha and Rāṇā periods, land was either state or communal. State land comprised agricultural land, which could be leased out. Public land, in contrast, was used for roads or government buildings, or was only marginally useful for agriculture, such as paths, fallow land, wasteland, or forests. The area used for agriculture consisted of land that the state had (a) itself leased out to peasants (*raikara*), (b) given to individuals in recognition of services, generally virtually tax-free (*birtā*), (c) allocated to religious organizations such as *guṭhīs*, (d) given to certain officials or soldiers as a form of payment (*jāgira*), (e) allocated to certain petty kings in return for declarations of loyalty and a flat tax (*rājya*), or (f) acknowledged as communally worked land (*kipaṭa*) for certain ethnic groups.

This state allocation of land came endowed with the exercise of certain sovereign rights. Some landlords had, for example, the patrimonial authority to pass judgment under both civil and criminal law; they could settle arguments, demand unpaid labor, or raise customs duties and other levies. In these cases, the state did not exact taxes from peasants until late in the nineteenth century, and, except for severe crimes, did not claim any policing rights. In the eighteenth and nineteenth centuries, peasants in their daily lives had little to do with the palace in Kathmandu directly. They were more closely connected with their landlord, and even more so with their headman, who collected the taxes for the state and generally enriched himself in so doing, meaning that he also functioned as a moneylender, collector of back rent, or middleman in trade. The consequences of this division of power were severe, for this weakened the government and created an elite of petty kings, powerful village men, landlords, and other title-holders of land. Holders or administrators of large areas of *birtā* or *jāgira* land, who enjoyed manifold usufructuary rights, could endanger the authority of the state.

Land as a Fief: The *Raikara* System

Raikara land was state land that was either taxed directly or granted or leased to private persons or landlords, either to work it themselves or to sublease it to peasants.[16] The task of collecting rent and tax on it was given either to salaried revenue officials or, after a competitive tender process, to non-governmental contractors, who had to be solvent and of good repute. *Raikara* land came with the right to determine the amount of rent to be paid and whether to take on or dismiss tenants. With few exceptions, the landlords could neither sell nor bequeath it. The contractors sometimes had the right to collect revenue generated from mines, mints, tolls, customs, or trade in certain goods. *Raikara* land developed into the most important category of land, and after 1951 the dominant one. Newly won land generally remained tax-free for a few years. The state secured in this manner the landlords' loyalty.

Taxes and levies were increasingly paid in cash after the middle of the nineteenth century on. In addition, tenants had to pay certain fees, especially in the hill areas; they did so, for example, annually through cash at the renewal of contracts or by giving regular amounts of clarified butter. Under this system, the harvest was divided among the state, landlords, and tenants, with any surplus generally going to the landlords. Few peasants had any land for which they did not have to make payments, and if they did, these properties were usually very small.

The criteria for calculating taxes were primarily based on the surface area and category of land. Basically, wet or easily "irrigated fields" (*kheta*) were used mostly for growing rice and wheat, while unirrigated land, especially on "sloping land" (*pākho*), was devoted to corn, millet, and upland rice. *Kheta* was clearly much more profitable and therefore taxed at a higher rate. On average, 50% of the crop was taken and this occurred two or three times per year, depending on the number of harvests. To be able to pay these high taxes, landlords had to exploit both types of farmlands as a rule, whereas peasants lived off the much lower yields of *pākho* land. As the *kheta* yields were more lucrative for the state, state controls over this type of land were stricter; exact measurements were taken and payment required in kind.

Peasants brought the landlord's harvest to the village, where a headman or district official took the state share. In the case of the peasants' *pākho* land, by contrast, the landlords tended to require a flat rate, which was calculated according to the number of farmsteads, or by how many oxen were set to the plow during the course of a day or half a day. When the land was divided among several farmsteads, taxes were higher. If no ox could be used and the land had to be worked by hand with a hoe (*kodālo*), the taxes were lower. This entire system of collecting essentially half the yield in taxes was called *adhiyā̃* or *adhiyā* ("half"), and the tenants were known as *adhiyāra*.

By 1830, a further system, called *kuta*, was put in place wherein the tenant agreed a fixed amount with the landlord or village headman, regardless of the actual harvest yield; the landlord or headman passed the tax revenue on to the government officer (*sāmanta*, *subbā*) for delivery to the central government. The palace in Kathmandu was naturally interested in predictable tax revenue, which the *adhiyā* system could not guarantee. The *kuta* system, which was particularly widespread in the hill and mountain regions, gave landlords the security of a fixed revenue, agreed upon before the harvest. Of course, the risk of a bad harvest or no harvest at all was now borne by the peasant. No wonder, then, that the *kuta* generated much resentment among them, since it often led to land being given up, to debt, or even to bonded labor. The peasants, unsurprisingly, often called for a return to the *adhiyā* system because, while it could impoverish, it only rarely ruined them.

Further, the landlords could increase levies if the yields proved to be particularly bountiful. But instead of considering the implications of all this, the government permitted landlords operating under the *kuta* system to introduce competition into the allocation of good land, namely on a contractual basis, with the one offering the most receiving it. This allowed landlords to bring in additional peasants or land laborers from outside if the peasants working the land hitherto had not fulfilled the lease requirements. Overall, the *kuta* system did not increase productivity and indeed contributed decisively to peasants becoming indebted and poor.

In order to remedy the injustices, and especially the mismatch between payments (rent and levies) and productivity, the Rāṇā refined an old system of four land classes in existence at least since the time of Sthiti Malla. These were calculated on the basis of the relation between the *murī* (or other measurements of volume) and *ropanī* (or other areas of land).[17] Table 7.2 shows the categories of land, taking the names of the first ordinal numbers in Persian.

In the late Rāṇā Period, the yields of the land classes were converted to monetary payments but registered in the traditional form. The rates of payment in cash or kind were abolished in 1963 in the mountain regions, and in 1966 in the Kathmandu Valley.

Table 7.2 Land Categories

Land category	Irrigation	Days of water standing in the fields	Amount produced (*murī* per *ropanī*)
abbala	Fully irrigable	2–3	3.5 plus
doyama	Three-quarterly irrigable	2–3	2.5 to 3.5
sima	Half-irrigable	1	1.75 to 2.5
cāhāra	Hardly irrigable	0	Less than 1.75

Land as a Reward: The *Birtā* System

One subcategory of *raikara* land was *birtā* land.[18] This was land entrusted by the state to individuals for their living, generally free of taxes and levies,[19] and granted on a long-term or even permanent basis to, as a rule, petty kings, Brahmins or priests, religious teachers, soldiers, and members of the aristocracy and the royal family.

This type of land followed a clear formal model when being conveyed. For example, a royal document (*lālamohara*) of 1833 mentions a "tax-free land grant" (*birtā-bitalapa*) to the "royal priest" (*rājaguru*) Raṅganātha Pauḍyāla, which he had received from King Rājendra's father for having recited a Purāṇa text during a festival.[20] It then lists the various categories—agricultural land along with woodland, caves, bluffs, building plots, and terraced fields—and their natural boundaries, such as paths and rivers. At the end, witnesses are named, among them Prime Minister Bhīmasena Thāpā and the priest who had recited the ritual enactment. Thus, these land donations had to be made with a ritual decision (*saṃkalpa*) binding together the king and his liegeman (the *birtā*-holder). The *birtā*-holder was bound to loyalty to his overlord, namely the state or king, but his local power was considerable. In general, *birtā* land gave the title-holder the right to sublet or, especially if the holder was a Rāṇā, even to bequeath, divide, sell, or mortgage the land, demand unpaid labor and other duties, or pronounce minor judgments. Further, offenders punished by enslavement became the property of the *birtā*-holder. The *Ain* establishes, with regard to marshland or barren land, that whoever worked wasteland or untended *raikara* land, thus developing it, should then receive a certain surrounding area as *birtā* land, thereby providing incentives for increased economic productivity.[21]

The *birtā* land created a class that enjoyed land use rights and that generally maintained loyalty toward the palace, in part because the palace did not much intrude upon their privileges. This formation of a feudal class meant a further hierarchy in society alongside the caste system.[22] Holding land meant social prestige, and the more one had, the higher one's social status. Conversely, land could be confiscated in cases of disloyalty and severe crimes, although *birtā* land generally stayed within the family, with only the current title-holder changing. Those who lost their land did receive compensation, for *birtā* land was protected to a degree, being something approaching private property. In every case, all land grants had to be confirmed anew by a new ruler, so that there was always a risk of losing it. It could only be alienated, too, with the permission of the palace. Every *birtā* grant had to be approved by the Rāṇā prime minister, which institutionalized the Rāṇā's power over land, the country's most important economic and political resource. The obligation to document everything was one reason why the number of documentation offices massively increased in the nineteenth and twentieth centuries, although there was no proper land registry office until 1965.[23]

Grants of *birtā* land weakened the country since they produced no tax income. But they were, at the same time, one of the most important means of strengthening the state, as they bound successful, commendable, or influential subjects to it: priests, victorious generals, leaders of social or ethnic groups, petty kings, and the Rāṇā and Śamśera aristocracy. For example, Vīra Śamśera claimed so much land for himself and his clan that by the mid-twentieth century the Śamśera had become the richest title-holders. On the other hand, losing power could result in loss of *birtā* land. Bhīmasena Thāpā and his family, for instance, were completely dispossessed in 1837,[24] but received major parts back when Bhīmasena Thāpā's nephew, Māthavara Siṃha Thāpā, became prime minister in 1843.

Land for Religious Services or Merit: The *Guṭhī* System

Guṭhīs (from Skt. *goṣṭhī*, originally "cow pen") are in most cases religiously motivated foundations or trusts provisioned with tax-exempt land. They date back to the Licchavi Period, but they really became widespread only in the Malla Period, when these foundations oversaw the duties of functionaries and administered the yields from donated land.

The *guṭhī* system regulates the activities of social and religious organizations: festivals or rites, temple services, maintaining sacred buildings, financing materials and animals needed for offerings, and building special processional chariots.[25] Schools, hospitals, and orphanages could also be the main beneficiaries of a *guṭhī* endowment. Temple *guṭhīs* were, as a rule, founded by the royal house or otherwise by private nobles or the wealthy. Such foundations usually involved donating a parcel of land, whose harvests were meant to pay for maintaining the *guṭhīs*. The land was often given to acquire religious merit and was registered in the donor's name. It could not be sold or modified, since as a rule it was an irreversible "religious gift" (*dāna*). *Guṭhī* land was also donated to set up foundations (*sadāvarta*) that gave alms to ascetics or beggars, or fed apes, cows, or bulls.

The state was not allowed to appropriate *guṭhī* land for its own purposes. Whoever confiscated such land, an 1817 deed of foundation by King Rājendra states, would be reincarnated as a worm and live for the next sixty thousand years in human excrement.[26] In the *Ain*, too, the ill-advised king or evil advisor who wishes to seize *guṭhī* land is threatened with the gate to heaven being shut on him but the way to hell remaining open. In a 1775 document, King Pratāpa Siṃha Śāha therefore properly returned *guṭhī* land belonging to the Taleju temple that had been misused as *jāgira* after the conquest of the Kathmandu Valley.[27]

Nevertheless, *guṭhī* land was not completely protected. The donor and any legal successors could change the beneficiary if the purpose of the donation was not being fulfilled. Likewise, the Śāha rulers could confiscate land if it was being misused. Occasionally, however, converting *birtā* land into *guṭhī* land could help donors ward off confiscation. If they did so, only a portion was designated as a donation for religious or charitable purposes, even if the whole property was declared as such. Given that provision, private *birtā* land was basically protected from the state's grasp.[28] Not even in the case of murder, when otherwise all property was seized by the state, could land of this category be confiscated.

Thanks to the *guṭhī* system, the Rāṇā were able to build a decentralized network of support for religious and charitable institutions, and thus increase their prestige among the population. However, the system led to many disputes. What was to be done if the land was washed away by floods, when other people laid claim to unjustified rights on the land, when there was a discrepancy between the pre-agreed and actual yields, or when someone wrongly declared *guṭhī* land to be *birtā* land and sold it?

The *guṭhī* system underwent many alterations, with both the state and its rulers throughout Nepal's history occupying or nationalizing *guṭhī*-endowed land for personal or state use. Thus, Rāṇā palaces, government buildings (including Singha Durbar), and a number of hospitals stand on what was once land under *guṭhī* control. Then, in 1964, all *guṭhī* land was transferred to a newly created semi-governmental Guṭhī Corporation (Guṭhī Saṃsthāna). The reason for the new administration was the intense criticism of the fact that the religious merit of the foundations only benefitted the donors, thus permitting a privileged class to exploit their land rights for their own sake, even though peasants produced the harvests. In addition, *guṭhī* land yielded virtually nothing for the state, and abuses were becoming ever more visible. The criticism was justified, but at the same time the *guṭhī* system was one reason for the variety of religious rituals and innumerable buildings built through an endowment, especially in the Kathmandu Valley and the Tarai. The Guṭhī Corporation became the biggest holder of land in Nepal, but it could not entirely replace the network of *guṭhī* activities. Many formerly privileged *guṭhīs* complained of missed payments, delayed payments, or underpayment, which resulted in festivals and rituals not being held and buildings not being maintained or renovated. Many a priest formerly employed by a *guṭhī* stopped revering the divinity, as the original *guṭhī* endowment stipulated, once the Guṭhī Corporation no longer paid him to do so.

Land as Remuneration: The *Jāgira* System

The category of land known as *jāgira* covered *raikara* land given to civil servants or military personnel by way of remunerative payment (*jāgira* also denotes a government post). King Pṛthvīnārāyaṇa Śāha knew how important suitable rewards and compensation were to his troops since it freed them from worrying about their families. In his *Divyopadeśa*, he stressed the need to pay soldiers according to their performance.[29] The *jāgira* system became for him one of the most important tools for buttressing his rapidly growing official and military apparatus. It had two advantages: those who received an award of land—the *jāgiradāras*—saw to state tasks and received the attendant remuneration. The other advantage was the development of agricultural land. *Jāgiradāras* preferred previously worked land, but often they received barren land, the exploitation of which increased not only their wealth but also that of the state. Generally, there was enough barren land readily available. With the increase in population and the loss of territory following the Anglo-Nepalese War (1814–16), however, land became scarcer.

In contrast to *birtā* land, *jāgiras* came with only the temporary right to yields on the property granted. *Jāgiradāras* did not farm this property themselves. Payments were calculated on the basis of annually revised documents, in which the amount and form of rent was listed: a "certificate" (*tirjā*) empowering the *jāgiradāras* to collect rent from their land, or a "receipt" (*purjā*) signed and handed over by the *jāgiradāra* to a tenant on receiving his rent. *Jāgiradāras* usually kept to the agreed conditions but collected much more. The calculation of rent was done in rupees and then converted to measures of grain.

There were clearly disadvantages to the *jāgira* system. Often the land was far from his place of work or residence, so that a *jāgiradāra* could not oversee it. The cost of any bad harvests through drought, landslides, floods, or insects was his to bear. From Candra Śamśera's time on, he could demand a salary instead of a *jāgira*, which had the advantage of regular payments instead of once or twice a year at harvest time. However, cash payments were not adjusted to the market. Even if grain prices rose, the salary remained the same.

The conversion of *raikara* to *jāgira* land was usually detrimental to a tenant. While the former system paid market prices by the state or the landlord, in the latter it was in the interest of the *jāgiradāra* to pay him less so that his own losses would not be too high. Increasingly, a kind of shadow economy began to develop in which *jāgiradāras* gave their *jāgira* certificates to middlemen or grain speculators (*dhokryā*), tasking them with collecting the annually reassessed rent. These middlemen were only allowed to accept an amount of money for the rent that corresponded to the market value. They did not, however, always do so. Either they came too early to a village, before the harvest, or much later, after the grain had already been sold but when the market price had risen much higher. The fifth article of the *Ain* ("Bālī bikrīko") deals with this problem.

Once a monetized system of economy was sufficiently established itself at the beginning of the twentieth century, the *jāgira* system had to collapse. For the state, this meant a loss of income. For example, in 1852/53, only about one percent of the proceeds on *jāgira* land in the mountainous region and Kathmandu Valley found its way into state coffers. Starting in 1846, the Rāṇā centralized the administration and deconstructed the feudal, decentralized *jāgira* system by confiscating land and paying officials. In this way, they increased state revenue and their private income many times over. Prime Minister Candra Śamśera was a particularly forceful proponent of salary payments, so much so that the shadow economy of middlemen dried up. In

1928, *jāgira* land in the central region and certain parts of the mountainous region was converted to neutral *raikara* land, with *jāgiradāras* receiving compensation. At the same time, however, the Rāṇā massively extended their own *jāgira* property. The result was a huge redistribution of wealth.

Land for Loyalty: The *Rājya* System

Rājya means "kingdom," but in the context of the tax system it referred specifically to certain minor kingdoms absorbed as tributaries into the Gorkha kingdom. Until the Rāṇā Period there were seven such minor kingdoms, and afterward a total of thirteen. The absorption often occurred without any warfare, but the petty kings were able to largely retain autonomy in internal matters only if they recognized Gorkha's sovereignty. These petty kings (*rājā*), who often received additional land, money, or other rewards for doing so, became the usufructuaries of the territories that were nominally allocated to them. They were not allowed either to transfer them or to divide them up.

The taxes and other levies were in some cases not very heavy. In 1791, for example, the *rājā* of Bajura paid only 500 rupees per year, and in 1769, the king of Jajarkot, Gajendra Śāha, only 701 rupees.[30] This minor king was also granted the right to pronounce death sentences, order caste degradations, confiscate *birtā* land, and collect fees on weights and measures. Later, in 1833, the king of Jajarkot, Dīpanārāyaṇa Śāha, even asked for a reduction in his tribute payments, inasmuch as his family had grown larger, land had been destroyed by landslides, and the peasants had become poor, and in 1835 he renounced almost his complete right to rule.[31]

Land as Communal Property: The *Kipaṭa* System

Kipaṭa land was the traditional communally used land of the Limbu, Rai, Sherpa, Danuvar, Sunuvar, Majhi, Newar, and other ethnic groups, especially in the mountainous and central hill regions. This category is fundamentally different from the *raikara* system, for the land, comprising fallow land, wasteland, and forests, was not the possession of an individual but of a community. *Kipaṭa* land could only be claimed if one was a member of the local community, even if (as was often the case) one no longer lived in the area. Landownership brought with it communal obligations and taxation, but less tax than in the case of *raikara* land. The government could only try to convince local communities to convert land to *raikara* and could not simply claim it.

The different forms of *kipaṭa*, and the attendant rights and duties, varied considerably from region to region. What united them was the fact that this land could not be sold or could only be sold within that particular population group. There thus was a sort of conservatism inherent to the *kipaṭa* category. As a rule, this was land that had belonged to the community for a very long time. Communal ownership did not mean, however, that the land was worked communally. Rather, it was generally allocated to individual families and cultivated or used by them in other ways. If someone was no longer able to work the land, it reverted to the community.

Kipaṭa land was not tax-free. If a peasant did not pay the required tax, the community would stand surety for him. Only if it, too, could not or would not pay could the state claim the land or enforce payment. But the state had its own problems with this category of land, as increasingly it had become impossible to tell who was obliged to pay tax and how large the plots of land were. The state therefore increasingly insisted on proof and registration. Absent that taxes were calculated on the basis of the number of oxen per farmstead instead of the size of the land. Rice land remained tax-free. Despite these complications, the state long hesitated to touch *kipaṭa* land. "If we should confiscate your land, then your ancestors and gods will destroy our kingdom," Pṛthvīnārāyaṇa Śāha declared in 1774 to a Limbu ruler.[32]

Still, the state tried repeatedly to convert *kipaṭa* land into *raikara* land, since the latter brought in greater tax revenue. Toward that end the state appointed village and district headmen, who received many privileges if they agreed to the conversion of at least portions of the *kipaṭa* land. In addition, the state supported the settlement of groups that did not belong to the local ethnic community. The privileged *kipaṭa* category did not apply to them, creating tensions between the two populations.

In time the state's requirements relating to *kipaṭa* land became more stringent. Usually, fixed sums were agreed upon, so that keeping such land diminished in profit. In addition, the prohibition on alienating the land became ever more riddled with loopholes, and in 1968 the category was completely abolished.

In summary, these traditional systems of land use were based on a fundamental exploitation of the peasantry, a step-by-step disempowerment of ethnic groups, and a disproportionate accumulation of farmland and forests in the hands of privileged groups—above all, the Rāṇā and Śāha. In 1861, Jaṅga Bahādura Rāṇā and his brothers received from King Surendra whole districts in the Tarai that had been returned to Nepal by British India for Nepalese help in the Great Mutiny of 1857.[33] In 1900, the British resident Henry Wylie observed a "tendency on the part of the [Prime] Minister to consider the whole of the surplus revenues of the state, after paying for the administration of the country, as his own private property".[34] By around 1950 some three-quarters of the *birtā* land, constituting about one-third of the country's agriculturally productive area, belonged to the Rāṇā.

The system of taxation was not really profitable for the state, since a large portion of land was granted to private persons either for their exclusive or near exclusive use. For example, according to historian Mahesh Chandra Regmi, the state received a bare million rupees in 1853, although the land figures suggested that it should have been double that.[35] In 1857, the state collected less in taxes in the Tarai than *birtā*-holders and other landlords. Apparently, there was no visible rise in productivity, no matter how much agricultural territory was developed. One could even say that the Gorkha kingdom was no more productive than the previous minor kingdoms had been.

The tenants carried all the risk of harvests in bad years, so that they often had to run up debts. Brahmins thus became not only landholders but also moneylenders. Often the peasants could only pay off their debts by unpaid (bonded) labor or even slavery. Frequently, they left in massive migrations to North India, Darjeeling, Sikkim, or Bhutan.[36] The statistics from Darjeeling in 1870 make this clear: some 32,350 Nepalese were living there, of whom 32,080 were Matvālī or Untouchables; there were no Brahmins or Chhetri among the migrants.

Labor and Slavery

Labor in Nepal means primarily labor on the land. While there were many other economic roles in a traditional village—among them traders, officials, blacksmiths, carpenters, craftsmen, basket weavers, butchers, tailors, priests, shamans, porters, and many others—the greater part of the labor was done by peasants. As only a small percentage of the peasantry had land of its own, they were burdened by high taxes and other levies and often could not make livings from the work of their own hands. Many people thus had to hire themselves out, in their own country or in another, so as to earn higher wages to pay off debts.

There was no lack of work in their own country. The population density was low and the need for labor grew steadily at the end of the eighteenth and throughout the nineteenth century, as construction and state formation under the Śāha and Rāṇā was labor-intensive. In the process, unfree forms of work arose, ranging from compulsory labor and bonded labor to slavery and child labor. Often the state enforced the *rakama* system, which was nothing more than compulsory labor for the state or the landholder, with no payment.[37]

The state needed unpaid labor for such public works as building roads, forts, dams, canals, and bridges.[38] It also needed bodies for military operations, the manufacture of ammunition and weapons, and maintaining horse and elephant stables and ferry services. Not least, the state had the population work for the convenience of its elite. For example, peasants transported to Kathmandu such luxury items as ice, which would be almost completely melted away by the time it arrived.

This form of obligatory unpaid labor, customarily called *jhārā*, was usually carried out for the government by working the land (*beṭha*) or performing regular services (*begāra*).[39] These latter had to be performed primarily by older boys and men, but sometimes involved entire villages. Thus, a 1796 document of Raṇabahādura Śāha stated that "all four caste classes and 36 caste groups"—a standard formula meaning all households—had to do compulsory labor to repair a river embankment that had been so badly damaged that water flowed into a low-lying palace. In the beginning, not even Brahmins were excused from such labor, although they generally did not have to perform any heavy physical work. Exceptions were made only for the aristocracy, high-ranking officials and military officers, and temple servants. In individual cases, freedom from such labor could be bought by instead producing goods. For example, in 1793 Raṇabahādura Śāha freed the goldsmiths in Kathmandu from compulsory menial labor as long as they minted gold coins for the palace.[40]

Most of the compulsory labor was needed to cultivate developed or fallow land belonging to the government. But it could also be required for the repair of palaces and temples. Upon occasion it might be called for the delivery of certain natural resources: coal, stones, wood, or (for the royal horses and elephants) grass and leaves. Men were usually not compensated or given food for the work, and they had to bring their own tools and provisions. Such compulsory labor could last for up to six months and involve marches of many days' or even weeks' duration. Beatings were common if work did not meet expectations.

From the start, these harsh requirements gave rise to discontent and complaints, especially because agricultural work had to be neglected during the compulsory labor, to the detriment of harvests. Abuse by officials requiring compulsory labor for their own private ends only made matters worse. The state began to issue ever more prohibitions to check abuses and started remunerating the work, at least within the porterage system.

An 1835 document of Rājendra Śāha, addressed to the nobles of Jumla, is typical.[41] In it he ordered that civilian and military state officials in the region should take only what the peasants gave voluntarily (specifically vegetables, fruits, and firewood), but they should not be forced to give these items. Rather, officials were to buy them at the usual market rates. Further, they were not to use the porterage system for the benefit of ordinary subjects without orders from above, unless it was a matter of transporting weapons or the ill. Any contravention was to be punished. The *Ain* bears witness to efforts to contain the excesses in Article 11 ("On Forced Labor"). It required a contractual basis for *jhārā* and prohibited government officials from forcibly demanding labor. In cases of contravention, those requiring unpaid labor were to pay workers four *ānās* per day, and porters were to be given meals.

Porters and the Postal System

In the past, those traveling Nepal's high hills could not avoid meeting porters, for nearly everything there had to be carried by man or beast (mules, horses, yaks, or goats). The porters often carried loads of over a hundred pounds and thus not infrequently their own weight. To do this, they used "bamboo panniers" (*ḍoko*), which were attached to a tumpline (*nāmlo*), and this was laid across the forehead so that the burden lay on the back.

Before 1956, when the first road from India to the Kathmandu Valley was opened, even cars were carried into the valley. The most famous example is a Mercedes-Benz 230 Pullman Landaulet, which Adolf Hitler allegedly presented to King Tribhuvan in 1940 or, according to other accounts, to the Śamśera Rāṇā prime minister.[42] It took sixty-four porters to transport the car on bamboo poles over the hills.

By 1791 a system of porters, called *hulāka*, was in place that developed into a system of mail runners, the precursor of the Nepalese postal service

(Nepāla Hulāka Ghara).[43] Porterage was one of the labor obligations (*jhārā*) owed for the most part by adult males (or sometimes whole villages) with the exception of Brahmins and select others, such as the Newars in Patan or Muslim glass bangle makers.[44] The *hulākī* laborers were privileged because they sometimes received some land as a *jāgīra*, which was protected from expropriation. They also enjoyed some reduced taxes and other levies, and were exempted from further labor obligations.[45]

In the beginning, the *hulāka* system mostly transported weapons and ammunition. Especially in the west of Nepal, it was organized into a network of fixed routes, so that porters only had to cover the distance between their village area and the next, where they could pass on the loads. The number of days it took the postal service to reach distant places, depending on whether or not goods were being delivered, were listed in the *Ain*.[46] If an office in Kathmandu required a response, thirty-five days were granted to prepare the document; to this were added the number of days it took to reach and return from the place starting "from Nepāla." In this manner, a fast service could function around the clock, which was one of the reasons for the military strength of the Gorkhali. By 1804 Bhīmasena Thāpā had it running on a countrywide level that reached even the far western parts of Nepal. Later, around 1878, it developed into a postal service used by the public, and from April 1881 on, one-, two- and four-*ānā* stamps were being introduced. From 1887 on prepaid post cards were also available, at two *paisās* each.

Porters were also needed in large numbers for military operations. To prepare for the second war with Tibet (1791–92), for example, 2,340 porters were indentured. The difference between paid soldiery and "unpaid porterage" (*begāra*) included a difference in status. In 1855, the Thakali in the Thak-Khola region of Mustang District complained that they were supposed to work as porters during preparations for the third Nepal-Tibet war, even though they had been recruited as soldiers under the Malla kings. Their point was conceded, and subsequently a Thakali regiment was set up.

A large number of porters were needed in 1911, too, when all electricity lines were laid from Pharping to Kathmandu. An official proclamation published in the *Gorkhāpatra* newspaper stated that all households between these two places were to supply the services of two porters.[47] Should they be unable to do so, they would have to bear a charge of two rupees per porter. Exceptions were made for households of minors, old people (over 60 years of age), the very poor, and widows. It was stated expressly that in other countries levies were raised for such tasks, but not in Nepal.

A group of scientists led by the Norwegian Norman Heglund examined porters in 2005 in Namche Bazaar and found that they worked very efficiently indeed, using less energy than the trekkers with their forty-four-pound rucksacks.[48] Apart from the way the burden was distributed, the porters used a slow but uniform back-and-forth gait, with pauses of up to forty-five seconds a minute. Remarkably, there was hardly any difference in energy consumption per pounds between men and women. The men, on average, bore 93% of their body weight, and the women between 60% and 70%. In 2005, the route from Kathmandu to Namche Bazaar, a distance of about 62 miles, took about a week. The return journey took two to three days.

Slavery, Compulsory Labor, and Bonded Labor

On November 28, 1924, Prime Minister Candra Śamśera had high-ranking officials and military men gather on the large open space of Tundikhel in the middle of Kathmandu. With him was the eighteen-year-old king, Tribhuvan.

Figure 7.3 Announcement of the end of slavery by Candra Śamśera on November 28, 1924, in Kathmandu. From Candra Śamśera, *Maharaja Chandra Shum Sher Jung Bahadur Rana's Appeal to the People of Nepal for the Emancipation of Slaves and Abolition of Slavery in the Country*. Kathmandu: Suba Pandit Rama Mani, 1925.

Candra climbed up to a platform beneath a large tree, sat down under an umbrella, and had the palace guru Hemraj Pande read out a long *Appeal to the People of Nepal for the Emancipation of Slaves and the Abolition of Slavery in the Country*. This begins with the following words:

> Gentlemen, To-day we meet to consider a delicate and difficult question. The world progresses and with it there is change, not only in our mode of living, in our relations with our neighbors, in our methods of administration and many things besides but in our domestic arrangements too. Our country and our people have now come much more to the fore than ever before. . . . Yet there rests on us, according to the present standard of the civilized world, a stigma, a slur on our name which diminishes its luster. They say we yet nurture the hated institution of slavery; we, who are so fiercely jealous of our independence, retain in vile bondage some of our own people and abandon them from generation to generation to continue in that state without lifting a little finger to sweep away custom unworthy of our glorious tradition.[49]

After these sentences followed a long justification for Candra Śamśera's proposal that his people should give up slavery. He appealed to Hindu tradition and its condemnation of slavery (technically not true, since slavery had long existed in India); he described the hopeless and despairing outlook of slaves and the shame of seventy-year-old slaves being subject to far younger "masters" in multi-generational households; and he demonstrated with detailed figures why it did not pay to keep slaves. He calculated that it costs 410 rupees to raise a slave child until the age of sixteen when he or she could work or be sold for 120 rupees; but if this sum had been lent out at 10%, 1,100 rupees would have been earned in the same period of time. Extensive tables based on the census of 1923 were attached as supporting evidence to the *Appeal*, showing that there were 51,519 slaves at the time, corresponding to a little more than one percent of the population, and 15,719 slave owners. Finally, he announced that his government would pay compensation for every slave freed.

Candra Śamśera's "appeal" was cautiously directed toward slave owners and the international public, which immediately applauded the prime minister's action. Likewise, Candra was vaunted by slaves, among whom a rumor circulated that he himself had married a slave woman.[50] The question of whether Candra Śamśera recommended giving up slavery for moral or humane reasons carries different meaning when the political situation at the time is considered. In 1923 Candra had signed a peace and friendship treaty with the British in which Nepal, in contrast to the minor kingdoms of India, was recognized as an independent nation. This status made it eligible to join the League of Nations, the predecessor of the United Nations. In 1924 this institution formed a commission for the abolition of slavery. The prime minister knew about this and likely wanted to make a favorable international impression. He therefore later had an English version of his *Appeal* made. On September 25, 1926, Nepal signed the League of Nations Convention on Slavery, which obliged all signatories to give up the slave trade.

Candra Śamśera's *Appeal* did not have the intended effect he hoped for, however. Not until September 2008 was the last form of slavery in Nepal, the *haliyā* system of bonded labor, abolished, thus ending a tradition dating at least to the Licchavi inscriptions.[51] However, such early testimony is rare, and what the tasks of these slaves (*dāsa*) were is not clear. The sources became more frequent in the Śāha and Rāṇā periods. The following outline is based on them.[52]

First, there were various forms of slavery, compulsory labor, and serfdom/servitude. According to the Slavery Convention of the League of Nations of 1926, a person can be called a slave when that person belongs to another and can be sold. In the case of bonded labor (i.e., serfdom), the person in question cannot be sold. The slave in the narrower sense, then, is somewhere between a human being and animal. The *Ain* makes this point clear when it equates the value of a slave with that of a four-footed domestic animal. The Nepālī terminology, as a rule, distinguishes between slaves (*kamārā*, *kamārī*), servants employed in the household (*kariyā*, *cākara*, *nokara*, *dāsa*), bonded laborers (*bā̃dhā*), laborers (*kāmakara*), and day laborers (*bhatuvā*); another term for slave was *gulāma*/*gulāmī*, from Arabic *gulām*, used especially in the Tarai but also in the Kathmandu Valley.[53]

The fate of actual slaves was deplorable. Female slaves were often sexually abused, small children and even babies were torn from their parents and sold, violence was most likely a daily occurrence, and food and shelter were minimal. Slaves had to work around the clock, cultivating land, herding animals, and fetching water or firewood. Those who were ill were cast out and did not have to be accepted back if they were away for forty-five days. Servants faced a somewhat better situation, but the differences between these categories were often ignored in daily practice. How far the humiliation of slaves could go is illustrated by a regulation from the *Ain*:

> If a master has put human excrement into the mouth of his male or female slave, the master shall not be entitled to get such a slave back. . . . If the master has put human excrement on other parts of the body than the mouth, he shall not be accused and blamed.[54]

In each and every case, being enslaved meant social death. Slaves lost their caste names, became strangers to their families and homes, were stripped of their ritual status, and became practically minors, the "children" of their master. Not only did they lose their liberty but most of all, they lost their own family. Slaves could be bequeathed, that is, passed on from generation to generation, thus becoming part of an enslaver's family network, especially if they were married to a female slave and had children, but this was no substitute for their own kin. And yet a slave who was integrated into a family was better off than a purely menial slave, who was traded and treated more or less as a commodity.

The reasons for bonded labor in a broader sense are manifold. One of the most frequent cases is when debts were not repaid.[55] When a slave or indentured debtor was sold, the state wanted documentation and wanted money. A debtor could hire out himself, his son, or a third party under exclusive exploitation rights until the debt had been paid off. In the *Ain*, the word "body" (*jyū, jīū*) was often used for pledges of human servitude. In fact, it was actual serfdom, of the kind practiced during Nepal's medieval period.[56] Under the *Ain*, the bondman had to give his agreement to the local authorities.

A further reason for servitude was the commission of crimes in breach of moral norms, especially sexual offenses (e.g., incest). According to the *Ain*, those so punished had to belong to an enslavable caste. Such punishment was severe, something close to capital punishment, and indeed sometimes explicitly imposed as a substitute when capital punishment was out of the question (e.g., for a Brahmin). Likewise, under certain circumstances the offering of alcohol could lead to enslavement (in contrast to consumption, which would lead to caste degradation).[57]

In individual cases, people were forced or tricked into slavery—for example, as a prisoner of war or a rebel—but also by use of vile means. Thus, a man asked by American anthropologist Timothy Whyte about his enslaved Thakuri grandfather said that his ancestor had been employed as a porter and had lived like a Brahmin, changing his clothes before entering the kitchen, for instance.[58] But when the landowner for whom he worked tore off his Sacred

Thread, he lost his caste status and became an "Enslavable Alcohol Drinker." There were cases, too, of voluntary enslavement, usually resulting from extreme neediness. The *Ain* deals with instances involving a liberated slave who returns to his former master, the latter being obligated to take him back. Private persons could also sell slaves to Muslims or Christians, knowing that they might be forcibly converted.

The most frequent reason for enslavement was as punishment for offenses or crimes. These rules are preserved in remarkable detail in the *Ain*.[59] They set forth how to deal with ill slaves, or those unable to work; with those who have run away and have been brought back (five rupees was the finder's reward); and those who helped others to run away. If a slave ran away and hired himself out elsewhere to someone who had no knowledge of his background, then no compensation had to be paid to the previous owner. Further, if a slave was sold by someone to whom he did not belong, then the latter had to pay compensation and fines. A regulation also covered the case of a master dissatisfied with the work of a slave; he was not permitted to simply lock the slave away or beat him, but first had to obtain permission to do so from a local authority.

According to the *Ain*, it was not possible, during a division of inheritance among brothers, to separate the children of a slave from their mother if they were under eleven years of age.[60] A minimum age for serfdom was also established: "Whoever takes on serfs under sixteen years of age, or offers such, must pay 10 rupees in fines in each case." A further article forbade the sale of children under twelve, a practice that was widespread at the beginning of the nineteenth century;[61] up to this age one was regarded as a minor. Nonetheless, a value was set for child slaves under litigation:

> Slave sons under 3: 20, slave daughters under 3: 25 rupees. Slave sons between 3 and 6: 30, slave daughters: 35 rupees. Slave sons between 6 and 12: 50, slave daughters: 55 rupees.[62]

The sale of slaves and types of payment were also precisely listed in the *Ain*. Thus, the price of a male slave aged between twelve and forty years was set at 100 rupees, and that of a female slave at 120 rupees. The work performed per day was calculated at 1 *ānā* (1/16 rupee) and an additional 1 *ānā* for the slave's food. This came to about 3.75 rupees per month and 45 rupees per year. However, the prices varied, depending on age, region, and sex, with fertile women fetching higher prices than men.

With these regulations, the state guaranteed the legal security of both slave owners and slaves. It established punishments to be imposed on officials of various magistracies and district offices when they illegally permitted enslavement or even engaged in such themselves. It was forbidden to manipulate caste status so as to enable enslavement. The distinction between Enslavable and Non-enslavable castes in the caste hierarchy in the *Ain* was itself an instrument of repression and exploitation, mainly of the peasantry and the impure castes or casteless. The state attended, too, to catching slaves who ran away. It further established the inheritance rights of slaves and regulated sexual relations between slaves and their masters.

From an economic point of view, the usefulness of slavery was questionable at best. The state claimed it gave easy access to labor through the system of "corvée" (*jhārā*), which avoided the need to care for slaves all their lives. It was a different matter when it came to the trade in slaves, especially in Garhwal, where an estimated 200,000 slaves were sold on to India in 1815.[63]

Efforts were repeatedly made already at the beginning of the Śāha and Rāṇā periods to check the extent of slavery. Simple citizens could and did liberate slaves. To do so, the slave took up a traditional "porter's basket" (*ḍoko*) onto his back, and when the master cut through the tumpline, the slave was free.

Liberating slaves was sometimes seen as being as meritorious as gifting slaves to a temple, as happened in 1695 when a Brahmin named Bālakṛṣṇa Deva Śarmā donated two female slaves to the Paśupatinātha temple, the deed of donation expressly stating that the Bhaṭṭa priests were not to have them at their beck and call.[64] Legal attempts to prohibit slavery, however, can only be observed regionally or in rudimentary form. There were thus extensive liberations on the occasion of the coronations of Deva Śamśera and Candra Śamśera. King Rājendra Śāha even issued one for the entire country, but it could not be imposed due to his weak position.

Mass liberations first occurred on April 23, 1925, when Candra Śamśera issued a legal prohibition of slavery. From then on trading in slaves was punishable by seven years in prison. Candra paid a total of 3,670,000 rupees to the slave owners—75 rupees per adult male slaves and 100 for females. These "liberated slaves" (*amalekha*, *ghartī*), whom the prime minister called Śivabhakta ("worshipers of Śiva"), received land to farm on in and around a village in the Tarai jungle which, in 1927, became an end station of the Indian railway. On June 15, 1929, the village was named Amlekhgunj ("the place of liberated slaves").[65] They were probably actually needed to cut timber for Indian railway ties. Basically, this resettlement program was a failure. No more than an estimated sixty households were established, no doubt because the place was in the middle of a malarial zone, but above all because the *ghartīs* did not gain social acceptance. The liberated slaves were long unable to form a group or caste of their own, find marriage partners, or integrate themselves into the working community. Many had bigger problems after liberation than before, finding work and housing only on the margins of society.

An economically damaging consequence of the enslavement of peasants was the neglect and decay of the land, with resulting shortfalls in the harvests. Thus, overall slavery in the nineteenth century contributed, if anything, to a stagnating economy. In private households, slaves or servants were not kept so much for profit as to gain prestige and demonstrate an owner's wealth.

On July 17, 2000, the system of debt bondage and forced labor was legally abolished and all debts were annulled. Around one hundred thousand men (*kamaiyā*) and women (*kamalarī*), but especially girls, were thereby freed, and, to some extent, even compensated and rehabilitated.[66] At the beginning many girls, particularly from the Tarai, were "sold on" by landholders to families in other parts of Nepal. Their parents, who had lost traditionally cultivated but unregistered land to inhabitants of the central regions, received meager compensation for their daughters and assurances they would be cared for. Despite being officially prohibited, this practice endured, but it was later largely stamped out following strong protests.

In sum, enslavement in nineteenth century Nepal must be seen as central to the loss of rights among the rural population and enslavable ethnic minorities, along with the so-called impure castes and the casteless. The laws made to this end exploited the Brahmanical ideas of purity and impurity in order to economically ruin and socially isolate a population already impoverished and marginalized after accusing them of moral offenses and imposing debt bondage. This chiefly affected the ethnic minorities, who did not observe Brahmanical purity regulations to begin with. The *Ain* directly benefited the ruling Bahun-Chhetri, especially the Rāṇā, in that it provided them with cheap labor as punishment for even minor "moral offenses."

Nothing shows this as clearly as the treatment of the Limbu, who, until their successful recruitment into the army in the third Nepal-Tibet war (1855–56), had belonged to the Enslavable castes, but thereafter were raised to the ranks of the Non-enslavable.[67] It was not some transformation in their way of life but rather purely political and economic Rāṇā interests that brought about this change. Agricultural debt and the pressure of high taxes and other levies of 50% and more were the reasons for the slavery and impoverishment of Nepal's small farmers.

Economy and Trade

Until well into the twentieth century foreign and domestic trade in Nepal was based on only a few resources, primarily agricultural products.[68] Artisanal and industrial products accounted for but a small portion of economic activity. Any surplus that could be exported to (British) India or Tibet consisted primarily of wood, rice, and wheat, and to a lesser extent of corn, molasses, wool, furs, ivory, jute, spices, medicinal herbs, and metalware, including bronze. Domestic trade mostly involved the exchange of salt, such dairy products as butter or clarified butter, honey, and animals (sheep, goats, ponies) and their wool, all from the mountainous regions, in return for grain, rice, and clothing from the lower-lying altitudes. Trade in timber occupied its own niche.

According to the *Divyopadeśa*, Pṛthvīnārāyaṇa Śāha did not want any trade with India or Tibet. He even forbade the wearing of clothing from other countries, thereby supporting the local weavers. He saw the flow of money to foreign countries as a loss to Nepal's productivity. The same idea is incorporated in the *Ain* as well; it explicitly recommends not to make any investments in India.[69] The British, by contrast, were interested in conducting trade with Nepal. They incorrectly assumed that great reserves of gold could be found there. Actually, the gold for coinage, including Nepalese specie, came from Tibet. The British needed timber and rice; both were consequently sold in great quantities to the East India Company. The British also assumed that they could sell the products of their wool industry better in Nepal than in India, an idea that only slowly took hold.

At the beginning of the nineteenth century, the state took on the role of trader, mostly in rice, and especially in the Tarai. As a result, private sellers had to subject themselves to prices dictated by the government or not sell their goods at all. The state was hardly interested in promoting business; on the contrary, it imposed numerous regulations on trade. Thus, in 1805 a regulation was issued stating that yogurt could only be sold in water-soaked clay vessels. Traders had to keep to certain routes. In some cases, restrictions were placed on where they could settle, and they were not permitted to sell any goods on which the state or its agents held a monopoly. In the Rāṇā period, this was the case for salt, oil, tobacco, and dried fish.

The state standardized weights and measures, attempted to prevent the adulteration of salt and milk, and made minimal preparations for bad harvests. When the prices for basic foodstuffs rose too high, it stepped in and ordered that all such items could only be sold at certain markets and only to state agents, who would then retail them at fixed prices. The state mint also did business, receiving silver and gold bars from Tibet and making a profit by minting copper coins as well.

A considerable part of state revenue was spent on weapons imports and the production of ammunition. Corresponding factories existed from 1793 on in the Kathmandu Valley and Tarai. As there was a lack of steel in Nepal, the imitations of British weapons never reached a sophisticated level of craftsmanship. The ammunition for firearms was a different matter, for sufficient amounts of saltpeter were available. Candra Śamśera also traded in Gorkha soldiers (mercenaries), whom he offered to the British in exchange for weapons.

What was trade like? Markets in which goods and wares could be offered for sale were rather rare, not least because there was still no extensive money economy at the beginning of the nineteenth century. While this was gradually becoming the norm in the Kathmandu Valley and in foreign trade, the north-south trade and domestic trade in the mountainous regions remained a barter economy into the twentieth century. Peasants took their products to their landlords or directly to their customers' households. In general, craftsmen produced only to order.

In addition, there was the problem of transporting goods, hindered by a lack of infrastructure and to some extent by internal levies—for instance, along the route from the Tarai to the Kathmandu Valley or to Tibet. The same is true of levies and duties on textiles or metalware, which sometimes had to be stamped with seals before they could be sold abroad. Transport involved days-long marches on foot and not all stretches could accommodate beasts of burden. Racing rivers had to be crossed, and steep, narrow paths along even steeper cliffs had to be negotiated. The high mountains could only be traversed over a few passes during the summer months. The main trade route went from Lhasa through Kuti to Patan, and from there continued southward through Hetauda to the Tarai. Another trade route joined Rasuwagadhi with Kirong in Tibet, and yet another led from Pokhara along the Kali-Gandaki River to Tibet, for which caravans with yaks and mules needed around a fortnight.

On March 1, 1792, a trade agreement was signed between Nepal and the East India Company, on the basis of which imports and exports were taxed at 2.5%. This meant a certain amount of protection for traders, but Nepal did not keep to the agreement, and it could not really be enforced. The same was true of a treaty of 1801. The British envoy Hodgson was of the opinion, however, that the agreement of 1792 had never been revoked and was thus still in force. He calculated the exports for 1830–31 at about one million rupees and the imports at about 1.6 million. In 1834, Prime Minister Bhīmasena Thāpā suggested a 4% duty on exports and imports, which was agreed to by both sides. Trade volume increased between 1830 and 1900 from an estimated three million rupees to forty million rupees.

During the Rāṇā Period, there was hardly any economic growth. Industrial or artisanal production remained limited to mainly clothing, wool blankets, arts and crafts, jewelry, and kitchen items. In principle, nothing changed until 1950. Offers by the British to produce new goods were not accepted. Nevertheless, the import of luxury goods from India continued to increase—above all, clothing made in the United Kingdom—as local manufacturers could not compete with them in quality.

Indian traders, including traders from the Tarai of (in the eyes of the palace and large parts of the populace) Indian descent, could move more or less freely within the country, but their businesses, too, were taxed. How this was done is revealed to some extent by a letter to an official (*jimmāvāla*) in the Tsum Valley sent by the regional general commander, Jagat Śamśera.[70] In this document, Jagat Śamśera reports that the Indian traders, who came every year to the upper Tsum Valley and paid the fee, long customary, of one pannier (*ḍoko*, approx. 55 pounds) of salt for six sheep and another one for a yak, still owed the said fee. The revenue had always been used to guarantee the security of the annual deployments of royal officials. By contrast, the traders from Tsum in India had always paid their fees. Jagat Śamśera therefore insisted that the nearest court should collect the outstanding fees.

Altogether, the Rāṇā Period was characterized by static agricultural activity and hardly any industrial production worth mentioning. The income from levies and duties mostly benefitted the Rāṇā elite, while the rural population remained in poverty or extremely modest circumstances. All of this was during a period when industrial production in India was making huge strides.

The economic structural weaknesses of the Rāṇā Period continue have an effect to the present day. Tax revenue in Nepal is still one of the lowest in Asia, there is still no industrial production worth mentioning, and there are still no necessary regulative mechanisms in place for economic progress.[71]

The consequences of this underdevelopment have been far-reaching. Nepal is one of the poorest countries on earth. It does not have enough work for its people, and the administrative apparatus hinders economic development, and particularly investment, through too much regulation. Regular blockades by India and strikes have a negative effect; corruption is endemic; there is no stable infrastructure; and education levels are far too low. Nonetheless, some progress can be charted. Economic growth has recovered, the provision of energy is increasing (especially with regard to electricity, there is real hope of sufficient supplies in the urban centers), road building is being expanded, and tourism and large amounts of development aid are stable, despite earthquakes and political unrest.[72]

The Legal and Administrative System

The legal system in Nepal, fixed in writing and codified, can be divided into three phases: (a) the legal system of royal decree in the pre-Rāṇā Period (before 1846), (b) the legal system of the *Ain* and its alterations in the Rāṇā Period (until 1951), and (c) the constitutional law of the modern monarchy (1951–63), the Panchayat Period (1963–90), and the period of multi-party democracy (since 1990).[73] Besides written law, there is much "customary law" (*loka- or deśadharma, deśācāra*) among the various ethnic groups and castes.

Apart from a few edicts, inscriptions, and manuscripts, all of the legal texts of Nepal until the mid-nineteenth century are more or less texts of classical Hindu law, Dharmaśāstras. Even the extensive *Nyāyavikāsinī* (fourteenth century), a Nevārī commentary on the *Nāradasmṛti* (a legal text from the fourth or fifth century), is more a translation of a Sanskrit commentary than an original work containing a divergent outlook on the law.

In the Licchavi, Malla, and pre-Rāṇā periods, the king was the highest legal authority, and he decided all important cases. He was aided by "royal priests" (*rājaguru*) and, from the nineteenth century on, by the "chief (religious) judge," the *dharmādhikārin*, who could co-decide in all matters of common law and morals, and in doing so often followed the norms of the Dharmaśāstras and customary laws. Thus, he could strip guilty persons of their caste, issue indulgences, charge fees, and impose prison sentences if someone had polluted himself by, for instance, engaging in illicit sexual intercourse. He could render those who had lost their caste status pure again—for example, by issuing them an indulgence in the form of a certificate of rehabilitation after specified atonement had been made and fees paid.

Ordeals were usual in gathering proof during court proceedings. In the late nineteenth century, the resident Brian H. Hodgson could still witness how accused persons were lowered into a deep tank or made to walk over fire to prove their innocence.[74] Among the punishments were death, imprisonment, branding, cutting off of a hand, confiscation of property, caste degradation or outcasting, and payment of fines.

In the Rāṇā Period, most cases were not decided by the king or prime minister but by various courts and offices.[75] In graver cases, however, the prime minister or else the Bhāradārī Kausala or Mulukī Aḍḍā still decided. Until the advent of Jaṅga Bahādura Rāṇā, though, the law remained unsystematically in the hands of the prime minister, local elders' councils, or caste committees.

In 1806, King Raṇabahādura Śāha issued a decree[76] that, for the first time, contained the idea of legal certainty, in that certain principles of state were now written down. Among these was the guarantee of house ownership, the prohibition of child slavery, the prohibition of exaggerated interest rates, and the right to fair treatment by local officials. Still, this document does show, as historian Ludwig Stiller writes, that "the administration was primarily concerned with revenue collection and that the villager's welfare was significant only in this context."[77]

Jaṅga Bahādura had many of these scattered regulations gathered together, improved, and summarized in the broad *Ain* of 1854. This text, which takes its name from the Persian word *āīn* for "law" (it received the epithet *mulukī* "royal, state" only in 1908), is a kind of constitution. Announced by Jaṅga Bahādura on January 6, 1854, in the name of King Surendra Vikrama Śāha, it was meant not least to systematize the caste system across the country, much to the distress of ethnic groups and other minorities for whom the fundamentally Hindu undertones of this law did not resonate. The *Ain* was often altered and shortened, especially under Vīra Śamśera, Candra Śamśera, and Juddha Śamśera. Under Mahendra Śāha (r. 1955–72), it was completely updated, and in 2016 it was revised for the last time before being renamed the *Nepāla Ain* in 2017.

The *Ain* of Jaṅga Bahādura Rāṇā incorporates many norms of classical Hindu law, but also of Indian Mogul administration and of "customary law." The importance of this text can be seen in, among other things, the fact that it was the first book printed in Nepal. It was compiled because, on his journey to Paris and London in 1850–51, Jaṅga Bahādura saw the printed book as an expression of Western superiority in an almost magical sense. It was said that the *Code Napoléon* of 1804 so impressed him that he established a "law council" (*Ain Kausal*), setting it the task of combining existing legal regulations into one homogeneous whole. The goal was to flaunt Nepal as the "only Hindu kingdom" where—in contrast to India, colonized or occupied by Muslims—cows, women, and Brahmins were protected, as stated at the beginning of the text. The goal too, however, was to dampen the contrast between the British rule of law and a haphazard feudal system.

The *Ain* is an extensive text with 163 articles, in which civil law is dealt with as much as criminal law. The great themes are landholdership, taxes and other levies, inheritance law, marriage and purity regulations, but also suttee, slavery, witchcraft, farting and spitting in public, and throwing chili powder into someone's eyes or onto their genitals—topics that show that priestly ideas of law and morals as well as the *vox populi* were listened to.

In the foreground is the hierarchy of castes, particularly the relationship between caste and status. "From now on, lower-ranking and higher-ranking subjects shall be punished equally according to guilt and caste," is stated at the beginning. This is actually a contradiction in terms, for on the one hand the law strives for the norm of equality, while on the other a distinction is drawn on the basis of caste. Ultimately, Jaṅga Bahādura Rāṇā was cementing the existing social hierarchy and the privileges of the aristocracy. Still, his intention to make binding legal principles that are in accordance with the rule of law is evident. An unusual number of documents supplement the legal norms set forth in the *Ain*. They are important, showing as they do how religious and legal norms were actually enforced.[78]

Indeed, the *Ain* strengthened legal certainty and social safeguards. Thus, it stipulates that the state must care for orphans or severely handicapped people. Corporal punishment was replaced to a great extent by fines. The trial by ordeals was abolished—such as waterboarding, in which the accused and the accuser (or two low-caste representatives of them) were thrown into a water tank, and the one who came up last was determined as being in the right. Some punishments did remain merciless: the death sentence (or, in the case of Brahmins, loss of caste) for killing a cow or for treason; enslavement and confiscation of property for many moral and property offenses; whipping for a first robbery, hacking off one hand for the second, and death for the third.

Law in Nepal, both prior to and within the *Ain*, differs from Western or Roman law primarily in the fact that the individual can hardly be separated from his or her social group. This is particularly true in cases of ritual impurity. A man who polluted himself, for example, through illicit sexual intercourse could be forbidden to have sexual intercourse with his own wife or dine with other family members. In addition, the pollution affected these peoples, too. But, above all, the law encoded in the *Ain* was not based on natural law. It was the law of the castes and the ethnic groups. What was punishable for one of them was not necessarily so for another, nor was the law distinguished from morality.

Perhaps the most important feature, however, is that the Hindu law of the *Ain* does not allow the king and the gods—state and religion—to be treated separately. The king also had religious power, inasmuch as the punishment he imposed could serve to expiate transgressions. Broadly speaking, religious punishment usually takes the form of an imposed atonement of some sort—for example, an oath to fast, a pilgrimage, prayers, or the offering of various gifts; secular punishment, by contrast, consists of prison, fines, and confiscations. Expiations involve absolution and the relation of a sinner to the gods and society; punishments involve public order and the rights of others. Atonement impacts another (e.g., one's next) life; punishment takes place in one's current life. Atonement is voluntary up to a point; punishments are not.

The *Ain* hardly distinguishes between atonement and punishment. Both were prescribed in certain cases. Caste degradation had severe social consequences. And yet there were cases in which the *Ain* declares "no punishment is to be imposed" (*khata lagdaina*), even though certain measures of expiation were foreseen: for example, rehabilitation (*patiyā*, *prāyaścit*); fines of atonement (*dastura*, *godāna*), which generally had to be paid to the *dharmādhikārin*; and certificates of indulgence (*patiyā-purjī*).[79] In truth, such a certificate could only be issued if a punishment had previously been imposed (prison, confiscation of property, branding, monetary fines), especially in cases of illicit sexual intercourse or offenses against consumption rules (e.g., eating together with casteless or other ritually impure persons or consumption of alcohol or other prohibited food items). Atonement could then be required in full or in part. If it had been imposed in a way that both cooked rice and water could again be accepted from caste and family members, then this signified a full re-integration into the caste. If it had been imposed only in relation to water, then the offending party was accepted only into a non-enslavable caste from which one might accept water.

From 1854 on, with the enactment of the *Ain*, a largely uniform legal and administrative system took shape. Soon after Jaṅga Bahādura Rāṇā's journey to Paris and London, English administrative concepts and titles (prime minister, commander-in-chief, lieutenant, colonel) would be introduced. The king or a "regent" (*nāyaba*) from the Śāha dynasty nominally oversaw the country, but the head of government was the *mukhtiyāra*, or prime minister. If there was a regent, he was senior to the *mukhtiyāra*. Certain families usually provided the prime minister: in the beginning particularly the Pā̃ḍe and Thāpā, and later the Kũvara Rāṇā and Śamśera Rāṇā. The power of the ruling families, however, was limited by an annual court day (introduced by Pṛthvīnārāyaṇa) featuring a "consultation" (*pajanī*), that all high-ranking officials and military officers had to attend. Occasionally they were fired, shunted off to other positions, or had their tasks reduced. Even the highest officials were not exempt from such outcomes. The dismissal of the powerful prime minister Bhīmasena Thāpā, for example, occurred in 1837 during such a consultation with Rājendra Śāha.

Apart from these positions, there were many subordinate or lesser civil service posts responsible for numerous special tasks. Under Candra Śamśera there were thirteen main offices and around sixty sub-offices in which there were many posts to be filled. In general, the higher ranks were reserved for the Rāṇā clan. Members of the *cautariyā* and respected Brahmins, Chhetri, Gurung, Magar, Limbu, and Newar could also receive posts, although mostly in the civil sections, and only up to the rank of *kājī* in the civil service and of colonel in the military. In many areas, the posts were virtually hereditary, the officials receiving *birtā* land that they could pass on to their sons.

The Rāṇā administration was an autocratic, despotic, strict system that conceded few liberties to its subjects. It was based on conformity, subordination, and currying favor. Relatives of the truly powerful occupied the higher ranks of officialdom. There was hardly any separation between civilian and military matters of administration. The administration rapidly grew into a paper-pushing bureaucracy in which everything had to be set down in writing. There were often no clear divisions of responsibility (one cause of corruption) and very high administrative fees. Above all, there was no political control over the administration, and of course no such thing as public control.

The Prohibition of Cow Slaughter

The Śāha and the Rāṇā virtually identified the prohibition against killing cattle as the Hindu definition of a state.[80] At the beginning of the *Ain*, for example, is stated: "In the Kaliyuga (i.e., the current, and worst, of the four eras of the world), this kingdom is the only Hindu kingdom, where cows, women, and Brahmins may not be killed." All three were held to be guarantors of religious purity. The Śāha dynasty left no doubt from the start that it regarded the cow as due special reverence and care. The name of their ancestral seat itself, Gorkhā (Skt. *gorakṣa*), means "protector of cows" and royal "cow sheds or cow pens" (*gośālā*) were set up in the foothills of the Himalaya, the Tarai, and the mountainous regions.[81]

How did the Śāha dynasty treat the numerous peoples under their rule who were not Hindu, some of whom consumed beef and even ritually killed cattle? Until recently, in the mountainous regions infertile or decrepit cows were pushed off a cliff and the act reported to the district supervisor as an accident. The Nepālī proverb "Does a fat cow die only because the tanner tells it to?" implies that not only hides were of interest. Did the Śāha kings let tolerance rule in such cases, or did they risk unrest through all too strict prohibitions? Were animals related to the cow, such as the yak, also categorized as holy? How were people treated who did not slaughter cows but did not refuse their meat?

Naturally, the prohibition against the killing of cattle could not be questioned.[82] It was valid without restriction over the whole of the kingdom and was part of the state ideology. Capital punishment was even imposed on occasion for breaches of it, as a letter from an Italian missionary in May 1740 makes clear. In 1805, Raṇabahādura Śāha decreed blanket capital punishment for this offense, presumably in order to make himself appear, in the wake of his erratic behavior, to be an exceptionally good Hindu.

From then on authorities were instructed to execute offenders in a particularly cruel manner. When word reached Kathmandu in 1806 that the local administration had absolved a tailor/musician (*damai*) in western Nepal suspected of having beaten a cow to death, the district headman was instructed to "cut flesh from the back (of the offender), to pour *cuk*, a kind of vinegar made from lemon-juice, and salt into the wound, to force him to eat his own flesh, and then to execute him." In Salyan in 1810 officials were told to skin those who killed oxen, or else to impale them or to hang them by their feet until they starved to death, and to enslave their immediate relatives. Later, in the *Ain*, the maximum penalty was changed to life imprisonment; in the ninth revision of the code, this was changed to twelve years.

Despite these intimidating examples, the full force of the law was not always applied. Yaks and hybrids between yaks and other cattle were not regarded in such extremely holy terms.[83] Whoever killed one at the start of the nineteenth century was not threatened with punishment, and certainly not capital punishment. Later, killers of yaks were also punished, even in the most remote regions of Nepal, but always provided that the central government had heard about the matter. Thus, in 1853 two Tibetan families living in the district of Humla in the extreme northwest of the kingdom were in such distress and so ill that they slaughtered four yak calves to survive. Afraid of the penalty, they fled to China. When Prime Minister Jaṅga Bahādura Rāṇā heard about this, he permitted the families to return after paying two rupees. In the *Ain*, a regulation on the killing of yaks was first added in the 1871 version, a violation that carried a fine of forty rupees; still, this was much less severe than life imprisonment, threatened in cases of the intentional killing of cows.

The Śāha and Rāṇā had other good reasons to overlook cases here and there. They needed cowhides for weapon covers and for transporting saltpeter. For this reason, certain ethnic groups or castes, such as the Limbu, Tibetans, Sherpa, Hayu, Lepcha, and Sarki, were repeatedly or regularly told to deliver the hides of buffalo, elephants, tigers, or other wild animals, but also cowhides, although they could sometimes buy their way free of this obligation.[84] The Gurung and Lama to the east of the Trishuli River were able to obtain exemption from such provisioning. However, in return they were required to enter the army and to promise to honor Brahmins and no longer eat beef. Both, the respect shown to Brahmins and abstinence from beef, were what made them, in the view of the rulers, upright and courageous soldiers.

The Śāha and Rāṇā rulers had recognized that it was more lucrative to raise taxes on certain vices than to constantly prohibit people from indulging in them. Consequently, those ethnic groups in the mountain regions and also some castes in the valleys who ate the meat of dead cattle, called *sinu* or *sino*, were forced to replenish state coffers. Under Gīrvāṇayuddha Śāha, certain groups were permitted to consume *sinu* if they delivered a portion of animal hides as compensation. Only if they did not comply with this obligation did they have to pay fines. In Solukhumbu, an area mainly inhabited by Sherpa, it was even possible, in return for an annual "expiatory payment" (*cokho-daṇḍa*), to eat the flesh of slaughtered cows.[85] Only when the central government in Kathmandu heard of this was a general prohibition against slaughtering cattle issued there too. Officials sent to the capital of this region, however, reported that very many inhabitants would have to be sentenced to death or enslaved if this prohibition were to be strictly enforced. It was then decided that only cases after 1804 would carry the capital sentence; all other offenders and their relatives were to be sold into slavery.

All of these various regulations were summarized in Article 66 ("On Cow Slaughtering") of the *Ain*, which shows that already by the middle of the nineteenth century a clear and general legal prohibition against slaughtering cattle was in place in Nepal. In India, this only came about in 1949 through Article 48 of the Indian Constitution, at first a very vague guideline in which any religious reasons were avoided, given the basic right to religious freedom important to, among others, Muslims.

The regulations of the *Ain* point to the well-known ambivalent attitude to the cow as a holy creature and as just a farm animal. The law attempts to give due consideration to both aspects. Whoever strikes a cow when working and injures it or unintentionally kills it has hardly anything to worry about; but whoever injures a cow with a weapon will be enslaved. The provisions of the *Ain* were unquestionably meant to protect the holiness and life of cows. The cow as a symbol of the king's orthodoxy and a unifying state ideology was foregrounded, not the animal as such.

The general protection of animals is no more the province of the *Ain* than is *ahiṃsā* (the obligation not to harm other beings) or vegetarianism. Kings, as members of the warrior class, were not obliged in any case to practice *ahiṃsā*, and in Nepal, moreover, the king was always an enthusiastic hunter. Still, there are signs of *ahiṃsā*. Thus, hunting and carrying out capital punishment are forbidden on certain holy days; and twenty years after the first *Ain*, the yak, too, was made a holy bovine, although limits were placed on punishment for offenses. Of course, animal sacrifices remain as exceptions. This certainly originated in the old teaching that a sacrificial animal gets liberated after being sacrificed. Sacrificial animals themselves accept their killing voluntarily, so it is said in Nepal, and they indicate this by shaking their bodies; that they are usually encouraged to do so by dripping water in their ear or on their head is a concern only for those of little faith.

The cow as a symbol and tool of nation-building through Hinduization—this is what often was foremost in mind when writing regulations into the law. It was not about actionable justice and the creation of legal certainty; it was above all a guarded and, when looked at more closely, rather symbolic protection of the cow. It appears that everyone could make do with the law: Brahmins had the legal guarantee that the cow was protected; rulers legitimized their rule in a religious guise and did not endanger it by issuing decrees of excessive harshness (e.g., forbidding the consumption of beef)—decrees that could not in any case be implemented in the more remote regions. And the heterogeneous population of Nepal could find enough loopholes in the law, if need be, to avoid deviating from custom.

Education and Traditional Learning

In traditional South Asia, education meant private or monastic training to become a priest or scholar. This was the case in Nepal, too. Sanskrit education was limited to certain classes of society and usually to males, mainly Brahmins and higher-ranking Chhetri. This education took place within the so-called Gurukula system, in which the pupil, from a young age, lives in the house-cum-school of the teacher and first acquires a certain basic knowledge through the frequent repetition of texts—a knowledge of grammar and also of Vedic texts, astronomy, "ritual texts" (*karmakāṇḍa*), and poetry. Those thus trained were sought after as officials since they could read and write, or else they became priests. In Buddhist circles, the education was similar, although the program was different and the teaching took mostly place in a monastery, where texts of the canon were memorized.

This traditional model of education is, then, a master-pupil relationship (*guru-śiṣya-sambandha*). Teaching takes place in a dogmatic fashion; personal opinions are not entertained. Knowledge in religious or spiritual communities is often regarded as a privilege passed on from the charismatic guru to his successor. The identification of the pupil or successor with the guru, master, or founder leads to a kind of "family" (*kula*), "school" (*śākhā*), or "congregation" (*saṃgha*), in which spiritual succession is of foremost importance.

These master-pupil arrangements provided the seedbed for the rise of outstanding scholarship. Nepal was at various times famous for its scholarship, and many monks from Tibet, China, and India made pilgrimages to active sites to recite, copy, and illustrate texts. The eleventh and twelfth centuries, in which the Nepalese-Tibetan monks Atīśa, Jñānakara, Marpa, and Ralo Dorje Drak came to the Kathmandu Valley, proved to be a particularly fertile period.

A Western-orientated system of education did not exist in Nepal before the end of the nineteenth century.[86] Daniel Wright, a physician at the British Residency, could still write in 1877: "The subject of schools and colleges in Nepāl may be treated as briefly as that of snakes in Ireland. There are none."[87] In contrast to India, Great Britain had only minor influence on the educational system in Nepal, one reason for the delay in modernization. Bhīmasena Thāpā permitted Bengalese teachers to instruct his family and received newspapers from England and India, but not until Prime Minister Jaṅga Bahādura Rāṇā did things begin to change. In the beginning he could neither read nor write, and later on he still had a child-like writing hand, but after his journey to England in 1851 he had a private school set up in the palace, and teachers brought from England primarily for his sons. In addition to English, this Darbar School offered history, geography, mathematics, Sanskrit, Hindi, Bengali, and Persian. The school was renamed Darbar High School in 1877. In 1891, it moved to a larger building west of the Rani Pokhari (pond), where it was opened increasingly to Śāha and Rāṇā children and, from 1902 on, to children from other social classes. The curriculum hardly included Nepal itself; the geography and history of Nepal were expressly forbidden subjects; and the language of instruction was English. At first, the school was affiliated with Kolkata University and then with Patna University. The few students who went to India through this channel received scholarships from the government. One of the first was Prime Minister Candra Śamśera, who passed his examinations in Kolkata in 1884.

A "Sanskrit school" (*pāṭhaśālā*) also operated in the same building that provided accommodations for the students. In these *pāṭhaśālās* the subjects taught included the Veda, grammar, astrology, and poetry. On the whole, however, Sanskrit instruction was not terribly respected by the Rāṇā, indicated by the low payments to pandits.

For a long time, Nepal did not have an institution of higher learning of its own, but on August 28, 1918, Prime Minister Candra Śamśera opened Trichandra College, in which natural sciences and English up to the intermediate level were taught and qualified students could then continue their education in India. King Tribhuvan attended the opening and Candra Śamśera supposedly said afterward that this would be the beginning of the end of the monarchy in Nepal. For the same reason, he also prohibited native newspapers from being read.[88] Indeed, students sent under state support to India in a private capacity brought back ideas that the government under Candra Śamśera did not like at all.[89] Thus, scholar Madhav Raj Joshi went to prison for two years and was later exiled, after he had represented, in the presence of both the king and the prime minister, the Indian reform movement Arya Samaj in a "public disputation" (*śāstrārtha*) in July 1905. At times he appeared to be gaining the upper hand in the disputation, but when the old pandits alleged that he held the position that Paśupati was only a stone, he was humiliatingly chased through town and arrested. Subsequently, the conditions placed upon receiving an education and even medical treatment abroad were hardened.

Gradually, Deva and Candra Śamśera set up further primary schools (*bhāṣā pāṭhaśālā*) throughout the entire country. Among other things, reading and writing in the Devanāgarī script, arithmetic, history, and applied geography were taught in them. In these schools, which did not require school fees, the language of instruction was Nepālī, taught according to standards set by the Gorkhā Bhāṣā Prakāśinī Samiti, a committee for the spread of the Nepālī language, even though at first there were no corresponding textbooks. One reason for this extension was the British need for Gurkha soldiers who could read and write. But implementing the more complex administrative regulations also required officials who were literate and had a better general education. To this end, "administrative schools" (*śrestā pāṭhaśālā*) were also opened; these concentrated exclusively on training administrators and personnel for the judiciary. From 1910 on, these institutions were supplemented by a special state institution, the Pāsajāñca Aḍḍā, under the control of the royal priest. Its teachers provided instruction in preparing documents, calculating, *dharmaśāstra*, bookkeeping, and other subjects including, later, "fingerprints" (*aũṭhā*). This last was certainly needed due to the many cases of forgery and also to the population's continuing low rates of literacy.

Almost all schools were inadequately equipped, as various documents from the early twentieth century strongly suggest. Thus, in 1940, one request was for mats for a school in Gorkha for pupils to sit on; in the same year, an order was issued by the prime minister to spend 604 rupees on a primary school, and three years later a further order to set up more schools in the same area. In 1921, Candra Śamśera issued an order to all revenue offices to use money from the Pāṭhaśālā Guṭhī to pay for school expenses, and there were repeated applications to move money to be used for the maintenance of schools.[90] On the whole, though, the Rāṇā held back from providing access to education for the populace. As a result, at the end of the Rāṇā Period, the illiteracy rate was an estimated 98%, including some members of the royal family.

Healing Systems and Shamanism

Health care as practiced in Nepal has left the first traces of its history in the Licchavi inscriptions, in which an *ārogyaśālā*, an institution for the care of the sick, is often mentioned.[91] In the Malla Period, Pratāpa Malla (r. 1641–74) distributed Ayurvedic medicine to the populace at the palace. Western medicine arrived in Nepal with the missionaries around 1660; they set up a small health post in Bhaktapur, even though they themselves were not doctors. Not much more information on health care in the Nepalese middle period is available.

The British brought physicians to their Residency: Francis Buchanan Hamilton (1762–1829), Henry Ambrose Oldfield (1822–71), Daniel Wright (1826–98?), and others, some of whom were also interested in healing plants. Oldfield reported such diseases as malaria, cholera, tuberculosis, and smallpox and noted the high rate of infant mortality. The medical knowledge these doctors possessed, though, almost exclusively benefitted the palace and high-ranking Rāṇā. Only from the 1930s on were some ordinary Nepalese treated in the British Legation Hospital, which received subsidies for this from Juddha Śamśera.

Hygienic conditions were poor due to a lack of clean water, canals, and vaccination campaigns. Epidemics easily and repeatedly broke out. In April 1898, for instance, bubonic plague struck, which led to ten days of strict quarantine for everybody coming from India to Nepal. No city administration existed to deal with such problems until 1919, at which time Keśara Śamśera, the son of Candra Śamśera, was appointed to head it.

Khokana Leper House, established in 1857, is said to have been the first hospital, although it served primarily to isolate leprosy patients. During the Rāṇā Period, prime ministers Vīra Śamśera and Candra Śamśera were behind the establishment of the first countrywide health service. Candra himself went to Kolkata several times for treatment of tuberculosis or had doctors come from the United Kingdom. In 1889, Vīra Śamśera had Bir Hospital in Kathmandu built in memory of Pṛthvī Vīra Vikrama Śāha. That same year later saw the construction of the Cholera Hospital in Teku, a leprosy hospital in Tripureshwar, and further hospitals in Birganj, Jaleshwar, Hanuman Nagar, Taulihawa, and Nepalganj. Candra Śamśera was responsible for the Chandra Lok Hospital in Bhaktapur, built in 1903, and the Prithvi-Chandra hospitals in Palpa, Palhi (Parasi), Doti, and Ilam. At the instigation of the then crown prince Tribhuvan Śāha (r. 1951–55), Tribhuvan-Chandra hospitals were built in Dhankuta, Bhadrapur, Sarlahi, and Rangeli. In 1918, the Naradevi Ayurvedic Hospital was added, in 1924 the Lalitpur Hospital in Patan, and in 1925 the Tri-Chandra Military Hospital in Kathmandu.

Documents show inadequate funds for hospital workers and equipment, along with qualified medical personnel, when these hospitals were set up. Drastic methods were sometimes used to solve these problems.[92] Thus, in 1890 Prime Minister Vīra Śamśera ordered that land be given to people whose properties were taken three years earlier for the construction of Bir Hospital. For a long time this hospital, severely damaged in the earthquake of 2015 and rebuilt by China in 2020–22, was the only hospital in the capital. In 1896, the queen (Sāhilā Baḍāmahārānī) supposedly donated 6,000 rupees to the hospital *guṭhī* from the sale of land.

An 1899 document outlining fifteen duties of hospital personnel shows that staff were expected to be present at the hospital around the clock, save for two to three months of holiday every three years. Doctors (Nep. *ḍākṭara*), among them several from India, had both medical and administrative duties, and all other personnel were subordinate to them and obliged to follow their orders. Personnel received a monthly salary, and doctors had to place timely orders at Bir Hospital for any medicine that needed to be imported.

Because of a lack of training and experience, native doctors often practiced a good deal of quackery. The *Ain* of 1854 attempted to prevent this by ordering that doctors personally had to take the medicine prescribed to or compounded for a patient when the latter died after taking it. If the doctor did not survive, it was considered that justice had been done.

* * *

Alongside state and allopathic health care are the various practices of traditional medicine: Ayurveda and local healers and shamans.[93] Ayurveda, literally "knowledge of (long) life," is an old holistic system of medicine, long fixed in writing, that has spread globally, including as a wellness method. It was developed and recorded in Sanskrit texts such as the *Suśrutasaṃhitā* (parts from the first millennium BCE) and the *Carakasaṃhitā* (sixth century CE, parts from 100–200 CE), and is based on a harmony of body, sense organs, spirit, and soul, as well as on the balance of the three "bodily humors" (*doṣa*), the elementary life energies: wind (*vāta*), fire/gall (*pitta*), and water/phlegm (*kapha*). Ayurveda further contains a fully developed botanically based therapy, comprehensive teachings on diet, and teachings on pediatrics, surgery, demonic possession, toxicology, and sex education or (in)fertility.

Nepal is home to a host of Ayurvedic hospitals, chemists, and doctors (*vaidya*). The traditional teacher-pupil training of doctors was supplemented in 1928 by a special school, the Nepal Rajakiya Ayurveda Vidyalaya, which was transferred in 1972 to the Ayurveda Campus of Tribhuvan University. The Singha Darbar Vaidya Khana, established by Juddha Śamśera, is an Ayurvedic pharmacy with over one hundred Ayurvedic medications. Originally only accessible to the Rāṇā, it was opened to all citizens by King Tribhuvan.

Local healers use a multitude of methods, the most frequent being exorcism, self-compounded medications, pulse diagnosis, rice oracles, mantras, and amulets.[94] Ayurvedic healers, charismatic healers, high-caste holy priests, and shamans are regarded as local healers. Often married women possessed by goddesses act as healers—the so-called Hāratīmātā or Ajimā. Holy priests (*gubhāju*, *lāmā*), ascetics, "astrologers" (*jyotiṣa*), and Brahmins usually do not hold healing séances and rarely give out medicines; rather, they perform rituals, such as text recitations or "fire sacrifices" (*homa*), to which healing powers are ascribed. "Illnesses" for which local healers tend to be consulted include spells, curses, unfavorable stellar configurations, the introduction of foreign substances into the body, lack of vitality, social conflicts (especially within families), and persecution by spirits and witches.

* * *

The largest group of healers is formed by shamans (*jhā̃krī*, *dhāmī*), who are found throughout Nepal, but especially in the mountain regions, and particularly among the Limbu, Rai, Sunuvar, Sherpa, Kami, Tamang, Gurung, Magar, Lapche, Chantel, and Hyolmo ethnic groups, but also among the Khasa-Arya.[95] They are usually males characterized by the ability to undergo possession, during which they can mediate between spirit forces of illness and patients. Shamans can call up spirits, negotiate with them, and give direct commands, which they do with the aid of a number of accessories, especially drums. But they can also go on journeys in the spirit world. Shamanism complements other religions in Nepal but does not question them.

One becomes a shaman through an experience of awakening and an initiation. A guiding teacher is necessary since a complex oral body of knowledge is transmitted, for example, through long songs and mantras. In individual cases, the shaman's calling can even be inherited. The central method of treatment is the night séance, conducted mostly in the house of the afflicted person and in the presence of family members. There the shaman falls into a trance and can, with the cooperation of the spirits and gods, see to the patient's welfare. Among the spirits, which are often to be found at crossroads, are local gods, animals or inanimate forces, the souls of people who

Figure 7.4 A *ramma*, "shaman," of the Magar in Taka, 1984, with his drum during a ritual journey in the course of a two-night séance of healing. Photo by Michael Oppitz.

died by suicide or some other unnatural death, the unquiet souls of dead relations, or the souls of other shamans. Not all of these spirits are malevolent. The shaman's expertise consists in knowing how to balance or satisfy these various forces. His most important instrument during his sessions is the drum.

The drums are used in healing séances. The shaman sends sound signals to the otherworldly beings, driving them away or pacifying them, thus warding off evil. With his drum, he sings the myths of creation or goes on journeys to the ancestors and gods, or into the nether world. He summons these beings with his drum and lets them enter him, so they can help him. With his drum, too, he is a healer: he diagnoses, devises therapies, and predicts the future. With the drum, he accentuates the meter of the songs, sets the beat for dances, passes into a trance, and signals the beginning and end of the songs. The drum is also the healer's companion on his journeys to the other world, and the vehicle on which he rides, flies, or otherwise travels. The shaman grows older together with his instrument, which accompanies him from ritual birth to his death—until, in the end, it hangs in a tree over the grave mound of its former wielder.

The repeated noise of the drum is also a warning to malevolent forces, which must be driven off because they beset the ill. Then the drum becomes something very like a weapon or shield, and the drumstick a threatening staff.

Many drums are painted, even though the original painted decoration may have smeared or faded. These decorations let people know about the shaman's universe, inhabited by people, deities, spirits, and mythical beings. The Magar use white chalk in liquid form for drawing, applying it with a stick and then drying the painted decoration in front of a fire. Laypeople, too, are permitted to do this if they are familiar with the pictorial repertoire, which includes such cosmographical content as the sun, the moon, or stars; animals; erotic motifs; and objects associated with ritual practice—even the drum itself.

Hunting and Elephants

Elephants have always been valued throughout Nepal's history. In the Śāha and Rāṇa periods they were used, for instance, as working animals, especially on hunting tours and in the timber industry, and by the military when patrolling the border.[96] A decree issued by King Gīrvāṇayuddha Śāha in 1813 and addressed to all those responsible for the elephant stables states: "If you yield so much as an inch of our territory, you commit a serious crime."

Most documents deal with elephants that were needed for hunting or the pleasure of royalty and the aristocracy. The Śāha and Rāṇā loved their hunting expeditions, which could last for weeks and employ hundreds of elephants. Prime Minister Jaṅga Bahādura Rāṇā was especially enthralled by these majestic animals. His fame partly derived from his supposedly having overcome a rampaging elephant with his bare hands during one hunt.

Royal hunting in the Rāṇā Period took place mainly in the Tarai, in the area of today's Chitwan National Park, and was staged on a grand scale, especially for foreign guests. A hunt organized by Candra Śamśera for King George V in December 1911 attracted particular attention. Within ten days, the hunting team shot dead eighteen rhinos, thirty-nine tigers and four sloth bears. The king is said to have killed eight rhinos and twenty-one tigers.[97]

Elephants were, in addition, a symbol of status and power. All elephants captured in Nepal belonged to the king. The association with the elephant-headed god Gaṇeśa brought with it the promise of good fortune and religious advantages. This could clearly last be seen in 1975 at the coronation of King Birendra Śāha and his wife Aiśvaryā, when these two led the procession on the backs of magnificently adorned elephants.

The wealth of elephants in Nepal gave rise to the habit among rulers to make gifts of them—for instance, at the weddings of high-ranking personages, on the occasion of the initiation of their sons, and as tokens of state hospitality.[98] Thus, the king of Morang had to send seven elephants to the Moguls as annual tribute, and the British laid claim to the same number in 1772 as a substitute for land in the Tarai that they had relinquished to Pṛthvīnārāyaṇa. The most unusual present is probably the elephant given in the *kāṭṭo-grahaṇa* ritual to a finely equipped and dressed Brahmin for taking upon himself the impurity of the king after the latter's death—allegedly, among other things, by eating a piece of the dead king's brain—and then leaving Nepal, or at least the Kathmandu Valley, on the animal.[99] This occurred in 2001 after the massacre in the royal palace, although the two chosen Brahmins remained in the country, some say after appealing to their rights as citizens; others claim because they had not received sufficient gifts.

The elephants were all given personal names, with the males often receiving the addition Prasāda (lit. "favor') and the females being named after the goddess Kālī. Some elephants became famous, such as Aḍaṅga Bahādura and Jala Prasāda, who was supposedly trained with the help of the prominent elephant Śrī Prasāda and enjoyed great respect. The "mahouts" (*māhuta*) sometimes gained recognition, too, occasionally receiving land from the king for their work.

The palace always apprised capturing and training elephants. As a rule, training was carried out with young elephants, who were made accustomed to hearing gun shots, and seeing fire or wild animals such as tigers and rhinoceros. The methods used in training were certainly cruel. Several people were involved: the mahouts, the "stable master" (*dāroga*), and the "master of the elephant grooms" (*rāuta*).

It is not clear how many elephants were under royal control in the nineteenth century. British major Orfeur Cavenagh reported that two hundred elephants were captured in 1850. In 1942, forester Evelyn Arthur Smythies spoke of several hundred animals, and in 1876 Britain's Prince of Wales, supposedly saw eight hundred animals. In 2011, between 109 and 142 wild and

208 tamed elephants were counted in Nepal.[100] At present, there are six state elephant stables, and the Nepalese government protects the wild elephants in five reserves.

The value of an elephant was comparable to that of a house. Elephants with only one tusk were considered especially valuable because of their resemblance to the god Gaṇeśa. In a Nepalese veterinary tract, these animals were proclaimed to be the kings of the elephants, and as such particularly pleasing to human kings. It goes on to say: "All problems vanish in the presence of such an animal. Wherever there is a one-tusked elephant, there pleasure and well-being are found."

Rāṇā Architecture

For reasons of prestige, the Śāha and Rāṇā spent a good deal of time looking after the royal towns (especially Kathmandu) and other places.[101] They introduced new ways of building and considerably altered the urban setting. But the Śāha did not start out as revolutionary innovators. The changes to the palace in Kathmandu during Pṛthvīnārāyaṇa's reign still retained many structural elements of Malla architecture. This is true also of the seven-story (originally nine-story) palace in Nuvakot, which was conquered by Pṛthvīnārāyaṇa Śāha in 1744 and renovated by him in 1762. It is true of the Gorkha palace, which received its present form around 1780; as well as the extension to the palace in Kathmandu and of Basantapur Tower, which was erected by Pṛthvīnārāyaṇa around 1770. The north wing added to the palace in Patan, probably by Raṇabahādura Śāha in about 1790, is indebted to Newar architecture in terms of material, although the encircling balcony, the glazed windows, and the Venetian blinds on the third story, together with the white-framed windows, are already a harbinger of architectural change. The Śāha and Rāṇā wanted to immortalize themselves by means of new, imposing imperial buildings and introducing a type of architecture that has come to be known as the Mogul or Lucknow style, commonly favored by the Nawabs of Oudh in North India. Nepal's rulers had intensive contacts with the administration and with traders in Lucknow, Kolkata, and Patna, to which they sent "ambassadors" (*vakila*) and brought back new ideas and many an architect.

The new architecture re-imagined the Islamic–North Indian tradition in the neo-classical style that the British East India Company had introduced in that region. Dating from 1880, it is characterized by entryways with

Corinthian columns and corresponding porticos or staircases, pargetting, glazed windows and window shutters, and onion-shaped domes. Thus arose monumental, whitewashed residences and domed temples, which contrasted with the red brick architecture of the Malla.

The new styles finally experienced their breakthrough under Prime Minister Bhīmasena Thāpā, who had accompanied Raṇabahādura Śāha to Varanasi. Starting in 1806, he had a residence built for himself in Lagan in southeast Kathmandu, the middle section of which was plastered and whitewashed. In 1820, he had Bagh Darbar built, again in the southeast, and then another residence in Chhauni, which later became an "arsenal" (*silkhānā*); then in 1860 a weapons museum; and finally, in 1930, the National Museum. These buildings, which were later altered and extended by Candra and Juddha Śamśera, are entirely in the Mogul style.

Among the great building complexes is an extensive palace that Jaṅga Bahādura Rāṇā and his brothers had built a few hundred meters further along the Bagmati River, between 1847 and 1877, of which, however, only a few individual sections have been preserved. Stylistically, it corresponds with the three-story north wing of the Hanuman Dhoka palace, which replaced an older building around 1822. Sometime around 1847 Jaṅga Bahādura's brother, Raṇoddīpa Siṃha Kũvara, seized Nārāyaṇahiti Palace, which had originally belonged to Fateh Jaṅga Śāha, who had been killed in the Koṭa Massacre. In 1881 the Rāṇā forced the Śāha to make this building henceforth their residence. In 1889 it was greatly extended, and in 1969 Mahendra had it replaced by a modern building planned by American architect Benjamin Polk (1916–2001). Like the old palace at Hanuman Dhoka, this new palace serves now as a museum.

Among the Śamśera Rāṇā, Vīra Śamśera was especially active in construction. At least fifteen new buildings in the Lucknow style are ascribed to him, among them the residences Seto Darbar (1890–92), Lal Darbar (1893), which later became the five-star hotel Yak and Yeti, Phora Darbar (1895), and Bahadur Bhavan (1889) on Kantipath, which later became the first hotel in Nepal. A further palace, Agni Bhavan, which was built in 1894 by Prime Minister Vīra for his brother General Jita Śamśera Rāṇā and later belonged to General Agni Śamśera Rāṇā, the son of Juddha Śamśera Rāṇā, was converted in 1964 into a hotel.

In 1903, Candra Śamśera had the largest palace in the Kathmandu Valley built, Singha Darbar, which originally had over 1,400 rooms and at the time was celebrated as one of the largest buildings in South Asia. It eventually became the seat of government and remains so to this day. But in 1973 it was almost completely destroyed by a devastating fire, and in 2015 became unusable in parts owing to that year's earthquake. Around 1913 Candra Śamśera also built Babar Mahal, part of which is now an elegant shopping arcade with boutiques and restaurants.

With regard to temples, Bhīmasena Thāpā introduced a new style: the domed temple. Among the earliest is Bhīmabhakteśvara in Kathmandu, built in 1823 to show that Bhīmasena was a true "devotee" (*bhakta*) of Śiva. Such temples, housing a *liṅga*, were built in large numbers and widely varying styles, especially around the Paśupatinātha temple, which had already received many such benefactions over the centuries, given that kings, nobles, and rich merchants wanted to immortalize themselves with a votive *liṅga* close to the patron deity of the land.

These votive *liṅgas* or Śivālayas ("abode of Śiva") rarely serve any clear-cut ritual function. As a rule, they are "quiet" shrines, where at best a priest will come in the morning to perform necessary acts of worship. One could call them a kind of memorial, since the shrines were erected in the name of the donor or of a deceased close relative. In the inscriptions the occasion is recorded: for the fame (*-prakāśeśvara*), on the liberation (*-mukteśvara*), or in devotional memory (*-bhaktīśvara*, *-bhakteśvara*) of the deceased, which epithets are attached to the name of the one so honored. The larger temples, often displaying pointed blind windows, ornamentation all around the building, tendrils, and—in front of the main entrance—bells, are sometimes surrounded by four smaller shrines at the corners of the platform.

Some of the largest temples in Deopatan belong to this type.[102] Jaṅga Bahādura Rāṇā began the trend in 1864 with Viśvarūpa in the middle of the Śleṣmāntaka woods east of the Paśupatinātha temple, nearly 100 feet high. In 1870, on the other side of the Bagmati River, the Pañcadevala was erected, comprising a group of five votive temples on a raised platform: the central Surendreśvara for the founder, Surendra Śāha (1829–81); Rājendreśvara for his father, Rājendra Śāha; Devarājeśvara for his two wives, Rājyalakṣmī and Sūryalakṣmī; and Trailokyeśvara for his son. The Śāha also commemorated themselves in the Guhyeśvarī temple area with further Śivālaya temples, among them Tripureśvara, the country's third-largest step temple, which Queen Lalitatripurasundarī had erected in 1817/18 in memory of her husband Raṇabahādura Śāha; it is still in the old Newar style.

The Rāṇā built some sixty votive *liṅgas*, among other things, in the Mṛgasthalī grove; they are placed around the *śikhara* temple of

Gorakhanātha, the legendary founder of Kanaphaṭṭā, whose followers are housed there. Another Rāṇā initiative is the complex of "fifteen Śivālaya" (*Pandhraśivālaya*) on the east bank of the Bagmati, which were built between 1859 and 1864 in memory of the victims of the Koṭa Massacre of 1846. The oval Jitajaṅgaprakāśeśvara, built in 1874 in his own name by Jaṅga Bahādura Rāṇā's second son, Jita Jaṅga, is one of a kind.

In addition, private persons had temples built from time to time, such as the Rāmacandra temple may that was erected in 1871 by Sanak Siṃha Lahūrī Ṭaṇḍan Chetrī in Battisputali near Deopatan.[103] Jaṅga Bahādura Rāṇā, who had married Sanak Siṃha's sister Kumārī Devī in 1839, promoted him immediately after the Koṭa Massacre to chief captain, and later, after he had stood with Jaṅga Bahādura in 1857 on the British side in Lucknow during the Great Mutiny, he was promoted to commanding colonel general.

The Legacy of the Śāha and Rāṇā Periods

For centuries, the geographical, social, and political situation of the country had not allowed for the formation of any durable power structures. Jaṅga Bahādura Rāṇā and some of his successors had provided some stability, but only in exchange for a despotic oligarchy with numerous victims and an arbitrary, fragile, and threatening style of rule. This Rāṇā era, which lasted until 1951, has been characterized as a century of tyranny that has entered history books as a dark time, a description that holds true for Śāha rule as well. However, this perception is deceptive,[104] for the Rāṇā were, at the same time, responsible for many modern developments, such as the unification of law, the prohibition of widow self-immolation and slavery, and the introduction of schools and hospitals. And until the middle of the twentieth century it was the Rāṇā, not the Śāha, who sought contact with the British.

Despite all their changes, the Rāṇā era inherited old structural weaknesses in three main areas: the country's geographical remoteness and political isolation, its scattered economic, social, and administrative organization, and political sharing of power. Indeed, in the Nepal of the nineteenth century, people lived for the most part cut off from the outside world, and were for the most part self-sufficient, lacking the fruits of the industrial successes in other parts of the world including India. However, despite the infrequent famine and massive levies, the population was usually able to cultivate enough rice, other grains, and vegetables. There was more than enough firewood. Textiles, agricultural machinery, and even pistols and rifles were all produced domestically. Trade with Tibet, China, and India brought in some additional items. A surplus facilitated a flowering of culture and craftsmanship.

Those who wished to leave the Kathmandu Valley had to be prepared for a difficult march on foot. News of events in the valley reached other parts of the country only with considerable delay. Conversely, rulers in the Kathmandu Valley did not always know what was happening in the other regions. Comprehensive control was virtually impossible. The administration under Jaṅga Bahādura Rāṇā, which made good use of the round-the-clock postal and courier service, was better organized than its predecessors, but the delivery chain often failed at some point, and hardly any decree ever reached all villages.

Nevertheless, paper documents were sent to nearly every corner of the land, not least in order to be able to more effectively collect taxes with the authority of the written word. This fiscal goal significantly increased the use of documents. In any case, the responsibilities of public administration were for the most part limited to military, fiscal, and—to a small extent—police tasks. Apart from protecting the royal house, officials had to collect fees, taxes, and other revenue, and maintain public order, including moral and religious standards. The great mass of paper documents has to do with such matters, and these are the sorts of things the *Ain*, Nepal's first constitution, deals with for the most part.

There was hardly any separation of the private from the public sphere. The Rāṇā administration governed right into the bedroom. The religious judge employed at the palace, the *dharmādhikārin*, demanded indulgences for all kinds of moral transgressions, such as offenses against food regulations and illicit sexual intercourse. Despite this exaggerated control on the part of the administration or state, there were hardly any state educational or medical facilities at the beginning of the Rāṇā era. There was a widespread lack of urban planning, irrigation systems, canalization, supraregional transport routes, and sufficient bridges.

People in the Kathmandu Valley were suspicious of almost everyone, particularly people from in the mountain regions and the Tarai. Every official had to be confirmed in the annual *pajanī* ceremony, and even loyal and proven people were not infrequently replaced. A life-long right to work in the administration, or at least a guarantee due to descent or status, was not to be expected. A rumor could start quickly, and within hours everyone in town would have heard it.

The careers of high-ranking and reputable families were not secure. This primarily had to do with the old Nepalese land rights, which recognized use rights for commoners but allowed ownership only to the king. As the right to use land was constantly changing, it was not possible for a European-style feudal class that might threaten the king to form.

The unification process in the Śāha and Rāṇā periods went hand in hand with the suppression of many classes, especially peasants and ethnic groups, along with the state adoption of the caste system leading to a hitherto unknown degree of hierarchization of society. Political, military, and economic power was mainly in the hands of a few families of the Bahun-Chhetri upper class, who enriched themselves through an exploitative system of landholdership, having secured these prerogatives under religious and legal mandates, and thereby created many privileges and monopolies.

This was the situation until the middle of the twentieth century. Nepal was by no means prepared to open up to the world, to dare to try new forms of political rule, or to reform itself socially and economically. And yet it slowly succeeded in entering the modern age following the renewed assumption of power by the Śāha and the increasing democratization and reform movements pursued in the footsteps of India.

8

From Monarchy to Republic, 1951–Present

During the Rāṇā Period, King Tribhuvan (Tribhuvana) Vīra Vikrama Śāha had shown cautious sympathy for the opposition movements that had formed in India since the 1930s and gained strength the 1940s. These groups represented a serious threat to the Śamśera Rāṇā. Tribhuvan felt isolated in his palace and strove to build back the influence of the Śāha kings. He demonstrated solidarity with the Nepali Congress (at first secretly and later openly), which the Indian government also supported. This did not go unnoticed by the Śamśera Rāṇā. Padma Śamśera Rāṇā, the last but two Rāṇā prime minister, cautiously attempted in 1948 to cement the prime minister's power for all time in a constitution, the Government of Nepal Act of VS 2004, but the future again belonged to the Śāha kings.[1]

The Restoration of the Śāhas

At first, however, the situation turned more threatening for Tribhuvan. On November 6, 1950, he took an opportunity and fled to India. Using the excuse of wanting to hunt, he, his eldest son Mahendra, his grandson Birendra (Vīrendra), and one of his daughters got into a car and left the palace, followed by other family members. But then the motorcade unexpectedly turned into the Indian Embassy and asked for asylum. The Śamśera Rāṇā maintained that Tribhuvan had left his kingdom and therefore had to be dethroned. Consequently, just one day later Prime Minister Mohana Śamśera placed Tribhuvan's second grandson, Gyanendra (Jñānendra), on the dragon throne in the Hanuman Dhoka palace. But Gyanendra was only three years old at the time and could hardly reign himself. Nonetheless, the Śamśera Rāṇā had coins minted with his name on them.

The Indians, in contrast to the British, had been reckoning with the end of Rāṇā rule for some time and gladly granted Tribhuvan asylum. On November 10, he and his family took an Indian aircraft to exile in Delhi. For the first time, the world took notice of Nepal to a significant degree. The

Nepal. Axel Michaels, Oxford University Press. English language edition © Oxford University Press 2024.
DOI: 10.1093/oso/9780197650936.003.0009

Śamśera Rāṇā tried and failed to persuade Tribhuvan to return. His flight meant a great loss of legitimation for them, as many people looked upon the king as the god Viṣṇu and the protector of the land.

Neither the Indian nor any other government recognized Gyanendra. Prime Minister Jawaharlal Nehru confirmed this in public on November 22, 1950, in parliament, declaring Tribhuvan to be Nepal's head of state. The majority of people in Nepal, too, wanted Tribhuvan's return and refused to accept Gyanendra. Violent protests broke out in both Nepal and India, and in November 1950 Birganj in the Tarai was taken by the Mukti Sena, a liberation army of the Nepali Congress. Nehru was furious upon hearing that the Nepali Congress and B. P. Koirala had been preparing for a military campaign without informing him even while King Tribhuvan was in Delhi, but he wanted to avoid an open confrontation with the Rāṇā. However, given the continued pressure from India, but also increasing democratic sympathies with democracy among younger Rāṇās, the Śamśera Rāṇā were already on the wrong side of history and had no choice but to agree to a party-based government led by the actual king. A compromise was reached in Delhi on January 8, 1951, between the Śamśera Rāṇā, Tribhuvan, and the Indian government, but without involving political parties in the matter.

On February 15, 1951, Tribhuvan returned to Kathmandu, where he received a triumphal reception. Thousands lined the road from airport to hail the promise of democracy and cheer the end of Rāṇā rule. On February 18, the new government was installed by royal proclamation. This day has been celebrated ever since as Democracy Day (Prajātantra Divasa). The government consisted of a coalition of Rāṇā and members of the Nepali Congress under the leadership of B. P. Koirala.

Ten days later, Tribhuvan announced a new constitution that for the first time would deserve the name democratic. The Interim Government of Nepal Act, which guaranteed certain basic rights, was passed by the cabinet on March 30. For a long time, however, individual pockets of resistance remained, and on November 12, the cabinet was dissolved, making a constitutional convention impossible. It would take another eight years before elections could take place due to interparty squabbles and resistance on the part of the Nepali Congress toward the Rāṇā role in administration, where they continued to occupy important official posts and to control various ministries. Also, civil unrest and violent rebellion had flared up in many regions outside the Kathmandu Valley, resulting in Indian Army intervention, especially in the Tarai. This led in turn to the first anti-Indian campaigns, stoked by the Śamśera Rāṇā under the pretext that foreign agents were causing disturbances in the country. Indeed, the Indian advisors who had accompanied Tribhuvan back to Nepal were constantly imposing their views upon him. Despite multiple cabinet shuffles, the country was still in turmoil.

Tribhuvan was torn between his own claim to power and his desire to let the people govern. In 1952 he seized power back in a move akin to an emergency law, to which the parties at first hardly reacted to because they were too busy quarreling among themselves. A year later he suddenly appointed M. P. Koirala, a half-brother of B. P. Koirala, as prime minister. The former had left the Nepali Congress and founded his own, very conservative party, the Rashtriya Praja Party. A year after that, the interim constitution was to allow for what was practically an absolute monarchy. In a proclamation of February 13, 1954, the monarch announced that from then on the highest authority in any and all matters lay with him. He was, however, he asserted, still striving for a constitutional monarchy. Tribhuvan did not live to see the democratic constitution that he had originally wanted; he died on March 13, 1955, in a Zurich hospital.

The first free elections took place on February 18, 1959. The Nepali Congress won a two-thirds majority, and its leader, the first freely elected prime minister, was B. P. Koirala. Some conservative parties, among them the Nepal Praja Parishad, Rashtriya Prajatantrik Party, and the Prajatantrik Mahasabha, allied themselves on June 1 to form the National Democratic Front. That month, India's Prime Minister Nehru visited Nepal. Everything seemed to be coming together for a democratic future.

In fact, Tribhuvan's push for democracy met with opposition, not only from the opposition parties but also from his son Mahendra, who had observed the instability of the 1950s with wariness. In the face of increasing criticism and numerous disturbances at the border and within the country, Mahendra, with the support of the opposition, dissolved the government and placed himself at the head of the cabinet on December 15, 1960. Basic rights were curbed, and several leading politicians were arrested. The constitutional monarchy only lasted for one short year, until January 1960, when the absolute monarchy returned, although the Indian government, in September 1962, attempted to unite the king and the democratic forces by means of an economic blockade.

Mahendra, probably the most far-sighted of the Śāha kings, instead introduced a new polity, the Panchayat system, which he regarded as a form of democracy particularly well suited for Nepal. The administration was based on Village Development Committees (VDC), whose members were determined locally and consisted of regional or national Panchayat members; in every case, the post was to be confirmed by the palace. At the same time, Mahendra dissolved the political parties, which he deemed self-serving, incompetent, and unsuitable because they bred communalism and strife. The press was censored, and the surveillance system strengthened. The king's portrait hung in every government office and many places of business.

Mahendra simultaneously fostered a pronounced nationalism. He had a new national anthem composed, and in the Panchayat Constitution of 1962 declared Nepal to be a Hindu state. He also contributed to unification by regularly traveling throughout the country in order to propagate a linguistic and national identity. Nepālī as the language of instruction and a uniform school curriculum were introduced throughout the country. Most strikingly, in schoolbooks—for instance, in the *Mahendra-Mālā* ("Garland of [King] Mahendra"), which was distributed throughout Nepal—the picture drawn was of a sovereign, prosperous, and territorially clearly delimited state, with a benevolent king at the top and harmony reigning among the tribes and ethnic groups. According to a slogan from this period, all Nepalese should have "one language, one style of clothing, one king, one country" (*eka bhāṣā, eka bheṣa, eka rāja, eka deśa*).[2] Mahendra improved the infrastructure, had east–west roads built, and opened the country in an unprecedented way, thereby bringing it onto the international stage. He repeatedly emphasized Nepal's difference from India, knowing that he had the people's support in this. The photographs of him and Queen Elizabeth II and other heads of state made news worldwide.

In the meantime, however, opposition was growing. In 1966–67 student protests erupted in the Kathmandu Valley and the Tarai, some of them violent. Mahendra did admit the need for comprehensive reform and released some opposition politicians, B. P. Koirala among them, from prison, but they refused to support the king's Panchayat system. The cabinet changed nearly every year.

Mahendra suffered from a heart attack in 1968 and died on January 30, 1972. He was succeeded by his eldest son Birendra, twenty-seven years old, educated in the United Kingdom and the United States. He did not at first change the system despite continuing unrest, murders of politicians, and attacks on the seat of government (Singha Darbar) and even on the king himself. Opposition to the Panchayat system increased, especially in educated circles. People demanded democratic reform. In 1979–80 mass protests were again staged and violently suppressed. On May 2, 1980, a national referendum was held, in which 54.7% voted to keep the Panchayat, although suspicions of manipulation were never entirely laid to rest.

The uncertain situation in Nepal was reflected in the life of B. P. Koirala. Prime minister in 1959, he was imprisoned in 1960 despite suffering from esophageal cancer and kept in prison until 1968 without a trial. As soon as he was freed, he went into exile in Varanasi, came back in 1976, was again arrested, and continued to be kept under various forms of detention, even though he was able to fly to the United States in 1977, 1978, and 1981 for medical treatment. In between he had attempted to persuade Birendra to take a conciliatory approach, in exchange for which he had even agreed to the referendum on the Panchayat system. When he died on July 21, 1982, he was so popular that an estimated half-million people honored him at his cremation.

Koirala had been only one of over forty prime ministers since 1951. On average, there was a new prime minister nearly every year, making it impossible to find political stability. Again and again, the social-democratic Nepali Congress replaced the communists and vice versa, the Maoist wing of the latter being much more radical than the Marxist-Leninist, which hardly represented left-wing politics any longer. The royalists never attained power; independent candidates, on the other hand, certainly did. Some prime ministers managed to hold office several times. The most frequent was Surya Bahadur Thapa, who served under various kings, led five governments (and was the first prime minister of the Panchayat era to serve four times in office), followed by the social democrat Girija Prasad Koirala, B. P. Koirala's brother.

Birendra did not have his father's charisma, but became very popular nevertheless. His politics were very ambiguous. On February 25, 1975, the day of his coronation, he presented a proposal, later signed by 130 nations, to the United Nations that Nepal be declared a Peace Zone. He said:

> As it's one of the most ancient civilizations in Asia, our natural concern is to preserve our independence, a legacy handed down by history. We need peace for our security, independence and for development. And if today, peace is an overriding concern for us, it is only because our people

> genuinely desire peace in the country, in our region and elsewhere in the world. It is with this earnest desire to institutionalize peace that I stand to make a proposition—a proposition that my country, Nepal, be declared a Zone of Peace. As heirs to a country that has always lived in independence, we wish to see that our freedom and independence shall not be thwarted by the changing flux of time, when understanding is replaced by misunderstanding, when conciliation is replaced by belligerency and war.[3]

Birendra also preserved his country's geopolitical neutrality, and significantly advanced its reputation through state visits.

At the same time, he was responsible for the suppression of unrest. To India's intense annoyance, he imported weapons from China and, in an argument over trade and transit issues, raised duties on imports from India. He was increasingly warned by the United Nations, the West, and educated youth to respect human rights.

In the mid-1980s, opposition to the Panchayat system grew from India, among other nations, which in 1989 instituted another economic blockade. Party leaders were arrested, bomb attacks and deaths occurred, the press was censored, and an assassination attempt made on journalist Padam Thakurathi, who had uncovered many scandals. On February 18, 1990, the Panchayat system collapsed during a "popular uprising" (*jana-āndolana*) and a party democracy was once again formed. On 1May 12, 1991, the first free election took place after thirty-two years of the democratic movement, and Girija Prasad Koirala became the first truly freely elected prime minister.

Shortly thereafter, Koirala came under pressure because of an unfavorable agreement with India over the regulation of water resources in the controversial Tanakpur Treaty. In July 1994 he resigned following a vote of no confidence, and for the first time a communist minority government came to power. Under the leadership of Man Mohan Adhikari, the new government introduced many reforms, such as lowering the previously very high prices for basic foodstuffs, a modest land reform, the repeal or improvement of disadvantageous treaties with India, and, for the first time, a rudimentary "state allowance for the elderly" (*vṛddhabhattā*). But on July 11, 1995, King Birendra dissolved Parliament and announced elections for November. However, these never took place, for the Supreme Court declared this decision to be unconstitutional. Between 1990 and 2000 there were ten governments, none of which was able to do anything about the party strife paralyzing the country's political life.

The Maoist Insurgency

In 1990 there were a total of fifty-four parties. The largest were the somewhat left-of-center Nepali Congress, catering to the middle class, and the more left-wing United Marxist-Leninist (UML), which sought land reforms and claimed to be fighting for the peasants. From 1951 the large parties were almost always led by Bahun-Chhetri, which frequently led to anger und unrest among other castes and the ethnic groups. Among the other more or less influential parties were the Maoist Communist Party of Nepal (Maoist Center); the conservative royalist Rashtriya Prajatantra Party; the right-wing conservative Rashtriya Janata Party Nepal; the Sanghiya Samajvadi Forum Nepal, which was particularly strong in the Tarai; the moderately left-wing Communist Party of Nepal (Marxist-Leninist); the likewise moderately left-wing Rastriya Janamorcha; and the far-left Communist Party of Nepal (United).

In the middle of the 1990s, a radical section separated from the United Left Front (ULF), a potpourri of numerous communist groups, and formed the Communist Party of Nepal (Maoist) under the leadership of Pushpa Kamal Dahal, also known as Prachanda ("the forceful or fierce one"), and Baburam Bhattarai. Thus an armed struggle against the establishment began, which became a ten-year civil war that claimed between 12,000 and 15,000 victims.[4]

Not long after the election in 1959, King Mahendra had begun to court the Communist Party of Nepal, which had only won four of 109 seats, in order to weaken the powerful Nepali Congress. But in so doing, he made the communists stronger than the vote count suggested. Marxist thought had arrived in Nepal earlier, with the Chinese Revolution, and was popular among workers and peasants. It may seem surprising that communism, including the Maoist variant of it, should have begun to take hold in Nepal so late, when it was already waning in Europe. The Maoists, however, maintained that communism in Europe had been betrayed, but that the teachings were still as relevant as ever. Nothing was more urgent than to found a workers' and farmers' state and eliminate social injustice.

On February 4, 1996, six years after the end of the Panchayat system, Baburam Bhattarai, the party chief, wrote a memorandum to the ruling prime minister. In it he complained of the increase in poverty, the differences between rural and urban development, the "imperialist" policies of the other parties, the criminal sale of the country's water resources, and the violent suppression of rebellions and protests. Then he set forty demands with deadlines, stipulating that failure to comply with them would unleash an armed struggle against the state. The demands had to do with (a) the question of nationality (e.g., the repeal of all discriminatory treaties with India, closure of the recruitment centers for Gorkha mercenaries, prohibition of vulgar Hindi films, dissolution of the "colonial and imperial" NGOs); (b) democracy (the disempowerment of the royal family, release of political prisoners, formation of a people's army and police force, abolition of untouchability, freedom of the press, the same rights for all languages and dialects); and (c) living conditions (giving land to the peasants, landless, and homeless, nationalization of the property of middlemen and compradors, full employment, minimum wages, free health care and education; drinking water, roads, and electricity for everyone; elimination of any and all corruption). What looked like a demand for an ideal state rather than violent upheaval necessarily led to the armed struggle, for the government did not concern itself with fulfilling any of the demands.

The injustices and discrimination highlighted in the memorandum were certainly one reason for the radicalization of Nepalese politics, but not the only reason, since these problems were longstanding. The leadership of the Maoist movement represented a supremely decisive catalyst of change: first and foremost Pushpa Kamal Dahal, a Brahmin and a student of agriculture, and Baburam Bhattarai, a Brahmin of the same age and a student of architecture and urban planning in Chandigarh who held a PhD from Jawaharlal Nehru University in Delhi. In India, Bhattarai had come into contact with a communist exile group led by activist Mohan Bikram Singh. Both were able to use the economic and ethnic discrimination in Nepal as propaganda for their aims. The often corrupt and incompetent political elite played into their hands.

The armed struggle first emerged in the western midland regions—in districts such as Rukum, Rolpa, Salyan, Jajarkot, and Dailekh. It began with a series of isolated attacks on several police stations in three districts (Rolpa, Rukum, and Sindhuli), initially with self-produced weapons and hand grenades. On February 13, 1996, for example, thirty-six Maoists attempted to attack the police station in Holeri in Rolpa district. The attack was unsuccessful, but the activists, as always, learned from their setbacks. Nepal's geography lends itself naturally to guerrilla warfare. The land is rugged, with areas that can quickly be retreated to. There are often only a few ways to access settlements, easily controllable from mountain ridges. The police and army maintained a presence only at a few strategically important places, and the poverty-stricken peasants, concerned mostly with managing their food supplies and shelter, were, at least at the start, openly inclined toward the Maoists fighting for them. Once the latter had taken a region, they began to exercise their power and use it in part on behalf of the poor. Thus, peasants were often conceded land rights, and old "loan deeds" (*tamasukha*) were destroyed. Now and then, too, booty from conquests was divided among the people.

The increasing violence, however, claimed more and more victims on both sides. Maoists taken prisoner were tortured and denied their right to defense, as Amnesty International and the International Red Cross complained from the start. Police did not exercise caution, firing shots at the least suspicion. There were reports, too, of plundering and rape. Every victim of the Maoists was declared a martyr. The attitude of the district officials was often that those who blatantly ignored the constitution had forfeited all rights themselves. Thus an attack by the Maoists was followed by a counter-attack by the state apparatus. Injustice fueled acts of revenge on both sides. The Maoists killed actual or alleged supporters of the state with their knives or rifles, often without any compunction, and frequently after humiliating them. It was reported that they made Brahmins eat beef or drink alcohol, and cut their identifying patrilinear "tuft of hair" (Skt. *śikhā*). Sometimes the forced abolition of caste and purity regulations was continued even after the Maoists had come and gone. These measures were seen by the Bahun-Chhetri as an "emergency situation" (*āpad*) and as such approved as in accordance with the Dharmaśāstra.[5] But afterward many groups continued to consume beef or carried on the custom of communal meals for all castes.

The fighting was at first limited to the countryside, but at the latest from 1997 on it moved into towns, and even the Kathmandu Valley. This took the form of targeted attacks, single bombings, and the creation of underground units by communist infiltrators—but, above all, general strikes. In July 1998, negotiations with the political parties were held with the help of mediators, but when these failed the re-ignited struggle attained a new level of intensity. On February 18, 2000, around 250 Maoists attacked a strongly defended police station in Ghartigaon in Rolpa District. At least fifteen policemen were killed in the attack, and substantial amounts of weapons and munition were taken. Such defeats demoralized the police. By mid-2000, only eight out of a total of thirty-nine police stations in the district were occupied.

For a long time the army did not interfere in the conflict. When in September 2000 the first attack took place in Dunai, the district capital of

Dolpa, located near an important pass to Tibet, a company of the Royal Nepalese Army (RNA) stationed nearby did nothing to help the hard-pressed law enforcement personnel, although this would have been easy to do by securing the only bridge providing access to the town. This incident increased the tension between the government and the army. The army distrusted the parties and regarded its enemy as the Nepali Congress and the parliamentary system. Some even supposed that the royal house and the army were secretly helping the Maoists so as to weaken the parties and any attempts to abolish the monarchy. The king and the army for their part would soon show themselves to be the only guarantors of a certain measure of law and order. The army was always in support of the royal house and let itself be misled into interfering in domestic politics when it served its own purposes. When Mahendra wanted to introduce the Panchayat system and dissolve parliament, it was the army that arrested B. P. Koirala and other party leaders. The king was and had always remained the supreme commander of the army.

In the early years, the Maoists operated covertly, often attacking at night, but they became increasingly visible. They also strengthened their propaganda campaign. Wherever they were, pamphlets and posters were distributed, house walls were painted with sayings and symbols, revolutionary songs were sung, and aggressive and motivating dramas were staged.

As if Nepal had not experienced enough tragedy, on June 1, 2001, a drama unfolded that heralded the final extinction of the monarchy: a horrendous massacre in the palace.[6] During King Birendra's reign, the royal family met every Friday in Narayanhiti Palace for an evening meal. As they wished to be undisturbed, personnel and guards were reduced to a minimum. Over dinner, there was small talk, rumors, and gossip. Naturally there was also some political discussion, but it was primarily a family gathering with women and children.

The Decline of the Monarchy and the Emergence of Democracy

On June 1, 2001, the men began, as always, with a drink in the early evening. Crown Prince Dīpendra raised a glass of whisky to his relations, but got into an argument with one guest while so doing and was reprimanded by his father. Soon he seemed quite drunk, and so his brother Nirājana and his sister—or, according to different reports, his cousin Pārasa, son of the once and future king Gyanendra (Jñānendra)—took him to his rooms. There he smoked a joint and called his girlfriend Devyānī Rāṇā, whom he wanted to marry, although his parents and the queen mother were against this, allegedly because of family politics under the control of Birendra's consort Aiśvaryā, or, it was also said, for astrological reasons. Faced with this vexing situation, he had fallen increasingly into despair. His girlfriend was worried about his state of mind.

Around 9 PM he dressed in military camouflage, took two combat firearms and a pistol (Dīpendra was a weapons enthusiast) and returned to the hall where the family had begun their meal. He approached his father stone-faced and shot at him with a SPAS-12 shotgun without saying a word. Then he went outside again, but immediately returned with the intention of shooting his father again. His uncle Dhīrendra tried to stop him, but Dīpendra shot him, too. After this, he shot his mother Queen Aiśvaryā Devī, his brother Nirājana, his sister Śrutī, his aunts Śānti and Śāradā, the latter's husband, and Birendra's cousin Jayantī. Four more relations were shot but survived.

The crown prince was silent during this massacre and occasionally shot into the backs of his relatives. Finally, he approached his cousin Pārasa with whom he was on cordial terms. Pārasa, who had been accused of being responsible for the death of popular folk musician Praveen Gurung in a traffic accident and other crimes, and was unpopular among the people owing to his luxurious lifestyle, told the crown prince that it was enough. Without a word, Dīpendra went out into the garden and shot himself in the head, holding the weapon in his left hand. He survived for three days in a coma, during which time he was declared king, and Gyanendra, the brother of Birendra, regent. Birendra's cremation took place according to Brahmanical court ritual at Āryaghāṭa inside the Paśupatinātha temple area, but no member of the royal family was present.

Not since the massacre of the Romanovs by the Bolsheviks had a royal family been wiped out in such a bloodbath. It did not take long, though, for doubts about the official version that the massacre happened in one fell swoop to surface. Why of all of them had Gyanendra's family survived, namely Pārasa, his mother Komala, and his sister Preraṇā? Was Gyanendra, who was in Pokhara at the time, behind the massacre? It was he, after all, who became king following Dīpendra's death. How believable is it that Dīpendra, allegedly very drunk and under the influence of drugs, was able to proceed so methodically? Why did Dīpendra shoot himself with his left hand, when he was known to be right-handed? Why had Gyanendra at first issued a statement that an automatic firearm had gone off on its own? None of these questions could be answered satisfactorily. As custom required that the corpses be immolated within twenty-four hours, an autopsy was not possible. The official investigating commission, led by the Supreme Court judge and the speaker of the House of Representatives, pieced together the official narrative after numerous interviews with many of those present at the massacre as eyewitnesses, but conspiratorial beliefs remain to this day.

With King Gyanendra on the throne, the attitude of the royal house toward the Maoists changed. If Birendra had harbored reservations and had hesitated to use the army against the rebels, Gyanendra was just waiting to seize absolute power in order to be able to fight the Maoists as ruthlessly as possible. Alleged supporters were killed at the slightest suspicion. The army shot blindly from helicopters at suspects. Soon the rebels were declared terrorists, and during the winter of 2001–2 more people died than in the six previous years combined. The result was further escalation, with fighting taking place in the capital, too, and there were many more victims. According to estimates, around two-thirds of the victims of this war were killed by state forces.

On May 22, 2002, Parliament was dissolved, and on October 4, 2002, Gyanendra dismissed Prime Minister Sher Bahadur Deuba. The formation of a new cabinet and the announcement of fresh elections was delayed, not least because an alliance of seven parties—Marxist-Leninist communists, social democrats, royalist conservative, and others—refused to participate in a transitional government without democratic legitimation.

Although the government received much support and weapons—for example, from the United States—it failed to bring the situation under control. Finally, on February 1, 2005, Gyanendra dismissed the transitional government, placed its members under house arrest, and declared a national emergency. Once again democracy had been suspended, and it remained so for some time, despite numerous protests by foreign governments, including India, the United States, and Germany. Gyanendra was of the opinion that he could better manage with direct rule, although by the end of 2002 the Maoists held power, or at least had a strong military presence, in fifty-five of Nepal's seventy-five districts.

The pressure from the parties and the streets increased. On April 7, 2006, the Seven Party Alliance called for a general strike that lasted more than two weeks. Hundreds of thousands demonstrated on the streets, and at least thirteen people were killed. Gyanendra was unable to withstand the domestic and foreign pressure. On April 24, he declared the immediate reopening of Parliament—a day that would become another Democracy Day holiday, this time called Lokatantra Divasa. Parliament decided first of all to limit the powers of the king by depriving him of the supreme command of the army, divesting him of the power to interfere in the executive branch, and withdrawing his immunity. When King Gyanendra was told to leave the palace immediately, he supposedly countered the argument that he was now an ordinary citizen and so enjoyed the usual eviction deadline. All royal symbols were removed, the banknotes with his portrait were gradually withdrawn from circulation, the obligatory royal portrait in offices was taken down, and the Royal Nepal Airlines was renamed Nepal Airlines. The fate of the king's absolute power and of the last Hindu kingdom on earth was sealed, although the king formally remained the head of state for another two years.

The question remained as to whether the alliance among the parties and the people would hold. After all, the people had been just as angry with the parties as they had been with the king. Members of Parliament were increasingly seen as corrupt and incompetent in equal measure. Many thought that at least they had known who was stealing from them in the case of the king, whereas afterward it was impossible to say.

Gyanendra, in any event, violated a cardinal principle of rule that is not based on force by neglecting the welfare of his people. Nepalese did not want to be ruled over but cared for. It was not enough to flex muscles, deploy soldiers and police, or hide inside Narayanhiti Palace. In two short television speeches, this ruler's coldness was made clear to his tormented people. In the first, on April 24, 2006, he had simply ignored the wish of the people for democratic elections and expressed no regret for victims killed in the demonstrations. In the second, a few days later, he made up for this, but it was too late. In the meantime, the press had reported that the victims had been hastily cremated without the suitable participation of their families. This was not only an affront to familial and religious feelings but also brought back troubling memories: after the palace massacre, too, Gyanendra had had the corpses of his brother's family immediately cremated, thus hindering autopsies and a reconstruction of the exact course of events. It was clear to most people that Gyanendra could not govern the country. His dour face at his enthronement lay like a shadow over his rule. He had few admirers, no foreign government except India invited him to visit, and fewer and fewer persons of rank took his side.

But it had also become clear that the Royal Nepalese Army had failed. Over all those years it had not succeeded in gaining victory over or perceptibly weakening some 15,000 active Maoist rebels supported by double that number of militia, although it had received considerable military aid. Even with helicopters and heavy weapons, the army seemed helpless in the rugged mountainous regions, where it was repeatedly exposed to bloody and costly attacks. The generals habitually justified themselves by saying that politicians had not let them attack the rebels right from the start. The soldiers did not dare to leave their camps and barracks at night. Even in the vicinity of the capital—for instance, in the small town of Banepa—they ventured out only by daylight, leaving the Maoists to move around and extort money at night. Having failed militarily and morally, the army had lost a considerable part of its international reputation. International organizations accused it of nearly as many human rights abuses as the Maoists were accused of. Any force that shoots from helicopters at anything that moves, or abducts and tortures prisoners, forfeits its credibility, even in an unusually long-suffering country such as Nepal.

Under such circumstances, there was a growing impression that the politics of the country had collapsed. Many were already speaking of a "failed state." The power relationships seemed muddled, the democratic structures had too recently been put in place, and the violence was difficult to contain. At least 70% of the country was in the hands of the Maoists, without anyone knowing who and how strong they really were. The government officially informed the embassies that it could not guarantee security outside the capital's Ring Road. For every external post in the country, the government needed many times more soldiers than personnel for the post's own security. Such centers were kept going at a cost to the population: the people were mercilessly exposed to marauding and terrorizing political groups. They suffered ever more from the collapse of vital infrastructure. No longer were hospitals and health posts being supplied, roads being built, potholes being fixed, or rubbish being removed; telephone lines were being cut and radio towers destroyed. Teachers dared not show up at school.

On April 25, 2006, Girija Prasad Koirala became prime minister for the fourth time. Although at age eight-five he was not a man of the future, his seniority lent him authority. Everything depended on whether he could succeed in bringing the Maoists to the table to negotiate. In February, Maoist leaders Pushpa Kamal Dahal and Baburam Bhattarai had already signaled their readiness in Delhi to representatives of the Seven Party Alliance and the international press, but they had also demanded a constituent assembly that would formally declare the end of the monarchy. On May 26, 2006, the new government under Prime Minister Koirala, under pressure from India and the United States, began peace talks with the Maoist rebels. Several hundred prisoners had been released beforehand, and a reform of the constitution had been promised. The goal was to end the civil war that had been going on for ten years. On November 21, 2006, an agreement to do so was signed by Koirala and Dahal.

The press had a large share in this decisive change. Despite constant censorship, threats, and arrests, young, courageous journalists had constantly reported on blatant grievances—sometimes hidden away in letters to the editor, sometimes with striking caricatures (in which even the king might be made fun of on front covers), and sometimes with sharp analyses of the situation. One of the most influential journalists, Kanak Mani Dixit, who himself had been arrested at the height of the unrest, encapsulated it all when, in a title story in the magazine *Himal South-Asian* he edited, he declared both the king and the Maoist leader Prachanda to be the "Great Chairmen" of the people. In this way, he cut the king down to size and made Prachanda a worthy adversary, whom one needed to trust. According to Dixit, the last king of Nepal had in the end done his land a service: "The Great Chairman Gyanendra," he wrote, "has done more in the past year than the Maoists to destroy the image of the monarchy, likewise he has done more to give energy to the 'democratic republic' than the rebels in the jungle."[7]

On December 28, 2007, 270 of 329 members of the transitional parliament voted for a federal and democratic republic as the form of state. On April 10, 2008, elections to the Constituent Assembly took place, which the Maoists won with a large majority, and in the opening session, on May 28, the king was formally stripped of his powers. Of the 564 members, 560 voted in favor. It was the end of the 240-year-old monarchy. Gyanendra left the palace on June 11. On July 23, Ram Baran Yadav was elected Nepal's first president, and on August 15 Pushpa Kamal Dahal was elected prime minister.

Dahal's political activities in the new republic were not always felicitous. He resigned as prime minister in the following May because no agreement had been reached as to how to integrate the Maoist rebels into the Nepalese army, and his attempt to dismiss the commander-in-chief had failed. He had also betrayed the trust placed in him. Many suspected that his new, more moderate political identity had long been his primary goal. He lost the next election, whereupon he nearly had to give up the chairmanship of his party and entered into a long-running quarrel with the new party chairman, Baburam Bhattarai. Meanwhile, despite ongoing allegations that he needs immunity because of the risk of being accused of war crimes and because he allegedly misappropriated funds intended for the integration of the Maoist guerillas into the regular army, Prachanda still sees himself as the leader of the poor and downtrodden, as a legitimate (if not legitimated) fighter against the ruling class.

From the founding of the republic, attempts were repeatedly made to enact a constitution on the basis of which free elections to a parliament could take place. There were many false starts, with the dates set being changed again and again, and tumultuous scenes in which representatives of the opposition threw chairs and microphones at their colleagues to prevent a threatening vote. But Nepal could not just ignore the question of a constitution. The citizens wanted their rights to be legally guaranteed, and they wanted political stability. Many Nepalese were stateless because they could not prove that they were citizens. If someone's father was unknown or had disappeared abroad, then a child could not receive citizenship or go to university. Repeated demonstrations took place demanding that mothers be accorded equal rights.

Not until November 19, 2013, did another election take place, once again for a new constituent assembly, as a constitution could not be ratified despite constant extensions of the deadline by the Constituent Assembly. A total of 143 political parties entered the fray, but no solution to the problems was forthcoming. The Maoists, who had won 229 seats in the April 2008 election, garnered only eighty-one seats; the Madhesi from the Tarai, too, saw their seats halved to forty from eighty-one. The centrist parties increased their proportions.

Among the points of disagreement throughout the whole process were the formation and exact delimitation of federal states along linguistic borders, between population groups, or between previously existing districts. Since all regions were populated by a multitude of different groups, a greater sticking point was the naming of the new provinces. Further points of difference were the distribution of power between the president and the prime minister, the election of MPs through party lists or direct candidacy, and what form the constitutional court would take.

While elements of the social democratic Nepali Congress, the Communist Party of Nepal (Marxist-Leninist), and the Rashtriya Prajatantra Party (Nepal) were in favor of a constitutional monarchy and a federal mixture of six or more ethnically mixed provinces, the Maoists, weakened in the election—or more precisely, the United Communist Party of Nepal (Maoist) together with thirty smaller parties—insisted on a model based on ethnic identity. The constitution they had in mind was meant to give marginalized castes and ethnic groups more rights. Women's rights groups, royalist Hindu nationalists, and other splinter groups fought in opposition for rights of their own. "They only know the language of terror and violence," said some; "they secretly want the monarchy back," said others.

Besides questions of ethnic and national identity were issues of concrete economic interests, and this is the point at which India and China came into the picture. Indian prime minister Narendra Modi visited Kathmandu shortly after his election on May 26, 2014; Chinese president Xi Jinping followed soon after. India wanted to build hydroelectric generators and China desired a railroad through the country so as better to access the Indian market.

The people of the fertile lowland area of the Tarai no longer wanted to be subject to the whims of (from their point of view) elitist officials in Kathmandu who patronized and exploited them. Most of the population there speak dialects of North Indian languages. But when, in July 2008, Vice President Paramananda Jha swore his oath of office in Hindī instead of the official language Nepālī, there was a storm of protest. After a decision by the Supreme Court, Jha had to repeat his oath a year later in Nepālī, a humiliation for the many speakers of Hindī in the country.

The question of delimiting and naming the provinces was by its very nature a difficult one to resolve, and anywhere this takes place there are regional and often "ethnic" interests and reservations. In Nepal, there were never any victorious foreign powers, but a jointly created political forum was formed to attempt to reach a political consensus. Despite all efforts, the peace process for a long time did not result in a generally accepted constitution. The pressure coming from within the Parliament and from the people was too great. This is why Subhash Chandra Nemwang, the somewhat inept chairman of the Constituent Assembly, did not in the end allow the drafts to be voted on in 2013. This assembly had been elected for four years, and while the failure to vote after only a year did not mean the end of an ongoing process, it was certainly a grave disappointment for the people, who were tired of being put off again and again. In such a situation, it was the uncompromising, power-hungry, self-serving actions of all the politicians, but especially the Maoists and members of the thirty parties, that frustrated people. Thus the citizens constantly called for general strikes and indiscriminately torched alleged strike-breakers' cars and motorcycles.

On September 20, 2015, the time had finally come. Parliament—despite the resistance of the Madhesi (who were a majority in Province no. 2) and the Janajati, as expressed in the form of massive protests in the Tarai that claimed almost fifty victims—ratified a constitution. There was broad agreement on its basic features, which declared Nepal to be a democratic, federal, and secular republic, with an independent judiciary, and certified the equality of all people and the freedoms of speech, assembly, and the press.

Individual constitutional problems of a technical nature, to be sure, remained. For example, there was the problem of proportional representation, which Nepal had decided on, in order to enable adequate representation of hitherto disadvantaged ethnic, religious, and social groups. This was a great step in this multi-ethnic, multireligious, and caste-based country. By law, the voting lists had to include the Dalit, the Adibasi Janajati (hill and mountain aborigines), the Khasa-Arya (a collective designation for the group with a relative majority in Nepal, who speak Nepālī and are divided into many castes), the Madhesi (the majority population of the Tarai), the Tharu, Muslims, women, and other groups.

The districts and seven provinces received more autonomy and also their own budgets, but the borders were drawn in such a way as to preserve the dominant Khasa-Arya almost everywhere as the majority. The Madhesi, in contrast, remained disadvantaged, having been turned into a minority in two provinces owing to the borders, instead of being able to form a dominant group. They therefore rejected this new constitution.

In February 2016, the protests increased again, especially in the Tarai, and, when India indirectly supported a frontier blockade, the country, already suffering from the aftermath of the 2015 earthquakes, suffered even more from a lack of gasoline, kerosene, propane, and pharmaceuticals. The big parties agreed to a rotational system for the office of prime minister: Prime Minister K. P. Oli, the leader of the Communist Party (Marxist-Leninist), was succeeded in August by Pushpa Kamal Dahal, who in turn was succeeded in June 2017 by Sher Bahadur Deuba.

Finally, on November 27 and December 7, 2017, the first elections under the new constitution took place, with a participation rate of 67%. This constitution provided for 165 directly elected members of the Federal Parliament and 110 elected proportionally (to the share of votes for the parties), which significantly reduced the previous number of 601 members. However, only those parties that had won more than 3% of the votes received seats. At the same time, seven provincial parliaments were elected. The two chambers of the Federal Parliament, namely the National Assembly (the upper house) and the House of Representatives (the lower house) elected the president and vice president. With the 753 local political representative bodies, city administrations, village councils, and Village Development Committees elected in 2017 in place, there was for the first time a Nepal that was completely democratically structured. In the elections, which were for the most part peaceful and whose result was accepted by all parties, a clear majority of the fifteen million registered voters decided in favor of a left-wing coalition of the Communist Party of Nepal / United Marxists-Leninists (CPN-UML) and the Communist Party of Nepal / Maoist Centre (CPN-MC). This coalition received a total of 116 first-past-the-post seats, the Nepali Congress a mere twenty-three, and the rest of the parties thirty-six seats.

The left-wing alliance won a majority, then, in both houses, and also in six out of seven provinces. A third of the seats are reserved for women, and there are also quotas for ethnic groups and minorities. Despite some inconsistencies and infractions of the voting laws, these elections represent a significant step forward in establishing Nepalese democracy. But they also presaged a further opening up toward China. One thing will probably remain unchanged, however. With twenty-six governments since 1990 and the rotational principle still being practiced for the premiership, including by the major parties, Nepal continues to be bound to the old model of divided rule.

On November 15, 2022, 17.9 million voters were asked to cast their ballots at over 22,000 polling stations to elect the 275-member House of Representatives, provincial legislatures, and a new prime minister, the twenty-eighth since democracy was introduced in 1990. There are two major mainstream political alliances: The Democratic Left Alliance led by the Nepali Congress and Prime Minister Deuba, aged seventy-six; with Communist Party of Nepal (Maoist Centre) led by the former Maoist guerrilla leader Pushpa Kamal Dahal ("Prachanda"), aged sixty-eight; and four other smaller parties. This alliance was opposed by a pro-Hindu, partly pro-monarchical alliance consisting of the Communist Party of Nepal (Unified Marxist–Leninist, CPN-UML) led by former Prime Minister K. P. Sharma Oli, aged seventy, and two other parties. The ideological party names do not say much. The mostly older party leaders are mainly concerned with maintaining their power.

The Communist Party of Nepal (UML) was the clear winner of votes but did not win a majority in the parliament to form the government. Other splinter parties were only able to win small shares of the vote. All the more surprising was the success of the new Rastriya Swatantra Party, led by former television presenter Rabi Lamichhane. Obviously, younger people in particular, especially in the cities and in the Tarai, wanted a turnaround, as it already became apparent in May 2022 with the election of Balendra Shah as the young independent mayor of Kathmandu. However, it remains to be seen whether this party will develop as a new influential political force.

With a hung parliament, the parties will likely continue their quarrels in building a coalition. It is likely that governments and prime ministers will change frequently. In any case, the challenge of the next government will be to tackle the long-standing problems such as corruption, federalism, secularism, labor market, administration, education, infrastructure, tourism, and balancing the relations with neighboring China and India.

Power and Authority: King, Prime Minister, and Maoist Leader

Although in Nepal the prerequisites for a strong monarchy existed, the political situation long remained unstable. This was primarily due to the ancient Indian system of dividing rule between the king and prime minister, and the problems of royal succession between 1777 and 1832. After 1856 the office of prime minister in Nepal also became hereditary, but the division of power among two or more nearly equal rulers, long practiced in South Asia, remained in place. The kings and prime ministers had shared power in Maratha and Vijayanagara empires. The Kathmandu Valley before the Śāha was ruled separately by three kings in the period from 1492 to 1768. As soon as one side showed itself to be weak, another was able to fill the power vacuum. This principle of divided rule was valid, basically, even after the integration of the Maoists into governing positions. To be sure, authority must legitimize itself by playing to people's notions of what lies beyond the world, while at the same time remaining effective within it, and so there are ever-shifting claims to power among various authoritative figures competing for it: king and Brahmin priest, king and prime minister, king (or prime minister) and Maoist leader, and Brahmin and ascetic—to name only a few.

Unstable conditions were of course caused not only by such tensions but also by the age of the kings or problems with succession. Between 1777 and 1832 the actual power lay with regents, usually the mothers of the kings or with the prime ministers. A further reason for the division of power was the custom of the Śāha kings to have at least two women as queens. They frequently attempted to assert their own sons as crown prince against other possible claimants.

Occasionally, wildly contradictory commands were issued from the palace on the same day—from the king, the prime minister, the regent, or the crown prince. It was often better for the people, and more so for officials, to do nothing than to do something wrong. Thus a climate of suspicion and envy, fear, and anxiety about property and possessions, life and limb, arose. With one exception, all prime ministers between 1777 and 1846 died unnatural deaths. Even Bhīmasena Thāpā, who held power for over thirty years, ended his days in great misery in prison. He had been accused of attempting to poison the crown prince—a popular accusation and doubtless a very useful one in a power struggle. Victory over rivals expressed itself in the rival being poisoned, assassinated, taken prisoner, exiled, demoted, or rendered a normal subject.

A certain measure of security was attainable through family connections and especially through marriage bonds. The first thing that Jaṅga Bahādura Rāṇā did after taking power was to ensure that all important army and administrative posts were occupied by his brothers and sons, regulated through a rule of succession according to which the eldest remaining brother in each case became prime minister, and then his own sons, whereas the Śāha kings' crown continued to fall to the eldest son.

The second thing he did was to get members of his family married into the royal family, whereby he obtained direct influence over the palace. To conform to caste rules, in 1849 he simply revised his origins upward, declaring that he was descended from high-caste Indian Rajputs from Merwar in Rajasthan. His son, Jagat Jaṅga, took the initiative and married a daughter of King Surendra Vikrama Śāha in May 1853. The wife of King Birendra Śāha, killed in 2001, came from the Rāṇā aristocracy. Crown Prince Dīpendra was apparently in love with a Rāṇā, albeit one whom the queen was not well disposed toward. After the court astrologer had predicted a destructive end to the alliance desired by the crown prince, and the queen had been able to persuade the king to oppose the match, the drama ending in the massacre at the Narayanhiti Palace played out.

The political power structure in Nepal from the eighteenth century on was complicated by the country's ethnic variety, rugged geography, and political isolation, all of which favored a polycentric division of power featuring more or less strong petty kingdoms, added to which was an overly fearful administration. Political dominance obviously required conquering centers of power. Whoever resided in the palace in Kathmandu, be it the royal palace or Singha Darbar, was the ruler. Still, the conquest of a power center by no means meant unlimited control of a clearly defined territory.

The result would not be particularly surprising, were not the kings of Nepal (as often in India) simultaneously regarded as all-powerful god-kings.[8] From the fourteenth century at the latest, they were called *deva* ("god") and identified with Viṣṇu or designated Naranārāyaṇa ("Nārāyaṇa [Viṣṇu] among men"). They were seen not only as the embodiment of the "divine order" (*dharma*) and as supreme warlords, but also as creators, the first and most distinguished of sacrificers. Their wives were called Rājyalakṣmī, that is, Lakṣmī of the Kingdom. The kings had to preside over many rituals.

The chronicles repeatedly make clear that the fate of Nepal depended on the kings. At the Matsyendranātha festival, it was the king who had to be shown the so-called small black vest (*bhoṭo*), as this promised to bring rain. Punishments handed down by the king were recognized as divine sanctions. The power of the king, then, expressed itself not only in having subjects at his disposal, in enjoying privileges, immunities, and the ability to limit others' freedom of decision, but also in its sacred functions. Coronation was deification,[9] and at his death it was not the "King" who died, only the earthly king.

This view of divine monarchy must naturally not be taken too far. The *Ain* makes clear that the power of the god-king was limited, as far as punishment and law were concerned. He was not even excepted from caste degradation, which he could undergo by law in cases of high treason.

In addition, the king is not the only "human" god. He has or had competition in the form of the Brahmins, who understand themselves as the embodiment of *brahman*, the absolute. Then there are the ascetics, who outstrip even the Brahmins, inasmuch as they regard themselves as liberated and thus free from cyclical rebirth, in contrast to Brahmins and the king. It is no accident that Hindu mythology and some chronicles are full of stories in which the power of the kings is challenged by Brahmins and ascetics.

Brahmin, ascetic, and king are then, in their different ways, as American anthropologist Richard Burghart made clear, rulers over different contexts and realms.[10] The Brahmin rules over the organic, the ascetic over the temporal, and the king over the terrestrial realm. The land and its subjects, seen from this perspective, become the extended body of the king, and every injury to land or people means an injury to the king. This applies too to the wielders of worldly power who have also competed with the king, as either prime ministers or Maoist leaders.

More important, however, is that the primacy of the king, the Brahmin, the ascetic, and the prime minister or Maoist leader is, in every case, relational. In traditional South Asia there is neither a religious nor a worldly absolute ruler; rather, there are types of superiority that manifest themselves in relation to types of dependency. For example, it is emblematic of higher rank that one may give another person a *ṭīkā*, the red spot on the forehead. Thus, normally a father gives his children a *ṭīkā*, as do teachers their pupils, a man a woman, and seniors juniors. Again, it was usually the king who gave his subjects a *ṭīkā*, for which they lined up in large numbers during the autumnal Dasaĩ festival. At the time of the Indrajātrā festival, however, the king went to the Kumārī, the girl who herself was a goddess, to receive a *ṭīkā* from her. If the king had not received the *ṭīkā* from Kumārī, then he would have been blamed for such calamities as earthquakes, bad harvests, or epidemics in the country. Interestingly, after the end of the monarchy, presidents have readily replaced the king as recipients of the Kumārī's *ṭīkā*.

The power that in the end distinguishes the king from Brahmins and ascetics, and that allows him to stand above them in various respects, is not his supposed secular status and his control of the territory—that would assume a distinction between politics and religion that only exists in a limited way in the Hindu context. Rather, it is a specific power of heroism that the king enjoys. The force of power and the power of force are emblematic of the king. Parasol and "rod" (*daṇḍa*), protection and punishment, are the foremost royal symbols. The Hindu king had punitive powers because he possessed religious authority and confirmed this ritually, not necessarily because he possessed any military power. On the contrary, the worldly power of the king frequently consisted of little more than royal insignia and oaths of loyalty.

The strength of the monarch, then, lay more in the king's inherited charisma and a system, based on it, of traditional oaths of loyalty sworn by the people. This charisma was expressed in the kingly privilege of granting titles, orders, land, and sinecures, or of founding identity-based temples and monasteries. In this way, the king became the giver and receiver of a series of gifts that could signify both higher rank (toward subjects) and dependency (on kings above him), according to the hierarchically structured ritual exchange of gifts in India.

The gift of land was the decisive criterion here. The monarch was owner and protector of the whole country; the distribution of land was one of his privileges, of which he made use, just as the Rāṇā prime ministers did, in order to create dependencies and to profit economically from land revenue. The subjected minor kings had to submit to this privilege, but they sometimes did retain local authority and power. Around three-quarters of the state budget in the mid-nineteenth century came from the revenue gained from possession of land and its rental. The king was thus hardly distinguishable from a feudal lord of the Middle Ages. What legitimized him was not only landownership but also power that was acquired and maintained through religious legitimation, as expressed in ritual. The Rāṇā aristocracy in Nepal owned much land, but they lacked heroic charisma. As a result, they constantly had legitimation problems, which they tried to compensate for by, among other ways, significantly expanding religious building. But they never approached the king when it came to charisma.

This charismatic power of the king is basically a transcendental power of life, which priests also embody. Both priests and kings are identified with this power thanks to their consecration or coronation, and thus attain a spiritual authority—with the result that they themselves are no longer entirely of this world. The first, and ideal, king, according to British anthropologist Maurice Hocart, is the "dead" king; the ideal Brahmin or priest is the "dead" ascetic, inasmuch as they have abandoned the world. This means that the more distant king and priest are from society, the purer they become, the more they embody the religious substance of the life-force per se. The life-force is not the king; he cannot be it, given that he dies, whereas his force, his power, must remain: the king is dead, long live the king. The life-force is the idea of power over life and of immortality, with which the king is identified at his coronation.

As the power of the king is also a religious power, it is not bound to any particular king. Only when territory is understood in the sense of mundane land, only when strength is reduced to political or military strength, does the king become a unique figure within the nexus of socio-religious power. But if land and strength are understood from the start as domains of action, then to be a king is to rule over those realms that can be won with heroic deeds. Among these deeds are heroic performances, submission to rulers (gods, kings, or gurus), the privilege of taking or giving, victories over evil forces (human, demonic, or inner enemies); but in the end, in Nepal as elsewhere, victory over death and mortality.

Building on these foundations, Maoist leader Pushpa Kamal Dahal has been able to use the ideals and religious power associated with the kingdom to his advantage by playing deftly on traditional patterns of power, while combining them with the call for renewal and for the new. For many mountain dwellers, he has kept his promise of social support and progress, always combined with announcements of final deliverance. He radically eliminated some abuses: slavery has been abolished, big landowners dispossessed, caste barriers torn down, the suppression of women outlawed, and alcohol abuse forbidden. In his camps, love marriages between castes were possible, as were communal meals among members of different castes. In addition, the ideal of a people's republic of Nepal, in which everyone would have the same rights, was highlighted, to a great extent. This did not fail to have an effect. Maoism in Nepal is not only the result of terror or economic oppression by the Śāha and Rāṇā rulers, but also the logical fulfillment of old royal heroic ideals and promises never followed through on.

The Maobadi, the "heralds (of the teachings) of Mao," as Prachanda's followers are called, were thus strong not only because they exploited the population through intimidation and oppression, but also because they skillfully used traditional and religious symbols for their own purposes. They organized their entry into villages as "ritual processions" (*jātrā*) and their gatherings as "ritual festivals" (*melā*). The red colors of their flags were the colors used on religious holidays, when women dress in their best saris and when temples are decorated. The Maobadi condemned the worship of gods and religious rituals, but at the same time they staged and celebrated their appearances as such. The broad red spot of vermilion on the forehead that one traditionally receives from the priest upon visiting a temple adorned many rebels in their camouflage suits, announcing a "pious" fighter.

Above all, Chairman Prachanda revived old ideals of heroism and purity. He is by origin a Brahmin, a caste group that has a particular idea of ritual and social purity. Indeed, Prachanda wanted to keep the country cleansed of what he thinks impure: corruption and arbitrary rule. In an interview with Li Ornesto published in the American communist newspaper *The Revolutionary Worker* on February 20, 2000, he said: "We also quoted comrade Mao about how the process of People's War is not only to crush the enemy, but also to clean our own dirtiness and all our bad habits—bad things we have had for a long time. To clean all these things, that is also the aim of the People's War."[11]

Prachanda has given his followers, who are mainly recruited from among the exploited and powerless peasants and mountain peoples, the chance to participate in the promise of deliverance. This is clear in, among other things, the martyrs' cult, which forms a notable source of identity within the Maoist movement. Pictures of rebels killed in fighting are constantly passed around. The courageous, loyal soldier who remained true to his ideal unto death was the myth that the royal army had itself created and maintained. Looked at from this point of view, the Maoist leader represented the continuation of the king-Brahmin alliance.

The country has come to terms with these competitive ideological struggles, its people having drawn their own conclusions about it all, as one modern myth told near the Paśupatinātha temple makes clear.[12] It is about the meeting between a king and a Maoist leader: In 1970, the Chinese government built the Ring Road around Kathmandu. This was one of the country's first big development projects and a symbol of its modernization. In Deopatan, however, the sanctuaries of the goddesses Maṅgalagaurī and Pīgāmāī were in the path of construction. The first temple could be moved a few meters to the north, as a Nepālī inscription on the temple bears witness. In the case of the goddess Pīgāmāī alias Vajreśvarī, however, there was a problem for the engineers: the goddess did not permit herself to be placed elsewhere. Until few years ago, the inhabitants near her shrine still remembered the reason:

> Some years ago, when this road was built, they wanted to move Vajreśvarī to the south. Everyone here was against this. But nobody listened to us, especially not the Chinese roadworkers. One of them rammed the big pipal tree behind the shrine of Vajreśvarī with his bulldozer. At that very moment, two snakes came creeping out of the tree. Well, what should I say! Three days later the poor man was dead. He died in horrible pain. At the same time there was a huge earthquake in China. Just at the moment when the tree was damaged. That was, of course, a damned difficult situation. I mean politically. The whole thing could only be solved because King Mahendra and Mao Zedong got together and discussed it. They decided, after long talks, that the goddess could stay here and the ring road should be built overhead to bypass her.[13]

And thus it came to pass. The peasant is probably saying that, in the end, nobody is stronger than the gods—neither kings, nor Brahmins, nor prime ministers, nor Maoists.

Administration and Law

In 1951, the Interim Government Act of Nepal, which confirmed the monarchy but permitted a parliament and political parties a voice in state matters, changed much in Nepal, including the bureaucratic structure of its government.[14] Although the king had absolute power, this constitution signified the beginning of a separation of the legislative, judicial, and executive powers. Something resembling a public that could think and act alongside the state developed, along with the idea that the state was responsible for law and order and for the basic needs of its citizens. This became obvious with the implementation of the first five-year plan (1956–61), as well as the establishment of a village development program (and the publication of these plans, their budgets, and laws in the newly created *Nepal Gazette*).

Land Reforms

It also became obvious by the fact that from 1951 on the *birtā* system was gradually modified, so that its use was increasingly subject to state regulation and title-holders were no longer able to demand unpaid labor or payments other than rent from peasants. From 1958 on they were no longer permitted to impose levies on alcohol, furs, or animal hides. In addition, all fallow and forested *birtā* land was nationalized without compensation. In December 1959, the *birtā* system was abolished, the land made equivalent to taxable *raikara* land, and all privileges associated with it declared null and void. The title-holders did receive compensation, which was calculated according to previous harvest yields. This was not really a land reform, since peasants gained virtually nothing by it. Basically, a feudal or landlord system was converted into a system that was equally unjust.

Similarly, the *guṭhī* system underwent many alterations, with both the state and its rulers throughout Nepal's history occupying or nationalizing *guṭhī*-endowed land for personal or state use. Thus, Rāṇā palaces, government buildings (including Singha Durbar), and a number of hospitals stand on what was once land under *guṭhī* control. Then, in 1964, all *guṭhī* land was transferred to a newly created semi-governmental Guṭhī Corporation (Guṭhī Saṃsthāna). The reason for the new administration was the intense criticism of the fact that the religious merit of the foundations only benefitted the donors, thus permitting a privileged class to exploit their land rights for their own sake, even though peasants produced the harvests. In addition, *guṭhī* land yielded virtually nothing for the state, and abuses were becoming ever more visible. The criticism was justified, but at the same time the *guṭhī* system was one reason for the variety of religious rituals and innumerable buildings built through an endowment, especially in the Kathmandu Valley and the Tarai. The Guṭhī Corporation became the biggest holder of land in Nepal, but it could not entirely replace the network of *guṭhī* activities. Many formerly privileged *guṭhīs* complained of missed payments, delayed payments, or underpayment, which resulted in festivals and rituals not being held and buildings not being maintained or renovated. Many a priest formerly employed by a *guṭhī* stopped revering the divinity, as the original *guṭhī* endowment stipulated, once the Guṭhī Corporation no longer paid him to do so.

The *jāgira* system was finally scrapped in 1951, when all such land became taxable *raikara* land. Most of the Rāṇā had lost the right to *jāgira* land by then in any case, since they were no longer employed as officials or accredited as such. This was the end of an exploitative system of land that privileged only the few, but it was not the end of suffering for the peasants.

Only from 1951 on would the land use system really be reformed.[15] In modern Nepal, only *raikara* land remains as officially registered land available for individuals or institutions. *Guṭhī* land has been preserved and is still administered by the Guṭhī Corporation. Traditional hereditary tenancies (*mohiyānī haka*), which were virtually equivalent to privately owned land, have been gradually dissolved. Public property (roads, paths, government sites, rivers, lakes, canals, wasteland, and other undeveloped land, along with certain forests, temples, and monasteries) is owned by the state and is labeled as such in the official government gazette (*Nepāla Rājapatra*). In the case of *raikara* land, there is an upper limit to private landownership: 6.7 hectares in the Tarai, 1.21 hectares in the Kathmandu Valley, and 3.5 hectares in the high mountainous regions. Foreigners may not acquire land.

Astoundingly, these asymmetric power relations led to few rebellions or separatist movements directed against the government in the Rāṇā Period, but instead were responsible for massive emigration, with people preferring the life of the industrial proletariat in the coal mines or on the tea plantations of India.

This situation of the peasantry has hardly been improved by recent changes. According to law, they are no longer arbitrarily dependent on landowners, they no longer have to perform unpaid labor, and they can acquire land, but in reality large segments of the peasantry are landless and dependent on landowners. Even when the peasants possess a little land, it is generally insufficient to provide a livelihood. With hardly any other work in rural areas, poverty and migration are common occurrences.

Administrative Reforms

After the end of the Rāṇā regime, almost the entire administration moved to Singha Darbar, the former residence of the Rāṇā prime ministers. The many posts were nearly all distributed among ten ministries. In June 1951, certain professional standards for government officials were also created, to be watched over by a Public Service Commission.

Prime Minister Tanka Prasad Acharya undertook an even more basic and professional reform of the administration in 1956 through the Civil Service Act, and in 1959 the first general election for the House of Representatives was held under the new constitution of that year. The prime minister thus elected, B. P. Koirala, introduced further reforms, including a trial period for officials, but many of these were fired by King Mahendra after he introduced the Panchayat (village council) system in 1962, retaining all legislative and executive rights for himself, so that the palace again became the country's political and administrative nerve center. A large number of officials were replaced because they did not appear loyal enough, and a new law did not permit them to formally complain about this. In 1961, Mahendra had also introduced a division of the country into five development regions, fourteen administrative zones (*añcala*), and seventy-five districts (*jillā*)—under Bhīmasena Thāpā there had been only ten districts—whose commissioners and chief district officers were, starting in 1965, directly subordinate to him. He reformed the training of officials and even had a course in public administration set up at Tribhuvan University. Local administration was based from the mid-1970s onward increasingly on Local Development Offices and the Village Development Committees (VDC). Since September 20, 2015, the country has been divided into seven provinces with seventy-seven districts.

Each province is further subdivided, with (among other things) some five hundred village councils.

With the end of the Panchayat system in 1990 and the enactment of the constitution of that year, a partition was again created between the palace and the government, whose prime minister was elected by members of parliament. The new prime minister, G. P. Koirala, created an Administrative Reforms Commission in 1991, which introduced a planning commission in all ministries, liberalized the marketplace, reduced administrative personnel by 15 to 20%, and simplified administrative processes. The VDCs became the central bodies for the control of funds in the rural parts of the country; later they received lump sums to administer on their own. In addition, a limit of thirty years on the duration of civil service was introduced. These changes became part of the Civil Service Act of 1992, which continues to form the basis for administration.

Legal Reforms

Since the fall of the Rāṇā, the law has been based on constitutions, first on the Interim Government of Nepal Act of 1951, then on the constitution of 1962. In both these constitutions Nepal, following the *Ain of 1854*, was declared to be a monarchic Hindu state. Likewise, the prohibition of missionary work remained in place. The *Mulukī Ain* of 1963 prohibited, in addition, discrimination against the casteless (Dalits) and legalized certain norms that contravened Hindu law—for example, cross-cousin marriages.

In 2008, after King Gyanendra was ousted, various drafts of the new constitution declared Nepal a multi-ethnic, multilingual, multireligious, and multicultural state. This principle of non-discrimination was carried into the constitution of 2015. Under it, Nepal became a secular federal republic, based on free elections and with the military subject to parliamentary control. Its self-image as a Hindu state, embodied in the *Ain*, was not retained in this constitution. Instead, the express right to freedom of religion was established (Article 26).

Public Education and Media

Only from 1951 onward did a state system of public education exist, making Nepal's one of the most recent in the world. At mid-twentieth century, some ten thousand pupils attended primary schools, and no more than two hundred students attended colleges. There was still no university worthy of the name. Nevertheless, at least a considerable number of Nepalese students were sent abroad under educational programs, primarily to India, but also to England and, from 1955 on, to the United States. Previously only six Nepalese students had been sent abroad, when Candra Śamśera sent them for technical education in Japan in 1902.[16]

Universal school attendance has been compulsory by law since 1975, which has raised the literacy rate to around 64%. Some 90% of children attend a school, with fewer girls than boys being registered, and with classes often being cut short, frequently due to agricultural labor. Most classes are overcrowded, and well-trained teachers are short in reply. Much value is placed on rote learning, much more so than on analytic understanding of lesson material.

Nepal is aware that economic growth requires a great deal of investment in education. Consequently, in 2016 around 11% of the Nepalese budget was spent on education. In 2017 there were some 40,000 public schools, 3,500 higher secondary schools, 1,400 colleges, and thirteen universities, four of which are officially accredited universities, among them Tribhuvan University, opened in Kirtipur in 1958. In 1986, the Sanskrit University was founded in Beljhundi (Dang District), and in 1991 Kathmandu University opened in Dhulikhel (Kabhrepalanchok District). Further, more than two hundred technical schools and numerous private colleges have been opened. Since 1975, Nepālī has been the language of teaching throughout the country. English skills have improved but have still not reached the level attained in India. However, there is still a stark contrast between urban and rural education.

As sociologist Benedict Anderson showed in his classic 1983 book, *Imagined Communities*, the modern national state was formed primarily by way of mass media, which form an essential part of education.[17] This occurred, and still does, through the publication of books and newspapers, particularly school textbooks, and increasingly by means of radio and television, and social media. A new sense of loyalty thereby challenges ties to village, clan, and family.

The first manually operated printing press, called the Gidde ("Eagle") Press, was brought to Nepal in 1851; the first electrically operated press arrived in 1912. The first book to be printed in Nepal was probably the *Ain*; the first journal, *Sudhāsāgara*, appeared in 1898; and the first newspaper, the *Gorkhāpatra*, started publishing on May 1, 1901.[18]

Until 1990, Nepal's media were under strict censorship.[19] The 2015 constitution guarantees the freedoms of speech, information, and the press, and the media landscape has since grown considerably. On the index of press freedom published by Reporters Without Borders, Nepal was 100th out of 180 countries in 2017.

Important media include the daily papers, among them *The Kathmandu Post* (*Kāntipura* in Nepālī), *Annapurna Post*, *MyRepublica*, and the government-owned newspapers *The Rising Nepal* and *Gorkhāpatra*. There are additionally some four hundred registered weekly papers. The diffusion of print media is limited, owing to logistical problems and the high rate of illiteracy. Television, which started broadcasting only in 1985, reaches only a comparatively small part of the Nepalese population. Besides the state-run Nepal Television, there are numerous private stations, such as Kantipur TV, Nepal 1, Sagarmatha TV, and Channel Nepal.

Radio has the greatest diffusion and the greatest influence on the formation of political opinion. Radio Nepal was founded in 1951, and in those days was on air only for four to five hours daily. On August 14, 1994, Radio Nepal started broadcasting in eight minority languages: Rai, Gurung, Limbu, and Magar, along with Bhojapurī, Avadhī, Tharū, and Nevārī. Today, Radio Nepal has eighteen broadcasting stations and is on air twenty hours a day in about twenty languages. Detailed news is given only in Nepālī and English, however, with summaries broadcast in other languages. Among the approximately one hundred private radio broadcasters are Himalaya Broadcasting, Hits FM, Radio Kantipur, Radio Lumbini, Image FM, and Radio Sagarmatha.

Public Health Care

From mid-twentieth century on, more health posts, hospitals and apothecaries were established during the Śāha Period: in Banepa (1954), Dailekh (1955), Ramnagar Bhutaha, and Biratnagar (1956), Chainpur and Dang (1957), and Baglung (1958). Kanti Hospital in Kathmandu opened in 1962. In the same period, the first health campaigns to fight malaria, smallpox, and leprosy were started, along with family planning programs. In 1963 there were twenty-three hospitals and 104 health centers. In addition, permission was given to NGOs and missionary organizations to enter the field of health care. Accordingly, more hospitals were built, such as Shanta Bhavan in Patan (1954), Suryabinayak Hospital in Bhaktapur, and others in Banepa (1957),

Kaski (1957), Gorkha (1957), Okhaldhunga (1963), Nawalparasi (1962), and Palpa (1954). Medical education was greatly improved with the opening of Tribhuvan Teaching Hospital (1986) and other teaching centers. Previously, most prospective doctors had to go to India for their medical schooling.

In the decades after 1962, comparatively large amounts continued to be invested in the health sector. In 2011/12, the health care budget in Nepal amounted to 5.8% of its GDP. According to the *Statistical Yearbook 2015*, in 2014/15 there were 116 hospitals with around 7,000 beds; 3,805 health posts; and 2,114 state-financed doctors, of whom only about 10%—mostly general practitioners—worked in rural areas.

Despite these efforts, health care in Nepal is still in need of development, especially in the countryside. Even in 2017, over half the population had no access to the most critical medicines, and there were on average twenty-one doctors for every 100,000 inhabitants. Many diseases are still widespread because of a lack of care or hygiene.

Unsurprisingly, among the most frequent illnesses are those of the digestive tract, along with covid-19, dengue, tuberculosis, typhus, malaria, rabies, and eye diseases. AIDS has a considerable presence as well. In 1990, the statistically leading causes of death were diarrhea, pneumonia, and tuberculosis; by 2013 they were such "civilizational" problems as diabetes, heart attacks, strokes, and lung diseases. Air pollution, especially in the Kathmandu Valley, is still in excess of World Health Organization recommendations, sometimes dramatically so. The valley's geography and unfiltered exhaust fumes contribute to this, as does, most significantly, the particulate pollution caused by unpaved streets and brick factories. In 1951 such air pollution was almost absent, when the manager of the legendary Hotel Royal, Boris Lisanevich, joked to a friend: "Look, where can I breathe such fresh air as here? If I live in Nepal, I'll live fifteen years longer!"

The Urbanization and Cultural Heritage of the Kathmandu Valley

With King Tribhuvan's return from exile in 1951 came the opening of the country and, with that, came tourism and rapid economic development, which in turn brought considerable change to the cities in the Kathmandu Valley. At first there were practically no hotels. The country's first international hotel to open was the legendary Royal Hotel, founded by Boris

Lisanevich, a former Russian dancer, friend of King Tribhuvan, Mahendra's chief of protocol, and a barkeeper in the Yak & Yeti Hotel.[20] Boris, as he was called by everyone, brought the first tourist group to Nepal in 1955 and thereby contributed much to the myth of Nepal as a kind of Shangri-La. At a time when there was hardly any electricity and no refrigerators in Nepal, Boris held celebratory banquets (among others, in 1961 for Queen Elizabeth II), entertained King Juan Carlos and his wife on their honeymoon, and hosted such celebrities as industrialists John D. Rockefeller III and Alfred Krupp, and film stars Vivian Leigh and Cary Grant. It was in this hotel that Prince Basundhara Śāha, Tribhuvan's son, met American journalist and author Barbara Adams, who became his mistress. Initially sent to write a piece for an Italian magazine on Elizabeth II's state visit, Adams ended up staying in Nepal for over five decades, during which time she founded one of Nepal's first travel agencies. Her extravagant parties and rides with the prince in an open Sunbeam Alpine cabrio marked the change in Nepal's aristocracy from Himalayan obscurity to global celebrity.

In the mid-twentieth century, the whole Kathmandu Valley was populated by some half million people. By 2018 the population had grown nearly five-fold mainly due to the Maoist insurgency, as many threatened people from the countryside migrated to Kathmandu. These figures evoke the rapid urban development both horizontal and vertical that has left modern towns with hardly anything in common with those in Erwin Schneider's famous aerial photos from the 1960s.[21] The former palaces and sacred buildings in the old towns have long since been surrounded by modern multistory structures. Starting at the end of the 1990s, after condominiums were legalized, residential buildings with up to sixteen stories arose on the periphery of the core towns. If Bauddha once consisted essentially of a *stūpa* visible from afar, this structure is now overshadowed by buildings that are taller than it.

The Kathmandu Valley has developed all the problems of a metropolis, particularly those endemic to every Asian metropolis. The triggers have been population growth, the opening up of the entire country to road traffic, and flight from the countryside.

In 1956, the first road connecting Nepal with India was completed, followed by one connecting Nepal with Tibet in 1966. Traffic and the transport of goods increased. The building boom has required labor and materials, especially steel for reinforcement. The first steel, which had been previously used for suspension bridges (1903), water hydrants (1905), utility poles (1911), and a ropeway (1922–25), was still carried on shoulders into the Kathmandu

Valley.[22] The first cars, too, were brought in this manner in 1920 to the capital. Today, trucks flow through to supply the town. Even water from artesian wells or rivers outside the Kathmandu Valley is transported in tanker trucks.

After the severe earthquake of 1934, Juddha Śamśera initiated a succession of changes starting with the construction of New Road in Kathmandu. For this, bricks and mortar were needed, both available in the valley. Over eighty brick kilns in the valley are still in full running capacity. In the 1960s, the first urban planners came as advisors; in 1964 a Town Development Committee Act was passed, and a year later the first town planning office was set up. One of the first advisors, Austrian Carl Pruscha, counseled not sacrificing too much agricultural land for the expansion of the city. There were further such plans—for example, in 1979 the Master Plan for the Conservation of the Cultural Heritage of the Kathmandu Valley by Austrian-American architect Eduard Sekler or that of the German Bhaktapur Development Project. But in all these plans the pre-industrial character of the towns was somewhat romanticized, and they were always being overtaken by the rapid development. The urbanization of the valley has continued, eating into the fields. The properties involved are, as a rule, hardly three hundred square feet in size. Highrise buildings and tiny back courtyards of some fifty square meters create an urban density that beggars the imagination. To this day, the towns suffer from lack of proper sewers and traffic infrastructure, not to mention earthquake-proof buildings.

How can Nepal's architectural heritage be preserved under these circumstances?[23] This is a question made all the more pressing by the earthquakes of 2015, and one vehemently argued about in public. The loss of significant architectural monuments of the sixteenth and seventeenth centuries was catastrophic, particularly for the Darbar Squares of the three old towns.

Nepal is used to earthquakes, and the old towns had always been rebuilt in the aftermath, but the situation was different following the 2015 earthquakes. This was true even though the rubble was quickly cleared away, usable bricks were stacked, and a large proportion of the statuary was taken to safety. The Kathmandu Valley Preservation Trust (KVPT) worked immediately following the earthquake, with the help of police, the military and the Department of Archaeology, to salvage and secure all architectural elements at the square in Patan. A few weeks after the earthquake, the best carpenters from Bhaktapur were already working to rebuild damaged parts and replace what had been lost.

For the reconstruction, however, the goals and strategy for monument maintenance necessarily changed. Originally, *guṭhīs* had seen to the maintenance, repair, and replacement of religious buildings. Inscriptions note the possession of land and the use of revenue from such land for such purposes. But the land reform of 1962 meant that the *guṭhīs*' revenue was taken from them, altering the way they managed the buildings and the rituals they hosted, such as payment of musicians and food for the poor. This gap was supposed to be filled by the state's care of monuments, which had been set up on the basis of the Ancient Monument Preservation Act of 1956, following the British-Indian model. From the start, preserving "archaeological" monuments was prioritized. This pertained to sites in the Tarai related to the Buddha's origins, but not to the thousands of Hindu or Buddhist buildings in towns dominated by the Newar. Not only was there a lack of resources for the state care of monuments at that time, but also a lack of expertise. The care of monuments, like urban planning, was seen as a Western, neo-colonial import and had been integrated into Nepal's administrative responsibilities in order to qualify for funding from international development organizations. Even the declaration in 1979 of seven sites in the valley as World Cultural Heritage Sites was due to one American expert's opinion, and to the fact that UNESCO was urgently seeking signatory states for the Convention of World Cultural Heritage. Finally, the paradoxical situation arose that three core areas of the World Cultural Heritage—the Taleju temples in Kathmandu, Patan, and Bhaktapur, the Paśupatinātha and Cāṅgunārāyaṇa temples, and the Nyatapola temple in Bhaktapur—which supposedly belong to all people, are only accessible to Hindus and are guarded by the army.

Not until the World Cultural Heritage of Nepal was entered on to the list of endangered sites in 2003 did officialdom increase the budget. In subsequent years, the authorities adopted new principles that went far beyond the 1964 Charter of Venice. Only traditional materials and techniques were to be used and—in alignment with the Eurocentric guidelines that have been in use in India since 1923—the replication of iconographic details was to be prohibited.

These regulations were again codified in the autumn of 2017, triggering heated controversies. With an eye to future earthquakes, an influential group of Nepalese architects and engineers who had been employed by the Department of Archaeology as advisors, ruled out the use of steel and concrete. The architects and engineers of the KVPT, in contrast, insist on the careful use of modern materials in areas not visible. The temples would not be entirely earthquake-proof, to be sure, but at least they would be safer.

Among the problems sparked by the controversy is that the law, repeatedly amended, still indiscriminately places all buildings older than one hundred years under protection. To this day there is no consistent idea of what a monument might actually be, and whether a monument loses its character when it is rebuilt. An examination of Nepalese history reveals that, despite fire, termites, or earthquakes, the cult buildings have basically remained attached to the place, even if their form and design have changed, especially in the decorative and iconographic details. It was important to give the gods their houses back. Broken cult images are dead; they cannot be used again.

On the square in Patan, the damaged buildings were exactly and painstakingly repaired with international funding so as to preserve as much "authentic" material as possible. More than 90% of the details in wood and a large proportion of the outer bricks were undamaged or only slightly damaged; badly damaged or missing elements were replaced with materials of a quality comparable to the original. The fragile elements were held together in most innovative ways with special bolts, steel banding, and stainless-steel pins.

The debate triggered by the earthquake makes clear that preserving cultural heritage is not a science per se but an attitude, even a system of beliefs, strongly bound to the experience of the craftsmen and architects who carry this out. Thus a host of dogmas relating to conservation, such as authenticity, originality, or aesthetic value, all drawing on orthodox restrictions and regulations, have had to contend with the desire for quick and practical implementation. At this point, insistence on traditional materials and methods becomes problematic, for tradition is then pitted against modernity. Tradition is not set down "in stone forever;" it, too, is always fluid and changing. This is true both of building techniques and the use buildings are put to. The local population has little difficulty with destroyed buildings being constructed in a different and perhaps more "beautiful" form. The debate is a textbook example of transcultural entanglements that will in time be resolved.

Literature, Art, and Music

Literature

In 1958, Nepālī was declared the sole national language was thereafter increasingly promoted at the expense of other languages and literatures. Much changed in Nepālī literature as a result. It was more oriented to fiction and opened up to new genres, such as the novella, short story, and crime novel. Above all, it became more critical, dealing with ever more political and social topics and conflicts, usually in a realistic style. Pahalamāna Siṃha Svāra had published his *Aṭala Bahādura* in 1907, a tragedy dealing with conspirative actions under the Rāṇā. Siddhicaraṇa Śreṣṭha, too, had written revolutionary poems against the Rāṇā and was sentenced in 1940 to eighteen years in prison for this, but was released five years later. In 1934, *Śāradā*, the first monthly literary journal, in which numerous other writers made their names, was begun. Among them was Gopāla Prasāda Rimāla, whose most famous poem, *Āmāko Sapanā* ("The Mother's Dream"), in which a mother dreams of her son conquering evil, shows how forward-looking and full of optimism the literature of the time was. Indeed, in 1951 the end of the Rāṇā regime was marked by Rimāla's poem *Parivartana* ("The Change").

Contemporary Nepālī literature is characterized by much experimentation, influenced in part by literature in Western languages, especially English. It has still not won over a mass public, but it has conquered new media, among them *Rūparekhā*, which became one of the leading journals for Nepālī literature, and the online magazine *Sāhitya*. Writers continually involve themselves in politics and write in a more intellectual and humorous style. In addition, ever more ethnic groups, not just Bahun-Chhetri, are writing in Nepālī. Poetry readings and poetry slams are frequently held, attended, as in the art scene, predominantly by younger Nepalese. This literature has yet to be extensively translated into English. Some writers, such as Manjushree Thapa (*Forget Kathmandu*, 2005) and Samrat Upadhyay (*Arresting God in Kathmandu*, 2001) do write mostly in English and have thus attracted international attention.

The Arts

Modern art and culture in Kathmandu engage in lively cross-border exchanges.[24] Newar artists were pioneers in Tibet of the spiritual and religious art known as *thangka* painting, and they shaped the Newar style of miniature and mural painting known as *paubhā*. Traditional painting, still practiced, deals mainly with Hindu and Buddhist themes and enjoys great international and national popularity. But it also displays a remarkable ability to transform itself. One outstanding representative of more recent *paubhā* painting is Lok Chitrakar, whose work betrays no break with tradition and showcases how topical and malleable contemporary art in Nepal is, despite European contexts deeming such art as folkloristic or traditional.

A brief historical overview provides insight into Nepal's variety of art production and the exchange of artistic ideas. In the nineteenth century, some Newar and other Nepalese artists began a discussion of the tradition of the Company School, which had arrived with the wave of British economic expansion and subsequent colonization of India, and was named after the British East India Company. One of its pioneers was Rajman Singh, the draftsman for British envoy Brian Hodgson.[25] In the 1830s and 1840s, he produced many drawings of architecture and landscape signed "Rājamān Siṃ Nepāla," of which fifty are preserved at the Royal Asiatic Society in London. Between 1850 and 1864, Henry Ambrose Oldfield, the physician at the British Residency, painted seventy-five watercolors especially featuring buildings and landscapes—held in the British Library, the Royal Geographic Society, and the Bavarian State Gallery.[26]

Another pioneer of this style was Bhajuman Chitrakar, who accompanied Prime Minister Jaṅga Bahādura Rāṇā in 1850 on his European tour to London and Paris and was able to familiarize himself with the historical paintings of the time. He introduced to Nepal the technique of oil painting on canvas in the vein of European historicism, as well as landscape and portrait painting as genres. As he never signed his work, it remains uncertain what can be attributed to him.

Many artists who, like Tej Bahadur Chitrakar, the court painter for Candra Śamśera, enjoyed a formal, Western-orientated education and training at the School of Art in Kolkata, founded by the British colonial rulers.[27] Others were self-taught or came from artists' families steeped in the *paubhā* tradition, which led, especially in the twentieth century, to sometimes blurred transitions between "European" modern and Nepalese traditional. Up into the 1930s, artists such as Dirghaman Chitrakar or Tej Bahadur Chitrakar were painting portraits in the European style, primarily of members of the aristocracy. Their works adorned, for example, the new palace, Singha Darbar, built by Candra Śamśera, who was especially fond of art in the "European" style.

The artists of this period were important cultural diplomats in a transnational space in which ideas of modernity and progress were being tested through art. Some of these artists shaped in turn art education in Nepal, as at Darbar High School, the Juddha Art School, and later the Lalitakala Academy.

The idea of an artistic education at a school of a secular type, founded for precisely that purpose, took hold in the first few decades of the twentieth century in Nepal and had a decisive impact on national education. The Royal Nepal Academy, founded in 1957 as the Nepal Academy of Literature and Art, and the Nepal Association of Fine Art (NAFA), founded in 1963, represented further steps in establishing a "national" art. Both institutions were funded by the royal family, who wished to promote Western art.

The 1960s were a period of artistically remarkable production and innovation and of cosmopolitan outlook in Nepalese art. Many of the artists considered to be in the modern school studied art in Varanasi. A few, such as Laxman Shrestha, made the leap to the Indian metropolises of Bombay and Delhi; even fewer were able to live and work in the centers of European modernism, such as London or Paris. Two artists in particular, by reason of their remarkable mobility and the shaping of a "Nepalese modernity," represent this swerve toward modern art in Nepal in the 1960s: Lain Singh Bangdel and R. N. (Rama Nanda) Joshi.

Bangdel's settling in Kathmandu in 1961, often called his return, marks that year as a key moment for the classical modern in Nepal.[28] He had actually never lived in Nepal, having grown up in Darjeeling. He studied first at the Academy of Fine Arts in Kolkata and then went to Paris in 1952 to study at the École des Beaux-Arts in Paris, where he wrestled intensively with the question of his identity as a "Nepali without Nepal." With his move to Kathmandu, Bangdel brought his experience of the European modern and of the metropolis to his "home country." His patron, King Mahendra, encouraged him to introduce abstract art to Nepal. In 1972, Bangdel was named head of the Royal Nepal Academy by King Bīrendra.

R. N. Joshi studied at the famous Sir J. J. School of Art in Bombay from 1959 to 1964.[29] He was probably one of the first artists to concern himself with art education and championed the founding of the first gallery for Nepalese art. Park Gallery was duly founded in 1968 in Kathmandu, and from it a whole series of international and national exhibitions and art workshops was organized. Joshi understood art to be a social and political as well as aesthetic activity, one that could help to lead Nepalese society out of what (for him) was a backward state into modernity. This explains his activities as a social worker and reformer, and his early environmental activity in campaigns on behalf of the Bagmati River. The works of R. N. Joshi cover such genres as watercolors, drawings, and paintings that feature landscapes, flora and fauna, rituals (e.g., the great procession of the deity

Matsyendranātha), and picturesque scenes of village life in the Kathmandu Valley, but also abstract *yantras*.

Park Gallery, now located in Patan, is still a central hub of Nepal's diverse art scene. This latter is primarily concentrated in the Kathmandu Valley and exhibits remarkable dynamism and vitality despite a minimal infrastructure of galleries, museums, collectors, and educational facilities. A classical school of art does exist at the Lalitakala Academy, and Tribhuvan University and Kathmandu University have departments of Arts and Design, but contemporary artists work in conditions of economic precarity. It is all the more surprising, then, that many young people from various social classes, castes, and ethnic groups, often with little financial backing or education, still choose the path of "free art."

The generation of artists born during and since the 1970s deserves particular attention. Some artists travel internationally, receiving grants and invitations from the United States, Japan, South Korea, or Europe; these include Hit Man Gurung and Sheelasha Rajbhandari, the two founders of the art collective ArTree Nepal. Art is developing into an ever more collaborative and interdisciplinary form, having begun to enter the public space from gallery and museum contexts. Artists have expressed themselves politically, commenting on the state of politics in Nepal, corruption, the decade-long civil war, and the situation of migrant workers in the Gulf States and South-East Asia. The works of female performance artists like Ashmina Rajit deal particularly with the role of women in a patriarchal environment like Nepal's. Many artists have occupied themselves with topics such as cultural heritage, migration, the role of women, democracy, climate change, and the representation of far-reaching social change, but also with the preservation of ritual and tradition.

The link between artistic activism and social, ecological, and political engagement proved especially close after the dramatic earthquakes of 2015.[30] The artist initiative CampHub, for instance, worked in the almost completely destroyed neighborhood of Thulo Byasi in Bhaktapur. Over a period of six months, artists from the group ArTree Nepal organized therapeutic workshops, cared for women, children, and older people, collected their stories, and transformed them in situ into a public exhibition project.

At the same time, the infrastructure of the small, yet dynamic art scene has gradually changed. On the initiative of Sangita Thapa, the owner of Siddhartha Gallery, which was founded in 1987 and exhibits both traditional and contemporary art, and of art historian and curator Dina Bangdel, international events like the Kathmandu International Art Fair (KIAF, renamed Kathmandu Triennale in 2017) have been established. Young artists receive the opportunity not only to present themselves and network through these events and other initiatives of the Siddhartha Arts Foundation or PhotoCircle, but also to undergo further training as cultural managers or curators and to learn critical writing and exhibiting skills. In these ways, the art scene of Nepal is internationalizing without forgetting its local roots and subject matter.

Museums, too, are increasingly opening up to young artists and innovative formats. For example, the Taragaon Museum at the Hyatt Regency Hotel, supported by the Saraf Foundation for Himalayan Traditions & Culture and designed in cooperation with Carl Pruscha in 1971, aims to spread knowledge of Nepal's architecture. The Patan Museum, which primarily exhibits the traditional art of Nepal, has opened its spaces to young artists and for contemporary photography. Given this simultaneity of different artistic directions and styles, the notion of traditional versus modern has to be rethought and refined in Nepal.

Music

Musical life in Nepal exists by means of *guṭhī* for festivals and rituals, or private groups for playing music at shrines. Groups organized according to caste, professional bands, and, more recently, private groups for jazz or other newer music are traditionally supported by sponsors, among whom were, in the past, the kings. Music is omnipresent in a diversity of musical pieces, performances, and instruments. Old men sit in groves and sing devotional songs, accompanied by drums, cymbals or a harmonium; drummers and flute players walk in processions and in rituals through the streets; concerts of classical (Indian) music are organized; musical groups play at festivals and dances; the shaman uses his drum to become entranced; bands accompany wedding parties; young musicians experiment with old and new instruments in new genres. Almost every ethnic group within the population has its own music style.[31]

On many ritual occasions, the traditional music of the *pañcaibājā* ("five instruments") is required; this can be extended to the *naumatī bājā* ("nine [or more] instruments").[32] These are ensembles of wind instruments, drums, and cymbals played by the low-caste Damai, almost without exception. The *pañcaibājā* is generally required for life-cycle rituals, with the exception of death and ancestor rituals. At contemporary weddings, it has more or less been replaced by modern brass bands, but on many other religious or worldly occasions it is still called upon, if only to announce the arrival of a politician as loudly as possible. The repertoire of the *pañcaibājā* comprises wedding music, folk songs, and various classical, seasonal, or ritual-dependent melodies (Skt. *rāga*), but also Bollywood hits. Often, the musicians dance to the music. In processions, the sound is often monotonous and precedes the procession. Whenever deities are underway, music is played.

The origins of the *pañcaibājā* lie in the Middle East, from which Muslim conquerors swept into India. Among their entourage were military bands; these spread throughout South Asia, arriving probably during the fourteenth century in Nepal, and no later than the eighteenth century, kings repeatedly commissioned this music.

While the *pañcaibājā* is mostly instrumental music, in *bhajana* or *dāphā* music, devotional song is in the foreground.[33] These are songs (*kīrtana*, *bhajana*, *vacana*, Hindī *satsang*), occasionally very old, composed by poet-saints, some of whom remain anonymous, that make up an essential part of the *bhakti* movements. *Dāphā* music is based on certain rhythms (*tāl*) given (or kept) by clapping, or with cymbals or drums, and on modi (*rāga*), wordless sung melodies that can be repeated and varied. A session will often begin with three strikes of the small kettle drums, followed by an instrumental introduction or invocation. There may only be an odd, not an even, number of songs; the first usually directed at Śiva.

A typical *dāphā* ensemble consists of men who play drums, large or small pairs of cymbals and sometimes bamboo flutes (*bãsurī*) or trumpets, and sing to this. The songs begin with an opening piece (*ālāpa*) or a refrain. Music is played in the inner courtyards of temples, half-open arcaded edifices (*pāṭī*, *sattala*), or outside on platforms (Nev. *dabū*, Nep. *ḍabalī*), usually in the morning and the evening, sometimes through the night, every day, or on certain occasions. Singing is done in choirs or choruses with refrains, with two groups of about the same size alternating. In contrast to the devotional songs of India, women do not participate in *dāphā* songs. The ensembles are, as a rule, organized in their own *guṭhī*.

Dāphā was originally court music, as manuscripts of *dāphā* songbooks make clear. The *āphā* groups generally have several such manuscripts,[34] written in Maithilī, Nevārī, and Sanskrit, or a mixture of these, often using an archaic language with its own linguistic constructions. Fundamental texts, often held together in leporello or *thyāsaphu* format, are, for example, the *Gītagovinda* or the *Saṅgītaratnākara* from the thirteenth century. The Malla, especially, were great patrons of the arts; they had around one hundred dramas and many songs written, or wrote these themselves, in Maithilī or Nevārī. In particular, Jaggajjyotir, Jagatprakāśa, Pratāpa and Jitāmitra Malla excelled in this; the *Gītapañcāśika* by Jaggajjyotir of 1628 or the *Mūladevaśaśidevavyākhyānanāṭaka* are especially significant. In the same vein, Raṇajit Malla, the last king of Bhaktapur, is supposed to have been a passionate composer of *dāphā* songs. His best-known song, *Hāya hāya Rāma Rāma*, was supposedly composed when he had to flee to India in exile after Pṛthvīnārāyaṇa Śāha had conquered the town. The Śāha and the Rāṇā took over the tradition of devotional song, perhaps because Pṛthvīnārāyaṇa had spent three years at the court of Raṇajit Malla and had learned to appreciate this tradition. Juddha Śamśera, in addition, decreed that musicians should be free of any kind of enforced labor.

A high-caste *dāphā* group at the Taleju temple in Bhaktapur survived into the 1980s. But *dāphā* music did not remain in higher or court circles, for the Newar peasants took it over and have preserved it. In this manner, this music became public music. In Bhaktapur it can be heard every evening at the Bhairava or the Dattātreya temples.

Hardly any other instrument has so many aspects and so many functions in Nepal as the drum. The inventory of this percussion instrument ranges from hand-held hourglass drums (*ḍamaru*) to the oversized kettle drums (*nagārā*) at the Hanuman Dhoka in Kathmandu; from the *tablā* of classical music to the great, bellied pipe drums (*dhimay*, *dhime*) of the Newar.[35]

* * *

The years following the Rāṇā regime opened Nepal to the world. They have brought many political changes to the country, above all freedom and democratization. Progress was made particularly in education and healthcare, less in terms of energy supply and industrialization. It was not until the 1990s that the infrastructure improved significantly through road construction, new forms of transport, and telecommunications. However, the political struggles between the power blocs and political parties have always hindered these processes. The second half of the twenty-first century has therefore hardly remedied the fundamental imbalance between the poor and rich sections of the population and between the Kathmandu Valley and the other regions, despite numerous five-year plans and a lot of economic aid. Between

1964 and 1990, average per capita income rose by only 295 rupees, and half of the population lived below the poverty line.[36] The influence of tourism is undoubtedly visible, but it has not necessarily contributed to improving the overall economic situation. Nepal, thus, continues to face major societal challenges: political instability, corruption, environmental problems, brain drain and migration, insufficient legality, slow and ineffective bureaucracy, strong population growth, and massive urbanization. Nonetheless, the opening of Nepal has shown an invigorating expansion and mixing in all cultural areas without sacrificing traditions and while maintaining ethnic diversity.

9

Alliances and Resistance

Ethnic Groups and Their Histories

In most works on the history of Nepal, the Kathmandu Valley occupies the foreground. Indeed, "Nepāla," as the valley also used to be called, forms the political, economic, and cultural center of the country. The center of power had shifted there at the latest by 1768/69, but this does not mean that the history of Nepal is just the history of this valley. The usual division into epochs—the Licchavi Period, Transitional Period, and the Malla and Śāha/Rāṇā periods—also neglects other regions or considers them only of secondary importance, especially since this division for the most part reflects the history of the Newar and Bahun-Chhetri up to 1768. Other regions and other ethnic groups are, as a rule, given short shrift in histories of Nepal, or, at worst, are simply erased from of the picture. This chapter represents an attempt at redressing this by looking from the fringes to the center. In the following, the histories of a few regions will be sketched by way of examples: in the south, the influential lowland region of Mithila and the stretch of the country from Palpa to the Tharu areas; in the north, the high mountain home of the Sherpa and Mustangi; and in the east, the region of the Kiranti (Rai and Limbu)—all areas of resistance to the spread of the Gorkhali.

Without question, a history of Nepal should include the histories of the Magar, Tamang, Gurung, Thakali, and many more ethnic groups, but the historical sources are often incomplete, shrouded in oral literature, scattered, or few in number.[1] The Magar, for instance, the third largest population group, settled from their first mention in the twelfth century in an area called Magarat, located roughly between Gorkha and Palpa, with confederations of up to twelve (*bahra magarat*) or—in the case of the Kham Magar—eighteen principalities.[2] Moreover, they are divided into many clans and subclans, and their status was subject to considerable social change. Examples include Rājendra Śāha's liberating the Gurung and Magar from enslavement and his exempting others from the state acquisition of "escheatable property"

Nepal. Axel Michaels, Oxford University Press. English language edition © Oxford University Press 2024.
DOI: 10.1093/oso/9780197650936.003.0010

(*aputālī*) or from the payment of fines for "illicit intracaste sexual relations" (*cākacakuī*).[3]

Similarly, it is difficult to write a history of the Tamang, the fifth largest population group. They are spread over large parts of the central region and have migrated partly to the Tarai or to Sikkim and Darjeeling. Also, they are divided into distinct groups that only rarely interact. Although the term "Tamang" can be found in Tibetan sources from the thirteenth century, the *Ain* does not mention them directly, not even by their clan names Murmi or Lama, which had been more common until then.[4] Instead, they there come under the pejorative collective category of Bhoṭe or Bhoṭyā for Tibetoid ethnic groups and are counted among the Enslavable Alcohol Drinkers. It was only in 1932 that various Bhoṭe groups, including Lama and Murmi, became officially known as Tamang.[5] It was just in relation to other ethnic groups and only in the nineteenth century that they acquired a measure of common identity based on language, religion (Buddhism), and rituals.[6] However, there are western and eastern subgroups called Nuppa and Shyarpa, respectively (the latter subdivided into Tamang and Ghale), and many other divergent features, ones concerning dietary and kinship rules, within the broad category comprising the Tamang.

The history of the Gurung, who are also divided into various groups and "clans" (*jāta*), is also difficult to reconstruct. In their oral myths and legends, they claim an origin from Mongolia, western China, Burma, and/or Mustang. According to other sources, Brahmins in the sixteenth century concocted false genealogies proving that the Gurung had an "Aryan" origin and came from northern India.

The Magar and Tamang, who, like the Gurung, typically consider themselves as the original inhabitants of Nepal, are closely associated with the Śāha and Rāṇā administrations by reason of their corvée work, slavery, or military service, during which they were shamelessly exploited and oppressed.[7] The Gurung and the Tamang (Lama), for instance, had to send one man from each household to fight on the western front of the expanding Gorkha empire.[8]

Thus the histories of the Tamang, Magar, and Gurung, who speak similar languages and share many social and ritual customs, overlap, the extent largely depending on often debated questions of origin and identity. The lack of historical sources is vexatious and demonstrates how much certain ethnic groups are virtually hidden within the history of Nepal. Their labor and taxes have contributed significantly to what today constitutes

Nepal, but at the same time they have long been excluded from decisive developments in education, administration, and the higher military ranks. American anthropologist Kathryn March has rightly called this an "internal colonization."[9]

The Tarai: From Mithila to the Madhesi Uprising

"Tarai" (also called Terai or Madesh), in Hindī and Nepālī, designates the humid, fertile Himalayan foreland stretching from the Siwalik Hills to the Gangetic plain.[10] It is rich in pastureland and forest, but also in swampland. In 1951 it was called the "Fever Hell of Nepal" by geophysicist, traveler, and writer Wilhelm Filchner because the subtropical climate and the geography favored the rapid spread of malaria. Five valleys in the Inner Tarai lead to the Himalaya: the Surkhet Valley, Dang Valley, Deukhuri Valley, Chitwan Valley, and Kamala Valley. In recognition of its remarkably varied flora and fauna, several national parks have been established in the Tarai; the best known is Chitwan National Park, established in 1973.

The western Tarai has been settled for ages by the Tharu, who came from India, some of whom settled in the valleys but who do not regard themselves as part of the current Madhesi Movement, and by the Dhimal and other indigenous groups who live further east.[11] The Maithili, the core population of the Madhesi (as the inhabitants of the Tarai are often called), are settled in central and eastern districts and in the Indian state of Bihar. Landless Dalit and Muslims are relatively strongly represented there, too. The Tarai is, then, by no means a culturally or ethnically homogeneous region.

The eastern part of the Tarai in particular is Nepal's breadbasket, while at the same time a small but important industrial region. It is thus essential to the country's prosperity, especially as it is home to more than half its population and contributes the most to the state's coffers. Despite this, the inhabitants are often regarded by the people in the hill regions and the high mountain areas as "Indian" or Madhesi (or Madise) rather than real Nepalese. Indeed, the Tarai is a border region with a frontier that is still largely open, and its residents have many family connections in India. Tensions between the lowlands and higher regions have flared up throughout history; they have increased in the last few years and even aroused separatist stirrings. Still, the Maithili and the Tharu in particular can look back at a long history of traditional bonds with the northern regions.

The first historical references to the Tarai are to Videha in the east, probably founded by King Janaka, who is repeatedly mentioned in the old Upaniṣads, and after whom the town Janakpur was named. Videha was a center of Vedic culture and became part of the Vajji Confederation, one of the large empires in North India around 600 BCE. Vaishali, the capital of the Licchavi, was also located in this region. According to various Sanskrit sources, Videha and Mithila were also known as the Tīrabhukti and Tirhut kingdoms, respectively. Mithila and Tirhut are therefore used for the most part as synonyms, and both India and Nepal claim to harbor the original homeland.

In the Tarai, too, lie places associated with the Buddha: Lumbini, where Gautama Buddha was born in the mid-fifth century BCE, and Kapilavastu, where his father Śuddhodana had a palace. Śuddhodana was probably actually the ruler of a small kingdom, of which there were several along the Himalaya. As the Pāli Canon says, the Buddha wandered through this region several times.

The Bengalese Pāla dynasty dominated the region from 711 to 1161; alongside and after it were various other dynasties, such as the Karnata (1087–1325), one of whose rulers, Nānyadeva, who originally came from Karnataka in South India,[12] set out and attacked the Kathmandu Valley, while their last king, Hara- or Harisiṃhadeva, fled with his family to the Kathmandu Valley, according to the chronicles, and asked for refuge in Bhaktapur. This dynasty could not effectively stand up under repeated pressure from the Moguls and thus became tributary. In 1324, by order of the sultanate of Delhi, Shams ud-dīn Ilyās attacked Mithila and then Bengal, and in 1349, having become the sultan of Bengal, he attacked the Kathmandu Valley. Several similar invasions of Mithila occurred later, but none into the Kathmandu Valley. It is not clear just how powerful Mithila's influence was in the valley, but its political and cultural connections expanded from the fourteenth century on. It also appears that a large part of the Karnata settled in Nepal. Sthiti Malla is supposed to have been a descendant of the Karnata king Harisiṃhadeva.

The Karnata dynasty was followed by the Oiniwara, whose first king, Kāmeśvara Ṭhākkura, was put on the throne in 1324/5 by Firuz Shah Tuglaq, the sultan of Delhi. This dynasty, too, remained tributary to the Muslim rulers in Delhi. The Oiniwara ruled until around 1530. After this, the power structure is unclear; the Muslims likely controlled the area more strongly than before. In 1577, Emperor Akbar appointed the Brahmin and "great landowner" (*zamindar*) of the Raj-Darbhanga dynasty Pandit Maheśa Ṭhākkura as regent. The royal status of this politically quite powerless dynasty, which ruled from the sixteenth into the twentieth century, is a matter of debate. By the mid-eighteenth century, following several battles, the Moguls had to a great extent lost their power in the Tarai. In 1765 they relinquished sovereignty and all remaining power to the East India Company.

The Sena dynasty (not to be mistaken for the Bengalese Sena) ruled sporadically over an area between the Gandaki River and the Kathmandu Valley, and were based in Makwanpur and Palpa.[13] The most famous of these rulers was Mukuṇḍa Sena I, who lived during the first half of the sixteenth century. The chronicles tell of him invading the Kathmandu Valley. Even though declared to be Magar in some documents, the Sena were Rajputs who in the fourteenth century had fled before the Muslims and had invaded the area around Butwal.[14] Mukuṇḍa Sena I weakened his kingdom by having it divided among his four sons after his death. Thus Palpa, Butwal, Tanahun, and Makwanpur became "independent principalities" (*parganna*) competing with such neighboring small kingdoms as Gulmi or Bettiah. For a long time, there were shifting alliances between the Sena kingdoms, but in the long run they could not resist being incorporated into the Gorkha polity.

At the beginning of the eighteenth century, the Sena submitted to the domination of the "governor" (Hindī *navāb*) in western Awadh but retained rights to the use of fertile land and commercially profitable forests. However, in general, the Sena became increasingly weak, so it was only a question of time before the Gorkhali, who were pressing westward after conquering the Kathmandu Valley, occupied larger parts of the Sena territory. In 1762, Makwanpur fell (it had temporarily split up into Chaudandi and Vijayapur), and in 1772 Tanahun. Palpa was still a dependency of both Awadh and the Gorkha in 1780, but in 1784 the Śāha occupied Palpa, so that its ruler, Mahadat Sena, briefly had to flee. A little later, however, he forged an alliance with Gorkha by marrying his daughter to the regent, Bahādura Śāha. By this means Palpa managed to retain a measure of sovereignty, while recognizing the pre-eminence of the Śāha. It supported them in their conquest of the western petty kingdoms, and thus remained independent for longer than the other such kingdoms. But in 1797 Palpa declared itself subject to Gīrvāṇayuddha Śāha, and in 1806 Pṛthivī Pāla, the last king of Palpa-Butwal, was summoned to Kathmandu and decapitated. Thus was the Palpa kingdom incorporated into Nepal.

Mithila remained a center of scholarship from the fourteenth to sixteenth century.[15] Jayadeva, author of the poem *Gītagovinda*, came from there, as did the mathematician and scholar Gaṇeśa Upādhyāya and philosopher

Vācaspati Miśra. Numerous important works on grammar, philosophy, and other subjects were written there, some of them in the Maithilī language itself. After the Muslim invasion of Mithila, many Brahmins fled to the Kathmandu Valley, but also to the Khasa kingdom, as can be gathered from an inscription of Jitāri Malla. They brought their manuscripts with them, many written in the Maithilī script, among them probably the oldest complete manuscript of a *Vājasaneyi-Saṃhitā*, a main text of the Veda, dating from 1428.[16] The Malla kings protected the Mithila culture and were particularly instrumental in supporting the writing of dramas in Maithilī. Such Maithili Brahmins as the Jha caste enjoyed considerable prestige at court. It is said that these Maithili Brahmins persuaded Sthiti Malla to officially introduce the caste system. In the mid-eighteenth century, the Śāha rulers looked upon the Maithili with suspicion, as the latter had helped the Malla, especially during the siege of Kirtipur, which had seemed hopeless at first.

The Tarai had always been a frontier area with open or at least porous borders between it and the petty kingdoms in the Himalaya and those in the Gangetic plain. Accordingly, there were many disputes over territorial issues and loyalties involving fluctuating claims to power, land, and taxing authority. At the beginning of the nineteenth century, there was no clear agreement on what belonged to Nepal, although the Śāha distinguished between the Tarai, which belonged to Nepal, and Mogul India (*muglāna*) including the Gangetic plain. Their claims upon this latter remained limited to a mixture of tribute and levies, along with territorial rights. But the same was claimed by the East India Company and other Indian states.

For the British, this situation was intolerable. They feared the densely forested and shadowy foothills on account of their deadly malaria and loathed the standoff—a situation that led eventually to the Anglo-Gorkha War (1814–16), the end of which brought a clear, straight frontier signifying the loss of the greater part of the western Tarai and nearly one-third of Nepal's entire territory, including Kumaon and Sikkim. If the area in the Tarai controlled by the Gorkhali until about 1810 had reached from Bhutan to the eastern part of Kangra, then at the end of the war there remained only a comparatively narrow strip. Gorkha, and more specifically Jaṅga Bahādura Rāṇā, did receive back a large area between the Mahakali and Karnali rivers in compensation for Jaṅga Bahādura's support of the British during the great Indian rebellion of 1857, but the Tarai was still smaller than it had been. Cartography played an important role during these border demarcations. The British insisted, time and again, on a straight border and the setting of immovable border stones and markers. The modern state required clear territorial frontiers that had never before existed in this form in Nepal.

Despite such cartographic and diplomatic clarifications, the Tarai remained a problematic, not fully integrated area, which led to constant friction. Many people felt that they belonged to both Nepal and India. After all, a large part of the population had come from North India. These conflicts flared up over questions of nationality, which continue to this day. After 1990, a Madhesi identity came into being; protests—some of them violent—were carried out by Khasa-Arya against discrimination and marginalization, and a strong sense of regionalism arose, spawning even separatist movements, the climax being the Madhesi Movement in 2007. The arguments brought forth against this discrimination—barriers to army enlistment, little consideration when assigning administrative and university posts, disproportionally few seats in Parliament, the unjust distribution of resources under infrastructure measures—are shared by the Madhesi with other Janajati. The Panchayat system, which had become firmly anchored in 1962 and apportioned political representation according to territorial criteria, had also led to great inequalities.

As long as no national identity had to be formed, the tensions were contained. But when the Nepal Citizenship Act of 1964 was announced, the question of which state one belonged to was revived. Thus it was often difficult for Madhesi to obtain a passport because of a lack of sufficiently credible documentation of having one's roots in Nepal. Birth and marriage certificates were missing or had been issued in India, and often there were and are strong family connections to India.

The question of national identity went no further for most people in the Tarai, however, than questions of national dress, national holidays, and the national language. In all these things, the inhabitants of the Tarai were and continue to be disadvantaged, especially following the declaration of Nepālī as the national language. This was done as a way to fence off India and the Hindī language, although most native tongues in the Tarai (e.g., Maithilī, Bhojapurī, and the Tharu languages) are related to Hindī, the lingua franca across the Tarai.

Is there such a thing as a Tarai or Maithila identity and political representation of all inhabitants of the Tarai?[17] Opinion continues to be divided on these questions. On the one hand, since the nineteenth century landless inhabitants of the hill and mountain regions have migrated into the foothills and the Tarai, with the encouragement of the Rāṇā. But this distresses the population there, who feel they are being invaded by foreigners and made landless. On the other hand, various ethnic groups and castes refuse to let themselves be compelled to take on a common Madhesi identity and instead on their own identities. This is especially true of the Tharu.

The Sherpa

Hardly any Nepalese people are so well known as the Sherpa.[18] This is owed to two things: the first ascent of Mt. Everest by the Sherpa Tenzing Norgay and Edmund (later Sir Edmund) Hillary on May 29, 1953, and that people's legendary readiness to help others—often taken advantage of—and their loyalty during expeditions. As early as 1907, Scottish physician and mountain climber Alexander Mitchell Kellas and Norwegians Carl Rubenson and Ingvald Monrad-Aas had each recruited Sherpas as porters for their climbs on Kangchenjunga. The Sherpa were quick to prove their worth by their performance, but also by their honesty, so that they have become nearly indispensable to this day for expeditions. The term "sherpa" in the meaning of assistant has found its way into the political lexicon, even if reducing this ethnic group to mere porters does not do justice to their complex social structure and history.[19]

The Sherpa (*shar pa*, meaning literally "those from the east part [of Tibet]") live for the most part in the highest regions of northeast Nepal, primarily in Khumbu, Solu, and Pharak. They immigrated into these areas in the late fifteenth and early sixteenth centuries, and thus speak a language (also called Sherpa) related to Tibetan, follow a mixture of Tibetan Buddhism and pre-Buddhist and shamanistic practices, and have settled in patrilinear clans and small villages. The census of 2011 counted about 113,000 Sherpa (including various ethnic groups that call themselves Sherpa). Many Sherpa have emigrated to India, too, especially to Darjeeling and to Sikkim.

Traditionally, the Sherpa have lived from agriculture (especially grain and potatoes), stock farming (yaks and cows), and trading in salt and rice between Tibet and the south of Nepal and India, where they have lived and worked on tea plantations or road construction sites. As they are good at handling yaks, which are suitable as pack animals for transporting wares over the high passes, they were popular as hired hands for caravans. More recently, they often work as porters and mountain guides, tourist guides, cooks, and trekking entrepreneurs. Their genetic adaptation to conditions at high altitudes has made them particularly suitable for alpine climbing and touring. Tourism has brought a certain degree of affluence.

The history of the Sherpa, for whom there are some written sources, in contrast to most other mountain peoples, is based primarily on histories written in Tibetan and documents in Nepālī preserved in monasteries and in Kathmandu, and which are accessible largely thanks to the work of anthropologists Michael Oppitz and Sherry B. Ortner. This is the source of the following briefly summarized preliminary and somewhat legendary description.

The Sherpa came probably from an area called Salmo Gang in the region of Kham in northeastern Tibet. Tibetan sources confirm that, among the

Figure 9.1 Sherpa Ngawang Tseten Lama of Metokpake, 1965, with the original manuscript of the *Rus yig* ("Report of the Bones"), a (hi)story of the Sherpa migration from Kham to Solu-Khumbu. Photo by Michael Oppitz.

migrants, there was a famous *lāmā* priest, Tertön Ratna Lingba, so that the migration can be dated to the fifteenth century. The reasons for this emigration are not known. Perhaps there were tensions between the Kham region and the Mongols, or else unknown religious or economic motives may have been key.

Emigration was restricted to four small patrilinear groups, protoclans, who are still regarded as the ancestors of the Sherpa alive today. These clans apparently did not migrate directly to the Khumbu region but went via a region around Tinkye District and south of Tsomo Tretung Lake; there they were probably driven out by troops of the Sultan Said Khan and his general Mirza Muhammad Haidar Dughlat, who had invaded south-central Tibet between 1531 and 1533.

The Sherpa then crossed the Nangpa La pass, one of the most important trade routes between China/Tibet and India, into Solukhumbu, which at the time appears to have been relatively free of settlement and to have been a hunting and pasturage area of the Rai. The sources do not report any large-scale conquests, at any rate. The protoclans distributed themselves across the entire region: the Minyagpa and Thimmi settled in the eastern and western parts of Khumbu, and the Serva and Chakpa went to Solu. Every clan laid claim to a clearly demarcated territory, in which the first villages and other subclans formed with the growth in population. This separation of places simultaneously established exogamous marriage borders.

Further Tibetan groups came to the Khumbu region at the beginning of the nineteenth century. They did not claim any origin from eastern Tibet, however, and did not keep any genealogical lists. In addition, members of other Nepalese ethnic groups, such as the Tamang, Gurung, Magar, Newar, Sunuvar, Rai, and groups originating in Bhutan, sometimes married Sherpa women. Their descendants were generally fully integrated into Sherpa culture and took on the corresponding clan names. A third group, the Khamba, came too. Immigrants from the Tingri District of Tibet, they were not regarded as pure Sherpa and therefore founded their own communities, mostly in Pharak. After the Chinese occupation of Tibet in 1959, even more Tibetan refugees came, who ended up staying for the most part.

The further history of the Sherpa is to a significant degree connected with foundations of temples and monasteries. Buddhist Sherpa priests (*lāmā*) had built smaller temples or shrines in early times, but larger public temples with "monasteries" (Tibetan *dgon pa*, *gompa*) were only added in the late seventeenth century. Between 1667 and 1720, four leading temples were built: Pangboche, Thami, Rimjung, and Zhung. Remarkably, they were no longer bound to clans and lay outside the settlements.

The first *gompa* arose in Pangboche, northeast of Namche Bazaar, probably between 1667 and 1672. It was likely intended primarily for noncelibate *lāmās*, who were different from the more ascetic *lāmās* in that they also conducted life-cycle rituals, while the former had primarily spiritual goals and performed Tantric or magic rituals. The Sherpa distinguish between the two groups by using the designations *gyudpi* for the married *lāmās* and *tolden* (= *yogin*) or *ngawa* ("wearers of black hats") for the ascetic *lāmās*.

The founder of Pangboche, Lama Sangwa Dorje, early on became a Sherpa cultural hero. It is said that all the annual *dumjes*, large exorcistic festivals, are basically rituals of commemoration for these *lāmās*. His reputation is based, among other things, on his having been sent to Kochag in Tibet as a small boy to study with a highly regarded teacher and master. His footprints are venerated at a cliff near Pangboche, where he supposedly slipped when he was searching for a suitable site for his temple foundation. In Sherpa cultural memory, Sangwa Dorje also had magical powers. He supposedly flew over Khumbu, and as a result of his meditations the god Gombu (Skt. Mahākāla) appeared as his patron divinity, for whom he had the temple built.

The Sherpa were very likely independent until the early eighteenth century, although their documents tell repeatedly of taxes paid to Tibet or Nepal. However, the indications of foreign domination are so scanty that the Sherpa were presumably controlled neither by Tibet nor by one of the smaller kingdoms in Nepal. This situation clearly changed in 1717, for there are indications in the oral tradition that they were subject to the Sena dynasty in Makwanpur for a time, supposedly because of an act of betrayal committed by a son of Zongnampha, Sangwa Dorje's great rival. Given the breakdown of the Sena dynasty its control over the Sherpa was, in any event, unlikely to have been strong.

The relations between the Sherpa and the Gorkha kingdom, which subdued them in the course of their conquests of eastern kingdoms between 1772 and 1774, were a mixture of contempt, non-interference, and mutual support. There were few open conflicts, but the Bahun-Chhetri regarded the Sherpa as lower in the hierarchy and classified them in the *Ain*, together with the Cepang, Danuvar, Hayu, Tharu, Rai, Limbu, and Tamang, as Bhote (Tibetoid ethnic groups) that fell within the category of the "Enslavable Alcohol Drinker" castes (*māsinyā matvālī*). The tendency to regard the Sherpa as impure and to propagate Hindu values of purity, however, strengthened rather than weakened their Buddhist-Lamaist identity. One conflict reflective of this concerned the Sherpa attitude toward slaughtering cows, which had been forbidden countrywide by the *Ain* under penalty of death. This conflict led to what is probably the first official journey of a Gorkha civil servant to Solukhumbu in 1805.

The Gorkhali introduced a new administrative structure, and new centers of trade arose. Nauje, renamed Namche Bazaar, grew into an important commercial town and a hub of the trade with Tibet. To collect taxes—mostly on "communal and collective land" (*kipaṭa*), parceled out to households—the Gorkhali created the position of *gembu* (Nep. *amālī*), who had the task of supervising the powerful regional administrator (*pembu*, Nep. *dvāre*). This figure was mentioned for the first time in a document from 1810. With this structure the government in Kathmandu could afford to concede to the Sherpa the monopoly on trade with Tibet, which meant that all other traders had to sell the goods they intended for Tibet to the Sherpa.

The Gorkhali faced a basic dilemma. On the one hand, they had to decentralize power; on the other hand, there was always the threat that those to whom such power was delegated could become too powerful and thus independent. Indeed, civil servants exploited their positions to enrich themselves. Thus, in 1892, some 450 Sherpa in Solukhumbu rebelled against the *dvāre* Jit Man Basnet, who had repeatedly demanded increased taxes, unjustifiably from the peasants' viewpoint, and did not hesitate to dispossess any farmer who did not pay. Eventually the protesters were officially judged to be in the right by Prime Minister Vīra Śamśera.[20]

The balance between the local and central powers, however, was always in danger, especially since peasants who felt oppressed often simply migrated to other regions where they had to pay less. Many documents thus call upon the tax collectors to rein themselves in and the renegades to return. A document from 1825 also directly states that the Sherpa do not have to give tax collectors additional free food or carry loads for them. "Neither the superintendent nor the government officials should cause the inhabitants any trouble," a further document declares.[21]

The Gorkhali presented themselves as the ones who ensured law and order, could end the tyranny of local powerful administrators, and therefore could be trusted. Thus, one of the earliest documents, dating from 1791, reads:

> You are loyal subjects, live loyally! Our "village superintendant" (*jeṭhābuḍhā*) and *dvāres* will not harass you. Our troops, too, will not harass

> you. Live loyally at your homes! Nobody will be permitted to plunder your possessions. If someone does harass you, come to Us, and We shall listen to the case and shall punish the harasser.[22]

The internal hierarchies were strengthened during Rāṇā rule, but there was an upswing in the economy, too, which led to the foundation of prestigious monasteries for celibate monks and nuns. These economic changes were related to the expansion of the British East India Company in eastern Nepal and northeastern India. The British had won back Sikkim through their victory in the war with Nepal but had also come to recognize that Nepal as a whole should not be conquered as long as the rulers in Kathmandu were not openly hostile. Since they did not want to give up their lucrative trade, they were looking for a trade route through Darjeeling and Sikkim. In addition, from 1841 on they created large tea plantations in Darjeeling, which made rapid strides thanks to new infrastructure. In 1866, Darjeeling was connected to the great network of roads in Bengal; in 1877, a road across the Jelap Pass in Sikkim was finished; and between 1855 and 1878 a railway was built between Kolkata and Darjeeling.

All of this required labor, and the Sherpa quickly saw an opportunity and seized it. They came in large numbers, as laborers and businessmen. Most of them remained in Darjeeling, but some returned wealthy. They likewise intensified their trade between Tibet and India through the Tarai, bringing Tibetan horses and ponies and fetching rice and other grain in exchange for them, or selling salt on the way to the southern regions.

A further source of wealth lay in serving some function within the state administration, preferably that of tax collector, a position that Sherpa exploited by having tenants work for them. Sometimes local administrators were given tax-free land (*birtā*) by the king or prime minister for special services rendered. This happened to one *lāmā* who supposedly was able to make it rain and who then founded the temple in Chalsa.

The Rāṇā administration did try to limit the status and power of tax collectors by paying them a salary instead of shares in land revenue, but this change was only moderately successful. The introduction of the *pajanī* system, probably by Pṛthvīnārāyaṇa, had been more influential; under it, all state employees had to have their rights and privileges confirmed once a year. In this way, the notoriously demanding *gempu* administrators, who were very unpopular among the Sherpa, were restrained to a certain extent.

Powerful people used some of their wealth to build monasteries for celibate monks and nuns in order to acquire prestige and respect and to legitimize that wealth. Sherpa society was basically founded on an egalitarian ethic, which expressed itself in equal rights of inheritance for children and all adult males' right to equal status and land of their own. Any economic inequality thus required justification, which was supplied by, among other things, the wealthy building or promoting the large monasteries in Rumbu (1902), Tengboche (1916), and Chiwong (1923), or the temple in Nauje (1905).

Boosted by new media, tourism provided the Sherpa with a further catalyst for growth from the 1960s on, but also brought far-reaching changes to their society. Today, even the Everest Base Camp has internet, and in April 2017 famed DJ Paul Oakenfold held the "highest (rave) party in the world" there. Goethe's exalted words "Mountains are mute masters who make for silent pupils" from *Wilhelm Meister's Journeyman Years* is still true in Nepal, but not everywhere there.

This historical sketch of the Sherpa is a good example of how many peoples—ones who, despite many commonalities, by no means form homogeneous communities—have developed in the high mountain regions. They have each lived in isolation, and again and again they have had to open up and adapt transculturally. At the same time, their only chance of preserving their identity is to emphasize their traditions and uniqueness. This more or less succeeds, at least when it comes to tourism, but not everywhere in Nepal's mountains are the conditions as favorable as they are in the Sherpa region. Many areas have been abandoned entirely or are inhabited only by the old, women, and children. Agriculture is no longer lucrative or even sustainable for survival. Work outside the fields is hard to come by, and if there is any, it is seasonal. The young men go where there is work: to the Kathmandu Valley, to India, or to the Gulf states. They send back money with which those left behind can see to their needs, buying American wheat, oil from Singapore, clothing from China, or smartphones from South Korea, while they themselves produce less and less.

Always swirling around the rather egalitarian "Tibetan" ethnic groups in the mountains, who traditionally know no castes, is the question of how far the long arm of Kathmandu reaches. They practice their folk religions, shamanism, Tibetan Buddhism, or the old Bön religion, and at the same time must defend themselves against the influences of what is largely Nepal's

Hinduistically shaped civil service and culture, whose structures and norms have been formed by the caste system. They speak among each other what for outsiders are barely comprehensible Tibetan dialects, but the educated usually also speak the official language, Nepālī. They live to some extent in extreme conditions, but have adapted to these, although they have been suffering from widespread rural depopulation. Their transregional trade activities often make them transcultural mediators. Very few have any documented history; instead they have a very detailed oral tradition in which much is as well preserved as it would have been in writing.

Mustang

The history of the Sherpa has already shown how much the high mountain regions are exposed to influences and attacks that cause the peoples there to create specific mechanisms by which to stand up for themselves. This is true in particular of the former kingdom of Mustang (from the Tibetan *smon-thang*, pronounced [*mœntang*]), a high mountain region stretching along the Kali Gandaki Valley to the Kora La Pass.[23] It is harsh terrain, where the temperature can fall to −22° F in winter, biting winds blow, and little precipitation falls. Agriculture is therefore only possible in the southern areas along the rivers.

The region is divided into a northern area (Upper Mustang), also known as Lo, and a southern area (Lower Mustang), consisting of the administratively and ethnically separate enclaves of Baragaon (also called "Lower Lo") and Shöyul (a group of five linguistically distinct villages, Panchgaon (a further ensemble of five villages—Thini, Shang, Tsherog, Cimang, and Marpha—whose non-Tibetan speaking population is counted as Thakali[24]), and Thak (or Thak Khola), in the main settled by Thakali. The distinction between Upper and Lower Mustang is fairly recent; it simply separates Lo from the other regions. The population of Lo, called Lopa, speaks a Western Tibetan language. Thakali and Gurung live there alongside them.

This region has many prehistoric caves and extensive cave systems, which were excavated into the cliffs at various levels up to 328 feet high. The caves appear to have served as tombs in prehistoric times (going back to about 1200 BCE), and later as living quarters, meditation sites, and places of refuge.[25] Numerous rock paintings depicting stylized hoofprints, animals, axes, scenes of sacrifice, and a few more recent Buddhist symbols and

Figure 9.2 Sketch of a cave drawing in Mustang. Sketch by Perdita Pohle.

reliquary shrines point to a long period of settlement. The region was settled by Tibetan ethnic groups starting in the seventh century, but the fortress of Muktinath was not constructed until the fourteenth century. Buddhism is archaeologically confirmed in this area from about 1000 CE. Furthermore, some twenty deserted sites of villages and fields, together with ruins of old fortresses and monasteries along rivers, testify to large-scale movements of populations.

Between Baragaon and Panchgaon lie Jomsom (the current district capital) and Kag (Nep. Kagbeni). Kag is the gateway to the eastern Muktinath Valley and, at 12,713 feet altitude, the temple of the same name. The small, multi-roofed temple is an important Hindu (and less so, Buddhist) pilgrimage destination. It contains a statue of Viṣṇu, honored as the "god of liberation," and numerous ammonites, likewise regarded as Viṣṇu. The temple is surrounded by 108 fountains for ritual baths. Buddhists in particular regard this water as holy, and the temple Chumig Gyatsa is called in Tibetan, "Hundred Fountains." They also regard the place as a seat of Avalokiteśvara, a stage along Padmasambhava's journey to Tibet where he is supposed to have

Figure 9.3 A fortress (*dzong*) in Mustang. Photo by Perdita Pohle.

meditated, and as one of the twenty-four Tantric places of the Ḍākinī, the heavenly dancers.

The formerly independent kingdom of Lo was a demilitarized zone until 1992 and was long looked upon as a place shrouded in secrets and cut off from the outside world. Only a few foreigners who paid a hefty fee for the privilege were permitted to enter Mustang. On October 7, 2008, it was absorbed administratively by Nepal, and so dissolved in a legal sense as a kingdom. The last official king, Jigme Dorje Palbar Bista, traced his dynasty back to Amepal, a noble from the neighboring Tibetan region of Gungthang who founded the Buddhist kingdom in the fifteenth century. Bista's son Agönpal extended the kingdom to cover nearly the entire area of the district created in 1962, with its capital Lo Manthang.

Recently Lo has begun increasingly to open up, both to tourism and to China. Both processes have been strongly energized by the construction of roads—one from the Chinese border to Lo Manthang, and another, traversable only by Jeep, from Pokhara through the Kali Gandaki Valley. In addition, the region is accessible by air thanks to an airport opened in Jomsom that was finished in 1962.

The people live by trade, raising livestock, and, increasingly, tourism. However, the rural exodus is considerable. In the long winter, people leave the thinly settled highland area for more low-lying regions. Trade is based for the most part on an old route from India/Nepal to Tibet/China across the comparatively low Kora La Pass, which was closed in 1950 after China's annexation of Tibet but was re-opened in 2001. Between the fifteenth and seventeenth centuries, the kingdom of Lo controlled this route, but in 1795 the kingdom was annexed by Gorkha and became tributary.

In Tibetan sources, Mustang is divided into two parts: Lo and Serib, a region shrouded in legend. Lo covered the area along the border with China up to the village of Gilling in Tibet's shadow, while Serib stretched from Jomsom to Cimang, a region of groups who do not speak Tibetan. The oldest Tibetan documents, above all the Dunhuang annals, report that King Songtsen Gampo conquered what is now West Tibet, including Lo and Serib, at the start of the eighth century. Serib apparently rebelled against Tibet in 705. Afterward Mustang repeatedly fell under the control of kingdoms surrounding it: Tibet from the seventh to nineth century; Khasa in the twelfth and thirteenth centuries; Gungthang in the thirteenth and fourteenth centuries; Jumla from the sixteenth to eighteenth century; and finally Gorkha at the end of the eighteenth century. In 1788, when the Gorkhali began their first war with Tibet, Jumla seized this opportunity to invade Lo. But the war was soon over, and in 1789 the Gorkhali conquered Jumla, so Lo also came under their control. When the Gorkha troops reached Lo, the inhabitants offered no resistance, and they were then allowed to preserve their local polity as long as they paid tribute.

The Rāṇā prime ministers brought momentous change by claiming a monopoly on the profitable salt trade along the Kali Gandaki. From the eighteenth century on, the right to trade had been auctioned off to traders licensed by the government, but under the Rāṇā the traders had to sell their salt to contractual buyers. As these latter were given far-reaching rights, the authority of the nobles and the autonomy of Lo both suffered considerably.

British anthropologist Charles Ramble has proposed a theory significant for the entire mountain region of Nepal.[26] Eschewing the usual separation of Buddhist and other, non-Buddhist traditions, Ramble shows that Buddhist ritual and indigenous popular traditions are two elements of a complex system of self-regulation, which, over the centuries, has taken on the character of a civil religion and thereby held its own against constant external and internal threats. The people of the village where he went for his fieldwork manifest unusual solidarity and cohesion, enabling them to stand together against regional and rival powers and villages, straighten out local disputes, forge strategies of cooperation, and clear up legal questions. The villagers' beliefs and practices are related primarily to divinities that are bound to the locality rather than to any universal idea; a highly developed legal tradition; and a form of government that provides for accountability through, for example, the democratic election of the village headman. Such institutions developed from the community, were created by the people, and have proven very pragmatic. To secure them, there is no need for religion, or at the most a need for a civil religion. Ramble thus sees elements of a civil religion developing even at the village level, something that had previously thought to be possible only at the state level. On a village level, Buddhism and non-Buddhist indigenous beliefs do not, therefore, enter into some kind of syncretism in which they complement each other, nor do they form a new, hybrid religion, but instead represent other areas of life that are significant more for the individual than for the community.

This analysis of a remote village in Mustang is so important because it shows what forms of social and cultural resilience can be developed by peoples of the mountain regions despite enormous transcultural influences. It also shows how local cultures can balance preservation and modernization by relying on social structures of their own. This is a serious alternative to the model of a uniformly imposed national system that weakens the responsibility of political leaders and exacerbates rather than dampens internal conflicts, and is an option that does not have to be at the expense of the many ethnic groups' diversity.

The Kiranti (Rai-Limbu) in Eastern Nepal

Kiranti (Kirānti) is the designation for an assemblage of ethnic groups, the main ones of which are the Rai (or Khambu) and the Limbu (or Yakthumba), who live for the most part in the eastern foothills but in the past occupied the area between the Tamakoshi and Tista rivers, and between Tibet and the Tarai.[27] To be more exact, the region of the Kiranti is divided into the "near" (*vallo*) Kirant area between the Sunkoshi River and the mountain Gaurishankar, mostly settled by the Sunuvar; the "central" (*mājh*) Kirant west of the Arun River, settled mostly by the Rai; and the "distant" (*pallo*) Kirant of the Limbu, lying to the east. These populations are divided into socially and linguistically smaller groups called *thars*. Thus the Rai are divided into more than two dozen sub-groups, such as the Mewahang Rai, Khaling Rai,

Chamling Rai, Thulung Rai, and Kulung Rai. Linguists have counted over fifty different Tibeto-Burman Rai dialects or languages; the Limbu language is more homogeneous. Not until the nineteenth century did the Rai (whose name means "king" or "prince" and is derived from Skt. *rājan*) amalgamate into one ethnic group and develop a shared identity, including shared political interests. Sometimes other groups speaking Tibeto-Burman languages are counted among the Kiranti, such as the Sunuvar or Hayu, or the Danuvar and Meche or Dhimal (both of which live in the Tarai), but not the Sherpa or Tamang, who came to Nepal from Tibet. According to the census of 2011, the Kiranti make up 3.1% of the population; today, only about one-third of the population of eastern Nepal is Kiranti.

Whether, and if so what, the Kiranti have to do with the old Kirāti or Kirāta mountain tribes named in Indian sources is still debated. This will probably never be finally clarified, but presumably before the Licchavi ruled in the Kathmandu Valley a Tibeto-Burman group related to the Kiranti held sway there. Interestingly, the Newar of Dolakha speak a Nevārī that is closer to Kiranti than Kathmandu Nevārī. But it may also be that the Kiranti were so named, or so called themselves, in order to emphasize their non-Hindu and indigenous origin.

Due to a lack of written sources, little is known about the older history of the Kiranti. However, the Rai-Limbu do have a strong oral tradition that preserves much relating to their origins. According to these myths, they came from the south into the eastern valleys and forged marriage alliances with Tibetoid groups in the north. Apart from earlier mention in Tibetan sources, written material first appears during the Makwanpur Sena dynasty The first firm eyewitness information comes from Francis Buchanan Hamilton, who reported in 1819 that the Sena had allied themselves with the Kiranti, who continued to assert their cultural and political autonomy, especially in the higher regions. This is echoed by the historian Kumar Pradhan, who wrote that "[t]he Kirats, although nominally under the rule of the Senas, enjoyed complete autonomy in the mountains."[28]

Indeed, the history of eastern Nepal, which, depending on the epoch, must include Darjeeling and parts of Sikkim and Tibet, is a history of constantly shifting alliances, loyalties, and rulers. The Tibetans, the Sena, the many small principalities, and later the British and the Gorkhali had competing claims and challenged or fought against each other. Sometimes there were simultaneous obligations to multiple alliances and corresponding payments of tribute to different rulers. Thus, in 1663 the Limbu (Tibetan Gtsong), Bhutia (the Lho, a Tibetoid group in modern Bhutan), and Lepcha (the Mon, the indigenous people of Sikkim) joined together in what is called the Lho-Mon-Tsong alliance, under the leadership of the Bhutia. It seems, though, that the Limbu were so oppressed by Tibet and the Bhutia that they fled in the eighteenth century to Limbuwan, their current area of settlement in Nepal, thereby cutting their ties to Sikkim. With the drawing of the border between the British and the Gorkhali in 1816, the Limbu were again severed culturally and religiously from their region of origin, for in Nepal Hinduism was propagated as the state religion, even as in Sikkim Buddhism had been. Again, the Limbu and other Nepalese who were constantly migrating to Sikkim in the nineteenth and twentieth centuries, along with the remaining Sikkimese Limbu, were treated as foreigners and correspondingly disadvantaged.

Hamilton reported that in the sixteenth century the ruler in Morang in southeast Nepal was Vijayanārāyaṇa, after whom the historically important town of Vijayapur (near Dharan) was named. This ruler took a Rai leader (*hang*) named Siṃha Rāi, who controlled the areas north of Morang, into his service, but had him killed shortly thereafter on the charge that he had forced a Hindu woman to eat beef. The son of the Rai leader—Hamilton calls him "Baju Ray"—then sought help from the Sena of Mawanpur. Lohanga, the son of the Sena king Mukuṇḍa Sena I, thereupon actually did conquer several small principalities in eastern Nepal, including Chaudandi and Morang. The Kiranti living in the hills, however, did not regard themselves as subjects of this ruler, although the Kiranti leader had been appointed as *cautariyā*, an office similar to a provincial governor and equal in rank with a prime minister. The extent of his area of influence remains unclear. This connection between a Hindu king and a leader of the Kiranti formed the basis for the later integration of the Kiranti into the Gorkha kingdom.

As this episode shows, the Sena presented themselves overtly as "protectors of Hinduism." That is indeed what they called themselves: *hindupati*. But after Mukuṇḍa Sena I they were at odds with each other and unable to establish a stable kingdom in the east. It was only the Śāha king Pṛthvīnārāyaṇa who managed to do so, after conquering eastern Nepal between 1772 and 1774. In a document of 1774, the king complained that many Kiranti had fled to India and Sikkim, so he was considering attacking Sikkim. Continuous resistance was expressed through a refusal to pay taxes, but in the end the military superiority of the Śāha king proved too great. The last pockets of Limbu resistance were destroyed in 1786. Pṛthvīnārāyaṇa granted the local rulers—as in the rest of the land—privileges and even a certain autonomy in matters of justice and taxation. In an order of 1774, he wrote to the Limbu ruler, Myang Hang Yang:

> We have received your reply to our previous letter. We desire peace and harmony. Our intent is good. We had afforded you refuge previously also. We have conquered your country by dint of our valor. The descendants of Tu Tu Myang Hang Yang were defeated and the country now belongs to us. But you [too now] belong to us and we undertake the protection of your kinsmen. We hereby pardon all of your crimes and confirm the customs and traditions, rights and privileges of your country. Join our Bharadars and render them assistance. Take care of the land as you did when it was being ruled over by your own chieftains. Enjoy the land from generation to generation as long as it remains in existence. You are different from the 900,000 Rai [of Majhkirat], because [their] chieftains are to be displaced, but not you. . . . In case we confiscate your land, may our ancestral gods destroy our kingdom.
>
> We hereby inscribe this pledge on a copper plate and also issue this royal order and hand it over to our Limbu brethren.[29]

In this proclamation, Pṛthvīnārāyaṇa mentions one particular feature of Rai-Limbu religion, namely its ancestral cult. For most Rai-Limbu, respect toward the ancestors and the spiritual relations based on it are a central concern. This is expressed in their "religion," which is actually more a repository of their tradition (called the Muddum or Mundhum) requiring neither meditation nor worship, but rather that the ancestors be honored and a specific way of living with them be followed, which distinguishes it from Hinduism (although this is widespread in Nepal and has also influenced the Kiranti). The Mundhum is a mythological corpus, transmitted orally and explaining many things: the origin of life, the first settlers, the villages and their relations to each other, natural phenomena, the culture and rituals, and the differences among the various social groups, which are very strongly oriented around "exogamous, patrilinear clans" (*thar*). In traditional Limbu clans, a wife was sought from another village. Another characteristic of the Kiranti religion is the division of religious duties between a priest-specialist, who primarily tends to relations with the ancestors, and a shaman, who can communicate with the spirits and the Hindu gods.

Pṛthvīnārāyaṇa also indirectly refers to the *kipaṭa* or communal land use system, which was dominant among the Kiranti. It was based on tribal customary law and meant that the land was used communally, while being allotted to the most powerful man in the village community (*rāi*, *subbā*, *jimmavāla*), who would later be named by the Gorkha king. The Rai then leased the land out to the peasants. Private ownership of this land did not exist, nor did state ownership of it. Consequently, the land was taxed per household, not by area. The Limbu strongly resisted the abolition of the *kipaṭa* system under the Rāṇā, but it could not survive in the long run after the intentional resettlement of other ethnic groups there, particularly Hindu castes that received fallow land from the state. Under the *Mulukī Ain* of 1888, *kipaṭa* land was formally transformed into *raikara* land, which in turn was completely abolished in the 1960s.

Until the constitution of 1990, ethnic groups in Nepal had little opportunity to express their identity. This has changed radically in the last few decades, with some groups even striving for independence or at least autonomous status—among them, radical Limbu, who have called for an autonomous state of Limbuwan. A pioneer of this movement was Mahāguru Phālgunanda Lingden (1885–1949), who was initially an adherent of a *bhakti* sect and then founded a new Kirāta religion, which instituted strict vegetarianism and the non-consumption of alcohol, abolished orthodox caste barriers, and above all attempted to strengthen Kiranti pride and nationalism. Phālgunanda, who fought as a soldier in Burma and Europe in the First World War, called this religion "religion of truth" (*satyadharma*), and indeed it did contain several of the purity features found in Hinduism, even if its followers did not regard it as a form of Hinduism. Phālgunanda combined his religious ideas with a pedagogical mission, setting up schools and spreading a script modeled on Devanāgarī called Śrījaṅga that is allegedly ancient, but which is documented only from the beginning of the nineteenth century on.

This new Kirānti religion spread quite rapidly, as can be seen from the many temples for Phālgunanda. The sense of Kiranti pride connected with it has gained numerous followers, not only among Phālgunanda's various successors, but also among intellectuals such as Iman Singh Chemjong (1904–1975), whose history of the Kiranti is one great glorification of the Rai-Limbu past.

From Empire to Nation State

The Śāha dynasty was unable to unify the country beyond a token Hinduization. Usually the kings were too weak, mentally too disturbed, or too young to rule the country. Between 1777 and 1950, six of the seven kings were between two and six years old at the time of their coronation; the last king, Gyanendra, was only three years old at the time of his first coronation. As a result, there were intense power struggles among regents, be they queens,[30] queen mothers, or prime ministers. Another consequence was massacres: in 1846, the Koṭa Massacre, when nearly the entire ruling elite was liquidated; or on June 1, 2001, when the crown prince killed his parents, siblings, and other relatives.

Moreover, for most of its history the country had a dual system of rule, and thus no clear center of power. Until the beginning of the twentieth century, it had no plainly demarcated territory with a secure border; even today, the border with India is porous and the citizenship of the people living along it is often unregulated or contested. The state consisted to a large extent of rights and privileges—both symbolic and material—exercised over land, labor, water, forests, markets, and the flow of goods and capital. These rights were granted by various authorities, mostly by the king, but also by aristocrats, officials, vassals, and other influential people. Thus wealth in the form of taxes came into the Kathmandu Valley, and privileges and prestige were granted to the favored local elites. Collectively the privileged few held the country together. Nepal in the sense of a modern state as a clearly defined space and identity existed to a minimal degree at best. In its place, there were powerful non-state forms of activity and political influence.

For example, Nepal did not have a uniform people to constitute the state in the form of a group who settled in its territory with some kind of state-defined and guaranteed membership in the community. As late as 1968, a husband-and-wife team of researchers could report:

> Some mountain tribes and villages in Nepal are still not conscious of there being a nation of Nepal. They see themselves as members of a different kind of ethnic grouping, and citizenship in a great organization is incomprehensible to them. *Nepal*, for them, simply designates the Kathmandu Valley.[31]

Nepal, that is, had many ethnic groups that enjoyed different types of power and whose identities were fluid. Among these was the model of "consensual rule" prevalent in the European Middle Ages and met with in the case of Mustang, a form of rule that does not deny "hierarchies or dependencies in commanding and obeying, but reflects the connection of monarchic rule to the medieval hierarchy of nobles and the cooperation of the estates."[32]

The question of independence thus engaged Nepal throughout the nineteenth and twentieth centuries. For a long time, the British did not officially regard the country as independent, but they nevertheless treated it as an almost independent state, for example signing treaties with it. In fact, the first treaties and agreements were not agreed upon with Nepal, but rather with whatever king was in power at the time. The East India Company surrounded the country on three sides, and in the north was the nearly impassable Himalaya. There was therefore no worry of Nepal becoming a power to reckon with. As late as 1903, the viceroy, Lord Curzon, wrote that Nepal was exclusively under the political influence and control of Great Britain. Although Nepal had never officially recognized the suzerainty of the British, it only officially declared itself independent in 1923, which was then acknowledged by the British.[33]

A monopoly on the application of force in the administration, judiciary, finance, and the military was claimed by the Kathmandu Valley (as the *Ain* shows), but remained limited in effect or powerless internally (the period of the Maoist rebellion once again threw this into sharp relief). Monopoly on the application of force externally, that is, waging war, was based on the recruitment of (at first) only a few loyal ethnic groups and castes, not on some general obligation to perform military duty. Other ethnic groups and the Tarai, which borders on the North Indian plain, had always had an ambivalent attitude toward the central government. Nepal remained an empire, albeit a small one, but without the dynamism of the modern European state. "Nepal was neither a nation in being, nor in hope," as historian Kumar Pradhan succinctly puts it.[34]

The Śāha kings were not primarily interested in a territorial state, but in loyalties and possessions (*muluk*) in an area the borders of which did not necessarily coincide with the state or territory.[35] There was no national strategy. Most social conflicts were not negotiated at the national level, but within castes and clans.[36] As in the medieval feudal system, the king owned the entire country and transferred to certain individuals titles to land of varying size and extent, ranging from a district or groups of people, to sometimes entire realms.[37] These land titles had to be confirmed annually during Dasaĩ, during a personal reception ceremony (*pajanī*). At the same time, the king recognized old rights of possession—for example, tribal rights in the communal land system (*kipaṭa*)—without, of course, giving up his fundamental claim to the land.

Pṛthvīnārāyaṇa and his successors were enabled, basically, to keep the country together only by this distribution of sinecures and privileges, by the application of force and the ideology of the allegedly unifying Hindu king, and by fostering a "Pahāḍī identity," with which the inhabitants of the hill regions were led to distinguish themselves from their fellow southern inhabitants in the Tarai (the Madhesi) and India.[38] The means were exploitative, the burden they posed resting to a horrifying extent on the peasants, Tibetoid and related ethnic groups, and the Dalits. There was the fundamental and discriminatory division of people into the "wearers of the Sacred Thread" (*tāgādhārī*)—the Brahmins, Thakuri, Chhetri and also some high-caste Newar—and the "Alcohol Drinkers" (*matvālī*)—the Tibetoid and such related groups as the Newar, Magar, Gurung, Sherpa, Rai, and Limbu, many of whom were assigned the status of Shudra. This hierarchization of the population took place according to law, the *Ain*, meaning that it was imposed. A process of Sanskritization was carried out, entailing, for example, an increase in prestige when local deities received Sanskrit-Brahmanical names and rituals. One regulation stated that ethnic groups had to pay for certain traditions, such as the consumption of beef when the animal had not been killed expressly for this purpose. Draconian measures, based on caste, followed: capital punishment, confiscation of property, degradation of one's caste status or exclusion from one's caste, exile, or slavery. Pejorative expressions were applied to ethnic groups, such as Murmi for the Tamang and Bhote for Tibetans or related groups. And certain groups were not considered for recruitment into the army.

The ruling Gorkhali either did not perceive the ethnic, linguistic, and religious diversity flourishing in their country, or else they attempted to suppress it. Some 123 languages are still being spoken in Nepal (according to Article 1.6 of the Constitution of 2015, they are all national languages), and 125 ethnic groups and castes are registered as such. This diversity, perhaps unique in the world, is a challenge that Nepal faces, and occasionally struggles with, but in doing so builds on it too.

In 1951, Nepal opened its international borders, and on December 14, 1955, it joined the world stage by becoming a member of the United Nations. In 1949, however, Russia and the Ukraine had voted against its membership, seeing Nepal more as a colony of India than an independent country. Nepal gradually developed into an internationally active nation state, and entered into modern global networks and bodies, such as the Universal Postal Union, the International Red Cross, and the International Olympic Committee.[39] Has this opening up strengthened the country's ability to function?

At first, Nepal attempted to force internal unity upon itself, meaning the dominance of the Khasa-Arya. All its people were to become Nepalese, dutiful subjects of the Hindu kingdom; Nepalese Tibetoid groups (Bhoṭiyā) and Muslims were not the only ones troubled by such a descriptor. There was no government office without a portrait of the Hindu king.

In addition, Nepālī was declared both the national and the official language. This was detrimental to several other languages that, being spoken by minorities, had little chance of becoming or remaining official languages, or at least of being promoted in schools. The motto of the Panchayat era was "one language, one style of clothing, one king, one country" (*eka bhāṣā, eka bheṣa, eka rājā, eka deśa*). The conscious aim was self-containment vis-à-vis India, since Maithilī and Bhojapurī, languages more closely associated with India, were rejected as official languages, even though a majority in Nepal speak them.

Furthermore, the typical Khasa-Arya garb became the national dress. This meant the sari for women and, for men, the long shirt (*daurā/labedā*), the trousers wide at the top and narrow at the bottom (*suruvāla*), and a cap (*ṭopī*). The *khukurī*, a distinctive knife with a curved blade, became a national symbol. Ethnicity was tolerated as such only in the form of folklore and in reaction to the Western preference for "authentic" culture. Public cultural events, such as dance or song evenings, and the increase in ethnic holidays bear witness to this tendency. There are now several New Year's festivals: Gyalpo or Bhotia Lhosar, Sonam or Tamang Lhosar, Tamu or Gurung Lhosar; in addition, there are celebrations on the occasion of calendrical change: Vikrama Samvat, Nepal Samvat, Hijri Calendar, the Gregorian Calendar, and Yele Samvat.

Equality under the law based on a unified notion of jurisprudence and the principle of universal equality has been in force in Nepal since 1990. Thus, centuries of oppression became a thing of the past, apart from the ten-year tyranny of the Maoist rebels. Secularization, too, had finally been achieved, although its limits have repeatedly been tested. For example, the tradition of the Kumārī child-goddess, who legitimated the authority of all kings once a year by giving them the red forehead mark, continued to be followed by all prime ministers and presidents, although Nepalese civil society has attempted for some years to forbid such "child labor." Neither a democratic national state as the executor of the unified will of the people nor a social welfare state has yet arrived, given the hindrances created by the caste system, but they are showing ever more signs of emerging.

Nepal has found itself, then, on the path to a modern nation state, which has made the problem of ethnicity particularly fraught. The Khasa-Arya of the Panchayat Period (1962–1990) skillfully played one side against the other. They favored nationality (*rāṣṭriyatā*) and regarded any shift of emphasis toward ethnicity as a step backward. Modernization for them meant overcoming ethnicity. This earned them the hostility of large parts of the Tarai, along with that of the ethnic minorities in the mountain regions and marginalized groups such as the Muslims and Dalits.

This shows that Nepal has followed a three-stage model of national unity:[40] It began with the "Empire" model of Pṛthvīnārāyaṇa Śāha, with different social hierarchies and legal systems, without any tendency to a unified culture. Under the leadership of Mahendra (and, to some extent, Bīrendra Śāha), the Panchayat system emerged as a symbol of a culturally unified nation in contemporary times. This system aimed to incorporate modern democratic principles, citizenship, efficient governance, and a commitment to ensuring equal treatment of all citizens under the law, while also safeguarding their well-being within a welfare state, along with a kind of unified national culture, with minority cultures simultaneously being suppressed or neglected. Finally, it moved to the Republic of Nepal's model of "pluricultural integration" after 1990, as ethnic minorities claim their political rights and see them becoming written into the constitution.

Conclusion

The recent past has not brought the streamlined unification that many had dreamt of for Nepal, namely a modern nation state embedded in today's globalized world. On the contrary, the more that nationalization has been propagated, the more minorities have become vocal. Ethnicity was suddenly no longer perceived as a relic of the deep past but as a resource. Indeed, ethnic groups collectively form a majority in some parts of the country. Even in the parliament of 1990, not only were Brahmins overrepresented compared to their proportion of the population but the Limbu, Gurung, Newar, and Thakali were too.[1] But the ethnic minorities were too weak, too divided, and too heterogeneous to secede from Nepal. This is true, in particular, of the Tarai, which could not cobble together a majority in favor of separation.

Nationalization has doubtless come at a price. Nepal has become a victim of the disenchanted modern world, particularly in areas affected by globalization: as a developing country in need of help; as a country overrun, spoiled, and littered by tourists; and as a country that loses its younger generation to foreign labor migration. Given the population growth, immigration from rural areas, environmental degradation, and political unrest, the impression that Nepal has not been coping well has gathered strength. This impression was considerably reinforced by the international media in the wake of the earthquakes of 2015. Nepal, long viewed as a Shangri La, has been increasingly described as a paradise lost, or worse yet, as a failed state. The main grounds cited are foreign labor migration, a lack of infrastructure (energy, water, transportation, communication, education, and health care), corruption, low economic growth, massive internal migration and urbanization, and violent conflicts between political parties and the Maoist movement and between castes or ethnic groups, along with the impact of development aid and tourism.

Aid has been being given to Nepal for around sixty-five years. According to the World Bank, more than a billion US dollars are allegedly promised to the country annually, in 2019 1,364 billion. Despite this, Nepal is still

Nepal. Axel Michaels, Oxford University Press. English language edition © Oxford University Press 2024.
DOI: 10.1093/oso/9780197650936.003.0011

one of the most underdeveloped countries in Asia. The reasons for this do not lie just with the Maoists, for the infrastructure destroyed during the civil war was relatively quickly restored. Far more responsible are corrupt state corporations, business syndicates, and the military exercising temporary monopolies on electricity, drinking water, gas, transport, and other necessities. One-quarter of all aid money is never spent; it just disappears. As long as the aid is not given by the donor with clear stipulations on its use, it will often not have the desired effect. One example is the money that was spent following the 2015 earthquakes.

As is well known, Nepal is an extremely popular destination for tourists because of its unique culture and natural landscape, including its national parks (20% of the country's area is protected). Tourists want a slice of untouched nature, but they themselves touch it and often leave it full of rubbish during Himalayan treks or at Mt. Everest. They want authenticity and turn away when the native population reconfigures, quite authentically, their cultural heritage as they understand it, or when, according to Western preconceptions, they disfigure it, such as by installing neon lights in old pagoda temples. Tourists want the old traditions and rituals, but are horrified when blood flows, for example, during the Dasaĩ festival, when animals are still sacrificed in front of almost every Hindu house. Tourists want to get away and experience something wholly different, but somehow it all needs to be as if they were still at home; they seek diversity, but not too much of it. Tourists, then, are the perfect expression of the present: they flee the inhospitable world that they themselves have created. Nepal pays the price for these incongruities.

Is Nepal a Failed State?

This is the crux of the problem. Have the factors created by Nepal's development into a nation state—factors in some cases connected with globalization—made Nepal a failed state?[2] The answer to this is simple. According to the usual criteria, a failed state—a questionable concept to start with, in that it turns the concept of the nation state, which only developed in the nineteenth century, into a universal norm—is one in which its territory can no longer be controlled, state power has eroded, public services and infrastructure no longer function, and state-to-state relations are no longer possible or have been frozen. None of this is true of Nepal, except to a limited extent the healthy operation of public infrastructure and services.

Nor has Nepal surrendered to a sense of fatalism in spite of the oft-repeated question *Ke garne* ("What can I/you/anyone do about it?!") and even people's belief that their life is "determined through a divine or powerful external agency."[3] Still, Nepal is a fragile state. This is demonstrated not only by the occasional shortages of vital necessities (water, electricity, heating gas, medications), the massive foreign labor migration due to a lack of supplies and care for rural areas, and the outbreaks of violence carried out by former Maoist rebels or ethnic groups. It is also demonstrated by Nepal's difficult path to becoming a nation state, which, in the eyes of the Bahun-Chhetri, is almost always based on the idea of a uniform culture and uniform politics. "Nationalism is a theory of political legitimacy, which requires that ethnic boundaries should not cut across political ones. . . . It follows that a territorial political unit can only become ethnically homogenous . . . if it either kills, or expels, or assimilates all non-nationals," as historian Ernest Gellner wrote.[4] Seen in this way, nationalism always means homogenization at the cost of ethnic, social, and cultural diversity.

Must it be this way? At first it would appear to be so. Indeed, independent cultures that have survived in the high Himalaya are regarded today as endangered. Among them are Buddhist tribal principalities or kingdoms, hereditary monastic communities, syncretistic forms of religious practice, and those with guarded claims to political sovereignty. Dutch anthropologist Willem van Schendel developed the so-called Zomia hypothesis from such realities, coined from *zomi*, a word widespread in Tibeto-Burman languages that designates dwellers in the high mountains.[5] The hypothesis refers to a continuous zone of highland culture that shares many common traits, has developed its own identities and forms of political action, and does not orientate itself toward the centralist nation state. American anthropologist James Scott expanded this theory, maintaining that highland cultures from Kashmir to Thailand share certain things and ideas—for example, low population density; historical isolation; a rejection of political dominance by a central state; great ethnic, religious, and linguistic diversity; or the lack of writing systems.[6] Anthropologist Sarah Shneiderman (2010) doubts this Zomia theory, however, and instead opines that different forms of state sovereignty and loyalty develop and exist side by side in a multistate space characterized by transregional trade and cultural contacts.

Is Nepal a Transcultural State Model?

Not enough attention has been paid to the many processes taking place in overlapping territories with no clear borders, which leads to competing claims to sovereignty within the same state. This was the case for the inhabitants of the Tarai in relation to India, but also for the Mustangi and Sherpa claims to free movement and trade in the border region of both Tibet and India. Similar processes can be seen in the cultural and religious syncretism within Nepal. It can be detected too in the resilience and resistance vis-à-vis the nation state claims, again, for instance, in Mustang or among the Sherpa.

Nepal has maintained itself in the shadow of the great "rocks," as Pṛthvīnārāyaṇa put it, of India and China, and it has not fallen to pieces. It was never colonized, and so its identity was never broken. There have never been any separatist movements worthy of mention; the individual kingdoms were too small and the ethnic groups too spread out to break away.

At the same time, since the mid-twentieth century, Nepal has resisted the often extremely dominant influence of Hinduism internally or accepted it in a tolerable form, and it has permitted the ethnic traditions to rise again to a certain extent. There is a common consciousness of the state, and egalitarian forms of living together have been developed, guaranteed by law, and increasingly put into practice notwithstanding still widespread remnants of the hierarchical caste system. Despite very deep religious differences, there have been almost no violent religious disputes among different parts of the population, and no religious wars broke out. Nepal's tolerance has allowed it to weather many a crisis, even the one caused by the Maoists.

Focusing on the nation state with its power center, the Kathmandu Valley, overlooks such factors, along with the different transcultural histories of the regions, the different political claims and forms of organization, the multiple and fluid identities, the cross-border transcultural, transreligious, and economic entanglements, and the mobile ways of life, all taking place in marginal zones, transit regions, and enclaves. Nepal is full of all of these, as this book has shown. If Nepal succeeds in continuing down this road, preserving its ethnic and cultural diversity, leaving the ethnic populations with a certain degree of autonomy, while at the same time integrating them into political decision-making processes, and if it manages the reforms needed for landownership, labor, education, and infrastructure, then the country can become a model for unity in diversity, even in the age of leveling globalization.

APPENDIX 1

An Essay on the Sources of Nepalese Historiography

The following sections focus on research on Nepal including historical studies by Nepalese scholars; on Nepal's languages and literatures; and on written historical sources, such as inscriptions, manuscripts, coins, and the many indigenous chronicles and paper documents from the eighteenth to twentieth centuries.

Research on Nepal

Apart from travel reports by Chinese and Tibetan monks who entered what is now Nepal as early as the late fourth century, and in larger numbers in the seventh century, research on Nepal does not start until the seventeenth century with the Jesuits and Capuchins, and with early adventurers.[1] From the nineteenth century on, other travelers from Europe followed.[2] It was a highly transcultural mix from which knowledge about Nepal was distilled. The Jesuits wanted to know everything they could so as to defeat the pagan with their own weapons. Back in Europe, the Encyclopedists wanted to know everything so as to defeat the clerical scholars with Enlightenment arguments.

In 1656, Austrian Jesuit Johann Grueber was given orders to find a land route from Europe to China. He stayed in Asia for over eight years, and on Christmas Eve of 1661 he arrived in the Kathmandu Valley via Lhasa and on his way to Patna in India. His impression of "Necpal," as he called the country, was not particularly good. Of the women of Nepal he wrote:

> The women of these kingdoms are so ugly that they seem more to be devils than human beings. For religious reasons they never wash themselves with water, but rather with a certain disgusting oil. Apart from its spreading an intolerable stench everywhere, they are so fouled by this oil that one might no longer hold them to be human beings but witches.[3]

Grueber had a telescope with him that allegedly so impressed King Pratāpa Malla that he believed he saw through it an enemy approaching. The king was thus well disposed toward the Jesuits and treated them as guests. But the relatively friendly reception of a group of Jesuits and Capuchin monks who arrived in the Kathmandu Valley in 1715 came to a sudden end when Pṛthvīnārāyaṇa Śāha conquered the valley in 1769.[4] Nepal remained for foreign missionaries a forbidden land until the mid-twentieth century.

From 1814 to 1816 war raged with the British East India Company. This Anglo-Nepalese war culminated in defeat for the Nepalese forces, who were forced to pull back from the Western Himalaya when the British arrived in Makwanpur, within striking distance of Kathmandu. As a result, the Śāha kings had to tolerate a British resident from this time on. This was the first opportunity for foreigners with no church affiliation to reside legally in Nepal, at least for a spell. After the short stays of the residents Captain Knox and his assistant Francis Buchanan Hamilton, Brian Houghton Hodgson arrived in 1820 as the assistant to the resident Edward Gardner. Hodgson remained only for two years at first, but returned in 1833 as Gardner's successor, and lived until 1843 in Kathmandu.[5]

Hodgson was the first Western visitor to collect and study texts and documents. Significant quantities of manuscripts, drawings, maps, and material objects later ended up in Cambridge, London, and Paris. In the main, though, his extensive collection is preserved in the British Library (over one hundred volumes or bundles of papers, 15,300 folios in all), and to a lesser extent in the Royal Asiatic Society, the Zoological Society of London, and the Bodleian Library in Oxford. Research on Nepal owes much to him, even though Indologist Sylvain Lévi went too far in his three-volume *Le Népal—étude historique d'un Royaume Hindou* (1905–8), stating: "Before Hodgson nearly everything had yet to be done; after him, his successors could only collect the gleanings."[6]

Hodgson marks the beginning of the use of sources written in indigenous languages. Famous researchers were to follow later in the nineteenth century. Among them were two doctors at the British Residency: Henry Ambrose Oldfield, who was in Nepal from 1850 to 1863/64, and who wrote an extensive report on his time there; and Daniel Wright, who produced a first history of Nepal for Western consumption, although it was actually an English translation of a native chronicle, the *Nepālikabhūpavaṃśāvalī*.

After a difficult journey lasting from 1844 to 1846, Prince Waldemar of Prussia managed to reach the Kathmandu Valley, where he was received on several occasions during his few weeks there by King Rājendra Śāha and the latter's son Surendra Śāha, and by Prime Minister Māthavara Siṃha Thāpā. Waldemar did not gain a favorable impression of the royal family and its conflicts, although he was given many gifts, but he was won over by the city of Kathmandu. He was especially impressed by the many temples and their striking roofs; also by the fact that the streets in the old town of Kathmandu were cobbled.

Indologist Sylvain Lévi, who stayed in the Kathmandu Valley between January 12, 1898 and March 10, 1899, collecting manuscripts all the while, produced the first great study of Nepal's cultural history, published in 1905. He extensively drew on Nepalese-Indian, Chinese, and Tibetan sources, among them twenty-one stone inscriptions, some of which he was the first to translate. Lévi is generally regarded as an Indologist, but he was also a historian, as anthropologist András Höfer has rightly pointed out.[7] Lévi recognized early on that Nepal represents India *in statu nascendi*, for features of old India are still palpably present, saying: "Le Népal c'est Inde qui se fait" (Nepal is India in the making).[8]

Some early British travelers in Nepal were interested not only in texts and inscriptions, but also in the country and its people, the mountains and valleys, the flora and fauna. Colonel Kirkpatrick and Francis Buchanan Hamilton, or even Brian Hodgson, hardly ever left the Kathmandu Valley; others, though, did travel through the higher mountain regions. In December 1850, Laurence Oliphant accompanied Jaṅga Bahādura Rāṇā to the prime minister's camp in the Tarai. Although he was dubbed by London's *The Spectator* magazine as "the oddest of Victorian oddballs," his report from 1852 seems to be truthful if not scholarly.

The travelers in Nepal collected whatever they could. Hodgson published 127 articles on nature in the Himalaya and discovered thirty-nine new species of flora and fauna, such as Hodgson's redstart (*Phoenicurus hodgsonsi*). Among the first researchers was adventurer, geologist, and natural scientist Herrmann von Schlagintweit-Sakünlünski, who travelled to Nepal in February and March of 1857. The eldest of five brothers, he produced nearly fifty volumes of reports and observations, hundreds of drawings and aquarelles, and more than fourteen thousand collected objects. A further researcher who should be mentioned was anthropologist and psychologist Gustave le Bon, famous for his book *The Crowd: A Study of the Popular Mind* (1895), and who in 1885 visited Nepal, among the first Frenchmen to do so.[9]

Following the opening up of Nepal to the wider world in 1951, intensified scientific interest manifested in the form of large research projects and expeditions. In 1959, the German Alpine Club planned an expedition under the leadership of zoologist Wolfgang Hellmich, later financed by the Fritz Thyssen Foundation, the results of which were published in the series *Khumbu Himal*, starting in 1965. One participant in these projects was Austrian Erwin Schneider, whose maps, based on early aerial photographs, long remained the most frequently used basis for spatial orientation in Nepal. The Thyssen House in Nepal developed into the Nepal Research Centre, financed by the German Oriental Society; it was inaugurated by Crown Prince Birendra in 1967, but had to close down in 2013 owing to a lack of financial support. These early institutions paved the way for excellent work in the areas of high mountain research, anthropology, Indology, art history, linguistics, and other disciplines. This work of Western researchers and institutions would be nothing, however, without the help of and cooperation with Nepalese scholars.

Nepalese Scholarship

Nepalese scholarship early on extended beyond the borders of the Kathmandu Valley.[10] The great achievement of Tibet in translating Buddhist and other texts from Sanskrit into Tibetan owes much to Newar scholars. Pandits from the Kathmandu Valley are accordingly mentioned and praised in Tibetan sources; for example, Vāgīśvarakīrti (956–1040), who is called "the Nepalese from Pharping" in the *Blue Annals*, was active at Vikramaśilā University. Samantaśrī, too, the author of one of the main texts of the Vajrayāna, the *Kālacakrayāna* (which he helped to translate into Tibetan), lived in Patan in the eleventh and twelfth centuries. Perhaps the most famous scholar of the time was Ratnakīrti, who wrote numerous works on logic, philosophy, and Buddhist epistemology. These and many other scholars are testimonial of the high level of intellectual connections between Nepal, India, and Tibet. Many scholars ended up teaching at universities in North India.

The Kathmandu Valley aside, Kapilavastu, Janakpur with its Maithili culture, and the Khasa-Malla heartland in the Karnali basin were all exceptional centers of traditional scholarship. It is only the Kathmandu Valley, though, that has maintained such a tradition down to the present day. Many Nepalese scholars were members of a group of researchers called Itihāsa Saṃśodhana-Maṇḍala ("History Correction Group"), which was founded in 1952 by Naya Raj Pant (1913–2002) and has included his sons Mahes Raj Pant and Dinesh Raj Pant, along with Gyan Mani Nepal, Dhanavajra Vajracharya, and others as members. This association of originally some twenty, mostly young researchers helped to correct the many errors in indigenous historical writing; worked primarily on texts, inscriptions, and documents of the Malla, Śāha, and Rāṇā Periods; and published their results mostly in Nepālī-language series or journals, such as *Pūrṇimā*. Most editions of Licchavi, Malla, and Śāha inscriptions are the fruits of this group's labors.

The (Itihāsa) Saṃśodhana-Maṇḍala united pupils under the *gurukula* system, which required great commitment on their part. During the eight-year course, students had to master Sanskrit (and often Nevārī) and to learn many texts by heart. Naya Raj Pant is said to have been a very strict teacher, but also one dedicated to his students. Born into a family that had provided royal priests in Kathmandu, he studied at a traditional Sanskrit school *pāṭhaśālā* in and later became a teacher at Tribhuvan University, from which he received an honorary doctorate. He made a name for himself as a highly qualified expert in the native fields of mathematics and astronomy, whose methods he tried to apply to historical material toward improving his understanding of Nepalese history in a way that was untainted by Western scholarship.

The life of Dhanavajra Vajracharya (1932–94) is perhaps typical of this learned circle. At the age of sixteen he was sent to Naya Raj Pant and underwent the latter's thorough training. In the ten years starting from 1961 he was the manager of the Itihāsa Saṃśodhana-Maṇḍala, but then in 1971 distanced himself from it when he joined the faculty of Tribhuvan University and helped to found the Institute of Nepal and Asian Studies. His excellent epigraphic education enabled him to publish in 1973 what is still the standard work on Licchavi inscriptions. He also wrote numerous other works on inscriptions in other parts of Nepal.

Even before Naya Raj Pant and his students, native scholars had gathered specialist knowledge relating to the cultural history of Nepal, among them Baburam Acharya (1888–1971) and Yogi Naraharinath (1913/15–2003) in particular. Acharya was educated as a pandit and collated many sources, which he gradually published or exploited, as in a four-volume work on Pṛthvīnārāyaṇa Śāha. He also claimed to have discovered that the original name of Mount Everest was Sagarmatha, although there is some doubt about this. Naraharinath was born Balbir Singh Hriksen Thapa in the Khasa region of western Nepal and became a *yogin* in the Gorakhanātha tradition and the Nepalese leader of the Nātha Sampradāya.[11] He learnt Sanskrit in India and supposedly published over one hundred books and pamphlets, among them *Itihāsa-Prakāśa*, a motley collection of sources. For most of his life he lived near the Paśupatinātha temple, where there is a monument to him. He was strongly engaged with social work, historiography, and Hindu ritual activism.

Another of the country's most educated scholars was palace guru Hemraj Pande (or Sharma) (1878–1953), who had a well-stocked private library of over eight thousand manuscripts, which was later transferred to the National Archives of Nepal. A second was highly respected and decorated Buddhist scholar Hemraj Shakya (1926–2010), who was trained in Kathmandu and Varanasi; was employed from 1951 until 1983, first in Bir Library and then in the National Archives of Nepal; established a library of his own in Patan, named Bhāratībhavana; and went on to work at the Nepal Research Centre after his retirement. His book on the Svayambhū Stūpa spawned many other studies. Among the most famous Buddhist scholars was Amritananda Vandya, who worked closely together with Brian Hodgson. He wrote, among other things, the *Dharmakoṣasaṃgraha*, *Chandomṛtalatā*, a Sanskrit-Nevārī lexicon, and a grammar of Nevārī. His grandson Gunananda helped the physician Daniel Wright with the latter's *History of Nepal*. Among other important Buddhist scholars Badri Ratna Vajracharya (1934–2016), whose course and book on Buddhist rituals received much recognition; Ratna Bahadur Vajracharya, a well-known priest and teacher; and Asha Kaji Vaidya, also known as Ganesh Raj Vajracharya, who wrote over thirty works on Buddhism, many of them translations of, or commentaries on, Sanskrit texts—only few of these texts, such as the *Daśakarmaviddhi*, have been translated into English.

The difficult examination and study of sources relating to land use was carried out, most notably, by Nepalese historian Mahesh Chandra Regmi (1929–2003). In 1957, he founded the private Regmi Research Centre, where a small group of Nepalese researchers copied and translated thousands of documents, of which the majority dealt with land rights and the tax and levy system. Equipped with this treasure trove of sources, Regmi wrote fourteen books on the economic history of Nepal. He financed his work by offering to embassies, international organizations, and scholars various services, such as a *Nepal Press Digest* and his *Regmi Research Series* (RRS), which appeared monthly between 1963 and 1968. Copies of the documents are preserved in his *Regmi Research Collection* (RRC). His publications, impressive though they are, occasionally lack philological reliability and consistency.

Dilli Raman Regmi (1913–2001), no relation to M. C. Regmi, received his training and his PhD in India, was a politician in the Nepali National Congress (which in 1950 merged with the Nepali Congress), participated fervently in the movement for democracy, became a minister of education and foreign affairs, and—a sideline, as it were—was one of Nepal's leading historians. He wrote, in English, monumental works that, while not always accurate, cover all periods.

Dor Bahadur Bista (born in 1928) is looked upon as the father of Nepalese anthropology. He was educated at Trichandra College in Kathmandu and worked from 1957 with Austro-British anthropologist Christoph von Fürer-Haimendorf, before becoming professor for anthropology at Tribhuvan University in 1978. His book *People of Nepal* (1972) on the groups and castes of Nepal is a classic; his *Fatalism and Development: Nepal's Struggle for Modernism* (1991) attacks with fierce engagement the oppressive influence of Brahmins in Nepal. In January 1996 he did not return from a trip to Jumla. The circumstances of his disappearance remain unexplained. In 2015, the filmmaker Kesang Tseten released the film *Castaway Man*, which deals with the tragedy of Dor Bahadur Bista.

Two Jesuits occupy something of a hybrid position: owing to their long stays in Nepal, their familiarity with the country, and their Nepalese citizenship, they can be counted as native scholars. John K. Locke, SJ (1933–2009) was born in Chicago and came to Nepal in 1959, where he took Nepalese citizenship in 1976. He worked as a teacher at St Xavier's Godavari School, and became one of the best researchers working on Newar Buddhist culture. His book on the Avalokiteśvara/Matsyendranātha cult is as fundamental as his study on the Buddhist monasteries in the Kathmandu Valley of 1985. He died in 2019, the same year as Father Ludwig F. Stiller, SJ (1928–2009), who had come to Nepal in 1953 and was employed at the same school. The latter worked as a historian, mainly on the Śāha and Rāṇā periods. Both men received their doctorates from Tribhuvan University.

From 1991 on, the private NGO Martin Chautari has developed into an intellectual center for social and cultural scientific debate in Nepal. It was founded by, among others, the Norwegian Martin Hoftun, who died in 1992 in an airplane crash. Like the Social Science Baha, founded in 2002, and the Nepal Research Bhavan, the successor of the Nepal Research Centre, Martin Chautari has a research library and conducts lectures, workshops, and conferences, and brings out numerous publications.

Despite many fears, traditional Sanskrit scholarship has not collapsed. The native system of education still produces some outstanding Sanskritists such as Diwakar Acharya who in 2016 took over the renowned Boden chair at Oxford. The state education system in the universities, however, has suffered from political unrest. Instruction was interrupted for long periods of time. Positions were granted on the basis of political favoritism, and the salary for teachers was not sufficient to prevent the best scholars in Nepal from leaving the country.

Not to be forgotten are art historian, scholar and novelist Lain Singh Bangdel and his daughter Dina, an art historian too. Lain Singh (1919–2002), the "Father of modern art in Nepal," as he is often called, was vice-chancellor of the Royal Academy of Nepal from 1962 until 1991. His book on the stolen art of Nepal excited much discussion. Dina Bangdel (1963–2017) was also an art historian, and worked in the US and latterly at the Virginia Commonwealth University in Qatar. She curated many exhibitions on the Buddhist and modern art of Nepal, such as "Built / Unbuilt: Home / City" for the Kathmandu Triennale in 2017. Shortly thereafter she died. Not much later, renowned archaeologist and art historian Sukra Sagar Shrestha also died. Lately, polymath Satya Mohan Joshi died on October 16, 2022, at the age of 122.

Languages and Literatures

According to Article 1.6 of the Constitution of 2015, "all languages spoken as mother tongues in Nepal are languages of the nation," even though Nepālī is the only official language, and has been the national language (*rāṣṭra bhāṣā*) since 1959.[12] That makes more than 120 languages, divided into five South Asian language groups, which are not, however, to be mistaken for ethnic borders.

The five major language families represented are the following:

(a) Among the Indo-Aryan languages, Nepālī is the most widespread (approx. 45% of native speakers according to the 2011 census). Originally called Khasakurā, it is written in the Devanāgarī script, like Sanskrit and Hindī, developed from Old Indian by way of Middle Indian idioms, and is spoken as a mother tongue for the most part by Brahmins and Chhetri. But Nepālī is also the second language and lingua franca of most other population groups. Further languages belonging to the

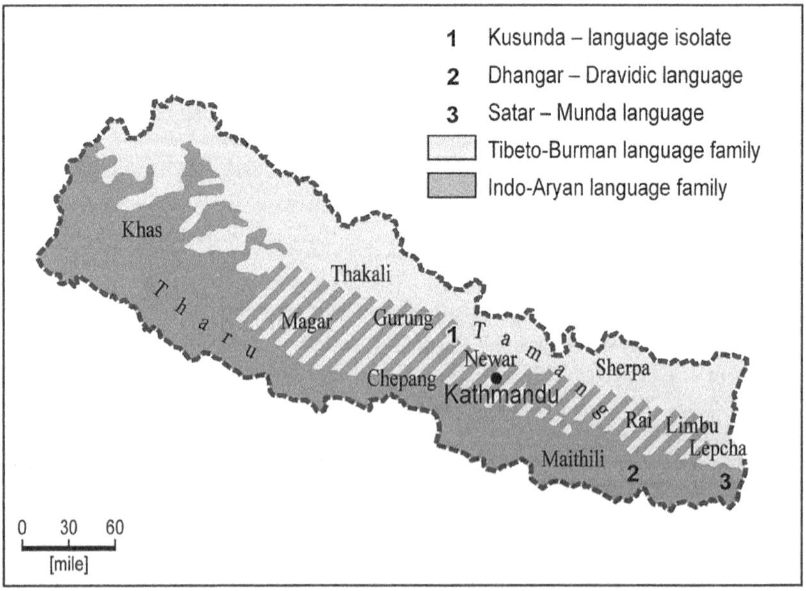

Figure A.1 Ethnic groups and languages of Nepal. Drawing by Nils Harm.

Indo-Aryan group are Maithilī (12%), Thāru (6%), Bhojapurī or Bihārī (6%), and Avadhī (2%), along with Bengalī, Hindī, and Sanskrit.

(b) The Tibeto-Burman or Sino-Tibetan languages: these are spoken by the Tamang (5%), Newar (3%), Magar (3%), Gurung (1%), Kiranti (Rai, Limbu: 3%), Sherpa, Bhotiya (Tibetan ethnic groups), Chepang, Dolpo, and Thakali.

Smaller language groups are represented by

(c) Austroasiatic (Munda), spoken by the Santhali or Satar in Jhapa and Morang districts;
(d) Dravidian, here the Kurukh language; and
(e) Kusunda, a language isolate with some links to Indo-Pacific languages, which has only a few native speakers left.[13]

Multilingualism has always been the norm in Nepal. English is a widespread foreign language, although not as common as in the colonized parts of South Asia. Refugees from Tibet have disseminated Tibetan quite a bit. Hindī is frequently understood, if more in the south than the north, because of its status as a cognate language, on the one hand, and owing to labor migration and Indian media, on the other.

Historically, primarily Sanskrit, Nevārī, Tibetan, Nepālī, Maithilī, and Avadhī are of greatest significance for texts, inscriptions, and documents. Sanskrit literature comprises the entire range of classical literature, intended essentially for priests, monks, scholars, and court circles. For some time Maithilī was also a court language, as evidenced by numerous dramas and poems written in it even by kings such as Jagajjyotir Malla, Jitāmitra Malla, or Bhūpatīndra Malla.

* * *

Classical Nevārī, also called Nepāla Bhāṣā or Nevā Bhāy ("language of Nepāla"), is a language predominantly spoken in the Kathmandu Valley and the only language in Nepal to possess a classical literature that can stand alongside those of Sanskrit, Maithilī, and Tibetan.[14] It has many lexical borrowings from Indo-Iranian languages (Sanskrit, Maithilī, Persian, Nepālī, Hindī, English), and some from Tibetan, due to the many connections that the Newar had with Tibet.

Aside from a few words in Licchavi inscriptions, this language is documented from 1114 CE in a palm-leaf manuscript,[15] from 1334 in a stone inscription at the Kāṣṭhamaṇḍapa in Kathmandu, and from the fourteenth century in various texts. Many early texts are bilingual, a mixture of Sanskrit and Nevārī. The earliest ones are the book of fables *Hitopadeśa* (1360); a medical text, the *Haramekhalā* (1374); a commentary on the legal text *Nāraḍasmṛti* (1380); a Sanskrit-Nevārī lexicon based on the *Amarakośa* (1382 and 1386); and the *Gopālarājavaṃśāvalī* or "Chronicle of the Gopāla Kings" (1389).

The Malla Period produced several dramas and poems in Nevārī, some of whose authors were women, and texts on the Āyurveda and the astral sciences, such literature being very imitative of Sanskrit models. Up to the sixteenth or seventeenth centuries, native developments are hardly discernible. But then creative energies broke loose, especially in drama and poetic writings. Jagajjyotir Malla marks the beginning with his *Saṅgītacandra*, a commentary on the *Nāṭyaśāstra*, an old text on dance and aesthetics. The first drama, the *Mūladevaśaśidevavyākhyānanāṭaka*, is ascribed to King Jagatprakāśa Malla. A particularly original facet of Nevārī literature can be seen in the texts praising certain (holy) places, above all the *Svayambhūpurāṇa* (1558 or earlier), probably the first text written entirely in Nevārī. Nevārī poems and songs (Skt. *Caryāgīta*, Nev. *cacā mye*) deserve mention, as do ritual texts reflecting Newar hybrid practice, and the lists of events (*thyāsaphu, ghaṭanāvalī*). An unusual class of documents is formed by the palm-leaf rolls, recording in the main donations of land and mortgages, and written in Sanskrit and Nevārī. Nevārī used in ritual contexts has developed its own mixture of Sanskrit and Nevārī with a great number of distinctive linguistic and grammatical features.[16]

Only a few Nevārī texts have so far been translated. Dane Hans Jørgensen made a start in 1921 with his translation of the *Vetālapañcaviṃśati*, and in 1931 with that of the *Vicitrakarṇikāvadānoddhṛta,* a collection of Buddhist legends from the eighteenth century. Jørgensen, who was the founder of Nevārī research in the West, also published a grammar and a dictionary of the language. He was followed by Austrian Indologist Siegfried Lienhard, who translated the *Maṇicūḍāvadānoddhṛta*, a Buddhist reincarnation story from the middle of the eighteenth century, and the *Nevārīgītīmañjarī*, a collection of one hundred poems collected in the period between Mahendra Malla und Pṛthvīnārāyaṇa Śāha.

After the Gorkhali conquest of the Valley, Nevārī was not recognized as an official language, and, in fact, was marginalized. Four writers who are well known as the "four pillars of Nepālabhāṣā" were even jailed for being active during the Rāṇā period: Niṣṭhānanda Vajrācārya, Siddhidāsa Mahāju, Jagata Sundara Malla and Yogavīra Siṃha Kaṃsākāra. From the twentieth century on, a renaissance of Nevārī literature set in during which, among other things, new Buddhist texts were written and journals published. Chittadhar Hridaya (1906–82), Siddhicharan Shrestha (1912–92), and Phatte Bahadur Singh (1902–83) were among the most prominent authors. In many cases, writers were exposed to hostility and persecution because they wrote in Nevārī and sometimes protested against the Rāṇā regime. Thus, Hridaya wrote his *Sugata Saurabha*, an epic poem on the life of the Buddha, in prison. Other notable Nevārī writers who wrote poems, short stories, or satire with themes taken from Nepal's culture and history include Satya Mohan Joshi (born 1920), Madan Mohan Mishra (1931–2013), and Durga Lal Shrestha (born 1937).

* * *

Nepālī or Khasakurā (or simply Khasa) is documented for the first time in western Nepal, in a few edicts from the eleventh or twelfth centuries; the designation Pahāḍī or Parvatīyā ("the speech of those living in the mountains") occurs as early as 1386 in a manuscript of the *Amarakośa*; other names for the language are Himālī, Gorkhā Bhāṣā, or (as Nepālī was officially called until 1930) Gorkhālī.

More extensive texts in manuscript form appear from the fourteenth century on. Among these are the *Bhāsvatī* (around 1333) and the *Khaṇḍakhādyaka* (around 1393), both of which are texts dealing with the astral sciences. Starting from the seventeenth century, Nepālī becomes well documented as a written language thanks to many works, mainly translations from the Sanskrit. Nepālī was used more and more in inscriptions, too, from 1641 onward—for example, in the Rani-Pokhari inscription of 1670;[17] this means that the language was not first introduced into the Kathmandu Valley by the Śāha dynasty.

Only with Bhānubhakta Ācārya (1814–68), called the "First Poet" (*ādikavi*), could Nepālī assert itself as having an independent literature of its own, however.[18] He translated the Sanskrit epic *Rāmāyaṇa* into a metric Nepālī version, thereby freeing himself from the constraints of Sanskrit literary genres.

From 1769 onward, Nepālī developed into the official language of administration, gradually replacing Sanskrit, Nevārī, and Maithilī. Accordingly, most documents of the Śāha and Rāṇā periods are written in Nepālī. In 1905, Candra Śamśera ordered that all documents be written in it. By the 1920s it had become the definitive official language of the country, but already in 1796 Raṇabahādura Śāha was rebuking the Nepalese emissary to Kolkata Dīnanātha Upādhyāya for writing a report in Persian: "You write in Persian, but as a Hindu you should write in Nāgarī letters [used for Nepālī]."[19]

In 1820, British officer James Alexander Ayton wrote his *Grammar of the Nepalese Language* at Fort William College in Kolkata. This is probably the first book to have Nepālī words printed in Devanāgarī script. The first book entirely in Nepālī and Devanāgarī script seems to be the Bible printed in 1821 by the Serampore Mission in Kolkata.

During the Rāṇā Period, numerous works in Nepālī were printed in Varanasi, as there were no printing houses in Nepal itself. Many writers were influenced by the rise of Hindī literature in North India, and in 1875 the Sahitya Academy in New Delhi recognized Nepālī as an Indian language of literature. Among the early Nepālī writers was Motīrāma Bhaṭṭa (1866–96), who published Bhānubhakta's *Rāmāyaṇa* in 1887 and a biography of him in 1891. Motīrāma gathered young authors around himself and encouraged them to engage in literary debate. He, like other poets, developed a taste for Urdu lyric poetry and devotional and erotic Śṛṅgāra literature, as evidenced in the anthology *Sūktisindhu* edited by Lekhanātha Pauḍyāla (Lekh Nath Poudyal). The literature could not be widely circulated, though, for lack of publishers and printers.

The situation changed with the arrival of the first newspaper in Nepal, the *Gorkhāpatra*, which Deva Śamśera permitted to start appearing in 1901. In 1913, Candra Śamśera established the Gorkhā Bhāṣā Prakāśinī Samiti ("Gorkha Language Publication Committee") to promote Nepālī literature; this was renamed in 1930 the Nepālī Bhāṣā Prakāśinī Samiti ("Committee for the Publication [of Works] in Nepālī"). To be sure, there was strict censorship. This led to many books continuing to be printed in Varanasi or Darjeeling. The Great Three, as the lyricists Lekhanātha Pauḍyāla (1885–1966) and Lakṣmī Prasāda Devakoṭā (1909–59) and the dramatist Bālakṛṣṇa Sama (1902–81) were called, wrote in a more conservative style. But increasingly, periodicals such as *Sundarī* (founded in 1906), *Mādhavī* (1908), *Gorkhālī* (1916) or, from 1932 on, the *Nepālī Sāhitya Sammelana Patrikā* ("Journal of the Association for Nepālī Literature") were appearing, in which poems and other works were published. Just how subtle criticism of the Rāṇā could be is illustrated by Lekhanātha's popular poem *Pījaḍāko Sugā* (A Parrot in a Cage) written at the beginning of the twentieth century, in which he addresses the soul trapped in the body, on the one hand, but also, if indirectly, his own situation as a priest and teacher under Bhīma Śamśera. Sama, too, whose original name was Bālakṛṣṇa Śamśera Jaṅga Bahādura Rāṇā, and who was thus one of the Rāṇā aristocracy, landed for a few months in prison because he sympathized with opponents of the regime. In contrast, Devakoṭā usually wrote in an interiorized and sometimes melancholy style. His admired metric work *Munā-Madana* of 1935 is characteristic. It is about a trader who goes to Tibet and stays there too long, although his wife had warned him precisely against so doing. When he finally returns, he finds that his wife and his mother have died.

* * *

Many myths and legends in the chronicles are based upon an oral tradition of the sort that is particularly well preserved in cultures that have not developed writing. While research into written traditions began relatively early on, work on oral traditions, which called for field work, only began to any mentionable extent in the 1970s.

At first, it was primarily fairy tales and fables that were collected and written down.[20] They entered such narrative literature as the *Hitopadeśa* or *Vetālapañcaviṃśati*, or else mythological texts such as the Purāṇas and Māhātmyas, and the chronicles as well. Above all, they have been passed down by word of mouth, now as in centuries past. It is true that there are hardly any longer professional bards or tellers of tales, but in villages one can quickly find old people, priests, or shamans who have no shortage of fairy tales, sagas, trickster tales, ghost stories, and legends to tell. These popular stories and tales go on distant journeys and can be found in many literary traditions. An example of a tale that has undoubtedly undergone a long period of wandering in oral form is the *Vetālapañcaviṃśati* (Twenty-Five [Tales] of a Vampire), a mixture of horror stories and erotic tales, of which there are many versions in Indian languages and in Nepālī.

A different group within oral literature is formed by creation and origin myths, which are told particularly during shamanistic séances. In these, for example, the deeds of the First Brahmin and the rise of humans, animals, and the rest of nature are dealt with. Equally important are ritual songs sung not so much to narrate as to support rites that have a mythical foundation. Anthropologists concentrated more at the beginning on the life and ritual practice of shamans, and less on the songs and texts transmitted by them. But interest grew in the 1980s, when anthropologists, too, began to turn to the languages and thought-worlds of the ethnic groups they were investigating. It was important thereby not to separate the text from its context.

Anthropologist Michael Oppitz captured this situation vividly in his 1980 film *Schamanen im blinden Land* (*Shamans of the Blind Country*), which documents the shamanism and life of the northern Magar. Later he also edited and published a large portion of the oral songs after translating and analyzing them. Similarly, ritual texts of several peoples in Nepal have been studied and edited.[21] Often a glimpse of pre-Buddhist or pre-Hindu traditions can be caught in these texts and in terms of a literary archaeology, archaisms and origins come to light.

Oral traditions often consist of a mixture of written and recited texts. This can be seen, for example, when the priest, Brahmin or *lāmā*, operates with written texts, while beside him a shaman (*jhā̃krī*, *bompo*) acts out his songs and recitations, and a ritual specialist goes about his task with his ritual handbooks. A neophyte usually learns the songs from his master. This requires memorizing long texts, for which certain mnemotechnical styles such as echo-like parallel structures or metric variation come to his aid.

Ritual texts often have the quality of written texts, since they are recited verbatim, with few variations. The Vedic texts were preserved in just this fashion. Despite this rigidity in wording and meter, orally transmitted texts differ from written ones in not being recited as a monologue, but in response to a context—for example, a healing séance. The situation into which the discourse plays thus becomes part of the performance of the text. Quite often the text consists of speech acts in which what is said is at the same time what is done, as in a marriage ceremony, where the word yes signifies agreement, the sealing of the marriage itself. The songs of the shamans are, in addition, frequently ritual journeys that follow the traces of a spirit or ancestor.

The linguistic policies of the Śāha and the Rāṇā rulers did not allow for ethnic languages and literatures to be nurtured. These had no place in schools, and books could not be printed in or devoted to them. Such has been possible only since 1990, and since then many literatures have developed with texts and schoolbooks of their own, whose purpose is often the discovery or rediscovery of an old or new ethnic identity.

Manuscripts and Documents

Nepal owns a huge store of traditional manuscripts.[22] The many Hindu pandits and Buddhist monks, often supported by kings, ensured a constant stream of teachers and pupils. Most manuscripts are written in Sanskrit, but around one-fifth are Tibetan woodblock prints. The cool climate of the Himalaya ensured that many texts were preserved in Nepal, whereas in India the manuscripts often fell victim to the heat, insects, or monsoon.

A preliminary catalogue of a small selection of these manuscripts was published by the Indian scholar Hara Prasad Shastri in 1905–6, forming the foundation for one of the most extensive indexes of manuscripts in South Asia. Among the precious items is an eighth-century palm-leaf manuscript of the *Lotus Sūtra* (*Saddharmapuṇḍarīka-Sūtra*), one of the most important early texts of Mahāyāna Buddhism, written in the first century; a manuscript of the expansive *Skandapurāṇa* dating from 811; and a medical text, the *Suśrutasaṃhitā*, going back to 878. A manuscript of the *Daśabhūmīśvarasūtra*, an early Mahāyāna text commented on by Vasubandhu, may even be from the sixth century. Moreover, the oldest surviving Vedic manuscript, part of the *Vājasaneyisaṃhitā* (ca. 1150), is preserved in Nepal along with old ritual handbooks such as the *Upakarmavidhi* (1060), *Vivāhasamuccaya* (1113), *Daśakarmapaddhati* (1176), and *Sandhyāvidhi* (1281).[23]

To this day, even an experienced priest will carry a notebook with him so as to be able to check the sequence of ritual commands or the key words for recitations. These manuscripts, generally in Sanskrit, Nevārī, or Nepālī, and a holdover from India's ancient ritual tradition, are scripts for the actions taken, even if more knowledge was transmitted orally from father to son, or from teacher to pupil. However, sons often no longer want to learn their fathers' traditional skills and knowledge and the copying of manuscripts no longer makes sense with the advent of new techniques such as photography or printing.

From the end of the seventeenth century, inscriptions and copperplates were increasingly supplemented by paper manuscripts (mostly *lokta* paper, also called "rice paper") in Nepālī or Nevārī. Earlier documents of the Malla Period are also often on sealed palm leaves.[24] These documents and manuscripts, preserved in the National Archives in Kathmandu, temple archives, Tribhuvan University, and private collections such as the *Regmi Research Collection*, form probably the most important interrelated assortment of historical texts of any South Asian region.[25] Within the framework of the Nepal-German Manuscript Preservation Project (NGMPP), financed by the German Research Council, a large part (approximately 180,000 items) of Nepal's wealth of manuscripts was microfilmed between 1970 and 2001. On the basis of a bilateral agreement between (then) His Majesty's Government of Nepal and the Federal Republic of Germany, copies of the microfilms are stored in the National Archives of Nepal and in the Oriental Department of the State Library in Berlin. The NGMPP was succeeded by a further long-term project of the DFG, the Nepalese-German Manuscript Cataloguing Project (NGMCP), which has produced a descriptive catalogue of some sections of this collection.

The cataloguing work of the NGMCP did not, however, include historical documents relating to particular temples and other holy places, or to legal history. Since 2014, this material has been systematically investigated within the project "Documents on the History of Religion and Law of Pre-modern Nepal" of the Heidelberg Academy of Sciences and Humanities. The emphasis here is on the Śāha and Rāṇā Periods. The document material includes decrees and edicts of kings that bear a red seal (*lālamohara*); other decrees (*sanada*, *rukkā*)—for instance, those of a prime minister, often with the emblem of a sword; land grants or sales, or else land donations and accompanying trust documents; pawn tickets and promissory notes; balances and lists; contracts and receipts; appointment letters; travel documents; missives; petitions; and writs of indulgence from a royal religious judge. This source material allows one to study how the social and religious institutions were transformed, new forms of collective identity coalesced, and bureaucratic structures were established in the eighteenth and nineteenth centuries. With the production of charters and other documents in the state administration, in temples, in jurisprudence, and in economic life, the act of writing took on a new quality.

Archaeology, Inscriptions, and Coins

Most excavations have taken place under the direction or supervision of the Department of Archaeology, which was established in 1953.[26] Among the early excavations, one under the leadership of Indian archaeologist P. C. Mukherjee in Tilaurakot near Lumbini revealed in 1899 remains of the capital city of the Śākya clan, to which the Buddha belonged. These finds were supplemented and confirmed by further excavations in Gotihawa and Pipri, again near Lumbini, by Indian scholar T. N. Mishra and a team under the direction of Italian archaeologist Giuseppe Verardi. The first excavations in the Kathmandu Valley, in the course of which ceramics, bricks, and coins of the Licchavi Period were found, but also the prehistoric bones of the first humans in this region, took place in 1965–66 in Handigaon, Lazimpat, and Dhumbarahi.[27] The results of such excavations are published regularly in the journal *Ancient Nepal*, put out by the Department of Archaeology.

Other excavations in Nepal have mostly only scratched the surface, as lack of experience, too little money, and insufficient technical apparatus have prevented all but a very few deeper excavations. One important technically adequate project, "Processes of Settlement and the Formation of States in the Tibetan Himalaya," carried out between 1992 and 1997, revealed that caves in the Mustang Valley contain prehistoric artifacts, which prove that people had already settled there three thousand years ago, and had contact both with India and Tibet.[28] It was also shown that the Muktinath Valley was settled around 500 BCE.

* * *

The history of Nepal's ancient period is based almost exclusively on stone inscriptions of the Licchavi dynasty, whose people settled mostly in the Kathmandu Valley; the epigraphy is in Sanskrit.[29] The earliest inscription, in Brāhmī script, is by Jayavarman from the year 184/5 CE. The longest Licchavi inscription is that of Mānadeva in Changu Narayana, dating from 464/5; this inscription is worthy of closer attention, as it is also the first historical proof of the custom of widow burning in South Asia.

The approximately 220 Licchavi inscriptions mostly contain royal edicts, land grants, temple foundations, and the like.[30] They are generally of a Brahmanical nature and show that the scribes were familiar with Sanskrit texts and their subjects: the Veda, scholarly textbooks (*śāstra*), the collections of myths (*purāṇa*), or poets such as Bāṇa or Kālidāsa. Not all of the inscriptions have been dated; many can only be roughly dated on paleographical grounds or through artistic comparison. Usually, these inscriptions are short texts on stelae, statues, *liṅgas*, *stūpas*, gargoyle waterspouts, sculptures, or bricks.

A peculiarity of the Malla inscriptions from the thirteenth to eighteenth century,[31] including those written on copper and gold plates, is the occurrence among them of multilingual texts. An extreme example is Pratāpa Malla's polyglot inscription at Hanuman Dhoka written in fifteen languages, among them English, French, and Persian. Inscriptions in two or three languages (Sanskrit, Nevārī, or Nepālī) are common; one rarity is the epitaph in Latin and Nevārī on the tombstone of Capuchin monk Francesco della Penna in Patan, dating from 1745.

The inscriptions, including those of the Malla Period, begin, as a rule, with praise (*praśasti*) of the donor, so that this material also forms a relatively reliable source of dates for the rulers. Several hundred copperplates and gold-plated inscriptions, which were used by court officials, among other things, to swear their loyalty to the king, are preserved, for example, in the treasuries of the Paśupatinātha temple, the national shrine of Nepal.

* * *

Coins are also important for historical research alongside inscriptions, given that they often mention the date of a ruler's crowning.[32] The earliest are Śākya coins of the fifth century BCE, which circulated just like other coins from the Maurya and Kushana Periods in the Tarai. Copper-iron coins of the Licchavi Period, however, only rarely have the name of the ruler, and are undated. The coins are round and relatively small, decorated with animal motifs, and have punched edges. The first such coin is ascribed to King Mānadeva.

For the Early Medieval Period (nineth to twelfth century) there are very few coin finds, but there are reports of a mint reform by Śivadeva, who introduced a silver coin with him portrayed as a lion. The use of currency was restricted in any case to the Kathmandu Valley and the trade routes to Tibet.[33]

Around 1534, a *mohara* coin was brought into circulation in Dolakha, which signals the start of a rich series of coins of the Malla Period, mostly minted in silver. They have inscriptions in Nevārī and are dated using the Nepāla Saṃvat chronology. A coin minted by Mahendra Malla called a *mahendramalli* and later similar coins were also used as currency in Tibet, and even occasioned wars between the two countries. On one side these coins bear the Śaiva trident, and on the other the Buddhist *vajra*. After these, there followed many other coins from Bhaktapur, Kathmandu, and Patan.

The Gorkha kings adopted the *mohara* system in 1749, their coins having the minting date on them in either the Śaka or Vikrama eras. Pṛthvīnārāyaṇa had a couple of silver coins minted before he conquered the Kathmandu Valley, but from 1690 onward most coins were minted in the valley. All other Śāha kings immortalized themselves on the later coins, which were usually of silver, copper, bronze, aluminum, or, in rare cases, gold. The coins were at first used mainly as a currency of reference in taxation, not as a general medium of payment. This latter first came about in the course of the nineteenth century, and much later in the mountain regions. In other words, in large parts of Nepal and long past the eighteenth century coins were used to appraise and reckon, but not as currency in the marketplace.

Under the Śāha dynasty, the situation gradually changed, albeit slowly. Increasingly the economy was being transformed from one of barter and exchange to one based on money. The gold and silver for the coinage usually came from Tibet, especially between

1788 and 1793, as a consequence of conquests and tribute payments. From 1775 on, Tibetan coins minted in Nepal were also in circulation, competing with the Śāha coinage. But in 1793 the Chinese built a mint in Lhasa, thus ending this particular business partnership.

In 1951, the Ministry of Finance created a Coin Design Board whose task was to come up with new coins and banknotes. Notable artists were members of this board. Thirty-one suggestions were entered, of which ten were chosen. The motifs were inspired by the struggle against the Rāṇā autocracy, and this was probably the reason that most of these coins were never minted. Still, from 1954 on, new coins that used some of the motifs of the planned coins did come into circulation. They usually had the image of the king on the obverse and innocuous motifs on the reverse, such as symbols of rulership (e.g., swords), temples, and *stūpas*, or else animals. These coins were made of an inexpensive alloy. Prime Minister M. P. Koirala said of this: "The design of the coins is of the people; for, it was for the first time, invited from them befitting the new era—the advent of democracy."[34] With the end of the monarchy in 2008, banknotes with the image of the king gradually disappeared.

Chronicles and Indigenous Historical Writing

A special category of texts of historiographical significance are the many chronicles (*vaṃśāvalī*, literally "genealogy") and eulogistic texts (*māhātmya*, *sthalapurāṇa*), in which there is a mixture of factual reporting and myths and legends. These chronicles are only of limited value as academic sources of history. This is clear from the deviations they display from the more secure dates in the Licchavi inscriptions, the great variation in the succession of rulers, and periods of rule that are sometimes much too long, especially in the old dynasties. However, the chronicles belie the oft-stated opinion that South Asia never produced historiographies.

In general, these Nepalese *vaṃśāvalīs* are divided into two groups: the older chronicles from the end of the fourteenth century are composed in a hybrid Sanskrit and in Old Nevārī. The *Gopālarājavaṃśāvalī*, for example, has three parts: the first, written in a corrupted Sanskrit, covers events up to 1386; the second, written in Old Nevārī and Sanskrit, runs from 1056/57 to 1275/76; and the third has entries for the years 1258/59 down to 1388/89. The sole manuscript of this chronicle is from the time of Sthiti Malla and was probably written by a court astrologer in Bhaktapur. It is one of the most significant sources of the Malla Period. It records important events such as the regnal periods of the kings, threats to the Kathmandu Valley, intrigues, the construction of temples, donations to temples (especially Paśupatinātha), and earthquakes or other natural disasters. This chronicle is supplemented by brief lists of events (*thyāsaphu*, *ghaṭanāvalī*) written in Nevārī, a sort of diary genre of the Malla Period.[35]

The second group of chronicles is more recent and considerably larger. The catalogue of the NGMPP alone lists 110 manuscripts, and the Hodgson Collection in the British Museum some eighteen. They were created for the most part toward the end of the eighteenth century and during the nineteenth, and, with few exceptions, are written in Nepālī. Standing alongside such Hindu chronicles as the *Bhāṣāvaṃśāvalī*, *Rājavaṃśāvalī*, *Rājabhogavaṃśāvalī*, or *Padmagiri's Chronicle*, is the so-called *Wright Chronicle*, a predominantly Buddhist chronicle and named after British physician Daniel Wright. The translation, however, is mostly by the native scholars "Shew Shunker Singh and Pandit

Shri Gunanand." The first edition of this important text, written around 1830 by a Buddhist scholar in Patan and entitled in the original *Nepālikabhūpavaṃśāvalī* ("Chronicle of the Kings of Nepal") together with a new translation appeared in 2015.

In substance, these chronicles attempt to document the history of the Kathmandu Valley and the sequence of its rulers from the mythical earliest times to the time of their composition, along with those rulers' activities and any special events during their rule. The greater part of these latter consists of the foundation of holy sites and reports of divine appearances, together with religious festivals and rituals. The *Nepālikabhūpavaṃśāv alī*, for instance, reads like a mixture of genealogies (*vaṃśāvalī*) of various dynasties and encomiums of localities (*māhātmya*). The text draws on excerpts of other eulogistic works such as the Buddhist *Svayambhūpurāṇa*, the Hindu *Himavatkhaṇḍa* of the *Skandapurāṇa*, or the *Nepālamāhātmya*.

The *Svayambhūpurāṇa* (Old History of Svayambhū) includes many myths and legends.[36] This popular text exists in Nevārī and Sanskrit prose and poetical versions from 1558 onward and translations into modern Nevārī and Tibetan.[37] The text has been constantly extended and altered over three centuries. In its core, however, it is probably a creation of the Nevārī Vajrayāna Buddhist school and describes the visits by four Buddhas from past ages, and thus the beginnings of the Kathmandu Valley. Ādibuddha, the Buddha's essence, appeared in the middle of a lake that covered the Kathmandu Valley, in a ray of light emanating from a lotus. The further narrative touches on, among other things, occurrences at numerous holy sites, holy figures (*siddha*), and monks. The poetic *Himavatkhaṇḍa* (Book of the Himalaya) and the *Nepālamāhātmya* (The Greatness of Nepāla, probably from the late seventeenth century) are texts with encomiums of holy sites in the Kathmandu Valley.

The chronicles have much to do with the political situation in the nineteenth century. One manuscript, for example, belonged to the collection of Sylvain Lévi and is preserved today in the Collège de France (Paris). To judge by the colophon, it was apparently commissioned by the palace in Kathmandu and then given to the scribe and translator Munsi Lakṣmīdāsa.[38] Later Lévi received it from the hands of Prime Minister Deva Śamśera Jaṅga Bahādura. This background shows the need the Śāha and Rāṇā rulers felt to legitimize their rule by having themselves placed in a glorious past accompanied by the blessings of the gods.

An historically important text is the *Divyopadeśa* or *Divya Upadeśa* (Holy Instruction), allegedly by King Pṛthvīnārāyaṇa Śāha.[39] However, it is highly questionable whether the work is really his. It is said that Pṛthvīnārāyaṇa delivered the "instructions" on his deathbed to his brothers and high-ranking officials (*bhārādāras*), among them Minister (*kājī*) Abhimāna Siṃha Basnet, after which they were copied and recopied. The text was first published 177 years later, in 1952, by Yogi Naraharinath in Varanasi on the basis of a manuscript that apparently came from village chief (*mukhiyā*) Bhakta Bahādura, a descendant of a clerk who used to work in the household of Minister (*kājī*) Abhimāna Siṃha. In the third revised edition of the *Divyopadeśa*, Baburam Acharya and Yogī Naraharinātha argue that the manuscript, which they used for their edition, could have been written around 1803. However, Newar scholar Kamal P. Malla argued that it was not a genuine text but created by Ācārya and (more particularly) Naraharinātha by joining fragmentary sayings. In fact, the *Divyopadeśa* differs in style considerably from Pṛthvīnārāyaṇa's letters, leading Malla to call the text a "literary harlequin's dress, pieced together by the heroic Gorkhali historians . . . from dusty fragments stored in the Basnet family . . . in the early 1950s."[40]

Archives and Museums

Most of the written material was stored, maintained, and copied in the homes of priests, or in temples and monasteries. Nepal's National Archives, for the construction of which India had donated money, was ceremonially opened on October 3, 1967, by King Mahendra. The organized archiving of texts in Nepal, however, goes way back to August 28, 1812, when King Gīrvāṇayuddha Śāha laid down how the palace library was to be set up.[41] He wrote to archivist and scholar Pandit Kedāranātha Jhā:

> We have given to you charge, from [VS] 1869 on, of the office containing all the books (*pustaka*) of our palace. Preserve all the books with a sense of dutifulness to yourself. Do not give any book to anybody without orders [from me]. If a book is useful for palace matters, put it to use it. Maintain the treasury [of funds for] the books as your own responsibility. Make corrections to books with [scribal] errors [in them]. Have books that are worn and torn recopied. Restore (books) as soon as they are damaged by mice, insects, water, or other [threats]. Upon orders [to do so], take money from the palace and have books copied that are not in the palace.[42]

He writes further that the archivist and a guard are to safeguard the texts, if necessary, copy them, and honor them with a series of rituals. In 1852, King Surendra Vikrama Śāha commanded that government documents be collected in the Jaisi Kotha, something along the lines of a foreign ministry in the old royal palace in Kathmandu, and which functioned as part of the Munsīkhānā established by Prime Minister Bhīmasena Thāpā. In 1874, however, Prime Minister Jaṅga Bahādura Rāṇā had the documents brought to his residence in Thapathali. Prime Minister Vīra Śamśera, finally, ordered the construction of a new building, later known as Ghaṇṭaghara Pustakālaya (Clock Tower Library), where the material was deposited in 1900. In 1962, this institution was renamed Bīra Pustakālaya Sarkāri Pustakakhānā (better known as Bir Library), but its major contents finally ended up in the National Archives.

In 2019, the National Archives (Rāṣṭriya Abhilekhālaya) became an independent department in Kathmandu under the Ministry of Culture, Tourism, and Civil Aviation of the Government of Nepal. Its most valuable section is made up of the contents of the former Bir Library, around twenty-two thousand manuscripts, along with the private library of the court priest (*rājaguru*) Hemraj Sharma (or Pande), containing some eight thousand manuscripts. These carefully sorted materials, often bound in cloth and surrounded by mothballs, demonstrate how much of a melting pot of literary figures, thinkers, and scholars the Kathmandu Valley was, from the Malla Period onward at the latest. Hardly any area of the comprehensive spectrum of Sanskrit literature went unattended. Scribes copied the texts over and over, writing them in ink on palm leaves or on local (*lokta*) and other kinds of paper.

Many archives have their origins in a private individual, one example being the Keshar (or Kaiser) Library. In 1937, the head of the military Keśara Jaṅga Bahādura Śamśera Rāṇā, together with his father, Candra Śamśera, visited the United Kingdom for the coronation of George VI (and in 1948 he would become ambassador there). Kaiser Shumsher, as he is also called (the name Kaiser is derived from *keśara*, "lion"), was so impressed by the libraries and museums that, after his return to Nepal, he built up his own archive, collecting over sixty thousand manuscripts and books, along with paintings, photos of meetings with high-ranking guests (such as Indologist Sylvain Lévi), and hunting trophies. This library remained in private hands until 1968, when Keśara Śamśera's second wife donated it to the Ministry of Education. Today the library, located next to the current Garden of Dreams in the Thamel quarter, is now a public one.

The Madan Puraskar Library also owes its existence to a private initiative. Starting with items belonging to writer Kamal Mani Dixit (1929–2016), the father of the journalists Kanak Mani and Kunda Dixit, the small archive underwent an expansion in 1956 thanks to a donation made by Jagadambā Kumārī Devī, the wife of Madana Śamśera Jaṅga Bahādura Rāṇā, another son of Candra Śamśera. The Regmi Research Centre is an equally important source for historical research. It was founded in 1969 by scholar and archivist Mahesh Chandra Regmi to facilitate study of administrative texts and documents, most of which kept at the Lagata Phāta ("Records Office") of the Department of Land Revenue in the Ministry of Finance, in other ministries or in the Guṭhī Saṃsthāna (a partly state-run institution for the administration and organization of religious foundations). This material he had translated into English and commercially published in the monthly *Regmi Research Series* (RSS) until 1989. A large part of his library is now housed in Martin Chautari, a center of modern intellectual pursuits. The Asha Archives in Kathmandu, too, were founded as a private initiative, by the Cvasā Pāsā organization. Named after Asha Man Singh Kansakar, the nucleus of the collection was donated by his son Prem Bahadur Kansakar, a Nevārī writer and an activist for democracy. The library, with over ten thousand manuscripts including over a thousand valuable palm-leaf manuscripts, was opened in 1987 and later painstakingly renovated and earthquake-proofed with the support of the Toyota Foundation and private donations.

The Central Library of Tribhuvan University, which suffered severe damage in the earthquake of 2015, possesses around five hundred thousand books, manuscripts, and other items; Kathmandu University (founded in 1990) for its part has nearly sixty thousand books. Besides these, there are numerous smaller college libraries.

Besides virtual archives, numerous digital resources and databases specifically concentrate on Nepal. Below is a curated list of the most significant ones:[43]

1. Cultural heritage: Endangered Archives Programme (keyword Nepal: Nepal), The Himalaya Archive Vienna, Opendatanepal;
2. Images: the Nepal Heritage Documentation Project (NHDP) with its Digital Archive of Arts and Monuments (DANAM) – a cooperation between Heidelberg University, Department of Archaeology and Saraf Foundation, NHDP's data are also in heidIcon—the image database of Heidelberg University, The Huntington Archive;
3. Journals and books: Archive.org (keyword: Nepal), Database of Nepalese Journals online;
4. Manuscripts: Cambridge Digital Library (keyword: Nepal), NGMPP/NGMCPDocumenta Nepalica ; Buddhist texts: A database of digital Sanskrit Buddhist texts from Nepal, Buddhist Digital Resource Centre (not only for Nepal, but contains a large collection of Nepal), Nepal-German Manuscript Cataloguing Project (NGMCP).

* * *

The history of museums in Nepal began in 1928 with the establishment of the Silkhāna ("Arsenal") Museum in a building which Prime Minister Bhīmasena Thāpā had had built in 1820 as his residence in the Chhauni quarter of Kathmandu. In 1930, Juddha Śamśera issued a printed edict forbidding the export of palm-leaf manuscripts and works of art that might redound to the country's glory,[44] and instead had them brought either to the Chhauni museum, which in Nepālī is called *myujīyama* (probably one of the first examples of the word "museum" being used in Nepal), or to the Bir Library. This was the first museum in Nepal based upon the tradition of the imperial museums in India. It was also known under the name of Cāuni Silkhāna, but in 1939 it was renamed "Nepal Museum" and opened to the public by Juddha Śamśera. Since 1967 it has been the National Museum (Rāṣṭriya Saṅgrahālaya) of Nepal. It houses sculptures, paintings, handicrafts, weapons, and coins, but also a natural sciences section and more. Among its greatest treasures is a life-sized statue of Jayavarman from the second century.

The National Museum, like all museums in Nepal, is under the supervision of the Department of Archaeology, which was established in 1953. This institution is primarily responsible for preserving the cultural heritage of Nepal. Since nearly the entire Kathmandu Valley is one great open-air museum, the task is huge. The objects, which are often still in ritual use, must be protected, restored, scientifically examined, and, above all else, simply registered, as there is still no comprehensive inventory.[45] Although the department works on the basis of the Ancient Monuments Preservation Act of 2013, giving its officials far-reaching powers to protect monuments, a lack of both funding and staff has led here, as elsewhere, to much being overlooked or neglected, which represents a serious threat to Nepal's cultural heritage.

One of the internationally best-known museums of Nepal is the Patan Museum,[46] which was constructed in the old palace of Patan according to designs by architect Götz Hagmüller, curated by American art historian Mary Slusser, first opened to the public in 1997, and redesigned in 2017. It contains sculptures, architectural drawings, and valuable woodcarvings. The last of these also forms the focus of the National Woodcarving Museum in Bhaktapur, opened in 1967. Further museums worth visiting are the Gurkha Memorial Museum in Pokhara and the Sherpa Museum in Namche Bazaar.

One of the more recent museums is the Narayanhiti Palace Museum in the former royal palace, which was built in 1963 according to a design by American architect Benjamin Polk. It is in the tradition of the Tribhuvan Memorial Museum at Hanuman Dhoka and primarily displays royal devotional objects.[47] The museum captures the Śāha's somewhat tarnished past glory: the audience halls, the opulent throne, and the rather modest private chambers. In the room in which the massacre of 2001 occurred one can still see the bullet holes in the walls. Otherwise, one finds stuffed animals from hunts, photographs of meetings with other state leaders or royalty such as Queen Elizabeth II, but also Romania's Nicolae Ceausescu and gifts from many countries.

* * *

The biggest museum, however, is the country itself, especially the Kathmandu Valley. With its countless temples and palaces, the statues of gods scattered everywhere, and its Buddhist *stūpas*, it is one vast open-air museum. It is not surprising that UNESCO declared the Kathmandu Valley as itself a world cultural heritage center, with seven sites ("Monument Zones") within it: the areas in and around the Darbar Squares in Kathmandu, Patan, and Bhaktapur, the two large stūpas Svayambhū and Bauddha, and the Hindu temples of Paśupatinātha and Cāṅgunārāyaṇa.

APPENDIX 2

Lists of Rulers, Prime Ministers, and British Envoys

Rulers of the Licchavi Period

CE	Ruler	Remarks
around 185	[Jayavarmā (also Jayadeva I)]	
	[Haridattavarman]	
	Vasurāja	Mentioned as an ancestor in an inscription of Dhruvadeva and Jiṣṇugupta
ca. 400	[Vṛṣadeva, Viśvadeva]	
ca. 425	Śaṅkaradeva I	
ca. 450	Dharmadeva	
464–505	Mānadeva I	
505–6	[Mahīdeva]	Mentioned only in Jayadeva II's Paśupatinātha stele
506–32	Vasantadeva	
	Manudeva	Only one undated inscription
538	Vāmanadeva	
545	Rāmadeva	
	Amaradeva	Mentioned on a brick
	Guṇakāmadeva	
560–65	Gaṇadeva	
567–ca. 590	Bhaumagupta, Bhūmigupta (?)	Probably not a king
567–73	Gaṅgādeva (1/2)	
575/6	Beginning of the Mānadeva Era	
575/6	[Mānadeva II]	Not mentioned in any inscription but inferred from the beginning of the Mānadeva Era
590–604	Śivadeva I	
605–21	Aṃśuvarman	
621	Udayadeva	Mentioned in Jayadeva's stele as the 13th king after Vasantadeva

(*continued*)

CE	Ruler	Remarks
624–25	Dhruvadeva	
631–33	Bhīmārjunadeva, Jiṣṇugupta	
635	Viṣṇugupta – Jiṣṇugupta	
640–41	Bhīmārjunadeva, Viṣṇugupta	
643–79	Narendradeva	
694–705	Śivadeva II	
713–33	Jayadeva II	
	Gaṇadeva (?)	
748–49	Śaṅkaradeva II	
756	Mānadeva III	
826	Balirāja	
847	Baladeva	
877	Mānadeva IV	

Rulers of the Early Medieval Period

CE	Ruler
	[Rudradeva]
	[Bālārjunadeva]
879	[Rāghavadeva]
920	Śaṅkaradeva I
987–90	Guṇakāmadeva I
998	Narendradeva I and Udayadeva
1004	Udayadeva
1005	Nirbhayadeva
1008	Nirbhayadeva and Rudradeva I
1011	Bhojadeva
1012	Rudradeva I and Bhojadeva
1015	Bhojadeva, Rudradeva I, and Lakṣmīkāmadeva I
1024–39	Lakṣmīkāmadeva I [Jayadeva]
1045–48	Bhāskaradeva

CE	Ruler
1048–60	Baladeva
1060–66	Pradyumnakāmadeva
1066–69	Nāgārjunadeva
1069–83	Śaṅkaradeva II
1083–85	Vāmadeva
1085–99	Harṣadeva
1099–1122	Siṃhadeva
1098–1126	Śivadeva (perhaps identical with Siṃhadeva)
1126–37	Indradeva
1137–40	Mānadeva
1140–46	Narendradeva II
1147–66	Ānandadeva I
1167–74	Rudradeva II
1174–78	Amṛtadeva
1178–83	Someśvaradeva
1185–95	Guṇakāmadeva II (perhaps in joint rule with Lakṣmīkāmadeva II and Vijayakāmadeva)
1192–97	Lakṣmīkāmadeva II
1192–1200	Vijayakāmadeva

Rulers of the Malla Period

Kathmandu Valley					
1200–16	Ari Malla I				
1216–55	Abhaya Malla				
1221	Raṇaśūradeva				
1256–58	Jayadeva				
1258–71	Bhīmadeva				
1271–74	Sīha Malla				
1274–1307	Ananta Malla et al.				
1295–1326	Rudra Malla				
1308–20	Ānandadeva II				
1320–44	Ari Malla II				
1347–61	Rājadeva				
1361–81	Arjunadeva				
1382–95	Sthiti Malla				
ca. 1395–1408	Dharma Malla				
1408–28	Jyotir Malla				
ca. 1428–82	Yakṣa Malla				
Kantipur (Kathmandu)		**Lalitpur (Patan)**		**Bhadgaon (Bhaktapur)**	
1482–1520	Ratna	1482–1519	Rāya et al.	1482–1504	Rāya et al.
1520–29	Sūrya	1546–56	Viṣṇusiṃha	1504	Vīra
1529–60	Amara = Narendra	1560–97	Purandarasiṃha	1505–19	Bhuvana

1560–74	Mahendra	1597–1619	Śivasiṃha of Kantipur	1519–22	Raṇa, Vīra, Jita
1575–81	Sadāśiva	1619–61	Siddhinarasiṃha	1522–23	Raṇa, Bhīma, Vīra, Jita
1578–1619	Śivasiṃha	1661–84	Śrīnivāsa	1524–48	Prāṇa
1619–41	Lakṣmīnarasiṃha and Raṇajitsiṃha	1684–1705	Yoganarendra	1548–60	Viśva
		1705–6	Lokaprakāśa	1561–1613	Trailokya, Tribhuvan et al.
1641–74	Pratāpa	1706–9	Indra (Purandara)	1614–37	Jagajjyotir
1674–80	Nṛpendra	1709	Vīranarasiṃha	1637–43	Nareśa
1680–87	Pārthivendra	1709–15	Mahindra	1643–72	Jagatprakāśa
1687–1700	Bhūpālendra	1715–17	Ṛddhinarasiṃha	1673–96	Jitāmitra
		1717–22	Bhāskara = Mahindrasiṃha		
1700–1722	Bhāskara = Mahindrasiṃha	1722–29	Yogaprakāśa	1696–1722	Bhūpatīndra
1722–34	Jagajjaya	1729–45	Viṣṇu	1722–69	Raṇajit
1735–46 and 1752–68	Jayaprakāśa	1745–58	Rājyaprakāśa		
1746–52	Jyotiprakāśa	1758–60	Viśvajit		
		1760–61, 1763–64	Jayaprakāśa of Kantipur		
		1762–63	Raṇajit of Bhaktapur		
		1764–65	Dalamardana (Śāha)		
		1765–68	Tejnarasiṃha		

Śāha and Rāṇā Periods

Reign	Ruler (lifetime)	Regent	Prime minister / *mukhtiyāra*
1559–70	*Dravya*		
	. . .		
1609–33	*Rāma*		
1633–45	*Dambara*		
1645–61	*Kṛṣṇa*		
1661–73	*Rudra*		
1673–1716	*Pṛthvīpati*		
1716–43	*Narabhūpāla* (1697–1743)		
1743–75	*Pṛthvīnārāyaṇa* (1723–75)		
1775–77	*Pratāpa Siṃha* (1751–77)		
1777–99	*Raṇabahādura* (1775–1806)	1777–85: *Rājyalakṣmī Devī* (mother)	
		1785–94: *Bahādura Śāha* (uncle, 1757–97)	
1799–1816	*Gīrvāṇayuddha* (1797–1816)	1799–1800: *Rājarājeśvarī* (wife of Raṇabahādura) 1800–1803: *Suvarṇaprabhā* (queen consort of Raṇabahādura) 1803–4: *Rājarājeśvarī*	1799–1804: Damodara Pāḍe
			1804–6: Raṇabahādura Śāha (father)
		1806–32 (Lalita-) Tripurasundarī (wife of Raṇabahādura)	1806–37: *Bhīmasena Thāpā*
			1837–38: *Raṅganātha Pauḍela*
			1838–40: *Raṇa Jaṅga Pāḍe*
			1840–43 and 1845–46: *Phatte (Fateh) Jaṅga Chautariyā*

1816–47	*Rājendra Vikrama* (1813–81)	1839–40: *Sāṃrājya Lakṣmī Devī*	1843–45: *Māthavara Siṃha Thāpā*
			1846–56 and 1857–77: *Jaṅga Bahādura Kūvara (Rāṇā)* (b. 1817, d. 1877)
			1856–57: *Bam Bahādura Rāṇā and Kṛṣṇa Bahādura Kūvara Rāṇā* (only 1 month)
1847–81	Surendra Vikrama (1829–81)		1877–85: *Raṇoddīpa Siṃha*
1881–1911	Pṛthvī Vīra Vikrama (1875–1911)		1885–1901: *Vīra Śamśera*
			1901: *Deva Śamśera*
1911–50	Tribhuvan Vīra Vikrama (1906–55)		1901–29 *Candra Śamśera*
			1929–32: *Bhīma Śamśera*
			1932–45: *Juddha Śamśera*
			1945–48: *Padma Śamśera*
1950–51 (3 months)	Jñānendra (Gyanendra) Vīra Vikrama (b. 1947)		1948–51: *Mohana Śamśera*
1951–55	Tribhuvan Vīra Vikrama (1906–55)		
1955–72	*Mahendra Vīra Vikrama* (1920–72)		
1972–2001	*Vīrendra* (Birendra) *Vīra Vikrama* (1945–2001)		
6/1–6/4/2001	Dīpendra Vīra Vikrama (1971–2001)	1/2001–4/6/2001: *Jñānendra* (Gyanendra) *Vīra Vikrama*	
2001–5/28/2008	*Jñānendra* (Gyanendra) *Vīra Vikrama* (b. 1947)		

Italics: the de facto ruler

Prime Ministers since 1951

	Name (Lifetime)	Ruling Period	Party
1.	Matrika Prasad Koirala (1912–97)	11/16/1951–8/14/1952	Nepali Congress
2.	Matrika Prasad Koirala	8/14/1952–4/11/1955	Rashtriya Praja Party
3.	Surya Bahadur Thapa (1928–2015) (1st)	4/11/1955-4/11/1955	Rashtriya Praja Party
4.	Tanka Prasad Acharya (1912–92)	1/27/1956–7/26/1957	Nepal Praja Parishad
5.	Kunwar Inderjit Singh (1906–82)	7/26/1957–5/15/1958	United Democratic Party
6.	Subarna Shamsher Rana (1910–77)	5/15/1958–5/27/1959	Nepali Congress
7.	Bishweshwar Prasad Koirala (1914–82)	5/27/1959–12/15/1960	Nepali Congress
Panchayat Era (1960–90)			
8.	Tulsi Giri (1926–2018) (1st)	4/2/1963–12/23/1963	Partyless
9.	Surya Bahadur Thapa (2nd)	12/23/1963–2/26/1964	Partyless
10.	Tulsi Giri (2nd)	2/26/1964–1/26/1965	Partyless
11.	Surya Bahadur Thapa (3rd)	1/26/1965–4/7/1969	Partyless
12.	Kirti Nidhi Bista (1927–2017)(1st)	4/7/1969–4/13/1970	Partyless
13.	Gehendra Bahadur Rajbhandari (1923–94)	4/13/1970–4/14/1971	Partyless
14.	Kirti Nidhi Bista (2nd)	4/14/1971–7/16/1973	Partyless
15.	Nagendra Prasad Rijal (1927–94)	7/16/1973–12/1/1975	Partyless
16.	Tulsi Giri (3rd)	12/1/1975–9/12/1977	Partyless
17.	Kirti Nidhi (3rd)	9/12/1977–5/30/1979	Partyless
18.	Surya Bahadur Thapa (3rd)	5/30/1979–7/12/1983	Rashtriya Prajatantra Party
19.	Lokendra Bahadur Chand (b. 1940) (1st)	7/12/1983–3/21/1986	Partyless
20.	Nagendra Prasad Rijal (2nd)	3/21/1986–6/15/1986	Partyless
21.	Marich Man Singh Shrestha (1942–2013)	6/15/1986–4/6/1990	Partyless
22.	Lokendra Bahadur Chand (2nd)	4/6/1990–4/19/1990	Rashtriya Prajatantra Party (Chand)
Constitutional Monarchy (1990–2008)			
23.	Krishna Prasad Bhattarai (1924–2011) (1st)	4/19/1990–5/26/1991	Nepali Congress
24.	Girija Prasad Koirala (1925–2010) (1st)	5/26/1991–11/30/1994	Nepali Congress

	Name (Lifetime)	Ruling Period	Party
25.	Man Mohan Adhikari (1920–1999)	11/30/1994–9/12/1995	Communist Party of Nepal (Unified Marxist–Leninist)
26.	Sher Bahadur Deuba (b. 1946) (1st)	9/12/1995–3/12/1997	Nepali Congress
27.	Lokendra Bahadur Chand (3rd)	3/12/1997–10/7/1997	Rashtriya Prajatantra Party (Chand)
28.	Surya Bahadur Thapa (4th)	10/7/1997–4/15/1998	Rashtriya Prajatantra Party
29.	Girija Prasad Koirala (2nd)	4/15/1998–5/31/1999	Nepali Congress
30.	Krishna Prasad Bhattarai (2nd)	5/31/1999–3/22/2000	Nepali Congress
31.	Girija Prasad Koirala (3rd)	3/22/2000–7/26/2001	Nepali Congress
32.	Sher Bahadur Deuba (2nd)	7/26/2001–10/4/2002	Nepali Congress
33.	Lokendra Bahadur Chand (4th)	10/11/2002–6/5/2003	Rashtriya Prajatantra Party
34.	Surya Bahadur Thapa (5th)	6/5/2003-6/3/2004	Rashtriya Prajatantra Party
35.	Sher Bahadur Deuba (3rd)	6/3/2004–2/1/2005	Nepali Congress
36.	Girija Prasad Koirala (4th)	4/25/2006–5/28/2008	Nepali Congress
Federal Democratic Republic of Nepal (2008–)			
37.	Girija Prasad Koirala (5th)	5/28/2008–8/18/2008	Nepali Congress
38.	Pushpa Kamal Dahal, aka Prachanda (b. 1954) (1st)	8/15/2008–5/25/2009	Unified Communist Party of Nepal (Maoist)
39.	Madhav Kumar Nepal (b. 1953)	5/25/2009–1/6/2011	Communist Party of Nepal (Unified Marxist–Leninist)
40.	Jhala Nath Khanal (b. 1950)	1/6/2011–8/29/2011	Communist Party of Nepal (Unified Marxist–Leninist)
41.	Baburam Bhattarai (b. 1954)	8/29/2011–3/14/2013	Unified Communist Party of Nepal (Maoist)
42.	Khil Raj Regmi (b. 1949)	3/14/2013–2/11//2014	Partyless
43.	Sushil Koirala (1939–2016)	2/11/2014–10/12/2015	Nepali Congress
44.	Khadga Prasad Sharma Oli (b. 1952) (1st)	10/12/2015–8/4/2016	Communist Party of Nepal (Unified Marxist–Leninist)
45.	Pushpa Kamal Dahal (2nd)	8/4/2016–6/7/2017	Unified Communist Party of Nepal (Maoist)
46.	Sher Bahadur Deuba (4th)	6/7/2017–2/15/2018	Nepali Congress
47.	Khadga Prasad Sharma Oli (2nd)	2/15/2018–7/13/2021	Communist Party of Nepal (Unified Marxist–Leninist)
48.	Sher Bahadur Deuba (5th)	7/13/2021–12/26/2022	Nepali Congress
49.	Pushpa Kamal Dahal (3rd)	12/26/2022–	Unified Communist Party of Nepal (Maoist)

N.B. In the temporal gaps, the king ruled directly. Ordinal numbers refer to the frequency of government periods.

British Residents

Tenure	Name
1816–29	Edward Gardner
1829–31	Brian Houghton Hodgson
1831–33	Thomas Herbert Maddock
1833–43	Brian Houghton Hodgson
1843–45	Henry Montgomery Lawrence
1845–47	John Russell Colvin
1847–50	Charles Thoresby
1850–52	James Claudius Erskine
1852–67	George Ramsay
1867–72	Richard Charles Lawrence
1872–88	Charles Edward Ridgway Girdlestone
1888–91	Edward Law Durand
1891–99	Henry Wylie
1899	Archibald Mungo Muir
1899–1901	William Loch
1901–2	Thomas Caldwell Pears
1902–5	Charles Withers Ravenshaw
1905–16	John Manners Smith
1916–18	Stuart Farquharson Bayley
1918–23	William Frederick Travers
Since 1923	"Envoys"

Notes

N.B. Literature marked by an asterisk (∗) refers to documents listed in the Documentary Sources section of the Bibliography.

Abbreviations

Ain	*The Mulukī Ain of 1854: Nepal's First Legal Code.* Introduced, translated, and annotated by Rajan Khatiwoda, Simon Cubelic, and Axel Michaels. Heidelberg: Heidelberg University Publishing, 2021.
BhV	*Bhāṣāvaṃśāvalī*
CNSt	*Contributions to Nepalese Studies*
DNA	Documenta Nepalica
EBHR	*European Bulletin of Himalayan Research*
GopV	*Gopālarāvaṃśāvalī*
HAdW	Heidelberger Akademie der Wissenschaften
H.M.G.	His Majesty's Government, Nepal
JNRC	*Journal of the Nepal Research Centre*
KVPT	Kathmandu Valley Preservation Trust
LA	Licchavi Abhilekha (Numbered after Dhanavajra Vajrācārya 1973c)
LIRI	Lumbini International Research Institute
MA	*Mulukī Ain*, cp. Ain
Manu	Mānava-Dharmaśāstra
NBhV	*Nepālikabhūpavaṃśāvalī*
NEFIN	Nepal Federation of Indigenous Nationalities
NHDP	Nepal Heritage Documentation Project
Nep.	Nepālī
Nev.	Nevārī
NGMPP	Nepal-German Manuscript Preservation Project
NS	Nepāla Saṃvat (starts 879 CE)
VS	Vikrama Saṃvat (starts 57 BCE)
RRC	*Regmi Research Collection* (vol. and page number)
RRS	*Regmi Research Series*
Skt.	Sanskrit
SINHS	*Studies in Nepali History and Society*
VDC	Village Development Committee

Introduction

1. *Divyopadeśa*, a text attributed to Pṛthvīnārāyaṇa, quoted from Stiller 1989: 39.
2. Dennis and Bhandari 2019.
3. Onta 1996a; K. L. Pradhan 2009.
4. S. B. Gyawali VS 2033; Onta 1996b; Whelpton 2017–18: 183.
5. See, for instance, D. R. Regmi 1975, 1: 100.
6. Risley 1896: viii.
7. Cf. Des Chene 2007; Michaels 2018a.
8. Whelpton 2005: 4.
9. Quoted from Michaels 2005b: 52.
10. Rose 1971: 8–9.
11. Pollock 2006.
12. Quoted from Uprety 1992: 94; cf. Whelpton 2005: 81.
13. Gellner 2016a.
14. Quoted from Kutzner 1857: 160.
15. *Ain* 1.1. All quotations from *Ain* are from the translation by E. Khatiwoda, S. Cubelic, and A. Michaels 2021.
16. Rupakheti 2016: 77.
17. *Divyopadeśa*, translation by P. R. Sharma 2008: 479. On the debate over this passage, see Stiller 1989: 44; D. Gellner 2008: 24; K. L. Pradhan 2009: xiii and 169–70.
18. Major overviews are Jayaswal 1936; D. R. Regmi 1960, 1965–1966, and 1975; B. R. Ācārya 1966 and 2013; Shaha 1990a and 1992; Slusser 1982, 1: 3–79; Whelpton 2005.
19. For a more detailed analysis of the theoretical implications of these chronicles, see Bajracharya and Michaels 2012; Michaels et al. 2016.
20. Cf. Gellner 2016a.

Chapter 1

1. On the toponymn and endonym "Nepāla,": LA 23; Lévi 1905–8, 1: 364; Dh. Vajrācārya and G. Nepāli 1953 (V.S. 2010); Burton-Page 1954; J. Nepālī 1983; Burghart 1984; M. R. Panta 2003; Bledsoe 2004: 69–70.; Gellner 2008; Whelpton 2008: 41; Malla 2015: 270–83; D. Acharya 2017.
2. Lévi 1905–8, 2: 63 (and Riccardi's translation 1975 of Lévi 1905: 12).
3. *Treaty with Nepal, November 1, 1860*: see *Sughauli Treaty of 1815*.
4. Whelpton 2008: 41.
5. For an overview of Nepal's infrastructure: Karan and Ishii 1996.
6. On the topography and flora: Miehe and Pendry 2015.
7. Most numbers are from the Government of Nepal 2011.
8. On the Himalayan mountains: Salisbury and Hawley 2011; website of Guenter Seyfferth: https://www.himalaya-info.org/index.htm (in German; last accessed June 21, 2021).

9. Quoted from Gutschow 2012: 106.
10. On Mount Everest: Ortner 1999; Gilman 2000; Unsworth 2000.
11. On Hawley: Choegyal and Dunham 2015.
12. On earthquakes in Nepal: A. Campbell 1833; M. R. Panta 2002b; B. S. J. B. Rana 2013; Bollinger et al. 2016; Raj and Gautam 2015; Asia Foundation 2016; Bajracharya and Michaels 2017; Brosius and Maharjan 2017; Brosius and Michaels 2020; see also the bibliographic resource guide by Baniya and Gautam 2019.
13. The dates from the thirteenth to eighteenth century are from chronicles and not wholly reliable.
14. GopV fol. 38.
15. On the 1934 earthquake, see also Prasad 1996: 63–86.
16. See *Nature* 592 (April 28, 2021): 726–31.
17. On the water problems in Nepal: Subba 2010; A. Adhikari 2014: 21–28.
18. Becker-Ritterspach 1982, 1995, and 1996; Gail 1997; Hegewald 2002; Furukawa 2010; G. Vajracharya 2016.
19. Hamilton 1928: 561–70.
20. See Rāma Śāha's Royal Edicts nos. 13–14; *Itihāsa-Prakāśa* 2: 419–26; Riccardi 1977: 51.
21. See Michaels 1994b, 1: 29–34, with further references.
22. ∗Anonymous 1905.
23. ∗Gīrvāṇayuddha Śāha 1803.
24. ∗Surendra Śāha 1847.

Chapter 2

1. All figures from Government of Nepal, 2023a.
2. Government of Nepal 2023b. The numbers do not sum up to 100% because the membership in the mentioned categories is disputed.
3. On Nepal's population and its subclasses: Bista 1972 and 1991; Nepali 1965; Toffin 1984; Gaborieau 1978; P. R. Sharma 2004; P. Sharma 2014; Gaenszle et al. 2015; and D. Gellner 1995, 2007, 2016a, 2016b, and 2019. For the population tables, see Whelpton 2008: 53–54 and D. Gellner 1992: 44 and 1995.
4. Government of Nepal 2023b. Cf. Rosser 1979 and B. G. Shrestha 2007 for the counting of castes and social groups.
5. On definitions of ethnic groups and ethnicity: Krämer 1996; Whelpton 2000: 46–47; and Gellner, Pfaff-Czarnecka, and Whelpton 2008: 12–17 (along with Gellner's articles mentioned above).
6. Whelpton 2005: 8–18 and 2017–18.
7. On theories that they rather came from the west or east: Witzel 1993; van Driem 1998; Whelpton 2000: 57–60 and 2017–18.
8. Whelpton 2000: 60.

9. On the Newar and Nevārī: Lévi 1905–8, 1: 220–22; D. R. Regmi 1965–66, 4: inscr. 52 [90–91], Slusser 1982, 1: 9–11.
10. Bista 1991: 37.
11. Ibid., 38.
12. Hitchcock 1979.
13. On migration: Sijapati and Limbu 2012; Government of Nepal 2015b; on early forms of migrant labor, see M. C. Regmi 1976: 13.
14. Cf. Gellner 2008.
15. Hamilton 1819: 23.
16. A text entitled *Jātimālā* containing 82 caste names has been published in *Rolamba* 1 (1): 7-8.
17. NBhV 19.41.
18. NBhV 19.48.
19. Höfer 1979a; Pfaff-Czarnecka 1989; for a summary of the *Ain*, see Khatiwoda, Cubelic, and Michaels 2021: Introduction.
20. Cf. Table 2.4 of the *Ain*; cf. Höfer 1979a: 45.
21. *Ain* 31.7.
22. On the position of women: Allen and Mukherjee 1982; Bennett 1983; Bista 1991: 62–66; Bennett, Sijapati, and Thapa 2013.
23. *Ain* 98.4.
24. On the *Svasthānīvratakathā*: Iltis 1985; Birkenholtz 2018.
25. Bista 1991: 62–63.
26. On the Kumārī: NBhV 19.3.61; Michaels 2009b with further references; Slusser 1982, 1: 311–16, Toffin 1984; M. R. Allen 1975; Letizia 2013; Tree 2014a and 2014b; for royal rituals performed by the Kumārī, see A. Zotter 2018 and 2021.
27. Oldfield 1880, 1: 251; Michaels 1992 (with further references), 1993a and 1994a; Maskey 1996: 64–85; M. R. Panta 1984; Mainali 2021.
28. Hamilton [1819] 1971: 23.
29. Cf. Hasrat 1970: 120 and 128, and ∗Rājendra Śāha 1841.
30. M. R. Panta 1977.
31. On *satī* in the case of concubines: ∗Rājendra Śāha 1822b and 1836b; see also the notes on ∗Rājendra Śāha 1836a.
32. On the practice of *satī* among Tamang, see March (2000: 21–22) based on a paper by B. H. Hodgson.
33. See ∗Candra Śamśera 1925: 45.
34. On secularization: Letizia 2012 and 2016.
35. Pfaff-Czarnecka 1999; P. R. Sharma 2008; Gellner, Hausner, and Letizia 2016.
36. On Dalits in transition: Gellner and Adhikari 2019.
37. On the NEFEN declaration: D. Gellner 2008: 20–21.

Chapter 3

1. Cf. Burghart 1984.
2. Lawoti 2005.
3. Slusser 1982: 1, 213–380; J. Ch. Regmi 1982a; van Kooij 1978; Levy 1990.
4. Briggs 1973; Unbescheid 1980; Bouillier 1986, 1993, and 2017.
5. D. R. Regmi 1965–66, 3: 31
6. C. Zotter 2022.
7. Gaborieau 1977; Siddika 1993; Sijapati 2011.
8. On Nepalese Buddhism: M. R. Allen 1973; Greenwold 1974; Ram 1977; Slusser 1982; K. Vaidya 1986; D. Gellner 1992; I. S. Bajracharya 2014; N. M. Bajracharya 1998; Lewis 2000; Lewis and Bajracharya 2016.
9. Brinkhaus 1987; von Rospatt 2009; Deeg 2016: 58–225 and 261–347.
10. Falk 1998 and 2012; Deeg 2003; Coningham et al. 2013; on early archaeological sources: Verardi 1992.
11. Hultzsch 1925: 164–65
12. According to new findings, this controversial researcher was not averse to falsifying evidence: see C. Allen 2008.
13. D. Acharya 2008: 43.
14. Cf. LA 1 and 98; D. Acharya 2008.
15. G. Vajrācārya 1973b; LA 77.
16. On Narendradeva's promotion of Buddhist monasteries: G. Vajrācārya 1973b; LA 77.
17. On the Sukhāvatī cult: D. Acharya 2008.
18. Petech 1984: 41–43; Davidson 2002: 130; Roerich 1996: 41–42; Lewis and Bajracharya 2016: 90–91.
19. On the Buddhist literature in Sanskrit: Mitra [1882] 1981; Tuladhar-Douglas 2006; Lewis and Bajracharya 2016: 173–75.
20. NBhV 14.23
21. Tuladhar-Douglas 2006.
22. Tuladhar-Douglas 2006: 205.
23. On the Matsyendranātha/Karuṇāmaya cult: N. Allen 1986; J. K. Locke 1980; Owens 1989.
24. Cf. M. Allen 1973; D. Gellner 1987; Lewis and Bajracharya 2016: 177; NBhV 19.3.
25. On Tibetan Buddhism in Nepal: Snellgrove 1987; Lewis 1996; on Theravāda Buddhism in Nepal: Kloppenburg 1977; LeVine and Gellner 2005.
26. On Newar Buddhism: Chattopadhyay 1980; D. Gellner 1992; Lienhard 1999; Tuladhar-Douglas 2006; Lewis and Bajracharya 2016.
27. Cf. Gellner 1992: 43.
28. On Buddhist life-cycle rituals: *Daśakarmavidhi*; Gutschow and Michaels 2008 and 2012.

29. M. Bajracharya 2006; Lewis and Bajracharya 2016: 138–41; D. Gellner 1991.
30. On my understanding and definition of Hinduism: Michaels 2004: 3–30.
31. Witzel 1976.
32. Witzel 1986 and 1992.
33. Toffin 2006.
34. On life-cycle rituals in Nepal: Gutschow and Michaels 2005, 2008, and 2012 with further references; Zotter and Zotter 2010; Gögge 2010; C. Zotter 2018b.
35. On immigrating Brahmins: D. R. Regmi 1965–66, 1: 271–93 and 640; Petech 1984: 113–17; Witzel 1985; Gögge 2007: 166–69.
36. On conversions, see Höfer 1979a: 158; D. Gellner 2005.
37. *Prasāda Gautama 1951.
38. Cf. Toffin 2012 and 2016; Gibson 2017; on the middle class in general: Liechty 2003; Lotter 2011; D. Gellner 2019.
39. On Śaivism in general: Sanderson 2009 and 2015; on Śaivism in Nepal: Slusser 1982, 1: 223–39.
40. Paurāṇic works such as the *Skandapurāṇa*, the *Himavatkhaṇḍa*, or the *Nepālamāhātmya* are full of praise for the many Śaiva shrines, as is the *Gopālarāja vaṃśāvalī*. Tantric Śaiva texts on lay practice, such as the *Śivadharmaśāstra*, the *Śivadharmottara*, or the late *Śivadharmasaṅgraha*, number in the thousands, some of them being rare manuscripts (e.g., *Niśvāsatattvasaṃhitā*, the earliest surviving Śaiva Tantra; *Jayākhyasaṃhitā*, the earliest extant Vaiṣṇava Pāñcarātra text; or the *Praśnavyākaraṇa*, the oldest surviving Jaina Tantra).
41. Ṭaṇḍana 1985, 1996, and 1999; Michaels 1994b and 2008 with further references.
42. On the Pāśupatas: D. Ācārya 1998 and 2005; Mirnig 2013 and 2016.
43. On Śivadharma manuscripts: de Siminis 2016.
44. Garbini 1997.
45. *Nepālamāhātmya* I.9–23.
46. Bakker 2014: 137–38.
47. On Licchavi *liṅgas*: Mirnig 2016.
48. On votive *liṅgas* at Paśupatinātha: Michaels 1994b, 1: 66–78.
49. Mentioned in NBhV 12.112–13.
50. Michaels 1996 and 2008: Chapter 10.
51. On early depictions of Śiva in Nepal: LA 53; Slusser 1982, 2: pls. 351–53.
52. Michaels 1993c, 2008: Chapter 9; G. Vajracharya 2020.
53. On Bhairava: LA 107; Slusser 1982, 1: 235–39 (especially Pacali Bhairava); Bühnemann 2013 (Nīlabhairava); Chalier-Visuvalingam 2013.
54. Briggs 1973; Unbescheid 1980.
55. D. R. Regmi 1965–66, 2: 569–70; Anderson 1971; J. K. Locke 1980; Owens 1989.
56. On Gaṇeśa: Slusser 1982, 1: 261–63; M. R. Shakya 2006.
57. Cf. D. R. Regmi 1965–66, 2: 621.
58. Slusser 1982, 1: 307–49; Tachikawa 2001.
59. On the difference between wild and mild goddesses: Michaels, Vogelsanger, and Wilke 1996: Introduction.
60. Dyczkowski 2001.
61. Flood 2011.

62. Pfaff-Czarnecka 2011; A. Zotter 2016 and 2018.
63. A. Zotter 2018.
64. Michaels 1984, 1994b: 191–240 and 2008: 79–106.
65. See LA 4; Gnoli 1956: no. 6.
66. On Vaiṣṇavism in Nepal: Pal 1970; Slusser 1982, 1: 239–58; Lienhard 1991; Jurami 2001; Pauḍyāla 2005; Gögge 2007; Mocko 2016.
67. Older names are Dolādri and Garuḍanārāyaṇa, and Dolāśikharasvāmin for the main deity.
68. On Changu Narayan: J. Ch. Regmi 1982a: 109; M. P. Khanāla n.d. (VS 2040.)
69. Gail 1984: 12–29; Gögge 2007: 28.
70. GopV fol. 20a and 30b; Hasrat 1970: 36–37; *Bhāṣāvaṃśāvalī* 1: 55 and 81.
71. Edited LA 148 and Gnoli 1956: 81.
72. See Pal 1970: 44–45; L. S. Bangdel 1989: 67–68; Slusser 1982, 1: 241.
73. Gögge 2007: 238–70; Burghart 2016.
74. Michaels 1995.
75. M. Jha 1971; Burghart 1978, 1985, and 2016; Burkert 2008.
76. On Kṛṣṇaism in Nepal: Lienhard 1992a, 1995; Gögge 2007: 162–211.
77. See LA 64 and 101.
78. Thyāsaphu E, fol. 7 in D. R. Regmi 1965–66, 3: 90 and 2: 296.
79. See G. Vajrācārya 1973a: 74–78.
80. On more recent developments of Kṛṣṇaism: *Prasāda Gautama 1951; Gögge 2007: 205–9.
81. D. R. Regmi 1965–66, 2: 558.
82. Lewis and Bajracharya 2016: 110–13.
83. Bühnemann 2010.
84. On festivals: Anderson 1971; P. Vajrācārya 1979; Goodman 1981; Vézies 1981.
85. On syncretism: Lienhard 1978a and 1978b; Bista 1991: 34; Brinkhaus 1996; D. Gellner 1997 and 2005.
86. On hybridity: Michaels 2018b.
87. Cf. D. Gellner 2005.
88. See Michaels 1996 (with further references) and 2006.

Chapter 4

1. On the prehistory of Nepal: Whelpton 2000; Corvinus 2007; Darnal 2016.
2. Cf. Dongol 1985; Sakai et al. 2006.
3. On the Kirāta or Kiranti: Chemjong 1967; Dh. Vajrācārya 1968b; Malla 1981; K. L. Pradhan 2009.
4. On the Kirāta influence in Licchavi history: Dh. Vajrācārya 1968b; for a particularly significant occurrence of *kirāti* in Licchavi inscriptions, see LA 91.
5. Nina Mirnig, personal communication; cf. also B. R. Ācārya 1963 and 1966.
6. On the land system of the Licchavis: P. R. Sharma 1983.

7. On Chinese pilgrims: Lévi 1905–8, 1: 149–92; Deeg 2016; on the influence of Newar scholars on Tibet: Lo Bue 1997.
8. On the Licchavi in India: H. N. Jha 1970.
9. On the influence of the Kushanas: Alsop and Tamot 1996/2001; Verardi 1992; T. N. Mishra 2000.
10. For the discussion of this point, cf. M. R. Panta and A. Sharma 1977; M. R. Panta 2003; D. Acharya 2017.
11. See D. R. Regmi 1983, 1 and 2: 2–3 (in both volumes); Riccardi 1989.
12. Riccardi 1989: 617.
13. Cuka Bāhā; see Petech 1984: 51–59.
14. D. Acharya 2009.
15. Witzel 1980.
16. D. Acharya 2009; cf. Riccardi 1980: 272.
17. Modified from D. Acharya 2017: 44–45.
18. Cf. Manu 4.26ff.
19. Gutschow 1997: 100–71.
20. Gutschow 1997, 2011, 1 and 2011, 2: 359.
21. Mirnig 2016: 314.
22. Snellgrove 1987, 2: 372.
23. Tucci 1962.
24. Petech 1984: 29.
25. D. R. Regmi 1965–66, vol. 1; Slusser 1982, 1: 41–51; Petech 1984.
26. de Siminis 2016: 257, cf. Petech 1984: 68.
27. Cf. Malla 2015: 203–8; N. R. Pant 1965: 4.
28. Petech 1984: 33–34.
29. On Guṇakāmadeva I: BhV II: 32; GopV fol. 23b; Petech 1984: 32–34.
30. Eltschinger 2019; I. S. Bajracharya 2014: 76–84.
31. Gutschow 2011, vol. 1.
32. Cf. Slusser 2010.
33. Petech 1984: 55.
34. Atkinson 1986; Tucci 1956; D. R. Regmi 1965–66, 2: 710–35; Pandey 1970 and 1997; P. R. Sharma 1972; Hitchcock 1979; Adhikary 1986 and 1988; Cüppers and Ehrhard 2007; Lecomte-Tilouine 2009a and 2009b, M. R. Panta 2009; T. B. Shrestha 2009; Andolfatto 2019: 37–71.
35. Dhungel 2002; Vitali 2012: 122–23.
36. See also M. P. Khanāla 1981/82 : 17–97.
37. Tucci 1956: 54–59.
38. Andolfatto 2019: 39.
39. NBhV 16.51–62.
40. D. R. Sharma 2012; Andolfatto 2019.
41. GopV fol. 26, pp. 129–30, transl. by K. P. Malla.
42. Cf. Gaborieau 1969; P. R. Sharma 1972; Winkler 1976.
43. See ∗Pṛthvīnārāyaṇa Śāha 1774a, RRS 1: 11.
44. Cf. D. R. Regmi 1975, 1: 1–18; Stiller 1975: 70–73.
45. Shaha 1990a, 1: 3–4.

46. D. R. Regmi 1975, 1: 18–26; Bista 1991: 37–38; Whelpton 2017–18: 174.
47. Cf. Stiller 1975: 33–62.
48. On the state as a *dhuṅgo*: Whelpton 2008: 43.

Chapter 5

1. Toffin 1984, 2005, and 2007; D. Gellner 1986 and 1992.
2. B. G. Shrestha 2015.
3. Petech 1984: 77.
4. Slusser 1982, 1: 53.
5. Cf. M. R. Pant and Sharma 1977.
6. D. R. Regmi 1965–66, 2: 474 and inscription no. LXLVII (3: 108–11).
7. D. R. Regmi 1965–66, 2: 423.
8. This was designed by terms derived from the Sanskrit verb root *bhuj* ("enjoy") and the pronoun *sva* ("self, own"): *bhoga* meaning "right of use" and *svatva* meaning "property." See Kölver and Śākya 1985.
9. Kölver and Śākya 1985; Gögge 2001.
10. Pant and Sharma 1977: 18.
11. Dh. Bajrācārya 1966.
12. Petech 1984: 183–88.
13. D. R. Regmi 1965–6, 2: 333–34; cf. Slusser 1982, 1: 64.
14. *Bhāskara Malla 1703.
15. NBhV 19/2.164.
16. Kathmandu Valley (Pruscha) 1975; Gutschow 1982 and 2011; Gutschow, Kölver, and Shresthacarya 1987; Gutschow and Kreutzmann 2013.
17. On Kirtipur: Herdick 1988; on Nuvakot: Gutschow 2011, 1: 154–66; on Panauti: Barré et al. 1981; on Sankhu: B. G. Shrestha 2012; on Thimi: Müller 1981; M. Pant 2002b.
18. Gutschow 2011, vol. 2.
19. On temple architecture: Bernier 1970 and 1979; Wiesner 1978; Korn 1979; Becker-Ritterspach 1982; Gutschow 1982, 1997, 2011, 2016, 2017, 2019; Gail 1984 and 1988; Hutt et al. 1994; Tiwari 2009; see also the Digital Archive of Nepalese Arts and Architecture (DANAM): https://danam.cats.uni-heidelberg.de/.
20. On *śikhara*-style and domed buildings: Gutschow 1986; Basukala, Gutschow, and Kayastha 2014.
21. On monasteries: J. K. Locke 1985; Gail 1991; D. Gellner 2001; Owens 2014.
22. See, for extent architectural studies, Gutschow 1997 and 2021.
23. On Svayambhū: GopV fol. 20b (cf. LA 18 and 96); Slusser 1982, 1: 276, and 1985; Ehrhard 1989 and 1991; Kölver 1992b; von Rospatt 2009, 2011, and Forthcoming; Gutschow 2011, 2: 681–706.
24. On Bhaktapur: Gutschow and Kölver 1975; Levy 1990; Gutschow 2017.
25. Müller[-Böker] 1981–82; S. Manandhar 1984; Kasten 2011.
26. Basukala, Gutschow, and Kayastha 2014.
27. D. Gellner 1992 and 1996; on the architecture of Patan: Gutschow 2011.

28. Mentioned in an inscription dated Saṃvat 107 (186 CE); see *Abhilekha Saṃgraha* 9: 24. Mary Slusser (1982, 1: 110–11) argues that this name is not to be derived from Mānagṛha (Mānadeva's palace), but from Nev. *māni* ("center") and *gvala* ("place").
29. Cf. Bühnemann 2010.
30. Slusser 1982, 1: 258–59.
31. For a very readable account on Kathmandu: Bell 2014.
32. Slusser 1982, 1: 92.
33. Cf. A. Zotter 2018.

Chapter 6

1. Hasrat 1970: 169–344; Stiller 1975, 1976, and 1993; S. B. Gyawali VS 2033; Dh. Vajrācārya and Ṭ. B. Śreṣṭha VS 2037 (1980/81); Riccardi 1977; D. R. Panta 1986–88; Shaha 1990a; Whelpton 1992 and 2005; Mocko 2016.
2. On Pṛthvīnārāyaṇa Śāha: Baral 1964; B. R. Ācārya (Acharya) 1967 and 1970a, D. R. Regmi 1975, 1: 88–270; Stiller 1975 and 1989.
3. B. R. Ācārya 1966: 36–41, Engl. transl. in RRS 4.9 (1972): 175–79; Y. Raj 2012; Bell 2018.
4. Bell 2018: 21.
5. Stiller 1989: 43.
6. See Giuseppe 1799; Kirkpatrick 1811: 383; NBhV 1: 134; Sukrasagar Shrestha 2016.
7. Sakya 1970: 49–50.
8. Hamilton [1819] 1971: 244; D. R. Regmi 1975, 1: 16; K. L. Pradhan 2009: 24.
9. Cf. Stiller 1976: 43.
10. Rupakheti 2016.
11. Cf. Whelpton 2007: 191.
12. Stiller 1975: 88.
13. Stiller 1975: 95.
14. Cf. M. C. Regmi 1999; Moran 2018.
15. ∗*Gorkhā Jājarkoṭa Dharma Sandhi* in: *Itihāsa-Prakāśa* 1, 4, English translation in RRS 2 (1970): 17 and Stiller 1975: 257–58.
16. W. D. Knox quoted from M. C. Regmi 1995: 9.
17. Stiller 1975: 219–51.
18. On Bhīmasena Thāpā: Ch. Nepālī 1956; K. L. Pradhan 2012.
19. Stiller 1975: 76–97.
20. K. L. Pradhan 2009.
21. See also Stiller 1975; D. R. Regmi 1975; M. C. Regmi 1999.
22. Bouillier 1991; C. Zotter 2018a.
23. Rupakheti 2016: 79.
24. Edwards 1975.
25. On the *munsī* see M. Bajracharya 2018.
26. Kshetri 1998: 25.

27. On the Anglo-Nepalese War: Chaudhuri 1960; Hussain 1970; Pemble 1971; Stiller 1975; Des Chene 1991; Michael 2013.
28. Pemble 1971.
29. Cf. Michael 1999.
30. *Gīrvāṇayuddha Śāha 1813, quoted from Stiller 1975: 246; emphasis in the original.
31. Stiller 1976: 7.
32. Reproduced in Stiller 1976: 22–24.
33. Stiller 1976: 48–49.
34. Cf. Gaige 1968.
35. Stiller 1976: 102–5.
36. Kshetri 1998: 47.
37. On Gurkha soldiers: Hamilton [1819] 1971: 14–55; Hodgson 1883; Tuker 1957; Caplan 1995 and 1991; Smith 1997; Onta 1997; Mulmi 2017.
38. From the preface of Turner's Nepali-English dictionary (1931: ix).
39. Kshetri 1998: 199.
40. Quoted from Des Chene 1991: 13.
41. Cf. Montgomery 1998; Des Chene 1991 and 1993.
42. Hodgson [1874] 1991: 40–41.
43. What it looks like when such a "non-effete" army is created can be seen even in present days, when thousands of young Nepalese come to be recruited but only around two hundred are accepted. The selection process starts immediately, according to size, age, hairstyle, and other criteria. Those that remain go through grinding tests, and in the end, standing in underclothes in front of British and Nepalese officers, a simple number is written by the officers on their upper bodies to tell them whether they have made it or not.
44. Cf. Onta 1997: 448.
45. For a more detailed description of the events, see Camman 1951; Dh. Vajrācārya and Nepāla 1957/1970; D. R. Regmi 1975, 1: 463–78; Rose 1971: 24–33; Killigrew 1979; Uprety 1980.
46. von Fürer-Haimendorf 1975.
47. T. P. Mishra 2003.
48. *Gīrvāṇayuddha Śāha 1804, also mentioned in NBhV 20.92 (p. 135) and Lévi 1905, 2: 181.
49. There are conflicting Chinese and Nepalese documents on the course of the war: For the Chinese sources, see Fang Lüeguan 1992 (*Official Summary Account of the Pacification of the Balebu*); *Chin-ting K'uo-er-k'a Chi lueh* (Peking, 1796): 54 plus 4 chuan in 8 vols., see Rose 1971: 303; Wei Yüan's report (English translation: Landon 1976, 2: 275–82). For the Nepalese sources, see the report of Raṇabahādura Śāha (Dh. Vajrācārya and Nepāla 1957); the unpublished "sandhi between the emperor of China and the king of Nepal signed after the war between two countries VS 1850" (*Documenta Nepalica* E_2730_0028). Cf. Camman 1951: chs. 5 and 6; Stiller 1975: 202–11; D. R. Regmi 1975, 1: 463–78.
50. NBhV 20.92 (p. 135)
51. Landon 1976, 2: 280.

52. Stiller 1975: 212.
53. Wei Yüan in Landon 1976, 2: 281.
54. The exact date and site of the signing ceremony are not clear. Rose (1971: 64) gives 30 September 1792 as the date (corresponding to that on the letter of the Chinese negotiator Fu K'ang-an stating the acceptance of conditions presented by the Nepalese government on September 27) and October 31as the date of the emperor's ratification. B. Acharya (2013: 251) gives October 6, 1792, for the latter.
55. On the relationship between Tibet, China, and Nepal, see Kirkpatrick 1811: App. 1; Camman 1951: chs. 5 and 6, Dh. Vajrācārya and Nepāla 1957; Rose 1971; Uprety 1980 and 1996.
56. Rose 1971: 11–12; Petech 1984: 213–23.
57. Cf. Vajrācārya and Nepāla 1957; T. R. Manandhar and Mishra 1986; V. K. Manandhar 2001.
58. T. R. Manandhar and Mishra 1986: 19–20; Petech 1996.
59. Hodgson 1880: 170–71.
60. Rose 1971: 65 n. 44.
61. Dh. Vajrācārya and Nepāla 1957: 71–72.
62. P. J. B. Rana 1909: 8; Stiller (1975: 212) comments that there is no indication "that this is an official treaty." Interestingly, however, this treaty was presented to the United Nations Organization in 1949 CE as additional proof of Nepal's independent and sovereign status (Stiller ibid.). For other primary and secondary sources on this issue, see Rose 1971: 59 n. 28 and 65 n. 44.
63. *Itihāsa-Prakāśa* 1: 121, my translation.
64. Pudma J. B. Rana 1909: 8; T. R. Manandhar and Mishra 1986; Uprety 1998: 41; V. K. Manandhar 2001; Michaels 2019.
65. See, for instance, *Phaṭya Śamśera 1893; cf. V. K. Manandhar 2001: 34.
66. *The Times*, December 25, 1896, quoted from Sever 1989: 205.
67. For detailed lists of the gifts, see Lévi 1905, 2: 191–92; Haenisch 1938: 35; T. R. Manandhar and Mishra 1986: 36 and appendices; V. K. Manandhar 2001: appendices to the chapters on the various missions.
68. Thornton to Wade, July 25, 1876, Foreign Secret Consultations, September 3, 1876, nos. 129–33, quoted from Dhanalaxmi 1981: 70.
69. See *Chin-Ting K'uo-er-k'a Chi lueh*, 25/42, pp. 13a–15a.
70. Sever 1989: 204.
71. Departmental Notes, Foreign Secret Consultations, October 8, 1877, nos. 149–50, quoted from Dhanalaxmi 1981: 70.

Chapter 7

1. On the Rāṇā Period: Kumar 1967; K. K. Adhikari 1984; Pramode S. Rana 1978 and 2004; Shaha 1990a; Whelpton 1983b, 1987, and 1992; Sever 1993; Prabhakar Rana, Pashupati Rana, and Gautam Rana 2003; S. Rana 2018.

2. On the administrative system of the Śāha and Rāṇā: Agrawal 1976; Kumar 1967; Caplan 1975; Edwards 1975 and 1977; K. K. Adhikari 1984; Gautama 2004; T. N. Shrestha 2005; Bhaṭṭarāī 2008.
3. K. K. Adhikari VS 2034 and 1984: 19–23; Shaha 1990a, 1: 217–21; Whelpton: 1992: 158–64; Stiller 1976: 78–94 and 1981; K. Pradhan 2012.
4. On Jaṅga Bahādura Rāṇā: K. K. Adhikari 1984; Shaha 1990a; Whelpton 1983b and 1992.
5. Oliphant 1852: 102–3.
6. Whelpton 1992: 175–76.
7. Landon 1976, 1: 135–56; Whelpton 1983b; Sanjukta Shrestha 2018.
8. ∗Dixit 1957/58. However, it is likely that Jaṅga Bahādura Rāṇā could sign his name but might not have been able to read or write.
9. Sanjukta Srestha 2018.
10. S. Rana 2018.
11. ∗Surendra Śāha 1849.
12. ∗Surendra Śāha 1856b.
13. ∗Surendra Śāha 1857.
14. J. F. Fisher 1997.
15. On land use and the tax system: M. C. Regmi (see Onta 2017 for a bibliography), in particular M. C. Regmi 1976, 1978a, and 1978b; D. R. Regmi 1965–66, 2: 494–537; Stiller 1976; S. Thapa 2000. Unless otherwise stated, the facts presented originate from these works—in particular, from M. C. Regmi 1976.
16. *Raikara* is probably derived from (Skt.) *rājya* "state" and (Skt.) *kara* "tax."
17. In the central regions and Kathmandu, one *murī* meant 48.77 kg. of rice, 68.05 kg. of wheat or corn, and 65.78 kg. of millet; a *ropanī* was 0.05 ha. See *Ain*, Article 40, for detailed breakdowns.
18. Also written *birttā* or *vīrttā*, derived from Skt. *vṛtti*, "livelihood."
19. For an exception, see the *potā* tax levied on *sunābirtā* land in ∗Surendra Śāha 1856b.
20. See ∗Rājendra Śāha 1833.
21. *Ain* 2.1, cf. 76.1 and ∗Surendra Śāha 1856b.
22. On the inappropriateness of applying the term feudalism to state formation in early South Asia: Whelpton 2000.
23. The Sadara Daphtara Khānā functioned as a "general office of Registry for all assignments in lieu of pay," not strictly as a land registry office (Edwards 1975: 112).
24. M. C. Regmi 1978a: 343.
25. On the *guṭhī* system: M. C. Regmi 1976: ch. 4; Toffin 2005; on *guṭhīs* in Licchavi inscriptions: LA 2, 24, and 70; on *guṭhīs* as a land category, see the *Ain* of 1854, Article 1. Newar *guṭhīs* (written *guthi* in Nevārī) are organizations set up along family or caste lines that conduct festivals and rituals in their communities. Such *guṭhīs* are only rarely funded by land donations.
26. cf. M. C. Regmi 1978a: 433–4.
27. ∗Pratāpa Siṃha Śāha 1775.
28. Burghart 1987: 250; cf. Bouillier 1993.
29. Stiller 1989: 44.

30. On the *rājya* documents of 1769 and 1791: M. C. Regmi 1978b: 42; *Pṛthvīnārāyaṇa Śāha 1769 and *Raṇabahādura Śāha 1791b.
31. *Dīpanārāyaṇa Śāha 1835.
32. M. C. Regmi 1978a: 626–27.
33. Cf. Aitchison 1863, 2: 182.
34. Kshetri 1998: 209.
35. M. C. Regmi 1978b: 46.
36. K. L. Pradhan 2009: 210–12.
37. On compulsory labor: M. C. Regmi 1999: 101–23 and 1976: chap. 9; Krauskopff 1999; Holmberg and March 1999.
38. On building roads: *Ain*, Article 53.
39. On the terminology for unpaid labor: Manik Bajracharya's commentary on *Rājendra Śāha 1847.
40. *Raṇabahādura Śāha 1793 und 1796b.
41. *Rājendra Śāha 1835.
42. Cf. Plachta and Tamang 2019.
43. M. C. Regmi 1999: 104–5; Stiller 1976: 52–4; RSS 11.5 (1979): 78 and 14.3–4 (1982): 50–53.
44. RRC_0011_0194, RRC_0007_0061, RRS 4.4 (1972): 18.
45. *Gīrvāṇayuddha Śāha 1807.
46. *Ain* 7.14.
47. *Gorkhāpatra* 10 Phālguna 1966 (21 February 1911) = RRS 11.9 (1979): 139–40.
48. Bastien et al. 2005.
49. *Candra Śamśera 1925: 1. The original speech read out was in Nepālī; it was titled *Śrī 3 mahārājabāṭa kariyāharūlāī amalekha garāune bāremā bakseko spīca.*
50. Whyte 1998: 321.
51. D. R. Panta 1997.
52. Landon 1976, 2: 163–72; M. C. Regmi 1999: 101–23, and 1978b: 156–69; Maskey 1996: 39–77; D. R. Panta 1997; Giri 2011; M. Bajracharya 2022.
53. *Gīrvāṇayuddha Śāha 1802a.
54. *Ain* 60.4.
55. Cf. *Lāla Bāhādura Khatrī Chetrī 1919.
56. See, for instance, the palm-leaf roll of the year 1051 (NS 172) in Kölver 1986d.
57. *Ain* 31.9.
58. Whyte 1998: 328.
59. In particular, in Articles 60, 87, 110, and 111.
60. *Ain* 83; on child slaves, see also Michaels 1986: 217–18.
61. RRS 1.1: 44
62. *Ain* 82.4.
63. On slavery in Garhwal: Atkinson 1984–86, 2: 620; Pradhan 2009: 195.
64. *Ḍaṅgola, Rājavaṃśī, and Vajrācārya 1984; *Bālakṛṣṇa Deva Śarmā 1773.
65. Whyte 1998.
66. Fujikura 2011.

67. Rupakheti 2017: 183–84.
68. On trade in Nepal: Hodgson 1971 (Chapter "On the Commerce of Nepal'); Kumar 1967: 132–41; M. C. Regmi 1999, 1975, and 1988; von Fürer-Haimendorf 1975; Bista 1980; Schrader 1988; Rankin 2004.
69. *Ain* 1.1.
70. *Jagat Śamśera 1890.
71. Cf. Rankin 2004.
72. For an overview of the infrastructure: Karan and Ishii 1996.
73. Adam 1934; K. K. Adhikari 1984: 273–320; D. B. S. Thapa 1985; Vaidya and Manandhar 1985; Fezas 1990; R. R. Khanāla 2002; Höfer 1979a; Michaels 2005a und 2009a; Klein 2015.
74. Hodgson 1992, 2: 220–23.
75. Cf. Sever 1989: App. 5; Khatiwoda, Cubelic, and Michaels 2021: Introduction.
76. *Raṇabahādura Śāha 1806; cf. D. R. Panta 1969.
77. Stiller 1976: 72.
78. See, for instance, T. R. Manandhar 1999: 28 and Khatiwoda 2017: 164.
79. For the latter, see Michaels 2005a: 42–43; Vajrācārya and Śreṣṭha VS 2032.
80. This section is partly based on Michaels 1997 (with further references).
81. *Raṇabahādura Śāha 1791a; M. C. Regmi 1976: 52; on the veneration of the cow and Lakṣmī (Kāmadhenu), see Kölver 1986a and Michaels 1997: Figure 4 (p. 84) with a depiction of Vīra Śamśera (dated VS 1989), who stands adoringly in front of a cow on whose body various deities are painted.
82. RRS 9.8 (1979): 126–28 (RRC 40: 165–68); D. R. Regmi 1965–66, 2: 538 (letter of a missionary).
83. On the relationship between cows and yaks: Oppitz 1997.
84. *Gīrvāṇayuddha Śāha 1805; RRS 11.2 (1979): 21–22.
85. RRS 8.8 (1979): 127–28; RRS 9.9 (1979): 129–30; see also RRS 1.1 (1969): 15–16 and 12.11 (1980): 169; Stiller 1975: 265.
86. On the Nepalese education system: Malla 1970; Bista 1991: 116–32; Maskey 1996; Raj and Onta 2014; Subedi and Uprety 2014; Parajuli, Uprety, and Onta 2021.
87. Wright 1877: 31.
88. Kshetri 1998: 255.
89. Stiller 1993: 136–37.
90. On Candra Śamśera's documents: *Anonymous 1921 und 1940.
91. Marasini 2003; Government of Nepal 2015a.
92. Documents: Raj, Aryal, and Mishra 2016; *Vīra Śamśera 1890; *Survey Office 1896; *Tribhuvana Śāha 1927; *Anonymous 1899, 1916a, 1916b, and 1945.
93. On traditional healing systems: Durkin-Longley 1982; Gewali 2008.
94. On local healers: Macdonald 1975; Wiemann-Michaels 1994; Dietrich 1998.
95. On shamanism: Hitchcock and Jones 1976; Oppitz 1979–80 (film), Höfer 1994 and 1981/1997; Sagant 1996; de Sales 2000; Maskarinec 1995 and 1999/2009; cf. also the *Ain of 1854*, section 74.
96. M. Bajracharya, Khatiwoda, and Michaels 2015.

97. Rookmaaker, Nelson, and Dorrington 2005; for a detailed description of such a hunt, see Sever 1993: 246–47.
98. On elephants as a form of tribute: Krauskopff and Meyer 2000; P. Locke 2006 and 2011.
99. Kropf 2002.
100. N. M. B. Pradhan, Williams, and Dhakal 2011.
101. On the Rāṇā monuments: Gutschow 2011, vol. 3.
102. On the monuments of Deopatan: Michaels 1994b and 2008; Michaels and Tandon 2017; Hutt et al. 1994.
103. Michaels 1995.
104. Rupakheti 2017.

Chapter 8

1. On post-Rāṇā politics: Gupta 1964; Joshi and Rose 1966; Pemble 1971; Shaha 1990b; Whelpton 2005; on the history of the constitutions: Gaenszle 1991b.
2. For variants, see Whelpton 2005: 183 and 2008: 49.
3. Duquesne 2011.
4. Ogura 1990; D. Thapa 2004; Upreti 2004; Hachhetu 2008–9; Lecomte-Tilouine 2013; A. Adhikari 2014; de Sales 2015, Zharkevich 2019.
5. Zharkevich 2017.
6. P. A. Raj 2001; Gregson 2002.
7. Dixit 2012.
8. Mocko 2016.
9. For the procedure of the Śāha coronation ritual, see Witzel 2022 and Michaels 2023.
10. Burghart 1984.
11. *The Revolutionary Worker*, no. 1043, February 20, 2000 (https://revcom.us/a/v21/1040-049/1043/interv.htm, accessed October 25, 2023).
12. Michaels 1993b.
13. Interview with a local Jyapu farmer in March 1982.
14. On the administrative system since 1951: Caplan 1975; Asia Foundation 2012.
15. Among modern laws relating to land use are: Country Code 1963; Land Survey and Measurement Act 1963; Act Concerning Land 1964; Guthi Corporation Act 1976; Land Acquisition Act 1977; Land Revenue Act 1978.
16. Barua 2002.
17. Sonntag 1995.
18. Devakoṭa VS 2074.
19. Hutt 2006.
20. On the Royal Hotel, Boris Lisanevich, and Barbara Adams: Peissel 1972; Adams 2004; Rai 2005; Liechty 2017: 37–44 and 64; Gill 2018.

21. On the modern architecture: Weiler 2010; Gutschow 2011, 3: 963–84 und 2012; on the historical photos of Erwin Schneider and others: Gutschow and Kreutzmann 2013.
22. On the ropeway: Gyawali, Dixit, and Upadhya 2004.
23. On the cultural heritage of Nepal: Amatya 1987; Kathmandu Valley Preservation Trust 2016; Weiler and Gutschow 2016; Tiwari 2016; Bajracharya and Michaels 2017.
24. D. Bangdel 2011; Alsop 2011; this section could not have been written without the strong input of Christiane Brosius.
25. Losty 2005; Gutschow 2015.
26. Partly printed in Oldfield 1880.
27. M. Chitrakar 2004.
28. Messerschmidt and Bangdel 2004.
29. B. Shrestha 2006.
30. Brosius and Maharjan 2017.
31. See, for instance, the special issue of EBHR 12–13 (1997).
32. Tingey 1990 and 1994.
33. Widdess 2013.
34. Lienhard 1992b.
35. Wegner 1986, 1988, and forthcoming.
36. Karan and Ishii 1996: 14.

Chapter 9

1. Thus, in the Documenta Nepalica catalogue there are only 41 documents in which Magar, 35 in which Tamang (or Murmi), and 132 in which Gurung are mentioned; the ambiguous name "Lāmā," which is also used as a title for Tibetan monks or priests and for Gurung and Magar clans, appears around 350 times.
2. Panta and Sharma 1977: 6.
3. ∗Rājendra Śāha 1823; ∗Rājendra Śāha 1822a; Fezas 1986.
4. Höfer 1979a: 147.
5. Kukuczka 2011: 399.
6. Holmberg 1996; cf. Campbell 2008.
7. Pignède 1993; Macfarlane 2008; Strickland 2018.
8. Pignède 1993: 490.
9. March 2000: 18.
10. Gaige 1968 and [1975] 2009; Michael 2011 and 2013; Guneratne 2011; Mathema 2011; D. Gellner 2013; Chaudhary 2015.
11. Müller 1999; Prashant 2015; Krauskopff 2018.
12. Petech 1984: 55.
13. On the Sena kings and Palpa: Ghimire 1988; Stiller 1989; Michael 2013: 57–59.
14. Whelpton 2005: 23.

15. On Mithila and Tirhut: S. M. Singh 1922; R. Chaudhary 1970; and Burghart 2016.
16. Witzel 1985.
17. Guneratne 2002; Burkert 2008.
18. von Fürer-Haimendorf 1964 and 1984; Oppitz 1968 and 1974; M. C. Regmi 1975; Ortner 1978, 1989, and 1999; Fisher 1990.
19. On the exciting history of interdependence and cultural conflicts between the "sahibs" and the Sherpas: Ortner 1999.
20. ∗Vīra Śamśera 1892 and Oppitz 1968: 64–66.
21. ∗Rājendra Śāha 1828.
22. Based on ∗Subba Purnanand 1791.
23. Tucci [1953] 1982; von Fürer-Haimendorf 1975; Jackson 1976, 1978, and 1984; Snellgrove 1987; Panta and Pierce 1989; Gutschow 1998; W. F. Fisher 2001; Dhungel 2002; Ramble and Vinding 1987; Schuh et al. 1999; Pohle 2000a, 2000b, and 2003; Ramble 2008 (with further references); Vitali 2012; Gutschow 2021: 65–398.
24. On the Thakali: Vinding 1998.
25. Cf. Eng and Aldenderfer 2011.
26. Ramble 2008.
27. Hamilton [1819] 1971; Chemjong 1967; Caplan 1970; McDougal 1979; Sagant 1982 and 1996; Gaenszle 1991b, 2002, and 2013; Pradhan 2009; Schlemmer 2004.
28. Pradhan 2009: 87.
29. ∗Pṛthvīnārāyaṇa Śāha 1774a and 1774b quoted from M. C. Regmi 1978a: 626p–q.
30. G. Karmacharya 2005.
31. Reed and Reed 1968: 5.
32. Schneidmüller 2018: 109.
33. Cf. Mulmi 2017.
34. K. Pradhan 2009: 168.
35. Burghart 1984 and 1987; Gellner 2016a.
36. Cf. Ch. Nepālī 1956: 185.
37. Gellner 2016a: 14.
38. Whelpton 2008 and 2017–18: 186.
39. Cf. Stiller 1976: 180–83.
40. Pfaff-Czarnecka 2004: 5; cp. Pfaff-Czarnecka 2023.

Conclusion

1. Cf. Lawoti 2005.
2. Cf. Panday 1999; Riaz and Basu 2010.
3. Bista 1991: 4.
4. E. Gellner 1983: 1–2.
5. van Schendel 2002; cf. Michaud 2010; Bergmann 2016.
6. Scott 2009.

Appendix 1

1. On the Jesuits, see Landon 1976, 2: 231–38.
2. Reports by and literature on early travelers to Nepal include: Kirkpatrick 1811; Hamilton 1819; Oliphant 1852; Hodgson [1874] 1971 and [1880] 1992; Oldfield 1880; Wright 1877; and Schlagintweit-Sakünlünski 1869–80; also Donner 2010; Jordan 2010; and Brescius, Kaiser, and Kleidt 2015.
3. Translated from Kircher [1667] 1985: 168.
4. Kalapura 2008; for the edition of the letters and reports of the missionaries, see Petech 1952–56 and his 1961 summary.
5. On Brian H. Hodgson, see Hunter [1896] 1991; March 2000; K. L. Pradhan 2001; Waterhouse 2005.
6. Lévi 1905–8, 1: 129.
7. Höfer 1979a.
8. Lévi 1905–8, 1: 128.
9. Le Bon [1886] 1981.
10. The following focuses on Nepal's past scholars. On early Newar scholarship, see Malla 1982; M. R. Panta 1979, 2002a and n.d. (2020); Y. Raj 2014. On Baburam Acharya: B. R. Ācārya 2013; on Dhanavajra Vajracharya: P. R. Sharma and Malla 1994; on learned Bajracharyas: Lewis and Bajracharya 2016: 155–66; on M. C. Regmi: Gaenszle 1992b; M. R. Panta 2002a; Onta 2003; Y. Raj 2014; on Dor Bahadur Bista: KC and Onta 2013; Bista 2015: 138–42 (with bibliography); on Prayag Raj Sharma: Kharel and KC 2016; on Father Locke: Sharkey 2009; Owens 2011; on Lain Singh Bangdel: Messerschmidt and Bangdel 2004. For further references to literature, see B. Gyawali 2018.
11. Stuparich 2016.
12. On the languages of Nepal: Sonntag 1995; van Driem 2001; Watters 2005.
13. Witzel 1993; Whitehouse et al. 2004.
14. On the Nevārī language and its literature: Jørgensen 1921, 1931, 1936, and 1941; Malla 1982 and 2015; Lienhard 1963, 1974, and 1992b; Tuladhar 2000; Lewis 2000; von Rospatt 2015.
15. Malla 1990.
16. Lewis 2000; Gutschow and Michaels 2005, 2008, and 2012; Michaels 2010.
17. Pokhrela et al. 1953; Clark 1957; cf. Birkenholtz 2018: 90.
18. J. Acharya 2011; on Nepālī literature: A. Subedi 1978; K. L. Pradhan 1984 and 1992; Hutt 1986, 1988, and 1991; Sinha 1997; M. L. Karmacharya 2005.
19. *Raṇabahādura Śāha 1796a.
20. *Aitihāsika Kathā-Saṃgraha* 1966; N. Sharma 1976; Kretschmar 1995.
21. Cf. Gaenszle 1992a. Texts of the Tamang have been edited and/or translated by Steinmann 1987, Holmberg 1996, and Höfer 1981 and 1997; of the Gurung, by Mumford 1989 and Strickland 2018; of the Rai-Limbu, by Sagant 1996, Gaenszle 1992a and 2002, as well as Vandenhelske and Gaenszle 2021; of the Magar, by de Sales 2000; and texts from the Bhuji Valley in western Nepal, by Maskarinec 1999–2009.
22. On Nepalese manuscripts: Bendall 1886; Shastri 1905–6 and 1917–57; Lévi 1905–8; D. R. Regmi 1965–66, 1: 38–42; Malla 1982.

23. The *Vājasaneyisaṃhitā* is edited by Witzel 2019.
24. Kölver and Śākya 1985.
25. On documents: Cubelic, Michaels, and A. Zotter 2018 (with further references).
26. On archaeology in Nepal: Mukherji 1969; Verardi 1992, 1997, and 2007; Darnal 2002 and 2016.
27. On Handigaon and Lazimpat: Deo 1968; Verardi 1992; on Dhumbarahi: Banerjee 1969.
28. Schuh et al. 1999; Pohle 2000b.
29. Indraji and Bühler 1880; Petech 1961; Dh. Vajrācārya 1968a; D. R. Regmi 1983; Verma and Singh 1994.
30. Dh. Vajrācārya 1973; D. R. Regmi 1983; Bledsoe 2004; D. Acharya 2008 and 2009; Mirnig 2013 (with further references) and 2016.
31. Dh. Vajrācārya 2011.
32. Walsh [1908] 1973; J. Ch. Regmi (ed.) 1982b; M. C. Regmi 1982; Rhodes 1989; Rhodes, Gabrisch, and Valdetaro 1989.
33. Petech 1984: 198–99.
34. Quoted from R. Shrestha 2007: 13.
35. Cf. M. R. Panta 1987.
36. See Shakya and Bajracharya 2010.
37. The addition *-purāṇa* ("old story") was added relatively late; other titles are *Gośṛṅgaparvata-Svayaṃbhūcaityabhaṭṭārakoddeśa*, *Bṛhatsvayaṃbhūpurāṇa*, or the *Svayambhū-Mahāpurāṇa*.
38. M. Bajracharya 2018.
39. On the *Divyopadeśa*: Stiller 1989; D. R. Panta 2016.
40. Quoted from Whelpton 2007: 190.
41. On archives: R. J. Thapa 1967 and Whelpton 1983a.
42. ∗Gīrvāṇayuddha Śāha 1812.
43. The following links are listed in the order of mention, all last accessed on November 11, 2023:

    (1) https://eap.bl.uk/search?f%5B0%5D=places%3ANepal%2C%20Asia or (collection type) Nepal: https://eap.bl.uk/search?query=nepal&f%5B0%5D=type%3ACollection, https://hav.univie.ac.at/, https://opendatanepal.com/;

    (2) https://danam.cats.uni-heidelberg.de/; https://heidicon.ub.uni-heidelberg.de/search (keyword (NHDP), https://huntingtonarchive.org/resources/lostStolen/nepal.php;

    (3) https://archive.org/search?query=nepal, https://www.nepjol.info/index.php/index;

    (4) https://cudl.lib.cam.ac.uk/search?fileID=&keyword=nepal&page=1&x=0&y=0, https://nepalica.hadw-bw.de/nepal/, https://www.dsbcproject.org/, https://www.bdrc.io/, https://www.aai.uni-hamburg.de/en/forschung/ngmcp.

44. ∗Juddha Śamśera 1930.
45. An attempt to at least document a large part of Nepal's monuments is the Digital Archive of Nepalese Arts and Architecture (DANAM).
46. Hagmüller 2002.
47. Whitmarsh 2018.

Bibliography

Primary Sources

Abhilekha Saṃgraha, edited by Rāmajī Tevārī et al. Kathmandu: Saṃśodhana-Maṇḍala, VS 2020 (1963).

Ācārya, Bhānubhakta. *Bhānukhaktako Rāmāyaṇa*. Kathmandu: Sajha Prakashan, 1982.

Ain (=[*Mulukī*] Ain of 1854):

Editions

Śrī 5 Surendra Bikram Śāhadevakā Śāsanakālamā Baneko Mulukī Ain. Kathmandu: Śrī 5 ko Sarkāra (Kānūna tathā Nyāya Mantrālaya), VS 2020 (1963).

Le Code Népalais (Ain), edited by Jean Fezas. 2 vols. Torino: Comitato per la Publicazione del Corpus Juris Sanscriticum, 2000 (1943).

Translation

The Mulukī Ain of 1854: Nepal's First Legal Code. With forewords by Patrick Olivelle and Saubhagya Pradhananga. Introduced, translated, and annotated by Rajan Khatiwoda, Simon Cubelic, and Axel Michaels. Heidelberg: Heidelberg University Publishing, 2021; https://heiup.uni-heidelberg.de/catalog/book/769?lang=en.

Aitihāsika Kathā-Saṃgraha, edited by Līlābhakta Munaṃkarmī. Kathmandu. 1966.

Bhāṣāvaṃśāvalī, edited by Nayanātha Pauḍela and Devīprasāda Laṃsāla. 2 vols. Kathmandu: Nepāla Rāṣṭriya Pustakālaya, VS 2020 and 2033 (1963 and 1976).

The Blue Annals by Gö Lotsawa, translated by George N. Roerich and Gendün Chöphel. 2 vols. Delhi: Motilal Banarsidass, [1949] 1996.

Bṛhatsaṃhitā of Varāmihira, edited by Acyutānanda. Vārāṇasī: Caukhambā Vidyābhavana, 1959.

Chin-ting K'uo-er-k'a Chi lueh (Official Summary Account of the Pacification of the Gorkhas), Peking, 1796, Book 13, Chuan 20, pp. 5b–13b / qin ding kuo er ka ji lüe by 西藏社會科學院西藏學漢文文獻編輯室. Beijing: 據方略館版影印, 1986.

Chronicle of the Kings of Nepal: see *Nepālikabhūpavaṃśāvalī*.

Daśakarmavidhi of Asha Kaji Vaidya (= Ganesh Raj Vajracharya). English translation by N. B. Bajracharya: *The Daśakarma Vidhi: Fundamental Knowledge on Traditional Customs of Ten Rites of Passage Amongst the Buddhist Newars*, edited by Michael Allen. Kathmandu: Mandala Book Point, 2010.

Divya-Upadeśa/Divyopadeśa of Pṛthvīnārāyaṇa Śāha: *Rāṣṭrapati Baḍamahārājādhirāja Śrī 5 Pṛthvīnārāyaṇa Śāhako Divya Upadeśa*, edited by Bāburāma Ācārya and Yogī Naraharinātha. 3rd rev. ed. Kathmandu: Prā. Śrīkṛṣṇa Ācārya, VS 2070 (2013; 1st ed., Vāranasī, 1952 CE [Gorakṣagranthamālā, 80]); English translation by Ludwig F. Stiller: *Prithivinarayan Shah in the Light of Dibya Upadesh*. Kathmandu: Himalayan Book Centre, 1989.

Dixit, Kamal, ed. VS 2014 (1957/58). *Jaṅga Bahādura Balāita Yātrā*. Lalitapura: Madana Puraskāra Pustakālaya.

Fang Lüeguan. 1992. *Qin ding Balebu ji lue [Official Summary Account of the Pacification of the Balebu]*. [Peking]: Quan guo tu shu guan wen xian suo wei fu zhi zhong xin: Fa xing Xin hua shu dian Beijing fa xing suo.

Gopālarājavaṃśāvalī, edited and translated by Dhanavajra Vajrācārya and Kamal P. Malla. Stuttgart: Steiner, 1985.

Gorakṣa-Śāha-Vaṃśa. Aitihāsika Mahākāvyam of Hariprasāda Śarmā. Kāśī, Pyūṭhān [etc.]: no publisher, VS 2022 (1965) (Gorakṣagranthamālā, 92).

Guṇakāraṇḍavyūha, edited by Min Bahadur Shakya. Lalitpur: Nagarjuna Institute of Buddhist Studies, 1992.

Hasrat, Bikram Jit, transl. 1970. *History of Nepal as Told by Its Own and Contemporary Chroniclers*. Hoshiarpur: V. V. Research Institute Press.

Himavatkhaṇḍa (Skandapurāṇamadhye). Kāśī: Gorakṣaṭillākāśī, VS 2013 (1956/57) (Gorakṣagranthamālā, 69).

Itihāsa-Prakāśa, edited by (Yogī) Naraharinātha. 2 vols. in 3 parts. Kathmandu: Itihāsa-prakāśa-saṃgha, VS 2010 (1953), VS 2012 (1955), and VS 2013 (1956/57).

Jātamālā/Jātīmālā (Garland of Castes): ed. in *Rolamba* 1 (1): 7–8.

Licchavikāla-ko Abhilekha, edited and translated by Dhanabajra Vajracharya. Kathmandu: Tribhuvana Viśvavidyālaya, 1973.

Mānava-Dharmaśāstra: Patrick Olivelle, *Manu's Code of Law: A Critical Edition and Translation of the* Mānava-Dharmaśāstra. New York: Oxford University Press, 2005.

Maṇicūḍāvadānoddhṛta: A Buddhist Re-birth Story in the Nevārī language, edited by Siegfried Lienhard. Stockholm: Almqvist and Wiksell, 1963.

Mūladevaśaśidevavyākhyānanāṭaka. Jagatprakāśamallas Mūladevaśaśidevavyākhyān anāṭaka: das älteste bekannte vollständig überlieferte Newari-Drama, edited by Horst Brinkhaus. Stuttgart: F. Steiner Verlag, 1987.

Mulukī Ain: see *Ain* and and Khatiwoda, Cubelic, and Michaels 2021.

Nepālamāhātmya, edited and translated by Jayaraj Acharya. Jaipur and New Delhi: Nirala Publ., 1992.

Nepālikabhūpavaṃśāvalī: History of the Kings of Nepal: A Buddhist Chronicle. Kathmandu: Himal Books, 2015–16. Vol. 1: Manik Bajracharya and Axel Michaels, *Introduction and Translation*; Vol. 2: Manik Bajracharya and Axel Michaels, *Edition*; Vol. 3: Niels Gutschow, *Maps and Illustrations*.

Padmagiris Chronik: see Hasrat 1970.

Paraśurāmopākhyānanāṭaka of Bhūpatīndramalla, edited by Ramawatar Yadav. Kathmandu: B. P. Koirala India-Nepal Foundation, 2011.

Rājabhogavaṃśāvalī = "Nepālko Itihāsa Rājabhogamālā." *Prācīna Nepāla* 7 (April 1969)–11 (April 1970).

Rājavaṃśāvalī = *Kāṭhmāṇḍu-Upatyakāko ek Rājavaṃśāvalī*, edited by Bālacandra Śarmā, *Prācīna Nepāla* 4 (July 1968)–6 (Jan. 1969).

Rāma Śāha, Royal Edicts of. *Svasti Śrī 9* [*sic*] *Mahārājadhirāja Rāma Śāhābāṭa Vādhi Vaksyāko Thiti*. In *Śrī 5 Surendra Bikram Śāhadevakā Śāsanakālamā Baneko Mulukī Ain*, edited by Śrī 5-ko Sarakāra [H.M.G]. Kathmandu: Kānuna tathā Nyāya Mantrālaya, VS 2022 (1965).

Saṃkalparatnāvalī of Harinātha Śarmā. Lucknow: Bhāratabhūṣana Press, VS 1980 (1923).

Sugata Saurabha: An Epic Poem from Nepal on the Life of the Buddha by Chittadhar Hridaya, translated by Todd T. Lewis and Subarna Man Tuladhar. New York: Oxford University Press, 2010.

Svasthānī-Vrata-Kathā, edited by Buddhisāgara Parājulī. Kathmandu: Ratna Pustaka Bhaṇḍāra, VS 2039 (1982).

Svayambhūpurāṇa: *Śrī Svayambhū Mahācaitya*, edited by Hem Raj Shakya. Kathmandu, 1977. English translation: *Śrī Svayambhū Mahācaitya. The Self-Arisen Great Caitya of Nepal*, translated from Nepalbhasa by Min Bahadur Shakya. Kathmandu: Svayambhu Vikash Mandal, 2004.

Vājasaneyi-Samhitā. The Two Oldest Veda Manuscripts: Facsimile Edition of Vājasaneyi Saṃhitā 1–20 (Saṃhitā- and Padapāṭha) from Nepal and Western Tibet (c. 1150 CE), edited by Michael Witzel and Qinyuan Wu. Cambridge, MA: Harvard Oriental Series, 2019.

Vetālapañcaviṃśati. A Nepali version of the Vetālapañcaviṃśati: Nepali Text and English translation with an Introduction, Grammar and Notes by Theodore Riccardi, Jr. New Haven, CT: American Oriental Society, 1971.

Witzel, Michael, ed. 2022. *The Rājyābhiṣeka Manual for the Coronation of King Birendra of Nepal (1975). Introduction and Facsimile Edition.* Cambridge, London: Harvard University, Department of South Asian Studies (Harvard Oriental Series, 100).

Wright, Daniel, ed. 1877. *History of Nepal*, translated from the Parbatiyā by Munshī Shew Shunker Singh and Pandit Shrī Gunānand. Cambridge: University Press.

Documents

Anonymous. 1899 (VS 1956). *Establishing hospital in Hanumannagar, Saptari*. In Yogesh Raj, Deepak Aryal, and Shamik Mishra. "Documents Related to the Early Hospitals in Nepal." *SINHS* 21 (2) (2016): 363–79.

Anonymous. 1905 (VS 1962). *A patra ordering that forest trees should not be randomly cut down (VS 1962)*. NGMPP, E 3136/5.

Anonymous. 1916a (VS 1973). *A note from Guthi Administration to Bhaktapur Hospital to find out whether the son of Harṣa Kumāra is squint-eyed (VS 1973)*. NGMPP, K 168/62.

Anonymous. 1916b (VS 1973). *A bid by contractors to the Guthi Administration in respect of the rate of clothes to be provided to the patients of the hospital (VS 1973)*. NGMPP, K 161/11.

Anonymous. 1921 (VS 1978). *An instruction to all revenue offices to draw school funds first from Pāṭhaśālā Guṭhī resources (VS 1978)*. NGMPP, K 196/58.

Anonymous. 1940 (1997). *A pratívedana by the General Administration to the commander-in-chief and prime minister to provide mats for the primary school of Gorkha (VS 1997)*. NGMPP, E 2778/31 and 39.

Anonymous. 1945. *Documents relating to contracting the supply of food to Pasupatinagar hospital (VS 2002–2003)*. NGMPP, DNA 8/1.

Bālakṛṣṇa Deva Śarmā (alias Upādhyā). 1773 (Śaka Saṃvat 1695). *A copperplate inscription recording the offering of two slave girls by Bālakṛṣṇa Upādhyā to serve Paśupatinātha*, edited and translated by Manik Bajracharya (with Ravi Acharya). Heidelberg: HAdW-DN), 2017; https://doi.org/10.11588/diglit.35143.

Bhāskara Malla. 1703 (NS 823). *An agreement on a copper plate between King Bhāskara Malla and Bhūpatindra Malla to maintain peace and amity (NS 823)*. NGMPP, PN_3/19.

Candra Śamśera. 1924 (VS 1981). *Saṃvat 1981 Sālka, mārga 14 gate, śukravārakā gina Śrī 3 Mahārāja Candrasaṃśera Jaśga Bahādura Rāṇā (...) bāṭa bhāradāra, āphisara ra bhalādmīharū jammbāgarī amalekha garne bāremā vicāra garnālāī ṭuṃḍikhelamā bakseko spīc*. Kathmandu.

Candra Śamśera. 1925. *Maharaja Chandra Shum Shere Jung Bahadur Rana's Appeal to the people of Nepal for the Emancipation of Slaves and Abolition of Slavery in the country*. Kathmandu: Suba Pandit Rama Mani.

Ḍaṅgola, Balarāmadāsa, Śaṅkaramāna Rājavaṃśī, and Pūrṇaratna Vajrācārya. 1984 (VS 2041). "Amalekha Garieka Kamārā Kamārīko Lagata." *Abhilekha* 2: 115–20.

Devagiri Gosaĩ. 1710 (NS 830). *Copy of a stone inscription of the Dattatreya Guṭhī*. NGMPP, K 149/57 (cp. K 271/16 and K 271/16).

Dīpanārāyaṇa Śāha. 1835 (VS 1892). *An arjī acknowledging receipt of a copperplate and a letter*, edited and translated by Simon Cubelic and Rajan Khatiwoda (with Manik Bajracharya). Heidelberg: HAdW-DN, 2014; https://doi.org/10.11588/diglit.36923.

Documents on ascetics. Heidelberg: HAdW-DN; https://www.hadw-bw.de/documents-ascetics.

Foreign Secret Records. 1800. *Intelligence from Benares dated 28 May (?) 1800*. National Archives India, Foreign Secret Records (1801–2), Copy of Tribhuvan University Central Library/NGMPP, T 32/11-12 (Transcript F. Stiller: NGMPP, T 36/21).

Gīrvāṇayuddha Śāha. 1802a (VS 1858). *A lālamohara of King Gīrvāṇayuddha emancipating a family of Patan from slavery (1858 VS)*, edited and translated by Manik Bajracharya (with Christof Zotter, Simon Cubelic, and Rajan Khatiwoda). Heidelberg: https://nepalica.hadw-bw.de/nepal/editions/show/135.

Gīrvāṇayuddha Śāha. 1802b (VS 1859). *A lālamohara from King Gīrvāṇa donating land to the Visaṅkhunārāyaṇa Guṭhī (VS 1859)*, edited by Ramhari Timalsina. Heidelberg: HAdW-DN, 2017; http://abhilekha.adw.uni-heidelberg.de/nepal/editions/show/786.

Gīrvāṇayuddha Śāha. 1803 (VS 1860). *A copy of a lālamohara from King Gīrvāṇa retaining the trust's right to collect firewood during the festival of Śrī 5 Devīnārāyaṇa (VS 1860)*. NGMPP, K 1/35A.

Gīrvāṇayuddha Śāha. 1804 (VS 1860). *A copy of a rukkā from King Gīrvāṇayuddha confirming Saṃkaradatta Vajhā to the office of priest (VS 1860)*, edited and translated by Astrid Zotter. Heidelberg: HAdW-DN, 2021; https://nepalica.hadw-bw.de/nepal/editions/show/27190.

Gīrvāṇayuddha Śāha. 1805 (VS 1862). "Regulations on taking the flesh of dead cattle, 1805." RRS 13.2 (1971): 31–32 (RRC 6: 180).

Gīrvāṇayuddha Śāha. 1807 (VS 1864). *A rukkā of the king directing twelve families of Māsau and Kimāḍi villages to operate a hulāka (VS 1864)*," edited and translated by Manik Bajracharya. Heidelberg: HAdW-DN, 2020; https://abhilekha.adw.uni-heidelberg.de/nepal/editions/show/715.

Gīrvāṇayuddha Śāha. 1812 (VS 1869). *A lālamohara from King Gīrvāṇayuddha placing Kedāranātha Jhā Paṇḍita in charge of manuscripts and books in the Kathmandu Palace (VS 1869)*, edited by Axel Michaels (with Manik Bajracharya). Heidelberg: HAdW-DN,2016; https://nepalica.hadw-bw.de/nepal/editions/show/839.

Gīrvāṇayuddha Śāha. 1813. "Letter to the governor general in Calcutta." In *The Rise of the House of Gorkha: A Study in the Unification of Nepal 1768–1816*, edited by Ludwig Stiller, 246. 2nd ed. Kathmandu: Ratna Pustak Bhandar, 1975.

Gīrvāṇayuddha Śāha. 1815 (VS 1872). *A lālamohara from King Gīrvāṇa commanding Nīlakanṭha Bhaṭṭa to handle the deity's forest for performing rituals (VS 1872)*, NGMPP, K_0495_0012; edited by Govinda Ṭaṇḍan, "Śrī Paśupatinātha Mandiramā Dakṣiṇātya Brāhmaṇa Pūjārīharūbāṭā Pūjā Garne Paramparā: Ek Adhyayana." *Abhilāṣa (Antarāṣṭriya Yātrā Varṣa 1985ko)*, Kathmandu, Jāeṇṭs Inṭarneṣanal, Pariśiṣṭa 2: 90–116.

Jagat Śamśera. 1890 (VS 1946). *A letter from Jagat Samsera ordering to enforce customary fees on mogalāniyā traders before trading in Pācapārvā of Syāra (VS 1946)*, edited and translated by Nadine Plachta and Rajendra Shakya. Heidelberg: HAdW-DN, 2017; http://abhilekha.adw.uni-heidelberg.de/nepal/editions/show/28164.

Jaṅga Bahādura Rāṇā, et al. 1853 (VS 1910). "Punishment for Eating Yak-Meat." RRS 4.11 (1972): 215 (RRC 33: 193–94).

Juddha Śamśera. 1930 (VS 1986). *An iṣṭihāra by the premier instructing the people not to export palm leaves, old books and works of art (VS 1986)*. NGMPP, E 2848/21.

Lāla Bāhādura Khatrī Chetrī. 1919 (VS 1976). *A mortgage of a slave borrowing money (VS 1976)*, NGMPP, K 241/45.

Phaṭya Śamśera. 1893 (VS 1950). *A copy of a letter from General Phaṭya Śamśera to Vakila Kulānanda ordering him to send articles from Calcutta to be presented to the emperor of China* (*VS 1950*), edited and translated by Axel Michaels (with Manik Bajracharya and Pabitra Bajracharya). Heidelberg: HAdW-DN, 2021 (E_2763_0075).

Prasāda Gautama. 1951 (VS 2008). *An inscription at the Karuṇāmaya Mandira in Bungamati commemorating a bhajana for Kṛṣṇa performed by Guru Kavi Prasāda Gautama* (*VS 2008*), edited and translated by Simon Cubelic. Heidelberg: HAdW-DN (NHDP_0001_0001).

Pratāpa Siṃha Śāha. 1775 (VS 1832). *A lālamohara from King Pratāpa Siṃha restoring guṭhī land to Śrī Taleju (VS 1832)*. NGMPP, DNA 12/50.

Pṛthivīnārāyana Śāha. 1769 (VS 1825). "Confirmation of Gajendra Shah as Raja of Jajarkot." RRS 2.1 (1970): 17 (= *Sandhipatrasaṃgraha*, p. 4).

Pṛthivīnārāyana Śāha. 1774a (VS 1831). *A letter from King Pṛthvīnārāyaṇa to Bhagavantanātha re personal and foreign affairs [VS 1831]*, edited and translated by Christof Zotter. Heidelberg: HAdW-DN, 2018; http://abhilekha.adw.uni-heidelberg.de/nepal/editions/show/23499.

Pṛthvīnārāyaṇa Śāha. 1774b (VS 1831). "Royal Order to the Limbus of Pallo-kirat, 1774." In M. C. Regmi 1978a, 626p–q.

Rājendra Śāha. 1817 (VS 1874). "Kush Birta." In *Land Tenure and Taxation in Nepal* by Mahesh Chandra Regmi, 433–34. Kathmandu: Ratna Pustak Bhandar, 1978.

Rājendra Śāha. 1822a (VS 1879). *A lālamohara of King Rājendra reconfirming the exemption of the Magars from maryoaputāli, cākacakui etc. (VS 1879)*, edited by Rajan Khatiwoda (with Christof Zotter). Heidelberg: HAdW-DN, 2017; https://abhilekha.adw.uni-heidelberg.de/nepal/editions/show/858.

Rājendra Śāha. 1822b (VS 1879). *An executive order from King Rājendra Sāha donating a house to Rādhāramaṇa Aryāla on the occasion of the satī of the juniormost concubine of King Raṇa Bahādura Sāha (VS 1879)*, edited and translated by Axel Michaels (with Manik Bajracharya and Rajan Khatiwoda. Heidelberg: HAdW-DN, 2017; http://abhilekha.adw.uni-heidelberg.de/nepal/editions/show/22627.

Rājendra Śāha. 1823 (VS 1883). *A lālamohara of King Rājendra reconfirming the exemption of Guruṅs, Ghales, Lāmās, the four jātas, the sixteen jātas etc. from aputālī, cākacakuī and pharneulo (VS 1883)*, edited and translated by Christof Zotter. Heidelberg: HAdW-DN, 2017; https://abhilekha.adw.uni-heidelberg.de/nepal/editions/show/987refpoint--3.

Rājendra Śāha. 1828 (VS 1885). "A letter to the Sherpas." In *Geschichte und Sozialordnung der Sherpa* by Michael Oppitz, 64. Innsbruck: Universitäts-Verlag Wagner.

Rājendra Śāha. 1833 (VS 1890). *A lālamohara from King Rājendra updating a VS 1863 land grant to Raṅganātha Pauḍyāla (VS 1890)*, edited and translated by Simon Cubelic (with Rajan Khatiwoda and Ramhari Timalsina). Heidelberg: HAdW-DN, 2017; http://abhilekha.adw.uni-heidelberg.de/nepal/editions/show/1042.

Rājendra Śāha. 1835 (VS 1892). "Forced Labor in Jumla." RRS 3.3 (1971): 59–60 (RRC 1: 818–19).

Rājendra Śāha. 1836a (VS 1893). *A lālamohara of King Rājendra establishing a guṭhī for the feeding of rice pudding to Paśupatinātha (VS 1885)*, edited and translated by Astrid Zotter (with Simon Cubelic, Rajan Khatiwoda, and Christof Zotter). Heidelberg: HAdW-DN, 2017; http://abhilekha.adw.uni-heidelberg.de/nepal/index.php/editions/show/884.

Rājendra Śāha.1836b (VS 1893). *A lālamohara from King Rājendra granting kheta-ghaḍeri to Indu Bhānsyā (VS 1893)*. NGMPP, DNA 13/86.

Rājendra Śāha. 1839 (VS 1896). "On the emancipation of slaves." In *Nepālamā Kariyāmocanako Itihāsa*, by Chittaranjan Nepali, 9–10. Kathmandu, 1964 (VS 2021).

Rājendra Śāha. 1841 (VS 1898). *A sales deed of the land donated to the Brahmin prior to committing satī by the senior queen of King Rājendra (VS 1898)*, edited and translated by Axel Michaels (with Rajan Khatiwoda and Raju Rimal). Heidelberg: HAdW-DN, 2017; http://abhilekha.adw.uni-heidelberg.de/nepal/editions/show/20393.

Rājendra Śāha. 1847 (VS 1903). *Copy of a rukkā issued by the king to Prime Minister Jaṅga Bahādura Kũvara permitting jhārā labour to be used to build a bridge at Āryaghāta (VS 1903)*, edited and translated by Manik Bajracharya (with Pabitra Bajracharya), HAdW-DN, 2019; https://nepalica.hadw-bw.de/nepal/editions/show/47509.

Raṇabahādura Śāha. 1783 (VS 1840). *A rukkā from the king exempting goldsmiths who mint coins from corvee (VS 1840)*. NGMPP, DNA 14/26.

Raṇabahādura Śāha. 1791a (VS 1848). "Royal Cattle Farms, 1791." RRS 6.7 (1974): 126–27 (RRC 5: 79–80 and 756–57).

Raṇabahādura Śāha. 1791 (VS 1848). "Bajura Rajya" [*Lālamohara* to Rāja Anantapāla of Bajura], RRS 6.1 (1974): 17 (RRC 19: 452).

Raṇabahādura Śāha. 1796a (VS 1853). "Raṇabahādura Śāha to Dīnanātha Upādhyāya." *Aitihāsika Patrasaṃgraha* 2: 99.

Raṇabahādura Śāha. 1796 (VS 1853). "Royal Order to (. . .) the town of Gorkhā," edited and translated by Mahes Raj Pant, *Ādārśa* 2: 106–7 (NGMPP, E 2430/2) = RRS 17 (1985): 175.

Raṇabahādura Śāha 1806 (VS 1862). "Svāmī Mahārāja Raṇabahādura Śāhako vi. saṃ. 1862 ko bandobasta," edited by Dineśarāja Panta, *Pūrṇimā* 24.6 (VS 2026): 238–67. English translation: RSS 3 (June 1971): 128–37 and in *The Silent Cry: The People of Nepal 1816–1839*, by Ludwig F. Stiller, 79–85. Kathmandu: Sahoyogi Press, 1976.

Raṇabahādura Śāha. 1816 (VS 1872). "Ban on Begar Labor." RRS 14.9 (1982): 134 (RRC 42: 186).

Raṅganātha Paṇḍita. 1837 (VS 1894). *A letter to the amālī of Patan regarding the term of boys who perform at the Kārttika dance 1838 (VS 1894)*, edited and translated by Simon Cubelic and Rajan Khatiwoda. Heidelberg: HAdW-DN, 2017; https://doi.org/10.11588/diglit.34875.

Subba Purnanand. 1791 (VS 1848). "A letter (*rukkā*) to Lama Kanchhinap Gumba, Yang Gumba." In *Geschichte und Sozialordnung der Sherpa*, by Michael Oppitz, 62. Innsbruck: Universitäts-Verlag Wagner, 1968.

Sughauli Treaty of 1815: "Full Text (and other treaties and memorandum that followed this Treaty"; http://nepaldevelopment.pbworks.com/w/page/34197552/Sughauli%20Treaty%20of%201815%3A%20Full%20Text (accessed August 19, 2020).

Surendra Śāha. 1847 (VS 1904). "Sleṣmāntaka Vana Bāreko Sanad," edited by H. M. G., Rāṣṭriya Abhilekhālaya, *Abhilekha* 2 (3): 19–21.

Surendra Śāha. 1848 (VS 1905). *A rukkā of the king forbidding abuse of porters and directing hulākī porters to carry the loads only for state purposes (VS 1905)*, edited and translated by Manik Bajracharya (with Pabitra Bajracharya). Heidelberg: HAdW-DN, 2019; https://abhilekha.adw.uni-heidelberg.de/nepal/editions/show/1342.

Surendra Śāha. 1849 (VS 1905). "*Lālamohara* regarding the title 'Rāṇā' to Jaṅga Bahādura Rāṇā." In *Rana Polity in Nepal: Origin and Growth*, by Satish Kumar, 158–59. London: Asia Publishing House, 1967 (also in *Nepal under Jung Bahadur 1846–1877*, by Krishna Kant Adhikari, 60–63. Vol. 1. Kathmandu: Sayayogi Press, 1984).

Surendra Śāha. 1850 (VS 1907). "Forced Labor in Jumla." RRS 15.5 (1983): 77–79 (RRC 79: 138–40).

Surendra Śāha. 1855 (VS 1912). "Recruitment of Gurungs." RRS 9.8 (1977): 116 (RRC 33: 244–45).

Surendra Śāha. 1856a (VS 1913). *A lālamohara from King Surendra directing Lakṣmī Narasiṅgha to build a water mill (VS 1913)*, edited by Rajan Khatiwoda (with Axel Michaels). Heidelberg: HAdW-DN, 2016; http://abhilekha.adw.uni-heidelberg.de/nepal/editions/show/1383.

Surendra Śāha. 1856b (VS 1913). "*Lālamohara* on the title 'Mahārāja von Kāski and Lamjung' addressed to Jaṅga Bahādura Rāṇā." In *Rana Polity in Nepal: Origin and Growth*, by Satish Kumar, 159–60. London: Asia Publishing House, 1967.

Surendra Śāha. 1857 (VS 1914). "Abstract Translation on the Maharaja of Nepal to Maharaja Jung Bahadoor Ranajee." In *Nepal under Jung Bahadur 1846–1877*, by Krishna Kant Adhikari, 63–64. Kathmandu: Sayayogi Press, 1984.

Survey Office. 1896 (VS 1953). *A purjī from the survey office to the Hospital Guṭhī re land donated by Sāhilā Badāmahārānī to the Hospital Guṭhī (VS 1953)*. NGMPP, K 372/2.

Tribhuvana Śāha. 1927 (VS 1979). *A lālamohara from King Tribhuvan providing substitute land for Degutale Guṭhī (VS 1979)*. NGMPP, K 62/22.

Vīra Śamśera. 1890 (VS 1947). *A document from the premier directing Sadara Daftar Khānā to substitute land affected guṭhī land (VS 1947)*. NGMPP, K 28/10.

Vīra Śamśera. 1892 (VS 1949). "Kipat Lands in Solukhumbu." RRS 6.8 (1974): 147–49 (RRC 57: 14–21).

Secondary Literature

Ācārya, Bābu Rāma (Acharya, Baburam). 1963 (VS 2020). "Kirāta nāma." *Nepālī* 16 (Śrāvaṇa): 1–31.

Ācārya, Bābu Rāma (Acharya, Baburam). 1966. *Nepālako Samkṣipta Vṛttānta*. Kathmandu: Pramod Shamsher and Nir Bikram "Pyasi."

Ācārya, Bābu Rāma (Acharya, Baburam). 1967 (VS 2024). *Śrī 5 Baḍamahārajādhirāja Pṛthvīnārāyaṇa Śāha*. Kathmandu: His Majesty's Press Secretariat.

Ācārya, Bābu Rāma (Acharya, Baburam). 1970. "King Prithvi Narayan Shah." RRS 10 (8): 121–25.

Ācārya, Bābu Rāma (Acharya, Baburam). 2013. *The Bloodstained Throne: Struggles for Power in Nepal (1775–1914)*. New Delhi: Penguin.

Ācārya, Divākara. 1998. "Prācīna Nepālamā Pāśupata mata." *Garimā* 191: 85–92.

Acharya, Diwakar. 2005. "The Role of Caṇḍa in the Early History of the Pāśupata Cult and the Image on the Mathurā Pillar Dated Gupta Year 61." *Indo-Iranian Journal* 48: 207–22.

Acharya, Diwakar. 2007. "Anuparama's *Dvaipāyanastotra* Inscription from the Early 6th Century: Text, Translation and Comments." *Journal of Indological Studies* 19: 29–53.

Acharya, Diwakar. 2008. "Evidence for Mahayana Buddhism and Sukhavati Cult in India in the Middle Period: Early Fifth to Late Sixth Nepalese Inscriptions." *Journal of the International Association of Buddhist Studies* 31 (1–2): 23–78.

Acharya, Diwakar. 2007. "Anuparama's *Dvaipāyanastotra* Inscription from the Early 6th Century: Text, Translation and Comments." *Journal of Indological Studies* 19: 29–53.

Acharya, Diwakar. 2017. *Nīpajana ra Nepāla: Euṭā Choṭo Ādya-Itihāsa*. Kathmandu: Martin Chautari.

Acharya, Jayraj. 2011. *Bhanubhakta Acharya: His Life and Selected Poems*. Kathmandu: Vidyarthi Pustak Bhandar.

Adam, Leonhard. 1934. "Recht und Sitte in Nepal: Angaben und Schilderungen von Angehörigen der Gurkha-Regimenter." *Zeitschrift für Vergleichende Rechtswissenschaft* 49 (1–2): 1–264.

Adams, Barbara. 2004. *Barbara's Nepal*. New Delhi: Adroit Publishers.

Adhikari, Aditya. 2014. *The Bullet and the Ballot Box: The Story of Nepal's Maoist Revolution*. London: Verso.

Adhikari, Krishna Kant. VS 2034 (= 1977/78). "Particulars Relating to the Massacre that Occurred at Kathmandu between 14th and 15th of September 1949." *Voice of History* 3: 31–39.

Adhikari, Krishna Kant. 1984. *Nepal under Jung Bahadur, 1846–1877*. Vol. 1. Kathmandu: BUKU.

Adhikari, Krishna Kant. 1995. "An Overview of Nepali Historiography: 1769–1950." In *State of Nepali Historiography*, edited by Tri Ratna Manandhar et al., 21–27. Kathmandu: CDH.

Adhikary, Surya Mani. 1986 (VS 2043/44). *Paścima Nepālako Aitihāsika Anveṣana*. Kathmandu: Research Centre for Nepal and Asian Studies.

Adhikary, Surya Mani. 1988. *The Khaśa Kingdom: A Trans-Himalayan Empire of the Middle Age*. Jaipur: Nirala Publications.

Agrawal, Hem Narayan. 1976. *The Administrative System of Nepal: From Tradition to Modernity*. New Delhi: Vikas Publishing House.

Aitchison, C. U. 1863. *A Collection of Treatises, Engagements, and Sunnuds relating to India and Neighbouring Countries*, Vol. 2: *NW Provinces, Oudh, Nipal, the Punjab and the States on the Punjab Frontier*. Calcutta: Bengal Printing Co.

Allen, Charles. 2008. *The Buddha and Dr. Führer: An Archaeological Scandal*. London: Haus Publications.

Allen, Michael R. 1973. "Buddhism without Monks: The Vajrayana Religion of the Newars of the Kathmandu Valley." *South Asia* 3: 1–16.

Allen, Michael R. 1975. *The Cult of Kumari: Virgin Worship in Nepal*. Kathmandu: INAS.

Allen, Michael R., and S. N. Mukherjee, eds. 1982. *Women in India and Nepal*. Canberra: Australian National University.

Allen, Nicholas. 1986. "The Coming of Macchendranāth to Nepal: Comments from a Comparative Point of View." In *Oxford University Papers on India*, edited by N. J. Allen et al., vol. 1, 75–102. New Delhi: Oxford University Press.

Alsop, Ian. 2011. "Traditional Religious Painting in Modern Nepal: Seeing the Gods with New Eyes." In *Nepal: Nostalgia and Modernity*, edited by Deepak Shimkada, 47–59. Mumbai: Marg Foundation.

Alsop, Ian, and Kashinath Tamot. 1996/2001. "A Kushan-Period Sculpture from the Reign of Jaya Varma, A.D. 184/185, Kathmandu, Nepal." http://www.asianart.com/articles/jaya/kings.html (accessed December 2, 2017).

Amatya, Shaphalya. 1987. "Nepal's Strategy on Heritage Conservation." In *Heritage of the Kathmandu Valley: Proceedings of an International Conference in Lübeck, 1987*, edited by Niels Gutschow and Axel Michaels, 95–103. Sankt Augustin: VGH Wissenschaftsverlag.

Anderson, Mary M. 1971. *The Festivals of Nepal*. London: Allen and Unwin.

Andolfatto, David. 2019. *Le Pays aux Cent-Vingt-Cinq-Mille Montagnes: Étude Archéologique du Bassinde la Karnali (Népal) entre le XIIe et le XVIe siècle*. Paris: Sciences de l'Homme et Société.

Asia Foundation. 2012. *A Guide to Government in Nepal: Structures, Functions, and Practices*. Kathmandu: Himal Kitab.

Asia Foundation. 2016. *Nepal Government Distribution of Earthquake Reconstruction Cash Grants for Private Houses*. Kathmandu, November 2016; https://asiafoundation.org/wp-content/uploads/2016/12/Nepal-Govt-Distribution-of-Earthquake-Reconstruction-Cash-Grants-for-Private-Houses.pdf (accessed October 30, 2017).

Atkinson, E. T. 1984–86. *Gazetteer of the Himalayan Districts of the North-Western Provinces of India*. Vols. 2 and 3. Allahabad: N.W. Provinces and Oudh Press.

Ayton, J. A. 1820. *A Grammar of the Nepalese Language*. Calcutta: Fort William College.

Bajrācārya, Dhana Bajra. See Vajrācārya, Dhanavajra

Bajracharya, Indra Siddhi. 2014. "Buddhism During Early Medieval Nepal (733 A.D.–1396 A.D.)." PhD dissertation. Kirtipur: Tribhuvan Unversity.

Bajracharya, Manik. 2006. "Gurumaṇḍala Pūjā." *Bunkenkai Kiyo – The Journal of the Graduate School of Humanities* 17: 130–46.

Bajracharya, Manik. 2018. "Munsīs in the Courts of Early Śāha and Rāṇā Rulers: The Career of Lakṣmīdāsa Pradhāna." In *Studies in Documents of India and Nepal*, edited by Simon Cubelic, Axel Michaels, and Astrid Zotter, 377–97. Heidelberg: Heidelberg University Publishing.

Bajracharya, Manik, ed. 2022. *Documents and Texts on Slavery and Unfree Labour in Nineteenth to Early Twentieth Century Nepal*. Heidelberg: Heidelberg University Publishing.

Bajracharya, Manik, and Axel Michaels. 2012. "On the Historiography of Nepal: The 'Wright' Chronicle Reconsidered." *EBHR* 40: 83–98.

Bajracharya, Manik, and Axel Michaels. 2017. "'Religious' Approaches to Heritage Restoration in Post-Earthquake Kathmandu." *Material Religion* 13 (3): 379–81.

Bajracharya, Manik, Rajan Khatiwoda, and Axel Michaels. 2015. "Six 19th–20th Century Documents on Elephants from the National Archives of Nepal." *Abhilekha* 32: 96–105.

Bajracharya, Naresh Man. 1998. *Buddhism in Nepal (465 B.C. to 1199 A.D.)*. Delhi: Eastern Book Linkers.

Bakker, Hans. 2014. *The World of the Skandapurāṇa*. Leiden: Brill Academic.

Banerjee, N. R. 1969. "Discovery of the Remains of Prehistoric Man in Nepal." *Ancient Nepal* 6: 6–9.

Bangdel, Dina. 2011. "Contemporary Nepali Art: Narratives of Modernity and Visuality." In *Nepal: Nostalgia and Modernity*, edited by Deepak Shimkada, 47–59. Mumbai: Marg Foundation.

Bangdel, Lain Singh. 1989. *Stolen Images of Nepal*. Kathmandu: Royal Nepal Academy.

Baniya, Jeevan, and Amit Gautam, eds. 2019. *Nepal Earthquake 2015 and Its Aftermath: A Bibliographic Resource Guide*. London: SOAS, University of London and Social Science Baha; https://sway.soscbaha.org/wp-content/uploads/2019/04/nepal-earthquake-2015-and-its-aftermath-1.pdf (accessed June 7, 2020).

Baral, Leelanatyashwar Sharma. 1964. "Life and Writings of Pṛthvīnārāyaṇ Śāh." PhD dissertation, University of London; http://himalaya.socanth.cam.ac.uk/collections/rarebooks/downloads/Baral_1964_thesis.pdf (accessed October 5, 2017).

Barré, Vincent, Patrick Berger, Laurence Feveile, and Gérard Toffin. 1981. *Panauti: Une ville au Népal*. Paris: Berger-Levrault. Reprint: Kathmandu: Vajra Publications, 2017.

Barua, Harendra B. 2002. *Pioneer Students in Japan: A Century Ago*. Kathmandu: Mandala Book Point.

Bastien, Guillaume J., et al. 2005. "Energetics of Load Carrying in Nepalese Porters." *Science* 308 (June 17, 2005): 1755.

Basukala, Bijay, Niels Gutschow, and Kishor Kayastha. 2014. *Towers in Stone: Śikhara Temples in Bhaktapur: Vatsalā and Siddhilakṣmī*. Kathmandu: Himal Books.

Becker-Ritterspach, Raimund O. A. 1982. *Gestaltungsprinzipien in der newarischen Architektur*. Berlin: Technical University.

Becker-Ritterspach, Raimund O. A. 1995. *Water Conduits in the Kathmandu Valley*. 2 vols. New Delhi: Munshiram Manoharlal.

Becker-Ritterspach, Raimund O. A. 1996. "Ḍhuṅge-Dhārās in the Kathmandu-Valley: Continuity and Development of Architectural Design." In *Change and Continuity: Studies in the Nepalese Culture of the Kathmandu Valley*, edited by Siegfried Lienhard, 393–412. Turin: Edizioni Dell'orso.

Bell, Thomas. 2014. *Kathmandu*. Gurgaon: Random House India.

Bell, Thomas. 2018. "What Happened to Captain Kinloch's Expedition to Nepal?" *EBHR* 50–51: 7–32.

Bendall, Cecil. 1886. *A Journey of Literary and Archaeological Research in Nepal and Northern India during the Winter of 1884–5*. Cambridge: Cambridge University Press.

Bennett, Lynn. 1983. *Dangerous Wives and Sacred Sisters: Social and Symbolic Roles of High-Caste Women in Nepal*. New York: Columbia University Press.

Bennett, Lynn, Bandita Sijapati, and Deepak Thapa. 2013. *Gender and Social Exclusion in Nepal: Update*. Kathmandu: Himal Books.

Bergmann, Christoph. 2016. "Confluent Territories and Overlapping Sovereignties: Britain's Nineteenth-Century Empire in the Kumaon Himalaya." *Journal of Historical Geography* 51: 88–98.

Bernier, Ronald M. 1970: *The Temples of Nepal: An Introductory Survey*. Kathmandu: Voice of Nepal.

Bernier, Ronald M. 1979. *The Nepalese Pagoda: Origins and Style*. New Delhi: S. Chand.

Bhaṭṭarāī, Ghanasyāma. 2008. *Nepālako Sthānīya Praśāsanako Itihāsa (1768 - 1951 ī. saṃ)*. Delhi: Adroit Publishers.

Bickel, Balthasar, and Martin Gaenszle, eds. 1999. *Cultural Horizons and Practices in Himalayan Space*. Zurich: Ethnological Museum of the University of Zurich.

Birkenholtz, Jessica Vantine. 2018. *Reciting the Goddess: Narratives of Place and the Making of Hinduism in Nepal*. New Delhi: Oxford University Press.
Bista, Dor Bahadur. [1967] 1972. *People of Nepal*. Kathmandu: Ratna Pustak Bhandar.
Bista, Dor Bahadur 1980. "Nepalis in Tibet." *CNSt* 8 (1): 1–19.
Bista, Dor Bahadur. 1991. *Fatalism and Development: Nepal's Struggle for Modernization*. Calcutta: Orient Longman.
Bista, Dor Bahadur. 2015. *Anthropology of Nepal: A Compilation of Dor Bahādur Bista's Articles*, edited by Naniram Khatri. Kirtipur: Tribhuvan University.
Bledsoe, Bronwen. 2000. "An Advertised Secret: The Goddess Taleju and the King of Kathmandu." In *Tantra in Practice*, edited by David G. White, 195–205. Princeton, NJ: Princeton University Press.
Bledsoe, Bronwen. 2004. "Written in Stone: Inscriptions of the Kathmandu Valley's Three Kingdoms." Vol. 1. PhD dissertation, University of Chicago.
Bollinger, L., P. Tapponnier, S. N. Sapkota, and Y. Klinger. 2016. "Slip Deficit in Central Nepal: Omen for a Repeat of the 1344 AD Earthquake?" *Earth, Planets and Space* 68; https://doi.org/10.1186/s40623-016-0389-1.
Bouillier, Véronique. 1986. "La caste sectaire des Kānphaṭā Jogī dans le royaume du Népal: L'exemple de Gorkhā." *Bulletin de l'Ecole française d'Extrême-Orient* 75: 125–68.
Bouillier, Véronique. 1991. "The King and His Yogi: Prithvi Narayan Sah, Bhagavantanath and the Unification of Nepal in the Eighteenth Century." In *Gender, Caste and Power in South Asia*, edited by J. P. Neelsen, 3–21. Delhi: Manohar.
Bouillier, Véronique. 1993. "The Nepalese State and Gorakhnathi Yogis: The Case of the Former Kingdoms of Dang Valley: 18–19th Centuries." *CNSt* 20 (1): 29–51.
Bouillier, Véronique. 2017. *Monastic Wanderers: Nāth Yogī Ascetics in Modern South Asia*. New Delhi: Manohar.
Bouillier, Véronique, Martin Brauen, and Charles Ramble, eds. 1993. *Anthropology of Tibet and the Himalaya*. Zurich: Ethnological Museum of the University of Zurich.
Brescius, Moritz von, Friederike Kaiser, and Stephanie Kleidt, eds. 2015. *Über den Himalaya: Die Expeditionen der Brüder Schlagintweit nach Indien und Zentralasien 1854 bis 1858*. Cologne: Böhlau.
Briggs, George Weston. 1973. *Gorakhnath and the Kanphata Yogis*. Delhi: Motilal Banarsidass.
Brinkhaus, Horst. 1987. *The Pradyumna-Prabhāvatī Legend in Nepal: A Study of the Hindu Myth of the Draining of the Nepal Valley*. Stuttgart: Franz Steiner Verlag.
Brinkhaus, Horst. 1996. "Tolerance and Syncretism in the Religious History of the Kathmandu Valley." In *Change and Continuity: Studies in the Nepalese Culture of the Kathmandu Valley*, edited by Siegfried Lienhard, 137–47. Turin: Edizioni Dell'orso (CESMEO).
Brosius, Christiane, and Sanjeev Maharjan. 2017. *Breaking Views: Engaging Art in Post-Earthquake Nepal*. Kathmandu: Himal Books and Social Science Baha.
Brosius, Christiane, and Axel Michaels. 2020. "Vernacular Heritage as Urban Place-Making: Activities and Positions in the Reconstruction of Monuments after the Gorkha Earthquake in Nepal, 2015–2020: The Case of Patan." *Sustainability* 12 (20); https://doi.org/10.3390/su12208720.
Buchanan, Francis. 1928. *An Account of the District of Purnea in 1809–10*. Patna: Bihar and Orissa Research Society.
Buchanan Hamilton: see Hamilton.
Bühnemann, Gudrun. 2010. "Complex Configurations: On the Iconography and Date of the Golden Gate Window of Patan." *Orientations* 41 (3): 24–30.

Bühnemann, Gudrun. 2013. "Bhairava and the Eight Charnel Grounds: On the History of a Monumental Painting at the Jayavāgīśvarī Temple, Kathmandu." *Berliner Indologische Studien* 21: 307–26.

Burghart, Richard. 1978. "The Disappearance and Reappearance of Janakpur." *Kailash* 6: 257–84.

Burghart, Richard. 1984. "The Formation of the Concept of Nation-State in Nepal." *Journal of Asian Studies* 44 (1): 101–25 (also in Burghart 1996: 193–225).

Burghart, Richard. 1985. "The Regional Circumambulation of Janakpur." *Puruṣārtha* 8: 121–47.

Burghart, Richard. 1987. "Gifts to the Gods: Power, Prosperity and Ceremonial in Nepal." In *Rituals of Royalty: Power and Ceremonial in Traditional Societies*, edited by David Cannadine and Simon Price, 237–70. Cambridge: Cambridge University Press.

Burghart, Richard. 1996. *The Conditioning of Listening: Essays on Religion, History and Politics in South Asia*. Delhi: Oxford University Press.

Burghart, Richard. 2016. *The History of Janakpurdham: A Study of Asceticism and the Hindu Polity*. Kathmandu: Himal Books.

Burkert, Claire. 2008. "Defining Maithil Identity: Who Is in Charge." In *Nationalism and Ethnicity in a Hindu Kingdom: The Politics of Culture in Contemporary Nepal*, edited by David Gellner, Joanna Pfaff-Czarnecka, and John Whelpton, 241–74. Reprint. Kathmandu: Vajra Publications.

Burton-Page, John. 1954. "The Name Nepal." *Bulletin of the School of Oriental and African Studies* 16: 592–97.

Camman, Schuyler. 1951. *Trade through the Himalayas: The Early British Attempts to Open Tibet*. Princeton, NJ: Princeton University Press.

Campbell, A. 1833. "Account of the Earthquake at Kathmandu." *Journal of the Asiatic Society of Bengal* 2: 564–67.

Campbell, Ben. 2008. "The Heavy Loads of Tamang Identity." In *Nationalism and Ethnicity in a Hindu Kingdom: The Politics of Culture in Contemporary Nepal*, edited by David Gellner, Joanna Pfaff-Czarnecka, and John Whelpton, 8–31. Reprint. Kathmandu: Vajra Publications.

Caplan, Lionel. 1970. *Land and Social Change in East Nepal: A Study of Hindu-Tribal Relations*. London: Routledge and Kegan Paul Limited.

Caplan, Lionel. 1975. *Administration and Politics in a Nepalese Town: A Study of a District Capital and Its Environs*. London: Oxford University Press.

Caplan, Lionel. 1991. "'Bravest of the Brave': Representations of 'The Gurkha' in British Military Writings." *Modern Asian Studies* 25 (3): 571–97.

Caplan, Lionel. 1995. *Warrior Gentlemen: "Gurkhas" in the Western Imagination*. Oxford: Berghahn Books.

Chalier-Visuvalingam, Elisabeth. 2013. *Bhairava: terreur et protection. Mythes, rites et fêtes à Bénarès et à Katmandou*. Brussels: Peter Lang.

Chattopadhyay, K. P. [1923] 1980. *History of Newar Culture*. Kathmandu: Educational Enterprise.

Chaudhary, Deepak. 2015. *Tarai/Madhesh of Nepal: Anthropological Study (Upgraded Version)*. Kathmandu: Ratna Pustak Bhandar.

Chaudhary, Radhakrishna. 1970. *History of Muslim Rule in Tirhut, 1206–1765 A.D.*, Varanasi: The Chowkhamba Sanskrit Office.

Chaudhuri, K.C. 1960. *Anglo-Nepalese Relations: From the Earliest Times of the British Rule in India till the Gurkha War*. Calcutta: Modern Book Agency.

Chemjong, Iman Singh. 1967. *History and Culture of the Kirat People*. Kathmandu: Puspa Ratna Sagar.

Chitrakar, Madan. 2004. *Tej Bahadur Chitrakar: Icon of Transition*. Kathmandu: TBC Studios.

Choegyal, Lisa, and Mikel Dunham, eds. 2015. *The Kathmandu Scene: Chronicles of Elizabeth Hawley 1988–2007*. 2 vols. Kathmandu: Vajra Publications.

Clark, T. W. 1957. "The Rānī Pokhrī Inscription." *Bulletin of the School of Oriental and African Studies* 20: 167–87.

Coningham, Robin A. E., et al. 2013. "The Earliest Buddhist Shrine: Excavating the Birthplace of the Buddha, Lumbini (Nepal)." *Antiquity* 87: 1104–23.

Corvinus, Gudrun. 2007. *Prehistoric Cultures in Nepal: From the Early Paleolithic to the Neolithic and the Quaternary Geology of the Dang-Deokhuri Dun Valleys*. 2 vols. Wiesbaden: Harrassowitz.

Cubelic, Simon, Axel Michaels, and Astrid Zotter, eds. 2018. *Studies in Documents of India and Nepal*. Heidelberg: Heidelberg University Publishing.

Cüppers, Christoph, and Franz-Karl-Ehrhard. 2007. "Die Kupferplatten der Könige Ādityamalla und Puṇyamalla von Ya-tshe." In *Tibetstudien: Festschrift für Dieter Schuh zum 65. Geburtstag*, edited by Petra Maurer and Peter Schwieger, 37–42. Bonn: Bier'sche Verlagsanstalt.

Darnal, Prakash. 2002. "Archaeological Activities in Nepal Since 1893 A.D. to 2002 A.D." *Ancient Nepal* 150: 39–48.

Darnal, Prakash. 2016. "Archaeology of Nepal." In *A Companion to South Asia in the Past*, edited by Gwen R. Schug and Susbhash R. Walimbe, 412–25. Chichester: Wiley Blackwell.

Davidson, Ronald. 2002. *Indian Esoteric Buddhism: A Social History of the Tantric Movement*. New York: Columbia University Press.

Deeg, Max. 2003. *The Places Where Siddhārtha Trod: Lumbinī and Kapilavastu*. Lumbini: LIRI.

Deeg, Max. 2016. *Miscellanae Nepalicae: Early Chinese Reports on Nepal. The Foundation Legend of Nepal in its Trans-Himalayan Context*. Lumbini: LIRI.

Dennis, Dannah, and Avash Bhandari. 2019. "Remembering and Remaking Nepal's Founder: A Visual History of Prithvinarayan Shah." *Tasveer Ghar – A Digital Archive of South Asian Popular Visual Culture*. March 18, 2019; http://www.tasveergharindia.net/essay/nepal-visual-prithvinarayan.html (accessed May 8, 2021).

Deo, Shantaram Bhalchandra. 1968. "Archaeological Investigation in the Nepal Tarai, 1964." Kathmandu: His Majesty's Government of Nepal, Department of Archaeology.

Des Chene, Mary Katherine. 1991. "Relics of Empire: A Cultural History of the Gurkhas, 1815–1987." PhD dissertation, Stanford University.

Des Chene, Mary Katherine. 1993. "Soldiers, Sovereignty and Silences: Gorkhas as Diplomatic Currency." *Comparative Studies of South Asia, Africa and the Middle East* 13 (1–2): 67–80.

Des Chene, Mary Katherine. 2007. "Is Nepal in South Asia? The Condition of Non-Postcoloniality." *SINHS* 12 (2): 207–23.

Devakoṭa, Grīṣma Bahādura. VS 2074 (1990/91). *Nepālako Chāpākhānā ra Patrapatrikāko Itihāsa*. Kathmandu: Sajha Prakashan.

Dhanalaxmi, Ravuri. 1981. *British Attitude to Nepal's Relations with Tibet and China (1814–1914)*. Chandigarh, New Delhi: Bahri Publications.

Dhungel, Ramesh K. 2002. *The Kingdom of Lo (Mustang): A Historical Study*. Kathmandu: Tashi Gephel Foundation.

Dietrich, Angela. 1998. *Tantric Healing in the Kathmandu Valley*. Delhi: Book Faith India.

Dixit, Kanak Mani. 2012. "Two Chairmen and a People." In *The Southasian Sensibility: A Himal Reader*, edited by Kanak Mani Dixit, 207–22. New Delhi: Sage.

Dongol, G. M. S. 1985. "Geology of the Kathmandu Fluvial Lacustrine Sediments in the Light of New Vertebrate Fossil Occurrences." *Journal of Nepal Geological Society* 3: 43–57.

Donner, Wolf. 2010. *Ins verbotene Land: Frühe Reisende in Nepal*. Berlin: Pro Business Verlag.

Duquesne, Isabelle. 2011. *Nepal, Zone of Peace: A Revised Concept for the Constitution*. Paris: Editions L'Harmattan.

Durkin-Longley, M. S. 1982. "Ayurveda in Nepal: A Medical Belief System in Action." PhD dissertation. Ann Arbor: University Microfilms International.

Dyczkowski, Mark S. G. 2001. *The Cult of the Goddess Kubjika: A Preliminary Comparative Textual and Anthropological Survey of a Secret Newar Goddess*. Wiesbaden: Franz Steiner Verlag.

Edwards, Daniel W. 1975. "Nepal on the Eve of the Rana Ascendency." *CNSt* 2: 99–116.

Edwards, Daniel W. 1977. "Patrimonial and Bureaucratic Administration in Nepal: Historical Change and Weberian Theory." PhD dissertation, University of Chicago.

Ehrhard, Franz-Karl. 1989. "A Renovation of Svayambhunath Stupa in the 18th Century and Its History." *Ancient Nepal* 114: 1–9.

Ehrhard, Franz-Karl. 1991. "Further Renovations of Svayambhunath Stūpa (from the 13th to the 17th Centuries)." *Ancient Nepal* 123–25: 10–20.

Eltschinger, Vincent. 2019. "Śāntarakṣita." In *Brill's Encyclopedia of Buddhism*, vol. 2, edited by Jonathan Silk et al., 383–90. Leiden: Brill.

Eng, J., and M. Aldenderfer. 2011. "Bioarchaeological Analysis of Human Remains from Mustang, Nepal 2010." *Ancient Nepal* 178: 9–32.

Falk, Harry. 1998. *The Discovery of Lumbini*. Lumbini: LIRI.

Falk, Harry. 2012. "The Fate of Aśoka's Donations at Lumbini." In *Reimagining Aśoka: Memory and History*, edited by Patrick Olivelle, 204–16. New Delhi: Oxford University Press.

Fezas, Jean. 1986. "The Nepalese Law of Succession: A Contribution to the Study of the Nepalese Codes." In *Recent Research on Nepal*, edited by Klaus Seeland, 159–86. Cologne: Weltforum Verlag.

Fezas, Jean. 1990 (VS 2047). "The Nepalese Juridical Tradition and Its Sources: A List of the *Ain* Books Kept in the National Archives." *Abhilekha* 8 (8): 121–34.

Fisher, James F. 1997. *Living Martyrs: Individuals and Revolution in Nepal*. New Delhi: Oxford University Press.

Fisher, James F. 1990. *Sherpas: Reflections on Change in Himalayan Nepal*. Berkeley: University of California Press.

Fisher, William F. 2001. *Fluid Boundaries: Forming and Transforming Identity in Nepal*. New York: Columbia University Press.

Flood, Gavin. 2011. "Body, Breath and Representation in Śaiva Tantrism." In *Images of the Body in India*, edited by Axel Michaels and Christoph Wulf, 70–83. New Delhi: Routledge.

Fujikura, Tatsuro. 2011. "Emancipation of Kamaiyas: Development of Social Movement, and Youth Activism in Post-jana andolan Nepal." In *The Tarai: History, Society, Environment*, edited by Arjun Guneratne, 54–69. Kathmandu: Himal Books.

Furukawa, Akira, ed. 2010. *Jarunhiti*. Kathmandu: Vajra Publications.

Gaborieau, Marc. 1969. "Note preliminaire sur le Dieu Maṣṭa." *Objets et Mondes* 9 (1): 19–50.

Gaborieau, Marc. 1977. *Minorités Musulmanes dans le Royaume hindou du Népal*. Nanterre: Société d'ethnologie.

Gaborieau, Marc. 1978. *Le Népal et ses Populations*. Brussels: Edition Complexe.

Gaenszle, Martin. 1991a. *Verwandtschaft und Mythologie bei den Mewahang Rai in Ostnepal: Eine ethnographische Studie zum Problem der ethnischen Identität*. Wiesbaden: Steiner.

Gaenszle, Martin. 1991b. "Blut im Tausch für Demokratie: Der Kampf um eine neue Verfassung in Nepal 1990." *Internationales Asienforum* 22 (3–4): 233–58.

Gaenszle, Martin. 1992a. "The Text Within: Studies of Oral Ritual Texts in Nepal in the Last Decade." *EBHR* 3: 5–16.

Gaenszle, Martin. 1992b. "On the Topicality of History: An Interview with Mahesh Chandra Regmi." *EBHR* 4: 40–46.

Gaenszle, Martin. 2002. *Ancestral Voices: Oral Ritual Texts and their Social Contexts among the Mehawang Rai of East Nepal*. Münster: Lit.

Gaenszle, Martin. 2013. "The Power of Script: Phalgunanda's Role in the Formation of Kiranti Ethnicity." In *Routeing Democracy in the Himalayas: Experiments and Experiences*, edited by V. Arora and N. Jayaram, 50–73. New Delhi: Routledge.

Gaenszle, Martin, Mark Turin, Will Tuladhar-Douglas, and Ram B. Chhetri. 2015. "People." In *Nepal. An Introduction to the Natural History, Ecology and Human Environment of the Himalayas: A Companion to the Flora of Nepal*, edited by Georg Miehe and Colin Pendry, 251–69. Edinburgh: Royal Botanic Garden.

Gaige, Frederick H. 1968 (VS 2025). "The Role of the Tarai in Nepal's Economic Development." *Vasudha* 11: 53–61.

Gaige, Frederick H. [1975] 2009. *Regionalism and National Unity in Nepal*. 2nd ed. Berkeley: University of California Press.

Gail, Adalbert J. 1984. *Tempel in Nepal (Band I): Ikonographie hinduistischer Pagoden in Pāṭan Kathmandutal*. Graz: Akademische Druck- und Verlagsanstalt.

Gail, Adalbert J. 1988. *Tempel in Nepal (Band II): Ikonographische Untersuchungen zur späten Pagode und zum Śikhara-Tempel*. Graz: Akademische Druck- und Verlagsanstalt.

Gail, Adalbert J. 1991. *Klöster in Nepal: Ikonographie buddhistischer Klöster im Kathmandutal*. Graz: Akademische Verlagsanstalt.

Gail, Adalbert J. 1997. "Religiöse Reliefs in Brunnen (*dhārā*, *hiti*) des Kathmandutales." *Annali dell'Università degli Studi di Napoli* 57 (3–4): 357–74.

Garbini, Riccardo. 1997. "Indo-Nepalese Epigraphy II: The Patan Inscription of Year 411 (= AD 489), an Example of the 'Compartement' Type." *AION* (Naples) 57 (3–4): 347–58.

Gautama, Rājeśa. 2004. *Rāṇakālīna Nepālako Praśāsanika, Śaikṣika ra Sāmājika Sudhāraharū*. Delhi: Androit Publishers.

Gellner, David N. 1986. "Language, Caste, Religion and Territory: Newar Identity, Ancient and Modern." *European Journal of Sociology* 27: 102–48.

Gellner, David N. 1987. "The Newar Buddhist Monastery: An Anthropological and Historical Typology." In *Heritage of the Kathmandu Valley*, edited by Niels Gutschow and Axel Michaels, 365–414. Sankt Augustin: VGH Wissenschaftsverlag.

Gellner, David N. 1991. "Ritualized Altruism, Devotion and Meditation: The Offering of the Guru Maṇḍala in Newar Buddhism." *Indo-Iranian Journal* 34: 161–207.

Gellner, David N. 1992. *Monk, Householder, and Tantric Priest: Newar Buddhism and its Hierarchy of Ritual*. Cambridge: Cambridge University Press.

Gellner, David N. 1995. "Introduction." In *Contested Hierarchies: A Collaborative Ethnography of Caste in the Kathmandu Valley, Nepal*, edited by David Gellner and Declan Quigley, 1–37. Oxford: Oxford University Press.

Gellner, David N. 1996. "A Sketch of the History of Lalitpur (Patan) with Special Reference to Buddhism." *CNSt* 23 (1): 125–57.

Gellner, David N. 1997. "For Syncretism: The Position of Buddhism in Nepal and Japan Compared." *Social Anthropology* 5 (3): 275–89.

Gellner, David N. 2001. *The Anthropology of Buddhism and Hinduism: Weberian Themes*. New Delhi: Oxford University Press.

Gellner, David N. 2005. "The Emergence of Conversion in a Hindu-Buddhist Polytropy: The Kathmandu Valley, Nepal, c. 1600–1995." *Comparative Studies in Society and History* 47 (4): 755–80.

Gellner, David N. 2007 "Caste, Ethnicity and Inequality in Nepal." *Economic and Political Weekly* 42 (20): 1823–28.

Gellner, David N. 2008. "Ethnicity and Nationalism in the World's Only Hindu State." In *Nationalism and Ethnicity in a Hindu Kingdom: The Politics of Culture in Contemporary Nepal*, edited by David Gellner, Joanna Pfaff-Czarnecka, and John Whelpton, 8–31. Kathmandu: Vajra Publications.

Gellner, David N. 2013. *Borderland Lives in Northern South Asia*. Durham, NC: Duke University Press.

Gellner, David N. 2016a. *The Idea of Nepal*. The Mahesh Chandra Regmi Lecture 2016. Kathmandu: Himal Books.

Gellner, David N. 2016b [with K.P. Adhikari]. "New Identity Politics and the 2012 Collapse of Nepal's Constituent Assembly: When the Dominant becomes 'Other.'" *Modern Asian Studies* 50 (6): 2009–40.

Gellner, David N. 2019. "Masters of Hybridity: How Activists Reconstructed Nepali Society." *Journal of the Royal Anthropological Institute* (N.S.) 25: 265–84.

Gellner, David N., and Krishna P. Adhikari, eds. 2019: "Nepal's Dalits in Transition." *Contributions to Nepalese Studies* 46 (2).

Gellner, David N, Joanna Pfaff-Czarnecka, and John Whelpton, eds. [1997] 2008. *Nationalism and Ethnicity in a Hindu Kingdom: The Politics of Culture in Contemporary Nepal*. Kathmandu: Vajra Publications.

Gellner, David, Sondra L. Hausner, and Chiara Letizia, eds. 2016. *Religion, Secularism and Ethnicity in Contemporary Nepal*. New Delhi: Oxford University Press.

Gellner, Ernest. 1983. *Nations and Nationalism*. Ithaca, NY: Cornell University Press.

Gewali, Mohan Bikram. 2008. *Aspects of Traditional Medicine in Nepal*. Toyama: University of Toyama, Institute of Natural Medicine.

Ghimire, Śrīrāma. 1988 and 1999 (VS 2045/46 and 2056/57). *Pālpā Rājyako Itihāsa*. 2 vols. Chitwan: Padma Ghimire.

Gibson, Ian. 2017. "Pentecostal Peacefulness: Virtue Ethics and the Reception of Theology in Nepal." *Journal of the Royal Anthropological Institute* (N.S.) 23: 765–82.

Gill, Michael. 2018. "Barbara Didi and Me." *ECS Nepal Magazine* (March), http://ecs.com.np/features/barbara-didi-me (accessed June 25, 2020).

Gilman, Peter, ed. 2000. *Everest: Eighty Years of Triumph and Tragedy*. London: Little Brown and Co.

Giri, Birendra R. 2011. "The Bonded Labor System in Nepal: Exploring *haliya* and *kamaiya* Children's Life-worlds." In *The Tarai: History, Society, Environment*, edited by Arjun Guneratne, 71–100. Kathmandu: Himal Books.

Giuseppe, Father. 1799. "Account of The Kingdom of Nepal." *Asiatic Researches* 2: 307–22.

Gnoli, Raniero. 1956. *Nepalese Inscriptions in Gupta-Characters*. Rome: Istitute Italiano per il Medio ed Estremo Oriente.

Gögge, Kathleen. 2001. "Nepalische Landdokumente: Kaufurkunden aus der Mallazeit." Masters thesis. University of Leipzig.

Gögge, Kathleen. 2007. *Viṣṇuitische Heiligtümer und Feste im Kathmandu-Tal/Nepal*. Heidelberg University: heiDok - The Heidelberg Document Repository.

Gögge, Kathleen. 2010. "Early Childhood Rituals Among the Newars and Parbatiyās in the Kathmandu Valley." In *Hindu and Buddhist Initiations in India and Nepal*, edited by Astrid Zotter and Christof Zotter, 87–136. Wiesbaden: Harrassowitz.

Goodman, Jim. 1981. *Guide to Enjoying Nepalese Festivals*. Kathmandu: Kali Press.

Government of Nepal. 2011. *National Population and Housing Census 2011*. Kathmandu: Central Bureau of Statistics, National Planning Commission Secretariat. Vol. 1.

Government of Nepal. 2014. *Population Monograph*, vol. 2. Kathmandu: Central Bureau of Statistics, National Planning Commission Secretariat.

Government of Nepal. 2015a. *2015 Statistical Year Book*. Kathmandu: Central Bureau of Statistics.

Government of Nepal. 2015b. *Labour Migration for Employment: A Status Report for Nepal: 2013/2014*. Kathmandu: Ministry of Labour and Employment, Department of Foreign Employment.

Government of Nepal. 2023a. *National Population and Housing Census 2021*. Kathmandu: Office of the Prime Minister and Council of Members, National Statistics office.

Government of Nepal. 2023b. *National Population and Housing Census 2021: National Report on caste/ethnicity, Language, Religion*. Kathmandu: Office of the Prime Minister and Council of Members, National Statistics office.

Greenwold, Stephen. 1974. "Buddhist Brahmans." *European Journal of Sociology* 15: 101–23.

Gregson, Jonathan. 2002. *Blood against the Snows: The Tragic Story of Nepal's Royal Dynasty*. London: Fourth Estate.

Guneratne, Arjun. 2002. *Many Tongues, One People: The Making of Tharu Identity in Nepal*. Ithaca, NY: Cornell University Press.

Guneratne, Arjun, ed. 2011. *The Tarai: History, Society, Environment*. Kathmandu: Himal Books.

Gupta, Anirudha. 1964. *Politics in Nepal: A Study of Post-Rana Political Developments and Party Politics*. London: George Allen and Unwin.

Gutschow, Niels. 1982. *Stadtraum und Ritual der newarischen Städte im Kathmandu-Tal: Eine Architekturanthropologische Untersuchung*. Stuttgart: W. Kohlhammer.

Gutschow, Niels. 1986. "Die Kuppelbauten des 19. Jh. im Kāṭhmāṇḍu-Tal." In *Formen kulturellen Wandels und andere Beiträge zur Erforschung des Himālaya*, edited by Bernhard Kölver, 283–310. Sankt Augustin: VGH Wissenschaftsverlag.

Gutschow, Niels. 1997. *The Nepalese Caitya: 1500 Years of Buddhist Votive Architecture in the Kathmandu Valley*. With Drawings by Bijay Basukala and an Introductory Essay on Newar Buddhism by David Gellner. Stuttgart: Menges.

Gutschow, Niels. 1998. "The Settlement Process in Lower Mustang (Baragaon), Nepal: Case Studies from Kag, Khyinga and Te." *Beiträge zur Allgemeinen und Vergleichenden Archäologie* 18: 49–145.

Gutschow, Niels. 2011. *Architecture of the Newars: A History of Building Typologies and Details*. 3 vols. Chicago: Serindia Publications.

Gutschow, Niels. 2012. *The Kathmandu Valley: New Buildings, Sites under Construction and Demolition, 1990–2011*. Kathmandu: Himal Books.

Gutschow, Niels. 2016. *The Portals in Newar Architecture: Tiered Temples in Nepal, 13th to 19th Centuries*. Kathmandu: Himal Books.

Gutschow, Niels. 2017. *Bhaktapur - Nepal: Urban Space and Ritual*. 2 vols. Berlin: DOM Publishers.

Gutschow, Niels. 2019. *The Sky Face: Kīrtimukha and Related Hybrid Creatures in the Architecture of Nepal, South- and South East Asia*. Kathmandu: Vajra Books.

Gutschow, Niels. 2021. *Chörten in Nepal: Architecture and Buddhist Votive Practice in the Himalaya in Dhading-Rasuwa, Dolpo, Humla, Manang, Mustang, Sindhupalchok-Dolakha*. Berlin: DOM Publishers.

Gutschow, Niels, and Ganesh Man Basukala. 1987. "The Navadurgā of Bhaktapur: Spatial Implications of an Urban Ritual." In *Heritage of the Kathmandu Valley: Proceedings of an International Conference in Lübeck, 1987*, edited by Niels Gutschow and Axel Michaels, 135–66. Sankt Augustin: VGH Wissenschaftsverlag.

Gutschow, Niels, and Bernhard Kölver. 1975. *Ordered Space: Concepts and Functions in a Town of Nepal*. Wiesbaden: Franz Steiner.

Gutschow, Niels, Berhard Kölver, and Ishwaranand Shresthacarya. 1987. *Newar Towns and Buildings: An Illustrated Dictionary Newārī–English*. Sankt Augustin: VGH Wissenschaftsverlag.

Gutschow, Niels, and Hermann Kreutzmann. 2013. *Mapping the Kathmandu Valley with Areal Photographs by Erwin Schneider*. Kathmandu: Himal Books.

Gutschow, Niels, and Axel Michaels. 2005. *Handling Death: The Dynamics of Death and Ancestor Rituals Among the Newars of Bhaktapur, Nepal*. With a film on DVD by Christian Bau. Wiesbaden: Harrassowitz Verlag.

Gutschow, Niels, and Axel Michaels. 2008. *Growing Up: Hindu and Buddhist Initiation Rituals among Newar Children in Bhaktapur, Nepal*. With a film on DVD by Christian Bau. Wiesbaden: Harrassowitz Verlag.

Gutschow, Niels, and Axel Michaels. 2012. *Getting Married: Hindu and Buddhist Marriage Rituals among Newars of Bhaktapur and Patan, Nepal*. With a film on DVD by Christian Bau. Wiesbaden: Harrassowitz Verlag.

Gutschow, Niels, Axel Michaels, Charles Ramble, and Ernst Steinkellner, eds. 2003. *Sacred Landscape of the Himalaya*. Vienna: Österreichische Akademie der Wissenschaften.

Gutschow, Niels, and Raju Roka, eds. 2017. *Patan Palace: The Restoration of Sundari Cok, 2006–2016*. Kathmandu: Kathmandu Valley Preservation Trust.

Gyawali, Bandana. 2018. *Bibliography of Early Twentieth Century Writings on Nepal*. Kathmandu: Martin Chautari.

Gyawali, Dipak, Ajaya Dixit, and Madhukar Upadhya, eds. 2004. *Ropeways in Nepal: Context, Constraints and Coevolution*. Lalitpur: Nepal Water Conservation Foundation.

Gyawali, Surya Bikram. VS 2033 (1976/77). *Pṛthvīnārāyaṇa Śāha* (in Nepālī). Darjeeling: Shyama Brothers.

Hachhetu, Krishna. 2008–9. "The Communist Party of Nepal (Maoist): Transformation from an Insurgency Group to a Competitive Political Party." *EBHR* 33–34: 39–71.

Haenisch, Erich. 1938. "Zwei Kaiserliche Erlasse: Vom Ausgange der Regierung Kienlung, Die Gorkha Betreffend." *Harvard Journal of Asiatic Studies* 3 (1): 17–39.

Hagmüller, Götz. 2002. *Patan Museum: The Transformation of a Royal Palace in Nepal.* London: Serindia Publications.

Hamilton, Francis Buchanan. [1819] 1971. *An Account of the Kingdom of Nepal and of Territories Annexed to this Dominion by the House of Gorkha.* New Delhi: Manjusri Publishing House.

Hamilton, Francis Buchanan. 1928. *An Account of the District Purnea 1809–10.* Edited by H. P. Jackson. Patna: Bihar and Orissa Research Society.

Hasrat, Bikram Jit: see Primary Sources.

Hegewald: Julia A. B. 2002. *Water Architecture in South Asia: A Study of Types, Developments and Meanings.* Leiden: Brill.

Herdick, Reinhard. 1988. *Kirtipur: Stadtgestalt, Prinzipien der Raumordnung und gesellschaftlichen Funktion einer Newar-Stadt.* Cologne: Weltforum Verlag.

Hitchcock, John. 1979. "An Additional Perspective on the Nepali Caste System." In *Himalayan Anthropology*, edited by James F. Fisher, 111–20. The Hague: Mouton.

Hitchcock, John, and Rex L. Jones, eds. 1976. *Spirit Possession in the Nepal Himalayas.* Warminster, England: Aris and Phillips.

Hodgson, Brian H. [1874] 1971. *Essays on the Languages, Literature and Religion of Nepal and Tibet together with further Papers on the Geography, Ethnology and Commerce of Those Countries.* London: Trübner and Co.

Hodgson, Brian H. [1880] 1992. *Miscelleanous Essays Relating to Indian Subjects.* New Delhi: Asian Educational Service, 1992.

Hodgson, Brian H. 1883. "Origin and Classification of the Military Tribes of Nepal." *Journal of the Bengal Asiatic Society* 2 (17): 217–34.

Höfer, Andras. 1979a. *The Caste Hierarchy and the State in Nepal: A Study of the Muluki Ain of 1854.* Innsbruck: Universitätsverlag Wagner.

Höfer, Andras. 1979b. "On Re-reading *Le Nepal*: What We Social Scientists Owe to Sylvain Levi." *Kailash* 7: 175–90.

Höfer, Andras. 1981 and 1997. *Tamang Ritual Texts.* 2 vols. Wiesbaden: Steiner.

Höfer, Andras. 1994. *A Recitation of the Tamang Shaman in Nepal.* Bonn: VGH Wissenschaftsverlag.

Holmberg, David H. 1996. *Order in Paradox: Myth Ritual, and Exchange among Nepal's Tamang.* 1st Indian ed. Delhi: Motilal Banarsidass.

Holmberg, David H., and Kathryn March. 1999. "Local Production/Local Knowledge: Forced Labour from Below." *SINHS* 4 (1): 5–64.

Hultzsch, Eugen. 1925. *Inscriptions of Asoka.* Oxford: Clarendon Press.

Hunter, William Wilson. [1896] 1991. *Life of Brian Houghton Hodgson, British Resident at the Court of Nepal.* New Delhi: Asian Educational Services.

Hussain, Assad. 1970. *British India's Relations with the Kingdom of Nepal, 1857–1947.* London: George Allen and Unwin.

Hutt, Michael. 1986. "Diversity and Change in the Languages of Highland Nepal." *CNSt* 14 (1): 1–24.

Hutt, Michael. 1988. *Nepali: A National Language and its Literature*. New Delhi and London: Sterling Publishers and School of Oriental and African Studies.

Hutt, Michael. 1991. *Himalayan Voices: An Introduction to Modern Nepali Literature*. Berkeley: University of California Press.

Hutt, Michael. 2006. "Things That Should Not Be Said: Censorship and Self-Censorship in the Nepali Press Media, 2001–2." *Journal of Asian Studies* 65 (2): 361–402.

Hutt, Michael, David Gellner, Axel Michaels, Greta Rana, and Govinda Tandan. 1994. *Nepal: A Guide to the Art and Architecture of the Kathmandu Valley*. Gartmore: Kiscadale Publications.

Iltis, Linda. 1985. "The Swasthānī Vrata: Newar Women and Ritual in Nepal." PhD dissertation, University of Wisconsin (UMI 8528426).

Indraji, Bhagvanlal, and Georg Bühler. 1880. "Inscriptions from Nepal." *Indian Antiquary* 9: 163–94.

Jackson, David P. 1976. "The Early History of Lo (Mustang) and Ngari." *CNSt* 4: 39–56.

Jackson, David P. 1978. "Notes on the History of se-rib, and Nearby Places in the Upper Kali Gandaki Valley." *Kailash* 6 (3): 195–227.

Jackson, David P. 1984. *The Mollas of Mustang*. New Delhi: The Library of Tibetan Works and Archives.

Jayaswal, K. P. 1936. "Chronology and History of Nepal, 600 B.C. to A.D. 880." *Journal of the Bihar and Orissa Research Society* 22: 157–264.

Jha, Hit Narayan, 1970. *The Licchavis (of Vaiśālī)*. Varanasi: Chowkhamba Sanskrit Series Office.

Jha, Makhan. 1971. *The Sacred Complex in Janakpur: Indological, Sociological, Anthropological and Philosophical Study of Hindu Civilization*. Allahabad: United Publishers.

Jordan, R. R. 2010. *From Missionaries to Mountaineers: Early Encounters with Nepal*. Kathmandu: Giridhar Lal Manandhar.

Jørgensen, Hans. 1921. "Ein Beitrag zur Kenntnis des Nevārī." *Zeitschrift der Deutschen Morgenländischen Gesellschaft* 75: 213–36.

Jørgensen, Hans. 1931. *Vicitrakarṇikāvadānoddhṛta: A Collection of Buddhistic Legends*. London: Royal Asiatic Society.

Jørgensen, Hans. 1936. *A Dictionary of Classical Newārī*. Copenhagen: Royal Danish Academy of Sciences and Letters.

Jørgensen, Hans. 1941. *A Grammar of Classical Newārī*. Copenhagen: Royal Danish Academy of Sciences and Letters.

Joshi, B. L., and J. Rose. 1966. *Democratic Innovations in Nepal: A Case Study of Political Acculturation*. Berkeley: University of California Press.

Jurami, Anne-Claire. 2001. "Architecture et iconographie de Viṣṇu dans le vallée de Kāṭhmāṇḍu, Népal." 3 vols. PhD dissertation, Université Paris III-Sorbonne.

Kalapura, Jose. 2008. "Nepal Inscribed: Christian Missionaries in Nepal in the 18th Century." *Proceedings of the Indian History Congress* 69: 881–903.

Karan, Pradyumna P., and Hiroshi Ishii. 1996. *Nepal: A Himalayan Kingdom in Transition*. Tokyo, New York, Paris: United Nations University Press.

Karmacharya, Ganga. 2005. *Queens in Nepalese Politics*. Kathmandu: Educational Publishing House.

Karmacharya, Madhav Lal, ed. 2005. *Nepalese literature*. Kathmandu: Royal Nepal Academy.

Kasten, Ani. 2011. "The Potters of Thimi: Village Ceramic Traditions in Flux." In *Nepal: Nostalgia and Modernity*, edited by Deepak Shimkada, 81–90. Mumbai: Marg Foundation.

Kathmandu Valley Preservation Trust. 2016. *Nepal, Patan Darbar: Earthquake Response Campaign. Documentation of the Work to Date.* Patan: KVPT.

KC, Gaurab, and Pratyoush Onta. 2013. *Bibliography of Social Scientific Writings by Dor Bahadur Bista.* Kathmandu Martin Chautari; http://www.martinchautari.org.np/files/DorBahadurBista-GaurabKC-POnta.pdf (accessed June 25, 2021).

Khadka, Narayan. 1997. *Foreign Aid and Foreign Policy: Major Powers and Nepal.* New Delhi: Vikash Publishing House.

Khanāla, Mohana Prasāda. 1981/82 (VS 2038). *Nepālī Bhāṣāko Hajāra Varṣa.* Kathmandu: Rāino Pablikesana.

Khanāla, Mohana Prasāda. n.d. (VS 2040, ca. 1983). *Cāṃgunārāyaṇakā Aitihāsika Sāmāgrī.* Kathmandu: Tribhuvana Viśvavidyālaya.

Khanāla, Revatī Ramana. 2002. *Nepālako Kānūnī Itihāsako Rūparekhā* (Nepal's Legal History: An Outline). Kathmandu: Author.

Kharel, Pranab, and Gaurab KC. 2016. *Bibliography of the Works of Prayag Raj Sharma.* Kathmandu: Martin Chautari.

Khatiwoda, Rajan. 2017. "Formation and Enforcement of the [Mulukī] Ain, Nepal's First Legal Code Containing the Edition and Translation of the Articles on Homicide in the [Mulukī] Ains of 1854 and 1870 Including Contemporaneous Legal Documents." PhD dissertation, Heidelberg University.

Khatiwoda, Cubelic, and Michaels 2021: see Primary Sources, *Mulukī Ain of 1854.*

Killigrew, John W. 1979. "Some Aspects of the Sino-Nepalese War of 1792." *Journal of Asian History* 13: 42–63.

Kircher, Anathasius. [1667] 1985. *China monumentis...*, Amsterdam 1667; German translation: *Johannes Grueber: Als Kundschafter des Papstes nach China 1656–1664. Die erste Durchquerung Tibets*, edited by Franz Baumann. Darmstadt: Wissenschaftliche Buchgesellschaft.

Kirkpatrick, Colonel. 1811. *An Account of the Kingdom of Nepaul Being the substance of observations made during a mission to that country in the year 1793.* London: William Miller.

Klein, Jan Niklas. 2015. "Nepal." In *Encyclopedia of Law and Religion*, edited by Gerhard Robbers. Leiden: E.J. Brill; http://dx.doi.org/ 10.1163/2405-9749_elr_COM_000115.

Kloppenburg, Rita. 1977. "Theravāda Buddhism in Nepal." *Kailash* 5 (4): 301–21.

Kölver, Bernhard. 1986a. "Der Staat und die Anderen: Formen institutioneller Auseinandersetzung." In *Formen kulturellen Wandels und andere Beiträge zur Erforschung des Himālaya*, edited by Bernhard Kölver, 19–32. Sankt Augustin: VGH Wissenschaftsverlag.

Kölver, Bernhard, ed. 1986b. *Formen kulturellen Wandels und andere Beiträge zur Erforschung des Himālaya.* Sankt Augustin: VGH Wissenschaftsverlag.

Kölver, Bernhard. 1986c. "Stages in the Evolution of a World Picture." *Numen* 32: 131–68.

Kölver, Bernhard. 1986d. "Zwei nepalische Dokumente zur Schuldknechtschaft (Documents from Nepal. 4)." *Zeitschrift der Deutschen Morgenländischen Gesellschaft* 136 (2): 434–49.

Kölver, Bernhard, ed. 1992a. *Seminar on German Research on Nepal in Kathmandu, March 12–15, 1990.* Kathmandu: Nepal Research Centre.

Kölver, Bernhard. 1992b. *Re-building a Stūpa: Architectural Drawings of the Svayambhūnātha*. Bonn: VGH Wissenschaftsverlag.

Kölver, Bernhard, and Niels Gutschow. 1975. *Ordered Space: Concepts and Functions in a Town of Nepal*. Wiesbaden: Franz Steiner.

Kölver, Bernhard, and Hemrāj Śākya. 1985. *Documents from the Rudravarṇa-Mahāvihāra, Pāṭan -1: Sales and Mortgages*. Sankt Augustin: VGH Wissenschaftsverlag.

Korn, Wolfgang. 1979. *The Traditional Architecture of the Kathmandu Valley*. Kathmandu: Ratna Pustak Bhandar.

Krämer, Karl-Heinz, 1996. *Ethnizität und nationale Integration in Nepal: Eine Untersuchung der ethnischen Gruppen im modernen Nepal*. Stuttgart: Franz Steiner Verlag.

Krauskopff, Gisèle. 1988. *Maîtres et possédés: Les rites et l'ordre social chez les Tharu (Népal)*. Paris: Editions du CNRS.

Krauskopff, Gisèle. 1999. "Corvées in Dang: Ethno-historical Notes." In *Nepal: Tharu and Tarai Neighbours*, edited by Harold O. Skar, 47–62. Kathmandu: Educational Enterprise.

Krauskopff, Gisèle. 2018. "The Silent History of the Tharu Farmers: Peasant Mobility and Jungle Frontiers in the Light of Written Archives." In *Studies in Documents of India and Nepal*, edited by Simon Cubelic, Axel Michaels, and Astrid Zotter, 351–76. Heidelberg: Heidelberg University Publishing.

Krauskopff, Gisèle, and Marie Lecomte-Tilouine, eds. 1996. *Célébrer le pouvoir: Dasain, une fête royale de Népal*. Paris: CNRS editions.

Krauskopff, Gisèle, and Pamela Deuel Meyer, eds. 2000. *The Kings of Nepal, and the Tharu of the Tarai*. Kirtipur: Centre for Nepal and Asian Studies.

Kretschmar. Monika. 1995. *Erzählungen und Dialekt aus Südmustang*. Sankt Augustin: VGH Wissenschaftsverlag.

Kropf, Marianna. 2002. "Katto Khuvaune: Two Brahmins for Nepal's Departed Kings." *EBHR* 23: 56–85.

Kshetri, Dil Bahadur. 1998. *Documents on Nepal: A Collection of Diplomatic Correspondences with British India, Sanads and Lalmohars*. Pokhara: Parbati Kshetri.

Kukuczka, Anne. 2011. "Negotiating Ethnic Identity in the Himalaya: The Tamang in Nepal." *Südasien-Chronik / South-Asia-Chronicle* 2011 (1): 393–437.

Kumar, Satish. 1967. *Rana Polity in Nepal: Origin and Growth*. London: Asia Publishing House.

Kutzner, Johann G. 1857. *Die Reise Seiner Königlichen Hoheit des Prinzen Waldemar von Preußen nach Indien in den Jahren 1844 bis 1846: Aus dem darüber erschienenen Prachtwerke im Auszuge*. Berlin: Verlag der Königlichen Geheimen Ober-Hofbuchdruckerei (R. Decker).

Landon, Perceval. [1928] 1976. *Nepal*. 2 vols. in one. Reprint, Kathmandu: Ratna Pustak Bhandar.

Lawoti, Mahendra. 2005. *Towards a Democratic Nepal: Inclusive Political Institutions for a Multicultural Society*. New Delhi: Sage Publications, and Kathmandu: Mandala Book Point.

Le Bon, Gustave. [1886] 1981. *Voyage au Népal*. Bangkok: White Orchid Press.

Lecomte-Tilouine, Marie. 2009a. "The Panchakoshi of Dullu: The Fire Frame of the Malla Imperial Capital." In *Bards and Mediums: History, Culture and Politics in the Central Himalayan Kingdoms*, edited by Marie Lecomte-Tilouine, 253–76. Almora: Almora Book Depot.

Lecomte-Tilouine, Marie. 2009b. "From the Bards' Grandeur to the Kings' Orders: History in Various Forms." In *Bards and Mediums: History, Culture and Politics in the Central Himalayan Kingdoms*, edited by Marie Lecomte-Tilouine, 173–88. Almora: Almora Book Depot.

Lecomte-Tilouine, Marie, ed. 2013. *Revolution in Nepal*. New Delhi: Oxford University Press.

Lecomte-Tilouine, Marie, and Pascale Dolfus, eds. 2003. *Ethnic Revival and Religious Turmoil: Identities and Representations in the Himalayas*. Oxford: Oxford University Press.

Letizia, Chiara. 2012. "Secularism in Nepal." *EBHR* 39: 66–104.

Letizia, Chiara. 2013. "The Goddess Kumari at the Supreme Court." *Focaal: Journal of Global and Historical Anthropology* 67: 32–46.

Letizia, Chiara. 2016. "Ideas of Secularism in Contemporary Nepal." In *Religion, Secularism and Ethnicity in Contemporary Nepal*, edited by David Gellner, Sondra L. Hausner, and Chiara Letizia, 35–76. New Delhi: Oxford University Press.

Lévi, Sylvain. 1905–8. *Le Népal: Etude historique d'un Royaume Hindou*. 3 vols. Paris: Ernest Leroux; English translation: *Ancient Nepal* (1973–90), 44 pts., and parts of vol. 2 translated by Theodore Riccardi in *Kailash* 3 (1975): 1–60.

LeVine, Sarah, and David N. Gellner. 2005. *Rebuilding Buddhism: The Theravada Movement in Twentieth-Century Nepal*. Cambridge, MA: Harvard University Press.

Levy, Robert. 1987. "How the Navadurgā Protect Bhaktapur: The Effective Meanings of a Symbolic Enactment." In *Heritage of the Kathmandu Valley: Proceedings of an International Conference in Lübeck, 1987*, edited by Niels Gutschow and Axel Michaels, 105–34. Sankt Augustin: VGH Wissenschaftsverlag.

Levy, Robert. 1990. *Mesocosm: Hinduism and the Organization of a Traditional Newar City in Nepal*. Berkeley: University of California Press.

Lewis, Todd. 1996. "A Chronology of Newar-Tibetan Relations in the Kathmandu Valley." In *Change and Continuity: Studies in the Nepalese Culture of the Kathmandu Valley*, edited by Siegfried Lienhard, 149–66. Turin: Edizioni Dell'orso.

Lewis, Todd. 2000. *Popular Buddhist Texts from Nepal: Narratives and Rituals of Newar Buddhism*. Translations in collaboration with Subarna Man Tuladhar and Labh Ratna Tuladhar. Albany: State University of New York Press.

Lewis, Todd, and Naresh Man Bajracharya. 2016. "Vajrayāna Traditions in Nepal." In *Tantric Traditions in Transmission and Translation*, edited by D. B. Gray and R. R. Overby, 87–198. New York: Oxford University Press.

Liechty, Mark. 2003. *Suitably Modern: Making Middle Class Culture in Kathmandu*. Princeton, NJ: Princeton University Press.

Liechty, Mark. 2017. *Far Out: Countercultural Seekers and the Tourist Encounter in Nepal*. Chicago: University of Chicago Press.

Lienhard, Siegfried. 1963. See Primary Sources, *Maṇicūḍāvadānoddhṛta*.

Lienhard, Siegfried. 1974. *Nevārīgītimañjarī: Religious and Secular Poetry of the Nevars of the Kathmandu Valley*. Stockholm: Almqvist and Wiksell.

Lienhard, Siegfried. 1978a. "Problème des syncrétismes religieux au Népal." *Bulletin de l'École Française d'Extréme Orient* 65: 239–70.

Lienhard, Siegfried. 1978b. "Religionssynkretismus in Nepal." In *Buddhism in Ceylon and Studies on Religious Syncretism in Buddhist Countries*, edited by Heinz Bechert, 146–77. Göttingen: Vandenhoeck and Ruprecht.

Lienhard, Siegfried. 1991. "Zur Frühgeschichte des Viṣṇuismus in Nepal." *Nachrichten der Akademie der Wissenschaften in Göttingen, Historisch-Philosophische Klasse* 3 (8): 351–61.

Lienhard, Siegfried. 1992a. "Kṛṣṇaismus in Nepal." In *Aspects of Nepalese Traditions*, edited by Bernhard Kölver, 227–34. Stuttgart: Franz Steiner Verlag.

Lienhard, Siegfried. 1992b. *Songs of Nepal: An Anthology of Nevar Folksongs and Hymns*. New Delhi: Motilal Banarsidass.

Lienhard, Siegfried. 1995. *The Divine Play of Lord Krishna: A Krishnalīlā Painting from Nepal: With Thirty-One Poems in Newari*. Bonn: VGH Wissenschaftsverlag.

Lienhard, Siegfried. 1999. *Diamantmeister und Hausväter: Buddhistisches Gemeindeleben in Nepal*. Vienna: Österreichische Akademie der Wissenschaften.

Lo Bue, Erberto. 1997. "The Role of Newar Scholars in Transmitting the Indian Buddhist Heritage to Tibet (c. 750 – c. 1200)." In *Les Habitants du Toit du Monde*, edited by S. Karmay and Ph. Sagant, 629–58. Nanterre: Société d'ethnologie.

Locke, John K. 1980. *Karunamaya: The Cult of Avalokitesvạra-Matsyendranath in the Valley of Nepal*. Kathmandu: Sahayogi Prakashan.

Locke, John K. 1985. *Buddhist Monasteries of Nepal: A Survey of the Bāhās and Bahīs of the Kathmandu Valley*. Kathmandu: Sahayogi Press.

Locke, Pierce. 2006. "History, Practice, Identity: An Institutional Ethnography of Elephant Handlers in Chitwan, Nepal." PhD dissertation, University of Kent.

Locke, Pierce. 2011. "The Tharu, the Tarai and the History of the Nepali Hattisar." *EBHR* 38: 59–80.

Losty, J. P. 2005. "'The Architectural Monuments of Buddhism': Hodgson and Buddhist Architecture of the Kathmandu Valley." In *The Origins of Himalayan Studies: Brian Houghton Hodgson in Nepal and Darjeeling, 1820–1858*, edited by David Waterhouse, 77–110. New York: RoutledgeCurzon.

Lotter, Stefanie. 2011. "Distinctly Different Everywhere: Politics of Appearance Amongst Rana Elites Inside and Outside of Nepal." *Comparative Sociology* 10: 508–27.

Macdonald, Alexander W. 1975. "The Healer in the Nepalese World." In *Essays on the Ethnology of Nepal and South Asia*, edited by Alexander W. Macdonald, 113–28. Kathmandu: Ratna Pustak Bhandar.

Macfarlane, Alane. 2008. "Identity and Change among the Gurungs (Tamu-mai) of Central Nepal." In *Nationalism and Ethnicity in a Hindu Kingdom: The Politics of Culture in Contemporary Nepal*, edited by David N. Gellner, Joanna Pfaff-Czarnecka, and John Whelpton, 185–204. Kathmandu: Vajra Publications.

Mainali, Sujita. 2021. *Satī: Itihāsa ra Mīmāṃsā*. Nepal: Kitab Publishers.

Malla, Kamal P. 1970. "The Intellectual in Nepalese Society." *Vasudha* 14: 5–6 (also in Malla 2015: 157–86).

Malla, Kamal P. 1981. "Linguistic Archaeology of the Nepal Valley: A Preliminary Report." *Kailash* 8 (1–2): 5–23.

Malla, Kamal P. 1982. *Classical Newari Literature: A Sketch*. Kathmandu: Educational Enterprise.

Malla, Kamal P. 1990. "The Earliest Dated Document in Newari: The Palm Leaf from Uku Bahah NS 234/AD 1114." *Kailash* 16 (1–2): 15–25.

Malla, Kamal P. 2015. *From Literature to Culture: Selected Writings on Nepalese Studies, 1980–2010*. Kathmandu: Himal Books.

Manandar, Sarala. 1984. "Teracotta Human Figuines from Tilaurakot: The Ancient Kapilvastu." *Ancient Nepal* 83: 1–12.

Manandhar, Tri Ratna. 1999 (VS 2056). "Sajāya Kāryānvayana Sambandhī Dastāveja." *Abhilekha* 17 (17): 25–28.

Manandhar, Tri Ratna, and Tirtha Prasad Mishra. 1986. *Nepal's Quinquennial Missions to China*. Kathmandu: Purna Devi Manandhar and Puspa Mishra.

Manandhar, Vijay Kumar. 2001. *A Documentary History of Nepalese Quinquennial Missions to China, 1792–1906*. Delhi: Adroit Publishers.

Marasini, B. R. 2003. "Health and Hospital Development in Nepal: Past and Present." *Journal of Nepal Medical Association* 42: 306–11.

March, Kathry. 2000. "Triangulating Tamang Ethnohistory: The Production of Identities in Colonial Encounters." *Himalayan Research Bulletin* 20 (1): 18–22.

Markham, Clements R., ed. 1971. *Narratives of the Mission of Georg Bogle to Tibet and the Journey of Thomas Manning to Lhasa*. New Delhi: Manjushri.

Maskarinec, Gregor. 1995. *The Rulings of the Night: An Ethnography of Nepalese Shaman Oral Texts*. Madison: University of Wisconsin Press.

Maskarinec, Gregor. 1999–2009. *Nepalese Shaman Oral Texts*. 2 vols. Cambridge, MA: Harvard University Press.

Maskey, Govinda. 1996. *Social Life in Nepal: From Tradition to Modernity (1901–1925)*. New Delhi: Anmol Publications.

Mathema, Kalyan Bhakta. 2011. *Madheshi Uprising: The Resurgence of Ethnicity*. Kathmandu: Mandala Book Point.

McDougal, Charles. 1979. *The Kulunge Rai: A Study in Kinship and Marriage Exchange*. Kathmandu: Ratna Pustak Bhandar.

Messerschmidt, Don, and Dina Bangdel, eds. 2004. *Against the Current: The Life of Lain Singh Bangdel – Writer, Painter and Art Historian of Nepal*. Bangkok: Orchid Press.

Michael, Bernado. 1999. "Statemaking and Space on the Margins of Empire: Rethinking the Anglo-Gorkha War of 1814–1816." *SINHS* 4 (2): 247–94.

Michael, Bernado. 2011. "The Tarai: A Part of Moghlan or Gorkha?" In *The Tarai: History, Society, Environment*, edited by Arjun Guneratne, 1–26. Kathmandu: Himal Books.

Michael, Bernado. 2013. *Statemaking and Territory in South Asia: Lessons from the Anglo-Gorkha War (1814–1816)*. London: Anthem Press.

Michaels, Axel. 1984. "Śiva's Wild and Wayward Calf: The Goddess Vatsalā, Her Temple and Yātrā." *Kailash* 9 (3–4): 105–47.

Michaels, Axel. 1986. "Der verstoßene Sohn: Nepalische *bālyogis* und der *deśāntara*-Ritus während der Initiation." In *Formen kulturellen Wandels und andere Beiträge zur Erforschung des Himālaya*, edited by Bernhard Kölver, 192–236. Sankt Augustin: VGH Wissenschaftsverlag.

Michaels, Axel. 1992. "Recht auf Leben und Selbsttötung in Indien." In *Recht zum Leben – Recht zum Töten im Kulturvergleich*, edited by B. Mensen SVD, 95–124. Sankt Augustin: Akademie Völker und Kulturen.

Michaels, Axel. 1993a. "Widow burning in Nepal." In *Nepal, Past and Present: Proceedings of the Franco-German Conference Art-et-Senans, June 1990*, edited by Gérard Toffin, 21–34. Paris: CNRS Editions.

Michaels, Axel. 1993b. "Gods versus Cars. On Moveable and Immoveable Gods at the Nepalese Paśupati Temple." *National Geographical Journal of India* 39: 151–59.

Michaels, Axel. 1993c. "Śiva under Refuse: The Hidden Mahādeva (Lukumahādyaḥ) and Protective Stones in Nepal." In *Flags of Fame: Studies in South Asian Folk Culture*, edited by Heidrun Brückner, Lothar Lutze, and Aditya Malik, 165–200. New Delhi: Manohar Publications.

Michaels, Axel. 1994a. "The Legislation of Widow Burning in 19th-Century Nepal. Edition and Translation of the Chapter *Satijānyako* of the Mulukī Ain." *Asiatische Studien* 118 (4): 1213–40.

Michaels, Axel. 1994b. *Die Reisen der Götter: Der nepalische Paśupatinātha-Tempel und sein rituelles Umfeld*. 2 vols. Sankt Augustin: VGH Wissenschaftsverlag.

Michaels, Axel, ed. 1995. *A Rāma Temple in 19th-Century Nepal: History and Architecture of the Rāmacandra Temple in Battīsputalī, Kathmandu*. Stuttgart: Franz Steiner Verlag.

Michaels, Axel. 1996 (with Nutan Sharma). "Goddess of the Secret: Guhyeśvarī in Nepal and Her Festival." In *Wild Goddesses in India and Nepal*, edited by Axel Michaels, Cornelia Vogelsanger, and Annette Wilke, 303–37. Bern: Peter Lang.

Michaels, Axel. 1997. "The King and the Cow: On a Crucial Symbol of Hinduization." In *Nationalism and Ethnicity in a Hindu Kingdom: The Politics of Culture in Contemporary Nepal*, edited by David Gellner, Joanna Pfaff-Czarnecka, and John Whelpton, 79–100. Reprint. Kathmandu: Vajra Publications.

Michaels, Axel. 2004. *Hinduism - Past and Present*. Princeton, NJ: Princeton University Press.

Michaels, Axel. 2005a. *The Price of Purity: The Religious Judge in 19th Century Nepal. Containing the Edition and Translation of the Chapters on the Dharmādhikārin in Two (Mulukī) Ains*. Turin: Corpus Iuris Sanscriticum et fontes iuris Asiae Meridianae et Centralis.

Michaels, Axel. 2005b. "*Saṃkalpa*: The Beginnings of a Ritual." In *Words and Deeds: Hindu and Buddhist Rituals in South Asia*, edited by Joerg Gengnagel, Ute Huesken, and Srilata Raman, 45–64. Wiesbaden: Harrassowitz Verlag.

Michaels, Axel. 2006. "Die Herrin des Verborgenen: Verwandlung und Identität im hinduistischen Pantheon." In *Verwandlungen*, edited by Aleida Assmann and Jan Assmann, 95–110. Munich: Fink.

Michaels, Axel. 2007. "Blutopfer in Nepal." In *Mythen des Blutes*, edited by Christa von Braun and Christoph Wulf, 91–107. Frankfurt/Main: Campus.

Michaels, Axel. 2008. *Śiva in Trouble: Festivals and Rituals at the Paśupatinātha Temple of Deopatan (Nepal)*. New York: Oxford University Press.

Michaels, Axel. 2009a. "Nepal." In *The Oxford International Encyclopedia of Legal History*, edited by Stanley N. Katz. Oxford: Oxford University Press.

Michaels, Axel. 2009b. "Macht und Ohnmacht einer lebenden Göttin: Die Kumārī im politischen Wechsel Nepals." In *Handlung und Leidenschaft: Jenseits von actio und passio*, edited by Klaus-Peter Köpping, Burkhard Schnepel, and Christoph Wulf, 164–76. Berlin: Akademie Verlag.

Michaels, Axel. 2010. "Newar Hybrid Ritual and Its Language in Hindu Initiations." In *Hindu and Buddhist Initiations in India and Nepal*, edited by Astrid Zotter and Christof Zotter, 137–50. Wiesbaden: Harrassowitz.

Michaels, Axel. 2013. "From Syncretism to Transculturality: "The Dīpaṅkara Procession in the Kathmandu Valley." In *South Asian Festivals on the Move*, edited by Ute Huesken and Axel Michaels, 317–42. Wiesbaden: Harrassowitz.

Michaels, Axel. 2016a. "Blood Sacrifice in Nepal: Transformations and Criticism." In *Religion, Secularism and Ethnicity in Contemporary Nepal*, edited by David Gellner, Sondra L. Hausner, and Chiara Letizia, 192–225. New Delhi: Oxford University Press.

Michaels, Axel. 2016b. *Homo ritualis: Hindu Ritual and Its Significance for Ritual Theory*. New York: Oxford University Press.

Michaels, Axel. 2017. "Rituals." In *Hinduism in India: The Early Period*, edited by Greg Bailey, 27–59. Los Angeles: Sage.

Michaels, Axel. 2018a. "Nepal in the World." Heidelberg: South Asia Papers, 2018; https://doi.org/10.11588/xarep.00004115.

Michaels, Axel. 2018b. "Hybridity." In *Engaging Transculturality: Concepts, Key Terms, Case Studies*, edited by Laila Abu-er Rub et al., 3–14. London: Routledge.

Michaels, Axel. 2019. "Lost in Transhimalayan Transculturality: Opium, Horses and an Englishman between China, Tibet and Nepal." In *China and the World—the World and China: Essays in Honor of Rudolf G. Wagner*, edited by Barbara Mittler et al., 79–88. Gossenberg: OSTASIEN Verlag.

Michaels, Axel. 2023. Review of Michael Witzel, *The Rājyābhiṣeka Manual for the Coronation of King Birendra of Nepal (1975). Introduction and Facsimile Edition.* (Cambridge, London: Harvard University.

Department of South Asian Studies (Harvard Oriental Series, 100). 2022. *Indo-Iranian Journal* 66, 385–394.

Michaels, Axel. Forthcoming. "Between Love and Power. The Dharma Drama of King Raṇa Bahādura Śāha (1775–1806)." In *Dharma in the Himalaya*, edited by Domenico Francavilla, Axel Michaels, and Florinda de Simini. Torino: Torino: Comitato per la Publicazione del Corpus Juris Sanscriticum.

Michaels, Axel, Cornelia Vogelsanger, and Annette Wilke, eds. 1996. *Wild Goddesses in India and Nepal: Proceedings of an International Symposium in Berne and Zurich, November 1994.* Bern: Peter Lang.

Michaels, Axel, Manik Bajracharya, Niels Gutschow, Madeleine Herren, Bernd Schneidmüller, Gerald Schwedler, and Astrid Zotter. 2016. "Nepalese History in A European Experience: A Case Study in Transcultural Historiography." *History and Theory* 55 (2): 210–32.

Michaels, Axel, and Govinda Tandon. 2017. *Paśupatikṣetra: A Historical Inventory.* Kathmandu: Himal Books.

Michaud, Jean, ed. 2010. "Zomia and Beyond." *Journal of Global History* 5 (2): 187–214.

Miehe, Georg, and Colin Pendry, eds. 2015. *Nepal: An Introduction to the Natural History, Ecology and Human Environment of the Himalayas: A Companion to the Flora of Nepal.* Edinburgh: Royal Botanic Garden.

Mirnig, Nina. 2013. "Favoured by the Venerable Lord Paśupati: Tracing the Rise of a New Tutelary Deity in Epigraphica Expressions of Power in Early Medieval Nepal." *Indo-Iranian Journal* 56 (3–4): 325–47.

Mirnig, Nina. 2016. "Early Strata of Śaivism in the Kathmandu Valley: Śivaliṅga Pedestal Inscriptions from 466–645 CE." *Indo-Iranian Journal* 59: 309–62.

Mishra, Tara Nanda. 2000. "Dated Figure of King Jayavarma: The Tradition of Figure Making and the Historical Importance of This Discovery." *Ancient Nepal* 146: 1–23.

Mishra, Tirtha P. 2003. "Nepalese in Tibet: A Case Study of Nepalese Half-Breeds (1856–1956)." *CNSt* 30 (1): 1–18.

Mitra, Rajendra Lal. [1882] 1981. *The Sanskrit Buddhist Literature of Nepal.* Reprint. New Delhi: Cosmo Publications.

Mocko, Anne T. 2016. *Demoting Vishnu: Ritual, Politics, and the Unravelling of Nepal's Hindu Monarchy.* New York: Oxford University Press.

Montgomery, Carina. 1998. "The Gurkhas and Colonial Knowledge: Habitat, Masculinity and the Making of a 'Martial Race,' c. 1760–1820." PhD dissertation, University of Calgary.

Moran, Arik. 2018. *Kingship and Polity on the Himalayan Borderland: The Reformulation of Rajput Identities during the Early Colonial Encounter*. Amsterdam: Amsterdam University Press.

Mukherji, Purna Chandra. 1969. *A Report on a Tour of Exploration of the Antiquities of Kapilavastu, Tarai of Nepal*. Delhi: Indological Bookhouse.

Müller[-Böker], Ulrike. 1981. *Thimi: Social and Economic Studies on a Newar Settlement in the Kathmandu Valley*. Giessen: Selbstverlag des Geographischen Instituts der Justus Liebig-Universität.

Müller[-Böker], Ulrike. 1981–82. "Pottery-Making in Thimi." *JNRC* 5–6: 177–91.

Müller, Ulrike. 1999. *The Chitawan Tharus in Southern Nepal: An Ethnoecological Approach*. Kathmandu, Stuttgart: Franz Steiner.

Mulmi, Amish Raj. 2017. "Why Did the British Not Colonize Nepal?" *The Record* 1.10.2017; https://www.recordnepal.com/wire/features/why-did-the-british-not-colonize-nepal/ (accessed December 10, 2017).

Mumford, Stan Royal. 1989. *Himalayan Dialogue: Tibetan Lamas and Gurung Shamans in Nepal*. Madison: University of Wisconsin Press.

Nepālī, Chittarañjana. 1956 (VS 2013). *General Bhīmasena Thāpā ra Tatkālin Nepāla*. Kathmandu: Nepal Cultural Association.

Nepālī, Jñānamaṇi. 1983 (VS 2040). *Nepāla Nirukta*. Kathmandu: Nepāla Rājakīya Prajñā-Pratiṣṭhāna.

Nepali, Gopal Singh. 1965. *The Newars: An Ethno-Sociological Study of a Himalayan Community*. Bombay: United Asia Publications.

Ogura, Kiyoko. 1990. *Kathmandu Spring: The People's Movement of 1990*. Kathmandu: Himal Books.

Oldfield, Henry Ambrose. 1880. *Sketches from Nipal, Historical and Descriptive, with Anecdotes of the Court Life and Wild Sports of the Country*. 2 vols. London: W.H. Allen.

Oliphant, Laurence. 1852. *A Journey to Katmandu: The Capital of Nepaul*. London: John Murray.

Onta, Pratyoush. 1996a. "Ambivalence Denied: The Making of Rastriya Itihas in Panchayat Era Textbooks." *CNSt* 23 (1): 213–54.

Onta, Pratyoush. 1996b. "Creating a Brave Nepali Nation in British India: The Rhetoric of Jati Improvement, Rediscovery of Bhanubhakta and the Writing of Bir History." *SINHS* 1 (1): 37–76.

Onta, Pratyoush. 1997. Review of *The Gurkha Connection: A History of the Gurkha Recruitment in the British Army* (Jaipur 1994). *Modern Asian Studies* 31 (2): 445–48.

Onta, Pratyoush. 2003. "The Death of a People's Historian: Mahesh Chandra Regmi (1929–2003)." *Himāl Southasian* 16 (8): 46–50.

Onta, Pratyoush. [2013] 2017. *Bibliography of Writings by Mahesh Chandra Regmi and a List of Reviews of Regmi's Books*. Kathmandu: Martin Chautari.

Oppitz, Michael. 1968. *Geschichte und Sozialordnung der Sherpa*. Innsbruck and Munich: Universitäts-Verlag Wagner.

Oppitz, Michael. 1974. "Myths and Facts: Reconsidering Some Data concerning the Clan History of the Sherpas." *Kailash* 2 (1–2): 121–32.

Oppitz, Michael. 1986. "Die Trommel und das Buch: Eine kleine und die große Tradition." In *Formen kulturellen Wandels und andere Beiträge zur Erforschung des Himālaya*, edited by Bernhard Kölver, 53–126. Sankt Augustin: VGH Wissenschaftsverlag.

Oppitz, Michael. 1991. *Onkels Tochter, keine sonst: Heiratsbündnis und Denkweise einer Lokalkultur des Himalaya*. Frankfurt am Main: Suhrkamp.

Oppitz, Michael. 1997. "The Bull, the Ox, the Cow and the Yak: Meat Division in the Himalaya." In *Les habitants du toit du Monde: Études recueillies en hommage à Alexander W. MacDonald*, edited by Samten Karmay und Philippe Sagant, 515–42. Nanterre: Société d'ethnologie.

Oppitz, Michael. 2007. *Trommeln der Schamanen*. Zurich: Völkerkundemuseum.

Oppitz, Michael. 2013. *Morphologie der Schamanentrommel*. 2 vols. Zurich: Edition Voldemeer and Springer.

Ortner, Sherry B. 1978. *Sherpas through Their Rituals*. Cambridge: Cambridge University Press.

Ortner, Sherry B. 1989. *High Religion: A Cultural and Political History of Sherpa Buddhism*. Princeton, NJ: Princeton University Press.

Ortner, Sherry B. 1999. *Life and Death on Mt. Everest: Sherpas and Himalayan Mountaineering*. Princeton, NJ: Princeton University Press.

Owens, Bruce. 1989. "The Politics of Divinity in the Kathmandu Valley: The Festival of Bungadya/Rato Matsyendranath." PhD dissertation, Columbia University.

Owens, Bruce. 2011. "Obituary for John K. Locke." *Himalaya, the Journal of the Association for Nepal and Himalayan Studies* 30 (1): 134–35.

Owens, Bruce. 2014. "Innovation in Traditions of Transformation: A Preliminary Survey of a Quarter Century of Change in the Bāhāḥs and Bahis of the Kathmandu Valley." *South Asia: Journal of South Asian Studies* 37 (1): 130–55.

Pal, Pratapaditya. 1970. *Vaiṣṇava Iconology in Nepal: A Study in Art and Religion*. Calcutta: Asiatic Society.

Panday, Devendraraj. 1999. *Nepal's Failed Development: Reflections on the Mission and Maladies*. Kathmandu: Nepal South Asia Centre.

Pandey, Ram Nivas. 1970. "The Ancient and Medieval History of Western Nepal." *Ancient Nepal* 10: 53–62 and 11: 45–60.

Pandey, Ram Nivas. 1997. *Making of Modern Nepal: A Study of History, Art and Culture of the Principalities of Western Nepal*. New Delhi: Nirala Publications.

Pant, Mohan. 2002. *A Study of the Spatial Formation of Kathmandu Valley Towns: The Case of Thimi*. Kyoto: Kyoto University.

Panta, Dineśa Rāja. 1986 (VS 2043)–1988 (VS 2045). *Gorkhāko Itihāsa*. 3 vols. Kathmandu: D.R. Panta.

Panta, Dineśa Rāja. 1969 (VS 2026). "Svāmīmahārāja Raṇabahādura Śāhako VS 1862 ko bandobasta." *Pūrṇimā* 24 (6.4): 238–67.

Panta, Dinesh Raj (Pant, Dinesh Raj). 1997. "The Institution of Slavery in Nepal and its Analysis Based on the Dharmaśāstras." In *Recht, Staat und Verwaltung im klassischen Indien*, edited by Bernhard Kölver, 135–58. Munich: R. Oldenbourg Verlag.

Panta, Dineśa Rāja. 2016 (VS 2073). *Śrī 5 Pṛthvīnārāyaṇa Sāhako Divyopadeśa ra Saṃkṣipta Jīvanī*. Kathmandu: Mañjarī Pablikeśana.

Panta, Maheśa Rāja. 1977 (VS 2024). "Mahendra Mallako viṣayako kehī kurā." *Pūrṇimā* 38: 74–89.

Panta, Maheśa Rāja (Pant, Mahes Raj). 1979. *On Sanskrit Education*. Kathmandu: the author.

Panta, Maheśa Rāja. 1987 (VS 2044). "Da. Gopālarājavaṃśāvalī sarasarī herdā." *Pūrṇimā* 72: 1–65.

Panta, Maheśa Rāja. 1984 (VS 2040). "Būḍhākājī Amarasiṃha Thāpā paraloka bhaeko kurā parekā, pāñcavaṭā tatkālika Aprakāśita patra." *Pūrṇimā* 58: 45–61.

Panta, Maheśa Rāja (Pant, Mahes Raj). 2002a. "Documents from the Regmi Research Collections I." *Ādarśa* 2: 61–152.

Panta, Maheśa Rāja (Pant, Mahes Raj). 2002b. "A Step toward a Historical Seismicity of Nepal." *Adarśa* 2: 29–60.

Panta, Maheśa Rāja. 2003 (VS 2060). "Prācīna kālamā nepālako vistārako viṣayamā euṭā nayā̃ lekha herdā." *Pūrṇimā* 112: 1–10.

Panta, Maheśa Rāja (Pant, Mahes Raj). 2009. "Towards a History of the Khasa Empire." In *Bards and Mediums: History, Culture and Politics in the Central Himalayan Kingdoms*, edited by Marie Lecomte-Tilouine, 293–326. Almora: Almora Book Depot.

Panta, Maheśa Rāja. n.d. (2020). *Nepālī Itihāsako Pariveśa: Kehī Aitihāsika ra Masījīvī*. Kathmandu: the author, no date [a collection of previous articles].

Pant, Mahes Raj, and Philip H. Pierce. 1989. *Administrative Documents of the Shah Dynasty Concerning Mustang and Its Periphery, 1789–1844 A.D.* Bonn: VGH Wissenschaftsverlag.

Pant, Mahes Raj, and Aishvarya Dhar Sharma. 1977. *The Two Earliest Copper-Plate Inscriptions from Nepal*. Kathmandu: Nepal Research Centre.

Panta, Naya Rāja. 1965 (VS 2022). "Licchavikālakā abhilekhamā dekhāparekhā 55 sammakā saṃvatkā aṅkako nirṇaya." *Pūrṇimā* 7: 1–7.

Parajuli, Lokranjan, Devendra Uprety, and Pratyoush Onta, eds. 2021. *School Education in Nepal: History and Politics of Governance and Reforms*. Kathmandu: Martin Chautari.

Pauḍyāla, Vīṇā. 2005 (VS 2062). *Kāṭhmāṇḍau Upatyakākā Viṣṇuvibhava Mūrti ra Citraharū*. Kathmandu: Tribhuvan University.

Peissel, Michael. 1972. *Tiger for Breakfast: The Story of Boris of Kathmandu; Adventurer, Big Game Hunter, and Host of Nepal's Famous Royal Hotel*. Bombay: Allied Publishers.

Pemble, John. 1971. *The Invasion of Nepal: John Company at War*. Oxford: Clarendon Press.

Petech, Luciano. 1952–56. *I Missionari Italiani nel Tibet e nel Nepal*. Vols. I–VII. Rome: Libreria dello Stato.

Petech, Luciano. 1961. "The Chronology of the Early Inscriptions of Nepal." *East and West* 12 (4): 227–32.

Petech, Luciano. 1984. *Mediaeval History of Nepal (c. 750–1480)*. 2nd rev. ed. Roma: Instituto Italiano per il Medio ed Estremo Oriente.

Petech, Luciano. 1996. "Chinese and Tibetan Materials on the Nepalese Quinquennial Missions." In *Change and Continuity: Studies in the Nepalese Culture of the Kathmandu Valley*, edited by Siegfried Lienhard, 167–88. Torino: Edizioni dell'Orso.

Pfaff-Czarnecka, Joanna. 1989. *Macht und rituelle Reinheit: Hinduistisches Kastenwesen und ethnische Beziehungen im Entwicklungsprozess Nepals*. Gruesch: Verlag Rüegger.

Pfaff-Czarnecka, Joanna. 1999. "Debating the State of the Nation: Ethnicization of Politics in Nepal – A Position Paper." In *Ethnic Futures: The State and Identity Politics in Asia*, edited by Joanna Pfaff-Czarnecka et al., 41–97. New Delhi, Thousand Oaks: Sage Publications.

Pfaff-Czarnecka, Joanna. 2004. "Demokratisierung und Nation-Building in geteilten Gesellschaften." In *Nation-Building: Ein Schlüsselkonzept für friedliche Konfliktbearbeitung?*, edited by Jochen Hippler, 4–69. Bonn: Dietz.

Pfaff-Czarnecka, Joanna. 2011. "Frictions, Frames and Fragments: Belonging and Ethnic Boundary-Making in Nepal's Contested Ritual Communication." In *Ritual, Conflict and Consensus: Case Studies from Asia and Europe*, edited by Gabriela Kiliánová, Christian Janoda, and Michaela Ferencová, 15–30. Vienna: Verlag der Österreichischen Akademie der Wissenschaften.

Pfaff-Czarnecka, Joanna. 2023. "The Language of Ethnicity: Indigenous Narratives in Nepal soon after the Peoples' War (1996–2006)." *International Quarterly for Asian Studies* 54 (3): 215-35.

Pfaff-Czarnecka, Joanna, and Gérard Toffin, eds. 2011. *The Politics of Belonging in the Himalayas: Local Attachments and Boundary Dynamics*. Los Angeles: Sage.

Pignède, Berbard. 1993. *The Gurungs: A Himalayan Population of Nepal*. Translated, edited, and annotated by Sarah Harrison and Alan Macfarlane. Kathmandu: Ratna Pustak Bhandar.

Plachta, Nadine, and Subas Tamang. 2019. "Labor Geographies: Uneven Infrastructures in Nepal's Rana Period." *Roadsides* 2: 25–33; https://doi.org/10.26034/roadsides-20190028.

Pohle, Perdita. 2000a. "Felsbilder und Wüstungen." *Archäologie in Deutschland* 1: 12–17.

Pohle, Perdita, 2000b. *Historisch-geographische Untersuchungen im Tibetischen Himalaya: Felsbilder und Wüstungen als Quelle zur Besiedlungs- und Kulturgeschichte von Mustang (Nepal)*. Giessen: Geographisches Intitut.

Pohle, Perdita. 2003. "Petroglyphs and Abandoned Sites in Mustang: A Unique Source for Research in Cultural History and Historical Geography." *Ancient Nepal* 153: 1–14.

Pokhrela, Śyāmaraja, Mohananātha Pāṃḍe, Bāburāma Nepāla, Kiśoramaṇi, and Suśīlakumāra Pokhrela. 1953 (VS 2010). "Kāntipurabhūpasya Śrī Pratāpamallasya Śilālekhaḥ [Vi. Saṃ. 1727]." *Saṃskṛta -Sandeśa* 1 (10–12): 55–58.

Pollock, Sheldon. 2006. *The Languages of the Gods in the World of Men: Sanskrit, Culture, and Power in Premodern India*. Berkeley: The University of California Press.

Pradhan, Kumar L. 1984. *A History of Nepali Literature*. New Delhi: Sahitya Akademi.

Pradhan, Kumar L. 1992. "Modern Nepali Literature." In *Modern Indian Literature: An Anthology*. Vol. 1: *Surveys and Poems*, edited by K. M. George, 185–96. New Delhi: Sahitya Akademi.

Pradhan, Kumar L. 2001. *Brian Hodgson at the Kathmandu Residency*. Delhi: Spectrum Publications.

Pradhan, Kumar L. [1991] 2009. *The Gorkha Conquests: The Process and Consequences of the Unification of Nepal, with Particular Reference to Eastern Nepal*. Kathmandu: Himal Books.

Pradhan, Kumar L. 2012. *Thapa Politics in Nepal: With Special Reference to Bhim Sen Thapa, 1806–1839*. New Delhi: Concept Publishing.

Pradhan, Narendra M. B., A. Christy Williams, and Maheshwar Dhakal. 2011. "Current Status of Asian Elephants in Nepal." *Gajah* 35: 87–92.

Prasad, Ishwari. 1996. *The Life and Times of Maharaja Juddha Shumsher Jung Bahadur Rana of Nepal*. New Delhi: Ashish Publishing House.

Prashant, Jha. 2015. *Battles of the New Republic: A Contemporary History of Nepal*. London: Hurst.

Pruscha, Carl, ed. 1975. *Kathmandu Valley: The Preservation of Physical Environment and Cultural Heritage, a Protective Inventory*. 2 vols. Vienna: Anton Schroll.

Rai, Dinesh. 2005. "Remembering Boris: As Inger Looks Back." *ECS Nepal Magazine* (November): 50–53.

Raj, Prakash A. 2001. *"Kay gardeko?" The Royal Massacre in Nepal*. New Delhi: Rupa and Co.

Raj, Yogesh. 2012. *Expedition to Nepal Valley: The Journal of Captain Kinloch (August 26–October 17, 1767)*. Kathmandu: Jagadamba Prakashan.

Raj, Yogesh. 2014. "Loss of Epistemic Diversity: Academic Historiography in Post-1950 Nepal." *SINHS* 19 (1): 1–39.

Raj, Yogesh, Deepak Aryal, and Shamik Mishra. 2016. "Documents Related to the Early Hospitals in Nepal." *SINHS* 21 (2): 347–400.

Raj, Yogesh, and Bhaskar Gautam. 2015. *Courage in Chaos: Early Rescue and Relief after the April Earthquake*. Kathmandu: Martin Chautari.

Raj, Yogesh, and Pratyoush Onta. 2014. *The State of History Education and Research in Nepal*. Kathmandu: Martin Chautari.

Ram, Rajendra. 1977. *A History of Buddhism in Nepal, A.D. 704–1396*. Patna: Janabhāratī Prakāśana.

Ramble, Charles. 2008. *The Navel of the Demoness: Tibetan Buddhism and Civil Religion in Highland Nepal*. Oxford: Oxford University Press.

Ramble, Charles, and Michael Vinding. 1987. "The Bem-chag Village Record and the Early History of Mustang." *Kailash* 13 (1–2): 5–47.

Rana, Brahma Shumsher Jung Bahadur. [1934] 2013. *The Great Earthquake in Nepal, 1934 A.D.* Translated by Kesar Lall. Kathmandu: Himal Books.

Rana, Prabhakar S. J. B., Pashupati S. J. B. Rana, and Gautam S. J. B. Rana. 2003. *The Ranas of Nepal*. New Delhi: Timeless Books.

Rana, Pramode Shamshere. 1978. *Rana Nepal: An Insider's View*. Kathmandu: Mrs. R. Rana.

Rana, Pramode Shamshere. 2004. *Rāṇāśāhasaṅko Bṛttānta*. Kathmandu: R. Rana.

Rana, Pudma Jung Bahadur. 1909. *Life of Maharaja Sir Jung Bahadur of Nepal*. Allahabad: Pioneer Press.

Rana, Sagar S. J. B. 2018. *Singha Durbar: Rise and Fall of the Rana Regime of Nepal*. 4th ed. New Delhi: Rupa.

Rankin, Katharine N. 2004. *The Cultural Politics of Markets: Economic Liberalization and Social Change in Nepal*. London: Pluto Press, 2004.

Reed, Horace B., and Mary J. Reed. 1968. *Nepal in Transition: Educational Innovation*. Pittsburgh: University of Pittsburgh Press.

Regmi, D. R. 1960. *Ancient Nepal*. Calcutta: Mukhopadhyay.

Regmi, D. R. 1965–66. *Medieval Nepal*. 4 vols. Calcutta: Mukhopadhyay.

Regmi, D. R. 1975. *Modern Nepal*. 2 vols. Calcutta: Mukhopadhyay.

Regmi, D. R. 1983. *Inscriptions of Ancient Nepal*. 3 vols. New Delhi: Abhinav Publications.

Regmi, Jagadish Chandra. 1982a (VS 2039). *Nepālako Dhārmika Itihāsa (Prācīna ra Madhyakāla)*. Kathmandu: Ratna Pustak Bhandar.

Regmi, Jagadish Chandra, ed. 1982b. "Malla Coins." *Nepal Antiquary* - Golden Jubilee Special Issue 46–50 (September).

Regmi, Mahesh Chandra. [1972] 1999. *A Study in the Nepali Economic History, 1768–1846*. Delhi: Adroit Publishers.

Regmi, Mahesh Chandra. 1975. "Landholding, Trade, and Revenue Collection in Solukhumbu." RRS 7 (7): 122–26.

Regmi, Mahesh Chandra. 1976. *Landownership in Nepal*. Berkeley: University of California Press.

Regmi, Mahesh Chandra. 1978a. *Land Tenure and Taxation in Nepal*. Kathmandu: Ratna Pustak Bhandar (Revised reprint of: Vol. 1: *The State as Landlord: Raikar Tenure*; Vol. 2: *Land Grant System: Birta Tenure*; Vol. 3: *The Jagir, Rakam, and Kipat Tenure Systems*; Vol. 4: *Religious and Charitable Land Endowment: Guthi Tenure*. Berkeley: Institute of International Studies 1963, 1964, 1965, and 1968).

Regmi, Mahesh Chandra. 1978b. *Thatched Huts and Stucco Palaces: Peasants and Landlords in 19th-Century Nepal*. New Delhi: Vikas.

Regmi, Mahesh Chandra. 1982. "Currency System in Nineteenth-Century Nepal." RRS 14 (5): 73–75.

Regmi, Mahesh Chandra. 1988. *An Economic History of Nepal, 1846–1901*. Varanasi: Nath Publishing House.

Regmi, Mahesh Chandra. 1995. *Kings and Political Leaders of the Gorkhali Empire, 1768–1814*. Hyderabad: Orient Longman.

Regmi, Mahesh Chandra. 1999. *Imperial Gorkha: An Account of Gorkhali Rule in Kumaun (1791–1815)*. Delhi: Adroit Publishers.

Rhodes, Nicholas Gervase. 1989. "The Monetization of Nepal in the 17th century." *Kailash* 10: 113–17.

Rhodes, Nicholas Gervase, K. Gabrisch, and P. D. R. Valdetaro. 1989. *The Coinage of Nepal from the Earliest Times until 1911*. London: Royal Numismatic Society.

Riaz, Ali, and Subho Basu. 2010. *Paradise Lost? State Failure in Nepal*. Lanham, MD: Lexington Books.

Riccardi, Theodore Jr. 1977. "The Royal Edicts of King Rama Shah of Gorkha." *Kailash* 5 (1): 29–65.

Riccardi, Theodore Jr. 1980. "Buddhism in Ancient and Early Medieval Nepal." In *Studies in the History of Buddhism*, edited by A. K. Narain, 365–281. New Delhi: R. Publishing.

Riccardi, Theodore Jr. 1989. "The Inscription of King Manadeva at Changu Narayan." *Journal of the American Oriental Society* 109 (4): 611–20.

Risley, H. H. [1896] 1992. "Introduction." In *Notes on Nepal* by Eden Vansittart, iii–ix. New Delhi: Asian Educational Services.

Roerich, George N. [1949] 1996. *The Blue Annals*. New Delhi: Motilal Banarsidass.

Rookmaaker, Kees, Barbara Nelson, and Darrell Dorrington. 2005. "The Royal Hunt of Tiger and Rhinoceros in the Nepalese Terai in 1911." *Pachyderm* 38: 89–97.

Rose, Leo. 1971. *Nepal: Strategy for Survival*. Berkeley: University of California Press.

Rosser, Colin. 1979. "Social Mobility in the Newar Caste System." In *The Anthropology of Nepal*, edited by Christoph von Fürer-Haimendorf, 68–139. Warminster: Aris and Philips.

Rupakheti, Sanjog. 2016. "Reconsidering State-Society Relations in South Asia: A Himalayan Case Study." *Himalaya, the Journal of the Association for Nepal and Himalayan Studies* 35 (2): 73–86.

Rupakheti, Sanjog. 2017. "Beyond Dharmashastras and Weberian Modernity: Law and State Making in Nineteenth-Century Nepal." In *Law Addressing Diversity: Pre-Modern Europe and India in Comparison (13th–18th Centuries)*, edited by T. Ertl and G. Kruijtzer, 169–96. Berlin: de Gruyter and Oldenbourg.

Sagant, Philippe. 1982. "L'hindouisation des Limbu." In *Les royaumes de l'Himālaya: Histoire et civilisation*, edited by A. W. Macdonald, 208–40. Paris: Imprimerie Nationale.

Sagant, Philippe. 1996. *The Dozing Shaman: The Limbus of Eastern Nepal*. Oxford: Oxford University Press.

Sakai, Tetsuya, Tomohiro Takagawa, Ananta P. Gajurel, Hideo Tabata, Nobuo Ooi, and Bishal N. Upreti. 2006. "Discovery of Sediments Indicating Rapid Lake-Level Fall in the Late Pleistocene Gokarna Formation, Kathmandu Valley, Nepal: Implication for Lake Terrace Formation." *The Quaternary Research* 45 (April): 99–112.

Sakya, Hemraj. 1970. *Medieval Nepal (Colophons and Inscriptions)*. Kathmandu: T. R. Vaidya.

de Sales, Anne. 2000. *Je suis né de vos jeux de tambours: La religion chamanique des Magar du Nord*. Nanterre: Societé d'ethnologie.

de Sales, Anne. 2015. "Identity Politics and the Maoist People's War in Nepal." In *Emancipatory Politics: A Critique*, edited by Stephan Feuchtwang and Alpa Shah, Chapter 6. Open Anthropology Cooperative Press; http://openanthcoop.net/press/emancipatory-politics-a-critique/ (accessed May 26, 2020).

Salisbury, Richard, and Elizabeth Hawley. 2011. *The Himalaya by the Numbers: A Statistical Analysis of Mountaineering in the Nepal Himalaya*. Kathmandu: Vajra Publications.

Sanderson, Alexis. 2009. "The Śaiva Age: An Explanation of the Rise and Dominance of Śaivism during the Early Medieval Period." In *Genesis and Development of Tantrism*, edited by Shingo Einoo, 41–349. Tokyo: Institute of Oriental Culture, University of Tokyo.

Sanderson, Alexis. 2015. "Tolerance, Exclusivity, Inclusivity, and Persecution in Indian Religion during the Early Mediaeval Period." In *Honoris Causa: Essays in Honour of Aveek Sarkar*, edited by J. Makinson, 155–224. London: Allen Lane.

Schendel, Willem van. 2002. "Geographies of Knowing, Geographies of Ignorance: Jumping Scale in Southeast Asia." *Environment and Planning D: Society and Space* 20: 647–68.

Schlagintweit-Sakülünski, Hermann von. 1869–1880. *Reisen in Indien und Hochasien: Eine Darstellung der Landschaft, der Cultur und Sitten der Bewohner in Verbindung mit klimatischen und geologischen Verhältnissen*. 4 vols. Jena: Hermann Costenoble.

Schlemmer, Grégoire. 2004. "New Past for the Sake of a Better Future: Re-inventing the History the Kirant in East Nepal." *EBHR* 25–26: 119–44.

Schneidmüller, Bernd. 2018. "Verklärte Macht und verschränkte Herrschaft: Vom Charme vormoderner Andersartigkeit." In *Macht und Herrschaft transkulturell: Vormoderne Konfigurationen und Perspektiven der Forschung*, edited by M. Becher, S. Conermann, and L. Dohmen, 91–121. Göttingen: V&R unipress GmbH.

Schrader, Heiko. 1988. *Trading Patterns in the Nepal Himalayas*. Saarbrücken: Verlag für Entwicklungspolitik.

Schuh, Dieter, et al. 1999. *Archaeological, Historical and Geographical Reports on Research Activities in the Nepal-Tibetan Border Area of Mustang During the Years 1992 and 1998*. Bonn: VGH Wissenschaftsverlag.

Scott, James C. 2009. *The Art of Not Being Governed: An Anarchist History of Upland Southeast Asia*. New Haven, CT: Yale University Press.

Sever, Adrian. [1989]. 1993. *Nepal under the Ranas*. 2nd ed. New Delhi: Oxford and IBH Publishing Co.

Shaha, Rishikesh. 1990a. *Modern Nepal: A Political History, 1769–1955*. 2 vols. New Delhi: Manohar.

Shaha, Rishikesh. 1990b. *Politics in Nepal, 1980–1990*. New Delhi: Manohar.

Shaha, Rishikesh. 1992. *Ancient and Medieval Nepal*. New Delhi: Manohar.

Shakya, Min Bahādur, and Shanta Harsha Bajracharya. 2010. *Svayambhū Purāṇa*. Nepal: Nagarjuna Institute of Exact Methods.

Shakya, Milan Ratna. 2006. *Gaṇeśa in Medieval Nepal*. New Delhi: Rupa.

Sharkey, Gregory. 2009. "Scholar of the Newars: The Life and Work of John K. Locke." *SINHS* 14 (2): 423–40.

Sharma, Dilli Raj. 2012. *Heritage of the Western Nepal: Art and Architecture*. Kirtipur and Kathmandu: Centre for Nepal and Asian Studies, Tribhuvan University.

Sharma, Nagendra. 1976. *Folk Tales of Nepal*. Reprint. New Delhi: Macmillan, 1990.

Sharma, Pitamber. 2014. *Some Aspects of Nepal's Social Demography: Census 2011 Update*. Kathmandu: Himal Books.

Sharma, Prayag Raj. 1972. *Preliminary Study of the Art and Architecture of the Karnali Basin, West Nepal*. Paris: Centre National de la Recherche Scientifique.

Sharma, Prayag Raj. 1983. "The Land System of the Licchavis of Nepal." *Kailash* 10 (1–2): 11–63.

Sharma, Prayag Raj. 2004. *The State and Society in Nepal: Historical Foundation and Contemporary Trends*. Kathmandu: Himal Books.

Sharma, Prayag Raj. 2008. "Nation-Building, Multi-Ethnicity, and the Hindu State." In *Nationalism and Ethnicity in a Hindu Kingdom: The Politics of Culture in Contemporary Nepal*, edited by David Gellner, Joanna Pfaff-Czarnecka, and John Whelpton, 471–532. Reprint. Kathmandu: Vajra Publications.

Sharma, Prayag Raj, and Kamal P. Malla. 1994. "Dhanavajra Vajracharya (1932–1994): A Tribute." *Himalayan Research Bulletin* 14: 2–5.

Shastri, Hara Prasad, ed. 1905–6. *Catalogue of Palm-leaf and Selected Paper Manuscripts belonging to the Durbar Library, Nepal*. 2 vols. Calcutta: Asiatic Society of Bengal.

Shastri, Hara Prasad. 1917–57. *A Descriptive Catalogue of the Sanskrit Manuscripts in the Government Collection of the Asiatic Society of Bengal*. Vol. I–XIV. Calcutta: Asiatic Society of Bengal.

Shneiderman, Sara. 2010. "Are the Central Himalayas in Zomia? Some Scholarly and Political Considerations across Time and Space." *Journal of Global History* 5 (2): 289–312.

Shrestha, Bal Gopal. 2007. "Castes among the Newars: The Debate between Colin Rosser and Declan Quigley on the Status of Shrestha." *EBHR* 31: 10–29.

Shrestha, Bal Gopal. 2012. *The Sacred Town of Sankhu: The Anthropology of Newar Ritual, Religion and Society in Nepal*. Newcastle upon Tyne, UK: Cambridge Scholars Publishing.

Shrestha, Bal Gopal. 2015. *The Newars of Sikkim: Reinventing Language, Culture, and Identity in the Diaspora*. Kathmandu: Vajra Books.

Shrestha, Banshi. 2006. *RN Joshi: Widening the Horizon of Nepalese Art*. Patan: Park Gallery.

Shrestha, Ramesh. 2007. *Nepalese Coins and Banknotes*. Kirtipur: Tribhuvan University.

Shrestha, Sanjukta. 2018. "Jung Bahadur's Love for British Guns." *Kathmandu Post*, January 20, 2018; http://kathmandupost.ekantipur.com/news/2018-01-20/jung-bahadurs-love-for-british-guns.html (accessed January 10, 2020).

Shrestha, Sukrasagar. VS 2067 (2016). "'Nāka Kāṭekai Ho' (Indeed the noses were cut off)." *Himal Khabar*, Jeṣṭha 26, 2067 (June 8, 2016); http://archive.himalkhabar.com/129497 (accessed February 1, 2017).

Shrestha, Tek Bahadur. 2009. "Dullu-Dailekh as Independent Principalities." In *Bards and Mediums: History, Culture and Politics in the Central Himalayan Kingdoms*, edited by Marie Lecomte-Tilouine, 277–92. Almora: Almora Book Depot.

Shrestha, Tulsi Narayan. 2005. *Nepalese Administration: A Historical Perspective*. Kathmandu: Ratna Pustak Bhandar.

Siddika, Shamina. 1993. *Muslims of Nepal*. Kathmandu: Gazzala Sikkika.

Sijapati, B., and Limbu, A. 2012. *Governing Labour Migration in Nepal: An Analysis of Existing Policies and Institutional Mechanisms*. Kathmandu: Himal Books.

Sijapati, Megan Adamson. 2011. *Islamic Revival in Nepal: Religion and a New Nation*. London and New York: Routledge.

de Siminis, Florinda. 2016. "Śivadharma Manuscripts from Nepal and the Making of a Śaiva Corpus." In *One-Volume Libraries: Composite and Multiple-Text Manuscripts*, edited by Michael Friedrich and Cosima Schwarke, 233–86. Berlin: de Gruyter.

Singh, Shyam Marayan. 1922. *History of Tirhut: From the Earliest Times to the End of the Nineteenth Century*. Calcutta: Baptist Mission Press.

Sinha, Gokul. 1997. "Nepali." In *Medieval Indian Literature: An Anthology*. Vol. 1: *Surveys and Selections*, edited by K. Ayyappa Paniker, 84–93. New Delhi: Sahitya Akademi.

Slusser, Mary Shepherd. 1982. *Nepal Mandala: A Cultural Study of the Kathmandu Valley*. 2 vols. Princeton, NJ: Princeton University Press.

Slusser, Mary Shepherd. 2010. *The Antiquity of Nepalese Wood Carving: A Reassessment*. Seattle: University of Washington Press.

Smith, E. D. 1997. *Valour: A History of the Gurkhas*. Gloucestershire: Spellmount.

Smythies, Olive. 1961. *Ten Thousand Miles on Elephants*. London: Seeley Service.

Snellgrove, David. 1987. *Indo-Tibetan Buddhism: Indian Buddhists and Their Tibetan Successors*. 2 vols. Boston: Shambala.

Sonntag, S. K. 1995. "Ethnolinguistic Identity and Language Policy in Nepal." *Nationalism and Ethnic Politics* 1: 108–20.

Steinmann, Brigitte. 1987. *Les Tamang du Népal: Usages et Religion, Religion de l'Usage*. Paris: Éditions Recherche sur les Civilisations.

Stiller, Ludwig F. [1973] 1975. *The Rise of the House of Gorkha: A Study in the Unification of Nepal, 1768–1816*. New Delhi: Manjusri Publishing House. 2nd ed. Kathmandu: Ratna Pustak Bhandar.

Stiller, Ludwig F. 1976. *The Silent Cry: The People of Nepal, 1816–1839*. Kathmandu: Sahoyogi Press.

Stiller, Ludwig F., ed. 1981. *Letters from Kathmandu: The Kot Massacre*. Kirtipur: Tribhuvan University, Research Centre for Nepal and Asian Studies.

Stiller, Ludwig F. [1968] 1989. *Prithivinarayan Shah in the Light of Dibya Upadesh*. Kathmandu: Himalayan Book Centre.

Stiller, Ludwig F. 1993. *Nepal: Growth of a Nation*. Kathmandu: Human Resources Development Centre.

Strickland, Simon S. 2018. *Materials for the Study of Gurung Pe*. Volume I and II. Cambridge, MA: Harvard Oriental Series.

Stuparich, Eloisa. 2016. "Treading the Frontiers of Hinduness: Yogi Naraharinath in 20th Century Nepal." PhD dissertation, Cornell University.

Subba, Bhim. 2010. "Water, Nepal and India." In *State of Nepal*, edited by Kanak Mani Dixit and Shastri Ramachandrandaran, 235–52. 10th ed. Kathmandu: Himal Books.

Subedi, Abhi. 1978. *Nepali Literature: Background, and History*. Kathmandu: Sajha Prakashan.

Subedi, Madhusudan, and Devendra Uprety. 2014. *The State of Sociology and Anthropology: Teaching and Research in Nepal*. Kathmandu: Martin Chautari.

Tachikawa, Musashi. 2001. *Mother-Goddesses in Kathmandu*. Delhi: Adroit Publications.

Ṭaṇḍana, Govinda. 1985 (VS 2042). "Śrī Paśupatinātha Mandiramā Bājā Sambandhi Vyavasthā: Eka Carcā." *Śaiva-Bhūmi* 3 (2): 25–41.

Ṭaṇḍana, Govinda. 1996 and 1999. *Paśupatikṣetrako Sāṃskṛtika Adhyayana*. 2 vols. Kathmandu: Jharendra Ṣamśer Ja. Ba. Rā. tathā Mañju Rāṇā.

Thapa, Depak, ed. 2004. *Understanding the Maoist Movement in Nepal*. 2nd ed. Kathmandu: Martin Chautari.

Thapa, Dhruba Bar Singh. 1985. "The Legal System of Nepal." In *Modern Legal Systems Encyclopedia*, edited by K. R. Redden, vol. 9, 121–47. Buffalo, NY: William S. Hein.

Thapa, Ramesh Jung. 1967. *The Archives Movement and Nepal*. Kathmandu: Department of Archaeology, His Majesty's Government, Nepal.

Thapa, Shankar. 2000. *Historical Study of Agrarian Relations in Nepal, 1846–1951*. Delhi: Adroit Publications.

Tingey, Carol. 1990. *Heartbeat of Nepal: The Pañcai Bājā*. Kathmandu: Royal Nepal Academy.

Tingey, Carol. 1994. *Auspicious Music in a Changing Society: The Damai Musicians of Nepal*. London: School of Oriental and African Studies.

Tiwari, Sudarshan Raj. 2009. *Temples of the Kathmandu Valley*. Patan: Himal Books.

Tiwari, Sudarshan Raj. 2016. "Material Authenticity and Conservation Traditions in Nepal." In *Authenticity in Architectural Heritage Conservation: Discourses, Opinions, Experiences in Europe, South and East Asia*, edited by Katharina Weiler and Niels Gutschow, 169–84. Heidelberg: Springer.

Toffin, Gérard. 1984. *Société et Religion chez les Néwar du Népal*. Paris: Editions du Centre National de la Recherche Scientifique.

Toffin, Gérard, ed. 1993. *Nepal, Past and Present: Proceedings of the Franco-German Conference Art-et-Senans, June 1990*. Paris: CNRS Editions.

Toffin, Gérard. 2005. *From Kin to Caste: The Role of Guthis in Newar Society and Culture*. Lalitpur: Social Science Baha (Mahesh Chandra Regmi Lecture, 2005).

Toffin, Gérard. 2006. "Construction et transformation d'un ratha urbain Népalais: L'Indrajātrā de Katmandou." In *Rites hindous, transferts et transformations*, edited by G. Colas and G. Tarabout, 97–251. Collection *Purusārtha* 25. Paris: Éditions de l'EHESS.

Toffin, Gérard. 2007. *Newar Society: City, Village, Periphery*. Kathmandu: Himal Books.

Toffin, Gérard. 2012. "The Propagation of a Hindu Sect in India and Nepal: The Krishna-Praṇāmī Sampradāy." *South Asia: Journal of South Asian Studies* 34 (1): 1–30.

Toffin, Gérard. 2016. "Neither Statues nor Ritual: An Analysis of New Religious Movements and Therapists in Nepal." In *Religion, Secularism and Ethnicity in Contemporary Nepal*, edited by David N. Gellner, Sondra L. Hausner, and Chiara Letizia, 115–49. New Delhi: Oxford University Press.

Tree, Isabella. 2014a. "A House for the Living Goddess: On the Dual Identity of the Kumari Chen in Kathmandu." *South Asia: Journal of South Asian Studies* 37 (1): 156–78.

Tree, Isabella. 2014b. *The Living Goddess: A Journey into the Heart of Kathmandu*. New Delhi: Penguin.

Tucci, Giuseppe. 1956. *Preliminary Report on Two Scientific Expeditions in Nepal*. Rome: Instituto Italiano per il medio ed Extremo Oriente (IsMEO).

Tucci, Giuseppe. 1962. "The Wives of Sron btsan sgam po." *Oriens Extremus* 9 (1): 121–26.

Tucci, Giuseppe. [1953] 1982. *Journey to Mustang, 1952*. Kathmandu: Ratna Pustak Bhandar.

Tuker, Francis. 1957. *Gorkha: The Story of the Gurkhas of Nepal*. London: Constable.

Tuladhar, Prem Shanti. 2000. *Nepal Bhasa Sahityaya Itihas: History of Nepalbhasa Literature*. Kathmandu: Nepal Bhasa Academy.

Tuladhar-Douglas, Will. 2006. *Remaking Buddhism for Medieval Nepal: The Fifteenth-Century Reformation of Newar Buddhism*. London: Routledge.

Turner, Ralph Lilley. 1931. *A Comparative and Etymological Dictionary of the Nepali Language*. London: Routledge and Kegan.

Unbescheid, Günter. 1980. *Kānphaṭā: Untersuchungen zu Kult, Mythologie und Geschichte śivaitischer Tantriker in Nepal*. Wiesbaden: Franz Steiner.

Unsworth, Walt. 2000. *Everest: The Mountaineering History*. 3rd ed. London: Baton Wicks.

Upreti, Bishnu Raj. 2004. *The Price of Neglect: From Resource Conflict to Maoist Insurgency in the Himalayan Kingdom*. Kathmandu: Bhrikuti Academic Publications.

Uprety, Prem R. [1980] 1998. *Nepal-Tibet Relations, 1850–1930: Years of Hopes: Challenges and Frustrations*. 2nd ed. Kathmandu: Ratna Pustak Bhandar.

Uprety, Prem R. 1992. *Political Awakening in Nepal: The Search for a New Identity*. New Delhi: Commonwealth.

Uprety, Prem R. 1996. "Treaties between Nepal and Her Neighbors: A Historical Perspective." *Tribhuvan University Journal* 19 (1): 15–24.

Vaidya, Karunakar. 1986. *Buddhist Traditions and Culture of the Kathmandu Valley (Nepal)*. Kathmandu: Sajha Prakashan.

Vaidya, Tulsi Ram, and Tri Ratna Manandhar. 1985. *Crime and Punishment in Nepal: A Historical Perspective*. Kathmandu: Bini Vaidya and Purna Devi Manandhar.

Vajrācārya, Dhanavajra 1966 (VS 2022). "Śamasuddīna-ko ākramaṇa." *Pūrṇimā* 8): 6–13.

Vajrācārya, Dhanavajra. 1968a (VS 2025). "Licchavi kālika vasti." *Pūrṇimā* 18 (5): 87–101.

Vajrācārya, Dhanavajra. 1968b (VS 2025). "Licchavikālako itihāsama kirāta kālako prabhāva." *Pūrṇimā* 17 (5,1): 1–8.

Vajrācārya, Dhanavajra, ed. 1973 (VS 2030). *Licchavi Kālakā Abhilekha*. Kathmandu: Tribhuvana Viśvavidyālaya.

Vajrācārya, Dhanavajra, ed. 2011 (VS 2068). *Pūrvamadhyakālakā Abhilekha*. Kathmandu: Centre for Nepal and Asian Studies.

Vajrācārya, Dhanavajra, and Jñānamaṇi Nepāla. VS 2010 (1953). "'Nepāla' ko artha 'nepāla khālḍo' ho." In *Itihāsa-Saṃśodhanako Pramāṇa-Prameya*, edited by Dhanavajra Vajrācārya, vol. 1, 21–28. Kathmandu: Itihāsa-prakāśa-saṃgha.

Vajrācārya, Dhanavajra, and Jñāna Mani Nepāla, eds. 1957. "Śrī 5 Raṇabahādura Śāhako Kumāũ gaḍhavāla vijaya garna gaekā bhārādāraharūlāī lekheko patra." In *Aitihāsika Patra Saṃgraha* (A Collection of Historical Letters), 1: 56–74. Kathmandu: Nepāla Saṃskṛtika Pariṣad, VS 2014; English translation: "An Official Nepali Account of The Nepal-China War: King Ran Bahadur Shah's Letter to Officials Sent for the Conquest of Kumaun Garhwal." RRS 2.8 (1970): 177–88.

Vajrācārya, Dhanavajra, and Ṭeka Bahādura Śreṣṭha. VS 2032 (1975/76). *Nuvākoṭako Aitihāsika Rūparekhā*. Kathmandu: Ratna Pustak Bhandar.

Vajrācārya, Dhanavajra, and Ṭeka Bahādura Śreṣṭha, eds. VS 2037 (1980/81). *Śāhakālakā Abhilekha*. Kathmandu: Tribhuvana Viśvavidyālaya.

Vajracharya, Gautamavajra. 1973. "Recently Discovered Inscriptions of Licchavi Nepal." *Kailash* 1 (2): 117–33.

Vajrācārya, Gautamavajra, ed. 1976 (VS 2033). *Hanumānḍhoka Rājadarabāra*. Kathmandu: Nepāl ra Eśiyālī Adhyayana Saṃsthāna.

Vajracharya, Gautama V[ajra]. 2016. *Nepalese Seasons: Rain and Ritual*. New York: Rubin Museum of Art.

Vajracharya, Gautama V[ajra]. 2020. "Three Licchavi Period Sculptures." *Orientations* 51 (2): 86–95.

Vajrācārya, Puṇyaratna. 1979 (VS 2036). *Hāmro Cāḍa-parva*. 4th ed. Kathmandu: Ratna Pustaka Bhaṇḍāra.

Vandenhelsken, Mélanie, and Martin Gaenszle. 2021. "Limbu Religion and the Remaking of Community." In *Brill's Encyclopedia of Religions of Indigenous People of South*

Asia, edited by Marine Carrin et al. Leiden: Brill; http://dx.doi.org/10.1163/2665-9093_BERO_COM_032248 (accessed March 19, 2021).

van Driem, George. 1998. "Neolithic Correlates of Ancient Tibeto-Burman Migrations." In *Archaeology and Language II: Correlating Archaeological and Linguistic Hypotheses*, edited by Roger Blench and Matthew Spriggs, 67–102. London: Routledge.

van Driem, George. 2001. *Languages of the Himalayas: An Ethnolinguistic Handbook of the Himalayan Region*. Leiden: Brill.

van Kooij, K. R. 1978. *Religion in Nepal*. Leiden: E. J. Brill.

Verardi, Giovanni. 1992. *Excavations at Hadigaon Kathmandu: Final Report*. Vol. 1: Text. Rome: Instituto Italiano per il medio ed Extremo Oriente (IsMEO).

Verardi, Giovanni. 1997. *Nepalese and Italian Contribution to the History and Archaeology of Nepal*. Rome: Istituto Italiano per l'Africa e L'Oriente (IsIAO).

Verardi, Giovanni. 2007. *Excavations at Gotihawa and Pipri, Kapilavastu District, Nepal*. Rome: Istituto Italiano per l'Africa e L'Oriente (IsIAO).

Verma, T. P., and Arvind Kumar Singh, eds. 1994. *A Corpus of the Licchavi Inscriptions of Nepal*. Delhi: Ramanand Vidya Bhawan.

Vézies, Jean-François. 1981. *Les fêtes magiques du Népal*. Paris: Editions Cesare Rancilio.

Vinding, Michael. 1998. *The Thakali: A Himalayan Ethnography*. London: Serindia Publications.

Vitali, Roberto. 2012. *A Short History of Mustang (10th–15th century)*. Dharamsala: Amnye Machen Institute.

von Fürer-Haimendorf, Christoph. 1964. *The Sherpas of Nepal: Buddhist Highlanders*. London: John Murray.

von Fürer-Haimendorf, Christoph. 1975. *Himalayan Traders: Life in Highland Nepal*. London: John Murray.

von Fürer-Haimendorf, Christoph, ed. 1979. *The Anthropology of Nepal*. Warminster: Aris and Philips.

von Fürer-Haimendorf, Christoph. 1984. *The Sherpas Transformed: Social Change in a Buddhist Society of Nepal*. New Delhi: Sterling.

von Rospatt, Alexander. 2009. "The Sacred Origin of the Svayambhūcaitya and the Nepal Valley: Foreign Speculation and Local Myth." *JNRC* 13: 31–86.

von Rospatt, Alexander. 2011. "The Past Renovations of the Svayambhūcaitya." In *Light of the Valley: Renewing the Sacred Art and Traditions of Svayambhu*, edited by Ts. P. Gellek and P. Dorje Maitland, 157–208. Cazadero, CA: Dharma Publishing.

von Rospatt, Alexander. 2015. "Local Literatures: Nepal." In *Brill's Encyclopedia of Buddhism*, vol. 1, *Literature and Languages*, edited by Jonathan Silk, Oskar von Hinüber, and Vincent Eltschinger, 819–30. Leiden: Brill.

von Rospatt, Alexander. Forthcoming. *The Svayambhū Caitya of Kathmandu and its Renovations*. Documenta Nepalica Book Series, vol. 5. Heidelberg: Heidelberg University Publishing.

Walsh, E. H. [1908] 1973. *The Coinage of Nepal*. Delhi: Indological Book House.

Waterhouse, David. 2005. *The Origins of Himalayan Studies: Brian Houghton Hodgson in Nepal and Darjeeling, 1820–1858*. New York: RoutledgeCurzon.

Watters, David E. 2005. "Kusunda: A Typological Isolate in South Asia." In *Contemporary Issues in Nepalese Linguistics*, edited by Y. Yadava et al., 375–96. Kathmandu: Linguistic Society of Nepal.

Wegner, Gert-Matthias. 1986. *The Dhimaybājā of Bhaktapur: Studies in Newar Drumming I*. Stuttgart: Steiner.

Wegner, Gert-Matthias. 1988. *The Nāykhi bājā of the Newar Butchers: Studies in Newar Drumming II*. Stuttgart: Steiner.

Wegner, Gert-Matthias. 2023. *Drumming in Bhaktapur: Music of the Newar People of Nepal*. Documenta Nepalica Book Series, vol. 4. Heidelberg: Heidelberg University Publishing.

Weiler, Katharina. 2010. *The Neoclassical Residences of the Newars in Nepal: Transcultural Flows in the Early 20th Century Architecture of the Kathmandu Valley*. Heidelberg: heiDok - The Heidelberg Document Repository.

Weiler, Katharina, and Niels Gutschow, eds. 2016. *Authenticity in Architectural Heritage Conservation, Discourses, Opinions, Experiences in Europe, South and East Asia*. Heidelberg: Springer.

Whelpton, John. 1983a. "Archives in Nepal." *South Asia Research* 3 (2): 78–84.

Whelpton, John. 1983b. *Jang Bahadur in Europe*. Kathmandu: Sahayogi Press.

Whelpton, John. 1987. "The Ancestors of Jung Bahadur Rana: History, Propaganda and Legend." *Contributions to Nepal Studies* 14 (3): 161–91.

Whelpton, John. 1992. *Kings, Soldiers and Priests: Nepalese Politics and the Rise of Jang Bahadur Rana, 1830–1857*. Kathmandu: Ratna Pustak Bhandar.

Whelpton, John. 2000. "From the Beginning: Themes in the Prehistory and Ancient History of Nepal." *Voice of History* 15 (2): 39–69.

Whelpton, John. 2005. *A History of Nepal*. Cambridge: Cambridge University Press.

Whelpton, John. 2007. "Response to Kamal Prakash Malla's Review of *History of Nepal*." *EBHR* 31: 186–93.

Whelpton, John. 2008. "Political Identity in Nepal: State, Nation, and Community." In *Nationalism and Ethnicity in a Hindu Kingdom: The Politics of Culture in Contemporary Nepal*, edited by David Gellner, Joanna Pfaff-Czarnecka, and John Whelpton, 39–74. Reprint. Kathmandu: Vajra Publications.

Whelpton, John. 2017–18. "The Limits of Nationalism: Political Identity in Nepal and the British Isles." *EBHR* 50–51: 161–96.

Whitehouse, Paul et al. 2004. "Kusunda: An Indo-Pacific Language in Nepal." *Proceedings of the National Academy of Sciences* 101 (15): 5692–95.

Whitmarsh, Bryony. 2018. "Reflecting Political Allegiances Through the Design of the Narayanhiti Royal Palace." *EBHR* 50–51: 112–44.

Whyte, Timothy. 1998. "The Legacy of Slavery in Nepal." *SINHS* 3 (2): 311–40.

Widdess, Richard. 2013. *Dāphā: Sacred Singing in a South Asian City. Music, Performance and Meaning in Bhaktapur, Nepal*. Farnham and Burlington, VT: Ashgate.

Wiemann-Michaels, Annette. 1994. *Die verhexte Speise: Eine ethnopsychosomatische Studie über das Depressive Syndrom in Nepal*. Frankfurt am Main: Peter Lang.

Wiesner, Ulrich. 1978. *Nepalese Temple Architecture, Its Characteristics and Its Relations to Indian Development*. Leiden: Brill.

Winkler, Walter. 1976. "Spirit Possession in Far Western Nepal." In *Spirit Possession in the Nepal Himalayas*, edited by John Hitchcock and Rex L. Jones, 144–62. Warminster: Aris and Phillips.

Witzel, Michael. 1976. "On the History and the Present State of Vedic Tradition in Nepal." *Vasudha* 15 (12): 17–24 and 35–39; https://doi.org/10.11588/xarep.00000087.

Witzel, Michael. 1980. "On the Location of the Licchavi Capital of Nepal. *Studien zur Indologie und Iranistik* 5–6: 311–67.

Witzel, Michael. 1985. "Regionale und überregionale Faktoren in der Entwicklung vedischer Brahmanengruppen im Mittelalter." In *Regionale Traditionen in Südasien*, edited by Hermann Kulke and Dietmar Rothermund, 37–76. Stuttgart: Franz Steiner Verlag.

Witzel, Michael. 1986. "Agnihotra-Rituale in Nepal." In *Formen kulturellen Wandels und andere Beiträge zur Erforschung des Himālaya*, edited by Bernhard Kölver, 157–87. Sankt Augustin: VGH Wissenschaftsverlag.

Witzel, Michael. 1992. "Meaningful Ritual: Vedic, Medieval, and Contemporary Concepts in the Nepalese Agnihotra Ritual." In *Ritual, State and History in South Asia: Essays in Honour of J. C. Heesterman*, edited by A. W. van den Hoek, D. H. A. Kolf, and M. S. Oort, 774–825. Leiden: E.J. Brill.

Witzel, Michael. 1993. "Nepalese Hydronomy: Towards a History of Settlement in the Himalayas." In *Nepal, Past and Present: Proceedings of the Franco-German Conference Art-et-Senans, June 1990*, edited by Gérard Toffin, 224–56. Paris: CNRS Editions.

Witzel, Michael. 2019. See Primary Sources, Vājasaneyi-Saṃhitā.

Witzel, Michael. 2022. See Primary Sources.

Zharkevich, Ina. 2017. "'Rules That Apply in Times of Crisis': Time, Agency, and Norm-Remaking during Nepal's People's War." *Journal of the Royal Anthropological Institute* (N.S.) 23: 783–800.

Zharkevich, Ina. 2019. *Maoist People's War and the Revolution of Everyday Life in Nepal.* Cambridge: Cambridge Univerity.

Zotter, Astrid. 2013. *Von Blüten, Göttern und Gelehrten: Die Behandlung von pūjā-Blüten im Puṣpacintāmaṇi. Text, Herkunft und Deutung eines nepalischen Kompendiums.* University of Leipzig; http://nbn-resolving.de/urn:nbn:de:bsz:15-qucosa-102174 (accessed June 26, 2021).

Zotter, Astrid. 2016. "The Making and Unmaking of Rulers: On Denial of Ritual in Nepal." In *The Ambivalence of Denial: Danger and Appeal of Rituals*, edited by Ute Huesken and Udo Simon, 221–56. Wiesbaden: Harrassowitz.

Zotter, Astrid. 2018. "Conquering Navarātra: Documents on the Reorganisation of a State Festival." In *Studies in Documents of India and Nepal*, edited by Simon Cubelic, Axel Michaels, and Astrid Zotter, 493–531. Heidelberg: Heidelberg University Publishing.

Zotter, Astrid. 2021: "Who Kills the Buffalo? Authority and Agency in the Ritual Logistics of the Nepalese Dasaĩ Festival." In *Nine Nights of Power: Durgā, Dolls, and Darbārs*, edited by Ute Huesken, Vasudha Narayan, and Astrid Zotter, 193–220. Albany: State University of New York Press.

Zotter, Astrid, and Christof Zotter, eds. 2010. *Hindu and Buddhist Initiations in India and Nepal.* Wiesbaden: Harrassowitz.

Zotter, Christof. 2018a. "Ascetics in Administrative Affairs: Documents on the Central Overseers of Jogīs and Saṃnyāsīs in Nepal." In *Studies in Documents of India and Nepal*, edited by Simon Cubelic, Axel Michaels, and Astrid Zotter, 445–92. Heidelberg: Heidelberg University Publishing.

Zotter, Christof. 2018b. *Asketen auf Zeit: Das brahmanische Initiationsritual der Bāhun und Chetrī im Kathmandu-Tal.* Heidelberg and Berlin: CrossAsia-ebooks.

Zotter, Christof. 2022. "Shades of Power: The Nātha Yogīs in Nepal." In *The Power of the Nāth Yogīs, Yogic Charisma, Political Influence and Social Authority*, edited by Daniela Bevilacqua and Eloisa Stuparich, 197–226. Amsterdam: Amsterdam University Press.

Films

Barkas, Geoffrey, and Ivor Mantagu. 1934. *Wings over Everest.* Great Britain 1934 (40 min.), USA (22 min.).

Bau, Christian, and Niels Gutschow. 2005. *Verabschiedung der Toten: Rituale der Newars in Bhaktapur*. Nepal: Thede filmproduktion/Verlag Peter Hess (66 min.).

Bau, Christian (camera), Niels Gutschow, and Axel Michaels. 2005. *Handling Death: A Newar Death Ritual in Bhaktapur, Nepal*. English/German. Video, DVD. Hamburg: thede filmproduktion (45 min.).

Bau, Christian (camera), Niels Gutschow, and Axel Michaels. 2008. *Growing Up: Hindu and Buddhist Initiation Rituals among Newar Children in Bhaktapur, Nepal*. English/German. Hamburg: thede filmproduktion (76 min.).

Bau, Christian (camera), Niels Gutschow, and Axel Michaels. 2012. *Getting Married: Hindu and Buddhist Marriage Rituals among Newars of Bhaktapur and Patan, Nepal*. English/German. Hamburg: thede filmproduktion (55 min.).

von Fürer-Haimendorf, Christoph. 1962. *Nepal, Mustang, Dolpo*. Silent black-and-white film. (1:23:40). (http://ethnoflorence.skynetblogs.be/village-humla-nepal/).

Grandits, Victor, and Jessica Krauß. 2007. *Mount Everest—Graveyard of My Friends / Mount Everest—Der Friedhof meiner Freunde*. Grandits Films / Südwestrundfunk (75 min.).

Lévi, Sylvain. 1920s. *Twenty-two Short Films Documenting Buddhist Rituals (mudras etc.) in Nepal, Filmed in the 1920s by A. A. Bake*. (https://salamandre.college-de-france.fr/audiovisuel-search-form.html).

Markowitz, Robert. 1997. *Into Thin Air: Death on Everest*. Sofronski Productions (90 min.).

Messner, Reinhold, and Peter Habeler. 2002. *Mount Everest—Todeszone/Death Zone*. 2002. Directed by Leo Dickinson. Studio: Film 101 DVD (50 min.).

Oppitz, Michael. 2017. *Schamanen im blinden Land / Shamans of the Blind Country*. German/English. Filmed 1979–80. With the accompanying book "Bewegliche Mythen / Mobile Myths" and the CD "Drei mythische Gesänge / Mythical Chants. 4 pts. Berlin: Arthouse.

Revill, Barny. 2006–7. *Everest: Beyond the Limit* (2006–7). TV production: Discovery Channel (50 min.).

Tseten Lama, Kesang. 2005. *On the Road with the Red God: Machhendranath*, produced by the filmmaker (kesang@homebase.wlink.com.np). Berne (Switzerland): Shunyata Film Production (75 min.).

Tseten Lama, Kesang. 2009. *In Search of the Riyal*, produced by the filmmaker (kesang@homebase.wlink.com.np). Berne (Switzerland): Shunyata Film Production (85 min.).

Tseten Lama, Kesang. 2010. *Saving Dolma*, produced by the filmmaker (kesang@homebase.wlink.com.np). Berne (Switzerland): Shunyata Film Production (62 min.).

Tseten Lama, Kesang. 2012. *Who Will Be a Gurkha*, produced by the filmmaker (kesang@homebase.wlink.com.np). Berne (Switzerland): Shunyata Film Production (72 min.).

Tseten Lama, Kesang. 2015. *Castaway Man*, produced by the filmmaker (kesang@homebase.wlink.com.np). Berne (Switzerland): Shunyata Film Production (82 min.).

For more films, see Digital Himalaya (http://www.digitalhimalaya.com/collections/films/).

Index

For the benefit of digital users, indexed terms that span two pages (e.g., 52–53) may, on occasion, appear on only one of those pages.

Tables and figures are indicated by an italic *t* and *f* following the page number.

The Index excludes names and terms found in the Preface, Acknowledgments, Notes, and Glossary. For kings and prime ministers and their families, consult the tables in Appendix 2, and for information on castes and ethnic groups, refer to Tables 2.1–2.4.

Ābhīra, 87, 91
Ācārya, Bandhudatta, 69
Acharya, Baburam, 1, 14–15, 298
Acharya, Diwakar, 10, 299
Acharya, Tanka Prasad, 168–69, 245–46
Adams, Barbara, 249–50
Adhikari, Man Mohan, 222
Adhiyā, adhiyā, 171–72
Ādibuddha, 8, 83, 86–87
Agni, 62, 212
Agriculture, 11–12, 169, 170, 224, 269–70, 275, 276
Ain (of 1854), 4–5, 6–7, 25–26, 32–33, 36–37, 38–39, 41–42, 47–48, 63, 143, 173, 175, 177, 182, 183, 186, 187–89, 190, 191, 194, 195–200, 201, 206, 215, 238, 247, 263, 272–73, 286, 287
ajimā, 70–71, 207
Akṣobhya, 55, 56, 122, 132–33
Alcohol, 32–33, 38–39, 68–69, 70, 74–75, 187–88, 197, 225, 241, 243, 263, 272–73, 284, 287
All-India Nepali Congress, 168–69
amālī, 273
amātya, 101, 110
Amitābha, 55, 56–57, 122
Amlekhgunj, 189–90
Amoghapāśa, 58
Amoghasiddhi, 22–23, 122
Aṃśuvarman, 56–57, 64, 65, 88, 91–92
Ānandadeva (I), 96–98, 125–26
Ancestors, 34, 35, 50, 87, 179, 187–88, 208–9, 258–59, 271, 283, 304
Anderson, Benedict, 247
Anglo-Nepalese (or -Gorkha) War, 151, 158, 163–64, 176, 267–68, 295–96
Animal sacrifice, 61, 71–73, 74–75, 93, 106, 201. *See also* Blood sacrifices
Anuparama, 92–93
Ar(a)niko Highway, 12, 153
Archaeology, 54, 89, 92, 100, 252, 276–77. *See also* Department of Archaeology (DoA)
Architecture, 22, 24–25, 78–79, 93–94, 98, 114, 115, 117, 118, 119, 211–12, 224, 255, 258
Archives, 298, 305, 310–11
Arjunadeva, 112
Army, 6–7, 31, 37, 52–53, 92, 103–4, 108, 110, 138–39, 142, 143, 145, 146, 149, 150, 152, 154, 155, 162, 164, 190–91, 200, 218–19, 223–26, 228–29, 230, 231–32, 237, 242, 252, 268, 287. *See also* Military; Soldiers, Soldiery
Art, 22, 57, 79, 93–94, 114, 253–61, 297, 299–300, 311–12
Arun River, 280–81
Ascetics, 5, 27–28, 41, 54, 55–56, 64, 65, 67–68, 69, 78–79, 87, 106, 111, 115, 118–19, 129, 132, 140, 143, 174–75, 207, 236, 238–39, 240, 272
Aśoka, 54, 86–87, 93–94, 115, 131

Aśoka Stūpa, 116*f*
Assam, 69
Aṣṭamātṛkā, 63, 74, 115, 130
Atīśa, 57–58, 202
Avalokiteśvara, 55, 56, 58, 59, 69–70, 81, 82, 83, 93–94, 98, 277–78, 299
Awadh, 266
Ayton, J. A., 303

Babar Mahal, 212–13
Bāghabhairava, 94–95, 114, 137
Bagmati River, 27, 65, 66–67, 68, 74–75, 77–78, 79, 108, 133, 212, 213–14, 256–57
bāhāḥ, bāhāla, bahī, 43–44, 58, 69–70, 80, 97, 98, 118, 120–21, 132–33
Bahun-Chhetri, 6–7, 29, 30–31, 32, 34–35, 42–43, 49, 62, 190, 216, 223, 225, 254, 262, 272–73, 292
Bajhang, 101
Bālagopāla, 80, 119, 132. *See also* Kṛṣṇa
Bālakumārī, 66, 117–18
Banepa, 95, 96–97, 102–3, 107, 112, 114, 230, 248
Bangdel, Dina, 257–58, 299–300
Bangdel, Lain Singh, 256, 299–300
Baragaon, 276, 277–78
bare chuyegu, 60
Barter, 192, 307–8
Basantapur, 120, 211
Bauddha. 61, 93–94, 250, 312. *See also* Bodhnath
Beijing, 105–6, 154, 156, 157
Bel tree, 26, 60–61
Belāyatyātrā, 163–64
Benares. *See* Varanasi (Benares)
Bengal, 21, 32–33, 52–53, 62–63, 80–81, 111, 148, 265, 274
Betravati, 156, 157
Bhadgaon, 1, 107, 112–13, 114, 124–25, 127*f*, 130*f*, *See also* Bhaktapur
Bhadrakālī, 38*f*, 71–73, 128–29
Bhagavatī, 63
Bhāgīrāma, 110
Bhairava, 63, 68–69, 74, 117–18, 128–29, 131, 134–35, 260
bhajana, 63–64, 80–81, 259
Bhaktapur, 1, 24–25, 26, 43–44, 46, 52–53, 62–63, 68–69, 70, 73–74, 75, 78, 79, 80, 81, 96–97, 107, 110, 111–13, 114–15, 117–19, 120, 124–27, 128–30, 131, 132–34, 135, 138, 204–5, 248, 251–52, 257, 259–60, 265, 307, 308, 312 . *See also* Bhadgaon
Bhaṇḍārī, Gagana Siṃha, 162
Bhānubhakta, 302, 303
bhāradāra, 139, 140, 143–44, 148–49, 309
Bhāskaradeva, 97
Bhasmeśvara, 94–95
Bhaṭṭa priests, 189
Bhaṭṭa, Motīrāma, 303
Bhattarai, Baburam, 223–24, 230–32
Bhaumagupta, 92–93
Bhīmasena temple, 117–18, 129, 132
Bhojapurī, 29, 248, 268, 288, 300–1
Bhojpur, 105
Bhote, Bhotiya, 30, 288, 301. *See also* Tibet
bhoṭo, 23–24, 69, 238
Bhṛkuṭī, 153
Bhutan, 33–34, 102–3, 180, 267–68, 271, 281–82
Bhutia, 281–82
Bhuvaneśvarī, 66
Bihar, 147–48, 264
Bīra Pustakālaya, 310
Biratnagar, 248
Birganj, 205, 218
birtā, 139–40, 170, 173–75, 177, 178, 179–80, 198, 274
Bisketjātrā, 26, 68–69, 125, 128–29, 133
Bista, Dor Bahadur, 32, 299
Blood sacrifices, 68–69, 70, 122–23. *See also* Animal sacrifice
Blue Annals, The, 57–58, 297
Boar, 77, 94
Bodhisattva, 53, 55–57, 58, 59, 60–61, 81, 82, 85, 93–94, 121, 123–24, 132–33
Bodhnath, 61, 93–94. *See also* Bauddha
Bogle, Georg, 153
Bonded labor. *See* Labor
Border, 4, 17–19, 21–22, 33, 108, 128–29, 137, 142, 145–47, 152, 153, 156, 157, 158, 168–69, 209, 219, 264, 267–68, 278, 279, 281–82, 285, 293

Brahmā, 3, 4, 20, 26, 87, 102, 129
Brahmins, 3–4, 5, 7, 27, 29–31, 32–33, 34–35, 37, 38–39, 47–48, 56, 60, 62–63, 64, 73, 79, 85–86, 93, 101, 104, 106, 109–10, 136, 138, 140, 141, 143–44, 164–65, 168, 173, 180, 181, 182–83, 187–88, 189, 195–96, 198–99, 200, 201–2, 207, 210, 224, 225, 236, 238–39, 240, 241–42, 243, 263, 265–67, 287, 290, 299, 300–1, 304
Bṛhatsaṃhitā, 19
Bridges, 26–27, 102, 155–56, 181, 215, 225–26, 250
British people, 2, 6, 12, 14, 110–11, 136–37, 138–39, 141, 145–49, 150, 151–52, 157, 158–59, 163, 164, 165, 166–67, 185–86, 191, 192, 193, 204, 205, 210, 214, 217–18, 267–68, 274, 281–82, 286, 295–96
Buddha, 4, 8, 13, 24, 52, 53–54, 55–56, 58, 59, 60, 61, 77, 81, 85, 86–87, 88, 93–94, 111, 122–24, 132–33, 153, 252, 265, 302, 306, 309
Buddhism, 3, 4, 5, 8, 13–14, 35, 43, 44, 52–61, 64, 69–71, 81–82, 85, 87, 88, 91, 92, 93–94, 95–96, 97, 98, 100, 102, 105, 115, 118–19, 120–21, 122–34, 202, 252, 254–55, 263, 269, 272–73, 275–77, 278, 279–80, 281–82, 292, 297, 298, 299–300, 302, 304, 305, 307, 308–9, 312. *See also* Mahāyāna Buddhism; Theravāda; Tibetan Buddhism; Vajrayāna Buddhism
Buddhists, 5, 24–25, 42, 44, 52, 53, 57, 60–61, 68, 69–70, 82, 83, 92–93, 97, 105, 111, 115, 120–21, 129, 271–72, 277–78, 279–80, 298, 305, 308–9
Buḍhānīlakaṇṭha, 22–23, 75–76, 80–81, 94
Buffalo, 44–46, 109, 200
Buṅgadyaḥ, 58, 59, 69–70, 98, 105
Bungamati, 59, 98, 114, 133
Burghart, Richard, 238–39
Burma, 105, 150, 158, 263, 284
Butwal, 102–3, 145–46, 266

Caitya, 56, 61, 93–94, 98, 101, 115, 121, 122, 132–33. *See also stūpa*
Calcutta. *See* Kolkata
Calcutta University, 202–3
Calendar, 23, 288
Caṇḍī, 71–73
Candragupta, 88–89
Capuchin monks, 53, 137, 295, 307
Cāranārāyaṇa (Car Narayan), 18*f*, 132, 134
Caravans, 192, 269–70
Caste, 13–14, 29–51, 35*t*–40*t*, 54, 56–57, 59–61, 62, 67–68, 81, 87, 89, 102, 111–12, 115–17, 129, 131, 138, 139–40, 151, 167–68, 173–74, 178, 181, 187–88, 189–91, 194–95, 196–97, 200–1, 207, 216, 223, 225, 232–33, 234, 237, 238, 241–42, 257, 258–59, 260, 266–67, 268–69, 272–73, 275–76, 283–84, 286–87, 288–89, 290, 293, 299
caturmukha, 65
cautārā, 109–10
cautariyā, 143–44, 149, 198, 282
Cavenagh, Orfeur, 210–11
Census, 29, 30–31, 36–37, 51, 52, 185, 269, 280–81, 300–1
Cereals, 153
Chabahil, 55–56, 70, 86–87, 93–94
Chalsa, 274
Chalukya dynasty, 31, 99
Chamling, 280–81
Chand, Dasarath, 168
Changu Narayana (Cāṅgunārāyaṇa), 52, 62, 64, 75, 76*f*, 79, 89–90, 94, 108, 115, 252, 306, 312
Channels, 25–26, 109
Chantel, 207
Chepang, 29, 301
Chhetri, 6–7, 29, 30–31, 32–33, 34–35, 42–43, 49, 50, 62, 78, 136, 143–44, 180, 190, 198, 202, 216, 223, 225, 254, 262, 272–73, 287, 292, 300–1
Child Goddess. *See* Kumārī
Child marriage, 41–42, 43
Children, 34, 46, 47–48, 70–71, 137, 141, 164, 185, 186, 187, 188, 195, 202–3, 226, 239, 247, 257, 275. *See also* Labor
China, 2, 4, 6, 7, 12, 13, 33–34, 56, 61, 88, 99–100, 105–6, 137, 140, 146, 150, 153–59, 165, 168, 199–200, 202, 206, 214–15, 222, 233, 235, 236, 242, 263, 271, 275, 278–79, 293, 295

Chitrakar, Bhajuman, 255
Chitrakar, Dirghaman, 255
Chitrakar, Lok, 254–55
Chitrakar, Tej Bahadur, 255
Chiwong, 275
Chobhar, 22, 53, 70, 85
Christians, 2, 4, 49–50, 52, 53, 63, 187–88
Chronicles, 7, 8, 19, 20, 22, 43–44, 47, 52, 53, 66–67, 69, 75, 77–78, 82–83, 85–87, 89, 92, 95–96, 97, 98, 100, 102–3, 106, 111–14, 125–26, 131, 238, 265, 266, 295, 296, 301, 303–4, 308–9
Chumbi, 158–59
Cimang, 276, 279
Cities, 1, 12, 54, 108, 112–13, 114, 127, 133–34, 138, 236, 249–50
Citizenship, 34, 232, 268, 285, 289, 299
Civil servant, 143, 176, 198, 245–46, 272–73, 275–76
Clarified butter, 171, 191
Clay, 23, 106, 109, 118, 191
Coins, 8, 70, 88–89, 107, 153–54, 181, 192, 217, 295, 306, 307–8, 311–12
Communists, 221, 222–23, 224, 225, 228, 232–33, 234–36, 241–42
Coningham, Robin, 54
Constitution, 5, 38–39, 49–51, 63, 168, 194, 195, 201, 215, 217, 218–20, 225, 230–31, 232–35, 243–46, 248, 284, 287, 289, 300
Copper, 118, 132–33, 192, 283, 307
Corn, 124–25, 138–39, 169, 171, 191
Coronation, 15, 107, 132, 139–40, 189, 210, 221, 238, 240, 284–85, 310–11
Corruption, 17–19, 60, 143, 193–94, 198, 223–24, 236, 241–42, 257, 260–61, 290
Corvinus, Gudrun, 84–85
Cows, 4–5, 44, 106, 109–10, 124–25, 174–75, 195–96, 198–202, 269–70, 272–73
Cow slaughter, 109–10, 196, 199, 200–1, 272–73
Craftsmanship, 98, 114, 115, 192, 214–15
Cultural heritage, 17, 251, 252, 253, 257, 291, 312
Curzon, Lord, 286
Customs duties, 154, 170
Cyāsiṃ Deval, 80
Dahal, Pushpa Kamal ("Prachanda"), 223, 224, 230–32, 234, 235, 241–42
Dakṣiṇakālī, 71–73
Dalai Lama, 154, 158–59
Dalits, 14, 29–30, 49–50, 234, 246, 264, 287, 289
Damai, 199, 258–59
dāna, 60, 174–75
Dance, 60, 68, 113–14, 115, 128–29, 130, 208–9, 258–59, 288, 301–2
Dang, 247–48, 264
Danuvar, 29–30, 178–79, 272–73, 280–81
dāphā, 259–60
Darbar (cf. Palace), 24, 120, 128, 202–3, 206–7, 212–13, 220–21, 238, 243, 251, 255–56, 312
Darbar High School, 202–3
Darjeeling, 1, 14, 33, 180, 256, 263, 269, 274, 281–82, 303
Dasaĩ, 5–6, 23, 44–46, 73, 126, 130, 239, 286, 291
Dattātreya, 112, 118–19, 129, 260
Debt. *See* Indebtedness
Degutale, 112, 134–35
Delhi, 52–53, 80, 217–18, 224, 230–31, 256, 265–66, 303
Democracy, 167–68, 194, 218, 219–20, 222, 223–24, 228–29, 235, 257, 289, 299, 308, 311
Deopatan, 26, 48–49, 65–66, 65*f*, 67*f*, 68–69, 74–75, 77–78, 80–81, 82–83, 86–87, 93–95, 108, 128, 141, 213, 214, 242
Department of Archaeology (DoA), 131, 251, 252, 253, 306, 312
Deuba, Sher Bahadur, 228, 234, 235
Devakoṭā, Lakṣmī Prasāda, 303
Devī, 39–41, 61–62, 71–73, 140, 148–49, 162, 164–65, 214, 227, 311. *See also* Goddess(es)
Devīmāhātmya, 71–73
Dharahāra Tower, 258–59
Dharmadeva, 56, 89
dharmādhikārin, 107–8, 109–10, 143–44, 194–95, 197, 215
Dharmaśāstra, 37–38, 42–43, 47, 64, 194–95, 204, 225
Dhimal, 29–30, 264, 280–81

Dhobi, 30
Dhumbarahi, 306
digudyaḥ, dugudyaḥ 105, 115–17
Dīpaṅkara, 55, 81
Districts, 26–27, 30, 100, 109, 110, 143–45, 164, 171–72, 179–80, 183, 189, 199–200, 224–26, 228, 232, 234, 245–46, 247, 264, 271, 277–78, 286, 301. *See also* Provinces
Divided rule, 105–35, 235, 236
Divyopadeśa, 1, 2, 4, 137, 138–39, 176, 191, 309
Dixit, Kamal Mani, 311
Dixit, Kanak Mani, 231, 311
Documents, 7, 19, 20–21, 26–28, 46, 73, 102–3, 109, 137, 144, 147, 156, 157, 164–65, 173–74, 175, 177, 181, 182, 183, 193, 195, 196, 204, 206, 209, 215, 266, 270, 272–73, 279, 282–83, 295, 296, 297, 298–99, 301–2, 303, 304, 305–6, 309, 310, 311
Dolakha, 102–3, 105, 144, 281, 307
Donations, 65, 175, 189, 311
Dorje, Lama Sangwa, 272
Doti, 101, 205
Drinking water, 24, 223–24, 290–91
Drums, 207–9, 258–59, 260
Dullu, 99–100, 104
Durgā, 39–41, 44, 63, 71–73, 74, 108–9, 115, 130

Earthquakes, 7, 14–15, 16–21, 22–23, 70–71, 105–6, 127, 131, 133–34, 168, 193–94, 206, 212–13, 234, 239, 242, 251, 252–53, 257, 290–91, 308, 311
East India Company, 10, 136–37, 141, 142, 147, 150, 191, 192–93, 211–12, 255, 265–66, 267, 274, 286, 295–96
Education, 33, 39, 41–42, 46, 143–44, 145, 152, 193–94, 202–4, 206, 215, 223–24, 236, 247–48, 255–57, 260–61, 263–64, 290, 293, 298, 299, 310–11
Elections, 168, 218–19, 222, 223, 228, 229, 231–33, 234–35, 236, 245–46, 279–80
Electricity, 12, 21–22, 166–67, 193–94, 223–24, 249–50, 290–91, 292
Elephants, 11, 25–26, 70, 110–11, 122, 128, 145, 157, 162, 181–82, 200, 209, 210–11
Elizabeth II, 15, 220, 249–50, 312
Empire, 5–6, 58–90, 110–11, 263, 286, 289
Eras, 4–5, 89, 95–96, 106, 168–69, 214, 221, 288, 308
Ethnicity, 32, 49, 136, 288, 289, 290
Everest, 11, 13, 14–17, 20, 269, 275, 291, 298

Failed state, 230, 290, 291–92
Fairy tales, 304
Fateh Jaṅga (Cautariyā), 149, 162, 212
Faxian, 88
Festivals, 5–6, 23–24, 26, 27, 42, 44–46, 56, 59, 62, 64, 67–68, 69, 73, 74–75, 82, 105, 111–12, 126, 128–29, 130, 133, 173, 238, 239, 291. *See also* Procession
Fiefs, 171
Filchner, Wilhelm, 264
Films, 4, 16, 249–50, 299, 304
Fire sacrifices, 48, 60–61, 207
Food, 17, 21, 34, 39, 41–42, 139–40, 181–82, 186, 188, 197, 215, 224–25, 252, 273
Folk religion, 52, 63, 105, 275–76
Forests, 11, 12, 13–14, 25–28, 67–68, 101, 170, 178–80, 244, 264, 266, 267–68, 285
Fortresses, 108, 120, 276–77, 278*f*
Foundations, 19, 27, 44, 56, 65–66, 77, 80, 117–18, 131, 134–35, 174–76, 241, 257–58, 271–72, 274, 297, 304, 305, 306–7, 309, 311
Fountain, 23, 24, 120, 277–78
Führer, Alois Anton, 54
FürerHaimendorf, Christoph von, 299

Gaṇeśa, 61–62, 63, 70, 77, 81, 102, 128, 210, 211, 266–67
Gardner, Edward, 145, 295–96
Garhwal, 99–101, 139–40, 145–46, 147–48, 189
Garlands, 37, 38, 58, 111–12, 220
Garuḍa, 24, 75, 76*f*, 81, 94, 118, 122, 129
Gaurī, 68

Gaurishankar, 280–81
Gautama, 53–54, 55, 265
Gellner, David, 4
Gellner, Ernest, 292
ghāṭa, 24, 65, 78, 94–95, 227
ghaṭanāvalī, 106, 301–2, 308
Gifts, 15, 23–24, 26, 174–75, 240. *See also* *dāna*; Donations
Goddess(es), 14–15, 39–41, 42, 43–46, 59, 61–62, 63, 64, 66, 68–69, 70–75, 78, 82–83, 88, 92, 105, 108–9, 112–14, 115–18, 119, 121, 122–23, 126–27, 128–29, 130–31, 132, 133, 134, 135, 207, 210, 239, 242, 288–89
Gokarna, 108
Gokarṇeśvara, 72*f*
Gold, 24, 53, 68, 78–79, 81, 97–98, 108–9, 118, 126–27, 131, 132–33, 153, 181, 191, 192, 307–8
Gopālarājavaṃśāvalī, 8, 19, 58, 66, 95, 100–1, 301, 308
Gorakhanātha, 23–24, 52, 69, 98, 213–14, 298
Gorkha, Gorkhali, 1, 33, 52, 78, 89–90, 103, 104, 114, 120, 136–59, 168–70, 178, 183, 192, 198–99, 204, 211, 223–24, 248–49, 262–63, 266, 267–68, 272–73, 278–79, 281–82, 283–84, 287, 302, 303, 307, 309
Gorkhā Rāj (kingdom), 1, 3–4, 32–33, 108, 136, 139–40, 145–46, 178, 180, 204, 263, 272–73, 282
Gorkhāpatra, 183, 247–48, 303
Gosainkund, 23
Great Britain, 152, 163–64, 202–3, 286
Greater Nepal, 138–39, 145–46, 147–48
Grueber, Johann, 295
Guhyeśvarī, 4–5, 66, 71–73, 81, 82–83, 213
Gūla, 60
GuṃVihāra, 56
Guṇakāmadeva (I and II), 22–23, 97–98, 133
Guṇakāraṇḍavyūha, 58
Gupta Period, 88–89, 92, 94, 95
Gurkha soldiers, 150–52, 204. *See also* Soldiers, Soldiery
Gurung, 29, 31, 37, 57, 102, 150, 198, 200, 207, 227, 248, 262–64, 271, 276, 287, 288, 290, 301
Gurung, Hit Man, 257
Gurung, Praveen, 227
guṭhī, 44, 87, 105, 109, 118–19, 141, 170, 174–76, 204, 206, 244, 252, 258, 259, 311
Guthi Samsthana (Guṭhī Saṃsthāna), 175–76, 244, 311
Gutschow, Niels, 38*f*–45*f*, 72*f*–76*f*, 90*f*, 93–94, 130*f*

Hagmüller, Goetz, 312
Hamilton, Francis Buchanan, 37, 46, 102–3, 205, 281, 282, 295–96
Handigaon, 56, 75, 91, 92–94, 306
Hanumān, 77–78, 134–35
Hanuman Dhoka, 68–69, 75–76, 94, 134–35, 160, 212, 217, 260, 307, 312
Haridattavarman, 77
Harisiddhi, 113–14
Harisiṃhadeva, 62–63, 265
Hārītī, 70–71, 88, 122–23
Harsha, 95
Hawley, Elizabeth, 16
Hayu, 200, 272–73, 280–81
Healer, 41, 206, 207, 208–9
Health service, 204–5, 206, 223–24, 247–48, 260–61, 290
Hearsey, Hyder Young, 151
Heglund, Norman, 184
Hellmich, Wolfgang, 297
Hetaura, (Hetauda) 192
Hierarchy, 29, 34–39, 40*t*, 59, 138, 157, 167–68, 173–74, 189, 196, 285
Hillary, Edmund, 15, 269
Himavatkhaṇḍa, 4–5, 111, 309
Hindī, 4, 26, 29–30, 202–3, 223–24, 233, 259, 264, 266, 268, 300–1, 303
Hiraṇyavarṇa Mahāvihāra, 132–33
Hodgson, Brian Houghton, 148–49, 151–52, 155–56, 192–93, 195, 255, 295–97, 298
Höfer, András, 296
homa, 60–61, 207
Horses, 77, 122, 162, 164, 181
Hospitals, 145, 174–76, 205, 206–7, 210, 214, 219, 230
Houses, 46, 70, 131, 195, 202, 207–8, 211, 291
  Construction, 23, 25–26

God-house (*dyaḥchē*), 74, 115–17, 126, 130
Royal House, 8, 44, 225–26, 228 (*see also* Palace)
House of Representatives, 227–28, 234–35, 245–46
Hridaya, Chittadhar, 302
Hsüan-tsang, 88
hulāka, 182–83
Humla, 57, 199–200
Humli, 29
Hyolmo, 207

Ihi ritual, 60–61
Ilam, 205
Imprisonment, 140, 195, 199–200. *See also* Prison, Prisoner
Impurity, 32, 38–39, 41–42, 46, 48, 74–75, 115–17, 189, 190, 196–97, 210, 272–73
Indebtedness, 141, 172, 180–81, 187, 190–91
Indo-Aryan (culture, people, languages), 29, 31, 50, 85–86, 88–89, 138, 150, 300–1
Indo-Parbatiyas, 29, 35*t*, *See also* Parbatiya
Indra, 62, 69, 81, 113, 135
Indrajātrā, 26, 44, 62, 68–69, 135, 239
Indrāyaṇī, 71, 72*f*
Indreśvara, 114, 120
Initiation, 32, 56–57, 60, 64, 112–13, 207–8, 210
Inscriptions, 3, 7, 8, 24–25, 31, 47, 54, 55–57, 62–63, 64, 65, 66, 69–70, 75–76, 77, 79, 80, 81, 84, 85–87, 89–96, 99–100, 101, 102, 106–7, 108–9, 110, 111, 113, 119, 121, 126–27, 128–29, 131, 132–33, 134–35, 186, 194, 204–5, 213, 242, 252, 266–67, 295, 296, 297, 298, 301, 302, 305, 306–7, 308
Islam, 7, 52–53, 57, 58, 63, 82, 211–12. *See also* Muslims

jāgira, 143, 146, 170, 175, 176, 182–83, 244
Jajarkot, 101, 139–40, 178, 224–25
Jalaśayana-Viṣṇu. *See* Śeṣanārāyaṇa
Janaipūrṇimā, 23
Janajati, 29–30, 31, 49–50, 51, 234, 268
Janakpur, 12, 78–79, 265, 297
Jātamālā, *Jātīmālā*, 37
Jayadeva, 266–67
Jayadeva I, 87
Jayadeva II, 77, 87, 89, 92
Jayatāri, 101
Jayavāgīśvarī, 66, 68–69
Jayavarman, 89, 90*f*, 94, 306, 311–12
Jesuits, 106, 295, 299
Jhā caste, 266–67
Jhā, Kedāranātha, 310
Jhā, Kulānanda, 66
Jhā, Paramananda, 233
jhārā, 146, 181, 182–83, 189
Jhokhang, 94
Jiṣṇugupta, 92
Jomsom, 277–78, 279
Jørgensen, Hans, 302
Joshi, Madhav Raj, 203–4
Joshi, Ramhari, 168
Joshi, R. N. (Rama Nanda), 256–57
Joshi, Satya Mohan, 299–300, 302
Judicial system, 104, 143, 165, 243. *See also* Law
Jumla, 100, 101, 139–40, 182, 279, 299
Jyapu, 37, 44

Kabhrepalanchok, 144, 247
Kagbeni, 277–78
Kaiser Library, 310–11
Kailāśakūṭa (-bhavana), 64, 92
Kailash (Kailāśa), 100
kājī, 108, 109–10, 140, 142, 153, 155–56, 162, 198, 298, 309
Kāla Bhairava, 68–69
Kalamochanghat, 78
kalaśa, 73–74
Kālī, 22, 61–62, 71–73, 77, 210
Kālidāsa, 306–7
Kālīhrada, 22
Kanga Ajimā, 71
Kali Gandaki, 192, 276, 278, 279
Kami, 30–31, 207
Kanaphaṭṭā, 213–14
Kangra, 145–46, 147–48, 267–68
Kaṅkeśvarī, 71–73
Kansakar, Asha Man Singh, 311
Kansakar, Prem Bahadur, 311
Kantipur (Kathmandu), 43–44, 112–13, 133, 248

Kapilavastu, 54, 297
Karkoṭaka, 22–24
Karmācārya, 105
Karnali, 32–33, 99–100, 102–3, 267–68, 297
Karnata dynasty, 108–9, 110–11, 265–66
Karuṇāmaya, 59, 69–70, 81, 105
Kāśī, 65–66. *See also* Varanasi (Benares)
Kaski, 139–40, 165, 166, 169, 248–49
Kāṣṭhamaṇḍapa, 69, 98, 99*f*, 113, 118–19, 129, 135, 301
Kathmandu. *See* Kantipur (Kathmandu)
Kathmandu Post, 248
Kathmandu University, 247, 257, 311
Kathmandu Valley Preservation Trust (KVPT), 131, 251
Kaumārī, 74
Kavīndrapura, 113, 118–19
Khaling, 280–81
Kham, 42, 262–63, 270–71, 270*f*
Khamba, 271
Khan, Sultan Said, 271
Khasa (Malla), 29, 32–33, 84, 95–96, 99–103, 104, 106, 111, 138, 139, 150, 266–67, 279, 297, 298
Khasa Arya, 29, 35, 37, 49–51, 207, 234, 268, 288, 289
khasakurā, 100, 300–1, 302
Khokana, 12, 205
Khumbu, 269, 271, 272, 297
Kinloch, George, 136–37
kipaṭa, 170, 178–79, 273, 283–84, 286
Kiranti, 85–86, 262, 280–81, 282–84, 301
Kirāta, 30, 31, 85–87, 89–90, 281, 284
Kirkpatrick, William J., 102–3, 296
Kirong, 192
Kirtipur, 94–95, 97, 114, 137, 138, 247, 266–67
Knox, W. D., 141, 295–96
Kolkata, 20, 46, 147, 163–64, 166–67, 168–69, 202–3, 205, 211, 221, 303
Kölver, Bernhard, 123*f*
Koirala, Bishweshwar Prasad, 3–4, 12, 168–69, 218, 219, 220, 221, 222, 225–26, 245–46
Koirala, Girija Prasad, 221, 222, 230–31, 246
Koirala, Matrika Prasad, 308
Kora La Pass, 276, 278–79
Koṭa Massacre, 67, 162, 163, 212, 213–14, 284–85
Kotwal, 22, 53
Kriyāsaṃgraha, 58
Kṛṣṇa, 63–64, 77, 79, 80–81, 94, 117–18, 119, 132
Kṛṣṇalīlā, 80
Kubjikā, 73
Kulung, 280–81
Kumaon, 62, 99–101, 139–40, 145–46, 147–48, 267–68
Kumāradevī, 88–89
Kumārī, 39–41, 43–46, 45*f*, 68–69, 81, 82, 105, 135, 239, 288–89
Kumārī Coka, 162
Kumbheśvara, 23, 70–71, 94–95, 132
Kushanas, 89, 94, 307
kuta-system, 172
Kuti Pass, 153, 154, 157, 192
Kũvara Rāṇā (cf. Śaṃśera Rāṇā), 161*t*, 162–66, 197–98
  Babara Jaṅga, 168
  Jagat Jaṅga, 166, 237
  Jaṅga Bahādura, 4, 20, 32, 38–39, 47–48, 134–35, 149, 152, 155–56, 160–61, 162–65, 163*f*, 166–67, 169, 179–80, 195–96, 197–98, 199–200, 202–3, 209, 212, 213–14, 215, 237, 255, 267–68, 296, 303, 309, 310–11
  Jit(a) Jaṅga, 213–14
  Juddha Pratāpa Jaṅga, 166
  Lakṣmīkāmadeva, 43–44, 97–98
  Lalitatripurasundarī, 142, 148–49, 213
Kvā Bāhāḥ, 80, 97, 98, 132–33

Labor, 103–4, 143, 152, 169–70, 173, 180–83, 236, 243, 247, 250, 259–60, 263–64, 274, 285, 293. *See also jhārā*; Slavery
  Bonded labor, 39, 46, 172, 180, 186, 187, 189, 190
  Child labor, 46, 181, 185, 188, 195, 288–89
  Labor migration, 290, 292, 301
Lagan, 212
Lahore, 142, 150
Lakṣmī, 39–41, 71, 133, 139–40, 238, 303

Lakṣmīdevī, 120
Lakṣmīśvara, 120
lālamohara 161, 169, 173, 305–6
Lama,
  Kyanche, 61
  Pasang Dawa, 13
  Sangwa Dorje, 272
  See also Dalai Lama
Lama (people), 200, 263
lāmā/lama (priest), 5, 57, 82, 207, 270–73, 274, 304
Lamjung, 136, 139–40, 165, 166, 169
Land categories, 173*t*
Land donations, 173, 305–6
Land ownership, 103–4, 146–47
Land reform, 222, 243, 252
Landlords, 109, 170–72, 180, 192
Lapche, 207
Law, 6–7, 42–43, 46, 92–93, 143, 144–45, 168, 170, 194–97, 199–200, 201–2, 214, 225–26, 234, 238, 243–46, 253, 273, 283–84, 287, 288–89, 293. *See also* Dharmaśāstra
Law, Edward, 149
Lazimpat, 75, 94–95, 306
Le Bon, Gustave, 296–97
Legation (residence), British, 205
Lévi, Sylvain, 296, 309, 310–11
Levies, 109, 139–40, 144–45, 146–47, 155–56, 169–70, 171, 172, 173, 178, 180–81, 182–83, 190–91, 192, 193, 196, 214–15, 243, 267
Levy, Robert, 125
Lhasa, 94, 153–54, 156, 158–59, 192, 295, 307–8
Licchavi period, 24–25, 31, 33, 55–56, 66, 68–69, 93–94, 95–96, 97, 107–8, 126, 131, 132–33, 153, 174, 262, 306, 307
Lienhard, Siegfried, 302
Life-cycle rituals, 34, 60–61, 62, 258–59, 272
Limbu, 29, 37, 42, 86, 150, 178–79, 190–91, 198, 200, 207, 248, 262, 272–73, 280–84, 287, 290, 301
Liṅga, 23, 65–68, 67*f*, 80, 82, 85, 94–95, 113, 128, 131, 213
Lingba, Tertön Ratna, 270–71
Lingden, Phālgunanda, 284
Lion, 44, 89–90, 122, 128, 307, 310–11
Lisanevich, Boris, 249–50
Literature, 5–6, 22, 42–43, 60–61, 105, 253–54, 255–56, 262–63, 301–2, 303, 304, 310
Locke, John K., 299
London, 163–64, 195–96, 197–98, 255, 256, 296
Lopa, 29, 276
Lucknow, 164, 211, 212, 214
Lūhiti, 24–25
Lukumahādyaḥ, 68, 115–17
Lumbini, 53–54, 81, 84–85, 86–87, 88, 248, 265, 306

Madhesi, 29–30, 232, 234, 264, 268–69, 287
Magar, 29, 30–31, 37, 42, 57, 102, 103, 139, 150, 198, 207, 209, 248, 262–64, 266, 271, 287, 301, 304
Mahābauddha, 119, 121
Mahābhārata, 80, 85–87, 100, 101, 129, 132
Mahāyāna Buddhism, 55–57, 59–60, 88–89, 91, 305
Mahendramalli (coin), 153–54
Māheśvarī, 44–46, 74
Mahiṣa, 73
Maithilī (language), 62–63, 113, 259–60, 266–67, 268, 288, 300–1, 303
Maithili people, 111, 264, 266–67, 297
Maitreya, 55, 56
Makara, 24–25
Makwanpur, 78, 102–3, 136–37, 139–40, 144, 266, 272, 281, 295–96
Malla, 5, 33, 37, 44, 52, 62–63, 73–74, 75–76, 84, 95–97, 98, 99–100, 101, 103–4, 106–7, 108–9, 112, 114, 119–20, 126, 129, 131, 136–37, 153–54, 183, 211–12, 259–60, 262, 266–67, 297, 307. *See also* Khasa (Malla)
  Ananta, 66
  Ari, 43–44, 73, 111–12
  Bhāskara, 112–13, 122
  Bhīma, 108, 112, 153
  Bhūpālendra, 66, 75
  Bhūpatīndra, 107–8, 112–13, 114–15, 125–27, 128–29, 301
  Cakravartendra, 24–25

Malla (*cont.*)
Jagajjyotir, 24, 259–60, 301–2
Jagatprakāśa, 112–13, 127, 259–60, 301–2
Jaya Prakāśa (Jayaprakāśa), 43–44, 136–37
Jayadharma, 107–8
Jayasthiti (*see* Malla: Sthiti)
Jitāmitra, 79, 110, 125–26, 128, 129, 259–60, 301
Jitāri, 100, 266–67
Lakṣmīnarasiṃha, 153
Mahendra, 134, 153–54, 302, 307
Mahindra, 107
Pārthivendra, 107
Pratāpa, 24–25, 44–46, 47, 61, 66, 67, 68–69, 80, 82–83, 96, 108, 112–15, 122–23, 134–35, 137, 204–5, 259–60, 295
Pṛthvī, 101, 102
Rāma, 43–44
Raṇa, 43–44, 112
Raṇajit, 125–27, 138, 259–60
Ratna, 43–44, 52–53, 111, 112, 134
Rāya, 112
Ṛiddhilakṣmī, 75
Rudra, 111–12
Siddhinarasiṃha, 80, 107–8, 113, 120–21, 131
Śivasiṃha, 66
Śrīnivāsa, 69–70, 81, 112–13, 131
Sthiti, 37–38, 43–44, 60, 62–63, 77–78, 96, 106, 107–9, 111–12, 125–26, 172, 265, 266–67, 308
Sūrya, 43–44
Trailokya, 43–44
Viṣṇu, 75–76, 76*f*, 131, 132
Viśva, 129
Yakṣa, 64, 107, 110, 112, 125–26, 128, 129
Yoganarendra, 24, 80, 107, 112–13, 132
Malla Period, 63, 73, 75–76, 77, 79, 106, 107–8, 110–11, 113, 114–15, 117–18, 119, 125–26, 132, 134, 174, 194–95, 204–5, 301–2, 305, 307, 308, 310
Mānadeva, 52, 56, 61, 62, 75, 89–90, 97–98, 306, 307
Mānagṛha, 91, 92
Māneśvarī, 108–9
Mangal Bazar, 80
Maṇihiti, 24–25, 131, 132
Mañjuśrī, 22, 53, 55, 59, 81, 82, 85, 98, 121
Manu, Mānavadharmaśāstra, 85–86, 93
Mao Dzedong, 241–42
Maoists, 21–22, 221, 223, 224, 230–33, 234–35, 236, 238–39, 241, 242, 250, 286, 288–89, 290, 292
March, Kathryn, 263–64
Marsyangdi, 136
Martin Chautari, 299, 311
Martyr, 225
Masks, 115–17, 134–35
Massacre, 67, 142, 158–59, 160, 162, 163, 210, 212, 213–14, 226, 227–28, 229, 237, 284–85, 312
Maṣṭā, 102
Maṭha, 118–19
Mathema, Dharma Bhakta, 168
Matsyendranātha, 23–24, 59, 69–70, 82, 98, 102, 105, 111–12, 114, 238, 256–57, 299
Matsyendranātha procession, 23–24, 59, 69–70, 82, 105, 111–12, 114, 238, 256–57
matvālī, 38–39, 180, 272–73, 287
Maurya dynasty, 307
Meat, 61, 199, 200–1
Merwar, 237
Mewahang, 280–81
Migration, 30–31, 33, 245, 257, 260–61, 270–71, 290, 292, 301
Military, 2, 103–4, 108, 110, 120, 136, 138–39, 142–44, 145, 147–48, 149, 150, 151–52, 155–56, 158–59, 160, 161, 162, 164, 165–66, 168, 176–81, 182, 183, 184, 197–98, 205, 209, 215, 216, 218, 227, 228, 230, 239, 240–41, 246, 251, 259, 263–64, 282–83, 286, 290–91, 310–11. *See also* Army; Soldiers, Soldiery
Mishra, Madan Mohan, 302
Mishra,Tara Nanda, 89, 306
Missionaries, 4, 53, 59–60, 63, 86–87, 112–13, 199, 204–5, 246, 248–49, 295. *See also* Capuchin monks
Mithila, 52–53, 62–63, 79, 99, 110–12, 262, 265, 266–67

Modi, Narendra, 233
Mogul, 78–79, 110–11, 161, 195–96, 211, 212, 267
mohara, 112–13, 307. *See also lālamohara*
Monasteries, 5, 56–57, 58, 59–60, 61, 64, 78, 81, 86–87, 88, 91, 97, 98, 111, 114–15, 118–19, 120–21, 122–23, 132–34, 145–46, 154, 157, 202, 239–40, 244, 270, 271–72, 274, 275, 276–77, 299, 310. *See also bāhāḥ, bāhāla, bahī*
Money, 19, 33, 152, 177, 178, 187, 191, 192, 204, 230, 275, 290–91, 306, 307–8, 310
Monks, 10, 55, 57–58, 60, 100, 307
Monsoon, 11, 12, 21, 22, 23, 305
Mountains, 11, 13*t*, 14–15, 16–17, 20, 22, 29, 33, 35, 57, 61–62, 68, 84, 138–39, 169, 172, 200–1, 207, 215, 224–25, 234, 241, 242, 262, 264, 268–70, 275, 276, 279–81, 285, 289, 296, 297, 307
Movie, 16
Mṛgasthalī, 27, 65–66, 213–14
Mucalinda, 24
Mukherjee, P. C., 306
mukhtiyāra, 139–41, 142, 149, 160–61, 162, 197–98
Muktinath, 276–78, 306
Mukuṇḍa, 43–44, 266, 282–83
Mulukī Ain. *See Ain* (of 1854)
Mundhum, 283
Museum, 24, 93–94, 129, 212, 257, 258, 308–9, 311–12
Music, 106, 124–25, 128–29, 258–60
Muslims, 2, 4, 30–31, 32, 33–34, 42, 49–50, 52–53, 62–63, 97, 101, 103, 111–12, 182–83, 187–88, 195–96, 201, 234, 259, 264, 265–67, 288, 289
Mustang, 13–14, 32, 57, 99–101, 104, 139–40, 183, 262, 263, 276, 277*f*, 278, 278*f*, 279, 280, 285, 293, 306

Nāga Pokharī, 24–25, 126
Nāgapañcamī, 23
Nāgarāja (person), 100
Nāgarāja (serpent king), 24–25
Nalanda, 57
Nandī, 118
Nangpa La, 271
Nānyadeva, 99, 265
Narabhūpāla, 47, 136–37
Nāradasmṛti, 194
Naraharinath, Yogi, 156, 298, 309
Narasiṃha, 77, 119
Nārāyaṇa, 63, 75–76, 77–78, 81, 89–90, 94–95, 108, 115, 120, 132, 238, 306. *See also* Viṣṇu
Narayanhiti Palace, 75–76, 226, 229, 237, 312
Narendradeva, 56, 69–70, 92, 125–26
Nāsaḥdyaḥ, 128–29
Nātha, 52, 69, 298
Nation, 1, 2, 5–6, 49–51, 73, 101, 185–86, 201–2, 285, 286, 287–88, 289, 290, 291–93, 300
National Archives, 298, 305, 310
Nauje, 273, 275
Nautale, 120
Navadurgā, 63, 74, 115, 130
Navagraha, 60
Navarātra, 73
Nehru, Jawaharlal, 168, 218, 219, 224
Nemuni, 10
Nepal Citizenship Act, 268
Nepal Federation of Indigenous Nationalities (NEFIN), 31, 49–50
Nepal-German Manuscript Preservation Project (NGMPP), 305, 308–9
Nepal Praja Parishad, 168, 219
Nepal, Gyan Mani, 297
Nepāla, 8, 10, 22, 57–58, 86–87, 88, 89–90, 97, 98, 99, 105–6, 108–9, 110–11, 113, 183, 244, 262, 301, 309
Nepāla Saṃvat, 95, 96, 307
Nepālamāhātmya, 65–66, 309
Nepālī (language), 1, 3–4, 14–15, 26–27, 29, 30, 33, 49, 100, 117, 138, 156, 157, 158–59, 186, 199, 204, 233, 234, 242, 247–48, 253–54, 256, 264, 268, 270, 275–76, 288, 297, 300–1, 302–3, 304, 305, 307, 308–9, 311–12
Nepali Congress, 168–69, 217, 218–19, 220, 221, 223, 225–26, 232–33, 234–35, 299
Nepālikabhūpavaṃśāvalī, 8, 20, 30–31, 43–46, 53, 58, 61, 62–63, 85, 100, 111–12, 155, 296, 308–9

Nevārī (language), 31, 57, 61, 68, 85, 86, 96, 105, 106, 112, 115–17, 131, 138, 194, 248, 259–60, 281, 297–98, 301–2, 303, 305, 307, 308, 309, 311
New Road, 168, 251
New Year's celebrations, 128–29
Newar, 6–7, 10, 23, 29, 30–31, 33, 35–37, 42, 44, 57, 58–61, 62, 63, 68–69, 70, 73, 74–75, 81–82, 83, 105–6, 115–17, 118, 119, 120–21, 122, 123–25, 128, 136, 138, 153–54, 178–79, 198, 211, 213, 252, 254–55, 260, 262, 271, 281, 287, 290, 297, 299, 301–2, 309
Newar (castes, population), 6–7, 10, 23, 29–31, 33, 35–38, 36*t*, 42, 44, 57, 105–6, 120–21, 124–25, 178–79, 260, 271, 287, 290
Newar Buddhism, 59–61, 81–82, 105. *See also* Vajrayāna Buddhism
Newspapers, 166–67, 183, 241–42, 247–48, 303
Norgay, Tenzing, 15, 269
Nuvakot, 10, 102–3, 112, 114, 120, 136–37, 138, 144, 155, 211
Nyātapola, 117–18, 128, 129, 130*f*, 132, 252
Nyāyavikāṣinī, 194

Ochterlony, David, 146, 150
Oldfield, Hemry Ambrose, 47, 126, 127*f*, 205, 255, 296
Oṃ maṇi padme hūṃ, 102, 122
Oppitz, Michael, 208*f*, 270, 270*f*, 304
Ordeal, 195, 196
Ortner, Sherry B., 270
Ottley, G. O. B., 163

Pāḍe family, 139, 148–49, 197–98. *See also* Pāṇḍe (Pāḍe) clan
Padmapāṇi-Avalokiteśvara, 59
Painting, 68–69, 80, 133, 254–55
pajanī, 143, 165, 197–98, 215, 274, 286
Pāla dynasty, 10, 32–33, 57, 58, 99, 265
Pāla, Pṛthivī, 266
Palace, 4–5, 22, 24–25, 26–27, 44–46, 63, 75–76, 79, 80, 81, 91, 92, 94, 96–97, 107–8, 109, 110, 114–15, 119–20, 125, 126–28, 127*f*, 131–33, 134–35, 142, 143–45, 149, 156, 160, 169, 170, 172, 173–74, 181, 185, 193, 202–3, 204–5, 210, 211, 212–13, 215, 217, 219–20, 226, 228–29, 231, 237–38, 245–46, 255, 265, 298, 309, 310, 312. *See also* Houses: Royal House; Narayanhiti Palace
Palpa, 43–44, 102–3, 111, 139–40, 145–46, 205, 248, 262–63, 266
Palm-leaf manuscripts, 97–98, 106, 109, 301, 305, 311–12
Panauti, 114, 120
Pañcadevala, 213
Pañcaibājā, 258–59
Panchayat system, 194, 219–21, 222, 223–24, 225–26, 245–46, 268, 288, 289
Panchen Lama, 154
Panchgaon, 276, 277–78
Pāṇḍe (Pāḍe) clan, 139, 143–44, 148–49, 197–98
Pande (Pāḍe), Damodara, 140–41
Pande (Pāḍe), Hemraj, 185, 298, 310
Pandhraśivālaya, 67, 213–14
Pangboche, 271–72
Pant(a), Dinesh Raj, 297
Pant(a), Mahes Raj, 297
Pant(a), Naya Raj, 297–98
Pāraskāragṛhyasūtra, 62
Parbatiya, 29, 61–62, 64
Paris, 163–64, 195–96, 197–98, 255, 256, 296, 309
Parliament, 42, 49, 50–51, 164, 218, 222, 225–26, 228–29, 231, 232, 233–35, 236, 243, 246, 268, 290. *See also* House of Representatives
Parties, political, 219, 222, 223, 232–33, 234–35, 236
  Communist Party (Marxist-Leninist) 234, 235–36
  Maoist Communist Party of Nepal (Maoist Center), 223, 235
  Nepali Congress 168, 217, 218–19, 221, 225–26, 299
  Rashtriya Praja Party, 219
  Seven Party Alliance, 228–29, 230–31
Pārvatī, 27, 65–66, 68, 83
Passes, mountain, 11, 33, 136–37, 138–39, 155, 192, 217–18, 269–70, 271
Passport, 268

Pāśupata, 65, 66, 70–71, 87
Paśupatinātha, 3–4, 27, 42, 48–49, 64, 65–66, 65*f*, 67–68, 74–75, 77, 81, 82–83, 85, 87, 94–95, 97–98, 102, 107, 111, 118, 128, 135, 140, 189, 213, 227, 242, 252, 298, 307, 308, 312
Patan, 1, 6–7, 24–25, 35, 43–46, 56, 57–58, 62, 69–71, 73–74, 77, 80, 81, 93–95, 96–97, 98, 107, 108, 112–13, 114–15, 117–18, 119, 120–21, 125–26, 129, 131, 132–34, 135, 137–38, 182–83, 192, 205, 211, 248, 251–52, 253, 257, 258, 297, 298, 307, 308–9, 312
Patan Museum, 24, 258, 312
pāṭī, 118–19, 259
Patna, 202–3, 211, 295
paubhā, 254–55
Pauḍyāla, Lekhanātha, 303
Pauḍyāla, Raṅganātha Paṇḍita, 173
Peasants, 23, 33–35, 37, 44, 103–4, 115, 124–25, 152, 169–72, 175–76, 178, 179–80, 181, 182, 189, 190, 192, 216, 223–25, 242, 243, 245, 260, 273, 283–84, 287
phalcā, 70, 118–19, 124–25
Pharak, 269, 271
Pharping, 52, 57–58, 69, 108, 112, 183, 297
Pig, 109, 124–25
Pīgāmāī, 66, 71, 242
Pilgrimage, 4–5, 22–23, 42, 53–54, 58, 67–68, 69–70, 77, 78, 81, 88, 99–101, 102, 111, 197, 202, 277–78
Pillar, 20, 86–87
Plants, Planting, 23, 27–28, 53–54, 85, 115–17, 205, 245, 269–70, 274
Platform (*ḍabali*), 115, 128, 132, 134, 213, 259
pīṭha, 4–5, 82–83, 115–17, 130
Places, 7, 8, 12, 23, 26, 44, 58, 70, 74, 78, 79, 80–81, 92, 93–94, 102, 108, 111, 115, 117, 118–19, 129, 165, 183, 211, 219–20, 224–25, 253, 265, 271, 276–78, 301–2, 305–6
Pohle, Perdita, 277*f*, 278*f*
Polk, Benjamin, 212, 312
Pollock, Sheldon, 3–4
Population density, 29, 181, 251, 292
Population growth, 29, 250, 260–61, 290
Pore caste, 37–38, 38*f*
Porters, 155–56, 162, 180–81, 182–84, 187–88, 189, 269–70
Pottery, 125
Poverty, 91, 137, 152, 193, 223–25, 245, 260–61
Prachanda. *See* Dahal, Pushpa Kamal ("Prachanda")
Pradhan clan, 138
Pradhan, Kumar, 281, 286
Pradyumna, 77
Pradyumnakāmadeva, 97
Prajñāpāramitā, 58, 59, 60
Priests, 3–4, 22–23, 24–25, 26–27, 29, 34–35, 37, 44, 47, 54, 56–57, 59–61, 69, 73, 74–75, 81, 82, 83, 102, 104, 105, 107–8, 109–10, 113, 138, 143–44, 173, 174, 175–76, 180–81, 189, 194–95, 196, 202, 204, 207, 213, 236, 239, 240, 241, 270–72, 283, 297–98, 301, 303, 304, 305, 310. *See also* Bhaṭṭa priests; Brahmins; *lāmā*/lama (priest); Vajracharya (priests)
Prison, Prisoner, 140, 148–49, 163–64, 187–88, 194–95, 197, 203–4, 220, 221, 223–24, 230–31, 237, 253–54, 302, 303. *See also* Imprisonment
Procession, 23–24, 58, 62, 64, 67–70, 74–75, 81, 106, 114, 115, 128–29, 130, 135, 174–75, 210, 241, 256–57, 258–59
Provinces, 144–45, 154, 169, 201, 232–34, 235, 245–46. *See also* Districts
pūjā, 43–44, 60–61, 63, 73, 106, 151–52
Pūjarī Maṭha, 129
Punishment, 20, 139–40, 164–65, 187, 188, 189, 190, 195, 196, 197, 199–200, 201, 238, 239, 287
  Capital punishment, 164–65, 187, 190, 199–200, 201
purāṇa, 173, 306–7

Qing dynasty, 155

Rādhā, 79, 80–81
Rai, 29, 30–31, 37, 42, 150, 207, 248, 262, 271, 272–73, 280–81, 282, 283, 284, 287, 301

Rāi, Siṃha, 282
raikara, 170, 173, 176, 177, 178–79, 244, 283–84
Rain, 7, 13–14, 21, 22–24, 59, 69, 81, 136–37, 238, 274, 318*t*
Raj-Darbhanga dynasty, 265–66
Rājarājeśvarī, 66–67, 74, 94–95, 140–41, 142
Rajasthan, 3, 32, 103, 237
Rajbhandari, Sheelasha, 257
Rajman Singh, 99*f*, 255
Rājopādhyāya, 60, 62, 73, 105, 109–10
Rajput, 29–30, 32–33, 103, 104, 237, 266
rājya, 102–3, 107, 170, 178
Rājyavatī, 90–91
Rāma, 39–41, 43–44, 63–64, 75–78, 79, 80–81, 96
Rāmānanda, 78
Rāmānandī, 78–79
Rāmāyaṇa, 77, 78, 80, 302, 303
Ramble, Charles, 279–80
Rāṇā(s). *See* Kūvara Rāṇā (cf. Śaṃśera Rāṇā)
Rāṇā Period, 1, 3, 5, 6–7, 25, 47, 63, 66, 77–78, 104, 109, 119, 133–34, 139, 143, 146–47, 152, 262, 263, 268–69, 274, 279, 283–84, 297, 299, 302, 303, 304–6, 308, 309
Rani Pokhari, 24–25, 202–3
Rashtriya Prajatantra Party, 219, 223, 232–33
Rasuwagardhi, 192
Ratnasambhava, 55, 122
Ratneśvara (*liṅga*), 66
Referendum, 221
Regmi, Dilli Raman, 112–13, 299
Regmi, Mahesh Chandra, 180, 298–99, 311
Regmi, Paśupati, 47
Resident, British, 148–49
Rhino, Rhinoceros, 11, 157, 209–10
Rice, 22, 23, 34, 39, 48, 68–69, 103, 124–25, 130, 138–39, 153, 169, 171, 179, 191, 200–1, 207, 214–15, 244, 269–70, 274
Rimāla, Gopāla Prasāda, 253–54
Risley, Herbert Hope, 1–2
Rituals. *See* Life-cycle rituals
Rivers, 13–14, 21, 22, 24–25, 65–66, 86, 94, 102–3, 118, 136–37, 142, 145–46, 147–48, 155–56, 173, 181, 192, 200, 244, 250, 266, 267–68, 276–77, 280–81. *See also* Bagmati River
Roads, 12, 25–26, 70, 102, 115–17, 129, 163–64, 170, 181, 182, 193–94, 220, 223–24, 244, 250–51, 260–61, 269–70, 274, 278
Ring Road, 183–84, 243
Rockefeller III, John D., 249–50
Roka, Raju, 18*f*
Rolpa, 224–25
Rukum, 224–25
Rumbu, 275
Rural exodus, 152, 169, 278–79

Sacred Thread, 32, 37, 38–39, 187–88, 287
Sacrifice, 27–28, 47–48, 54, 62, 74–75, 91, 101, 103–4, 201, 207, 238, 276–77, 291. *See also* Animal sacrifice; Blood sacrifices; *homa*; *Satī*
Sagarmatha, 11, 298. *See also* Everest
Śāha Period, 104, 122, 248
Śāha
  Aiśvaryarājyalakṣmī, 210, 226–27
  Bahādura, 139–40, 154, 155
  Basundhara, 249–50
  Birendra (Vīrendra), 66, 129, 139–40, 154, 155, 210, 217, 220–21, 222, 226–27, 228, 237, 256, 289, 297
  Dīpendra, 226–28, 237
  Gajendra, 178
  Gīrvāṇayuddha, 26–27, 47, 140, 142
  Gyanendra (Jñānendra), 217, 226–27
  Mahendra, 5–6, 12–13, 66, 139, 195, 212, 217, 219–21, 223, 225–26, 242, 245–46, 249–50, 256, 287, 310
  Parasa, 226–28
  Pratāpa Siṃha, 126, 139–40, 154, 175
  Pṛthvīnārāyaṇa, 1, 2, 3, 4, 5–6, 26–27, 38–39, 44, 47, 53, 96–97, 100, 102–3, 104, 114, 120, 125–26, 136–40, 143, 144, 153–54, 176, 179, 191, 197–98, 210, 211, 259–60, 274, 282–84, 287, 289, 293, 295, 298, 302, 307, 309
  Rājyalakṣmī Devī, 139, 149, 162, 213, 238

Raṇabahādura, 47, 68–69, 79, 120, 139, 140–42, 154–55, 162, 181, 195, 199, 211, 212, 213, 303
Raṇoddīpa Siṃha, 152, 166, 212
Raṇoddyota, 140
Saṃrājyalakṣmī Devī, 148–49
Surendra, 27, 149, 162, 164–65, 179–80, 195, 213, 237, 296, 310
Suvarṇaprabhā, 47, 140, 142
Tribhuvan(a), 20, 139, 182, 184, 203–4, 205, 206–7, 217–19, 245–46, 249–50
Vīrendra (*see* Śāha: Birendra (Vīrendra))
Śaivism, 52, 61–62, 64, 65, 68, 71
Śakti, 56–57, 61–62, 70–71
śakti, 39–41, 83, 115
Śākyamuni, 53, 56, 132–33
Salt, 30–31, 138, 153, 191–92, 193, 199, 269–70, 274, 279
Salyan, 104, 139–40, 199, 224–25
Sama, Bālakṛṣṇa, 303
Samantaśrī, 297
Śamśera Rāṇā, 166–67, 182, 197–98, 212, 217–19
Agni, 161*t*, 212
Bhīma, 77–78, 166, 167–68, 303
Candra, 12, 49, 79, 152, 166–68, 167*f*, 177–78, 184, 185–86, 189–90, 192, 195, 198, 202–4, 205, 209, 212–13, 255, 303, 310–11
Deva, 166–67, 189, 204, 303, 309
Dhīra, 127, 166
Juddha, 20, 166, 168, 195, 205, 206–7, 212, 251, 259–60, 311–12
Kāntivatī, 140, 141
Keśara, 168, 205, 310–11
Madana, 311
Mohana, 166, 168, 217
Padma, 156, 166, 168, 217
Vīra, 25–26, 166, 174, 195, 205–6, 212, 217, 273, 310
Samudragupta, 10, 85–86, 88–90
Śaṅkara, 52, 94–95, 98
Śaṅkaradeva, 66–67, 89, 97–98
Sankhu, 56, 108, 114
Sannyasi, 29
Sanskrit language, 3–4, 42–43, 52, 54, 57, 58, 68–69, 86, 92–93, 96, 100, 106, 111, 202–3, 206, 247, 259–60, 265, 287, 297–98, 299, 300–3, 305, 306–7, 308, 310
Sanskrit texts, 305–6
Śāntipura, 22–23
Sarasvatī, 59, 71, 82, 121
Sarki, 30, 200
Satī, 27–28, 46–49, 91. *See also* widow burning
Schendel, Willem van, 292
Schneider, Erwin, 297
Schools, 202–3, 255–57, 299
Schrom, Thomas, 116*f*
Sculptures, 24, 57, 72*f*–76*f*, 75, 94, 98, 100, 113, 121, 125, 131, 306–7, 311–12
Sekler, Eduard, 251
Sena dynasty, 43–44, 78, 102–3, 111, 266, 272, 281–83
Sena, Mahadat, 266
Sena, Mukuṇḍa, 43–44, 266, 282–83
Serfdom, 186, 187, 188
Serib, 279
Serpents (*nāga*), 22–25, 53, 69, 71, 79, 81, 94, 115
Śeṣanārāyaṇa, 22–23, 115
Seto Darbar, 212
Seven Party Alliance, 228–29, 230–31
Sexual intercourse, 194–95, 196–97, 215
Shakya, 44, 59–60, 61, 120–21, 133
Shakya, Hemraj, 298, 310
Shamanism, 5, 102, 180–81, 206–9, 208*f*, 258, 269, 275–76, 283, 304
Shams ud-dīn Ilyās, 52–53, 111, 265
Sharma, Hemraj, 185, 298, 310
Shastri, Hara Prasad, 305
Shastri, Shukra Raj, 168
Shigatse, 145–46, 154
Sherpa, 14–16, 29, 31, 42, 57, 153, 178–79, 200–1, 207, 262, 269–76, 270*f*, 280–81, 287, 293, 301, 312
Sherpa
Tensing Norgay, 15
Ngawang Tseten Lama, 270*f*
Shneiderman, Sarah, 292
Shrestha, Durga Lal, 302
Shrestha, Ganga Lal, 168
Shrestha, Laxman, 256
Shrestha, Shukrasagar, 137, 299–300

Shrestha, Siddhicharan, 302
Shrestha caste, 37
Shudra (*śūdra*), 34–35, 37, 287
Siddhilakṣmī, 128
Sikh, 150
Śikhara Style, 80, 94, 119, 121, 122–23, 128, 132, 213–14
Sikkim, 33, 102–3, 105, 139–40, 145–46, 147–48, 158–59, 180, 263, 267–68, 269, 274, 281–83
Silk, 157
Silk Road, 88
Silkhana, 311–12
Silumahādyaḥ, 127
Silver, 66, 97–98, 153–54, 157, 192, 307–8
Simraongarh, 99
Sindhupalchok, 136–37, 144
Singh, Mohan Bikram, 224
Singh, Phatte Bahadur, 302
Singha Darbar, 206–7, 212–13, 220–21, 238, 243, 255
Sinja, 100
Sino-Nepalese War, 153, 155
Sītā, 39–41, 71, 77–79
Sītalā, 70–71, 122–23
Śiva, 4, 26, 27, 56, 59, 61–62, 63, 64–65, 66, 67–71, 74–75, 81, 82, 83, 92, 94–95, 96, 97–98, 102, 115–17, 118, 119, 127, 129, 132, 189–90, 213, 259. *See also* Śaivism
Śivadeva, 91–92, 97–98, 307
Śivadharma, 65, 96, 97–98
Śivarātri, 67–68
Skandapurāṇa, 66, 70, 111, 305, 309
Slavery, 184*f*, 185–90, *See also* Labor
Śleṣmāntaka, 213
Slusser, Mary, 312
Smārta, 62–63, 81
Snakes, 20, 23, 75–76
Soldiers, Soldiery, 33, 102, 110, 111, 136–37, 138–39, 141, 143, 145, 146, 147–48, 150, 151–52, 154, 156, 158–59, 164, 165, 170, 173, 176, 183, 192, 200, 204, 229–30, 242, 284
Solukhumbu, 57, 200–1, 271, 272–73
Someśvara I, 99
Songtsen Gampo, 94, 95, 153, 279
Stiller, Ludwig, 138–39, 147, 195, 299
Stones, religious, 68–69, 70, 115–17, 119, 128–29, 203–4
Squares, 24–25, 80, 119, 125, 127, 127*f*, 128–29, 131, 132, 133, 251, 253
stūpa, 55, 116*f*, 121, 122–24, 123*f*, *See also* Bauddha; Svayambhū (Caitya, Stūpa)
subbā, 143–45, 172, 283–84
Sunaḍhokā, 126–27
Sunkoshi, 280–81
Sunuvar, 29, 150, 178–79, 207, 271, 280–81
Svāra, Pahalamāna Siṃa, 253–54
Svasthānīvratakathā, 42
Svayambhū (Caitya, Stūpa), 22–23, 53, 70–71, 88, 93–94, 101, 102, 112, 122, 123–24, 123*f*, 135, 280–81, 298, 312
Svayambhūpurāṇa, 8, 22, 58, 301–2, 309
Syncretism, religious, 81–83, 279–80, 293

Taleju, 43–46, 63, 73–74, 81, 82, 108–9, 112–13, 117–18, 119, 126–27, 128, 131, 132, 134, 175, 252, 260
Tamakoshi, 280–81
Tamang, 4, 29, 31, 36–37, 42, 57, 82, 86, 207, 262–64, 271, 272–73, 280–81, 287, 288, 300–1
Tanahun, 102–3, 266
Ṭaṇḍana, Sanak Siṃha Lāhūrī, 214
Tantrism, 22–23, 52, 60, 61, 62, 63, 64, 65–66, 68–71, 73, 74–75, 81, 83, 93, 97–98, 105, 113–14, 117, 122–23, 128, 131, 132, 272, 277–78
Tārā, 44, 59, 83, 89
Tarai, 11–13, 25–26, 29–30, 34–35, 42, 52–53, 61, 62–63, 78, 86, 99–101, 103–4, 111, 136–37, 140, 142, 146–48, 149, 164, 166, 168, 169, 175–76, 179–80, 186, 189–90, 191, 192, 193, 198–99, 209, 210, 215, 218–19, 220, 223, 232, 233, 234, 236, 244, 252, 263, 264–65, 267–69, 274, 280–81, 286, 287, 289, 290, 293, 296, 307
Tashilunpo, 145–46, 154, 157
Tathāgatas, 56, 121, 122
Teku, 120, 205
Television, 248
Tengboche, 275
Terai. *See* Tarai

Thakali, 29, 31, 37, 153, 183, 262–63, 276, 290, 301
Ṭhakuri caste, 29, 30, 32, 37, 187–88, 287
Thami, 29, 271–72
thangka, 105–6, 254–55
Thankot, 141
Thāpā, 142, 197–98
  Amara Siṃha, 66, 142, 144
  Bhīmasena (Bhimsen), 47, 66, 126, 134–35, 139, 140, 142, 147–49, 173, 174, 183, 192–93, 202–3, 212, 213, 245–46, 310, 311–12
  Māthavara Siṃha, 162, 174, 197–98, 237, 296
Thapa, Balbir Singh Hriksen, 298
Thapa, Manjushree, 254
Thapa, Sangita, 257
Thapa, Surya Bahadur, 221
Thapathali, 310
Tharu, 29–31, 33, 36–37, 42, 234, 262, 264, 268–69, 272–73
Tharū language, 248, 300–1
Theravāda, 59–60, 81
Thimi, 114, 117–18, 125, 138
Thulung, 280–81
thyāsaphu, 106, 259–60, 301–2, 308
Tibet, 1–2, 4, 14, 15, 33–34, 61, 88, 94, 95, 99–101, 102, 105–6, 108, 124–25, 133–34, 136–37, 145–46, 148, 153–59, 165, 183, 190–91, 192, 202, 225–26, 250, 254–55, 269–71, 272–73, 274, 277–79, 280–82, 293, 297, 301, 303, 306, 307–8
Tibetan Buddhism, 61, 121, 269, 275–76
Tibetan language and literature, 279, 281, 296, 297, 301, 309
Tibeto-Burman languages, 10, 13–14, 29, 31, 37, 57, 102, 105, 138, 280–81, 292, 301
Tiger, 11, 128, 200, 209, 210
ṭīkā, 39, 44, 46, 107, 239
Tilaurakot, 306
Tilganga, 94
Tirhut, 99, 265
tirjā, 177
Tista, 145–46, 280–81
Tourism, 65, 249–50, 269–70, 290, 291, 310
Trade (route), 2, 11–12, 88, 102, 103–4, 105–6, 108, 115, 129, 132, 133–34, 136–37, 138–39, 146, 148, 153–54, 155–56, 158–59, 170–71, 185–86, 191–93, 214–15, 222, 271, 273, 274, 275–76, 278–79, 292, 293, 307
Traffic, 12, 125, 145, 227, 250–51
Transitional period, 262
Trees, 25–28
Tribhuvan Airport, 12–13
Tribhuvan University, 206–7, 245–47, 257, 297–98, 299, 305, 311
Tribute payments, 103–4, 110–11, 146–47, 154, 157, 158, 178, 210, 267, 279, 281–82, 307–8
Tripura, 96–97
Tripurasundarī, 74, 126
Triśūlajātrā, 26
Tseten, Kesang, 299
Tsum, 29, 193
Tuladhar-Douglas, Will, 58
Turner, Ralph Lilley, 150
Tusāhiti, 24–25
Tutelary deities, 32, 94, 108–9, 112

Umāmaheśvara, 68, 94–95, 114
UNESCO, 252, 312
Untouchable castes, 30, 37, 38–39, 38*f*, 180. *See also* Dalits; *matvālī*
Upadhyay, Samrat, 254
Upādhyāya, Gaṇeśa, 266–67
Upādhyāya, Dīnanātha, 303
Uray, 61

Vaidya caste, 23–24, 37, 206–7
Vaidya, Asha Kaji, 298
Vairocana, 55, 122
Vaishali, 88–89, 265
Vaiṣṇavism, 52, 61–62, 64, 71, 75–76
Vaishya, 34–35
Vājasaneyisaṃhitā, 62, 305
Vajji Confederation, 88–89, 265
vajra, 122–24, 307
Vajracharya caste and priests, 44, 60–61, 120–21
Vajracharya (priests), 36*t*, 44, 60–61
Vajracharya, Badri Ratna, 298
Vajracharya, Dhanavajra, 297, 298

Vajracharya, Ganesh Raj, 298
Vajracharya, Ratna Bahadur, 298
Vajrapāṇi, 55, 56, 81
Vajrayāna Buddhism, 56–57, 58–59, 61, 81, 97, 105, 122–24, 297, 309
Vajrayoginī, 81, 82, 93–94, 114
Vajreśvarī, 66, 71, 242
Vaṃśagopāla temple, 80
vaṃśāvalī. *See* Chronicles
Vandya, Amṛtānanda, 298
Varanasi (Benares), 54, 65–66, 80, 138, 140–41, 212, 221, 256, 297–98, 303, 309
Varman clan, 101
varṇa, 6, 34–35, 38–39
Vasantadeva, 75, 91–92
Vāsuki, 4–5
Vatsalā, 64, 65*f*, 74–75, 94–95, 128
VDC (Village Development Committee), 219–20, 245–46
Veda, Vedic, 10, 43–44, 49, 52, 54, 62, 64, 73, 81, 83, 92–93, 101, 202, 203, 265, 266–67, 304, 305, 306–7
Verardi, Giuseppe, 306
Vetālapañcaviṃśati, 302, 304
Victoria, Queen, 164
Videha, 265
Virāṭeśvara, 66–67, 67*f*, 94–95
Viśaṅkhunārāyaṇa, 115
Vishnumati, 133
Viṣṇu, 26, 52–53, 56, 63, 64, 75–77, 81–82, 94–95, 102, 129, 132, 134, 169, 217–18, 238, 277–78. *See also* Nārāyaṇa; Śeṣanārāyaṇa
Viṣṇugupta, 77–78, 92
Viśvarūpa, 79, 213
Viśveśvara, 117, 118, 132
Vow, 48, 91
Vṛṣadeva, 56, 89

Wade, Thomas, 158
Waldemar of Prussia, 4, 296
Wang Xuance, 88
War, 86–87, 110, 128–29, 142, 146, 148, 150, 152, 154–55, 157, 164, 165, 183, 187–88, 190–91, 221–22, 223, 228, 230–32, 257, 267–68, 274, 279, 286, 295–96
Wasteland, 12, 170, 173, 178–79, 244, 275
Water, 11, 12, 16–17, 21–26, 32, 37, 38–39, 42, 48, 53, 59, 67–68, 73, 82–83, 85, 102, 109, 112, 169, 186, 197, 201, 222, 223–24, 250, 277–78, 292, 295
Water architecture, 24–25, 115, 117–18, 120, 132, 181, 196, 205, 250
Weapons, 108, 136–37, 150, 164, 181, 182, 183, 192, 212, 222, 224–25, 227, 228, 230, 295, 311–12
Weber, Max, 6–7
Wedding, 79, 111–13, 129, 258–59
Wei Yüan, 155
Wheat, 169, 171, 191
Widow burning, 27, 166–67, 306. *See also Satī*
Window, 81, 126, 131, 211–12
Witchcraft, 196
Women, 4–5, 37–38, 39–43, 46, 47–48, 49, 120, 153, 184, 188, 190, 195–96, 207, 226, 235, 237, 241, 257, 259, 295, 301–2
Wood, 12, 25–26, 27, 60–61, 98, 118, 181–82, 191, 253
Wood carving, 26, 118
Wright, Daniel, 8, 202–3, 205, 296, 298, 308–9. *See also Nepālikabhūpavaṃśāvalī*

Yakṣeśvara, 120, 128
Yaśodharā, 58
Yoginī, 82
Younghusband, Francis, 158–59
yuga, 8

Zomia, 292
Zhung, 271–72